THE PAPERS OF ULYSSES S. GRANT

THE PAPERS OF

ULYSSES S. GRANT

Volume 13:
November 16, 1864–February 20, 1865

Edited by John Y. Simon

ASSOCIATE EDITOR
David L. Wilson

EDITORIAL ASSISTANT
Sue E. Dotson

SOUTHERN ILLINOIS UNIVERSITY PRESS
CARBONDALE AND EDWARDSVILLE

Library of Congress Cataloging in Publication Data (Revised)

Grant, Ulysses Simpson, Pres. U.S., 1822–1885.
  The papers of Ulysses S. Grant.

  Prepared under the auspices of the Ulysses S. Grant Association.
  Bibliographical footnotes.
  CONTENTS: v. 1. 1837–1861—v. 2. April–September 1861.
—v. 3. October 1, 1861–January 7, 1862.—v. 4. January 8–March 31,
1862.—v. 5. April 1–August 31, 1862.—v. 6. September 1–December 8, 1862.—v. 7. December 9, 1862–March 31, 1863.—v. 8.
April 1–July 6, 1863.—v. 9. July 7–December 31, 1863.—v. 10.
January 1–May 31, 1864.—v. 11. June 1–August 15, 1864.—v. 12.
August 16–November 15, 1864.—v. 13. November 16, 1864–February 20, 1865.
  1. Grant, Ulysses Simpson, Pres. U.S., 1822–1885. 2. United
States—History—Civil War, 1861–1865—Campaigns and battles
—Sources. 3. United States—Politics and government—1869–1877
—Sources. 4. Presidents—United States—Biography. 5. Generals—
United States—Biography. I. Simon, John Y., ed. II. Wilson, David
L. 1943–. III. Ulysses S. Grant Association.
E660.G756 1967   973.8'2'0924   67–10725
ISBN–0–8093–1197–6 (v. 13)

115360

To Oliver W. Holmes (1902–1981)

Ulysses S. Grant Association

Contents

═══

Maps and Illustrations

MAPS

ILLUSTRATIONS

Frontispiece

Introduction

══════

O N NOVEMBER 16, 1864, Lieutenant General Ulysses S. Grant prepared to leave City Point for a week, first visiting with his family in Burlington, N.J., then consulting with Secretary of War Edwin M. Stanton in Washington before returning to the army so long encamped before Petersburg. Also on November 16, Major General William T. Sherman left Atlanta on a journey of his own, taking an army of some 60,000 across Georgia to the sea. Relative inactivity at Petersburg annoyed Grant, even though he recognized that the stalemate was a necessary component of his strategy. The Army of Northern Virginia under General Robert E. Lee, defending Richmond and Petersburg, constituted the last truly dangerous striking force of the South; while Grant immobilized Lee, the other U.S. armies could gut the Confederate heartland. Grant was prepared "to take the odium of apparent inactivity" before Petersburg, believing that eventual victory would result.

So Grant urged vigorous movement of his armies elsewhere, as he and the other officers at City Point moved from tents to wooden cabins for the winter. When Sherman marched toward the sea, Confederate General John B. Hood advanced his forces into Tennessee, hoping that a Confederate offensive might force Sherman northward. Grant believed that Major General George H. Thomas at Nashville commanded an army adequate to meet and defeat Hood, and for weeks he urged Thomas to take the offensive, growing more impatient as Thomas insisted on careful preparation. Admitting "I could stand it no longer," Grant gave peremptory orders for an attack, again without immediate response. Grant finally sent a replacement to Nashville, and even started for Nashville himself just as Thomas struck decisively, shattering the Army of Tennessee. Hood's defeat ended the Confederate threat in the middle theater of war and vindicated federal strategy. After the fall of Savannah on December 20, Grant planned to march Sherman's army northward through the Carolinas toward an eventual union of armies at Richmond.

During the winter, Grant found opportunity to rid himself of two commanders who had long troubled him. Major General William S. Rosecrans, commanding at St. Louis, had refused to cooperate in any grand strategy, instead insisting that his own department lay under imminent threat. By reorganizing the department as part of a military division under Major General John Pope, Grant arranged to send Rosecrans home to await orders for the rest of the war. Major General Benjamin F. Butler, commanding nearly half of the forces before Richmond and senior to Major General George G. Meade, commanding the Army of the Potomac, had amply demonstrated his incapacity as a field commander, yet his vital political connections thwarted Grant's efforts at removal. Butler bungled badly while commanding an expedition against Fort Fisher and Wilmington, N.C., placing all hope for breaching the walls of the fort on the explosion of a powder-laden vessel. This created much noise and nothing else; Grant later testified that "the gunpowder plot" had the same effect as "firing feathers from muskets." Butler then returned to Virginia rather than commencing the siege Grant had ordered. This disobedience justified Butler's removal, and Grant was further vindicated by the fall of Fort Fisher a few weeks later to a similar expedition commanded by Major General Alfred H. Terry. As Grant put it, "The failure at Fort Fisher was not without important and valuable results." Grant replaced Butler with Major General Edward O. C. Ord, who had also replaced Major General John A. McClernand, a similar threat, in June, 1863, at Vicksburg.

Through the winter, then, Grant had refined his commanders, ousting Butler and Rosecrans, and allowing Thomas to survive only because he smashed a Confederate army. Dissatisfied with Major General Edward R. S. Canby's slowness in campaigning against Mobile, Grant might have removed him also had not the approach of an end to war turned his attention elsewhere. The arrival of three Confederate peace commissioners, including Vice President Alexander H. Stephens, at City Point at the end of January revealed Southern weakness, even though the discussions with Lincoln proved unproductive. Belief in the approaching end to war resulted in Grant's willingness to resume the exchange of prisoners, since Confederates would probably have no time to return to active service.

By February 20, Grant could order Major General Philip H. Sheridan to take his cavalry to Lynchburg, destroy the railroad link to Richmond, and prepare to move south to join Sherman, then "eating out the vitals of South Carolina." On the same day, Grant proposed to send part of Meade's cavalry in the same direction. Sherman's success had convinced Grant that Confederate military power had crumbled to the point that cavalry alone might end the war.

In fall, 1864, Grant began to employ "Philp & Solomons' Highly Improved Manifold Writer," a device for making one or more copies of correspondence through the use of a stylus on double-faced carbon paper inserted between sheets of thin yellow writing paper. As a result, a greater proportion of Grant documents in his own hand exist for the closing months of the war, occasionally two copies of the same document. Although clerical copies prepared at headquarters rarely deviated in substantive matters from Grant's originals, handwritten documents with false starts, alterations, and idiosyncratic spellings have a greater immediacy and sometimes disclose thought patterns otherwise unrecoverable.

We are indebted to W. Neil Franklin and Karl L. Trever, both recently deceased, for searching the National Archives; to Mary Giunta, Anne Harris Henry, and Sara Dunlap Jackson for further assistance in the National Archives; to Harriet Simon for proofreading; to Karen Biggs and Patricia Ann Owens, graduate students at Southern Illinois University, for research assistance.

Financial support for the period during which this volume was prepared came from Southern Illinois University and the National Historical Publications and Records Commission. We acknowledge with special gratitude research grants from the Lincoln National Life Foundation and the Robert R. McCormick Foundation.

JOHN Y. SIMON

February 20, 1984

Editorial Procedure

1. Editorial Insertions

A. Words or letters in roman type within brackets represent editorial reconstruction of parts of manuscripts torn, mutilated, or illegible.

B. [. . .] or [— — —] within brackets represent lost material which cannot be reconstructed. The number of dots represents the approximate number of lost letters; dashes represent lost words.

C. Words in *italic* type within brackets represent material such as dates which were not part of the original manuscript.

D. Other material crossed out is indicated by ~~cancelled type~~.

E. Material raised in manuscript, as "4ᵗʰ," has been brought in line, as "4th."

2. Symbols Used to Describe Manuscripts

AD	Autograph Document
ADS	Autograph Document Signed
ADf	Autograph Draft
ADfS	Autograph Draft Signed
AES	Autograph Endorsement Signed
AL	Autograph Letter
ALS	Autograph Letter Signed
ANS	Autograph Note Signed
D	Document
DS	Document Signed

Df	Draft
DfS	Draft Signed
ES	Endorsement Signed
LS	Letter Signed

3. *Military Terms and Abbreviations*

Act.	Acting
Adjt.	Adjutant
AG	Adjutant General
AGO	Adjutant General's Office
Art.	Artillery
Asst.	Assistant
Bvt.	Brevet
Brig.	Brigadier
Capt.	Captain
Cav.	Cavalry
Col.	Colonel
Co.	Company
C.S.A.	Confederate States of America
Dept.	Department
Div.	Division
Gen.	General
Hd. Qrs.	Headquarters
Inf.	Infantry
Lt.	Lieutenant
Maj.	Major
Q. M.	Quartermaster
Regt.	Regiment or regimental
Sgt.	Sergeant
USMA	United States Military Academy, West Point, N.Y.
Vols.	Volunteers

4. *Short Titles and Abbreviations*

ABPC	*American Book-Prices Current* (New York, 1895–)
CG	*Congressional Globe* Numbers following represent the Congress, session, and page.

J. G. Cramer	Jesse Grant Cramer, ed., *Letters of Ulysses S. Grant to his Father and his Youngest Sister, 1857–78* (New York and London, 1912)
DAB	*Dictionary of American Biography* (New York, 1928–36)
Garland	Hamlin Garland, *Ulysses S. Grant: His Life and Character* (New York, 1898)
HED	*House Executive Documents*
HMD	*House Miscellaneous Documents*
HRC	*House Reports of Committees* Numbers following *HED, HMD,* or *HRC* represent the number of the Congress, the session, and the document.
Ill. AG Report	J. N. Reece, ed., *Report of the Adjutant General of the State of Illinois* (Springfield, 1900)
Johnson, Papers	LeRoy P. Graf and Ralph W. Haskins, eds., *The Papers of Andrew Johnson* (Knoxville, 1967–)
Lewis	Lloyd Lewis, *Captain Sam Grant* (Boston, 1950)
Lincoln, Works	Roy P. Basler, Marion Dolores Pratt, and Lloyd A. Dunlap, eds., *The Collected Works of Abraham Lincoln* (New Brunswick, 1953–55)
Memoirs	*Personal Memoirs of U. S. Grant* (New York, 1885–86)
O.R.	*The War of the Rebellion: A Compilation of the Official Records of the Union and Confederate Armies* (Washington, 1880–1901)
O.R. (Navy)	*Official Records of the Union and Confederate Navies in the War of the Rebellion* (Washington, 1894–1927) Roman numerals following *O.R.* or *O.R.* (Navy) represent the series and the volume.
PUSG	John Y. Simon, ed., *The Papers of Ulysses S. Grant* (Carbondale and Edwardsville, 1967–)
Richardson	Albert D. Richardson, *A Personal History of Ulysses S. Grant* (Hartford, Conn., 1868)
SED	*Senate Executive Documents*
SMD	*Senate Miscellaneous Documents*
SRC	*Senate Reports of Committees* Numbers following *SED, SMD,* or *SRC* represent the number of the Congress, the session, and the document.
USGA Newsletter	*Ulysses S. Grant Association Newsletter*

Young John Russell Young, *Around the World with General Grant* (New York, 1879)

5. *Location Symbols*

CLU University of California at Los Angeles, Los Angeles, Calif.
CoHi Colorado State Historical Society, Denver, Colo.
CSmH Henry E. Huntington Library, San Marino, Calif.
CSt Stanford University, Stanford, Calif.
CtY Yale University, New Haven, Conn.
CU-B Bancroft Library, University of California, Berkeley, Calif.
DLC Library of Congress, Washington, D.C. Numbers following DLC-USG represent the series and volume of military records in the USG papers.
DNA National Archives, Washington, D.C. Additional numbers identify record groups.
IaHA Iowa State Department of History and Archives, Des Moines, Iowa.
I-ar Illinois State Archives, Springfield, Ill.
IC Chicago Public Library, Chicago, Ill.
ICarbS Southern Illinois University, Carbondale, Ill.
ICHi Chicago Historical Society, Chicago, Ill.
ICN Newberry Library, Chicago, Ill.
ICU University of Chicago, Chicago, Ill.
IHi Illinois State Historical Library, Springfield, Ill.
In Indiana State Library, Indianapolis, Ind.
InFtwL Lincoln National Life Foundation, Fort Wayne, Ind.
InHi Indiana Historical Society, Indianapolis, Ind.
InNd University of Notre Dame, Notre Dame, Ind.
InU Indiana University, Bloomington, Ind.
KHi Kansas State Historical Society, Topeka, Kan.
MdAN United States Naval Academy Museum, Annapolis, Md.
MeB Bowdoin College, Brunswick, Me.
MH Harvard University, Cambridge, Mass.
MHi Massachusetts Historical Society, Boston, Mass.

MiD	Detroit Public Library, Detroit, Mich.
MiU-C	William L. Clements Library, University of Michigan, Ann Arbor, Mich.
MoSHi	Missouri Historical Society, St. Louis, Mo.
NHi	New-York Historical Society, New York, N.Y.
NIC	Cornell University, Ithaca, N.Y.
NjP	Princeton University, Princeton, N.J.
NjR	Rutgers University, New Brunswick, N.J.
NN	New York Public Library, New York, N.Y.
NNP	Pierpont Morgan Library, New York, N.Y.
NRU	University of Rochester, Rochester, N.Y.
OClWHi	Western Reserve Historical Society, Cleveland, Ohio.
OFH	Rutherford B. Hayes Library, Fremont, Ohio.
OHi	Ohio Historical Society, Columbus, Ohio.
OrHi	Oregon Historical Society, Portland, Ore.
PCarlA	U.S. Army Military History Institute, Carlisle Barracks, Pa.
PHi	Historical Society of Pennsylvania, Philadelphia, Pa.
PPRF	Rosenbach Foundation, Philadelphia, Pa.
RPB	Brown University, Providence, R.I.
TxHR	Rice University, Houston, Tex.
USG 3	Maj. Gen. Ulysses S. Grant 3rd, Clinton, N.Y.
USMA	United States Military Academy Library, West Point, N.Y.
ViHi	Virginia Historical Society, Richmond, Va.
ViU	University of Virginia, Charlottesville, Va.
WHi	State Historical Society of Wisconsin, Madison, Wis.
Wy-Ar	Wyoming State Archives and Historical Department, Cheyenne, Wyo.
WyU	University of Wyoming, Laramie, Wyo.

Chronology

NOVEMBER 16, 1864–FEBRUARY 20, 1865

═══

Nov. 16. USG at City Point as the siege of Petersburg continued.

Nov. 16. Maj. Gen. William T. Sherman left Atlanta with some 60,000 men to begin his march across Ga. to the sea.

Nov. 17. USG started for Burlington, N.J., to visit his family.

Nov. 19. USG at Burlington.

Nov. 19. USG directed Maj. Gen. Philip H. Sheridan to consider an attempt to cut the Virginia Central Railroad.

Nov. 20. USG at New York City.

Nov. 21. C.S.A. Gen. John B. Hood advanced into Tenn.

Nov. 23. USG at Washington consulted with Secretary of War Edwin M. Stanton.

Nov. 24. USG returned to City Point and instructed Maj. Gen. George H. Thomas to move against Hood.

Nov. 25. USG requested the removal of Maj. Gen. William S. Rosecrans from command in Mo. He also conferred with Maj. Gen. George G. Meade about operations at Petersburg.

Nov. 27. USG encouraged Thomas to take the offensive against Hood.

Nov. 28. USG again requested Rosecrans's replacement.

Nov. 29.   USG conferred with Maj. Gen. Benjamin F. Butler and Rear Admiral David D. Porter about the expedition to capture Fort Fisher and Wilmington, N.C.

Nov. 30.   USG proposed to place Maj. Gen. John Pope in command of the Military Div. of the Mo., making a formal request to President Abraham Lincoln on Dec. 7.

Nov. 30.   Hood failed to break U.S. lines during the battle of Franklin, Tenn., and Maj. Gen. John M. Schofield withdrew toward Nashville during the night.

Dec. 1.   USG arranged relief for U.S. prisoners of war in the South.

Dec. 2.   USG requested Stanton to relieve Rosecrans, and again suggested that Thomas take the offensive.

Dec. 3.   USG planned an expedition down the Weldon Railroad which started on Dec. 7 under command of Maj. Gen. Gouverneur K. Warren.

Dec. 5.   USG again suggested offensive movements to Thomas.

Dec. 6.   USG ordered Thomas to attack Hood.

Dec. 7.   USG informed Stanton that it might be necessary to relieve Thomas.

Dec. 8.   USG directed Maj. Gen. Henry W. Halleck to issue orders relieving Thomas, suspending the order later in the day.

Dec. 9.   USG informed Thomas that he had suspended the order for his relief.

Dec. 10.   USG directed Maj. Gen. Edward O. C. Ord to be prepared for a possible C.S.A. attack north of the James River.

Dec. 10.   Sherman's army emerged near Savannah, Ga.

Dec. 11.   USG pressed Thomas to attack Hood.

Dec. 13.   USG sent Maj. Gen. John A. Logan to Nashville with orders to relieve Thomas.

Dec. 13.   Sherman reached the sea, capturing Fort McAllister, Ga.

Dec. 14. USG started from City Point for Nashville to oversee operations and reached Washington the following day. He stopped there after learning that Thomas had attacked Hood.

Dec. 15–16. Thomas won the battle of Nashville, virtually destroying Hood's army.

Dec. 17. USG (at Burlington) instructed Logan not to continue to Nashville.

Dec. 18. USG at Washington decided not to bring Sherman's army to City Point by water because of lack of transportation; instead, Sherman would march northward through the Carolinas.

Dec. 19. USG at City Point informed Sherman about rumors that C.S.A. President Jefferson Davis was in poor health.

Dec. 20. USG testified before the Joint Committee on the Conduct of the War concerning the battle of the Crater.

Dec. 20. C.S.A. forces evacuated Savannah and Sherman presented the city to Lincoln for Christmas on Dec. 22.

Dec. 22. USG ill.

Dec. 24. USG arranged to send blankets and clothing to U.S. prisoners in Richmond.

Dec. 25. Frederick Dent Grant, USG's son, arrived at City Point for a visit, returning home on Jan. 1.

Dec. 25. Butler failed to capture Fort Fisher and returned to Hampton Roads, Va., even though USG had directed him to begin siege operations if the attack failed.

Dec. 28. Lincoln issued a pass to Francis P. Blair, Sr., to travel to Richmond on a peace mission to Davis. Blair finally conferred with Davis on Jan. 12 with inconclusive results.

Dec. 29. USG at Fort Monroe.

Dec. 30. USG prepared to send a second expedition against Fort Fisher and Wilmington under the command of Bvt. Maj. Gen. Alfred H. Terry. He also directed that U.S. forces hold Fort Smith, Ark.

1865

JAN. 2. USG continued preparations for the second expedition to
Fort Fisher, planning to embark troops by Jan. 6.

JAN. 3. USG instructed Terry about the expedition to Fort Fisher.

JAN. 4. USG requested Stanton to relieve Butler from command,
and, upon learning that Stanton had left for Savannah, asked
Lincoln on Jan. 6. The following day Ord replaced Butler as
commander of the Dept. of Va. and N.C.

JAN. 4. USG directed Maj. Gen. Edward R. S. Canby to move
against Mobile.

JAN. 4. USG thanked the citizens of Philadelphia for giving him a
furnished house.

JAN. 5. USG at Fort Monroe to see off the Fort Fisher expedition,
spending the night at Norfolk.

JAN. 6. USG instructed Sherman to organize Negro troops to garrison forts and islands along the coast of Ga. and S.C.

JAN. 7. USG decided to transfer Schofield and his corps from Tenn.
for duty in N.C.

JAN. 8. USG directed Maj. Gen. Irvin McDowell to move into Mexico if used by C.S.A. forces as a base of operations.

JAN. 10. USG arranged to buy property in Mo. owned by his
brother-in-law John C. Dent for back taxes.

JAN. 13. U.S. forces landed near Fort Fisher, capturing the fort on
Jan. 15.

JAN. 15. USG continued to seek means to provide relief for U.S.
prisoners in the South.

JAN. 17. USG learned of the capture of Fort Fisher and immediately
recommended Terry for promotion.

JAN. 18. USG informed Halleck that he believed Thomas incapable
of directing rapid offensive movements.

JAN. 20. USG traveled to Washington to confer the following day
with Halleck and Stanton about future operations.

JAN. 21.   USG at Annapolis Junction, Md., agreed to accept Robert Todd Lincoln, the President's son, on his staff with the rank of capt.

JAN. 21.   USG sent Maj. Gen. Lewis Wallace on a mission to Tex. to determine if C.S.A. forces might surrender in the region.

JAN. 21.   USG authorized negotiations to arrange for the exchange of all prisoners.

JAN. 23.   USG at City Point urged the confirmation of Meade as maj. gen. Confirmation came on Feb. 2.

JAN. 24.   C.S.A. rams moved down the James River to attack City Point. The attempt failed. USG requested the relief of the U.S. Navy commander on the James because he failed to take precautions even after a warning of C.S.A. plans on Jan. 21.

JAN. 26.   USG decided to visit Fort Fisher accompanied by Schofield and Asst. Secretary of the Navy Gustavus V. Fox, leaving Hampton Roads the following day.

JAN. 31.   USG returned to City Point to find three informal C.S.A. peace emissaries, a result of Blair's discussions with Davis.

FEB. 1.   USG recommended that the President meet the C.S.A. peace emissaries, and Lincoln held an unproductive conference at Hampton Roads on Feb. 3.

FEB. 2.   USG continued negotiations for the exchange of prisoners, and instructed Ord to examine ways to attack Richmond.

FEB. 4.   USG informed Stanton that he did not want to begin final offensive operations at Petersburg until Schofield and Sherman were in place in N.C. USG also directed Meade to move west of Petersburg the following day.

FEB. 5.   USG completed arrangements to begin exchanging prisoners.

FEB. 5–7.   U.S. forces extended the siege lines west of Petersburg during the battle of Hatcher's Run.

FEB. 6.   USG directed Meade not to attack entrenched positions.

FEB. 8. USG renewed instructions to Sheridan to attempt to cut the Virginia Central Railroad and the James River Canal.

FEB. 9. USG left City Point, arriving in Washington the following day.

FEB. 11. USG testified before the Joint Committee on the Conduct of the War about Butler's failure to take Fort Fisher.

FEB. 12. USG at Fort Monroe on his return to City Point.

FEB. 13. USG informed that the government was having difficulty raising enough money to pay the army.

FEB. 16. USG arranged to supply Sherman's army when it arrived in N.C.

FEB. 17. Sherman captured Columbia, S.C., forcing C.S.A. evacuation of Charleston which U.S. forces occupied the following day.

FEB. 20. USG instructed Sheridan to prepare a cav. raid and ordered a one hundred gun salute in honor of the occupation of Columbia and Charleston.

The Papers of Ulysses S. Grant
November 16, 1864–February 20, 1865

To Maj. Gen. Henry W. Halleck

City Point 8 p. m
Novr 16th 1864

MAJ. GENL H W HALLECK
CHF OF STAFF

If Major Macree has been tried and found wanting I do not want him [pl]aced on duty. Knowing him when I first entered the army [and] receiving a letter from him requesting to be placed on duty I referred it with the endorsement you received. I never served with the Major therefore know nothing of his qualifications

U S GRANT
Lt Genl

Telegram received (at 8:10 P.M.), DNA, RG 107, Telegrams Collected (Bound); copies, *ibid.*, Telegrams Received in Cipher; *ibid.*, RG 108, Letters Sent; DLC-USG, V, 45, 70, 107. On Nov. 12, 1864, Maj. Gen. Henry W. Halleck wrote to USG. "On presenting Major Macrae's letter, with your endorsement, to the Adjt Genl., I was informed that the Major had been tried in several positions, as mustering, disbursing, comg a post, &c., and found to be worse than useless in each, and that the Dept would be embarrassed by his services in any position whatever. I have no personal acquaintance with the Major beyond a single interview, but from all I can learn, he would be troublesome in almost any command. He has written to the War Dept several times for a position, but the Secty does not seem inclined to give him one. I presume, however, that he will put him on some duty if you particularly desire it, and will designate what post you wish him to have." ALS, DNA, RG 108, Letters Sent (Press).

On Oct. 17, Maj. Nathaniel C. Macrae, Cincinnati, wrote to USG. "You may be surprised to find me writing to you on business wholly interesting to myself. I presume to do this upon our former association. I was 'retired' in 1861 very much against my inclination, & although on duty since, at long intervals, I find myself not at ease. I desire to perform *duty* as long as I hold a commission. This letter, though private is intended to request you to order me on duty. I can perform duty as well now as I could before this war. I would prefer duty in this Dept: with this place as my home. 1st. To report to Genl. Hooker as inspector of Hospitals &c—2d. To command this city or Newport & Covington—3d. To command some Fort on the Sea board or Lakes—as Ft Niagara or the Forts below Detroit. 4th. To be Supt. Rcg Service West. And, there is a Board in this city of U S. officers & Surgeons, Genl. Slemones is presiding over this board; upon which I might be placed. with some interest to the Service. I beleive this

Board examines officers & Soldiers as to their capacity for Service. My going on duty will not, I think, prove injurious to the public interest. I desire to say—I find my expenses so great—incident to increased price of provisions & expense of my children, as to make it my duty to myself, and, to my children and to save my feelings towards my country, *to ask for duty*. If I ask for what should not be given me please forget that I ventured this presumption. Offering you my sincere congratulations on your own successes . . ." ALS, *ibid.*, Letters Received. On Oct. 24, USG endorsed this letter. "Forwarded to Maj. Gn. Halleck, Chief of Staff of the Army. I would be very glad to have Maj. Ma[cra]e assigned to duty if his services can be made useful." AES, *ibid.* Macrae, USMA 1826, was appointed to serve on a military commission in Dec., 1864.

To Maj. Gen. John A. Dix

(Cipher)   Nov. 178th *1864*. 8 *o'clock*, 30 A *M*.
MAJ. GN. DIX, NEW YORK,

If you can spare abo a regiment of regulars order them to report to Gn. Wallace in Baltimore. You need not send any of the regulars to City Point.

U. S. GRANT
Lt. Gn.

ALS (telegram sent), CSmH; telegram received (sent from Baltimore), DNA, RG 393, Dept. of the East, Hd. Qrs., Letters Received. *O.R.*, I, xliii, part 2, 644. On Nov. 18, 1864, Maj. Gen. John A. Dix, New York City, telegraphed to USG. "The 18th and 11th U. S. infantry were about to embark when I received your telegram of this morning. They have together 600 men As the transportation was provided I thought best not to separate them and I have ordered them both to report to Gen Wallace at Baltimore The steamer will touch at Ft Monroe. The 14th infantry—aggregate 375 men—was to embark tomorrow for City Point; I detain it for your orders. I can spare it." Telegram received (at 5:00 P.M.), DNA, RG 107, Telegrams Collected (Bound); (at Burlington, N. J., 8:00 P.M.) *ibid.*, RG 108, Letters Received; copies, *ibid.*, RG 107, Telegrams Received in Cipher; *ibid.*, RG 393, Dept. of the East, Telegrams Sent. *O.R.*, I, xliii, part 2, 645.

To Edwin M. Stanton

(Cipher)   Burlington [*Nov. 19, 1864, 1:30* P.M.]
HON. E. M. STANTON, SEC. OF WAR

I intend to go to New start to New York at 3 p. m. If there is any reason by for my not going please telegraph me, or if you think

I should be at the front let me know and I will get there as fast as possible. As any train I would have to take from here to Washington starts from New York I would likely get there as soon from the latter place as from here.

U. S. GRANT
Lt. Gn.

ALS (telegram sent), CSmH; telegram received (at 2:00 P.M.), DNA, RG 107, Telegrams Collected (Bound). *O.R.*, I, xlii, part 3, 658. On Nov. 19, 1864, 2:15 P.M., Secretary of War Edwin M. Stanton telegraphed to USG. "~~Your telegram just received.~~ There ~~is a~~No reason why you should not go to New York. Let me have your address there." ALS (telegram sent), DNA, RG 107, Telegrams Collected (Bound); telegram received, *ibid.*, RG 108, Letters Received. At 7:30 A.M., USG had telegraphed to W. H. Gatzen, Camden and Amboy Railroad. "I would like to go to New York on the train which passes Burlington at 1.28 p. m. taking my family with me. Will return on train leaving New York at 12 m on Monday [*Nov. 21*]." ALS (telegram sent), CSmH.

On Nov. 17, 9:00 A.M., USG, City Point, telegraphed to Maj. Gen. Henry W. Halleck. "I leave this morning for Burlington N. J. Will have with me a Cipher operator." ALS (telegram sent), *ibid.*; telegram received (at 9:50 A.M.), DNA, RG 107, Telegrams Collected (Bound); *ibid.*, Telegrams Collected (Unbound). *O.R.*, I, xlii, part 3, 632. On the same day, USG telegraphed to Maj. Gen. George G. Meade. "Please telegraph me in cipher any thing important that may occur in my absence" Telegram received, DNA, RG 393, Army of the Potomac, Cav. Corps, Letters Received; copies (2), Meade Papers, PHi. *O.R.*, I, xlii, part 3, 632.

On Nov. 18, 4:00 P.M., Stanton telegraphed to USG. "Please ~~make it~~ come this way if possible on your return" ALS (telegram sent), DNA, RG 107, Telegrams Collected (Bound); telegram received, *ibid.*, RG 108, Letters Received. At 8:30 P.M., USG telegraphed to Stanton. "I will be in Washington Teusday morning. Will go to New York with my family and remain until Monday." ALS (telegram sent), CSmH; telegram received (on Nov. 19, 11:00 A.M.), DNA, RG 107, Telegrams Collected (Bound). *O.R.*, I, xlii, part 3, 638.

To Maj. Gen. Philip H. Sheridan

Burlington N. J. Nov. 19th/64 [*9:00* A.M.]

MAJ. GEN SHERIDAN, NEWTOWN VA.

It is reported from Richmond that Early has been recalled from the valley.[1] If you are satisfyied this is so send the 6th Corps to City Point without delay. If your Cavalry can cut the Va. Central road now is the time to do it.

U. S. GRANT
Lt. Gn

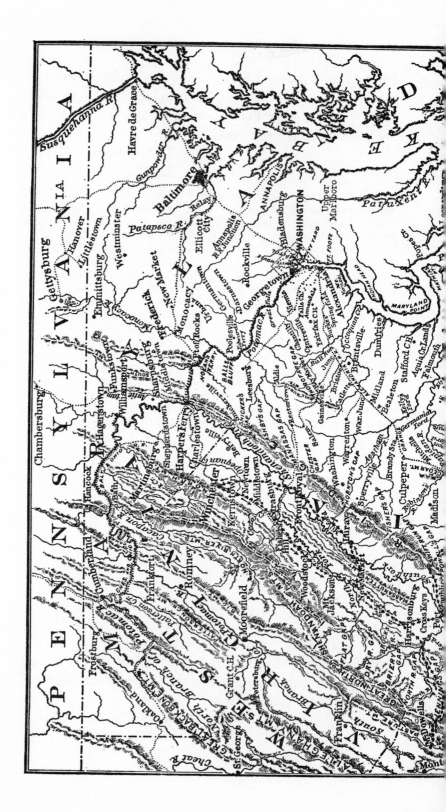

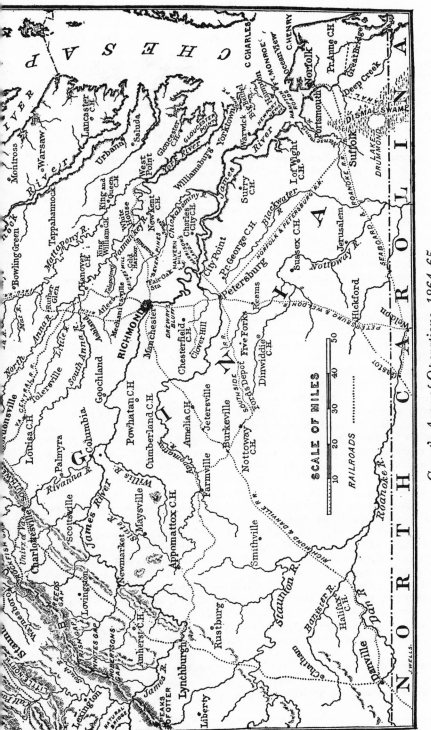

Grant's Area of Operations, 1864–65

From Memoirs (*revised ed.; New York, 1909*), II, between pp. 136–37

ALS (telegram sent), CSmH; copies, DLC-USG, V, 45, 70, 107; DNA, RG 108, Letters Sent. *O.R.*, I, xliii, part 2, 645.

On Nov. 12, 1864, 10:00 P.M., Maj. Gen. Philip H. Sheridan, Kernstown, Va., telegraphed to USG. "Yesterday evening the enemys cavalry made a demonstration on my front south of Newtown and my scouts reported a large Infantry force having moved down the pike to Middletown with the intention of attacking—This morning I had everything ready, but no attack was made—About one p m moved Custer's Div. of cavalry up the back road and the middle road. Pennington's Brigade met two Brigades of Rosser's cavalry on the back road, charged them, and drove them at a run, four or five miles and across Cedar Creek capturing some prisoners—While this was going on Genl Powell's Division moved on the Front Royal pike and thence across towards Middletown—At Nineveh he met Lomax' cavalry, increased to what is called 'John Morgans cavalry, charged it, captured all of Lomaxs Artillery, two pieces with caissons horses, Artillery men &c, and his ammunition train, and ran his cavalry up the Luray Valley for a distance of eight or nine miles—One Brigade of Merritts Division moved up the pike late this evening but nothing important occurred. Col Dudleys Brigade of the Nineteenth corps moved out to demonstrate in this cavalry movement, also some sharpshooters of the Sixth corps Our losses are very slight—I have to regret the loss of Col Hull of Penningtons Brigade who was killed while gallantly leading a charge.—Powell captured fourteen 14 commissioned officers two hundred 200 privates and two 2 battle flags, killed several officers and brought in thirty five wounded. As yet I have seen no Infantry, and think the report of the Scouts untruthful" Telegram received (on Nov. 13, 7:15 A.M.), DNA, RG 107, Telegrams Collected (Bound); copies (2), *ibid.*, Telegrams Received in Cipher; (2) DLC-Philip H. Sheridan. Printed as received on Nov. 13, 7:00 P.M., in *O.R.*, I, xliii, part 1, 36; *ibid.*, I, xliii, part 2, 611. On Nov. 13, Lt. Col. Theodore S. Bowers telegraphed to USG. "Sheridan reports that he today sent Custars Division to look after Enemys Cavalry that hung round his front last Evening—Penningtons Brigade met two (2) Brigades of Rossers Cavalry, Charged & drove them five (5) miles and across Cedar Creek capturing some prisoners. Genl Perrell met Lennox's Cavalry, drove it Eight or nine (9) miles up Lunay Valley Capturing two (2) Guns all he had with Caissons horses and Artillerymen, Ammunition train, fourteen (14) Commissioned officers, Two hundred (200) Privates, Two (2) Battle Flags Killed several officers & brought in thirty five (35) wounded, our loss slight—Gen Thomas reports that Hatch finds the Enemy still in force in their position—Shoal Creek still very high—Smith not yet heard from." Telegram received, CtY. On Nov. 14, 11:00 A.M., Sheridan telegraphed to USG. "The reconnoissance made by the Cavalry yesterday enables me to give you definite information of the recent movement of the enemy here—Early moved with whole army from New Market on the same day that I moved back from Cedar Creek under the impression, so prisoners say, that a large number of the troops here had been sent north on account of the election. He came down to the north side of Cedar Creek on the 12th—The information given by my scouts was correct in every particular —Earlys cavalry having been driven in and broken on both flanks, he fell back in great haste on the night of the 12th inst and according to reports of prisoners has gone back to New Market—Gen Torbert pushed on to Strasburg yesterday driving the enemy out of town and up to Fishers hill—The cavalry fight of Powell and Custar was very creditable—Merritt was but slightly engaged after dark with the enemys Infantry on the pike   The result of the days operation was twenty commissioned officers, 225 men, two pieces of artillery three Caissons, two battle flags and four ammunition wagons captured and the complete rout of the enemys cavalry—Our loss was only two killed seven wounded and seven captured—The railroad will soon be finished to the crossing of the Opequan Creek, I can then get long forage for our animals—They are now suffering very much from the cold weather & insufficiency of food" Telegram received (at 8:30 P.M.), DNA, RG 107, Telegrams Collected (Bound); copies, *ibid.*, Telegrams Received in Cipher; (2) DLC-Philip H. Sheridan. Printed as received at 10:00 P.M. in *O.R.*, I, xliii, part 1, 36; *ibid.*, I, xliii, part 2, 624. On Nov. 15, 12:30 P.M., Sheridan, Newtown, Va., telegraphed to USG. "Earlys Army did not stop at Fishers Hill, but continued its retreat during the night of the 12th back to New Market. From the report of prisoners and citizens the Army was stampeded by the attack of our cavalry on his extreme flanks, I regret that I could not get sufficient positive information of Early's presence but all the prisoners captured early in the day were cavalry men & were positive that no infantry had come this way   This incorrect information was true as far as they knew, as they had [tr]aveled on the side roads, and could not see any of the infantry—Citizens report Imboden, Morgans, cavalry about twelve hundred strong as the only organized reinforcement that Early has received; but that the Army has been increased by conscripts detailed men, and men of the second class farmers   They report Earlys Army very much increased in numbers—" Telegram received (at 10:30 P.M.), DNA, RG 107, Telegrams Collected (Bound); copies (marked as sent at 12:30 A.M.), *ibid.*, Telegrams Received in Cipher; (2) DLC-Philip H. Sheridan. Printed as sent at 12:30 A.M. in *O.R.*, I, xliii, part 1, 37; *ibid.*, I, xliii, part 2, 630.

On Nov. 20, 1:00 A.M., Sheridan, Kernstown, telegraphed to Brig. Gen. John A. Rawlins. "There has been none of the enemys force within reach in my front for a distance of forty (40) miles since the last advance of Early and his hasty retreat—The report in reference to Earlys army having left the Valley entirely, is somewhat contradictory. I will comply with the request of the Genl in chief as soon as I can definitely ascertain the true condition of affairs—Steps have been taken to ascertain the facts in the case" Telegram received, DNA, RG 107, Telegrams Collected (Bound); (at 2:45 P.M.) *ibid.*, RG 108, Letters Received; copies, *ibid.*, RG 107, Telegrams Received in Cipher; (2) DLC-Philip H. Sheridan. *O.R.*, I, xliii, part 2, 649. On Nov. 21, 9:00 A.M., Sheridan telegraphed to Rawlins. "I haven't any positive information—reports are very conflicting—It was reported to me on the 17th that Earlys whole army moved from New Market to Staunton—On the 18th I heard that only one Division moved (Breckenridges old Division commanded by Horton [*Wharton*]) and it moved to East Tennessee—On the 18th I received a letter from Early at New Market—Yesterday I heard that Earlys army was moving to Richmond then again I heard that he was going to Staunton to go into winter quarters—None of my scouts sent out have returned   they must have been captured—I moved out this morning all the cavalry and will be able to ascertain definitely—Kershaws Div I think is not more than 5000 strong   it must have made very fast time to have gotten to Richmond—It was at Middletown on the 12th and ᵗʰleft that place on the night of the 12th—From Middletown to Staunton is 77 miles which it had to march—My impression is that Early has gone to Staunton and will probably go to Richmond with a portion of his troops—If such is the case I will move the 6th corps as rapidly as possible. I would like to be a little more certain than I am at present before I send it off" Telegram received, DNA, RG 107, Telegrams Collected (Bound); (2—at 8:30 P.M.) *ibid.*, RG 108, Letters Received; copies, *ibid.*, RG 107, Telegrams Received in Cipher; (2) DLC-Philip H. Sheridan. *O.R.*, I, xliii, part 2, 653. On Nov. 22, 10:00 A.M., Rawlins telegraphed to Sheridan. "Genl Butler reports that Kershaws division has come into his front and that deserters report that another division of Earlys command is coming. The latter he does not believe—Deserters who come into Genl Meades front state that it was reported in Petersburg that Earlys command was returning to Richmond" Telegram received (at 11:10 A.M.), DLC-USG, V, 70; DNA, RG 107, Telegrams Collected (Bound); copies, *ibid.*, Telegrams Received in Cipher; *ibid.*, RG 108, Letters Sent; DLC-USG, V, 45, (misdated Nov. 23) 70, 107; (misdated Nov. 23) Rawlins Papers, ICHi. *O.R.*, I, xliii, part 2, 658.

1. On Nov. 18, 11:00 A.M., Rawlins telegraphed to Sheridan. "The following is sent for your information: Scouts who left Richmond yesterday afternoon state that the day before all the transportation that could be spared from other railroads was put upon the Central, and sent North; that wagon trains were also sent in that direction, and that it was understood in the City that these preparations were made for the return of Early's forces. Are there any ~~Jno~~ indications in your front confirmatory of this" Telegram sent, Rawlins Papers, ICHi; telegram received (at 3:00 P.M.), DNA, RG 107, Telegrams Collected (Bound); *ibid.*, Telegrams Collected (Unbound). *O.R.*, I, xliii, part 2, 641. At 4:20 P.M., Rawlins telegraphed to USG. "Scouts who left Richmond yesterday afternoon report that the day before all the rolling stock that could be spared from other railroads was put on the Central, and sent North; that wgon trains were sent in the same direction; and that it was understood in the city that they were sent for the purpose of bringing Early back. There was very sharp picket firing last night along the Bermuda front ~~A rebel~~ ~~picket~~ ~~informed~~ Gen. Graham ~~learned~~ ~~from~~ was told by a rebel picket to-day that the enemy tried to attack this line last night, but his men would not come up, and that the attack was deferred until to-night also, that Lee intended to evacuate Petersburg to-night." Telegram sent, Rawlins Papers, ICHi; telegram received (at 7:50 P.M.), DNA, RG 107, Telegrams Collected (Unbound). *O.R.*, I, xliii, part 2, 640–41.

To Brig. Gen. John A. Rawlins

(Cipher)   Burlington N. J.
                                                                 Nov. 19th/64 [*11:30* A.M.]

GN J. A. RAWLINS, CITY POINT,
I left directions for the troops to be in readiness to move in case the enemy should detach largely to the South.[1] Should such a thing occur telegraph me and I will get back as fast as steam can carry me. If it is true that Early is going back it behooves Gen. Meade

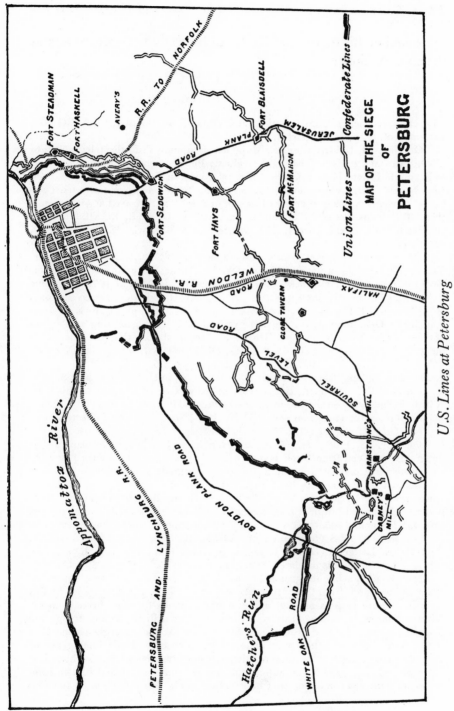

U.S. Lines at Petersburg

From *William Conant Church, Ulysses S. Grant . . . (New York, 1897), between pp. 308–9*

to be well on his guard and Butler to be ready to reinforce him at the shortest notice.

U. S. GRANT

Lt. Gn

ALS (telegram sent), CSmH; copies, DLC-USG, V, 45, 70, 107; DNA, RG 108, Letters Sent. *O.R.*, I, xlii, part 3, 658–59.

On Nov. 18, 1864, 1:00 P.M., Maj. Gen. Benjamin F. Butler telegraphed to USG. "All quiet to day   Last night Grahams Pickets were driven in ~~to~~ on ~~front of~~ Bermuda Front   Have reinforced him by a veteran Brigade   Troops all back from North" ALS (telegram sent), DNA, RG 107, Telegrams Collected (Unbound); telegram received (marked as sent at 2:00 P.M., received at 4:00 P.M.), *ibid.*, Telegrams Collected (Bound); (at 8:00 P.M.) *ibid.*, RG 108, Letters Received. *O.R.*, I, xlii, part 3, 652. See telegram to Edwin M. Stanton, Nov. 15, 1864.

On Nov. 19, 3:00 P.M., Butler telegraphed to USG. "All quiet to this hour. The enemy have got a portion of the picket line near Ware bottom church but have made no further advance" Telegram received, DNA, RG 107, Telegrams Collected (Unbound); (at 8:00 P.M.) *ibid.*, RG 108, Letters Received; copy, *ibid.*, RG 107, Telegrams Received in Cipher. *O.R.*, I, xlii, part 3, 664. At 5:00 P.M., Brig. Gen. John A. Rawlins telegraphed to USG transmitting a telegram of 11:00 A.M. from Maj. Gen. George G. Meade stating that the lines were quiet. Telegram received (at 6:15 P.M.), DNA, RG 107, Telegrams Collected (Unbound); *ibid.*, RG 108, Letters Received; copy, *ibid.*, RG 107, Telegrams Received in Cipher. Printed as received at 6:30 P.M. in *O.R.*, I, xlii, part 3, 659.

On Nov. 21, 2:30 P.M., Butler telegraphed to USG. "All quiet to this hour A little Picket firing on the Bermuda line last night. Raining very heavily   Roads impassible" ALS (telegram sent), DNA, RG 107, Telegrams Collected (Unbound). *O.R.*, I, xlii, part 3, 676.

On Nov. 23, 1:00 P.M., Meade telegraphed to Rawlins. "I forward a despatch just received from Genl. Hancock which is all the intelligence I have to communicate at present. Johnson has a So. Ca—brigade in his Division formerly commanded by Evans now by Elliott.—If any troops are detached by Lee it would probably be So. Ca—& Georgia troops   If they have been sent they have undoubtedly gone by Rail & intelligence of their departure ought to be received thro our Richmond scouts. Have you any information of the probable return of the Lt. Genl—?" ALS (telegram sent), DNA, RG 393, Army of the Potomac, Cav. Corps, Letters Sent; telegram received, *ibid.*, RG 108, Letters Received. The enclosure is misdated Nov. [11] in *O.R.*, I, xlii, part 3, 600. On Nov. 23, 1:30 P.M., Rawlins telegraphed to USG. "General Meade forwards here the following despatch from Genl Hancock, and says it is all the intelligence he has to communicate at present, that Johnson has a South Carolina brigade in his Division, formerly commanded by Evans, now by Elliott. If any troops are detached by Lee it would probably be South Carolina and Georgia troops, that if they have been sent they have undoubtedly gone by rail and intelligence of their departure ought to be received through our Richmond scouts. I have had no information from General Butler, suppose you have instructed him to communicate with you direct and that he is acting in obedience thereto,   I have informed General Meade you will be here tomorrow." ALS (telegram sent), Rawlins Papers, ICHi; telegram received (at 6:15 P.M.), DNA, RG 107, Telegrams Collected (Bound); *ibid.*, Telegrams Collected (Unbound). *O.R.*, I, xlii, part 3, 686. Another enclosure is *ibid.*, pp. 686–87.

1. See letters to Maj. Gen. Benjamin F. Butler and to Maj. Gen. George G. Meade, Nov. 15, 1864.

To Maj. Gen. Henry W. Halleck

(Cipher)　　　　　　　　　　　*New-York*, Nov. 20th *1864* [*9:30* P.M.]

MAJ. GEN. HALLECK, WASHINGTON

Dispatches from City Point, making it evident that much of Early's force is going to Richmond, I think it advisable to send the 6th Corps there at once. One Division of Cavalry should also go unless they can get through to cut the Central road & canal.

U. S. GRANT
Lt. Gen.

ALS (telegram sent on Astor House stationery), CSmH; telegram received (on Nov. 21, 1864, 12:25 A.M.), DNA, RG 107, Telegrams Collected (Bound). *O.R.*, I, xlii, part 3, 665; *ibid.*, I, xliii, part 2, 648.

On Nov. 20, 11:20 A.M., Brig. Gen. John A. Rawlins telegraphed to USG, sending copies to Secretary of War Edwin M. Stanton and to Maj. Gen. Philip H. Sheridan. "Our Agent who left Richmond at 5 o'clock last evening brings the following information: 'Kershaws Division began to arrive in Richmond on friday afternoon at 4 p m—Some of it passed through during the night and also yesterday—By the rough calculation of citizens who send us the information it was supposed that the Division amounted to nearly 10,000 men—The fact of its arrival is undoubted—The markets in Richmond yesterday were filled with Kershaws men and one of our agents a market man had his stall robbed by them —the troops passed through to the South side—They said themselves that they were going to Chesterfield Citizens in Richmond in talking about it said they were on their way to Longstreet—Their arrival gave rise to considerable discussion in Richmond as to whether Lee expected to attack or to be attacked— For two or three days an order has been in force that the Central Road would not be open except for military purposes It is reported in Richmond that the greater part of Sheridans forces have arrived here, That the first of his regiments began to debark on the north side of the James on thursday last, that Sheridan himself has remained in the valley with a small part of his army Yesterday afternoon it was reported in Richmond that more troops would come from the valley but whether this rested upon any fact other than that the order in regard to the Central RR. is still in force is not known it was also reported in

Richmond that such of Earlys men as remain in the valley were to fall back to Mount Jackson and go into winter quarters there.' More torpedoes have been placed in front of Fort Darling" Telegram received (marked as sent at 1:30 P.M., received at 3:00 P.M.), DNA, RG 107, Telegrams Collected (Bound); *ibid.*, Telegrams Collected (Unbound); copies, *ibid.*, Telegrams Received in Cipher; (incomplete) Rawlins Papers, ICHi. Printed as sent at 1:30 P.M. in *O.R.*, I, xlii, part 3, 666. At 5:50 P.M., Maj. Gen. Benjamin F. Butler telegraphed to USG. "All remains quiet here—Kershaws Division passed Richmond Friday—Deserters report that two (2) Brigades of it are encamped at Chaffins farm and the rest of it at Chesterfield—It is possible there may be an attempt to break through our lines—we will endeavor to watch it. Richmond papers insist that Sheridans forces have arrived and are encamped on the North Side of the James—Have ordered two (2) regiments of Colored troops of the Ninth (9th) Corps to the Bermuda lines Have not sent back the two (2) regiments of Pennsylvania troops because of Kershaws movements—It is reported at Richmond that the remainder of Earlys troops have gone into winter quarters at Mount Jackson—We are in the midst of a very severe storm which has lasted thirty six (36) hours Roads nearly impassible" LS (telegram sent), DNA, RG 107, Telegrams Collected (Unbound); telegram received (marked as sent at 4:30 P.M., received at 8:00 P.M.), *ibid.*, Telegrams Collected (Bound); (on Nov. 21) *ibid.*, RG 108, Letters Received. Printed as sent at 4:20 P.M. in *O.R.*, I, xlii, part 3, 669.

On Nov. 21, Rawlins telegraphed to Butler and to Maj. Gen. George G. Meade. "Have you any information of any changes or movements of the Enemy in your front? If so please communicate the same to these Head Qrs." Telegram received (at 8:00 P.M.), DNA, RG 393, Army of the Potomac, Cav. Corps, Letters Received; copies (2), Meade Papers, PHi. *O.R.*, I, xlii, part 3, 673. At 7:50 P.M., Butler telegraphed to Rawlins. "I have no information of any change save what I have communicated by Telegraph to the Lt General that is to say that Kershaws dvision have come in our front and in front of Bermuda. Deserters report nothing else—I have sent you the Richmond papers of day but they have nothing—It is reported however that another division from Early is coming in on our extreme right—near Darby town Road but I think it is part of Kershaw" ALS (telegram sent), DNA, RG 107, Telegrams Collected (Unbound); telegram received, *ibid.*, RG 108, Letters Received. *O.R.*, I, xlii, part 3, 676. At 8:00 P.M., Meade telegraphed to Rawlins. "I have no information of any movement or change on my front. The Pickets on my extreme left reported un-usual running of cars last night on the South side Rail Road—trains reported moving apparently both ways into & out of Petersburgh—Deserters state a report was in circulation that Early's forces were returning to Richmond.—" ALS (telegram sent), DNA, RG 393, Army of the Potomac, Cav. Corps, Letters Received; telegram received, *ibid.*, RG 108, Letters Received. *O.R.*, I, xlii, part 3, 673.

On Nov. 22, 11:00 A.M., Meade telegraphed to Rawlins. "I have nothing to report this morning beyond the fact observed last night again of the constant running of trains on the Southside RR reported as before as apparently going both ways & stopping in the presumed vicinity of the enemys lines. I am unable to form any judgment from this report as to whether the enemy is reinforcing his right or sending away troops—Deserters report no movements but say it was generally understood Earlys troops were all running back." Telegram received, DNA, RG 108, Letters Received. Printed as sent at 1:25 P.M. in *O.R.*, I, xlii, part 3, 680. At 5:00 P.M., Butler telegraphed to USG. "All quiet—Two Divisions of Earlys men reported on the Darbytown Road" ALS (telegram sent), DNA, RG 107, Telegrams Collected (Unbound); telegram received, *ibid.*, Telegrams Collected (Bound). *O.R.*, I, xlii, part 3, 685.

To Mrs. Mary M. Bergholz

New-York, Nov. 20th *1864*

MRS. MAY M. BERGHOLZ,

I have just learned from Gen. Dix that your husband has been released and sent to City Point to see me. I at once telegraphed to the Provost Marshal at Baltim[ore] to stop him if it was not to late and to say to him that I would be in Washington on Teusday.[1] I fear however my dispatch will reach Baltimore too late to intercept him.

I arrived here with my family last night. Will remain until 2 P. m. to-morrow. So many persons are calling to see me that I can not get out. If you will call at the Aster House, Parlor and send your name to my room I will be glad to see you.

Gen. Dix was not aware of the arrest of your husband until he received my letter. Do you not see now that I have been able to befriend you? It iafforded me great pleasure though I was sorry you should need friendly aid. I am satisfied there was no reason why Mr. B. should be arrested.

Yours Truly
U. S. GRANT
Lt. Gn.

ALS (on Astor House stationery), DLC-USG, I, B. On Nov. 21, 1864, USG telegraphed to Brig. Gen. John A. Rawlins. "mister bergholtz has been sent to city Point to give me some information please entertain him at Hedqrs until eye get back" Telegram received (in cipher), DNA, RG 107, Telegrams Collected (Unbound). On Nov. 25, Lt. Col. Ely S. Parker issued Special Orders No. 136. "Brig. Gen. Patrick, Provost Marshal General &c., will order paid to W. R. Bergholz the sum of two hundred ($200) dollars, for information given the Lieutenant General, and secret services rendered the Government." Copies, DLC-USG, V, 57, 62, 63, 64.

1. Nov. 22.

To Edwin M. Stanton

———

Washington, D. C. Nov. 23d, *1864.*

THE HON. EDWIN M. STANTON
SECRETARY OF WAR
SIR.

I have the honor to submit the following list of Major and Brigadier Generals of Volunteers, whom I recommend to be mustered out of service. I do not, however, insist upon such action being taken, though of opinion, that the public interest, will be benefitted by it: Major General[*s*] Franz Sigel, John A. McClernand, Rob't H. Milroy, James S. Negley, John M. Palmer, James G. Blunt, Julius H. Stahel, Carl Schurz, Brigadier General[*s*] Henry H. Lockwood George W. Morell S. D. Sturgis N. B. Buford Ben Alvard Eleazer Paine, A. von Steinwehr, Thomas J. McKean, John Cook, Jacob G. Lauman, Speed S. Fry, Nathan Kimball, Max Weber, Neal Dow, Benjamin S. Roberts, Fitz Henry Warren, Henry D. Terry, Mason Brayman, Francis B. Spinola, Solomon Meredith, Alfred W. Ellet, Sullivan A. Meredith, Joseph F. Knipe, Frank S. Nickerson, Edward H. Hobson, Joseph T. Copeland, Thomas A. Rowley, Egbert B. Brown, Daniel Ullman, Alfred N. Duffie, Clinton B. Fisk, James H. Ledlie, Byron R. Pierce,

I also recommend the following Brigadier Generals, to be brought before the Retiring Board: Brigadier General[*s*] H. M. Judah, A. J. Slemmer, G. R. Paul,

Many of these Generals it might be advisable to notify, so as to give them the opportunity of *resigning if they elect to do so.* Conspicuous among this class I would name Maj. Gen. Jno. Palmer and Brig. Genl. Thomas J McKean. The former has rendered good service in the past, but unfortunately for his record threw up the command of an Army Corps in the presence of the enemy. The latter is only incapacitated by age from doing his duties well as a General. I understand he is fully conscious of this fact and has heretofore asked to be placed back on duty as paymaster. With regard to all the General Officers named in this list I am satisfied the good of the service will be advanced by their withdrawal from service.

Very respectfully
Your ob't serv't.
U. S. GRANT
Lieut. Gen'l.

LS, DNA, RG 94, Letters Received, 1361A 1864. This letter is transcribed without reproducing the original columnar format. On Nov. 23, 1864, Col. Edward D. Townsend wrote to USG. "I enclose a draft of a letter embracing the names of officers spoken of by you for muster out, this morning—I have put all the names in the list and if it was not your intention to include some of them, they can be stricken out. I also enclose a copy of the Special Orders issued to-day assigning certain Generals to duty—" ALS, *ibid.*, RG 108, Letters Received. The enclosed list included just those officers listed in USG's letter.

On March 23, 1865, USG wrote to Secretary of War Edwin M. Stanton. "The following named Officers, were among those recommended in my letter of date Nov, 23d 1864, for muster out of service   Major General[*s*] Franz Sigel James S, Negley   Brigadier General[*s*] Henry H, Lockwood   George W, Morell S, D, Sturgis   N. B. Buford   Ben. Alvord   Eleazer Paine   A, Von Steinwehr John Cook   Jacob G, Lauman   Speed S, Fry   Max Weber   Benjamin S, Roberts Fitz Henry Warren   Mason Brayman   Francis B, Spinola   Solomon Meredith Joseph F, Knipe   Alfred W, Ellett   Sullivan A, Meredith   Frank S, Nickerson Edward H, Hobson   Joseph T, Copeland   Thomas A, Rowley   Egbert B, Brown Daniel Ullman   Alfred N, Duffie   Byron R, Pierce" Copies, DLC-USG, V, 46, 75, 108; DNA, RG 108, Letters Sent. This letter was also in columnar format.

On Nov. 23, 1864, Governor Francis H. Peirpoint of Va. wrote to President Abraham Lincoln. "It would be a great relief to me to see you and Gen. Grant together for a short time. I think the object worth the request. I will await your decision at the Kirkwood House this P.M." Laurence C. Affron Autographs, winter, 1966–67. On the same day, Lincoln endorsed this letter. "My time is of indespensable importance to me now, but I will see Gov. Pierpoint with Gen. Grant *now* if ~~they~~ he calls—" *Ibid.* Lincoln, *Works* (*Supplement*), p. 267.

To Maj. Gen. George H. Thomas

[*Washington, D. C., Nov. 23, 1864*]

The bearer of this, Mr. Gier is a Union citizen of Ala. to whom I have furnished a pass to come and go at pleasure over our roads and rivers within your command. Mr. G. is very earnest and it is his desire to bring back to the Union all he can of his Southern brethren and especially those of his own state (Alabama). The principal object he has in view in travelling back and forth is to

forward this object. I would be pleased if you would extend to him
a pass to travel back and forth on our army Gunboats plying below
Bridgeport . . .

Josiah H. Benton sale, American Art Association, March 12–13, 1920; *The
Flying Quill: Autographs at Goodspeed's* (Jan.–April, 1959), no. 65. See Lincoln, *Works*, VIII, 112. On Jan. 26 and Feb. 6, 1865, Jean Joseph Giers, Decatur, Ala., and Nashville, wrote at length to USG discussing his efforts to restore
loyalty in northern Ala. ALS, DNA, RG 108, Letters Received. *O.R.*, I, xlix,
part 1, 590–92, 659. With his first letter, Giers enclosed a letter of Feb. 1 from
Governor Andrew Johnson of Tenn. to USG introducing and praising Giers.
Ibid., pp. 592–93. After the war, Giers wrote to Johnson and others about his
continuing efforts to serve the U.S. in Ala. *Ibid.*, I, xlix, part 2, 473–74, 485,
706; DLC-Andrew Johnson. On Nov. 14, Giers wrote a similar letter to USG.
ALS, DNA, RG 109, Union Provost Marshals' File of Papers Relating to Individual Civilians. On June 25, 1866, USG endorsed an application of Giers for
appointment as tax commissioner for Ala. "Mr. Giers is a man of undoubted
loyalty and ability, and rendered our army without recompense valuable services
during the war." Copies, *ibid.*, RG 56, Collector of Customs Applications; *ibid.*,
RG 108, Register of Letters Received. On Nov. 5, 1867, Giers wrote to USG
recommending Thomas N. Bailey for appointment to USMA. ALS, *ibid.*, RG 94,
Cadet Applications. Bailey was appointed a year later.

To Maj. Gen. Henry W. Halleck

(Cipher)   City Point Va. Nov. 24th *1864*. [*4:00* P.M.]
MAJ. GN. HALLECK, WASHINGTON

The President proposed sending Burnside to Ky. to relieve
Burbridge and I concented to it. On reflection I think it a bad selection. Burbridge should be removed and Thomas had better be
directed to find him employment elswhere and substitute a commander himself for Ky.

U. S. GRANT
Lt. Gn.

ALS (telegram sent), CSmH; telegram received (at 5:30 P.M.), DNA, RG
107, Telegrams Collected (Bound). *O.R.*, I, xlv, part 1, 1015.
   On Nov. 9, 1864, Governor Thomas E. Bramlette of Ky. wrote to USG.
"I have this day written to Maj Genl. W. T. Sherman requesting for important
reasons stated, the removal of Brevet Maj Genl. S. G. Burbridge from command
in the District of Kentucky. The disturbed condition of communications with
Genl. Sherman, and the necessity of immediate action occasion this letter; to
you, hoping that you will take action under the circumstances. All my ingenuity
and watchfulness have been taxed to the utmost for sometime to foil the evil

effects of Genl. Burbridges, weakness and mischeveous acts in this Military District. The importance of maintaining quiet in Kentucky ias indispensable to the
security of our noble armies down with Sherman, and securing the permanency
of his position you well understand. Genl. Burbridges course for some weeks has
been to irritate and exasperate the minds of the loyal people of Ky. His out-
rageous and indiscriminate arrests of persons purely on account of their favoring
the election of McClellan; treating as rebels all who are opposed to Mr. Lincolns,
re-election—threatening and bullying the Citizens—and menacing the Civil authorities and Officers of the State—laying unjust political restrictions upon the
business and necessary trade of the Country—seeking out inventions by which to
harrass, oppress and injure those who differ with him in politics, has produced
a very bad state of feeling which has required all my skill to keep from manifest-
ing itself in open violence. He keeps it up. Yesterday he arrested many Citizens
for no offence except the *disloyalty* as they term it of being opposed to Mr. Lincoln's re-election. He arrested and I am informed by letter has sent off to be carried
South of our lines, one of our prominent men—Genl. Jno B. Huston of Lexington
(formerly of Clarke County). The rumors are rife of many others to be sent to
glut political vengeance. In a word he is making more enemies to our safety than
much prudence can overcome. He has in various ways sought to provoke collision
with the Civil authorities, but in this I have uniformly foiled him; for no such
collision shall be brought about which I can prevent by any prudence, foresight
wisdom—or by any personal sacrifices. It would be too hazardous to the cause
of our Country for such an evil to occur, I will prevent it if in the power of man
in the exercise of a prudent action with a clear foresight of the evils. Genl.
Burbridge has not capacity to comprehend the evils which he is prompted to
provoke. He is instigated by men who do comprehend and intend them, and who
work upon his weakness through his vanity to accomplish them. He is wholly
unfit for any command where there is anything at stake, which requires either,
intellect, prudence firmness of purpose, justice or the manliness of the Soldier to
accomplish—Fearing that Maj Genl. Sherman may not get my communication
in time to save us from much injury I earnestly beseech you to interpose your
authority and arrest the malevolent acts which through the weakness and vanity
of Genl Burbridge, have been and are being inflicted upon the loyal Citizens of
your Native State" LS, DNA, RG 107, Letters Received from Bureaus. *O.R.*,
I, xxxix, part 3, 724–25. On Nov. 14, USG endorsed this letter. "Respectfully
forwarded to the Secretary of War. I do not know how far Gov. Bramlette ought
to be conciliated. But I have from the start mistrusted Gen. Burbridge's ability
and fitness for the place he now occupies. I had selected Gen. Ammon for the
command of Kentucky, and placed him there in orders. At the time however,
Gen. A. was engaged as member of a Court Martial which was likely to hold for
some weeks. Gen. Burbridge being available at the time was assigned to the temporary command and has managed to retain it ever since. I have had many unofficial complaints of Gen. Burbridge's course, and do think that the best interests of the service require that a sensible soldier, one perfectly free from prejudice
and party influence should be sent to relieve him. Gen. Dodge if not on other
duty, would make a suitable commander for Kentucky. I sent a staff officer to
Kentucky last week to investigate complaints, and before knowing that the
Governor of the State found Gen. Burbridge objectionable." ES, DNA, RG 107,
Letters Received from Bureaus. *O.R.*, I, xxxix, part 3, 725.

   On Nov. 28, T. S. Bell and U.S. District Judge Bland Ballard, Louisville,
wrote to USG. "There are various rumors respecting the supercedure of Brevet

Major General Burbridge in the command of the District of Kentucky, and while we are far from giving them credit, they have assumed a shape that renders it incumbent upon us to say something to you on the subject, This we owe to that duty of fidelity which we acknowledge is due to you from every loyal person. Under instructions from a telegram from the Secretary of War the undersigned waited upon you at the Galt House in this city and requested as a great means towards successful engineering of the policy of the Administration, in Kentucky, that General Burbridge should be retained in command in this District. We feel that it is due to ourselves to say that we have not been disappointed in our expectations from General Burbridge He has performed his difficult duties with energy, fidelity, discretion and wisdom. He is singularly just and kind in his disposition and in handling probably as refractory material as this continent holds, he has been eminently successfull The first signer of this paper has had unusual opportunities of knowing the minute details of the administrative acts of General Burbridge. He was appointed by the Union State Convention, Chairman of the State Executive committee and as such was brought into intimate intercourse with the working loyal men of every part of the state. As Surgeon of the Board of Enrolment of the 5th Congressional Dist. of the State he is intimate with the machinery of military affairs in the State, especially with the enrolment, drafting and enlistment of the able-bodied negroes and from both of these sources of knowledge for a reliable judgement, he has no hesitation in saying that loyalty in Kentucky enjoyed a motor force in Genl Burbridge that it could scarcely have received from any other quarter. That he has sometimes made mistakes is undoubtedly true, but it would be difficult to point out any one who has not. He has excited enmities because of his loyalty, in some quarters, and in other quarters, among a few loyal men by refusing to permit himself to be used as their tool. But as a patriot, a devoted enemy to the rebellion and as a military man thoroughly acquainted with the tortuous ways of things in Kentucky, he has been singularly free from errors His integrity is unsullied and he enjoys the love, the confidence and the devotion of loyal men of Kentucky, beyond any other Military man who has had command of this District., General Sherman only excepted. If this were not the case we should not only be willing but desirous for his removal We have not a particle of personal feeling in this matter. Our whole being is involved in the utter extinction of this rebellion and in the 1 complete triumph of the rights of all men We do not desire to see any one in a position of command and of influence who cannot aid in this great work, We feel that on our continent the battle now waged is a battle for all mankind and that upon its conclusion hang the future destinies of our race, And this brings us to the point that forms a part of our apology for this letter. As chairman of the State Executive Committee one of the signers of this letter is now preparing Kentucky for her final position in the struggle for freedom, He has called a convention of the loyal men of the state for the purpose of bringing all possible influence to bear upon our Congressmen and legislature to induce them to place Kentucky among the three fourths majority for an amendment of the Constitution forbidding involuntary servitude save for crime. As Chairman of this Committee he is in active intercourse with the prominent men of Kentucky, on the subjects and he does not know any one of these men who is not anxious that General Burbridge shall retain his position as commander of the District. He will be of infinite value to our great civic enterprise, and we wish to rivet Kentucky to her right position in this matter, because that will sweep the platter clean. With her in the majority we shall have twenty seven States, a three fourths majority including John Van Buren's 'erring sisters' Now, inasmuch as you greatly assisted us by placing General Burbridge in command of this District, we pray for your continued assistance in the great work before us? You should know us too well to suspect that we have any motive ~~in~~ for deceiving you. Our desire is for the triumph of the government, no matter what that triumph may do with us individually, and for that reason we could not ask for any personal benefit to any one, except for the benefit of the public interest General Burbridge is absent now upon a military expedition, and we have had no intercourse with him for some time, but whether he is present or absent we know that he is endeavoring to do his whole duty . . . P. S. We wish to add one thought to a mere reference made in the body of this letter. We spoke then of the refractory material which General Burbridge has had to manage, and we add the conviction that just in proportion to the faithful discharge of National duties in Ky by a military commander, in that ratio will be dissatisfaction, grumbling and complaint, and this, too, among some who profess to be loyal. Paul knew people of this kind in his day. He said 'all are not Israel who are of Israel.'" LS, DNA, RG 108, Letters Received.

On Dec. 2, 9:30 P.M., USG telegraphed to Secretary of War Edwin M. Stanton. "If you agree with me I would like that Thomas be directed to assign Couch to the command of Ky. The reports from there show conclusively that Burbridge should not be retained." ALS (telegram sent), Samuel M. Clement, Jr., Collection, PHi; telegram received (at 10:10 P.M.), DNA, RG 107, Telegrams Collected (Bound). O.R., I, xlv, part 2, 16. The word "there" is not in USG's hand; "Kentucky" appears instead in the telegram received. On Dec. 3, 10:00 A.M., Stanton telegraphed to USG. "Couch is ~~about the worst man we could select for Kentucky.~~ not a good administrative officer for Kentucky. I would prefer Stoneman to him. The President would like to see the reports about Burbridge to which you refer. Thesre ~~b~~ is no disposition to retain him ~~against~~ if there be any well grounded complaints but if the Military authority is surrendered to a sympathiser with Bramlette, ~~it will be as~~ Dr Breckenridge says it will be necessary to conquer Kentucky." ALS (telegram sent), DNA, RG 107, Telegrams Collected (Bound); telegram received, ibid., RG 108, Letters Received. O.R., I, xlv, part 2, 28.

To Maj. Gen. George H. Thomas

"Cipher"   City Point, Va. Nov. 24, 1864. [4:00 P.M.]
MAJ. GEN. THOMAS, NASHVILLE, TENN.

I send you the following proclamation from Beauregard just taken from Savannah paper of the 21st. Do not let Hoods[1] forces get off without punishment.

U. S. GRANT. Lieut. Gen.

"Corinth Nov. 18th via Selma Nov. 18."
"To the people of Georgia. Arise for the defence of your native

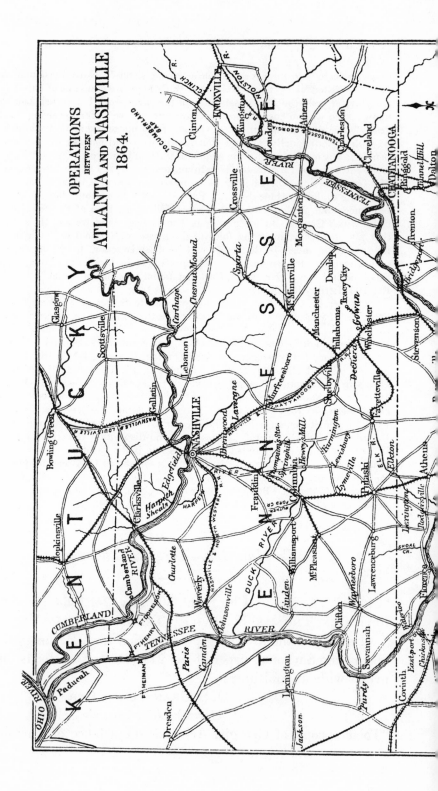

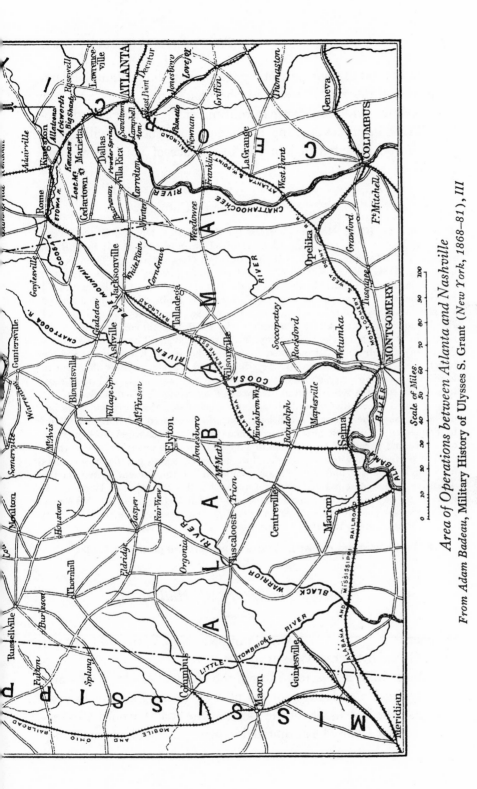

Area of Operations between Atlanta and Nashville

From Adam Badeau, Military History of Ulysses S. Grant (New York, 1868–81), III

soil. Rally around your patriotic government and gallant soldiers, obstruct and destroy all roads in Sherman's front, flank and rear and his Army will soon starve in your midst. Be confident and resolute. Trust in our overruling providence and success will crown your efforts. I hasten to join you in defence of your homes and fire-sides.

G. T. BEAUREGARD"
Gen'l. Com'd'g.

Telegram sent, ICHi; telegram received (at 5:40 P.M.), DNA, RG 107, Telegrams Collected (Bound). Printed as received on Nov. 25, 1864, in *O.R.*, I, xlv, part 1, 1014. On Nov. 25, 11:00 A.M., Maj. Gen. George H. Thomas telegraphed to USG. "Your dispatch of 4 P. M yesterday just recieved—Hoods entire army is in front of Columbia and so greatly outnumbers mine at this time that I am compelled to act on the defensive—None of Genl Smith's troops have arrived yet although they embarked at St Louis on tuesday last—The transportation of Hatch's and Grierson's Cavly was ordered by Genl Washburn I am told to be turned in at Memphis which has crippled the only Cavalry I have at this time— All of my Cavalry was dismounted to furnish horses to Kilpatrick's division which went with Genl Sherman My dismounted Cavalry is now detained in Louisville awaiting arms and horses horses are arriving slowly and arms have been detained some where enroute for more than a month. Genl Grierson has been delayed by conflicting orders in Kansas and from Memphis and it is impossible to say when he will reach here. Since being placed in charge of affairs in Tennessee I have lost nearly fifteen thousand men discharged by expiration of service and permitted to go home to Vote—My gain is probably twelve thousand of perfectly raw troops—So therefore as the enemy so greatly outnumbers me both in Infantry and Cavly I am compelled for the present to act on the defensive The moment I can get my Cavalry I will march against Hood and if Forrest can be reached he will be punished—" ALS (telegram sent), MH; telegram received (at 3:00 P.M.), DNA, RG 107, Telegrams Collected (Bound); (at 7:00 P.M.) *ibid.*, RG 108, Letters Received. *O.R.*, I, xlv, part 1, 1034.

1. In the telegram received, "Forrests" appeared in place of "Hoods."

To Maj. Gen. Henry W. Halleck

(Cipher)   City Point, Va, Nov. 25th *1864*. [*noon*]
MAJ. GEN. HALLECK, WASHINGTON,

Whilst in Washington I urged the removal of Rosecrans and the substitution of Dodge for his place. I would like you to urge this upon the President. In the Dept. of the Ark. I would also recommend that Canby be authorized to place Reynolds in command[1] and to put Steele in his place if he thinks the good of the service demands it. Steele I do not think quite equal to the efficient command of a Dept. whilst he is a first class commander of troops in battle. I would suggest leaving this change entirely to Canby's judgement

U. S. GRANT, Lt. Gn

ALS (telegram sent), CSmH; telegram received (at 12:30 P.M.), DNA, RG 107, Telegrams Collected (Bound). *O.R.*, I, xli, part 4, 672–73. On Nov. 25, 1864, 3:00 P.M., Maj. Gen. Henry W. Halleck telegraphed to USG. "Authority was given to Genl Canby some days ago to make such changes as he deemed best in Dept of Arkansas. Genl Thomas reports that Genl Dodge is well and available for duty." ALS (telegram sent), DNA, RG 107, Telegrams Collected (Bound); telegram received, *ibid.*; (at 5:00 P.M.) *ibid.*, RG 108, Letters Received. *O.R.*, I, xli, part 4, 673. At 6:00 P.M. and 7:30 P.M., USG telegraphed to Halleck. "I see no objection to Gen. Canby's recommendation to have Gen. Dana's command made into a Department. It embraces much territory and is as much a Department in command as either of the others composing Canby's Division." "I think it advisable to send orders to Mo. that all the troops coming from there shall receive their directions from Gen. Thomas and not listen to conflicting orders." ALS (telegrams sent), CSmH; telegrams received (at 6:00 P.M. and 7:30 P.M.), DNA, RG 107, Telegrams Collected (Bound). *O.R.*, I, xli, part 4, 673. The second is also *ibid.*, I, xlv, part 1, 1034.

1. On Nov. 15, 12:30 P.M., USG telegraphed to Halleck. "I would advise that orders be sent assigning Maj. Gn. J. J. Reynolds to the command of the Trans-Miss. Division during the disability of Gen. Canby." ALS (telegram sent), CSmH; telegram received (at 1:00 P.M.), DNA, RG 107, Telegrams Collected (Bound). *O.R.*, I, xli, part 4, 568.

To Maj. Gen. George G. Meade

By Telegraph from City Point 2.15 P. M
Dated Nov 25 *1864.*

To MAJ GEN MEADE

Finding you are not at my Head Qrs yet 2 P. M. I suppose you are not coming down today. Tomorrow I shall go up the James River—and out to Genl Butler's Head Q.rs & if you feel like it would be glad to have your company.

U S GRANT
Lt Genl

Telegram received (at 2:25 P.M.), DNA, RG 393, Army of the Potomac, Cav. Corps, Letters Received; copies, *ibid.*, RG 108, Letters Sent; DLC-USG, V, 45, 70, 107; Meade Papers, PHi. *O.R.*, I, xlii, part 3, 703. On Nov. 25, 1864, 9:00 A.M. (sent at 9:15 A.M.), Maj. Gen. George G. Meade telegraphed to USG. "I have nothing of importance to communicate.—If you are going to be at home this morning I propose to visit City Point.—" ALS (telegram sent), DNA, RG 393, Army of the Potomac, Cav. Corps, Letters Received; copies, *ibid.*, Army of the Potomac, Letters Sent; Meade Papers, PHi. *O.R.*, I, xlii, part 3, 702. On the same day, USG telegraphed to Meade. "I shall be at home all day." *Ibid.*, p. 703. On the same day, Brig. Gen. Seth Williams telegraphed to USG. "Your telegram of 2:15 p m is received. General Meade is now on his way to your Head Quarters." Copy, DNA, RG 393, Army of the Potomac, Letters Sent. Printed as sent at 2:45 P.M. in *O.R.*, I, xlii, part 3, 703.

On Nov. 24, Meade had telegraphed to Brig. Gen. John A. Rawlins. "I have just examined an intelligent non-commissioned officer from Harris Brigade Mahones Divn who came into our lines this morning. He says he was in Petersburg yesterday and in Bushrod Johnstons Divn. and that he heard nothing of a Brigade having been moved or sent away and he feels sure no troops have been detached from Lee's army. Other deserters from Johnstons Div since the one who reported the fact do not confirm the withdrawal of any brigade or regts of that Div. The non-commissioned officer says A Shlip was issued from the Petersburg Paper yesterday announcing the occupation without resistance of Macon by Genl Sherman." Telegram received, DNA, RG 108, Letters Received. Printed as written at 1:00 P.M., sent at 1:25 P.M., in *O.R.*, I, xlii, part 3, 696.

To Julia Dent Grant

City Point, Va. Nov. 25th *1864.*

DEAR JULIA,

We reached here yesterday morning all well. If you desire to do so you may come down here and spend a week as early as you please after next week. I wish you would write to Mrs. Rawlins and ask her to come with you. Gen. Rawlins would be pleased if you would do so and would regard it as a compliment. Her address is Danberry Conn. You might make your visit immediately after the meeting of Congress which will be next Monday week.[1] I do not want you to come next week because it is likely that I may be away for several days. Do not mention this because it indicates a movement.—On my arrival here I found about a peck of letters I have read them all but have not yet got through answering.—Have you read how I was mobbed in Phila?[2] It is a terrible bore to me that I cannot travel like a quiet citizen.

If you come before Christmass you will of course only bring Jess with you. Fred and Buck are old enough to travel alone and can come down during the Holidays. Let me know in time and I will meet you either in Washington or Baltimore and will send you a pass over the road from Philadelphia. I have been so busy that I have not yet looked up Lewis Dent's matters but will try to do so to-morrow and will also write to your father. Love and kisses for you and the children. I found three letters from you on my return.

ULYS.

ALS, DLC-USG.

    1. Dec. 5, 1864.
    2. See *New York Herald*, Nov. 23, 25, 1864; Benjamin P. Thomas, ed., *Three Years with Grant as Recalled by War Correspondent Sylvanus Cadwallader* (New York, 1955), pp. 269–70.

To Maj. Gen. Henry W. Halleck

(Cipher)   City Point, Va, Nov. 27th *1864*. [*12:30* P.M.]
MAJ. GEN. HALLECK, WASHINGTON,
    Please inform Gens. Thomas & Sheridan that it is not expected of them to give the Major Generals ordered to report to them commands of more than Divisions. I think also it will be well to break up the Dept. of the Susquehanna and attach it to the Middle Dept.

U. S. GRANT
Lt. Gn.

ALS (telegram sent), CSmH; telegram received (at 2:20 P.M.), DNA, RG 107, Telegrams Collected (Bound). *O.R.*, I, xliii, part 2, 676–77.

To Maj. Gen. George H. Thomas

(Cipher)   City Point, Va, Nov. 27th *1864*. [*9:00* P.M.]
MAJ. GEN. THOMAS, NASHVILLE TENN.
    Savannah papers just received state that Forrest is expected in rear of Sherman and that Breckenridge is already on his way to Georgia from East Tenn.

If this proves true it will give you a chance to take the offensive against Hood and to cut the rail-roads up into Va with a small cavalry force.

U. S. GRANT
Lt. Gn

ALS (telegram sent), CSmH; telegram received (at 9:30 P.M.), DNA, RG 107, Telegrams Collected (Bound); Seward Papers, NRU. *O.R.*, I, xlv, part 1, 1083; (incomplete) *ibid.*, p. 1107. On Nov. 28, 1864, 10:00 A.M., Maj. Gen. George H. Thomas telegraphed to USG. "Your dispatch of 9. P. M yesterday received—We can as yet discover no signs of the withdrawal of Forrest from Tennessee, but he is closely wathed, and our movements will commence against Hood as soon as possible whether Forrest leaves Tennessee or not—My information from E Tennessee leads me to believe that Breckenridge is either falling back to Va or is on his way to Ga—He now holds Bulls Gap but Stoneman is moving on that place from Kno~xville ~whilst~ Burbridge from Cumberland Gap —Stoneman already has orders to destroy the R R into Va if he possably can." ALS (telegram sent), MH; telegram received (at 3:20 P.M.), DNA, RG 107, Telegrams Collected (Bound); (at 7:00 P.M.) *ibid.*, RG 108, Letters Received. *O.R.*, I, xlv, part 1, 1104.

To Maj. Gen. Henry W. Halleck

(Cipher)   City Point, Va, Nov. 28th *1864*. [*2:30* P.M.]
MAJ. GEN. HALLECK, WASHINGTON,

I approve Gen. Canby's recommendation of releiving Steele with Reynolds most heartily. I hope the order will be made at once.[1] Steele should be ordered to report to Canby to take Reynolds place. He is a better commander of troops, leaving off the responsibilities of a Department, than any General now left with Canby. Whilst this work of changing is going on I would like to see a change made in Mo. and in the Dept. of the South giving Dodge the former[2] and Pope the latter. Foster is not fit for duty. I would like to see him appointed Brig. Gen. in the regular Army and retired.

U. S. GRANT
Lt. Gn.

ALS (telegram sent), CSmH; telegram received (at 3:00 P.M.), DNA, RG 107, Telegrams Collected (Bound). *O.R.*, I, xli, part 4, 702.

1. See *ibid.*, pp. 674, 711.

2. See *ibid.*, p. 749. On Feb. 18, 1865, Maj. Gen. William S. Rosecrans, Cincinnati, wrote to USG. " 'Agate', Washington correspondent of the 'Cincinnati Gazette', a man of character and Librarian of Congress, in a letter published in the Daily Gazette of the 16th. Inst. under the caption *Why Rosecrans was removed* says, 'Genl Grant himself freely stated his ground for the removal in a recent conversation. ' "I ordered him to transfer his troops to Thomas after Sherman had started to Savannah. He could have done it in three days. He spent thirty at it. There was no occasion for the delay; there had been no serious campaign in his Dept, and the talk of an enemy then dangerous was preposterous. So I ordered his removal".' This widely published statement affects my military character and even your own. As I take it you are not the man to say that behind the back of a brother officer which you would decline to say to his face. I therefore discharge a duty I owe to you as well as mysel by informing you of this statement and asking, 1. Have you, 'freely' or otherwise 'in conversation' avowed 'yourself the auther of my removal from the command of the Dept. of the Missouri? 2. Have you directly or impliedly stated that I took thirty days to transfer my troops when it could have been done in 'three' or any other number of days materially less than was actually taken? 3. Have you directly or by implication said that there had been no serious campaign in Mo.? 4. Have you directly, or impliedly, said that I ever wrote or talked, as an excuse for delay in forwarding troops to Genl Thomas, that there was a dangerous enemy to hinder, or made any other statement that you have called 'preposterous' or which has not been amply verified by facts and events? In addressing you this personal note I act on the same principle as in 1862 when, parting with you at Jackson Tenn, on learning that men for selfish ends, had been leading you to believe that which I knew to be wholly false, I *asked* and *gave* explanations which you declared, as I considered them, 'perfectly satisfactory'. That principle is, 'never to permit a brother officer, nor suffer myself, to be injured from neglect to ask and give explanations on grave matters'. Trusting I shall be met in the same spirit, and receive prompt and frank replies to my questions, . . ." ALS, USG 3. On July 29, 1871, Rosecrans noted on his copy of this letter that USG had never answered it. Rosecrans Papers, CLU.

To Maj. Gen. Henry W. Halleck

(Cipher)   City Point, Va, Nov. 28th 1864 [*6:30* P.M.]
Maj. Gn. Halleck, Washington

If the 6th Corps is moved here please send all the Inf.y before forwarding a single piece of Artillery or wagon. I do not care for the Artillery coming here at present if it can be used elswhere. The wagon train can follow after all the troops are transported without the use of other transports than those now in service.

U. S. Grant
Lt. Gn.

ALS (telegram sent), CSmH; telegram received (at 6:00 P.M.), DNA, RG 107, Telegrams Collected (Bound). *O.R.*, I, xlii, part 3, 725; (incomplete) *ibid.*, I, xliii, part 2, 682.

To Maj. Gen. Henry W. Halleck

(Cipher)   City Point, Va, Nov. 28th/64 [*8:30* P.M.]
MAJ. GEN. HALLECK, WASHINGTON

There is no evidence of any of Early's forces having come here except Kershaw's Division. Up to Saturday[1] certainly none others had. It is highly probable however that Early may have been sending troops to Ga by way of Lynchburg, Burkesville & Danville. This report from Sheridan looks as if the 6th Corps could now be spared.

U. S. GRANT
Lt. Gen.

ALS (telegram sent), CSmH; telegram received (at 9:00 P.M.), DNA, RG 107, Telegrams Collected (Bound). *O.R.*, I, xlii, part 3, 725; *ibid.*, I, xliii, part 2, 682.

1. Nov. 26, 1864.

To Maj. Gen. George G. Meade

(Cipher)   City Point, Va, Nov. 28th *1864.* [*9:30* A.M.]
MAJ. GEN. MEADE,

The movement which I spoke of for Thursday[1] next will not take place owing to change of plan which I will tell you of when wee meet. It is advisable however that the 5th Corps should be got out of the line ready for any immergency.

U. S. GRANT
Lt. Gn.

ALS (telegram sent), CSmH; telegrams received (2), DNA, RG 107, Telegrams Collected (Unbound); *ibid.*, RG 393, Army of the Potomac, Cav. Corps, Letters Received. *O.R.*, I, xlii, part 3, 726. On Nov. 28, 1864, 11:00 A.M., Maj. Gen. George G. Meade telegraphed to USG. "I have taken no steps in reference to future movements beyond conferring with Gen Warren and sending a scouting party this morning towards Stony Creek to examine the condition of the roads. Gen Warren stating that he could withdraw easily the night before he moved it was thought better not to disturb him as it might attract the attention of the enemy; and now if there will be a few days before you propose to move I would suggest relieving the 2d Corps by the 9th. This would give us the 2d and fifth for a movement leaving the 9th to hold the lines. The 2d Corps have been so long in their present position it is entitled to be relieved & the 9th Corps is the one I should prefer leaving in a defensive position" Telegram received (at noon), DNA, RG 108, Letters Received; copies, *ibid.*, RG 393, Army of the Potomac, Letters Sent; Meade Papers, PHi. Printed as sent at 11:45 A.M. in *O.R.*, I, xlii, part 3, 725–26. A telegram from USG to Meade appears to answer the telegram above. "Make the transfer of Places Between the 2d & 9th Corps proposed" Telegram received (dated Nov. 27—received at 1:03 P.M.), DNA, RG 393, Army of the Potomac, Cav. Corps, Letters Received; copy (dated Nov. 25) Meade Papers, PHi; (dated Nov. 9) DLC-USG, V, 45, 70, 107; DNA, RG 108, Letters Sent. Printed as sent on Nov. 28 in *O.R.*, I, xlii, part 3, 726.

On Nov. 28, USG telegraphed to Brig. Gen. Charles K. Graham. "Heavy firing is heard is apparently on your front does it appear to be an attack of the enemy" Telegram received, DNA, RG 393, Army of the Potomac, Telegrams Received; copies, *ibid.*, RG 108, Letters Sent; DLC-USG, V, 45, 70, 107. *O.R.*, I, xlii, part 3, 737. On the same day, Graham telegraphed to USG. "The firing on my front has entirely ceased—The enemy had advanced on the right this afternoon in a portion of the woods where there has been no contest before—We have ~~strengthened~~ straightened our line and are now strengthening it. The colored Division is in fine spirits and if the line is attacked which I do not apprehend will give a good account of itself" ALS (undated telegram sent), DNA, RG 107, Telegrams Collected (Unbound); telegram received, *ibid.*, RG 108, Letters Received. *O.R.*, I, xlii, part 3, 737. Two undated telegrams sent by Graham, the first addressed to Lt. Col. Theodore S. Bowers, the second to USG, may have been sent on Nov. 28. "The firing on my front is simply picket firing. If any advance is made I will telegraph" "The enemy advanced their picket line about forty yards in one point of the line to-day—We have driven them back & the firing has almost entirely ceased" ALS (telegrams sent), DNA, RG 107, Telegrams Collected (Unbound). On the same day, 8:00 P.M., Lt. Col. Cyrus B. Comstock telegraphed to Brig. Gen. Henry W. Benham. "Their appear to be an attack ~~on~~ upon the Bermuda Hundred front. Please hold your Command in readiness to move at short notice, if it should become necessary." Copies, DLC-USG, V, 45, 70, 107; DNA, RG 108, Letters Sent.

1. Dec. 1.

To Maj. Gen. Philip H. Sheridan

(Cipher)   City Point Nov 28[1] *1864.* [*5:30* P.M.]
MAJ. GEN. SHERIDAN, KEARNSTOWN VA.

My impression now is that you can spare the 6th Corps with impunity. I do not want to make the order for it imperative but unless you are satisfied that it is necessary for the defence of the

Valley I would like to get it here as early as possible. I do not care particularly for the Artillery belonging to the Corps, but the Inf.y alone and wagon trains to follow.

U. S. GRANT
Lt. Gn.

ALS (telegram sent), CSmH; telegram received (at 6:00 P.M.), DNA, RG 107, Telegrams Collected (Bound). *O.R.*, I, xliii, part 2, 683. On Nov. 28, 1864, 8:00 P.M., Maj. Gen. Philip H. Sheridan telegraphed to USG, sending a copy to Maj. Gen. Henry W. Halleck. "I will send the 6th Corps to you by Divisions, with intervals of one day, commencing on the (30) thirtieth—They can be shipped from Stevensons Depôt (4½) four & a half miles from Winchester by railroad to Washington" Telegram sent, DNA, RG 107, Telegrams Collected (Unbound); telegram received (at 8:00 P.M.), *ibid.*, Telegrams Collected (Bound); (addressed to Halleck) *ibid.*, RG 108, Letters Received. *O.R.*, I, xliii, part 2, 683.

1. Dateline not in USG's hand.

To Edwin M. Stanton

City Point, Va. Nov. 30th *1864.*

HON. E. M. STANTON,
SEC. OF WAR,
SIR:

I would respectfully recommend the promotion, by Brevet, of Capt. Michael R. Morgan, C. S. regular Army, and Lt. Col. & Chief Com.y of the Armies operating against Richmond, to the rank of Colonel in the regular Army.

Col. Morgan is well known as one of the most efficient officers in his Department and has been kept out of promotion by his efficiency as a Staff officer making it objectionable to let him be placed in command of troops.

He is an officer that it will always be desirable should have Brevet rank above many of his seniors so as to make him available for responsible and important positions. It will require three brevets to give him the grade asked.

I would further request that the promotion here asked be given at once so that it may go into the Senate early after the meeting of

Congress, or with the first appointments sent to that body for confirmation.

Very respectfully
your obt. svt.
U. S. GRANT
Lt. Gen.

ALS, DNA, RG 94, ACP, 1330 1882. *O.R.*, I, xlii, part 3, 747. Michael R. Morgan, born in 1833 in Halifax, Nova Scotia, USMA 1854, held the rank of 1st lt. before the Civil War. Appointed capt. and commissary as of Aug. 3, 1861, he served in the Dept. of the South on the staff of the 10th Army Corps with the rank of lt. col. until advanced to chief commissary of the Armies operating against Richmond as of June 16, 1864. See Morgan, "From City Point to Appomattox with General Grant," *Journal of the Military Service Institution of the United States*, XLI, 149 (Sept.–Oct., 1907), 227–55. On Jan. 20, 1865, 11:00 A.M., USG telegraphed to Secretary of War Edwin M. Stanton. "I notice in the papers a long list of names sent into the Senate for brevet promotions but dont see that of Lt Col M. R. Morgan. I would like, if his name has not gone in, to have it sent in at once" Telegram received (at 11:10 A.M.), DNA, RG 94, ACP, 1330 1882; *ibid.*, RG 107, Telegrams Collected (Bound); copies, *ibid.*, Telegrams Received in Cipher; DLC-USG, V, 72. *O.R.*, I, xlvi, part 2, 183.

To Maj. Gen. Henry W. Halleck and Maj. Gen. George H. Thomas

City Point Va.
11.30 a. m. Nov. 30. 1864

MAJ GEN H. W. HALLECK,
CHF OF STAFF
COPY TO GEN THOMAS NASHVILLE—

The Richmond Enquirer of yesterday says that it is no longer contraband to state that Breckenridge's command is now marching on a campaign that will fill Ky with dismay and that probably by this time Burbridge has felt the shock, The Richmond papers of the 28th stated that Breckenridge was at Bristol in person on the 25th.

U S GRANT
Lt General

Telegram received (at 12:30 P.M.), DNA, RG 107, Telegrams Collected (Bound); copies, *ibid.*, Telegrams Received in Cipher; *ibid.*, RG 108, Letters Sent; *ibid.*, RG 393, Dept. of the Cumberland, Telegrams Received; (marked as sent at 11:15 A.M.) DLC-USG, V, 45, 70, 107. *O.R.*, I, xlv, part 1, 1166. On Nov. 29, 1864, 8:30 P.M. (sent at 9:05 P.M.), Lt. Col. Theodore S. Bowers telegraphed to Brig. Gen. John A. Rawlins. "The Richmond Enquirer of today says that it is no longer contraband to state that Gen. Breckinridges troops are now marching on a campaign that will soon make Kentucky ring with the shouts of his men if Burbridge has not already felt the shock of his steel. It says further that intelligence from Augusta of the 26th states that the Macon train arrived on the previous night at the usual time & that the rumor that the Central Road had been cut was incorrect. The Augusta papers of the 25 says the Whig report that Gen Wayne had whipped Kilpatricks cavalry division at the Oconee. Wheeler with many thousand men has intercepted the enemy at a point at present unmentionable & is giving them no rest night or day. The Richmond papers all assert that Grant is moving heavy colums to our left with a view of seizing the RRd & deserters from Grant report great activity among his troops They also claim that Mahone captured from 60 to 70 prisoners from the Bermuda Line on Monday night. Gen Bragg assumed command of North Carolina with HdQrs at Wilmington on the 17th." Telegram received, DNA, RG 107, Telegrams Collected (Unbound); (press) *ibid. O.R.*, I, xlii, part 3, 738. On Nov. 30, 6:00 P.M., Maj. Gen. George H. Thomas telegraphed to USG. "Your despatch 11 30 a m recd. I have notified Gen. Stoneman who will notify Burbridge Gen Stoneman telegraphed me yesterday that Breckenridge was at Morristown with a force by no means formidable and I feel confident Breckenridge cannot get much the start of him should he attempt any movement" Telegram received (at 8:10 P.M.), DNA, RG 107, Telegrams Collected (Bound); (at 9:30 P.M.) *ibid.*, RG 108, Letters Received; copies, *ibid.*, RG 107, Telegrams Received in Cipher; *ibid.*, RG 393, Dept. of the Cumberland, Telegrams Sent. *O.R.*, I, xlv, part 1, 1166–67. On Dec. 1, 8:00 A.M., Thomas telegraphed to USG. "I sent your despatch of 11.30 a m yesterday to Maj Genl Stoneman at Knoxville. He telegraphs in reply that he can not learn from any source that Breckenridge has more than three or four thousand men. He also reports that a woman who had come through the enemy's lines says that she was told by one of Breckendge's Officers that Lee was evacuating Richmond and that his advance was at Dublin Station or New River. I have no further news from Genl Schofeild—but feel sure every thing goes well" ALS (telegram sent), MH; telegram received (marked as sent on Nov. 30, 8:00 P.M., received on Dec. 1, noon), DLC-John M. Schofield; DNA, RG 107, Telegrams Collected (Bound); (marked as sent on Dec. 1, 8:00 A.M.) *ibid.*, RG 108, Letters Received. *O.R.*, I, xlv, part 2, 3.

To Maj. Gen. Henry W. Halleck

City Point Va
Nov 30th 1864 7.30 P. M

MAJ GEN H. W. HALLECK
CHIEF OF STAFF.

Is it not practicable now to spare from five 5 to ten 10 thousand of the Veteran Reserve Corps for the field? The latter number

could now be advantageously used so as to give an equal number
for duty in the field of able bodied men,   They could garrison Ft
Monroe, Norfolk Wilson's wharf, Powhatan & City Point

U S GRANT
Lt Genl

Telegram received (at 8:35 P.M.), DNA, RG 107, Telegrams Collected
(Bound); copies, *ibid.*, Telegrams Received in Cipher; *ibid.*, RG 108, Letters
Sent; DLC-USG, V, 45, 70, 107. Printed as received at 8:30 P.M. in *O.R.*, I,
xlii, part 3, 747. On Dec. 1, 1864, 10:30 A.M., Maj. Gen. Henry W. Halleck
telegraphed to USG. "There are no Veteran Reserves available. On the contrary
the [fo]rce is so reduced by expiration of enlistments, that other troops are
called for to guard prisoners of war & drafted men." ALS (telegram sent), DNA,
RG 107, Telegrams Collected (Bound); telegram received, *ibid.*; *ibid.*, RG
108, Letters Received. *O.R.*, I, xlii, part 3, 766.

To Maj. Gen. Henry W. Halleck

Headquarters Armies of the United States.
City Point. Va. Nov. 30th 1864.

MAJ GENL H. W. HALLECK.
CHIEF OF STAFF OF THE ARMY.
GENERAL;

I have just despatched to you requesting that the Depts of the
North west. Mo. & Kansas, be erected into a Military Division and
that Genl Pope be assigned to the command.[1] I think it highly essential that the territory embraced in these three Depts should all
be under one head. The importance of this change is much increased because of the inefficiency of two of the commanders of
Depts, named, one of whom I suppose cannot be well removed. I
do however think it of very great importance that Gen Rosecrans
should be removed.

There is no fault with Genl Canby that induces me to recommend a curtailment of his command, but being at such a distance
from Mo. he cannot direct affairs there as well as it can be done
from Washington. I wish you would lay this matter before the Sec
of War and urge that the change be immediately made. With
Pope in command we secure at least two advantages we have not

heretofore had, namely, subordination, and intelligence of administration.

> Very respectfully,
> Your obt Servt.
> U. S. GRANT,
> Lt. Genl.

Copies, DLC-USG, V, 45, 70, 107; DNA, RG 108, Letters Sent; *ibid.*, Letters
Received. *O.R.*, I, xli, part 4, 716.

1. On Nov. 30, 1864, 3:00 P.M., USG had telegraphed to Maj. Gen. Henry
W. Halleck. "Genl Pope is here and has objections to the command which I
proposed for him that I think well founded and will not urge it further. I would
be glad however to have the Dept of the Missouri taken from the command of
Genl Canby being so distant from him in [point] of ~~communication~~ time it takes
to communicate and have it with the Dept of North West & Kansas put into a
Military Division under Pope" Telegram received (at 4:00 P.M.), DNA, RG
107, Telegrams Collected (Bound); copies, *ibid.*, Telegrams Received in Cipher;
ibid., RG 108, Letters Sent; DLC-USG, V, 45, 70, 107. *O.R.*, I, xli, part 4, 717.

To Rear Admiral David D. Porter

Cipher   Nov. 230th *1864* [*10:00* P.M.]
ADML. D. D. PORTER, FT. MONROE
Southern papers show that Bragg with a large part of his force
has gone to Ga. If we can get off during his absence we will stand
a good chance ~~to~~ not only to carry Ft Fisher but to take Wilmington. ~~I wil~~ The troops will be ready to start the moment you are
ready.

> U. S. GRANT
> Lt. Gn.

ALS (telegram sent), CSmH; copies, DLC-USG, V, 45, 70, 107; DNA, RG 108,
Letters Sent. *O.R.*, I, xlii, part 3, 750; *O.R.* (Navy), I, xi, 110.
On Nov. 28, 1864, 10:30 A.M., USG telegraphed to Maj. Gen. Benjamin F.
Butler. "Will you be at Ft. Monroe all day to-morrow? If so I will meet you and
the Admiral there at 3 p. m." ALS (telegram sent), CSmH; telegram received,
DLC-Benjamin F. Butler. *O.R.*, I, xlii, part 3, 735. At 11:40 A.M., Butler tele-
graphed to USG. "I will await your coming and notify the Admiral—Please
telegraph me when you leave so that I may be sure & meet you—" ADfS, DLC-
Benjamin F. Butler; telegram received, DNA, RG 107, Telegrams Collected
(Unbound). *O.R.*, I, xlii, part 3, 736. On Nov. 29, USG telegraphed to Butler.
"I will leave here at ten (10) A. M." Telegram received, DNA, RG 107, Tele-
grams Collected (Bound). On the same day, USG telegraphed to Maj. Gen.

George G. Meade. "I leave here at ten A. M. for fortress Monroe. will be back early in the Morning." Telegram received (at 8:31 A.M.), *ibid.*, RG 393, Army of the Potomac, Cav. Corps, Letters Received; copy, Meade Papers, PHi. *O.R.*, I, xlii, part 3, 738. Also on Nov. 29, Rear Admiral David D. Porter, Hampton Roads, telegraphed to USG. "What time may I expect you here." LS (telegram sent), DNA, RG 107, Telegrams Collected (Unbound). *O.R.*, I, xlii, part 3, 738.

On Nov. 30, Porter twice telegraphed to USG. "Can start in three days on the original arrangement of twelve thousand men—Will take a little longer to fit Powder vessel—" LS (telegram sent), DNA, RG 107, Telegrams Collected (Unbound); telegram received (marked as sent on Dec. 1, 12:30 A.M.), *ibid.*, RG 108, Letters Received. Printed as received on Dec. 1, 12:30 A.M., in *O.R.*, I, xlii, part 3, 750; *O.R.* (Navy), I, xi, 110. "I will be up on the Second ~~Nove~~ December—would come up sooner but my machinery is apart—If you are coming down will wait here." ALS (telegram sent), DNA, RG 107, Telegrams Collected (Unbound); telegram received (marked as sent on Dec. 1, 1:30 A.M.), *ibid.*, RG 108, Letters Received. *O.R.* (Navy), I, xi, 110; (dated Dec. 1, 1:30 A.M.) *O.R.*, I, xlii, part 3, 767. On Dec. 1, USG telegraphed to Porter. "I will be at home to-morrow." ALS (telegram sent), Kohns Collection, NN; telegram received, DNA, RG 107, Telegrams Collected (Bound). *O.R.*, I, xlii, part 3, 767. On Dec. 2, 3:00 P.M., Porter signaled to USG. "I am coming up." Signal received, DNA, RG 107, Telegrams Collected (Unbound). On Dec. 2, 11:30 A.M., USG telegraphed to Meade. "I shall be at Hd Qrs. all day. Adml. Porter will be here also." ALS (telegram sent), Kohns Collection, NN; copies, DLC-USG, V, 45, 70, 107; DNA, RG 108, Letters Sent. *O.R.*, I, xlii, part 3, 776.

To Maj. Gen. Benjamin F. Butler

By Telegraph from Hdqrs City Pt,
Dated Nov 30 1864. [4:30 P.M.]

To MAJ GEN BUTLER

I observe Savannah & Augusta papers sent me by Col Mulford from which I gather that Bragg has gone to Georgia taking with him what I judge to be most of the forces from about Wilmington —it is therefore important that Weitzel should get off during his absence & if succesful in effecting a landing he may by a bold dash also succeed in capturing Wilmington   make all the arrangemt for his departure so that the navy will not be detained one ~~movement~~ moment for the [army.]

Did you order Palmer[1] to make the movement proposed yesterday—it is important that he should do so without delay

U S GRANT
Lt Genl

Telegram received, DLC-Benjamin F. Butler; copies, DLC-USG, V, 45, 70, 107; DNA, RG 108, Letters Sent. *O.R.*, I, xlii, part 1, 970–71; *ibid.*, I, xlii, part 3, 760. On Nov. 30, 1864, 8:45 P.M., Maj. Gen. Benjamin F. Butler telegraphed to USG. "Orders will go down tomorrow to General Palmer to make the move ~~on Rainbow~~ Bluff of which we spoke—I have been busy all day endeavoring to ascertain the truth ~~of~~ as to the movement of troops from here—Deserters say that Fields Hokes and Kershaws Divisions have all moved each giving a different one but gone towards Petersburg—My signal officer reports a train of Six (6) cars loaded with troops and Six (6) open cars loaded with artillery passing from Petersburg toward Richmond to day—I am inclined to believe that the movement is of Hokes Division to Petersburgh only because of a difficulty and a very angry discussion which has sprung up between Hoke and Field in regard to thier failure at Battery Harrison on the 30th of September last, which appeared in the Richmond papers—and that Kershaw is to take Hokes place here—We have had literally no deserters for two (2) days—We have nearly perfected the plan of organization of the corps—With your leave I will be down in the morning for the necessary orders—I have spared every thing I can from the Hospital ~~boats~~ and ~~all~~ other boats in the Department to move troops—The Navy shall not wait for me a single hour and we will make the push if it is possible" LS (telegram sent), DNA, RG 107, Telegrams Collected (Unbound); telegram received (at 9:00 P.M.), *ibid.*, RG 108, Letters Received. *O.R.*, I, xlii, part 3, 760; (incomplete) *ibid.*, I, xlii, part 1, 971. On the same day, USG telegraphed to Butler. "I shall be at Hd Qrs tomorrow & will be glad to see your here" Telegram received, DLC-Benjamin F. Butler. *O.R.*, I, xlii, part 3, 760. At 9:15 P.M., USG telegraphed to Butler. "Did you receive a cipher despatch from me today?" Telegram received (at 9:15 P.M.), DNA, RG 94, War Records Office, Miscellaneous War Records. At 9:20 P.M., Butler drafted his answer at the foot of the telegram received. "Yes and have answere it fully" ADf, *ibid.* On Nov. 29, Lt. Col. Theodore S. Bowers telegraphed to Brig. Gen. John A. Rawlins four times, the third and fourth at 3:30 P.M. and 7:30 P.M. "Col Sharpe reports as follows   Deserters who came in yesterday to the Army Potomac say that rumors prevail in the different camps that troops have been sent to Georgia   Some say that Kershaws others Fields Division had gone. On Gen. Butlers front no deserters came in yesterday showing great care on the part of the enemy to prevent our getting information   It is also reported in Gen Butlers command that Hokes Division has left their front   All this is rumor but it comes from so many sources that it is worth attention" "Files of Richmond papers of the 28th just recd. The Examiner says the tenor of the news from Georgia so far as it has reached us is cheering. Our readers must be content with this simple announcement in regard to the present status of affairs in Georgia   Gen Beauregard has issued a proclamation in which he says he is hastening to their assistance   The dispatch it was pretty well ascertained that the left wing of Sherman Army when it reached Madison numbered 16.000 men. They burnt the town when they left   The Enquirer says the Augusta Chronicle of Sunday has the following. It is stated that a large Cavalry force has left Greenville S C & is moving across the country in the direction of Atlanta probably with a view off the Yankee Column which is moving down the Georgia R Rd in this direction   A reliable gentleman who reached Augusta on thursday from Stone Mountain reports that the Yankee column moving down the Georgia R Rd divided at Decatur one half going down the Covington Road & the other the Rockbridge Road. At Stone Mountain they burned all the unoccupied houses comprising some two thirds of the town & were laying waste the Country as they progressed. They march in hollow squares their trains in centre They united at Bakers Hill near Covington & it was not known whether they would strike for Eatonton or Athens He describes the view from the summit of Stone Mountain of the Conflagration of Atlanta as awful beyond description The gate city was an ocean of flame as the feiry waves rose & fell throughout the whole extent." "The Examiner says that Sheridan is sending large bodies of troops to join Grant & when they arrive Grant will certainly attack the lines of Richmond—The dispatch learns that Grant is massing troops on his left Gen Breckinridge was at Bristol Tenn in person on the 25th Thirteen thousand federal prisoners confined at Salisbury N C attempted to make their escape on the 24. The enemy brought artillery on them killed 40 & wounded a large number when the prisoners submitted." "Capt Leets scouts report that only Kershaws Division of Earlys Command has gone to Richmond. It is rumored that Early will withdraw all his force from the Valley. A Battle is expected shortly at Richmond and women and children are being moved from there and Petersburg to other points for safety" Telegrams received, *ibid.*, RG 107, Telegrams Collected (Bound). On Nov. 30, USG telegraphed to Butler. "Have you had information through deserters to know whether Kershaw's or Fields Div. has gone South?" ALS (telegram sent), CSmH; telegram received (at 8:00 P.M.), DNA, RG 107, Telegrams Collected (Unbound). Printed as sent at 8:00 P.M. in *O.R.*, I, xlii, part 3, 761. At 11:30 P.M., Butler telegraphed to USG. "Two deserters just in from Hokes Division say there is no movement of that Division—They also say that Field is on our right where he has been— They further say it is Heths Division which has gone from Petersburg Have furnished this information to Col. Sharp" LS (telegram sent), DNA, RG 107, Telegrams Collected (Unbound). *O.R.*, I, xlii, part 3, 761.

On Nov. 30, Butler wrote to Rawlins. "I have the honor to request of the Lieut. General Commanding the Armies of the United States, that the following changes may be made in the organization of the Army of the James. It is proposed that the 18th and 10th Corps be discontinued, that the White Infantry troops of the 18th and 10th Corps, now with the Army of the James, be consolidated under the direction of the Major General Commanding the Dept. of Va. and No. Ca. and they constitute a new Corps to be called the 24th Corps. That the Colored Troops of the Dept. of Va. and No. Ca. be organized into a new Corps, to be called the 25th Corps, that the Artillery of the 18th Corps, be transferred to the 24th Corps and that the Artillery of the 10th Corps be transferred to the 25th Corps. The present 18th Corps Staff to be transferred to the 24th Corps and the present 10th Corps Staff to be transferred to the 25th Corps. That Major General E. O. C. Ord may be assigned to the command of the 24th Corps, and Major General G. Weitzel, may be assigned to the 25th Corps." LS, DNA, RG 108, Letters Received. *O.R.*, I, xlii, part 3, 761. USG wrote at the top of this letter: "By telegraph to Adj. of the Army" and at the end "Approved." AES, DNA, RG 108, Letters Received; telegrams received (2—dated Dec. 1), *ibid.*, RG 107, Telegrams Collected (Bound).

Earlier on Nov. 30, USG had telegraphed to Maj. Gen. Godfrey Weitzel. "Please inform me if Genl Butler has returned" Telegram received, *ibid.*, Telegrams Collected (Unbound). At 3:35 P.M., Weitzel drafted his reply at the foot of the telegram received. "Gen Butler has returned" ADfS, *ibid.*

1. Innis N. Palmer, born in 1824 in Buffalo, N. Y., USMA 1846, served in the Mexican War and reached the rank of capt. before the Civil War. Appointed

brig. gen. as of Sept. 23, 1861, he commanded a brigade in the peninsular campaign, and after Dec., 1862, held a series of commands in N. C. For his expedition, see letter to Maj. Gen. George G. Meade, Dec. 5, 1864.

To Maj. Gen. George G. Meade

City Point, Va, Nov. 30th/64

MAJ. GEN. MEADE,

I am just in receipt of news from Savannah to the 26th. Augusta papers announce the ~~arrival~~ approach there of Hamptons Cavalry. It also gives the following dispatch. Hd Qrs. Cav.y ~~200~~ Nov. 24th To COMD.G OFFICER AUGUSTA, Please insert this in all papers in Augusta. All men of my Command now in Ga. will rendezvous forthwith in Augusta & those in South Carolina at Columbia and await orders, signed WADE HAMPTON. ~~I~~

U. S. GRANT
Lt. Gn

ALS (telegram sent), DNA, RG 107, Telegrams Collected (Unbound); copy, Meade Papers, PHi. Printed as sent at 11:40 A.M. in *O.R.*, I, xlii, part 3, 748.

To Maj. Gen. George G. Meade

(Cipher)   Nov. 230th *1864.* [*noon*]
MAJ. GEN. MEADE,

Try to ascertain how much force Hampton has taken from here with him. He has gone him self beyond doubt. If the enemy has reduced his Cavalry much we must endeavor to make a raid upon the Danville road. Bragg has taken most of the troops from Wilmington to Ga. which will aid an expedition which I have ordered from Newberne to cut the Weldon road south of the Roanoke.

U. S. GRANT
Lt. Gn.

ALS (telegram sent), CSmH; telegram received, DNA, RG 393, Army of the Potomac, Cav. Corps, Letters Received. *O.R.*, I, xlii, part 3, 748. On Nov. 30, 1864, Maj. Gen. George G. Meade telegraphed to USG. "Deserters this morning

report that all the dismounted cavalry about one thousand (1000) in number
have been sent to Georgia it being understood they were to be remounted there
no other part of the cavalry force has gone so far as our information extends   It
is probable Hampton has been sent to organize these & other mounted he coming
from that section of the country   Greggs scouting party returned day before
yesterday having gone within 2 miles of stoney creek bringing back some few
prisoners contrabands & refugees & capturing 6 wagons loaded with wheat.
from these persons it was learned that the cavalry occupied their old positions the
main body at Dinwiddie C. H   no departure of any troops south was reported
all is quiet on the lines. The exchange of position between the 9th & 2d corps
will be accomplished today" Telegram received (at noon), DNA, RG 108,
Letters Received; copies, *ibid.*, RG 393, Army of the Potomac, Letters Sent;
Meade Papers, PHi. Printed as written at noon, sent at 12:10 P.M., in *O.R.*, I,
xlii, part 3, 748. At 2:00 P.M., Meade telegraphed to USG. "The best way in
my judgement to ascertain whether Hamptons has taken away any considerable
part of his force will be to send Greggs cavalry over towards Dinwiddie C. H.
and make them develope their force. The only difficulty is that if Hamptons force
is not reduced he so largely outnumbers Gregg it is hard for the latter to find
out anything positive; still, if you think it worth while I will send him   We generally get the earliest and most precise information from deserters and refugees"
Telegram received (at 3:00 P.M.), DNA, RG 108, Letters Received; copies,
ibid., RG 393, Army of the Potomac, Letters Sent; Meade Papers, PHi. *O.R.*, I,
xlii, part 3, 748–49.

To Maj. Gen. George G. Meade

Nov. 30th 1864

MAJ. GN. MEADE,

The information obtained from deserters just sent by the Provost Marshel[1] satisfies me that only Hampton in person & his dismounted Cavalry have gone to Ga. There will be no use therefore
of sending out the Cavalry to ascertain what force of the enemy
have left. The enemy evidently think however that we are about
making a grand attack and if this idea can be kept up by sending
the Cavalry out it would be well to do so send them.

U. S. GRANT
Lt. Gn.

ALS (telegram sent), CSmH; telegram received (at 3:55 P.M.), DNA, RG
393, Army of the Potomac, Cav. Corps, Letters Received. *O.R.*, I, xlii, part 3,
749. On Nov. 30, 1864, 7:00 P.M., Maj. Gen. George G. Meade telegraphed to
USG. "A Scout of the enemy belonging to Butlers Cavy Brigade was Captured
this A m by Some of the Cavy and has just been sent in. It has been positively

ascertained from him that Gen Hampton was in Camp near Burgess Mill on the 27th inst his wife being with him on a visit. Hampton is known to have a son now in S C who was recently wounded in Hoods army. If his name is wade it may account for the proclamition in the Augusta papers. The prisoner will not answer directly whether any of the Cavy has gone South but the inference from his examination is that no mounted force has gone. I have ordered Gregg to move with all his avaiable force tomorrow and endeavor to ascertain if the enemy is building a Rail Road from Stoney Creek and try to find out whether any forces have gone South. I have replied to Maj Gen Wilcox that the Same reasons which interfered with his asking his Commanding Genls interposition will prevent my returning private R. A. Pryor Vize the impossibility of sanctioning this irregular & unauthorized intecourse. I have more-over informed him I have recommended the dismissal from the Service of Capt Burrage of a Massachusetts Regt who a few days ago allowed himself to be Captured in the Same manner as Mr Pryor was taken" Telegram received, DNA, RG 108, Letters Received; copies, *ibid.*, RG 393, Army of the Potomac, Letters Sent; Meade Papers, PHi. Printed as sent at 7:40 P.M. in *O.R.*, I, xlii, part 3, 749–50. On Nov. 29, Meade wrote to USG. "The accompanying sealed letter was received by a flag of truce that came to our pickets on the right of Fort Cumming about 1 p m to day—" Copies, DNA, RG 393, Army of the Potomac, Letters Sent; Meade Papers, PHi. On Nov. 29, C.S.A. Maj. Gen. Cadmus M. Wilcox had written to USG. "I take the liberty of writing to you with reference to an incident that occurred between the picket-lines of the two armies on Sunday, the 27th instant, about 2 p. m., and after my explanation of the affair I trust that the request that I make may be granted, believing that my statement will be confirmed by the reports of the officers and men of your forces. The affair that I refer to is the capture of Private Roger A. Pryor, Third Virginia Cavalry, on the 27th instant, by the pickets of the troops under your command, and under the following circumstances, viz: At the time mentioned above this soldier rode up to our picket-line and looked for awhile at the opposite line through his glass, then dismounted from his horse, and taking from his pocket a newspaper waved it toward a group of Federal officers. One of these responded to this with a paper in a similar manner, and the two mutually approached for the exchange of papers. Private Pryor asked the pickets on our side not to fire. Upon meeting each other they shook hands and exchanged papers. The Federal officer then seized Pryor by the arm and led him off to the rear. Upon reaching the line in rear a crowd gathered around them and seemed to regard him as a prisoner, and since then he has not been seen. I feel much interest in the case of this soldier, but cannot ask of the commander of our forces to intercede for him, for it is against his positive orders to exchange papers with the Federals, and doubtless there are like orders from yourself. It is, however, well known that papers are exchanged, and as above indicated, and when not actually engaged in deadly strife men from both armies are anxious and willing, and very naturally so, to hold communication and to exchange papers. This soldier is, I believe, thoroughly imbued with a sentiment of honor, and could not have approached your lines with any sinister purpose; and though at this time a private in the ranks from choice, has been both a colonel and a brigadier-general in our army and filled both grades with credit to himself. Should my statement be corroborated by that of your officers I believe that this man's case will be favorably regarded by you, and [that he] will soon be returned to our lines, to his friends and family." *O.R.*, I, xlii, part 3, 739. On Nov. 30,

USG endorsed this letter. "Respectfully referred to Maj. Gen. George G. Meade for such answer as he may deem proper, if it is deemed necessary to answer at all." *Ibid.*

Also on Nov. 30, USG. wrote to Meade. "One division of the Sixth Corps leaves Stephenson's Station at 11 a. m. to-morrow for Washington, and will embark and be on its way here by the morning of the 2d. The other two divisions will follow, a day intervening between the departure of divisions. I would suggest that the Sixth Corps be put in the line to relieve the Fifth Corps." *Ibid.*, p. 750.

On Dec. 1, 11:00 A.M., Meade telegraphed to USG. "I have nothing of importance to report, beyond the disgraceful fact that Sixteen men of the 61st N. Y. Vols 1st Divn. 2d corps deserted to the enemy last night from the picket line.—" ALS (telegram sent), DNA, RG 94, War Records Office, Army of the Potomac; copies, *ibid.*, RG 393, Army of the Potomac, Letters Sent; Meade Papers, PHi. *O.R.*, I, xlii, part 3, 767.

1. On Nov. 30, 2:00 P.M., Meade endorsed a telegram to USG. "I Forwardies the above just received.—" AES, DNA, RG 108, Letters Received; telegram received, *ibid.* Text altered in *O.R.*, I, xlii, part 3, 749. The enclosure is *ibid.*

To Maj. Gen. George G. Meade

City Point, Va., November 30, 1864.

Respectfully returned.

In the assignment of Maj. Gen. A. A. Humphreys to the command of the Second Corps no reflection upon or disrespect to Major-General Gibbon was intended. General Humphreys has long desired the command of troops and it has been promised him. When General Hancock left it was understood that he was permanently relieved and separated from the corps, and General Humphreys, being the oldest major-general in the Army of the Potomac, was placed in command of it. The wording of the order of assignment might have been made less objectionable. There was, however, no intention of in any way reflecting upon General Gibbon, and it was expected that the temporary assignment would be made permanent by the President. It is hoped that General Gibbon will accept this explanation as satisfactory. I have full confidence in General Gibbon as a commander of troops, and believe him entirely capable of commanding a corps. I should not like to spare his services from this army; but if after this explanation he continues dissatisfied he will, on his application, be relieved.

U. S. GRANT,
Lieutenant-General.

O.R., I, li, part 1, 1191. Written on a letter of Nov. 26, 1864, from Maj. Gen. John Gibbon to Brig. Gen. Seth Williams, adjt. for Maj. Gen. George G. Meade. "The assignment of Major-General Humphreys to the command of the Second Corps temporarily, during the absence on leave of the permanent commander, I regard as a direct reflection upon me. I have the honor to request that I may be at once relieved from my present command." *Ibid.*, I, xlii, part 3, 714. On Nov. 27, Meade endorsed this letter. "Respectfully forwarded to headquarters Armies of the United States. The assignment of Major-General Humphreys to the command of the Second Corps was made in pursuance of the instructions of the lieutenant-general commanding, and the assignment was necessarily announced in the order as temporary, a permanent assignment requiring the sanction of the President. It is understood that General Gibbon would have made no objection to serving under General Humphreys as the permanent commander of the corps, but thinks that pending such permanent assignment the command of the corps should have been devolved on him. I do not consider that General Gibbon has any just cause to complain of the phraseology of the order assigning General Humphreys to the command of the Second Corps, especially as it is believed it was well known in the corps that General Hancock was not to return to this army. As, however, he asks to be relieved from further service here, I have no objection to offer to the granting of his application." *Ibid.*, I, li, part 1, 1191. See *ibid.*, I, xlii, part 3, 730–31, 788, 988; Henry H. Humphreys, *Andrew Atkinson Humphreys: A Biography* (Philadelphia, 1924), pp. 262–64.

To Julia Dent Grant

City Point, Va, Nov. 30th *1864.*

DEAR JULIA,

We are having delightful weather here now which I hope will continue until your visit, if you make it, is over. I wrote you not to come this week because I expected to make a move and fight a battle which would take me away from City Point for a day or two or three. Owing to changes in my plan this will not now take place. The moment I receive your letter saying you are coming I will write to the rail-road manager in Phila to give you rail-road accomodations and will go to Washington to meet you. The enemy here seem very restive and full of expectation of a general attack.

This has probably prevented them from detaching from here against Sherman. It is understood the people are all leaving Richmond & Petersburg but of this I am not certain.

Love and kisses for you and the children.

Of course I am not displeased with you for purchasing your furs now. I give you $500 00 per month and you can buy whatever you wish with it.

ULYS.

ALS, DLC-USG.

To Maj. Gen. Henry W. Halleck

City Point, Va, Dec. 1st *1864.*

MAJ. GEN. HALLECK, WASHINGTON,

Greggs Cavalry was sent South this morning on a reconnoisance move particularly to discover if the enemy were moving troops South. The following dispatch is just received in relation to it.[1]

U. S. GRANT
Lt. Gn.

ALS (telegram sent), CSmH; telegram received (at 9:00 P.M.), DNA, RG 107, Telegrams Collected (Bound). *O.R.*, I, xlii, part 1, 24; *ibid.*, I, xlii, part 3, 766.

1. USG enclosed a telegram of Dec. 1, 1864, 8:00 P.M., from Maj. Gen. George G. Meade to USG. "I have just heard from Genl. Gregg—His despatch is dated 3.45. P. M.—He reports having captured stoney creek station—which was defended by infantry & cavalry in works with artillery.—He captured two pieces of artillery, but had no means of bringing them off—so spiked them & destroyed the carriages.—He has 190 prisoners 8 wagons & 30 mules—burnt the depot with 3000 sacks of corn—500 bales of hay—a train of cars—large amount of bacon clothing ammunition and other government stores—destroyed all the shops & public buildings—The 2d brigade Col. Gregg Comg. had the advance, and is reported as most gallantly carrying the enemys position.—Genl. Gregg is now returning to camp—No information could be obtained of the passing of any force Southward either cavalry or infantry—The bed of the branch road from stoney creek was seen—graded but no rails laid.—At Duval station south of

stoney creek much property was destroyed, and a large amount of railroad iron found, which an effort was made to destroy by burning.—When the staff officer who brought the despatch left, the enemy were showing signs of having concentrated & were following, but he thinks Genl. Gregg will be in camp by midnight.—" ALS (telegram sent), DNA, RG 94, War Records Office, Army of the Potomac; telegram received (at 8:25 P.M.), *ibid.*, RG 108, Letters Received; DLC-Benjamin F. Butler. *O.R.*, I, xlii, part 1, 24; *ibid.*, I, xlii, part 3, 766–67. On Dec. 2, 11:30 A.M., Meade telegraphed to USG. "The Provost Marshall reports 170 prisoners as received from Genl. Gregg including 7. comd. officers, among them Maj. Fitzhugh of Hamptons staff in charge of construction party engaged in building branch Rail Road—This number of prisoners is 20 less than Gregg reported last night, tho it is not certain all have yet come in as I have no report this morning from Genl. Gregg.—I propose visiting your Hd. Qrs during the course of the day unless you are going to be absent." ALS (telegram sent), DNA, RG 94, War Records Office, Army of the Potomac; telegram received, *ibid.*, RG 108, Letters Received. *O.R.*, I, xlii, part 3, 776.

To Maj. Gen. Henry W. Halleck

(Cipher)   City Point, Va, Dec. 1st *1864* [*5:30* P.M.]
MAJ. GEN HALLECK, WASHINGTON

I think it had better be announced in orders that all contributions of clothing and provisions for our prisoners in Southern hands will be received by Lt. Col. Mulford Asst. Agt. of Exchange and also where they will be received.

Some regulation should be made as to what articles will be received. If the Sec. of War will notify me who from among our prisoners he would like paroled to receive contributions and distribute them I will ask his parole. Two names had better be submitted.

U. S. GRANT
Lt. Gn.

ALS (telegram sent), IHi; telegram received (on Dec. 2, 1864, 6:20 A.M.), DNA, RG 107, Telegrams Collected (Bound). *O.R.*, II, vii, 1174. On Dec. 2, Maj. Gen. Henry W. Halleck endorsed a copy of this telegram. "Respectfully referred to Brig Genl Wessels to report names of several officers deemed competent for the duty proposed, also list of articles which should be sent." AES, DNA, RG 249, Letters Received. *O.R.*, II, vii, 1174.

To Maj. Gen. Henry W. Halleck

City Point
Dec 1st 1864 [*5:30* P.M.]

MAJ GEN HALLECK
CHF OF STAFF

I will not have the battalion of Mass Cavalry ordered from the Dept of the South unconditionally—I do not see however the use of Cavalry there, if there is a real need of it—I will send a reduced regiment to that Dept and bring the four Companies above mentioned to the other regiment

U S GRANT
Lt Genl

Telegram received (on Dec. 2, 1864, 6:00 A.M.), DNA, RG 107, Telegrams Collected (Bound); copies, *ibid.*, Telegrams Received in Cipher; *ibid.*, RG 108, Letters Sent; DLC-USG, V, 45, 70, 107. On Dec. 1, 11:30 A.M., USG had telegraphed to Maj. Gen. Henry W. Halleck. "4th Mass. Cavalry has Eight companies here and four companies in the Dept. of the South. Please order these latter here." ALS (telegram sent), Kohns Collection, NN; telegram received (at 1:45 P.M.), DNA, RG 107, Telegrams Collected (Bound). At 3:15 P.M., Halleck telegraphed to USG. "Genl Foster has no other cavalry than the battalion of 4th Mass, which is now reduced to one hundred men. He asks for the 8 companies with 10th corps. If I order as you direct, it will leave not a single mounted man in the Dept of the south. Is this your intention?" ALS (telegram sent), *ibid.*; telegram received, *ibid.*; (marked as sent at 3:00 P.M.) *ibid.*, RG 108, Letters Received.

To Maj. Gen. Benjamin F. Butler

City Point, Va, Dec. 1st *1864.*

MAJ. GEN. BUTLER,

The French Man of War Adonis is here. Will proceed to Aikins Landing in the morning with the French Consul on his way to Richmond to effect the transfer of French subjects from rebeldom. Please have an Ambulance at the Landing and an officer to conduct Mr. Paul,[1] the Consul, through the lines. If rebel authorities agree to let French subjects through please arrange where they will be received.

U. S. GRANT
Lt. Gn.

ALS (telegram sent), CSmH; copies, DLC-USG, V, 45, 70, 107; DNA, RG 108, Letters Sent.

On Nov. 24, 1864, Secretary of State William H. Seward wrote to USG. "I enclose, for your information and for any opinion which you think proper to express, a translation of the instructions which Mr. Geofroy, the Chargé d'Affaires of France, proposes to give to Captain Manigault [*Marivault*], of the French Navy, and Mr. Paul, the French Consul at Richmond in regard to the removal within our lines of the subjects of France now within the lines of the insurgents." LS, *ibid.*, Letters Received. *O.R.*, I, xlii, part 3, 693. The enclosures are *ibid.*, pp. 693–94.

On Nov. 30, 11:00 A.M., Rear Admiral David D. Porter telegraphed to USG. "Is there any objection to the French Sloop of War coming up to City Point" LS (telegram sent), DNA, RG 107, Telegrams Collected (Unbound). *O.R.* (Navy), I, xi, 110. At 11:00 A.M., USG telegraphed to Porter. "Your Dispatch received. There is no objection to the French Sloop of War coming to City Point. Let it come." Telegram sent, DNA, RG 107, Telegrams Collected (Unbound); telegram received, *ibid.*, Telegrams Collected (Bound).

On Dec. 1, Maj. Gen. Benjamin F. Butler forwarded to USG a signal message reporting art. moving by railroad toward Richmond. AE (telegram sent), *ibid.*, Telegrams Collected (Unbound). *O.R.*, I, xlii, part 3, 775.

1. Alfred Paul, French consul at Richmond during the Civil War, was especially concerned about the export of tobacco. See Lynn M. Case and Warren F. Spencer, *The United States and France: Civil War Diplomacy* (Philadelphia, 1970), pp. 526–44; letter to William H. Seward, Dec. 14, 1864; telegram to Edwin M. Stanton, Feb. 21, 1865.

To Maj. Isaac S. Stewart

City Point, Va, Dec. 1st *1864*

DEAR MAJOR,

Your favor of the 29th ultimo enclosing draft for $47.50 and accounts for signature is just received. As I draw forage in kind I am not entitled to the $50 00 per month for horses. The accounts upon which you paid are therefore correct. Enclosed you will please find the draft returned.

The following is a discriptive list of my servants which you can have inserted in the accounts paid upon to perfect them

		ft	in	Eyes	Hair
James Guard,	White	5.	11	Dark	
William[1]	Black	5.	7	"	
Douglass	"	5.	9	"	
Georgianna	"	5.	4	"	

I am under obligations to you Major for your concideration and favor.

Yours Truly
U. S. GRANT
Lt. Gen

To MAJ. I. S. STEWART
PAYMASTER U. S. A.

ALS, IHi.

1. See letter to Julia Dent Grant, Sept. 25, 1864.

To Edwin M. Stanton

From City Point 1 p m Decr 2d *1864.*

HON EDWIN M STANTON
SECY OF WAR

Immediately on receipt of Genl Thomas' dispatch I sent him a dispatch which no doubt you read as it passed through the office. Rosecrans will do less harm doing nothing than on duty. I know no Department or Army Commander deserving such punishment as the infliction of Rosecrans upon him. His name could well go on the list I sent up a few days ago[1]

U S GRANT
Lt Genl

Telegram received (at 2:00 P.M.), DNA, RG 107, Telegrams Collected (Bound); copies, *ibid.,* Telegrams Received in Cipher; *ibid.,* RG 108, Letters Sent; DLC-USG, V, 45, 70, 107. *O.R.,* I, xli, part 4, 742–43; (incomplete) *ibid.,* I, xlv, part 2, 16. On Dec. 2, 1864, 10:30 A.M., Secretary of War Edwin M.

Stanton twice telegraphed to USG. "Where shall Rosecranz be assigned or sent by the order placing Dodge in command of the Department of Missouri." "The President feels solicitious about the disposition of Thomas to lay in fortifications for an indefinite period 'until Wilson gets equipments.' This looks like the Mc-Clellan & Rosecranz strategy of do nothing and let the rebels raid the country. The President wishes you to consider the matter." ALS (telegrams sent), DNA, RG 107, Telegrams Collected (Bound); telegrams received, *ibid.*, RG 108, Letters Received. *O.R.*, I, xli, part 4, 742; *ibid.*, I, xlv, part 2, 15–16.

1. See letter to Edwin M. Stanton, Nov. 23, 1864.

To Edwin M. Stanton

(Cipher)   City Point, Va, Dec. 2d 1864 [*7:30* P.M.]
HON. E. M. STANTON, SEC. OF WAR,

Do you not think it advisable to authorize Wilson to press horses & mares in Ky. to mount his Cavalry, giving owners receipts so they can get their pay? It looks as if Forrest will flank around Thomas until Thomas is equal to him in Cavalry.

U. S. GRANT
Lt. Gn.

ALS (telegram sent), James S. Schoff, New York, N. Y.; telegram received, DNA, RG 107, Telegrams Collected (Bound). *O.R.*, I, xlv, part 2, 16. On Dec. 2, 1864, 9:00 P.M., Secretary of War Edwin M. Stanton telegraphed to USG. "General Thomas ought to seize horses and every thing else he needs. It has been heretofore and he surely cannot be hesitating about it. The officer in command at Louisville should also seize or Thomas send some one to do so for him." ALS (telegram sent), DNA, RG 107, Telegrams Collected (Bound); telegram received (marked as sent at 9:30 P.M., received at 10:00 P.M.), *ibid.*, RG 108, Letters Received. *O.R.*, I, xlv, part 2, 16.

On Dec. 5, 3:30 P.M., Maj. Gen. Henry W. Halleck telegraphed to USG. "The records show that there have been issued at Louisville Lexington & Nashville, since Sept 20th, twenty two thousand cavalry horses. This number is exclusive of the cavalry horses previously issued and brought into the Dept by Grierson & others, and the commands of Burbridge and Garrard, and those sent to Sherman. If this number, without any campaign, is already reduced to ten thousand mounted men, as reported by Genl Wilson, it may be safely assumed that the cavalry of that army will *never* be mounted, for the destruction of horses in the last two months has there alone been equal to the remounts obtained from the entire west. None are issued to Rosecrans, Steele or Canby." ALS (telegram sent), DNA, RG 107, Telegrams Collected (Bound); telegram received, *ibid.*; *ibid.*, Telegrams Collected (Unbound); *ibid.*, RG 108, Letters Received. *O.R.*, I, xlv, part 2, 55.

To Maj. Gen. Henry W. Halleck

(Cipher)   City Point, Va. Dec. 2d/64 [*10:00* P.M.]
Maj. Gen. Halleck,

Is it not possible now to send reinforcements to Thomas from Hooker's Dept.? If there are new troops, organized state Militia or anything that can go now is the time to annihilate Hood's Army. Gov. Bramlett might put from five to ten thousand horsemen into the field to serve only to the end of the campaign. I believe if he was asked he would do so.

U. S. Grant

Lt. Gn.

ALS (facsimile telegram sent), Parke-Bernet Sale No. 715, Dec. 4, 1945, p. [11]; telegram received (at 10:45 P.M.), DNA, RG 107, Telegrams Collected (Bound). *O.R.*, I, xlv, part 2, 16–17. On Dec. 3, 1864, 2:00 P.M., Maj. Gen. Henry W. Halleck telegraphed to USG. "Every available man from Hooker's & other western Depts have been sent to Genl Thomas. Hooker [is] already calling for more troops to be sent to him to guard his prisoners, & Genl Fry is getting all he can from the hospitals. Thomas was authorised some time [ago] to call on the Governors of any western state for militia, if he wanted them. He himself says that no more troops should be sent [fr]om Kentucky. Loyal Kentuckians say that if Bramlett's militia are armed a large portion of them will join the rebels. All cavalry horses that could be procured in the western states have been sent to Nashville to the entire neglect of other Depts. I believe that every possible effort has been made to supply Genl Thomas' demands and wants so far as the means at the disposition of the government permitted. Genl A J. Smith's command was thirty-one days, after Genl Rosecrans recieved [the] orders, in reaching Nashville." ALS (telegram sent), DNA, RG 107, Telegrams Collected (Bound); telegram received, *ibid.*; (marked as sent at 1:30 P.M.) *ibid.*, RG 108, Letters Received. *O.R.*, I, xlv, part 2, 28–29.

To Maj. Gen. Benjamin F. Butler

~~Nov~~ Dec. 2d 1864

Maj. Gen. Butler,

I understand that Pollard,[1] the Southern Historian, is at Fortress Monroe paroled and going about the Wharf and elswhere with freedom. The imprudence of many of our officers in telling all they know to every one makes this objectionable, particularly if he is to be exchanged. I would suggest close confinement for him until the time comes for exchanging. I would also suggest that if he is exchanged Richardson & Brown,[2] two correspondents that were captured running the Vicksburg blockade, be demanded for him.

U. S. GRANT
Lt. Gn.

ALS (telegram sent), CSmH; telegram received (at 9:35 P.M.), DLC-Benjamin F. Butler. *O.R.*, I, xlii, part 3, 782. On Dec. 2, 1864, 9:20 P.M., Maj. Gen. Benjamin F. Butler telegraphed to USG. "I will attend to the matter of Mr Pollard I did ~~k~~ not know that he was ~~to come up—He is not to~~ at large—He is not to be exchanged unless Richardson and Brown are given up—" LS (telegram sent), DNA, RG 107, Telegrams Collected (Unbound); telegram received, *ibid.*, RG 108, Letters Received. *O.R.*, I, xlii, part 3, 782. See telegram to Edwin M. Stanton, Dec. 21, 1864.

On Dec. 31, 12:30 P.M., Butler telegraphed to USG. "Is there any reason now why Pollard may not be sent through the lines to effect the exchange of Richardson the Tribune correspondent as there is no movement at present of which he can speak" Telegram received (at 1:10 P.M.), DNA, RG 108, Letters Received; copy, *ibid.*, RG 107, Telegrams Collected (Unbound). On the same day, USG telegraphed to Butler. "I would [be] very glad to exchange Pollard for Richardson. I think Brown who was captured at the same time should be released." Telegram received, *ibid.*; copies, *ibid.*, RG 108, Letters Sent; DLC-USG, V, 45, 71, 107.

1. Edward A. Pollard, born in 1832 in Va., on the staff of the *Richmond Examiner* during the Civil War, wrote a *Southern History of the War* published in annual volumes during the war. Captured while running the blockade in 1864, he was first imprisoned at Boston, then allowed to visit relatives in Brooklyn. Jack P. Maddex, Jr., *The Reconstruction of Edward A. Pollard: A Rebel's Conversion to Postbellum Unionism* (Chapel Hill, 1974), pp. [3]–5.

2. Correspondents Junius H. Browne and Albert D. Richardson of the *New York Tribune* and Richard T. Colburn of the *New York World* were captured on May 3, 1863, while attempting to run the Vicksburg batteries. Junius Henri Browne, *Four Years in Secessia . . .* (Detroit, 1866), pp. 231–39; Albert D. Richardson, *The Secret Service, the Field, the Dungeon, and the Escape* (Hartford, 1865), pp. 337–45. Because of their strong dislike of the *Tribune*, C.S.A. authorities soon released Colburn but refused to discuss the exchange of the others. On Dec. 18, 1864, Richardson and Browne escaped.

To Maj. Gen. George H. Thomas

(Cipher)   City Point Va. Dec. 2d *1864.* [*11:30* A.M.]
MAJ. GEN. THOMAS, NASHVILLE TENN.

If Hood is permitted to remain quietly about Nashville you will loose all the road back to Chattanooga and possibly have to abandon the line of the Tenn. Should he attack you it is all well but if he does not you should attack him before he fortifies. Arm and put in the trenches your Qr. Mr. employees, citizens &c.

U. S. GRANT
Lt. Gn.

ALS (telegram sent), Elkins Collection, Free Library of Philadelphia, Philadelphia, Pa.; telegram received (marked as sent at 11:00 A.M., received at 2:00 P.M.), DNA, RG 107, Telegrams Collected (Bound). *O.R.*, I, xlv, part 2, 17.

To Maj. Gen. George H. Thomas

City Point Va
Dec. 2nd 1864 1.30 P. M

MAJ GEN GEO H. THOMAS
NASHVILLE TENN.

With your citizen employees all armed you can move out of Nashville with all your army and force the enemy to retire or fight upon ground of your own chosing. After the repulse of Hood at Franklin[1] it looks to me that instead of falling back to Nashville we should have taken the offensive against the enemy, at this distance however I may err as to the best method of dealing with the enemy. You will now suffer incalculable injury upon your Rail Roads if Hood is not speedily disposed of, put forth therefore every possible exertion to attain this end. Should you get him to retreating give him no peace

U. S. GRANT
Lt Genl.

Telegram received (at 2:10 P.M.), DNA, RG 107, Telegrams Collected (Bound); copies, *ibid.*, Telegrams Received in Cipher; *ibid.*, RG 108, Letters Sent; *ibid.*, RG 393, Dept. of the Cumberland, Telegrams Received; DLC-USG, V, 45, 70, 107; DLC-John M. Schofield. On Dec. 2, 1864, 10:00 P.M., Maj. Gen. George H. Thomas telegraphed to USG. "Your two telegrams of 11 A M and 1.30 P M to day recd—At the time that Hood was whipped at Franklin I had at this place but about five thousand men of Gen. A. J. Smith's command which added to the force under Schofield would not have given me more than twenty five thousand men, besides Schofield felt convinced that he could not hold the enemy at Franklin until the five thousand could reach him— As Gen Wilsons cavalry force also made only about one fourth that of Forrest, I thought it best to draw troops back to Nashville, and wait arrival of the remainder of Gen A J. Smith's force, and also force of about five thousand commanded by Gen Steedman, which I had ordered up from Chattanooga. The Division of A J Smith arrived yesterday morning and Steedman's arrived last night I now have Infantry enough to assume the offensive, if I had more cavalry, and will take the field any how as soon as remainder of Gen McCooks Division cavalry reaches here, which I hope will be in three or four days We can neither get reinforcements or equipments at this great distance from the north very easily, and it must be remembered that my command was made up of the two weakest corps of Gen Sherman's army, and all the dismounted cavalry, except one Brigade, and task of reorganizing & equiping has met with many delays, which have enabled Hood take advantage my crippled condition I earnestly hope however that in few more days shall be able give him fight—" Telegram received (on Dec. 3, 1:15 A.M.), DNA, RG 107, Telegrams Collected (Bound); *ibid.*, RG 108, Letters Received; DLC-John M. Schofield; copies, *ibid.*; DNA, RG 107, Telegrams Received in Cipher; *ibid.*, RG 393, Dept. of the Cumberland, Telegrams Sent. *O.R.*, I, xlv, part 2, 17–18.

1. On Dec. 1, USG telegraphed to Maj. Gen. George G. Meade. "The following dispatch just received from General Schofield—thro Genl Thomas. . . . Franklin Tenn. November 30th 1864. The enemy made a heavy and presistent attack with about two Corps, commencing at about four (4) o'clock this afternoon, and lasting until after dark. He was repulsed at all points with very heavy loss, probably five (5) or six (6) thousand men—Our loss is probably not more than one tenth that number. We have captured about one thousand (1000) men including one (1) Brig. Gen'l (Sgd) J M SCHOFIELD MAJ. GEN'L" Copies, DNA, RG 393, Army of the Potomac, Telegrams Received; Meade Papers, PHi. See *O.R.*, I, xlv, part 1, 1171.

To Julia Dent Grant

City Point, Va. ~N~Dec. 2d *1864*

DEAR JULIA,

I have just received your letter saying that you would start in a few days to pay me a visit. On reflection I will not write to the Manager of the rail-road to send you a ticket. Fred. can get your ticket before you leave Burlington so that you will have no trouble. I will meet you in Washington with a special boat. As you start so soon I will write no more letter to you. I will however write to the children every two or three days. Have you heard anything further from your house in Phila? You will be here so soon however that it is not necessary to answer any questions. Love and kisses for you and the children.

ULYS.

ALS, DLC-USG.

To Maj. Gen. George G. Meade

By Telegraph from City Point 1 30 P M
Dated Decr 3d *1864*.

To MAJOR GEN MEADE

The sixth (6th) Corps will probably begin to arrive here tonight or in the morning.—As soon as it does get here I want you to move with the Second (2d) and about two (2) Divisions of the Fifth (5th) Corps down the Weldon railroad destroying it as far to the South as possible. Four (4) guns to each Division I think will be the greatest abundance to take and six (6) days rations

U S GRANT
Lt Genl

Telegram received, DNA, RG 94, War Records Office, Army of the Potomac; copies, *ibid.*, RG 108, Letters Sent; DLC-USG, V, 45, 70, 107; Meade Papers, PHi. *O.R.*, I, xlii, part 3, 784. On Dec. 3, 1864, 3:00 P.M. (sent at 3:15 P.M.), Maj. Gen. George G. Meade telegraphed to USG. "I would suggest, the relieving the whole of the 5th corps by the 6th on its arrival—then sending the 5th corps with one or two divisions of the 2d on the expedition proposed—I should myself think one division would be sufficient with the cavalry—as this would give Warren nearly 25,000 men—My object in making this suggestion is as Warren ranks Humphreys & would take the command it is better for him to have his whole corps—Humphreys would not go unless two divisions of his Corps are sent.—" ALS, DNA, RG 94, War Records Office, Army of the Potomac; telegram received, *ibid.*, RG 108, Letters Received. *O.R.*, I, xlii, part 3, 784–85.

To Maj. Gen. George G. Meade

By Telegraph from City Point 5 30 P M
Dated Dec 3d *1864*.

To MAJOR GENERAL MEADE

If but one (1) Corps goes on the expedition mentioned in my despatch of this morning I would as soon General Humphreys would command it as any other officer; thinking it however it ~~however~~ better to take a larger force I named relieving part of the Fifth (5th) Corps because I would sooner trust Warren in command than Wright—I think there should be a force of twenty thousand (20.000) infantry and then all the reserves that possibly be spared from the lines should be held ready to go after the enemy if he follows—I will write my views more fully before the expedition starts

U S GRANT
Lt Genl

Telegram received, DNA, RG 94, War Records Office, Army of the Potomac; copies, *ibid.*, RG 108, Letters Sent; DLC-USG, V, 45, 70, 107; Meade Papers, PHi. *O.R.*, I, xlii, part 3, 785.

To Maj. Gen. William T. Sherman

City Point, Va, Dec. 3d *1864.*

MAJ. GEN. W. T. SHERMAN,
COMD.G ARMIES NEAR SAVANNAH, GA,
GENERAL,

The little information gleaned from the Southern press indicating no great obsticle to your progress I have directed your mails, which had previously been collected in Baltimore by Col. Markland, Spl. Agt. of the P. O. Dept. to be sent as far as the Blockading Squadron off Savannah to be forwarded to you as soon as heard from on the Coast. Not liking to rejoice before the victory is assured I abstain from congratulating you and those under your command until bottom has been struck. I have never had a fear however for the result.

Since you left Atlanta no very great progress has been made here. The enemy has been closely watched though and prevented from detaching against you. I think not one man has gone from here except some twelve or fifteen hundred dismounted Cavalry. Bragg has gone from Wilmington. I am trying to take advantage of his absence to get possession of that place. Owing to some preparations Admiral Porter and Gen. Butler are making to blow up Fort Fisher, and which, whilst I hope for the best, do not believe a particle in, there is a delay in getting this expedition off. I hope they will be ready to start by the 7th and that Bragg will not have started back by that time.

In this letter I do not intend to give you anything like directions for future action but will state a general idea I have and will get your views after you have established yourself on the Sea Coast. With your veteran Army I hope to get controll of the only two through routes, from East to West, possessed by the enemy before the fall of Atlanta. This condition will be filled by holding Savannah and Augusta, or by holding any other port to the East of Savannah, and Branchville. If Wilmington falls a force from there can co-operate with you.

Thomas has got back into the defences of Nashville, with Hood close upon him. Decatur has been abandoned and so has all the roads except the Main one leading to Chattanooga. Part of this falling back was undoubtedly necessary and all of it may have been. It did not look so however to me. In my opinion Thomas far outnumbers Hood in Infantry. In Cavalry Hood has the advantage in morale and numbers. I hope yet Hood will be badly crippled if not destroyed.

The general news you will learn from the papers better than I could give it.

After all becomes quiet and roads up here so bad that there is likely to be a week or two of ~~quiet~~ that nothing can be done I will run down the Coast and see you. If you desire it I will ask Mrs. Sherman to go with me.

Yours Truly
U. S. GRANT
Lt. Gen.

ALS, DLC-William T. Sherman. *O.R.*, I, xliv, 611–12.

On Nov. 20, 1864, Brig. Gen. John A. Rawlins telegraphed to Secretary of War Edwin M. Stanton, sending a copy to USG, transmitting news of Maj. Gen. William T. Sherman's movements from the *Richmond Dispatch*. Telegram received (at 1:00 P.M.), DNA, RG 107, Telegrams Collected (Bound). On Nov. 21, 4:00 P.M., Rawlins telegraphed to USG and Stanton transmitting additional news about Sherman from the Richmond paper. Telegram received (at 4:45 P.M.), *ibid.*; (at 5:00 P.M.) *ibid.*, RG 94, War Records Office, Dept. and Army of Ga. *O.R.*, I, xliv, 506–7. At 4:30 P.M., Rawlins telegraphed to USG. "Perhaps it would be well not to take official notice of this summary of news from the

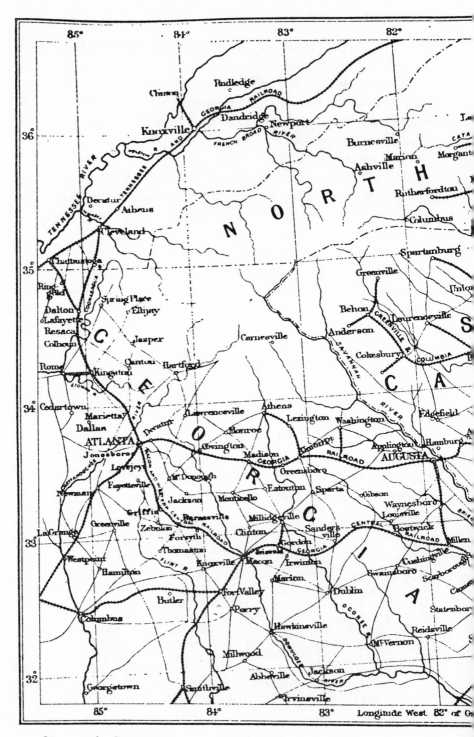

Sherman's Campaigns through Georgia and the Carolinas, 1864–65

SHERMAN'S MARCHES
THROUGH
GEORGIA AND THE CAROLINAS
1864-5.

Richmond papers lest the rebel authorities prohibit the publication of news from
Sherman altogether." Telegram received (at 6:00 P.M.), DNA, RG 94, War
Records Office, Dept. and Army of Ga.; *ibid.*, RG 107, Telegrams Collected
(Bound); *ibid.*, Telegrams Collected (Unbound); copies, *ibid.*, Telegrams Received in Cipher; Rawlins Papers, ICHi. *O.R.*, I, xliv, 507. On Nov. 22, 7:00
P.M., Rawlins telegraphed to USG, sending a copy to Stanton, transmitting news
of Sherman. Telegram received (at 7:30 P.M.), DNA, RG 107, Telegrams Collected (Bound); copy, *ibid.*, Telegrams Collected (Unbound). *O.R.*, I, xliv, 518.
On Nov. 23, Rawlins twice telegraphed to USG, the second time at 9:30 P.M.,
transmitting news of Sherman. Telegrams received (at 3:10 P.M. and 9:25
P.M.), DNA, RG 107, Telegrams Collected (Bound). On Nov. 24, 10:30 A.M.,
Rawlins telegraphed to Stanton transmitting a telegram from Maj. Gen. George
G. Meade which reported that deserters stated that Sherman had captured
Macon. Telegram received (at 8:30 P.M.), *ibid.*; copies, *ibid.*, Telegrams Received in Cipher; *ibid.*, RG 108, Letters Sent; DLC-USG, V, 45, 70, 107. *O.R.*,
I, xlii, part 3, 693. The telegram received from Meade is in DNA, RG 108,
Letters Received.

On Dec. 1, 10:30 P.M., USG telegraphed to Stanton. "The Richmond Examiner of to-day idmits that Sherman will succeed in reaching the Sea coast.
Other papers admit that he has crossed the Oconee." ALS (telegram sent),
IHi; telegram received (at 11:15 P.M.), DNA, RG 107, Telegrams Collected
(Bound).

On Dec. 3, USG telegraphed to Maj. Gen. Benjamin F. Butler. "Please
telegraph me if there is any news from Sherman in the Richmond papers of
today." Telegram received, DLC-Benjamin F. Butler. At 8:00 P.M., Butler telegraphed to USG. "There is absolutely no news in the Richmond papers from
Sherman—An extract fom Savannah News says Oconee Bridge is burnt Nov 20th
and that on Tuesday the Enemy made his appearance at Griswoldville bunt the
Town had a battle & were repulsed—And that a raiding party had Approached
Warrenton But all this seems to be only accounts of skirmishes Send papers"
ALS (telegram sent), DNA, RG 107, Telegrams Collected (Unbound); telegram received (at 8:30 P.M.), *ibid.*, RG 108, Letters Received.

On Dec. 5, 1:40 P.M., Butler telegraphed to USG. "Richmond papers just
in. Sherman reached Milledgeville on the 20th, and left with his main body 25th.
They cannot make out where he is or where he is going. Dates of Georgia papers
to the 30th. Orderly on the way with papers." *O.R.*, I, xlii, part 3, 816.

On Dec. 7, 1:30 P.M., Butler telegraphed to USG. "Richmond papers just in
The augusta Chronicle of third (3) says, The Enemy broke his camp at Louisville & moved towards no 9 on central Road the fourteenth (14) & twentieth
(20) army Corps in advance and further says by reference to Map that Millen
is fifty seven (57) miles from savannah & one hundred and twenty (120) from
Charleston and ninety seven (97) from Darien to which place it is thought he
is moving, Sherman left Atlanta on twelfth (12th) of November reaching Millen
on second (2d) Dec he has traversed one hundred & sixty five (165) miles in
twenty (20) days travelling at same rate he would reach savannah on nineth
(9th) or if to Darien he would reach that place on the 15th" Telegram received, DNA, RG 108, Letters Received.

To Maj. Gen. Henry W. Halleck

Cipher   City Point, Va, Dec. 4th *1864*. [*9:30* A.M.]
MAJ. GEN. HALLECK, WASHINGTON,

Lieut. Dunn of my Staff starts this morning for New York with dispatch for Gen. Sherman. Col. Markland[1] will leave N. Y. at the same time with the accumulated Mails for Gen. Sherman's Army. Any information desirable to communicate to Gen. Sherman, up to Teusday[2] morning next, if sent to Lieut. Dunn at the Aster House, New York will be in time to be taken by him.

The Richmond papers of yesterday having no news from Sherman except what they can glean from Augusta papers as old as those already received by us argues favorably for us.

U. S. GRANT
Lt[. Gen.]

ALS (telegram sent), IHi; telegram received (marked as sent at 10:30 A.M., received at 11:20 A.M.), DNA, RG 107, Telegrams Collected (Bound).

1. On Dec. 4, 1864, 5:15 P.M., Post Office Agent Absalom H. Markland, Fort Monroe, telegraphed to USG. "The Captain of U. S transport Genl Lyon just arrived from Savannah having left there Thursday night. Sherman was then at Millen with his whole force. People at Savannah badly scared." ALS (telegram sent), *ibid.*, Telegrams Collected (Unbound).
2. Dec. 6.

To Maj. Gen. Benjamin F. Butler

(Cipher)   City Point, Va, Dec. 4th 1864 [*10:00* A.M.]
MAJ. GN. BUTLER,

I feel great anxiety to see the Wilmington expedition off both on account of the present fine weather, which we can expect no great continuance of, and because Sherman may now be expected to strike the Sea Coast any day leaving Bragg free to return. I think it advisable for you to notify Admiral Porter and get off without any delay with or without your powder boat.

U. S. GRANT
Lt. Gn.

ALS (telegram sent), PPRF; telegram received (at 11:00 A.M.), DNA, RG 107, Telegrams Collected (Unbound). *O.R.*, I, xlii, part 1, 971; *ibid.*, I, xlii, part 3, 799.

On Dec. 4, 1864, 11:15 A.M., Maj. Gen. Benjamin F. Butler telegraphed to USG. "I will leave for you Hd Qrs in few minutes" Telegram received, DNA, RG 107, Telegrams Collected (Unbound).

At 2:30 P.M., USG telegraphed to Brig. Gen. Rufus Ingalls. "Get transportation for 6.500 Inf.y and ~~twelve guns~~ two six gun batteries, without horses, at Fortress Monroe by the morning of the seventh. Vessels able to go to sea will be required." ALS (telegram sent), CSmH; telegram received (at 3:30 P.M.), DNA, RG 107, Telegrams Collected (Bound).

To Maj. Gen. Philip H. Sheridan

(Cipher) City Point, Va. Dec. 4th *1864.* [*8:00* P.M.]
MAJ. GEN. SHERIDAN, KEARNSTOWN VA.

Do you think it possible now to send cavalry through to the Va. Central road? It is highly desirable this be done if it is possible. I leave the practicability of this to be determined by you.

U. S. GRANT
Lt. Gen.

ALS (telegram sent), Maine Historical Society, Portland, Maine; telegram received (at 9:00 P.M.), DNA, RG 107, Telegrams Collected (Bound). *O.R.*, I, xliii, part 2, 740. On Dec. 5, 1864, 12:30 P.M., Maj. Gen. Philip H. Sheridan, Kernstown, Va., telegraphed to USG. "I have contemplated a Cavly: raid on the Central rail road; intending to go myself, when things are satisfactory here: but from all the light which I have, I have not estimated the braking of the road as very important—I am satisfied that no supplies go over the road towards Richmond from any point north of the road; or from the Shenandoah Valley—on the contrary the rebel forces here, (in the valley) have drawn supplies from the direction of Richmond—To break the road at Charlottesville, and up to Gordonsville Gordonsville, would only be breaking the circuit—the supplies south of the road, and between it and the James river could be hauled on straight lines to the road, and run in both directions—via: Louisa C. H. and via: Lynchburg to Richmond—I have the best of evidence to show, that there is no depôts at Gordonsville, or Charlottesville; and that the trains passing through those places are only burdend by necessities for Early's Army—I think that the Rebels have looked at this matter about as I do—and they have not been at all fearful of my going in that direction; as the temporary distruction would only inconvenience them—and would be of no great value to me—I will make the raid soon, if it is made at all—and will only go myself, if all affairs here are in a healthy condition —" Telegram sent, DNA, RG 107, Telegrams Collected (Unbound); telegram received (at 1:00 P.M.), *ibid.*, Telegrams Collected (Bound); (on Dec. 6) *ibid.*, RG 108, Letters Received. *O.R.*, I, xliii, part 2, 743–44.

On Dec. 4, 1:30 P.M., USG telegraphed to Sheridan. "If you think it necessary to retain a Division of the 6th Corps for a few days do so." ALS (telegram sent), CSmH; telegram received (at 2:30 P.M.), DNA, RG 107, Telegrams Collected (Bound). *O.R.*, I, xliii, part 2, 739. At 3:00 P.M., Sheridan telegraphed to USG. "I would like to keep Gettys Div: here for a few days—if it will not very much interfere with your desires—If this Divisions remains here for a few days; it gives me security—and the movement of the other two Divs: forces the enemy to move one way, or the other—" Telegram sent, DNA, RG 107, Telegrams Collected (Unbound); telegram received (at 3:40 P.M.), *ibid.*, Telegrams Collected (Bound); *ibid.*, RG 108, Letters Received. *O.R.*, I, xliii, part 2, 739.

On Dec. 8, 3:30 P.M., Sheridan telegraphed to USG. "I send tomorrow morning the remaining division of the 6th Corps. No troops of the enemy have left the Valley except Kershaws division. I did expect that the movement of the two divisions of the 6th Corps would cause a movement on the part of the enemy but up to the present time it has not" Telegram sent, DNA, RG 107, Telegrams Collected (Unbound); telegram received (at 6:00 P.M.), *ibid.*, Telegrams Collected (Bound); *ibid.*, RG 108, Letters Received. *O.R.*, I, xliii, part 2, 756.

To Edwin M. Stanton

City Point 1 30 p m
Decr 5th 1864

HON. EDWIN M STANTON
SECY OF WAR

I am not in favor of using officers who have signally failed when entrusted with command in important places, again, as a general rule where an officer is entrusted with the command of a Department he ought to be allowed to use the material given him in his own way.

I would simply suggest the transmission of this dispatch to Schofield and leave it discretionary then with him to employ Stoneman or relieve him from duty as he deems best

U S GRANT
Lt Genl

Telegrams received (2—at 2:00 P.M.), DNA, RG 107, Telegrams Collected (Bound); copies, *ibid.*, Telegrams Received in Cipher; (marked as sent at 1:00 P.M.) *ibid.*, RG 108, Letters Sent; *ibid.*, RG 393, Army of the Ohio, Telegrams Received; DLC-USG, V, 45, 70, 107; (2) DLC-John M. Schofield. Printed as sent at 1:00 P.M. in *O.R.*, I, xlv, part 2, 54. On Dec. 5, 1864, 11:55 A.M., Secretary of War Edwin M. Stanton telegraphed to USG. "It appears from an order of Schofields that he had assigned Stoneman to duty as second in command of the Department of the Ohio. General Thomas and Schofield both wish him to hold that position. If you approve of his so doing I ~~will~~ am content although I think him one of the most worthless officer in the service and who has failed in everything entrusted to him. Please say whether he had better be restored to the command given by Schofield or whether Ammon should not be the chief in command in Schofields absence. If so send the order to Adjt Gen Townsend." ALS (telegram sent), DNA, RG 107, Telegrams Collected (Bound); telegram received, *ibid.*, RG 108, Letters Received. *O.R.*, I, xlv, part 2, 54.

To Maj. Gen. Henry W. Halleck

(Cipher)   City Point Va. Dec. 5th/64 [*8:30* P.M.]
MAJ. GN. HALLECK,

The enemy report having captured 800 prisoners, 1500 horses & mules, 200 wagons & ambulances 8 guns and to have destroyed a greatdeel of public property at New Creek. Is there anything of this?

U. S. GRANT
Lt. Gn

ALS (telegram sent), CSmH; telegram received (on Dec. 6, 1864, 7:25 A.M.), DNA, RG 107, Telegrams Collected (Bound); *ibid.*, Telegrams Collected (Unbound). See *O.R.*, I, xliii, part 2, 745–46. On Dec. 6, 1:00 P.M., Maj. Gen. Henry W. Halleck telegraphed to USG. "Genl Sheridan was ordered [s]ome days ago to report in [re]gard to New Creek disaster. The movements asked for by Genl Thomas against Mobile & Ohio R. R. were ordered by Genl Canby on the 25th & 26th ultimo, & these orders have [be]en repeated." ALS (telegram sent), DNA, RG 107, Telegrams Collected (Bound); telegram received, *ibid.*; *ibid.*, Telegrams Collected (Unbound); *ibid.*, RG 108, Letters Received.

To Maj. Gen. George G. Meade

City Point Va. Dec. 5th 1864

MAJ. GEN. G. G. MEADE
COM'D'G. A. P.
GENERAL,

You may make immediate preperations to move down the Weldon railroad for the purpose of effectually destroying it as far

South as Hicksford, or farther if practicable. Send a force of not less than 20.000 Infantry sixteen or twenty guns and all your disposable cavalry. Six days rations and twenty rounds of extra amunition will be enough to carry along. The Infantry amunition, I think, it will be advisable to carry in ambulances, six boxes to each team to avoid heavy trains as far as possible.

General Palmer probably started from New Berne yesterday or to day, with a force of from three to four thousand men to cut the same road, south of the Roanoke. His route is up the Chowan in steamers as far as he can get. The enemy are known to be fortifying about Rainbow. Gen. Palmer will endeavor to turn this position and capture the negroes and few troops engaged in the works. If successful he will then strike for the nearest point of the railroad south of Weldon and work on down the road to Goldsboro, or until driven off by a superior force. If he succeeds in reaching Goldsboro, he will move from there directly to New Berne.

The force you send should endeavor to destroy the railroad iron collected about Stony Creek either by fire or by twisting. After reaching Hickford it will probably be advisable to return by roads East of the Weldon road.

Whilst the expedition is out, reduce the number of men in the line to the lowest maximum. Hold all the reserves thus obtained in readiness to move south if their services should be required. Each reserve can be held in the rear of the Corps to which it belongs.

I avoid details, for the execution believing they can be better arranged by the officers who go in command of the troops—.

Very Resplly, Your Obt. Servt
U. S. GRANT
Lt. Genl.

Copies, DLC-USG, V, 45, 71, 107; DNA, RG 108, Letters Sent; (2) Meade Papers, PHi. *O.R.*, I, xlii, part 3, 804–5.

On Dec. 4, 1864, 11:30 A.M. (sent 11:50 A.M.), Maj. Gen. George G. Meade telegraphed to USG. "Genl. Parke yesterday afternoon opened his batteries on some working parties of the enemy in front of Fort Sedgewicke—From deserters who came in last night he is informed that the rebel General Gracie was killed by one of our shells.—Genl Gregg reports that about 2 o'clock this morning his outpost at Davenport Church was attacked by a dismounted force of the enemy & driven in losing one killed nine wounded & five missing, out of a strength of Twenty five—With the small force of cavalry & great extent of country to watch it is impossible to provide against these surprises of the advanced posts—Genl. Gregg immediately took measures to re-establish his post & pursue the assailants. With the above exceptions, all else has been quiet.—A report was brought by a deserter yesterday that Mahone with 10,000 men had gone to stoney creek, but no confirmation of this statement has been made, nor any evidence of the withdrawal of so considerable a body of the enemy from their lines.—" ALS (telegram sent), DNA, RG 94, War Records Office, Army of the Potomac; telegram received, *ibid.*, RG 108, Letters Received. *O.R.*, I, xlii, part 3, 794. On Dec. 5, 1:00 P.M., Meade telegraphed to USG. "Nothing of importance to report—A Deserter confirms the reported death of the confederate General Archibald Gracie.—Wheaten's division of 6th corps has arrived & is relieving Crawfords of the 5th   the divisions of the 5th corps as they are releived will be moved ~~in rear~~ outside of the rear line of works between the Weldon R. Rd. & the Jerusalem plank road.—"   ALS (telegram sent), DNA, RG 94, War Records Office, Army of the Potomac; telegram received, *ibid.*, RG 108, Letters Received. *O.R.*, I, xlii, part 3, 804. On the same day, USG telegraphed to Meade. "I read in a Richmond paper a full account of the death of Gen. Gracie. The same shot killed a Captain & private and wounded one other." ALS (telegram sent), CSmH; telegram received (at 1:30 P.M.), DNA, RG 94, War Records Office, Army of the Potomac. *O.R.*, I, xlii, part 3, 804.

On Dec. 4, Brig. Gen. John A. Rawlins telegraphed to Meade. "The advance of the 6th Corps is now debarking here   you will please send them necessary orders for the front. They are without transportation." Telegram received (at 1:14 P.M.), DNA, RG 94, War Records Office, Army of the Potomac; copies (2), Meade Papers, PHi. *O.R.*, I, xlii, part 3, 794. On the same day, Meade telegraphed to Rawlins. "I shall direct that the troops of the 6th Corps as fast as they arrive relieve the troops of the 5th A. C. in the position now held by the latter and that the 5th Corps on being relieved concentrate in some suitable position between the Halifax road and the Plank road (Jerusalem)"   Telegram received, DNA, RG 108, Letters Received; copy, Meade Papers, PHi. Printed as sent at 3:40 P.M. in *O.R.*, I, xlii, part 3, 795. On Dec. 5, Rawlins telegraphed to Meade. "A portion of the 3rd Division 6th Corps with Genl T Seymour in command arrived this morning, and have nearly completed their debarkation. The remainder of the Division will reach here this afternoon"   Copies (2), Meade Papers, PHi. Printed as received at 1:30 P.M. in *O.R.*, I, xlii, part 3, 805. At 1:45 P.M., Rawlins telegraphed to Meade. "At Gen. Sheridans request the order for Gettys division to return here has been suspended for a few days in which time he hopes to have more satisfactory information as to the intention of Early"   Telegram received, DNA, RG 94, War Records Office, Army of the Potomac; copies, *ibid.*, RG 108, Letters Sent; DLC-USG, V, 45, 70, 107; (2—misdated Dec. 6) Meade Papers, PHi. *O.R.*, I, xlii, part 3, 805. At 3:15 P.M., Meade telegraphed to USG. "Does the detention of Gettys division, make any suspension of your previous orders—If not I will place another division of the 2d corps in the front line so as to withdraw the whole of the 5th; but if you do not propose any movement before the arrival of Getty I will leave the Division of the 5th he is to releive in the line till he comes.—" ALS (telegram sent—misdated Dec. 15), DNA, RG 94, War Records Office, Army of the Potomac; telegram received (at 5:00 P.M.), *ibid.*, RG 108, Letters Received. *O.R.*, I, xlii, part 3, 805. At 6:30 P.M., USG telegraphed to Meade. "We will not wait for Getty's Division. How soon can you move troops? I have been waiting to get off troops in down the coast but as Palmer has already moved from Newbern will wait here no longer. I will go out to see you in the morning" ALS (telegram sent), CSmH; telegram received, DNA, RG 94, War Records Office, Army of the Potomac. *O.R.*, I, xlii, part 3, 806. At 9:30 P.M. (sent at 9:45 P.M.), Meade telegraphed to USG. "Genl. Seymour says it will take all day tomorrow to get his division up—if so by tomorrow night the 5th corps will be moved ready to move the next day—the cavalry & if required one division of the 2d corps can move at the same time—No orders or intimations of any have yet been given or will be till the last moment, so as to prevent the information getting to the enemy.—" ALS (telegram sent), DNA, RG 94, War Records Office, Army of the Potomac; telegram received (at 9:45 P.M.), *ibid.*, RG 108, Letters Received. *O.R.*, I, xlii, part 3, 806.

On Dec. 11, USG telegraphed to Meade. "Major Gen Wright is here and expects the arrival of his last Div tonight and Early in the morning At what point on the railroad will you have them debark" Telegram received (at 10:00 P.M.), DNA, RG 94, War Records Office, Army of the Potomac; copies (2), Meade Papers, PHi. *O.R.*, I, xlii, part 3, 953. At 10:15 P.M., Meade telegraphed to USG. "Maj. Genl. Wrights 3d. Division should debark on the Rail Road at Parke Station.—" ALS (telegram sent), DNA, RG 94, War Records Office, Army of the Potomac; copies, *ibid.*, RG 393, Army of the Potomac, Letters Sent; Meade Papers, PHi. *O.R.*, I, xlii, part 3, 953.

To Maj. Gen. George H. Thomas

(Cipher)   City Point, Va, Dec. 5th *1864*. [*8:00* P.M.]
MAJ. GEN. THOMAS, NASHVILLE TENN.

Is there not danger of Forrest moving down the ~~Tenn.~~ Cumberland[1] to where he can cross it? It seems to me whilst you should be getting up your cavalry as rapidly as possible to look after Forrest Hood should be attacked where he is. Time strengthens him in all probability as much as it does you.

U. S. GRANT
Lt. Gen.

ALS (telegram sent), CSmH; telegram received (on Dec. 6, 1864, 7:20 A.M.), DNA, RG 107, Telegrams Collected (Bound); *ibid.*, Telegrams Collected (Unbound). *O.R.*, I, xlv, part 2, 55. A copy is dated Dec. 6, 6:30 P.M., in DNA, RG 393, Dept. of the Cumberland, Telegrams Received. On Dec. 6, 8:00 P.M., Maj. Gen. George H. Thomas telegraphed to USG. "Your telegram of 6 30 P M Dec 5th just recieved. As soon as I can get up a respectable force of cavalry I will march against Hood. Gen Wilson has parties out now pressing horses and I hope to have some six or 8000 cavalry mounted in three days from this time. Gen Wilson has just left me having recd. instructions to hurry the cavalry remount

as rapidly as possible. I do not think it prudent to attack Hood with less than
6000 cavalry to cover my flanks because he has under Forrest at least 12000. I
have no doubt Forrest will attempt to cross the river but I am in hopes the gunboats will be able to prevent him. The enemy has made no new developments
today. Breckenridge is reported at Lebanon Tenn with 6000 men but I cannot
believe it possible" Telegram received (at 11:45 P.M.), *ibid.*, RG 107, Telegrams Collected (Bound); (on Dec. 7) *ibid.*, RG 108, Letters Received; copies,
ibid., RG 107, Telegrams Received in Cipher; *ibid.*, RG 393, Dept. of the Cumberland, Telegrams Sent; DLC-John M. Schofield. *O.R.*, I, xlv, part 2, 70.

1. Not in USG's hand. Tennessee appeared in the telegram as sent.

To Brig. Gen. Rufus Ingalls

City Point Va
Dec. 5th 1864. 11 30 A. M

BRIG GEN'L RUFUS INGALLS
CHF QR MR.

One division of troops have arrived, transports are unloaded
and sent back. Twenty three and half (3½) days grain and one
(1) days hay on hand. Pipe has not arrived for the hospitals yet,
its much needed. Bradley[1] says two (2) additional side wheel tugs
like the "Stevens" are much needed. Col Wise[2] was asked for them
some time since

U S GRANT
Lt Genl

Telegram received (at noon), DNA, RG 107, Telegrams Collected (Bound);
copy, *ibid.*, Telegrams Received in Cipher.

1. George W. Bradley of N. Y., appointed capt. and q. m. as of Nov. 26,
1862, assigned as lt. col. as of Sept. 17, 1864. On Nov. 5, Brig. Gen. Rufus
Ingalls wrote to Lt. Col. Theodore S. Bowers requesting that Bradley be placed
in charge of the City Point Depot with the rank of col. and that Capt. Henry B.
Blood be assigned as act. chief q. m., 10th Army Corps, with the rank of lt. col.
ALS, *ibid.*, RG 94, ACP, Q108 CB 1864. On Nov. 5, USG endorsed this letter.
"Respectfully forwarded to the Secretary of War. The assignments within re-
quested have been made. I recommend that Leiut. Col. George W. Bradley be
promoted to the grade of Colonel, and Capt. H. B. Blood to that of Leiut.enant
Colonel." ES, *ibid.* See *O.R.*, I, xlii, part 3, 518. On Nov. 15, Bvt. Maj. Gen.
Alfred H. Terry wrote to Ingalls. "Although I can hardly flatter myself that you
will recollect me, I trust that you will permit me to take advantage of the intro-

duction which I had to you about a year since to address you privately upon an official matter. I am very desirous that Captain William V. Hutchings should receive the appointment of Chief Quartermaster of this Corps and although by General Grant's Order Captain Blood has been assigned to that duty yet as I suppose that the appt. has not been made absolute by his promotion to be a Lt. Colonel I beg permission to present Captain Hutching's name for your consideration. Captain H. is a most excellent and faithful officer, & he has been connected with this corps for nearly two years, & he has repeatedly acted as chief. I have no doubt that Capt. Blood is a good officer. I know that were he not such he would not have been assigned to the position, but I am confident that he can be no more competent than Captain Hutching's if such be the case, it seems to me that the last named officers long & faithful service in the corps gives him a greatly superior claim to such promotion as may take place within it, & that he will have great reason to be disappointed if a stranger from another army is brought into the place. I have myself a high regard & esteem for Captain H & I should be extremely gratified if he could receive the promotion which I think is due to him. Should you find it possible consistently with your views of the public interest to reconsider the matter and make the appointment in accordance with these suggestions you would confer very great obligations on Your Most Obt. Sevt." ALS, DNA, RG 94, ACP, 601T CB 1864. On the same day, USG endorsed this letter. "Respectfully forwarded to the Secretary of War with the request that Capt. William V. Hutchings, Asst. Q. M. of Vols, be promoted to the grade of LieutenantColonel, and assigned as Chief QuarterMaster of the 10th Army Corps, vize Lieut. Col. Bradley appointed Colonel and assigned to the City Point Depot." ES, *ibid.* Also on Nov. 15, 9:00 P.M., USG telegraphed to Col. Edward D. Townsend. "On the fifth (5) inst I forwarded a communication from Gen Ingalls asking that Capt H. B. Blood Asst Quartermaster be promoted to the grade of Lieut Col & assigned as Chief Quartermaster of the tenth (10) Army Corps. I now withdraw the recommendation in this case and do not desire the promotion or assignment of Capt Blood" Telegram received (at 11:00 P.M.), *ibid.*, B169 CB 1864; *ibid.*, RG 107, Telegrams Collected (Bound); copies, *ibid.*, RG 94, ACP, T601 CB 1864; *ibid.*, RG 108, Letters Sent; DLC-USG, V, 45, 70, 107.

2. George D. Wise, appointed capt. and q. m. as of Sept. 28, 1861, and assigned as col. as of Aug. 2, 1864.

To William P. Fessenden

City Point, Va, Dec. 6th *1864.*

Hon. W. P. Fessenden,
Sec. of the Treasury,
Dear Sir:

The bearer of this, W. D. W. Barnard, is desirous of entering into such business as may be consistent with Treasury and Military regulations at such sea port as may be opened up by Gen. Sherman's expedition.

I have known Mr. Barnard for many years and will say for him what I have declined to say, universally, for the many others who have asked me for similar letters; *he will comply with all regulations, civil & Military, without watching.* I bespeak for Mr. Barnard such privileges as your Dept. think proper to grant loyal persons in the quarter here mentioned.

> I have the honor to be
> Very respectfully
> your obt. svt.
> U. S. GRANT
> Lt. Gn.

ALS, DNA, RG 56, Div. of Captured and Abandoned Property, Letters Received. See *PUSG*, 1, 342.

To Maj. Gen. Benjamin F. Butler

———

> *By Telegraph from* City Pt
> *Dated* Dec—6 *1864.* [3:00 P.M.]

To MAJ GEN BUTLER

A movement will commence on the left tomorrow morning—make immediate preparations so that your forces can be used north of the River if the Enemy withdraw, or South if they should be required —let all your men have 2 days cooked Rations in havresacks— during tomorrow night withdraw to the left of your line at Bermuda the force you propose sending South unles otherwise ordered —it would be well to get ready as soon as you ~~eavly~~ can to ~~blows~~ out the end of the canal.

> U S GRANT
> Lt Genl

Telegram received, DLC-Benjamin F. Butler; copies, DLC-USG, V, 45, 71, 107; DNA, RG 108, Letters Sent. *O.R.*, I, xlii, part 3, 834.

To Maj. Gen. Benjamin F. Butler

City Point, Va, Dec. 6th *1864.*

MAJ. GEN. B. F. BUTLER,
COMD.G ARMY OF THE JAMES,
GENERAL,

The first object of the expedition under Gn. Weitzel is to close
to the enemy the port of Wilmington. If successful in this the second will be to capture Wilmington itself. There are reasonable
grounds to hope for success if advantage can be taken of the absence of the greater part of the enemy's forces, now looking after
Sherman in Georgia. The directions you have given for the numbers and equipment of this expedition are all right except in the
unimportant matters of where they embark, and the amount of
intrenching tools to be taken. The object of the expedition will be
gained by effecting a landing on the main landing between Cape
Fear River and the Atlantic, North of the North entrance to the
river. Should such landing be effected whilst the enemy still hold
Fort Fisher, and the batteries guarding the entrance to the river,
then the troops should intrench themselves and by co-operating
with the Navy effect the reduction and capture of those places.
These in our hands the Navy could enter the harbor and the port
of Wilmington would be sealed. Should Fort Fisher, and the point
of land on which it is built, fall into the hands of our troops, immediately on landing, then it will be worth the attempt to capture
Wilmington by a forced march and surpris[e]. If time is consumed
in gaining the first object of the expedition the second will become
a matter of after concideratio[n.] The details for execution are
entrusted to you and the officer immediately in command of the
troops.

Very respectfully
your obt. svt.
U. S. GRANT
Lt. Gen.

P. S. Should the troops under Gen. Weitzel fail to effect a landing at or near Fort Fisher they will be returned to the Army operating against Richmond without delay.

U. S. G.

ALS, DLC-Benjamin F. Butler. *O.R.*, I, xxxiv, part 1, 40; *ibid.*, I, xxxvi, part 1, 43–44; *ibid.*, I, xxxviii, part 1, 32–33; *ibid.*, I, xlii, part 1, 971–72; *ibid.*, I, xlii, part 3, 835; *O.R.* (Navy), I, xi, 149–50.

Maj. Gen. Benjamin F. Butler had transmitted to USG a copy of his instructions of Dec. 6, 1864, to Maj. Gen. Godfrey Weitzel which Butler endorsed. "Respectfully forwarded to Lt General Grant for his information and with the earnest request that he will make any suggestion that may occur to him in aid of the equipment." AES, DNA, RG 108, Letters Received. *O.R.*, I, xlii, part 1, 973. The instructions are *ibid.*, pp. 972–73; *ibid.*, I, xlii, part 3, 837–38. At 4:00 P.M., USG telegraphed to Butler. "I had sent you a cipher dispatch before receiving copy of your instructions to Gn. Weitzel. I think it advisable all embarkation should take place at Bermuda. The number of intrenching tools designated I think should be increased three or four times." ALS (telegram sent), CSmH; telegram received, DNA, RG 107, Telegrams Collected (Unbound). *O.R.*, I, xlii, part 1, 973; *ibid.*, I, xlii, part 3, 834. At 6:25 P.M., Butler prepared a telegram to USG which was not sent. ALS, DNA, RG 393, Dept. of Va. and N. C., Telegrams Sent (Press). *O.R.*, I, xlii, part 3, 834. At 7:15 P.M., Butler telegraphed to USG. "Cipher despatch recievd Orders will be given to carry it out the orders contained in it" ALS (telegram sent), DNA, RG 107, Telegrams Collected (Unbound). *O.R.*, I, xlii, part 3, 835.

On Dec. 7, USG telegraphed to Butler. "Let Gen. Weitzel get off as soon as possible. We dont want the Navy to wait an hour." ALS (telegram sent), CSmH; telegram received (at 8:40 P.M.), DNA, RG 107, Telegrams Collected (Unbound). *O.R.*, I, xlii, part 1, 973; *ibid.*, I, xlii, part 3, 859. On the same day, Butler telegraphed to USG. "Gen Weitzels command is encamped at Signal Tower near Point of Rocks and awaits Orders—Admiral Porter telegraphs he will be ready by tomorrow" ALS (telegram sent), DNA, RG 393, Dept. of Va. and N. C., Telegrams Sent. *O.R.*, I, xlii, part 1, 973; *ibid.*, I, xlii, part 3, 858.

To Maj. Gen. William T. Sherman

Confidential—   City Point, Va, Dec. 6th *1864*.
MAJ. GEN. W. T. SHERMAN,
COMD.G MIL. DIV. OF THE MISS.
GENERAL,

On reflection since sending my letter by the hands of Lieut. Dunn I have concluded that the most important operation towards closing out the rebellion will be to close out Lee and his Army. You have now destroyed the roads of the South so that it will probably take three months, without interruption, to reestablish a through line from East to West. In that time I think the job here will be effectually completed. My idea now then is that you establish a base on the sSea Coast. Fortify and leave in it all your Artillery and Cavalry and enough Infantry to protect them, and at the same time so threaten the interior that the Militia of the South will have to be kept at home. With the balance of your command come here by water with all dispatch. Select yourself the officer to leave in command, but you I want in person.

Unless you see objections to this plan which I can not see use every vessel going to you for purposes of transportation.

Hood has Thomas close in Nashville. I have said all I could to force him to attack without giving the possitive order until to-day. To-day however I could stand it no longer and gave the order without any reserve. I think the battle will take place to-morrow. The result will probably be known in New York before Col. Babcock, the bearer of this, will leaves New York. Col. B. will give you full information of all operations now in progress.

> Very respectfully
> your obt. svt.
> U. S. GRANT
> Lt. Gn.

ALS, DLC-William T. Sherman. Printed as received on Dec. 15 in *O.R.*, I, xliv, 636–37. On Dec. 16, 1864, Maj. Gen. William T. Sherman, "Near Savannah," wrote to USG. "I received, day before yesterday, at the hands of Lieut. Dunn, your letter of Dec 3d and last night at the hands of Col. Babcock, that of Dec 6th. I had previously made you a hasty scrawl from the tug-boat 'Dandelion' in Ogeechee River, advising you that the Army had reached the sea coast, destroying all rail-roads across the State of Georgia, and investing closely the City of Savannah, and had made connection with the fleet. Since writing that note I have in person met and conferred with Genl. Foster and Admiral Dahlgren, and made all the arrangements which I deemed essential to reducing the city of Savannah to our possession. But, since the receipt of yours of the 6th I have initiated measures looking principally to coming to you with 50.000 or 60.000 Infantry and incidentally to take Savannah, if time will allow. At the time we carried Fort McAllister by assault so handsomely—with its 22 guns and entire garrison, I was hardly aware of its importance: but since passing down the river with Genl. Foster and up with Admiral Dahlgren, I realize how admirably adapted are Ossabaw Sound and Ogeechee river to supply an Army operating against Savannah—Sea-going vessels can easily come to Kings Bridge,—a point on Ogeechee River 14½ miles due West of Savannah—from which point we have roads leading to all our camps. The country is low and sandy and cut up with marshes which in wet weather will be very bad, but we have been so favored with weather that they are all now comparatively good, and heavy details are constantly employed in double corduring the marshes, so that I have no fears even of a bad spell of weather. Fortunately also, by liberal and judicious foraging, we reached the sea coast abundantly supplied with forage and provisions, needing nothing on our arrival except bread: of this we started from Atlanta provided with from eight (8) to twenty (20) days supply per Corps and some of the troops only had one (1) days issue of bread during the trip of thirty days: and yet they did not want—for sweet potatoes were very abundant, as well as corn meal, and our soldiers took to them naturally. We started with about 5.000 head of cattle and arrived with over 10.000—of course consuming mostly turkeys, chickens, sheep, hogs and the cattle of the country. As to our mules and horses we left Atlanta with about 2.500 wagons, many of which were drawn by mules which had not recovered from the Chattanooga starvation, all of which were replaced, the poor mules shot, and our transportation now is in superb condition—I have no doubt the State of Georgia has lost, by our operations, 15.000 first rate mules. As to horses, Kilpatrick collected all his remounts, and it looks to me in riding along our column, as though every officer had three or four horses and each regiment seems to be followed by at least fifty negroes and foot-sore soldiers, riding on horses and mules. The custom was for each Brigade to send out daily a foraging party of about fifty men, on foot, who invariably returned mounted, with several wagons loaded with poultry, potatoes, &c, and as the army is composed of about forty Brigades, you can estimate approximately the quantity of horses collected. Great numbers of these were shot by my orders, because of the disorganizing effect on our Infantry of having too many idlers mounted. Genl Easton is now engaged in collecting statistics in this line, but I know the Government will never receive full accounts of our captures—although the result arrived at was fully attained—viz: to deprive our enemy of them. All these animals I will have sent to Port Royal, or collected behind Fort McAllister, to be used by Genl. Saxton in his farming operations, or by the Quarter Masters Department after they are systematically accounted for. Whilst Genl. Easton is collecting transportation for my troops to James river, I will throw to Port Royal Island all our means of transportation I can, and collect the balance near Fort McAllister, covered by the Ogeechee River and intrenchments to be erected and for which Capt Poe my chief Engineer is now reconnoitering the ground—but in the mean time, will act as I have begun, as though Savannah City were my objective,—namely, the troops will continue to invest Savannah closely, making attacks and feints whenever we have firm ground to stand upon—and I will place some 30 lb Parrots, which I have got from Genl. Foster, in position, near enough to reach the centre of the city, and then will demand its surrender. If Gen Hardee is alarmed or fears starvation, he may surrender, otherwise, I will bombard the city but not risk the lives of my men by assaults across the narrow causeways by which alone I can now reach it. If I had time, Savannah with all its defendant fortifications, is already in our positsession, for we hold all its avenues of supply. The enemy has made two desperate efforts to get boats from above to the city, in both of which he has been foiled—Genl. Slocum whose Left flank rests on the river—capturing and burning the first boat, and on the second instance driving back two gunboats and capturing the steamer 'Resolute' with seven Naval officers and a crew of 25 seamen. Genl. Slocum occupies Argyle Island, and the upper end of

Hutchinson Island, and has a Brigade on the South Carolina shore opposite, and
he is very urgent to pass one of his Corps over to that shore—But in view of the
change of plan made necessary by your order of the 6th I will maintain things *in
Statu-quo* till I have got all my transportation to the rear & out of the way and
until I have Sea transportation for the troops you require at James River, which
I will accompany and command in person. Of course I will leave Kilpatrick with
his cavalry—Say 5.300—and it may be a Division of the 15th Corps, but before
determining this I must see Genl. Foster, and may arrange to shift his force,
(now near about the Charleston R. R. at the head of Broad River) to the Ogeechee, where, in co-operation with Kilpatricks Cavalry he can better threaten the
State of Georgia than from the direction of Port Royal. Besides I would much
prefer not to detach from my regular Corps any of its Veteran Divisions, and
would even prefer that other less valuable troops should be sent to reinforce
Foster from some other quarter. My four Corps full of experience and full of
ardor coming to you *en-masse*, equal to 60.000 fighting men, will be a reinforcement that Lee cannot disregard. Indeed, with my present command I had
expected, upon reducing Savannah, instantly to march to Columbia S. C. thence
to Raleigh, and thence to report to you. But this would consume, it may be, six
weeks time after the fall of Savannah—whereas, by Sea, I can probably reach
you with my men and arms before the middle of January. I myself am somewhat
astonished at the attitude of things in Tennessee—I purposely delayed at Kingston until Genl. Thomas assured me that he was *all ready*; and my last despatch
from him, of the 12th November, was full of confidence: in which he promised
me that he would 'ruin Hood' if he dared to advance from Florence,—urging me
to go ahead and give myself no concern about Hoods' army in Tennessee—Why
he did not turn on Hood at Franklin after checking and discomfiting him; sur-
passes my understanding. Indeed, I do not approve of his evacuating Decatur,
but think he should have assumed the offensive against Hood from Pulaski in the
direction of Waynesburgh [*Waynesboro*]. I know full well that Gen. Thomas is
slow in mind and in action: but he is judicious and brave, and the troops have
great confidence in him—I still hope that he will out-manoeuvre & destroy Hood.
As to matters in the South-east, I think Hardee in Savannah has good artillerists,
some 5000 or 6000 good Infantry, and it may be a mongrel mass of 8.000 or
10.000 Militia and fragments. In all our marching thro' Georgia he has not
forced me to use anything but a skirmish line, though at several points he had
erected fortifications and tried to alarm us by bombastic threats. In Savannah he
has taken refuge behind in a line constructed behind swamps & overflowed ricefields, extending from a point on the Savannah River about three miles above the
city, around by a branch of the Little Ogeechee—which stream is impassable
from its Salt marshes and boggy swamps, crossed only by narrow causeways or
common corduroy roads—There must be 25.000 citizens men, women, and children, in Savannah, that must also be fed; and how he is to feed them beyond a
few days, I cannot imagine, as I know that his requisitions for corn on the interior counties were not filled, and we are in possession of the rice fields and
mills which could alone be of service to him in this neighborhood. He can draw
nothing from South Carolina, save from a small corner down in the South-West
East, and that by a disused wagon road. I could easily get possession of this but
hardly deem it worth the risk of making a detachment which would be in danger
by its isolation from the main army—Our whole Army is in fine condition as to
health, and the weather is splendid. For that reason alone I feel a personal dislike

to turning North-ward. I will keep Lt Dunn here until I know the result of my demand for the surrender of Savannah, but whether successful or not, shall not delay my execution of your orders of the 6th, which will depend alone upon the time it will require to obtain transportation by sea—" LS, DLC-Edwin M. Stanton. *O.R.*, I, xliv, 726–28. On Dec. 20, USG endorsed this letter. "Respectfully forwarded to the Secretary of War, for his information." ES, DLC-Edwin M. Stanton. On Dec. 20, 2:00 P.M., USG telegraphed to Secretary of War Edwin M. Stanton. "Col. Babcock of my Staff has just returned from bearing dispatches to Sherman. As he visited and saw all the Army with Sherman I have thought it might prove interesting to you to see ~~the Col.~~ him. He will leave in the Mailboat in the morning with a copy of Sherman's letter." ALS (telegram sent), CSmH; telegram received (at 3:00 P.M.), DNA, RG 107, Telegrams Collected (Bound). *O.R.*, I, xliv, 765. On Dec. 18, 8:00 P.M., Sherman wrote to USG. "I wrote you at length by Col Babcock on the 16th inst. As I therein explained my purpose, yesterday I made a demand on Genl. Hardee for the surrender of the city of Savannah, and to-day received his answer, refusing: copies of both letters are herewith enclosed. You will notice that I claim that my lines are within easy cannon-range of the heart of Savannah: but General Hardee claims we are four and a half miles distant—But I myself have been to the intersection of the Charleston and Georgia Central Railroads, and the three mile post is but a few yards beyond, within the line of our pickets. The enemy has no pickets outside of his fortified line, which is a full quarter of a mile within the three (3) mile post: and I have the evidence of Mr R. R. Cuyler, President of the Georgia Central Railroad, who was a prisoner in our hands, that the mile-posts are measured from the Exchange, which is but two squares back from the river. But by tomorrow morning I will have six 30 pounder Parrots in position, and Gen. Hardee will learn whether I am right or not—From the left of our line, which is on the Savannah River, the spires can be plainly seen: but the country is so densely wooded with pine and live oak, and lies so flat, that we can see nothing from any other portion of our lines. Genl Slocum feels confident that he can make a successful assault at one or two points in front of the 20th Corps, and one or two points in front of Genl Davis' (14th) Corps. But all of Genl. Howards troops—the right wing,—lie behind the Little Ogeechee, and I doubt if it can be passed by troops in the face of an enemy—Still we can make strong feints, and if I can get a sufficient number of boats, I shall make a co-operative demonstration up Vernon River, or Warsaw [*Wassaw*] Sound—I should like very much indeed to take Savannah, before coming to you—but as I wrote to you before, I will do nothing rash or hasty, and will embark for the James River as soon as Genl Easton,—who is gone to Port Royal for that purpose,—reports to me that he has an approximate number of vessels for the transportation of the contemplated force—I fear even this will cost more delay than you anticipate, for already the movement of our Transports and the Gun-boats has required more time than I had expected—We have had dense fogs, and there are more mud-banks in the Ogeechee than were reported;—and there are no pilots whatever—Admiral Dahlgren promised to have the channel buoyed and staked, but it is not done yet—We find only Six (6) feet water up to King's Bridge at low tide, about ten (10) up to the rice-mill, and Sixteen to Fort McAllister—All these points may be used by us, and we have a good strong bridge across Ogeechee at Kings, by which our wagons can go to Fort McAllister, to which point I am sending the wagons (not absolutely necessary for daily use,)—the negroes, prisoners of war, sick &c, en-route for Port Royal—In relation to Savannah, you will remark that Genl Hardee refers to his still being in communication with his War Department—This language he thought would deceive me, but I am confirmed in the belief that the route to which he refers,— namely, the Union plank-road, on the South Carolina shore, is inadequate to feed his Army and the people of Savannah, for Genl. Foster assures me that he has his force on that very road near the head of Broad river, and that his guns command the Railroad, so that cars no longer run between Charleston and Savan- nah—We hold this end of the Charleston Rail-road, and have destroyed it from the three (3) mile post, back to the Bridge—about twelve (12) miles. In an- ticipation of leaving this country, I am continuing the destruction—of their Rail- roads, and at this moment have two-Divisions and the Cavalry at work breaking up the Gulf Railroad from the Ogeechee to the Altamaha, so that even if I do not take Savannah, I will leave it in a bad way—But I still hope that events will give me time to take Savannah, even if I have to assault with some loss. I am satisfied that unless we take it, the Gun-boats never will: for they can make no impression upon the batteries which guard every approach from the Sea—And I have a faint belief that when Col Babcock reaches you, you will delay opera- tions long enough to enable me to succeed—With Savannah in our possession, at some future time, if not now, we can punish South Carolina as she deserves, and as thousands of people in Georgia hoped we would do. I do sincerely believe that the whole United States, North and South, would rejoice to have this Army turned loose on South Carolina, to devastate that State in the manner we have done in Georgia: and it would have a direct and immediate bearing on your campaign in Virginia—" LS, DNA, RG 108, Letters Received. *O.R.*, I, xliv, 741–43.

To Maj. Gen. George H. Thomas

(Cipher)   City Point Va. Dec. 6th *1864.* [*4:00* P.M.]
MAJ. GEN. THOMAS, NASHVILLE TENN.

Attack Hood at once and wait no longer for a remount of your Cavalry. There is great danger of delay resulting in a campaign back to the Ohio river.

U. S. GRANT
Lt. Gen.

ALS (telegram sent), PHi; copies, DLC-USG, V, 45, 71, 107; DLC-John M. Schofield; DNA, RG 107, Telegrams Received in Cipher; *ibid.*, RG 108, Letters Sent; *ibid.*, RG 393, Dept. of the Cumberland, Telegrams Received. *O.R.*, I, xlv, part 2, 70. On Dec. 6, 1864, 9:00 P.M., Maj. Gen. George H. Thomas tele- graphed to USG. "Your telegram of 4 P M this day ~~recd~~ just received. I will make the necessary disposition and attack Hood at once, agreeable to your orders though I believe it will be hazardous with the small force of cavalry now at my service" Telegram received (on Dec. 7, 12:25 A.M.), DNA, RG 107, Tele- grams Collected (Bound); *ibid.*, RG 108, Letters Received; copies, *ibid.*, RG

107, Telegrams Received in Cipher; *ibid.*, RG 393, Dept. of the Cumberland, Telegrams Sent; DLC-John M. Schofield. *O.R.*, I, xlv, part 2, 70.

To Abraham Lincoln

(Cipher)   City Point, Va, Dec. 7th 1864 [*3:30* P.M.]
A. LINCOLN, PRESIDENT, WASHINGTON,
    The best interests of the service require that the troops of the Northwest, Departments of the N. W. Mo. & Kansas, should all be under one head. ~~and~~ pProperly they should all be in one Department. Knowing however the difficulty of displacing Department commanders I have recommended these Departments be ~~placed~~ ·thrown together into a Military Division and Gen. Pope put in command. This is advisable for the fact that as a rule only one point is threatened at a time and if all that territory is commanded by one man he can take troops from one point to satisfy the wants of another. With separate Department commanders they want to keep what they have and get all they can. This will not be the case with Dodge who has been apponted to command Mo. nor will it be with Pope.
                                        U. S. GRANT
                                        Lt. Gn

ALS (telegram sent), Lamon Papers, CSmH; telegram received (marked as sent at 4:00 P.M., received at 7:00 P.M.), DLC-Robert T. Lincoln; DNA, RG 107, Telegrams Collected (Bound). *O.R.*, I, xli, part 4, 784–85.

To Edwin M. Stanton

Cipher   City Point, Va, Dec. 7th/64 [*1:30* P.M.]
HON. E. M. STANTON, SEC. OF WAR,
    You probably saw my order to Thomas to attack? If he does not ~~does~~ it promptly I would recommend superceeding him by Schofield, leaving ~~S~~Thomas subordinate. Steele is an admirable

Corps commander and I would say order him to report to Canby until there is an opening to put him in command of a Corps. I would have no objection, would like, Steele appointed to command of 9th Corps and Parke ordered to report to Canby.

U. S. GRANT
Lt. Gen.

ALS (telegram sent), Broadcast Music, Inc., New York, N. Y.; telegram received (at 2:10 P.M.), DNA, RG 107, Telegrams Collected (Bound). *O.R.*, I, xlv, part 2, 84. On Dec. 7, 1864, 10:20 A.M., Secretary of War Edwin M. Stanton telegraphed to USG. "You remember that when Steele was relieved by Canby he was ordered to Cairo to report to this Department. What shall be done with him. The order ~~removing~~ superseding Rosecranz by Dodge has been issued. Thomas seems unwilling to attack because it is hazardous as if all war was any thing but hazardous. If he waits for Wilson to get ready, Gabriel will be blowing his last horn." ALS (telegram sent), DNA, RG 107, Telegrams Collected (Bound); telegram received (marked as sent at 10:00 A.M.), *ibid.*, RG 108, Letters Received. *O.R.*, I, xlv, part 2, 84.

To Maj. Gen. Henry W. Halleck

(Cipher)   City Point, Va. Dec. 7th/64 [*3:30* P.M.]
~~Hon. E. M.~~ MAJ. GN. HALLECK,

Every day I receive letters from rebel deserters who, in the absence of employment, have enlisted and now find themselves confronting their old regiments or acquaintances. I wish you would ask the sec. of War to give me discretionary authority to transfer such as I think deserving of it.

U. S. GRANT
Lt. Gn.

ALS (telegram sent), CSmH; telegram received (marked as sent at 4:00 P.M., received at 4:00 P.M.), DNA, RG 107, Telegrams Collected (Bound). Printed as sent at 4:00 P.M. in *O.R.*, I, xlii, part 3, 842. On Dec. 8, 1864, 3:00 P.M., Maj. Gen. Henry W. Halleck telegraphed to USG. "The Secty of War authorises such transfer of rebel deserters as you may deem proper. The transfers should be reported to Adjt Genl of the Army to be noted on rolls. There are still over two thousand enlisted rebel prisoners at Rock Island who have recieved bounties, but are of no use." ALS (telegram sent), DNA, RG 107, Telegrams Collected (Bound); telegram received, *ibid.*; *ibid.*, RG 108, Letters Received. *O.R.*, I, xlii, part 3, 863.

To Maj. Gen. Henry W. Halleck

(Cipher)   City Point, Va, Dec. 7th/64 [*10:00* P.M.]
MAJ. GN. HALLECK, WASHINGTON,

   Gen. Warren with a force of about 22,000 Infantry, six batteries and 4,000 cavalry started this morning with the view of cutting the Weldon rail-road as far South as Hicksford. Butler at the
same time is holding a threatening attitude North of the James to
keep the enemy from detaching from there. To-night he has moved
6.500 Infantry and two batteries across James River to be embarked at Bermuda to co-operate with the Navy in the capture of
the mouth of Cape Fear River. Palmer has also moved, or is supposed to have moved, up the Roanoke to surprise Rainbow, a place
the enemy are fortifying and to strike the Welon road if successful
South of Weldon. To-day Gen. Butler sent some troop[s] across the
river above Dutch Gap, and captured the pickets, and now holds the
opposite side of the river. It being a long bend, overflown by high
tide, with no outlet except along the levees on the bank, I think he
will be able to hold it. This may prove of advantage in opening the
Canal and is a decided advantag[e] in holding the enemy who have
long been expecting an attack when it is opened. It is calculated to
keep the enemy "at home" whilst Warren is doing his work.
                                       U. S. GRANT
                                       Lt. Gn.

ALS (telegram sent), IHi; telegram received, DNA, RG 107, Telegrams Collected (Bound). *O.R.*, I, xlii, part 1, 24; *ibid.*, I, xlii, part 3, 842.

To Maj. Gen. Benjamin F. Butler

                                   By Telegraph from City Pt 2.10 P M
                                       Dated Dec 7. *1864.*
To MAJ GEN BUTLER
   Good for Ludlow.[1] Is it possible now to take advantage of the
lodgement effected by him to carry the heights south of the river?

Please have this matter looked into. Warren moved at daylight this
morning.

U. S. GRANT

Lt Genl

Telegram received, DLC-Benjamin F. Butler; copies, DLC-USG, V, 45, 70, 107;
DNA, RG 108, Letters Sent. *O.R.*, I, xlii, part 3, 858. On Dec. 7, 1864, 2:00
P.M., Maj. Gen. Benjamin F. Butler telegraphed to USG. "Brig. Gen Ludlow
made a dash upon the other side of the River opposite Dutch Gap and captured
a half Dozen of the enemies Pickets and drove the rest away We now hold that
bank and Maj Michie is engaged in making his Surveys and Soundings preparatory to openig the Canal" ALS (telegram sent), DNA, RG 107, Telegrams
Collected (Unbound); telegram received, *ibid.*, RG 108, Letters Received. *O.R.*,
I, xlii, part 3, 858.

Also on Dec. 7, Butler endorsed to USG a telegram of 3:30 A.M. reporting
C.S.A. movements across the James River. *Ibid.*, p. 861. At 2:20 P.M., Butler
telegraphed to USG further news of C.S.A. movements. Telegram received,
DNA, RG 108, Letters Received. *O.R.*, I, xlii, part 3, 858.

1. Benjamin C. Ludlow, born in 1831 in Hamilton County, Ohio, graduated
in 1854 from the University of Pennsylvania with a degree in medicine, which
he practiced in New York City, Calif., Mexico, and Cincinnati. Appointed capt.,
4th Mo. Cav., as of Sept. 23, 1861, and maj. as of Oct. 14, 1862, he served on
the staff of Maj. Gen. Joseph Hooker as aide, on the staff of Maj. Gen. George
G. Meade as inspector of art., and in Feb., 1864, was appointed chief of cav. by
Butler. Appointed bvt. brig. gen. as of Oct. 28, for services at Dutch Gap and
Spring Hill, Va., he was assigned to command the cav. brigade, 25th Army
Corps, on Dec. 2. *Ibid.*, p. 783.

To Maj. Gen. George G. Meade

City Point, Va, Dec. 7th/64

MAJ. GN MEADE,

Has Gen Warren been heard from since he started? I know
that if any thing important had been heard it would have been reported. But I am anxious to learn even where there is no obsticle
to his advance.

U. S. GRANT

Lt. Gn.

ALS (telegram sent), CSmH; telegram received (at 5:15 P.M.), DNA, RG 94,
War Records Office, Army of the Potomac. *O.R.*, I, xlii, part 3, 843. On Dec. 7,
1864, 5:25 P.M. (sent at 5:32 P.M.), Maj. Gen. George G. Meade telegraphed

to USG. "I have received A despatch dated 11½ A m from Warren's adjt. Genl. and written at the crossing of Warwick Swamp by the Jerusalem plank road—reported the infantry nearly all passed at that time the column moving briskly & no detention or obstacle reported from the front.—This is all the news I have received—Warren will strike the road below stoney creek to prevent being detained by the works at that place.—A single gun supposed to be a signal gun by the enemy was heard here between 12 & 1. P. M—No indications of any movement as yet.—" ALS (telegram sent), DNA, RG 94, War Records Office, Army of the Potomac; telegram received, *ibid.*, RG 108, Letters Received. *O.R.*, I, xlii, part 3, 843–44.

At 10:30 A.M., Meade had telegraphed to USG. "Maj. Genl. Warren in command of 4. Divisions of Infantry the cavalry & Five batteries of artillery moved this morning at day light to execute your instructions received yesterday. —Had the present weather been anticipated I should have postponed the move- ment As it is if we are to have continued bad weather, it is as well it should be at the commencement ~~the~~ of the expedition rather than a later period.—The weather prevents our signal officers observing any movement of the enemy.— The lines are now held in such manner, that at short notice they can be left to the enclosed works & the picket line.—Maj. Genl. Crittenden reported yesterday & has been assigned to duty ~~with~~ under Maj Genl. Parke in the 9th corps." ALS (telegram sent), DNA, RG 94, War Records Office, Army of the Potomac; tele- gram received, *ibid.*, RG 108, Letters Received. *O.R.*, I, xlii, part 3, 842. On the same day, USG telegraphed to Meade. "The Pro Mar Richmond Agent brings information that Wilcoxs Div went South on Thursday last—Have you any in- formation to corroborate this" Telegram received (at 10:50 A.M.), DNA, RG 94, War Records Office, Army of the Potomac; copies, *ibid.*, RG 108, Letters Sent; DLC-USG, V, 45, 70, 107; (2) Meade Papers, PHi. *O.R.*, I, xlii, part 3, 843. At 11:20 A.M., Meade telegraphed to USG. "Our information from de- serters, contrabands & others is conclusive that Wilcox is in my front—deserters from two of his brigades, having been reported yesterday.—" ALS (telegram sent), DNA, RG 94, War Records Office, Army of the Potomac; copies, *ibid.*, RG 393, Army of the Potomac, Letters Sent; Meade Papers, PHi. *O.R.*, I, xlii, part 3, 843. At 6:45 P.M., Meade telegraphed to USG. "I forward despatch Just recd from Signal officers. The Cox Road runs nearly parallel to the s side R R & between & it & the Boydton plank. The movement reported is I think to meet an expected attack on the s side road." Telegram received, DNA, RG 108, Letters Received; copy, *ibid.*, RG 393, Army of the Potomac, Letters Sent. *O.R.*, I, xlii, part 3, 844. The enclosure is *ibid.*

To Maj. Gen. George H. Thomas

From City Point 5 p m Dec 7th *1864.*

MAJ GEN G H THOMAS NASHVILLE

The Richmond Sentinel of today, has the following—

"Intelligence received yesterday from East Tennessee an- nounces the advance of Burbridge from Kentucky which was met on part of Breckenridge by a retrograde movement to Greenville in order to protect his communications with the rear"

U. S. GRANT
Lt Genl

Telegram received (at 7:00 P.M.), DNA, RG 107, Telegrams Collected (Bound); copies, *ibid.*, Telegrams Received in Cipher; *ibid.*, RG 108, Letters Sent; DLC-USG, V, 45, 70, 107. Printed as received at 10:00 P.M. in *O.R.*, I, xlv, part 2, 84. On Dec. 7, 1864, 10:00 P.M., Maj. Gen. George H. Thomas telegraphed to USG. "Your despatch of 5 P M today just recd. Gen Stoneman telegraphed me yesterday that Breckenridge had fallen back. I have directed Stoneman to pursue him as far as he can into Va breaking & destroying 25 or 30 miles rail road and also to destroy the Salt works if possible" Telegram received (on Dec. 8, 3:30 P.M.), DNA, RG 107, Telegrams Collected (Bound); *ibid.*, RG 108, Letters Received; copies, *ibid.*, RG 107, Telegrams Received in Cipher; *ibid.*, RG 393, Dept. of the Cumberland, Telegrams Sent; DLC-John M. Schofield. *O.R.*, I, xlv, part 2, 84.

To Maj. Gen. Henry W. Halleck

(Cipher)   City Point, Va, Dec. 8th *1864*. [*4:00* P.M.]
MAJ. GEN. HALLECK, WASHINGTON

Please direct Gen. Dodge to send all the troops he can spare to Gen. Thomas. With such an order he may be relied on to send all that can pr[op]erly go. ~~Gen.~~ They had probably better be sent to Louisville for I fear either Hood or Breckinridge will get into the Ohio river. I will submit whether it is not advisable to call on Ohio Ia. & Ill. for Sixty thousand men for thirty days. If Thomas has not struck yet he ought to be ordered to hand over his command to Schofield. There is no better man to repel an attack than Thomas— but I fear he is too cautious to ever take the initiative.

U S GRANT
Lt Gen

ALS (incomplete facsimile telegram sent), Hanzel Galleries, Inc., Sept. 23–24, 1973; telegram received (at 5:30 P.M.), DNA, RG 107, Telegrams Collected (Bound). *O.R.*, I, xlv, part 2, 96. See following telegram. On Dec. 8, 1864, 1:20 P.M., Maj. Gen. Henry W. Halleck telegraphed to USG. "Last returns from Dept of Missouri exhibit a force present for duty (exclusive of A J Smith's forces) of about nineteen thousand men, of which about six thousand were in & around St Louis. Requisitions have just been recived for twenty thousand dol-

lars to construct new barracks for the accomodation of troops in St Louis.
[Fr]om all the information I can get St Louis is in no more danger of an insur-
rection than Chicago, Philadelphia or New York, and that troops are required
there [on]ly for the defence of the public stores, & for prison guards. Moreover,
that Missouri is not in the slightest danger of an invasion this winter. I therefore
respectfully suggest, that, now the commanding officer has been changed, five
thousand men from that Dept can be sent to Genl Thomas at Nashville. In case
of any real difficulty in Missouri they can readily be returned. As Genl Rawlins,
your chfofstaff, has recently visited St Louis, I submit the matter for your consideration." ALS (telegram sent), DNA, RG 107, Telegrams Collected (Bound);
telegram received, *ibid.*; *ibid.*, RG 108, Letters Received. *O.R.*, I, xli, part 4,
797–98; *ibid.*, I, xlv, part 2, 96.

To Maj. Gen. Henry W. Halleck

(Cipher)   City Point, Va, Dec. 8th *1864*. [*10:00* P.M.]
MAJ. GEN. HALLECK, WASHINGTON,

    Your dispatch of 9 p. m just received. I want Gen. Thomas
reminded of the importance of immediate action. I sent him a dispatch this evening which will probably urge him on. I would not
say relieve him until I hear further from him.

U. S. GRANT
Lt. Gn.

ALS (telegram sent), Mrs. Donald L. Burhans, Peoria, Ill.; telegram received,
DNA, RG 107, Telegrams Collected (Bound). *O.R.*, I, xlv, part 2, 96. On Dec.
8, 1864, 9:00 P.M., Maj. Gen. Henry W. Halleck telegraphed to USG. "If you
wish Genl Thomas relieved from command, give the order. No one here will, I
think, interfere. The responsibility, however, will be yours, as no one here, so
far as I am informed, wishes Genl Thomas' removal." ALS (telegram sent),
DNA, RG 107, Telegrams Collected (Bound); telegram received, *ibid.*; *ibid.*,
RG 108, Letters Received. *O.R.*, I, xlv, part 2, 96.

To Maj. Gen. George G. Meade

Dec. 8th/64

MAJ. GEN. MEADE,

    Hokes Division left Gen. Butlers front towards Petersburg last
night.[1] I suppose there is no doubt about this fact. I hope your Cav-

alry will be able to learn whether there has been any movement towards Warren. When this is known we will know what to do.

U. S. GRANT

Lt. Gn.

ALS (telegram sent), CSmH; telegram received (at 8:38 P.M.), DNA, RG 94, War Records Office, Army of the Potomac. Printed as received at 8:30 P.M. in *O.R.*, I, xlii, part 3, 866.

On Dec. 8, 1864, 8:30 A.M. (sent at 8:55 A.M.), Maj. Gen. George G. Meade telegraphed to USG. "The accompanying despatch was received after midnight last night. It is forwarded for your information—Warren will strike the road lower down than I designed.—" ALS (telegram sent), DNA, RG 94, War Records Office, Army of the Potomac; telegram received, *ibid.*, RG 108, Letters Received. *O.R.*, I, xlii, part 3, 864. The enclosure is *ibid.*, p. 855. At 10:20 A.M. (sent at 10:35 A.M.), Meade telegraphed to USG. "I forward for your information two despatches just received. I have made arrangements to hold my lines with about 11,000 men leaving about 22,000 men & 30 guns available for any movement." ALS (telegram sent), DNA, RG 94, War Records Office, Army of the Potomac; telegram received (undated), *ibid.*, RG 108, Letters Received. *O.R.*, I, xlii, part 3, 865. The enclosures are *ibid.*, pp. 869, 871. At 10:45 A.M., Meade telegraphed to USG. "I have about 700 mounted men whom I will push out on the left on the Vaughan road to see if they can ascertain or hear any thing of the movements of the enemy." ALS (telegram sent), DNA, RG 94, War Records Office, Army of the Potomac; telegram received, *ibid.*, RG 108, Letters Received. *O.R.*, I, xlii, part 3, 865. At 10:50 A.M., USG telegraphed to Meade. "If the enemy send off two Divisions after Warren what is there to prevent completing the investment of Petersburg with your reserves?" ALS (telegram sent), CSmH; telegram received (at 10:55 A.M.), *ibid.*, RG 94, War Records Office, Army of the Potomac. *O.R.*, I, xlii, part 3, 865. At 11:15 A.M. (sent at 11:50 A.M.), Meade telegraphed to USG. "I dont think the information of the sending of two divisions after Warren is as yet sufficiently positive to justify an attempt to complete the investment of Petersburgh—It would appear that Mahone only had moved tho it was reported Wilcox was to—at sundown yesterday he had not—Besides there is as yet no evidence that Mahone has gone after Warren—He was in reserve & may have moved only to cover an expected attack on the South side road—The cavalry I ~~have~~ am sending out will perhaps bring us positive information of any considerable movement against Warren.— Unless there is such, and even then, I hardly think my reserves will be sufficient to complete the investment & hold the new line against the forces in front and against a probable attack in the rear from the troops detached after Warren should they return on being advised of the danger.—I should therefore be in favor of waiting more positive information before making a movement.—" ALS (telegram sent), DNA, RG 94, War Records Office, Army of the Potomac; telegram received, *ibid.*, RG 108, Letters Received. *O.R.*, I, xlii, part 3, 865. At noon, Meade telegraphed to USG. "Forwarded for your information I judge from these & ~~th~~ preceding reports the the whole Rebel force in my front is ordered to be on qui vive with 3 days rations but as yet there is no positive indication of any movement except a concentration on their right ~~I~~ to wait developements" Telegram received, DNA, RG 108, Letters Received. *O.R.*, I, xlii, part 3, 869.

The enclosure is *ibid.*, pp. 868–69. At 1:30 P.M., USG telegraphed to Meade. "I would not favor moving to the left unless the most possitive evidence was had that the enemy had moved a very conciderable force away from Petersburg. Then it would be uncertain whether it would not be better to attempt to force a weak place in his lines." ALS (telegram sent), CSmH; telegram received (at 1:35 P.M.), DNA, RG 94, War Records Office, Army of the Potomac. *O.R.*, I, xlii, part 2, 866. At 7:20 P.M., Meade telegraphed to USG. "I send you all the information received since last despatch—You will see how conflicting it is Troops reported coming in cars from Richmond to Petersburgh—then reported moving from Petersburgh to Butlers front—again moving westward to the Cox & Boydtown Plank and then others reported leaving the lines near lead works & going in to Petersburgh—No large bodies reported moving in any direction.—I have not yet heard from the cavalry sent down the Vaughn road. A squadron of cavalry has just come in from the Nottoway river, where they were left by Warren till his column should pass & then directed to return here collecting stragglers   The Comd. officer reports the pontoon bridge over the Nottoway was taken up just before daylight when he immediately left—He brings in 850 stragglers—He estimates the distance to the bridge 20 miles—He has no news other than above—saw & heard nothing of the enemy on his return.—" ALS (telegram sent), DNA, RG 94, War Records Office, Army of the Potomac; telegram received, *ibid.*, RG 108, Letters Received. *O.R.*, I, xlii, part 3, 866.

1. On Dec. 8, Maj. Gen. Benjamin F. Butler transmitted to USG two signal messages, endorsing the second. "Respectfully forwarded for the information of Lt Genl Grant   Deserters Say that Hokes Division moved away last night but they did not know where   The enemy are strenghtenig their forces opposite Dutch Gap" AES (telegram sent), DNA, RG 107, Telegrams Collected (Unbound). *O.R.*, I, xlii, part 3, 886–87.

To Maj. Gen. George G. Meade

(Cipher)   City Point, Va, Dec. 8th *1864.* [*10:00* P.M.]
MAJ. GEN. MEADE,

Your dispatch received. I think it will be well to send out a Division of Infantry to help forcing a crossing of Hatcher's Run and find out what the enemy are doing. Send them in the morning. The enemy are playing a game of bluff with us now and as we hold the strong hand we want to take advantage of it. Any further movement than that in support of the Cavalry crossing Hatcher's Run will depend upon developments.

U. S. GRANT
Lt. Gen.

ALS (telegram sent), PPRF; telegram received, DNA, RG 94, War Records
Office, Army of the Potomac. *O.R.*, I, xlii, part 3, 867. On Dec. 8, 1864, 9:00
P.M. (sent at 9:40 P.M.), Maj. Gen. George G. Meade telegraphed to USG.
"The cavalry have returned—they found a force at the crossing of Hatchers run
by the Vaughn road, said to be Youngs brigade of cavalry—which prevented his
any further progress, and as it was nearly dark, when they reached there the
officer withdrew—with a loss of some 5 or 6 wounded. I have directed to start at
daylight tomorrow & try the Halifax road crossing which is lower down, but his
force is so small, that if the enemy undertakes to hold Hatchers run with his
cavalry, he can easily bar the passage to my small command which is only about
a regiment I think it very probable Hoke has come over this side—leaving Field
& Kershaw north of the James—I am quite satisfied Lee will offer a stubborn
resistance to any attempt on the South side road—I dont think he can detach a
force so far as will at all jeopardise Warren he may harrass & interrupt the
work of destroying the Rail Road but Warren has roads to the Eastward with
means of crossing the Nottoway at any point and can always withdraw.—The
difficulty of taking advantage of Lee's detaching against Warren is to get positive information of in the fact in time—The only certain information will be
Warren's report—unless deserters should come in tonight or tomorrow morning.
—I send you the last report from signal officer—" ALS (telegram sent), DNA,
RG 94, War Records Office, Army of the Potomac; telegram received, *ibid.*, RG
108, Letters Received. *O.R.*, I, xlii, part 3, 866–67. The enclosure is *ibid.*, pp.
873–74.

     At 10:30 P.M. (sent at 10:40 P.M.), Meade telegraphed to USG. "Brig.
Genl. Ledlie, after an absence of four months on sick leave has today returned to
this army.—After the reported conduct of this officer at the assault on the enemy's line on the 30th of July last, where it is well understood, he failed to accompany his Division when it advanced & for other reasons, I am constrained to
request he be relieved from duty with this army." ALS (telegram sent), DNA,
RG 94, War Records Office, Army of the Potomac; telegram received, *ibid.*, RG
108, Letters Received. *O.R.*, I, xlii, part 3, 867. At 11:00 P.M., USG telegraphed
to Meade. "Gen. Ledlie has been recommended by me for muster out of service.
Order him to his home to await orders and communicate to him the fact that he
cannot have here again another command." ALS (telegram sent), CSmH; telegram received (at 11:10 P.M.), DNA, RG 94, War Records Office, Army of the
Potomac. *O.R.*, I, xlii, part 3, 867.

To Maj. Gen. George H. Thomas

(Cipher)   City Point, Va, Dec. 8th/64 [*8:30* P.M.]
MAJ. GN. THOMAS, NASHVILLE TENN.

     Your dispatch of yesterday received. It looks to me evident the
enemy are trying to cross the Cumberland river and are scattered.
Why not attack at once? By all means avoid the contingency of a
footrace to see which, you or Hood, can beat to the Ohio. If you

think necessary call on the Governers of states to send a force into Louisville to meet the enemy if he should cross the river. You clearly never should cross except in ~~his~~ rear of the enemy. Now is one of the farest opertunities ever presented of destroying one of the three Armies of the enemy. If destroyed he can never replace it. Use the means at your command and you can do this and cause a rejocing that will resound from one end of the land to another.

U. S. GRANT
Lt. Gn.

ALS (telegram sent), Elkins Collection, Free Library of Philadelphia, Philadelphia, Pa.; telegram received, DNA, RG 107, Telegrams Collected (Bound). *O.R.*, I, xlv, part 2, 97. On Dec. 9, 1864, 1:00 P.M., Maj. Gen. George H. Thomas telegraphed to USG. "Your dispatch of 8 30 P. M of the 8th is just received I had nearly completed my preparations to attack the enemy tomorrow morning, but a terrible storm of freezing rain has come on to-day which will make it impossible for our men to fight to any advantage. I am therefore compelled to wait for the storm to break and make the attack immediately after. Admiral Lee is patrolling the river above and below the city and I believe will be able to prevent the enemy from crossing—There is no doubt but Hoods forces are considerably scattered along the river with the view of attempting a crossing —But it has been impossible for me to organise and equip the troops for an attack at an earlier time—Maj Genl Halleck informs me that you are very much dissatisfied with my delay in attacking I can only say I have done all in my power to prepare, and if you should deem it necessary to relieve me I shall submit without a murmur." ALS (telegram sent), MH; telegram received (at 4:10 P.M.), DNA, RG 107, Telegrams Collected (Bound); *ibid.*, RG 108, Letters Received. *O.R.*, I, xlv, part 2, 115.

To Edwin M. Stanton

———

(Cipher)   City Point, Va. Dec. 9th/64 [*1:00* P.M.]
HON. E. M. STANTON, SEC. OF WAR,

The names of Brig. Gen. J. C. Veatch and Brig. Gen. W. Vandiver[1] should be added to the list of Generals who should be mustered out of service or forced to resign. Veatch can not be got to do duty in the field and Vandiver is a drawback where he does serve. This was not Veatches character at the begining of the war but became so after leaving him in Memphis for a time.

U. S. GRANT
Lt. Gn.

ALS (telegram sent), CSmH; telegram received (marked as sent at noon, received at 1:40 P.M.), DNA, RG 94, Letters Received, 1361A 1864; *ibid.*, RG 107, Telegrams Collected (Bound).

1. William Vandever, born in 1817 in Baltimore, moved to Ill. in 1839 and to Iowa in 1851, where he practiced law and was elected a Republican U.S. Representative in 1858. He retained his seat in Congress when appointed col., 9th Iowa, as of Sept. 24, 1861, and brig. gen. as of Nov. 29, 1862.

To Edwin M. Stanton

City Point, Va, Dec. 9th *1864.*

HON. E. M. STANTON,
SEC. OF WAR,
SIR:

I would respectfully recommend Lt. Col. Wm T. Clark, A. A. Gen. Army of the Tenn. for promotion to Brig.adier Generalcy. There has been fewer promotions given to the Armies in the West than to those in the East recently. Col. Clark I know has been recommended for this promotion by the officers under whom he has served and once before I recommended him. I have been personally acquainted with his services from the advance on Corinth to the time I left Vicksburg in 1863. I know him to be eminently qualified for the position to which he is now recommended.

Hoping this promotion, so richly earned by long and valuable services, will be given, I remain,

Very respectfully
your obt. svt.
U. S. GRANT
Lt. Gn.

ALS, deCoppet Collection, NjP. William T. Clark, born in Conn. in 1831, practiced law in Davenport, Iowa, when the Civil War began. Appointed 1st lt. and adjt., 13th Iowa, as of Nov. 2, 1861, he was appointed capt. and adjt. as of March 6, 1862. On Oct. 11, Brig. Gen. Thomas J. McKean, Corinth, wrote to USG. "I wish to recommend in advance of the Official Report of the Battles of the 3rd & 4th inst the promotion of the following named Officers of my Staff 1st Capt Wm T. Clark Asst Adjutant Genl. Capt. Clark is an intelligent industrious and faithful Officer, and during the late Battle his conduct was distinguished for Zeal & Bravery—2nd—Lieut Mortimer A. Higley Qr. Mr. 15th Regt.

Iowa Vols. (Actg. Division Qr. Mr. during the battles of 3rd & 4th inst.)—Lieut
Higley is an energetic and business like Officer and saved the Division Equipage
on the 3rd inst by his good judgment & energy—And I recommend that he be
made 'Commissary of Subsistence with the rank of Captain' in Vol. service—"
ALS, DNA, RG 94, ACP, C1507 CB 1865. On Oct. 16, USG endorsed this
letter. "I would respectfully recommend that Capt. Wm T. Clarke Asst. Adj.
Gen. to Gen. McKean be promoted to the rank of Maj. and be attached to the
Staff of Maj. Gen. J. B. McPherson. Also that Lieut. Mortimore A. Higley,
R. Q. M. 15th Iowa Vols. be promoted to the rank of Capt. and C. S." AES,
ibid. Both men received appointments, and Clark advanced to lt. col. as of Feb.
10, 1863. On Jan. 30, 1865, Clark was nominated (and on Feb. 20 confirmed)
as bvt. brig. gen. to rank from July 22, 1864.

To Maj. Gen. Henry W. Halleck

(Cipher)   City Point Va. Dec. 9th *1864*. [*11:00* A.M.]
MAJ. GEN. HALLECK, WASHINGTON.

Dispatch of 8 p. m, last evening from Nashville shews the
enemy scattered for more than seventy miles down the river and
no attack yet made by Thomas. Please telegraph orders relieving
him at once and placing Schofield in command. ~~He~~ Thomas should
be directed to turn over all orders and dispatches received since
the battle of Franklin to Schofield.

                                                                    U. S. GRANT
                                                                    Lt. Gn.

ALS (telegram sent), CSmH; telegram received (at 1:45 P.M.), DNA, RG 107,
Telegrams Collected (Bound); (incomplete) InFtwL. *O.R.*, I, xlv, part 2, 115–
16. For orders drafted incorporating this telegram, see *ibid.*, p. 114. On Dec. 9,
1864, 4:10 P.M., Maj. Gen. Henry W. Halleck telegraphed to USG. "Orders
relieving Genl Thomas had been made out when his telegram of this P M. was
recieved. If you still wish these orders telegraphed to Nashville, they will be forwarded." ALS (telegram sent), DNA, RG 107, Telegrams Collected (Bound);
telegram received, *ibid.*; *ibid.*, RG 108, Letters Received. *O.R.*, I, xlv, part 2, 116.

To Maj. Gen. Henry W. Halleck

(Cipher)   City Point, Va. Dec. 9th *1864*. [*5:30* P.M.]
MAJ. GEN. HALLECK, WASHINGTON.

Gen. Thomas has been urged in every way possible to attack
the enemy even to the giving the possitive order. He did say he

thought he would be able to attack on the 7th but did not do so nor has he given a reason for not doing it. I am very unwilling to do injustice to an officer who has done as much good service as Gen. Thomas has, however and will therefore suspend the order relieving him until it is seen whether he will do anything.

U. S. GRANT

Lt. Gen.

ALS (facsimile telegram sent), Sotheby Parke Bernet, Elsie O. and Philip D. Sang Foundation sale, Nov. 14, 1978, no. 412; telegram received (at 6:00 P.M.), DNA, RG 107, Telegrams Collected (Bound). *O.R.*, I, xlv, part 2, 116.

On Dec. 10, 1864, 10:30 P.M., USG telegraphed to Maj. Gen. Henry W. Halleck. "I think it probably will be better to bring Winslow's cavalry to Gen Thomas until Hood is driven out. So much seems to be awaiting the raising of his cavalry force that everything should be done to supply this want—" Telegram received (at 11:00 P.M.), DNA, RG 107, Telegrams Collected (Bound); copies, *ibid.*, Telegrams Received in Cipher; *ibid.*, RG 108, Letters Sent; DLC-USG, V, 45, 70, 107. *O.R.*, I, xlv, part 2, 130.

To Maj. Gen. Benjamin F. Butler

———

By Telegraph from City Point

Dated Dec 9 *1864.* 2 p m

To MAJ GEN BUTLER—

The Steamer Empire City is loaded with ordnance stores bound for New Orleans   A telegraph from Washington just received shows that it is important that these Stores be forwarded   If you can dispense with this Vessel let her go on   if not the moment troops are debarked from her send her forward on her way

U. S. GRANT

Lt Gen.

Telegram received, DLC-Benjamin F. Butler; (press) DNA, RG 107, Telegrams Collected (Bound); copies, *ibid.*, RG 108, Letters Sent; DLC-USG, V, 45, 70, 107. See *O.R.*, I, xlii, part 3, 1080.

To Maj. Gen. George G. Meade

By Telegraph from City Pt
Dated Dec 9 *1864.*

To MAJ. GEN MEADE

Genl. Canby has releived Gen. Steele from the command of the dept. of Arkansas for failing to supply Fort Smith & his western posts in season   As it might not be pleasant for steele to serve under a division commander who releived him from the command of a department I have expressed a willingness that Parke should be ordered to report to Canby and Steele placed in command of the ninth (9) Corps—Steele is one of the best of commanders of troops in hand—

U S GRANT
Lt Gn.

Telegram received (at 12:[1]5 P.M.), DNA, RG 94, War Records Office, Army of the Potomac; copies, *ibid.*, RG 108, Letters Sent; DLC-USG, V, 45, 70, 107; (2) Meade Papers, PHi. *O.R.*, I, xlii, part 3, 890. On Dec. 9, 1864, 1:00 P.M., Maj. Gen. George G. Meade telegraphed to USG. "Your despaehtch in regard to proposed change in command of the 9th corps is received, and I have to state the same is satisfactory to me.—" ALS (telegram sent), DNA, RG 94, War Records Office, Army of the Potomac; telegram received, *ibid.*, RG 108, Letters Received. *O.R.*, I, xlii, part 3, 890.

To Maj. Gen. George G. Meade

By Telegraph from City Pt 2 15 P M
Dated Dec 9 *1864.*

To MAJ GEN MEADE

Your instructions to Gen Humphreys are satisfactory—If the enemy move against Miles he can be supported—In any event he can save himself by moving Eastward & then fall back—With the reinforcement the enemy is now receiving from the valley he may be strong enough to detach heavily by tomorrow—The remaining Div of the sixth corps starts tomorrow to join your command

U S GRANT
Lt Gen

Telegram received, DNA, RG 94, War Records Office, Army of the Potomac; copies (marked as sent at 2:25 P.M.), *ibid.*, RG 108, Letters Sent; DLC-USG, V, 45, 70, 107. Printed as sent at 2:15 P.M., received at 2:25 P.M., in *O.R.*, I, xlii, part 3, 891. On Dec. 9, 1864, USG had telegraphed to Maj. Gen. George G. Meade. "It is highly desirable that we should learn what the enemy are doing but Gen. Miles will have to be left with discretionary powers as to the Method of forcing the Crossing of Hatchers Run—I would simply say to him that the object is to learn if the enemy have detached against Warren and with what forces and leave him to select the way to do it" Telegram received (at 1:45 P.M.), DNA, RG 94, War Records Office, Army of the Potomac; copies, *ibid.*, RG 108, Letters Sent; DLC-USG, V, 45, 70, 107; (2) Meade Papers, PHi. Printed as sent at 1:45 P.M. in *O.R.*, I, xlii, part 3, 890. At 2:00 P.M., Meade telegraphed to USG. "I forward you a despatch from Maj. Genl. Humphrys & my reply therto which will explain existing condition of affairs & ~~will~~ answer yours of 1.45 P. M—" ALS (telegram sent), DNA, RG 94, War Records Office, Army of the Potomac; telegram received, *ibid.*, RG 108, Letters Received. *O.R.*, I, xlii, part 3, 890. The enclosures are *ibid.*, pp. 890–91.

At 9:00 A.M. (sent at 9:20 A.M.), Meade telegraphed to USG. "I send two reports received this morning.—The reconnaissance of the cavalry & a division of infantry moved this morning early but have not yet reported; progress.—" ALS (telegram sent), DNA, RG 94, War Records Office, Army of the Potomac; copies, *ibid.*, RG 393, Army of the Potomac, Letters Sent; Meade Papers, PHi. *O.R.*, I, xlii, part 3, 889. The enclosures are *ibid.*, pp. 894, 917. At 9:15 A.M. (sent at 9:30 A.M.), Meade telegraphed to USG. "The above just receivd is sent for your information.—" AES (telegram sent), DNA, RG 94, War Records Office, Army of the Potomac. *O.R.*, I, xlii, part 3, 889. The enclosure is *ibid.* At 11:15 or 11:45 A.M. (sent at 11:50 A.M.), Meade telegraphed to USG. "I transmit two despatches just recieved.—Miles has been advised to move cautiously after crossing Hatchers run—His right flank by the Duncan road & the one Hancock took is open & he is nearer to the enemy than to us—Humphrys has been ordered to hold another command in readiness to move to his support if neccessary.—" ALS (telegram sent), DNA, RG 94, War Records Office, Army of the Potomac; copies, *ibid.*, RG 393, Army of the Potomac, Letters Sent; Meade Papers, PHi. *O.R.*, I, xlii, part 3, 889. The enclosures cannot be positively identified. At 12:10 P.M. (sent at 12:30 P.M.), Meade telegraphed to USG. "I forward despatch just received. I fear the obstacles presented to Miles will check him sufficiently long to enable the enemy to send infantry to the point threatened as Miles is nearer the enemys lines than he is to ours—His right flank is besides open to a movement down the Duncan road.—I have rather anticipated as the result of our last movement, that Hatchers run would be found next time more strongly guarded.—" ALS (telegram sent), DNA, RG 94, War Records Office, Army of the Potomac; telegram received (at 12:30 P.M.), *ibid.*, RG 108, Letters Received. *O.R.*, I, xlii, part 3, 889–90. The enclosure is *ibid.*, p. 900.

At 6:00 P.M., Meade telegraphed to USG. "I send you the latest despatches received—I will have the mail carrier carefully examined when he comes in A contraband living at Armstrongs who was at the Boydtown plank road yesterday south of Hatchers run says Heth & Wilcox, two of Hills Divisions passed there yesterday & the day before this would confirm the mail carriers report that Hill had gone to Dinwidie." ALS (telegram sent), DNA, RG 94, War Records Office, Army of the Potomac; copies, *ibid.*, RG 393, Army of the Potomac, Letters Sent;

Meade Papers, PHi. *O.R.*, I, xlii, part 3, 891. According to *O.R.*, the enclosures are *ibid.*, pp. 895, 905, but the second of these was enclosed in a telegram of 8:45 P.M. from Meade to USG. "I expect we have all the information we will get from our reconnaissance which is that Hill's corps probably all of it went yesterday to Dinwiddie C. H—undoubtedly to meet Warren's movement, which Lee may have thought was for the south side R. Road—When the cavalry report Warren on the Welden road Hill will follow after & try to drive him off—Giving him 15,000 infantry & 8000 cavalry he is not Warren's superior & without fortifications, if Warrens men will fight, and we have any luck, Warren ought to repulse him—If however the fortune of war is against him he can always retire to the Eastward & cross the Nottoway—I dont see what we can do to assist Warren—Lee has sent away 3 divisions & received 3. viz—Hoke—Gordon & Pegram—so that his force in my front is about equal to what it was before detaching—I on the contrary have sent off 20,000 & received only 8000, so that I am 12,000 proportionately weaker—Under these circumstances a flank movement I think would be hazardous Lee would hold his lines & act on the defensive, until he heard from Hill & the latter, even if he failed to drive Warren—would when Warren withdrew of his own accord which he will do after exhausting his supplies—Hill could return and threaten our rear either of the flank movement or of the lines, the latter being necessarily open. I instructed to Warren to communicate with me & hoped to have heard to day—He was ordered positively to send a party in advance on his return to report his route—it would probably be well to hold a command in hand to meet him in case any intelligence should be received rendering this necessary.—Do you wish Miles to remain out tomorrow, he will not be withdrawn without your orders.—" ALS (telegram sent), DNA, RG 94, War Records Office, Army of the Potomac; telegram received (at 9:30 P.M.), *ibid.*, RG 108, Letters Received. *O.R.*, I, xlii, part 3, 891–92. The second enclosure in this telegram was a copy of a telegram of 4:00 P.M. from Col. Benjamin F. Fisher, chief signal officer, to Meade. "The Avery house station reports 3.20 P. M a train of 21 wagons followed by a column of the Enemys Infantry between 4 & 5000 have just moved towards Petersburg on road N W of Pocahontas coming from direction of Richmond I have inquired more particularly about the numbers given & if over estimated will report according" Copy, DNA, RG 108, Letters Received. At 9:15 P.M., Meade telegraphed to USG. "Just as I sent my last despatch the following was received—You will note that only a part of Hills corps is here reported as moving to Dinwiddie—This corroborates the contrabands statement that Heth & Wilcox passed down yesterday.—" ALS (telegram sent), *ibid.*, RG 94, War Records Office, Army of the Potomac; copies, *ibid.*, RG 393, Army of the Potomac, Letters Sent; Meade Papers, PHi. The enclosure cannot be positively determined. At 10:00 P.M., USG telegraphed to Meade. "Miles may be withdrawn to-morrow after noon. It will be well as you say to be in readiness to move o+ut to meet Warren if he should require assistance." ALS (telegram sent), NHi; telegram received (at 10:05 P.M.), DNA, RG 94, War Records Office, Army of the Potomac. *O.R.*, I, xlii, part 3, 892. At 10:30 P.M., Meade telegraphed to USG. "I forward despatch just received.—The fighting referred to was probably Hamptons Cavalry disputing our possession of the rail road.—" ALS (telegram sent), DNA, RG 94, War Records Office, Army of the Potomac; telegram received (at 10:35 P.M.), *ibid.*, RG 108, Letters Received. *O.R.*, I, xlii, part 3, 892. The enclosure is *ibid.*, p. 908.

To Maj. Gen. Philip H. Sheridan

(Cipher)   City Point, Va, Dec. 9th 1864 [*1:30* P.M.]
MAJ. GEN. SHERIDAN, KEARNSTOWN VA.

Deserters in to-day shew that Gordons & Pegram's[1] Divisions left early last Wednsday[2] morning. We have deserters from Terry's[3] Brigade of Gordon's Division. This only leaves Rhodes[4] & Whartons Divisions[5] with the Cavalry, in the Valley. If the weather holds favorable you can now make a successfull offensive campaign. Try it if you can.

U. S. GRANT
Lt. Gn.

ALS (telegram sent), CSmH; telegram received (at 3:00 P.M.), DNA, RG 94, War Records Office, Miscellaneous War Records; *ibid.*, RG 107, Telegrams Collected (Bound). *O.R.*, I, xliii, part 2, 765. On Dec. 10, 1864, 7:30 P.M., Maj. Gen. Philip H. Sheridan, Kernstown, Va., telegraphed to USG. "A Deserter from the Enemy who came into my lines, confirms the movement of Pegram's, and Gordon's Divisions on the 7th inst: We are now having here very bad weather. (7) seven inchs of snow and very cold—" Telegram sent, DNA, RG 107, Telegrams Collected (Unbound); telegram received (marked as sent at 7:20 P.M.), *ibid.*, RG 108, Letters Received. Printed as sent at 7:20 P.M. in *O.R.*, I, xliii, part 2, 772.

1. John Pegram, born in 1832 in Petersburg, Va., USMA 1854, resigned from the U.S. Army as 1st lt. as of May 10, 1861. He served as a C.S.A. staff officer before appointment as brig. gen. as of Nov. 7, 1862. At the time USG wrote, Pegram commanded Early's Div., 2nd Army Corps. *Ibid.*, pp. 877, 927.
   2. Dec. 7, 1864.
   3. William Terry, born in 1824 in Amherst County, Va., graduated from the University of Virginia (1848), practiced law and edited a newspaper. Entering the Civil War as 1st lt., 4th Va., he was appointed brig. gen. as of May 19, 1864; in Dec., he commanded a brigade in the div. of Maj. Gen. John B. Gordon, 2nd Army Corps.
   4. Robert E. Rodes, born in 1829 in Lynchburg, Va., graduated from the Virginia Military Institute (1848), where he taught until resigning (1851) to become an engineer. Rising to C.S.A. maj. gen., he was mortally wounded at the battle of Winchester, Sept. 19, 1864.
   5. Gabriel C. Wharton, born in 1824 in Culpeper County, Va., graduated from the Virginia Military Institute (1847), then practiced engineering. He commanded the 51st Va. before his appointment as brig. gen. as of July 8, 1863. In Dec., 1864, he commanded a div., 2nd Army Corps.

To Maj. Gen. George H. Thomas

(Cipher)   City Point, Va, Dec. 89th 1864 [7:30 P.M.]
MAJ. GN. THOMAS, NASHVILLE TENN.

Your dispatch of 1 P. M. to-day received.[1] I have as much confidence in your conducting a battle rightly as I have in any other officer. But it has seemed to me that you have been slow and I have had no explaination of affairs to convince me otherwise. Receiving your dispatch to Gen. Halleck[2] of 2 p. m. before I did the one to me, I telegraphed to suspend the order relieving you until we should hear further. I hope most sincerely that there will be no necessity of repeating the order and that the facts will show that you have been right all the time.

U. S. GRANT
Lt. Gn.

ALS (telegram sent), Elkins Collection, Free Library of Philadelphia, Philadelphia, Pa.; telegram received (at 9:00 P.M.), DNA, RG 107, Telegrams Collected (Bound). *O.R.*, I, xlv, part 2, 115. On Dec. 9, 1864, 11:30 P.M., Maj. Gen. George H. Thomas telegraphed to USG. "Your despatch 7 30 P m is just received. I can only say in further explanation why I have not attacked Hood that I could not concentrate my troops and get their transportation in order in shorter time than it has been done and am satisfied I have made every effort that was possible to complete the task" Telegram received (misdated as sent on Dec. 8, 11:30 P.M., received on Dec. 9, 12:45 A.M.), DNA, RG 107, Telegrams Collected (Bound); *ibid.*, Telegrams Collected (Unbound); (on Dec. 10) *ibid.*, RG 108, Letters Received; copies, *ibid.*, RG 107, Telegrams Received in Cipher; DLC-John M. Schofield. *O.R.*, I, xlv, part 2, 115.

1. See telegram to Maj. Gen. George H. Thomas, Dec. 8, 1864.
2. See *O.R.*, I, xlv, part 2, 114.

To Maj. Gen. George G. Meade

By Telegraph from City Point 12 10 1.20 P. M
Dated Dec 10th *1864.*

To MAJ GEN MEADE
I think it advisable to move with all the force you can to Warrens relief. Benham will be ordered up as you suggest

I dont think there should be any delay in starting out reenforcements to Warren

U S GRANT.
Lt Genl

Telegram received (at 1:30 P.M.), DNA, RG 94, War Records Office, Army of the Potomac; copies, *ibid.*, RG 108, Letters Sent; DLC-USG, V, 45, 70, 107; (2) Meade Papers, PHi. *O.R.*, I, xlii, part 3, 921. On Dec. 10, 1864, 1:00 P.M., Maj. Gen. George G. Meade telegraphed to USG. "I send you two despatches all the information received this morning—Eight men deserted to the enemy yesterday & last night from the 2d. corps—Two men were ordered to be hung at 12. today convicted of desertion to the enemy.—I have directed Maj. Genl. Humphrey to commence withdrawing the troops under Miles at 2. P M today— the men having suffered very much from the storm of last night I wished to give them time to get in their camps before dark—I have directed Maj Genl. Parke to hold his available reserves about 8000 ready on the Jerusalem plank road to move at a moments notice without trains to Warrens relief if necessary—The cavalry will accompany this command. Should this contingency arise, before the arrival of the division of the 6. corps I propose to move up Genl. Benhams command to support Parkes line—If this meets with your approval I would be glad that Genl. Benham should be so notified.—" ALS (telegram sent), DNA, RG 107, Telegrams Collected (Unbound); copies, *ibid.*, RG 393, Army of the Potomac, Letters Sent; Meade Papers, PHi. *O.R.*, I, xlii, part 3, 921. The enclosures are *ibid.*, pp. 925, 927. At 1:10 P.M., Meade telegraphed to USG. "The above just recd. this is undoubtedly warren." Telegram received (at 1:15 P.M.), DNA, RG 108, Letters Received. The enclosure is in *O.R.*, I, xlii, part 3, 927. At 1:28 P.M., USG telegraphed to Meade. "What point will you have Benham sent to He will be sent out by rail as soon as he ~~he~~ can be got off." Telegram received (at 1:32 P.M.), DNA, RG 94, War Records Office, Army of the Potomac; copies, *ibid.*, RG 108, Letters Sent; DLC-USG, V, 45, 70, 107; (2) Meade Papers, PHi. *O.R.*, I, xlii, part 3, 921. At 1:50 P.M., Meade telegraphed to USG. "Genl. Benham can be moved by rail and landed at Meade station, from whence he can report to Genl. Parke.—" ALS (telegram sent), DNA, RG 94, War Records Office, Army of the Potomac; telegram received, *ibid.*, RG 108, Letters Received. *O.R.*, I, xlii, part 3, 922.

To Maj. Gen. George G. Meade

By Telegraph from City Pt
Dated Dec 10 *1864.* [*2:10* P.M.]

To MAJ GEN MEADE

I sent to Gen Shepley at Norfolk to know if he has heard from Warren & to try & communicate with him—I have also notified Shepley that it is barely possible Warren may be forced to make into Suffolk & if so he will want rations & forage immediately[1] Has your ₱Provost Marshal got a scout who by working Eastward might reach Warren. If so send him orders to avoid danger by going to Suffolk if necessary—

U S. GRANT
Lt Gen

Telegram received (at 2:20 P.M.), DNA, RG 94, War Records Office, Army of the Potomac; copies, *ibid.*, RG 108, Letters Sent; DLC-USG, V, 45, 70, 107; (2) Meade Papers, PHi. *O.R.*, I, xlii, part 3, 922. On Dec. 10, 1864, 3:00 P.M., USG telegraphed to Maj. Gen. George G. Meade. "Do the enemy keep such a force between you and Warren as to prevent your Cavalry from pushing out to see and lean the movements of the enemy and our own troops?" ALS (telegram sent), NHi; telegram received (at 3:03 P.M.), DNA, RG 94, War Records Office, Army of the Potomac. *O.R.*, I, xlii, part 3, 922. At 3:00 P.M. (sent at 3:35 P.M.), Meade telegraphed to USG. "I will send a scout with Genl. Potter Comd. troops sent to Warren's support, who will leave Potter at the Nottoway & try to make his way to Warren   In the mean time Sharpe from City Point and Shepley from Norfolk might send one if they can from Suffolk—Warren was directed to return by way of Jerusalem which is on the road from Hicksford to Suffolk.—If he takes that route it will be risky for Potter to go too far from here.—I have just received your despatch of 3. P. M—I do not know what there is between Warren & this Army—the road to the crossing of the Nottoway was open on the day after Warren left, when a squadron of cavalry returned with his stragglers.— The handful of cavalry I have have been on the extreme left & are now returning, and will be sent with Genl. Potter & pushed in advance to obtain information by which his movements will be guided.—" ALS (telegram sent), DNA, RG 94, War Records Office, Army of the Potomac; telegram received (at 3:30 P.M.), *ibid.*, RG 108, Letters Received. *O.R.*, I, xlii, part 3, 922.

1. See telegrams to Brig. Gen. George F. Shepley, Dec. [*10*], 1864.

To Maj. Gen. George G. Meade

————

By Telegraph from City Pt
Dated Dec 10 *1864.* [*7:30* P.M.]

To MAJ. GEN MEADE

Gen. Ord reports on information of deserters that Hokes division is still in his front. Was it not supposed that this division had gone to Petersburg. There has been an attack threatened all P. M. north of the James—

U. S. GRANT
Lt. Gen

Telegram received, DNA, RG 94, War Records Office, Army of the Potomac; copies, *ibid.*, RG 108, Letters Received; DLC-USG, V, 45, 70, 107; (2) Meade Papers, PHi. *O.R.*, I, xlii, part 3, 923. On Dec. 10, 1864, 7:40 P.M. (sent at 7:45 P.M.) and 8:25 P.M. (sent at 8:45 P.M.), Maj. Gen. George G. Meade telegraphed to USG. "I forward despatches from Signal officer, and from Genl. Miles, who just before withdrawing had some skirmishing with the enemy across Hatchers run.—Genl. Potters column moved at 6. P. M He has orders to march all night & not to halt till he gets to the Nottoway. A regiment of Engineers with a canvass bridge accompanies him.—The cavalry required time to get ammunition rations & forage but as soon as supplied will be pushed after him.—Your despatch of 7.35 just received—I have presumed Hoke to be in my front but believe the information came from you—I suppose thro Genl. Butler I will enquire, if any deserters have reported him here.—" "On application to the Prov. Mar. Dept—I find there has been no information received here of Hoke being in our front—A report existed at one time that he had gone to No. Ca. but was not considered reliable—The intelligence of his being South of the Appomatox, having come from you, I presumed it was based on information from Genl. Butlers line & was undoubted—You will perceive the Signal officers continued to report today as they have for several days past the movement of troops into Petersburgh from the direction of Richmond—If these are all of Earlys army he can not have left many in the valley—" ALS (telegrams sent), DNA, RG 94, War Records Office, Army of the Potomac; telegrams received, *ibid.*, RG 108, Letters Received. *O.R.*, I, xlii, part 3, 923. The enclosures are *ibid.*, pp. 925, 928.

To Maj. Gen. Edward O. C. Ord

By Telegraph from City Point
Dated Dec 10th. *1864.*

To GENL ORD.

There is very good evidence that hokes Division went south several days ago. If so Field & Kershaws are The only Two left. You can reinforce by taking a part of your force from Bermuda Your lines are very strong and by rapidly moving your reserves from where they are not wanted to where they are I think you will be able to hold against the enemy. It is hardly likely they will mass much force on your extreme right and endanger being cut off from Richmond. Great vigilance however will be necessary in your whole line and especially so about daylight in the morning It might be a proper precaution to send all your surplus teams south of the river or inside the fort at Deep Bottom.

U S. GRANT
Lt Gen

Telegram received (at 4:00 P.M.), Ord Papers, CU-B; copies, DLC-USG, V, 45, 70, 107; DNA, RG 108, Letters Sent. *O.R.*, I, xlii, part 3, 942. On Dec. 10, 1864, 6:30 P.M., Maj. Gen. Edward O. C. Ord telegraphed to USG. "Genl Kautz reports at 5½ P M that a prisoner of the 8th North Carolina represents that Kershaw has taken post in front of Fort Harrison—and that Hokes and Fields divisions recieved orders at 1 (one) O-Clock last night and marched out on the Charles City and Darby Town roads to our right with three days rations —to our right—two deserters came in last night from the piquet to the right of Ft Harrison and state that they belong to the Colquetts brigade Hokes Division, which they Division they say marched to the James river a few days since but did not cross—turned around and came back   I have made the best arran desposition I could and have small reserves ready to march to threatened points—at dark dropping shots were still being fired on the signal hill front—" ALS (telegram sent), DNA, RG 107, Telegrams Collected (Unbound); telegram received, *ibid.*, RG 108, Letters Received. *O.R.*, I, xlii, part 3, 941–42.

On Dec. 10, Bvt. Maj. Gen. Alfred H. Terry telegraphed to Lt. Col. Theodore S. Bowers. "The enemy have driven in our cavalry pickets at the Johnson farm & are moving in what is reported to be a heavy force down the Darbytown road toward our right. I think it must be merely a reconnaisance. I will report again as soon as the object of the movement is develloped" ALS (undated telegram sent), DNA, RG 107, Telegrams Collected (Unbound); telegram received (at 12:20 P.M.), *ibid.*, RG 108, Letters Received. *O.R.*, I, xlii, part 3, 942. At 1:00 P.M., USG telegraphed to Terry. "It is more than likely The enemy suspect we have weakened our lines North of the James much more than we have & the object of the present move is to find out   but be prepared if there should be an attack on any part of your lines." Telegram received (at 1:00 P.M.), DNA, RG 107, Telegrams Collected (Unbound); copies, *ibid.*, RG 108, Letters Sent; DLC-USG, V, 45, 70, 107. *O.R.*, I, xlii, part 3, 942. At 1:20 P.M., USG telegraphed to Brig. Gen. John W. Turner. "Is Gen Ord in Command North side of the river —a dispatch just rec'd from Gen Terry would indicate that he was—answer quick as I want to give directions to the officer in command" Telegram received, DNA, RG 94, War Records Office, Army of the Potomac; copies, *ibid.*, RG 108, Letters Sent; DLC-USG, V, 45, 70, 107. *O.R.*, I, xlii, part 3, 938. At 1:28 P.M., Turner telegraphed to USG. "Gen Ord is in command, he arrived this morning" ALS (telegram sent), DNA, RG 107, Telegrams Collected (Unbound); telegram received, *ibid.*, RG 108, Letters Received. *O.R.*, I, xlii, part 3, 938.

On Dec. 10, 9:20 A.M., Ord telegraphed to Brig. Gen. John A. Rawlins. "The following dispatch just recd from Gen Terry. 'Gen Foster reports to me that the enemy have withdrawn from the signal Hill & Camp Holly front. Col West of the Cavy has re established his picket line' " Telegram received (at 9:30 A.M.), DNA, RG 108, Letters Received. *O.R.*, I, xlii, part 3, 970.

At 1:24 P.M., USG telegraphed to Ord. "Have your command under Arms ready to receive an attack and reserves ready to move to any part of the lines most threatened. The enemy may think you enough weakened to justify them in a general attack." ALS (telegram sent), NHi; telegram received, Ord Papers, CU-B. *O.R.*, I, xlii, part 3, 941. At 2:00 P.M., Ord telegraphed to USG. "The dispositions are made and men under arms—Enemy in considerable A force— perhaps 2 Brigades are reported by Genl Kautz as in front of Camp Holly and spring hill—they are skirmishing with our Cavalry—a few casualties so far— another Kautz says another force crossing enemies is advancing down the four mile Creek—strength of the enemy not know but the cavalry report it much superior to their force   Richmond papers state we will probably attack them (the rebels) today—hence This may be only a reconnaissance—" ALS (telegram sent), DNA, RG 107, Telegrams Collected (Unbound); telegram received, *ibid.*, RG 108, Letters Received. *O.R.*, I, xlii, part 3, 941. At 3:00 P.M., USG telegraphed to Ord. "The enemy have probably ~~detachment~~ detached so heavily from the north side that they have become nervous lest we attack them there. If they do not attack you I think it will be well to push out a force and see what the enemy have got"   Telegram received, Ord Papers, CU-B; copies, DLC-USG, V, 45, 70, 107; DNA, RG 108, Letters Sent. At 3:20 P.M., Ord telegraphed to USG. "Genl Terry on my right reports that ~~the~~ Prisoners taken say that Fields division is advancing on the Interfval between Spring Hill and Signal Hill—the indications are that I have three divisions in my front besides ~~citizen~~ Richmond defenders—and my line is too long—~~can you send me~~" ALS (telegram sent), *ibid.*, RG 107, Telegrams Collected (Unbound); telegram received, *ibid.*, RG 108, Letters Received.

To Brig. Gen. George F. Shepley

(Cipher)   City Point, Va, Dec. 9th [*10*] 1864 [*11:00* A.M.]
GEN. SHEPLEY, NORFOLK, VA.

Gen. Warren has been out five days on the Welden road and nothing heard from him since the evening of the first day. Have you heard through scouts via Suffolk any thing from him? I wish you would send out and see if information can be got. It may be possible that Gen. Warren will have to fall back by way of Suffolk and if he does forage and provisions will have to be sent to him.

U. S. GRANT
Lt. Gn.

ALS (telegram sent), NHi; telegram received (dated Dec. 10, 1864), DNA, RG 94, War Records Office, Army of the Potomac. *O.R.*, I, xlii, part 3, 950. On Dec. 10, 8:00 P.M., Brig. Gen. George F. Shepley telegraphed to USG. "Your telegram is received. I have heard nothing of Gen Warren. A Cavalry expedition will start at day light in the morning for the information you desire. Please notify me when you hear of Gen Warren." ALS (telegram sent), DNA, RG 107, Telegrams Collected (Unbound); telegram received, *ibid.*; (on Dec. 11) *ibid.*, RG 108, Letters Received. *O.R.*, I, xlii, part 3, 950.

To Brig. Gen. George F. Shepley

City Point, Va, Dec. 9th [*10*] *1864.* [*1:00* P.M.]
BRIG. GEN. SHEPLEY, NORFOLK, VA.

Please send a trusty scout by way of Suffolk, or such other route as you deem best, to try to communicate with Gen. Warren who is between Stoney Creek and Hicksford. Have him notify Gn. Warren for me that it is my desire that he should avoid battle as much as possible. If necessary he can come into Suffolk, get rations and forage there, and return here by such route as may then be deemed best.

U. S. GRANT
Lt. Gen.

ALS (telegram sent), Washington and Jefferson College, Washington, Pa.; copies (dated Dec. 10, 1864), DLC-USG, V, 45, 70, 107; DNA, RG 108, Letters Sent. *O.R.*, I, xlii, part 3, 950. On Dec. 10, 8:00 P.M., Brig. Gen. George F. Shepley telegraphed to USG. "Your second telegram of this date is recd. I shall make immediate arrangements to communicate with Gen Warren" Telegrams received (2), DNA, RG 107, Telegrams Collected (Unbound); (on Dec. 11) *ibid.*, RG 108, Letters Received. *O.R.*, I, xlii, part 3, 951.

On Dec. 11, 4:30 P.M., Shepley telegraphed to USG. "I have sent a scout towards Hicksford also three companies of cavalry in the same direction also a like force of cavalry and two pieces of artillery to South quay to hold the crossing of the Blackwater & move in the direction of Weldon Rations and forage will be ready at a moments notice to be at Suffolk if wanted" Telegram received, DNA, RG 107, Telegrams Collected (Unbound); *ibid.*, RG 108, Letters Received. *O.R.*, I, xlii, part 3, 971. At 7:30 P.M., USG telegraphed to Shepley. "Warren is at the Notaway. Will return to-morrow." ALS (telegram sent), OClWHi; telegram received, DNA, RG 107, Telegrams Collected (Unbound). *O.R.*, I, xlii, part 3, 971.

To Edwin M. Stanton

City Point, Va. Dec. 11th *1864.*
HON. E. M. STANTON
SECRETARY OF WAR.
WASHINGTON, D. C.

About the first of November, Col. Henry G. Thomas,[1] 19th Regiment U. S. Colored Troops claimed a Brigade in Gen. Ferrero's Division on the ground of seniority. Generals Parke and Ferrero would not give him one because in their judgement he was incompetent for such a command, and applied to Maj. Gen Meade to relieve him from duty in the Division. This Gen. Meade did not feel authorized to do. He was however disposed of for that time by being placed on Gen. Ferrero's Staff as Inspector. After a time another Brigade was formed in the Division to which, by reason of his rank, Col. Thomas was assigned. Thus a Brigade was made and given to an incompetent Commander, to retain two good ones. Yesterday Thomas presented himself at Gen. Meade's Headquarters with the appointment of a full Brigadier General, claiming that he was appointed to fill Neal Dow's vacancy.[2]

There is no doubt of the incompetency of Henry G. Thomas for the position to which he has been appointed, and had the President been aware of the facts, he certainly would not have made the appointment. I therefore respectfully ask that his appointment be revoked.

> I have the honor to be, Sir,
> Very Respectfully
> Your Ob't Servant
> U. S. GRANT
> Lieut. General

LS, DNA, RG 94, ACP, 3426 1871. On Dec. 11, 1864, Maj. Gen. George G. Meade wrote to USG. "(Confidential—& Private) . . . During our last movement to the left, I was appealed to by Maj. Genl. Parke to relieve from duty a Col. Thomas comdr. a colored regiment, on the ground of his being senior to the brigade comdr. in Ferero's division & claiming one of the brigades, when in the judgement of Ferero & Parke he was not competent for the command.—I declined to relieve him unless the matter was put in writing & I believe the affair was compromised by Ferero's taking him on his Staff as Inspector—Subsequently a third brigade was organised to which he was assigned by virtue of his rank as Col—in this manner the two good brigade comdr. were retained altho' a brigade had to be given to an incompetent comdr.—I knew nothing personaly of Col Thomas & no more than what transpired at the time I refer to—. Yesterday Col Thomas presented himself at these Hd. Qrs with the full commission of *Brigadier General* & assigned to this army—He saying he had been appointed to fill Neal Dow's vacancy—Now I *dont think this is right* & dont suppose you knew of the circumstances—I think you ought to insist on having a word to say on filling these vacancies, and they ought to be filled as I am sure you will fill them with the distinguished & meritorious officers in the field & not the incompetent—I take it for granted nothing was known of Col Thomas at Washn but what his friends averred in his behalf & but I think in the cases of officers in the field a refrence should be made to their superiors before the appt. power commits itself—I take the liberty of mentioning these circumstances—not that I desire any action in the case of Col. Thomas, but to advise you of the facts—because I deem it due to the officers whom I have recommended for promotion that these claims should be urged." ALS, PHi.

1. Henry G. Thomas, born in 1837 in Portland, Maine, graduated from Amherst College and practiced law in Maine before the Civil War. Appointed capt., 5th Maine, as of June 24, 1861, and capt., 11th Inf., as of Aug. 5, he was appointed col., 19th Colored, as of Jan. 16, 1864, and brig. gen. as of Nov. 30.
2. Neal Dow, born in 1804 in Portland, Maine, a successful businessman twice elected mayor of Portland, was best known as a temperance advocate. Appointed col., 13th Maine, as of Nov. 23, 1861, and brig. gen. as of April 28, 1862, he was captured near Port Hudson, imprisoned for eight months, and resigned his commission for health reasons as of Nov. 30, 1864.

To Maj. Gen. Henry W. Halleck

(Cipher)   City Point, Va, Dec. 11th 1864 [4:00 P.M.]
MAJ. GEN. HALLECK, WASHINGTON,

There has been no news from Warren since the evening after he left.[1] The Richmond papers however contain no news of any engagement with him beyond a rumored fight between Hamptons Cavalry and some of his forces. A force of some 8,000 men were sent South yesterday under Gen. Potter to secure his return. The latest news contained in Richmond papers of yesterday from Shermans army says that on the 7th he was East of the Ogechee twenty-five miles from Savannah moving on that place. On the 6th he had marched his Army Eighteen miles.

U. S. GRANT
Lt. Gen.

ALS (telegram sent), PPRF; telegram received (marked as sent at 4:30 P.M., received at 8:40 P.M.), DNA, RG 107, Telegrams Collected (Bound). *O.R.*, I, xlii, part 1, 24–25; (printed as received at 9:00 P.M.) *ibid.*, I, xlii, part 3, 951.

1. On Dec. 11, 1864, 5:45 P.M. (sent at 6:00 P.M.), Maj. Gen. George G. Meade telegraphed to USG. "I transmit despatches just received from Maj—Genl. Warren—I understand from the officer who brings it that no opposition was met except from Cavalry till they reached Hicksford, where artillery was found in position on the other side of the *Meherien*. On the return the cavalry met some infantry near Jarrats but no great force—From all I can gather Hill

either did not leave Dinwiddie, or else pushed for Hicksford thinking Welden was Warrens objective—" ALS (telegram sent), DNA, RG 94, War Records Office, Army of the Potomac; telegram received (at 6:00 P.M.), *ibid.*, RG 108, Letters Received. *O.R.*, I, xlii, part 3, 953. At 8:30 P.M., USG telegraphed to Maj. Gen. Henry W. Halleck. "The following dispatch from Warren has just been recd from Genl Meade— . . . 'Sussex C House 11 a m Decr 11th 1864 MAJ GEN MEADE I have completely destroyed the Rail road track from the Nottoway to Hicksford and my command is all at the crossing of the Nottoway— Time did not allow me to go in between the Nottoway and Stony Creek but it can be done at any time—I have met but trifling opposition or annoyance but the rain, and working night and day has been very fatigueing and the weather very un- comfortable, the men have however stood it all in good spirit, and we have made the best marching I have ever seen, The roads are now in very bad condition—I propose to return tomorrow' " Telegram received (on Dec. 12, 3:30 P.M.), DNA, RG 107, Telegrams Collected (Bound); copies, *ibid.*, Telegrams Received in Cipher; *ibid.*, RG 108, Letters Sent; DLC-USG, V, 45, 71, 107. *O.R.*, I, xlii, part 1, 25; *ibid.*, I, xlii, part 3, 951.

To Maj. Gen. George G. Meade

By Telegraph from City Point 7 P M
Dated Dec 11th *1864.*

To MAJOR GENERAL MEADE
Your cipher despatch just received—The plan you propose I think well of and wish you would make all the preparations for carrying it into effect.—It will be of the greatest importance to select the right officer for taking the advance

U S GRANT
Lt Gen

Telegram received, DNA, RG 94, War Records Office, Army of the Potomac; copies, *ibid.*, RG 108, Letters Sent; DLC-USG, V, 45, 71, 107; (2) Meade Papers, PHi. *O.R.*, I, xlii, part 3, 953. On Dec. 11, 1864, 1:00 P.M. (sent be- tween 2:10 P.M. and 2:25 P.M.), Maj. Gen. George G. Meade telegraphed to USG. "Two deserters have just come in to our left They report Gordon & Pe- grams Division as holding the lines previously held by Heth & Wilcox.—This gives as the force in my front Johnston—Gordon & Pegram probably not over 15,000 men—The lines must therefore be comparatively weak tho as they are much shorter than my lines, they are perhaps held stronger than Parke holds his —From all the reports of signal officers, I should judge the enemy were stronger on the left, as troops have been constantly seen moving that way and as the enemy are expecting an attack on the S. Side R. Rd—Miles movement would draw all their available reserves there.—Hill undoubtedly went to Dinwiddie C. H whether he moved the whole of his force beyond that point against Warren, or whether he only sent the cavalry & part of his infantry is a point about which I am in doubt His position at Dinwiddie is favorable either for operations against Warren, or to meet Warren in case he moved on the South Side road or to attack in rear any force I should send in that direction—These considerations together with the absence of any bad news from Warren lead me to infer that Hill has perhaps not moved with his whole force against Warren, for had there have been heavy & severe fighting I think Potter would either have heard something of it or would certainly have encountered some fugitives or stragglers from the field as they would naturally return by the road they marched which Potter is on.—Under the supposition above indicated in case we hear of Warren's returning in good order, I think there is a chance of carrying by a coup-de-main the centre of Lee's weakened lines—For this purpose I would mass the reserves of the 6th corps about 5000, in the woods between Forts Howard & Alex Hays—and when Warren's column is within supporting distance, make an assault on the enemys line between the Jerusalem plank road & the Welden R. Rd—to be followed if successful by Warrens whole column—This operation is undoubtedly hazardous & will be dependant on the fact of whether or not we surprise the enemy—Should the first dash fail, the idea should be abandoned and the troops withdrawn—If successful in breaking thro the lines and followed by Warrens column, we ought to be able to secure Petersburgh—I make these suggestions for your consideration If the 3d Division of the 6th corps reaches in time it would be added to the assaulting column.—The 2d corps would hold the left & look out for an attack from Hill, who should be expected in that direction & possibly in our rear up the Welden Road, as of course on Warrens with drawing, if he does not follow him he will try to play the same game I am proposing viz to strike our weakened lines before Warren can get back.—It will therefore be necessary that Warren should be close up to us before it will be prudent for us to attempt the offensive from the front.—" ALS (telegram sent), DNA, RG 94, War Records Office, Army of the Potomac; telegram received, *ibid.*, RG 108, Letters Received. *O.R.*, I, xlii, part 3, 952–53.

At 10:15 A.M. (sent at 10:25 A.M.), Meade had telegraphed to USG. "I send a despatch just received from Genl. Potter—The orderly bringing it says the cavalry were arriving when he left, so that I hope during the course of the day to receive positive intelligence of Warren—I can hardly think Warren was at Allen's bridge last night, because his orders were positive to report his return & route in advance, and if he had started back I should have heard from him.— If he has had much fighting stragglers from his command may have found their way to Allens bridge.—Considering the weather & the night Potter & his command are entitled to great credit for the march they have made—The fact that Potter does not report any stragglers or fugitives at Freemans bridge which is where Warren crossed & where those taking to the rear would be likely to be found looks favorable for Warrens success.—" ALS (telegram sent), DNA, RG 94, War Records Office, Army of the Potomac; telegram received (at 10:15 A.M.), *ibid.*, RG 108, Letters Received. *O.R.*, I, xlii, part 3, 951–52. The enclosure is *ibid.*, pp. 967–68.

At 10:45 P.M. (sent at 11:00 P.M.), Meade telegraphed to USG. "I forward a despatch which looks as if the enemy were returning to their lines.—" ALS (telegram sent), DNA, RG 94, War Records Office, Army of the Potomac; telegram received, *ibid.*, RG 108, Letters Received. *O.R.*, I, xlii, part 3, 954. The enclosure is *ibid.*, p. 962.

To Maj. Gen. George H. Thomas

(Cipher)   City Point, Va, Dec. 11th *1864*. [*4:00* P.M.]
MAJ. GEN. THOMAS, NASHVILLE, TEN

If you delay attack longer the mortifying spectacle will be witnessed of a Rebel Army moving for the Ohio River and you will be forced to act, accepting such weather as you find. Let there be no further delay. Hood cannot stand even a drawn battle so far from his supplies of Ordnance stores. If he retreats and you follow he must loose his Material and much of his Army. I am in hopes of receiving a dispatch from you to-day announcing that you have moved. Delay no longer for weather or reinforcements.

U. S. GRANT
Lt. Gn.

ALS (telegram sent), Elkins Collection, Free Library of Philadelphia, Philadelphia, Pa.; telegram received (at 8:40 P.M.), DNA, RG 107, Telegrams Collected (Bound). *O.R.*, I, xlv, part 2, 143. On Dec. 11, 1864, 10:30 P.M., Maj. Gen. George H. Thomas telegraphed to USG. "Your despatch of 4 P M this day just recd. Will obey the order as promptly as possible howevermuch I may regret it as the attack will have to be made under every disadvantage. The whole country is covered with a perfect sheet of ice & sleet and it is with difficulty the troops are able to move about on level ground. It was my intention to attack Hood as soon as the ice melted and would have done so yesterday had it not been for the storm" Telegram received (on Dec. 12), DNA, RG 107, Telegrams Collected (Bound); *ibid.*, Telegrams Collected (Unbound); *ibid.*, RG 108, Letters Received; copies, *ibid.*, RG 107, Telegrams Received in Cipher; *ibid.*, RG 393, Dept. of the Cumberland, Telegrams Sent; DLC-John M. Schofield. *O.R.*, I, xlv, part 2, 143.

To Maj. Gen. Henry W. Halleck

City Point Va
11 30 P M Dec 12th 1864

MAJ GEN H W HALLECK
GENL IN CHIEF

There are at Springfield Illinois a large number of recruits for Sherman's Army

Please order the whole camp removed from camp Butler, to

Nashville. At the latter place they will be of use whilst waiting an opportunity to join the Regiments to which they belong—

U S GRANT
Lt Gen

Telegram received (on Dec. 13, 1864, 12:15 A.M.), DNA, RG 107, Telegrams Collected (Bound); copies, *ibid.*, Telegrams Received in Cipher; *ibid.*, RG 108, Letters Sent; DLC-USG, V, 45, 71, 107. *O.R.*, I, xlv, part 2, 155.

To Maj. Gen. George G. Meade

City Point, Va, Dec. 12th/64 [*1:00* P.M.]

MAJ. GEN. MEADE,

Your dispatch just received. I would not advise the attack suggested by you unless with a good prospect of it succeeding. But if you are prepared for it act on your best judgement when Warren gets back and the time comes for making the attack.

U. S. GRANT
Lt. Gn.

ALS (telegram sent), deCoppet Collection, NjP; telegram received (at 1:00 P.M.), DNA, RG 94, War Records Office, Army of the Potomac. *O.R.*, I, xlii, part 3, 972. On Dec. 12, 1864, noon (sent at 12:30 P.M.), Maj. Gen. George G. Meade telegraphed to USG. "In the absence of any positive intelligence of Hills position, after a careful examination of the ground by Engineers & reliable officers—the intelligence of the signal officers & Picket officers of the return of the enemy to his works—the condition of the troops now returning from the expedition to Hicksford on which they have from the weather suffered very much— from all these considerations I am constrained to advise giving up my suggestion of yesterday to attack the enemys line on the ground that I have no reason to believe it will be successful, and am not disposed to engage in such an operation except under the most favorable circumstances—I will however have every thing in readiness awaiting your decision.—" ALS (telegram sent), DNA, RG 94, War Records Office, Army of the Potomac; telegram received (at 3:40 P.M.), *ibid.*, RG 108, Letters Received. *O.R.*, I, xlii, part 3, 972.

At 10:40 A.M., Meade had telegraphed to USG. "Deserters report Kershaws division South of the Appomatox Have you any information of its being withdrawn from Butlers front.—" ALS (telegram sent), DNA, RG 94, War Records Office, Army of the Potomac; copies, *ibid.*, RG 393, Army of the Potomac, Letters Sent; Meade Papers, PHi. *O.R.*, I, xlii, part 3, 971. At 10:50 A.M., USG telegraphed to Meade. "The last information placed Kershaws Div. in front of Fort Harrison. I will enquire of Gen. Ord if it hass gone." ALS (telegram sent), Kohns Collection, NN; telegram received (at 10:50 A.M.), DNA, RG 94, War Records Office, Army of the Potomac. *O.R.*, I, xlii, part 2, 972. At 11:00 A.M.,

USG telegraphed to Maj. Gen. Edward O. C. Ord. "Gen. Meade says Kershaws
Div. is reported South of the Appomattox Have you heard of its withdrawel
from your front?" ALS (telegram sent), Williams College, Williamstown,
Mass.; telegram received, DNA, RG 94, War Records Office, Army of the Potomac. *O.R.*, I, xlii, part 3, 981. On the same day, USG telegraphed to Ord.
"Please telegraph any news from Sherman the Richmond papers of to day may
contain." Copies, DLC-USG, V, 45, 71, 107; DNA, RG 108, Letters Sent. At
3:30 P.M. and 4:30 P.M., Ord telegraphed to USG. "The Richmond examiner
of to day says—'Our last advices from Georgia represent that Sherman was advancing towards Savannah by three parallel roads. He must be in the vicinity of
the city by this time— . . . Generals Beauregard, Hardee, Smith, and we believe
Taylor are in command of our forces' This is all of interest in to day's papers—
Two deserters in to day, one of thinks some troops moved towards the river
yesterday—this not reliable as the man was on piquet—he says the rumor was
that it was Kershaws Division" ALS (telegram sent), DNA, RG 107, Telegrams Collected (Unbound); telegram received (at 4:00 P.M.), *ibid.*, RG 108,
Letters Received. *O.R.*, I, xlii, part 3, 981–82. "The Richmond Whig of to day
says—'The advance of Shermans Army was within twenty miles of Savannah
yesterday afternoon—The fight for the possession of the city may be progressing
to day—'" ALS (telegram sent), DNA, RG 107, Telegrams Collected (Unbound). On the same day, USG telegraphed to Meade. "The only information
Gn. Ord has of movement of troops from his front is from a deserter off pickett.
He heard a report that some troops had moved towards the river yesterday. Understood it was Kershaw's Div." ALS (telegram sent), Kohns Collection, NN;
telegram received (at 4:05 P.M.), DNA, RG 94, War Records Office, Army of
the Potomac. *O.R.*, I, xlii, part 3, 972.

At 4:45 P.M., Ord telegraphed to USG. "Genl. Butler left orders for an expedition to the country between the Piankatank and Potomac to burn and break
up sundry places—the officer going proposes to take the companys of cavalry at
Harrison's landing and one from Williamsburg with a force of Infantry—as part
of this cavalry was ~~just~~ posted by your order I ask if it can be now removed"
ALS (telegram sent), DNA, RG 107, Telegrams Collected (Unbound); telegram received (at 6:00 P.M.), *ibid.*, RG 108, Letters Received. *O.R.*, I, xlii,
part 3, 982. On the same day, USG telegraphed to Ord. "There is no objection
to taking the Cavalry from Harrisons Landing & Williamsburg for the expedition ordered by Gen'l. Butler" Copies, DLC-USG, V, 45, 71, 107; DNA, RG 108,
Letters Sent. *O.R.*, I, xlii, part 3, 982. At 11:10 P.M., Ord telegraphed to USG.
"Gen Fererro telegraphs movements within the enemys lines on his front which
he is inclined to think indicates an attack—I think it more probable the enemy
are detaching a portion of his forces" ALS (telegram sent), DNA, RG 107,
Telegrams Collected (Unbound); telegram received (at 11:10 P.M.), *ibid.*, RG
108, Letters Received. *O.R.*, I, xlii, part 3, 982.

On Dec. 13, 10:00 A.M., USG telegraphed to Ord. "I shall start soon to
visit you. Please send two ambulances to Aikin's. The ladies will be with me."
Typescript, Eliot Davis, Vancouver, Wash.; telegram received, DNA, RG 393,
Dept. of Va. and N. C., Telegrams Received. *O.R.*, I, xlii, part 3, 992.

On Dec. 14, Ord telegraphed to USG. "I learned today from prisoners in
yesterday morning that Kershaws troops are Still in my front" Telegram received (at 7:55 P.M.), DNA, RG 108, Letters Received. *O.R.*, I, xlii, part 3,
1005.

To Maj. Gen. Philip H. Sheridan

(Cipher)   City Point, Va, Dec. 12th/64 [*10:30* P.M.]
MAJ. GEN. SHERIDAN, KEARNSTOWN VA.

I think there is no doubt but that all of Gorden's & Pegram's Divisions are here. The inhabitants of Richmond are supplied exclusively over the roads North of James River. If it is possible to destroy the Va. Central road it will go far towards starving out the garrison of Richmond. The Welden road has been largely used until now notwithstanding it has been cut to stoney creek. It is now gone to Hicksford and I think can be of no further use. If the enemy are known to have retired to Staunton you will either be able to make a dash on the communications North of the James or spare a part of your force. ~~Let me know your view as to the practicability of moving this Winter and also as to the propriety of detaching troops~~

Let me know your views as to the best course, to make a dash on the Central road & canal or to detach from your command.

U. S. GRANT
Lt. Gn.

ALS (telegram sent), PPRF; telegram received, DNA, RG 107, Telegrams Collected (Bound). *O.R.*, I, xlii, part 3, 972–73; (received at 11:25 P.M.) *ibid.*, I, xliii, part 2, 778. On Dec. 12, 1864, 6:00 P.M., Maj. Gen. Philip H. Sheridan had telegraphed to USG. "The reports up to this evening are as follows—Early moved a portion, or all his Infantry back towards Stanton, commencing the movement last friday. The soldiers sayid that they were going into Winter Quarters there—I can not get any confirmation of the movement of of Gordons, and Pegrams Divisions, other than the report of (1) one deserter—All others state that Pegram did not move, previous to last friday: and knew nothing of the movement of Gordons Div: I have been unable to do anything towards determining absolutely these movements, on account of the snowstorm, and the intenely cold weather now prevailing here" Telegram sent, DNA, RG 107, Telegrams Collected (Unbound); telegram received (at 7:30 P.M.), *ibid.*, Telegrams Collected (Bound); *ibid.*, RG 108, Letters Received. *O.R.*, I, xliii, part 2, 778. On Dec. 13, 8:30 P.M., Sheridan telegraphed to USG. "Your telegram of yesterday recd to day—I strongly advise the withdrawal of more of the Infy: force of this command—(1) one Division can now be spared, and perhaps (2) two, in a very short time. It is impassible to do any thing towards the central Road, until the present inclement weather is over—The snow is now (7) seven inches deep, and the cold intense; it is very wintery—I will break the RailRoad if possible as soon as the weather will permit—(2) Two deserters from Gordons

Division came in to day, they are from the 10th Louisiana (Reb) Infy—they report that they left the Division at Harrisonburg on last thursday the 8th inst— that this Div: (Gordons) with Pegrams was marching to Fishersville, apoint between Stanton, and Waynes boro, and as they suppose to take the cars for Richmond—My information goes to prove that no supplies go from the south side of the Central Road, or from the Shenandoah Valley—and I usually question Refugees & prisoners my self—I saw more supplies growing in the neck down about King & Queen C. H. North of the Mattapony River last summer, than in any other section of Virginia—If that country could be cleand out it would be important In reference to what troops should go from here to join you, I would advise the removal of the troops known as Western Virginians; they are too near their homes, and should go among strangers. The New Creek affair and at every other point where guerrillas have given any annoyance—it was from a surprise of these troops of the border. If you prefer the 19th Corps I will send it by Divisions—I believe that every thing should be used this winter to give no rest to the enemy; and if it causes a concentration of Troops on the part of the Enemy at Richmond, it only causes greater Embarrassment in their supplies—We are a long ways from Richmond here; and for any permanent occupation at vital points, a very large portion of any command would have to be used in protecting the line of communication—The movemt of Early with the balance of his force to Stanton is not yet confirmed" ALS (telegram sent), DNA, RG 107, Telegrams Collected (Unbound); telegram received (at 10:00 P.M.), *ibid.*, Telegrams Collected (Bound); (on Dec. 14) *ibid.*, RG 108, Letters Received. *O.R.*, I, xliii, part 2, 780. On Dec. 14, noon, USG telegraphed to Sheridan. "Your dispatch of last evening rec'd. You may select the troops and number of them you send here. I would prefer separate regiments, Brigades or Divisions to a Corps because then I could attach them to Corps already organized and not increase the number of Hd Qrs." ALS (telegram sent), CSmH; telegram received (at 12:30 P.M.), DNA, RG 107, Telegrams Collected (Bound). Printed as received at 1:00 P.M. in *O.R.*, I, xliii, part 2, 785.

On Dec. 19, 11:00 A.M., Sheridan, Kernstown, Va., telegraphed to USG. "I sent off this morning for City Point (1) one Div: of Genl: Crooks Command —it will number about (3500) thirty-five hundred men—On wednesday I will forward the Pro: Div: numbering about 3000—The weather has been very bad, and is still so. I sent out the Cavly: this morning—(2) two Divisions to cross through 'Chester Gap' and strike the RailRoad, if possible—The other Div: goes up the valley pike towards Stanton—and stays out as long as its forage will last —The weather is so very bad that I am not sanguine of success in getting to the Rail Road—My Scouts report that the two Divisions, Rodes & Hortons [*Wharton's*], commenced moving up the valley last ~~wednesday~~ Friday from their camp between Harrisonsburg, and New Market—I will probably know to night or to morrow if any have gone to Richmond—" ALS (telegram sent), DNA, RG 107, Telegrams Collected (Unbound); telegram received (at 1:00 P.M.), *ibid.*, Telegrams Collected (Bound); *ibid.*, RG 108, Letters Received. *O.R.*, I, xliii, part 2, 804. At 10:00 A.M., Brig. Gen. John A. Rawlins had telegraphed to Sheridan. "The following is forwarded for your information 'Scouts returned this a. m. bringing Richmond dates to 18th—Rhodes Division has arrived from the valley passed directly through Richmond and either went to Lee or further South —They came into Richmond during Friday and Saturday last and were not permitted to hold any conversation with the citizens or if they knew, to tell where they were going—This informant reports that Early is still in the valley and has

Rossers and Imbodens cavalry and one Division of Infantry If he has a Div of
Infantry I can not tell what Division it is unless it may be one made up of scattered Virginia Commands We are credibly informed that on Saturday last Jeff
Davis made a second attempt to poison himself and came near succeeding in his
attempt—It was considered an even chance whether he recovered or not yesterday morning—It is said that the news from Georgia has a depressing influence
on the spirits of Jefferson It was rumored in the city of Richmond yesterday
that Gen Sherman had captured Savannah' J M McENTEE CAPT &c'" Telegram received (at 11:30 A.M.), DNA, RG 107, Telegrams Collected (Bound);
copy, *ibid.*, Telegrams Received in Cipher. *O.R.*, I, xliii, part 2, 804–5. At 4:00
P.M., Sheridan telegraphed to Rawlins. "Your telegram just recd *Good*—
'Jeff's poisoning', is in large letters on the Bulletin board in this Rebel town—
its splendid!! I gave Thomas 200 guns and Sherman will only be limited by a
due regard for Economy in powder In my despatch of this a. m. I informed the
General of the movement of Rodes D̶i̶v̶. and Hortons Divisions—Rodes Div has
not passed through Richmond One of my best men lay in their Camp south of
New Market." Telegram sent, DNA, RG 107, Telegrams Collected (Unbound);
telegram received (at 5:00 P.M.), *ibid.*, Telegrams Collected (Bound); *ibid.*,
RG 108, Letters Received. *O.R.*, I, xliii, part 2, 805.

To Edwin M. Stanton

From City Point Va Decr 13th *1864.*

HON E M. STANTON
SEC'Y OF WAR—Richmond papers of today contain the following
U. S. GRANT
Lt Genl

"Richmond Dispatch says—'Sherman is near Savannah probably
not five miles distant, has not yet made an attack. It is still doubtful
whether he will do so or make for the coast south east of the city. It
is very certain he has not yet opened communication with the coast
though he may do so very soon. *Later*—A telegraphic dispatch received from below Charleston states that Sherman was in line [o]f
battle (we will not say where) confronted by [a] strong confederate force. Another paper states there has been no direct communication with Savannah for several days, but we apprehend the wires
have been cut between that place and Charleston"[1]

Telegram received (at 5:35 P.M.), DNA, RG 107, Telegrams Collected
(Bound); *ibid.*, Telegrams Collected (Unbound); DLC-Benjamin F. Butler. On
Dec. 13, 1864, 3:00 P.M., Secretary of War Edwin M. Stanton telegraphed to
USG. "We have here The Richmond Despatch of yesterday containing the fol-
lowing paragraph. 'Shermans Movements. The latest news from Sherman is that

on staurday he was at Bloomingdale on the central Georgia R. R. fifteen miles west of savannah. It was not absolutely certain whether it was in his programme to attack the city to slide away down to the coast or endæeavor to force a passage of the savannah river enroute for pPort Royal. our pasition at savannah is difficult as involving the necessity of protecting both the city & some ten 10 miles of the savannah and charleston R. R. which leaving the city on the west curves to the north & crosses the River eight 8 miles above. Sherman since he left Millen has been felling timber behind him and otherwise obstructing the Roads to protect his rear from the remorseless ravages of wheeler who has hunted and hung upon him like a bloodhound.' Not knowing whether the paper has reached you I send the paragraph" ALS (incomplete telegram sent), DNA, RG 107, Telegrams Collected (Bound); telegram received (at 3:30 P.M.), *ibid.*, Telegrams Collected (Unbound); *ibid.*, RG 108, Letters Received.

1. On Dec. 13, Maj. Gen. Edward O. C. Ord telegraphed to USG conveying the information quoted. ALS (telegram sent), *ibid.*, RG 107, Telegrams Collected (Unbound).

To Maj. Gen. Cadwallader C. Washburn

City Point, Va, Dec. 13th *1864*

MAJ. GEN. C. C. WASHBURN,
COMD.G DIST. OF VICKSBURG,
DEAR GEN.

The bearer of this, Judge Lewis Dent, a Brother-in-law of mine, has been a Government Lesee of plantations in La. between Vicksburg and Lake Providence for the last two years. Judge Dent I think you will find has complied with all the regulations governing lesees. He has several times been raided upon and lost most or all of his stock each time. I think he has never had any restored to him by recapture. What the regulations are now in this matter I do not know but hope the same favors will be extended to Judge Dent as are extended to other loyal citizens engaged in planting.

I will be pleased to have you make the acquaintanc[e] of my brother-in-law who you will find an inteligent and agreeable gentleman.

Yours Truly
U. S. GRANT
Lt. Gn.

ALS, James S. Schoff, New York, N. Y.

To William H. Seward

City Point, Va. Dec. 14th. 1864.

Hon. W. H. Seward
Sec. of State,
Sir!

Your communication of the 12th inst. enclosing translation of one from the French Consul at Richmond Va. is received.

The Consul, and Cap't. Maryvault of the French Navy, were exceedingly anxious to send their vessels directly up to Richmond. I explained to them, that obstructions placed in the river by us would prevent this. They feared that objection might be raised to allowing French subjects leaving the South, unless they passed directly from the "Rebel Flag." I unfortunately replied that this could be obviated by sending them by way of Fredericksburg. The Consul at once seized upon this to open the question of getting out their tobacco by that route apparently forgetting his French subjects. In my conversation I stated that if I had my way they should not have a hogshead of tobacco purchased since the breaking out of the rebellion. Since however, as an act of courtesy, their right to all purchased prior to a certain date, had been conceded to them, they should be protected to that, I recollect also of advising them to remove their tobacco to Fredericksburg, as a safer place to keep it than Richmond. Richmond is a besieged city and it may be destroyed either as an act of the enemy or in battle for possession of the place. I am very certain I expressed no willingness for their vessels to run beyond our blockading vessels except for the single purpose of bringing out their subjects. What I then stated was in conversation without previous reflection on the subject, I will now state, in mature reflection that I will not, by my advice, permit a foreign vessel to pass our Military occupation into rebel ports, for any purpose whatever.

If we allow French vessels to run in after tobacco, may not the English claim the same previlege for running in after cotton?

Should it be the order of the President to order, what I would not advise, his wishes will be carried out.

> I have the honor to be
> Very respectfully
> Your ob't. serv't.
> U. S. GRANT. Lt. Gn'l.

Copies, DLC-USG, V, 45, 71, 107; DNA, RG 108, Letters Sent. On Dec. 12, 1864, Secretary of State William H. Seward wrote to USG. "I enclose a translation of a Memorandum sent hither by the French Charge d'Affaires of a reported conversation between the agents of that government for the removal of Frenchmen from insurgent territory and yourself. It is therein stated that you intimated to them that their government might remove their tobacco by the way of Fredericksburg and the Rappahannock. I will thank you for a report of your views on this subject. The French government as you are aware, is anxious to get its tobacco, and it is desirable that this wish should be complied with sofar as the public interests may allow." LS, *ibid.*, Letters Received. Seward enclosed a document headed "(Translation.)" "In the conversation which he had with the Agents of H. I. M on the subject of embarking the French who wish to leave the the South, Lieut General Grant, himself made the remark, that if the existing arrangement was on the part of the hostile authorities, the object of some objections, Fredericksburg would perhaps be, under the circumstances, the most favorable point for effectuating the direct transfer of such French to our Flag. This city, he said, is at present in the hands of the enemy, who has repaired the railroad and placed it in direct communication with Richmond. It is not within the range of our present operations, and the very facility we would have for taking possession of it, if that entered into our views, renders it but little likely that it may be the theater of direct hostilities. I would not on my part, said he, make any objection to French Vessels ascending the Rappahannock as near to that city as their draft of water will permit. The General added on this occasion, that the same point appeared to him to offer a possibility for the export of Tobacco's, interrupted by the present operations. Without indicating, be it understood, anything on the subject of his own ulterior movements, he thinks the transport of Tobacco from Richmond to Fredericksburg by the RailRoad would offer at the same time, the best chance of security, and the greatest probability of not meeting with interruptions to the shipment." Copy, *ibid.*

On Dec. 12, 2:30 P.M., USG telegraphed to Maj. Gen. Edward O. C. Ord. "Please notify the Comd'r of the french Vessel at Aikens Landing that they must return to the mouth of James River by friday next, up to that time all foreign subjects presenting themselves on our Lines will be passed through to his Vessel where they will be required to remain until out of the River" Telegram received (marked as sent at 3:45 P.M.), *ibid.*, RG 393, Army of the Potomac, Telegrams Received; copies, *ibid.*, RG 108, Letters Sent; DLC-USG, V, 45, 71, 107. Printed as sent at 3:45 P.M. in *O.R.*, I, xlii, part 3, 982. On Dec. 17, Seward wrote to USG introducing Lt. Ede Miot, commanding the French vessel *Adonis*. Stan. V. Henkels, Catalogue No. 1194, June 8, 1917, p. 91.

On Dec. 18, Seward wrote to USG. "I have received your letter of the 14th instant relating to the transfer of French subjects from insurgent territory and to the tobacco belonging to the French Government. I yesterday addressed to M L de Geofroy the Charge d'Affaires of France a note a copy of which I inclose from which you will perceive that the course recommended by you has been adapted." LS, DNA, RG 108, Letters Received. The enclosure is *ibid*.

To Edwin M. Stanton

(Cypher)   City Point, Va, Dec. 14th *1864*. [*8:00* P.M.]
HON. E. M. STANTON, SEC. OF WAR, WASHINGTON

I would respectfully recommend the promotion of Brevet Maj. Gen. W. H. Emory and Brevet Maj. Gen. Jeff. C. Davis to the full rank of their brevets. The resignation of General Crittenden[1] makes one vacancy and it is to be hoped that vacancies will be made to occur so as to give the rank of Major General to officers commanding Corps. I do not make this recommendation in opposition to Commanders under whom these officers have been serving but I beleive in furtherance of their previous recommendations.

U. S. GRANT
Lt. Gen.[2]

AL (telegram sent), CSmH; telegram received (at 9:00 P.M.), DNA, RG 107, Telegrams Collected (Bound). *O.R.*, I, xliii, part 2, 785. No appointments followed.

1. On June 7, 1864, Maj. Gen. Thomas L. Crittenden wrote to USG. "I do not believe that my services here are of any value to the Country and I therefore request most respectfully, to be relieved from duty with this Army. My devotion to our institutions is undeminished my hostility to rebellion the same as when the war begun. It is not my desire to relieve any of the distinguished officers in this Army who are my juniors and who have such Commands as I think I am fairly entitled to, by every rule which has heretofore governed in the Army. An order which sent me to a Division marching against the enemy the ordinary pride of a soldier compelled me to obey without a protest I have obeyed the order fought the Division for nearly a month and now there is a Brigadier General in the Command entirely competent to take charge of it, and I feel that I am consenting to my own degradation by holding longer my present position. I sincerely trust that my services may be made available in such position as I ought to have by my rank without placing me in immediate contact with a whole Army of juniors who hold higher Commands." LS, DNA, RG 94, Letters Received, 714C 1864. On the same day, Maj. Gen. George G. Meade endorsed this letter. "Respectfully forwarded for the action of the Lt. Genl Comdg. I can not approve of this application as a matter of principle, and can not but consider the time chosen for its presentation as in-opportune.—" AES, *ibid*. Also on June 7, USG

endorsed this letter. "Respectfully forwarded to the Secretary of War   Gen Crittenden has been relieved from duty on the within request, and ordered to report to the Adjutant General of the Army   A Division is all the Command a Major General can claim as a right, and this was given to Gen Crittenden and in a Corps Commanded by his senior. In selecting Gen. Crittenden from among the Major Generals who were without commands, and who it was inconvenient to assign to duty, I did it out of consideration for his personal bravery and patriotism, and the high appreciation I had formed of his whole character from heresay and a slight acquaintance during this war. It is my conviction that no Command can now be given Gen. Crittenden other than the command of a Division without prejudice to the service"   ES, *ibid*. On the same day, Lt. Col. Theodore S. Bowers issued Special Orders No. 30. "Maj. Gen T. L. Crittenden, U. S. Vols. is at his own request, relieved from duty in the 9th Army Corps, Army of the Potomac, and will proceed to Washington, D. C. and there report to the Adjutant General of the Army for orders." DS, *ibid*. At 7:30 P.M., Maj. Gen. Ambrose E. Burnside telegraphed to USG. "An application was made to you this morning from Maj Genl Crittenden to be releived from duty with this command   Under the circumstances I am Satisfied that ~~the interests of the public would~~ it would be better [to] releive him—If proper I would be glad to have an answer that I can make ~~such~~ proper arrangements—You can ~~deem~~ consider this dispatch confidential or otherwise, as you think the interests of the Service demands"   Copies, *ibid*., RG 107, Telegrams Collected (Unbound); *ibid*., RG 393, 9th Army Corps, Telegrams Sent. *O.R.*, I, xxxvi, part 3, 683. On the same day, USG telegraphed to Burnside. "The order has been made & is on its way to your Hd. Qrs. for the relief of Genl Crittenden"   Telegram received, DNA, RG 94, Generals' Papers and Books, Burnside. *O.R.*, I, xxxvi, part 3, 684.

On Dec. 3, Crittenden, Metropolitan Hotel, Washington, D. C., telegraphed to USG. "I am here under your order to report to Genl: Mead,   If not needed at once would like a day or two to equip, as I am without an outfit for the field" ALS (telegram sent), DNA, RG 107, Telegrams Collected (Unbound). On the same day, USG telegraphed to Crittenden. "Your despatch of this date is received. Permission to remain in Washington a day or two (2) *granted* you" Telegram received (press), *ibid*., Telegrams Collected (Bound); copies, *ibid*., RG 108, Letters Sent; DLC-USG, V, 46, 76, 108.

On Dec. 7, Crittenden wrote to Brig. Gen. Lorenzo Thomas resigning as maj. gen. ALS, DNA, RG 94, ACP, C1296 CB 1864. On the same day, Meade endorsed this letter. "Respectfully forwarded—Maj Genl. Crittenden ranks all the officers of this army of his grade—There was no position at my disposal that would have been satisfactory to him—Maj. Genl—Crittenden having once before, asked to be relieved from this army, owing to the insufficiency of his command (a division) his tender of resignation is now considered as a matter of deliberation & based on his well considered views of the prerogatives of his rank. Under these circumstances tho, from the high character I have always heard of Maj. Genl Crittenden, I regret extremely, he should deem it necessary to give up his commission, I feel I can not withhold my approval & therefore recommend its acceptance—"   AES, *ibid*. On the same day, USG endorsed this letter. "Approved and respectfully forwarded to the Secretary of War"   ES, *ibid*. At 11:30 A.M., Meade telegraphed to USG. "Maj. Gen Crittenden tenders his resignation and asks for a leave pending action on it. Shall I grant the leave?" Telegram received, *ibid*., RG 108, Letters Received. *O.R.*, I, xlii, part 3, 843. On the same day, USG telegraphed to Meade. "~~Accept~~ Grant Gn. Crittenden a leave of absence." ALS (telegram sent), OClWHi; copies, DLC-USG, V, 45, 70, 107; DNA, RG 108, Letters Sent. *O.R.*, I, xlii, part 3, 843. See *ibid.*, pp. 689, 847, 998.

    2. Signature not in USG's hand.

To Edwin M. Stanton

———

City Point, Va. Dec. 14. 1864.

HON. E. M. STANTON
SEC. OF WAR,
SIR!

    I would respectfully request, the promotion of Cap't. Geo. K. Leet, A. A. Genl. either to the rank of Maj. or Lieut. Col. in his Dep't. He is eminently worthy of the latter rank. Cap't. Leet has rissen from the ranks on his merits alone, to his present rank. Promotion has not spoiled him. Since I have been commanding the Armies Cap't. Leet, has been in charge of the Office in Washington, where I doubt not he has won the respect and esteem of all with whom he has come in contact.

                       Very Respectfully
                       Your ob't. servant.
                       U. S. GRANT Lt. Gen.

Copies, DLC-USG, V, 45, 71, 107; DNA, RG 108, Letters Sent. George K. Leet received an appointment as maj. as of Feb. 25, 1865.

To Maj. Gen. Henry W. Halleck

———

(Cipher)   City Point, Va, Dec. 14th *1864*. [*10:00* A.M.]
MAJ. GEN. HALLECK, WASHINGTON

    What has been done with Steele? He is too good a soldier immediately in command of troops to leave idle. As Canby asked for his removal I think it will be better to order Steele here in command of the 9th Corps and send Parke to Canby.

                       U. S. GRANT
                       Lt. Gen.

ALS (telegram sent), CSmH; telegram received (at 11:30 A.M.), DNA, RG 107, Telegrams Collected (Bound). Printed as sent at 9:30 A.M. in *O.R.*, I, xli, part 4, 851; *ibid.*, I, xlii, part 3, 993. On Dec. 14, 1864, 2:00 P.M., Maj. Gen. Henry W. Halleck telegraphed to USG. "Genl canby ordered Steele to [C]airo before he recieved the orders of the War Dept or my letter. By these orders Steele was to report to him at New Orleans. I think from canby's letter that that arrangement will suit him. [I] would not change the order [ti]ll Canby is heard from after recieving [the] Genl order, as he has very [few] good officers & I think will want Steele's services." ALS (telegram sent), DNA, RG 107, Telegrams Collected (Bound); telegram received, *ibid.*; *ibid.*, RG 108, Letters Received. *O.R.*, I, xli, part 4, 851; *ibid.*, I, xlii, part 3, 994.

To Maj. Gen. Benjamin F. Butler

(Cipher)   City Point Va. Dec. 14th/64 *[10:00* A.M.*]*
MAJ. GEN. BUTLER, FORTRESS MONROE, VA,

What is the prospect for getting your expedition started? It is a great pity we were not ten or twelve days earlyer. I am confident it would then have been successful. Have you heard from Palmer? The Richmond papers give no account of any Federals on the Roanoke or Welden road South of Welden.

U. S. GRANT
Lt. Gn.

ALS (telegram sent), CSmH; telegram received (at 10:00 A.M.), DLC-Benjamin F. Butler. *O.R.*, I, xlii, part 1, 974; *ibid.*, I, xlii, part 3, 1004–5. On Dec. 14, 1864, 10:45 A.M., Maj. Gen. Benjamin F. Butler, "On Board Ben Deford," telegraphed to USG. "Porter started yesterday Transport fleet are at Cape Henry. I am Just starting The weather for the last six days has been such that it would be useless to be on the Coast. Expedition left Plymouth Wednesday last. You will remember that you have cut communication between Weldon & Petersburgh. Every thing is off in the best time possible" ALS (telegram sent), DLC-Benjamin F. Butler; telegram received (marked as sent at 10:35 A.M.), DNA, RG 108, Letters Received. *O.R.*, I, xli, part 1, 974–75; *ibid.*, I, xlii, part 3, 1005.

On Dec. 10, 11:45 A.M., Butler, Fort Monroe, telegraphed to USG. "Has been bloing a gale ever since we arrived. Is clearing up a litle. We are all ready waiting for the navy—Any news from Warren or Sherman" ALS (telegram sent), DNA, RG 107, Telegrams Collected (Unbound); telegram received, *ibid.*; (marked as sent at noon) *ibid.*, RG 108, Letters Received. *O.R.*, I, xlii, part 1, 974; *ibid.*, I, xli, part 3, 938. At 8:30 P.M., USG telegraphed to Butler. "Nothing from Sherman or Warren. Heavy cannonading was heard South of Petersburg very distant this forenoon." Telegram received (at 8:30 P.M.), DLC-Benjamin F. Butler; copies, DLC-USG, V, 45, 70, 107; DNA, RG 108, Letters Sent. *O.R.*,

I, xlii, part 3, 938. On Dec. 11, 6:00 P.M., Butler telegraphed to USG. "Gale still continues. Clouds Just breaking away—All ready and Waiting One of Mulfords steamers Just in Charlestown Mercury of Decr 6th says—Sherman was reported yesterday at Station No 6 on the Georgia Road about 60 miles from Savannah—making for that city No other News—Have telegraphed this to Sec'y of War—" ALS (telegram sent), DNA, RG 107, Telegrams Collected (Unbound); telegram received, *ibid.*, RG 108, Letters Received. *O.R.*, I, xlii, part 1, 974; *ibid.*, I, xlii, part 3, 969. At 8:30 P.M., USG telegraphed to Butler. "Richmond papers of the 10th, show that on the 7th Sherman was East of the Ogachee, and within twenty five miles of Savannah, having marched eighteen miles the day before. If you do not get off immediately you will loose the chance of surprise and weak garrison." Copies, DLC-USG, V, 45, 71, 107; DNA, RG 108, Letters Sent. *O.R.*, I, xlii, part 1, 974; *ibid.*, I, xlii, part 3, 969.

To Maj. Gen. George G. Meade and
Maj. Gen. Edward O. C. Ord

(Cipher)   City Point, Va, Dec. 14th *1864.*
MAJ. GEN. ORD & MEADE

I am unexpectedly called away. Please address all dispatches for me to Gen. Rawlins at these Hdqrs and they will be forwarded.[1]

U. S. GRANT
Lt. Gn.

ALS (telegram sent), CSmH; copies, DLC-USG, V, 45, 71, 107; DNA, RG 108, Letters Sent. *O.R.*, I, xlii, part 3, 995.
On Dec. 13, 1864, 5:30 P.M., USG telegraphed to Maj. Gen. George G. Meade. "Will you please give me a summary of Warren's operations on the expedition from which he has just returned." ALS (telegram sent), NHi; telegram received (at 5:33 P.M.), DNA, RG 94, War Records Office, Army of the Potomac. *O.R.*, I, xlii, part 3, 985. At 6:00 P.M. and Dec. 14, noon, Meade telegraphed to USG. "I have received no report from Genl. Warren other than the despatch already transmitted to you—I have called on him for one more in detail.—" "Altho Warren was called upon last evening on receipt of your telegram & again this morning, I am yet without any further details than those transmitted in his despatch of the 11th—In the absence of a report from Warren, I have made a resumé of the operations from my personal knowledge which I send for your consideration—As soon as Warren's report is received, it will be transmitted." ALS (telegrams sent), DNA, RG 94, War Records Office, Army of the Potomac; copies, *ibid.*, RG 393, Army of the Potomac, Letters Sent; Meade Papers, PHi. *O.R.*, I, xlii, part 3, 985, 994; (2) *ibid.*, I, xlii, part 1, 37. On Dec. 14, 11:00 A.M., Meade had written to USG reporting the expedition of Maj. Gen. Gouverneur K. Warren. Copies, DNA, RG 393, Army of the Potomac, Letters Sent; (2) Meade Papers, PHi. *O.R.*, I, xlii, part 1, 37–38.

At 3:00 P.M., USG telegraphed to Meade. "I wish you would have special attention directed to ascertaining if Hill's Corps has gone South. It looks much as if it had." ALS (telegram sent), Knox College, Galesburg, Ill.; telegram received (at 3:00 P.M.), DNA, RG 94, War Records Office, Army of the Potomac. *O.R.*, I, xlii, part 3, 994. At 4:30 P.M. (sent at 4:45 P.M.), Meade telegraphed to USG. "Deserters came in this A M & last night—belonging to Pegrams division, who report their division being relieved last evening by ~~Lawles~~ Lawes brigade of Hills corps—They were of the opinion & from reports that all of Hills corps had returned or were returning to their old position—their Division Pegrams they said was moved further to the right on being relieved.—This is all the information we have of Hill's movements.—" ALS (telegram sent), DNA, RG 94, War Records Office, Army of the Potomac; telegram received (at 4:45 P.M.), DNA, RG 108, Letters Received. *O.R.*, I, xlii, part 3, 994. At 6:20 P.M. (sent at 6:30 P.M.), Meade telegraphed to USG. "The above despatch forwarded for your information—I should judge there was no doubt of the return of Hill's corps—altho' a part may perhaps have been left behind or sent further south.—" ALS (telegram sent—misdated Dec. 13), DNA, RG 94, War Records Office, Army of the Potomac. *O.R.*, I, xlii, part 3, 995. The enclosure (dated Dec. 14) is *ibid.* At 8:00 P.M., Meade telegraphed to USG. "If the foregoing statement can be relied on Hills whole corps has returned" Telegram received (at 8:05 P.M.), DNA, RG 108, Letters Received; copy, Meade Papers, PHi. *O.R.*, I, xlii, part 3, 999. The enclosure is *ibid.*

On Dec. 15, Maj. Gen. Edward O. C. Ord telegraphed to Brig. Gen. John A. Rawlins. "Gen Fererro commanding Bermuda Defences reports his command very weak   his men have to go on picket duty every other night   Can the 28 U S C belonging to his command and now at city Point be ordered to him." ALS (telegram sent), DNA, RG 107, Telegrams Collected (Unbound); telegram received, *ibid.*, RG 108, Letters Received. *O.R.*, I, xlii, part 3, 1011. On the same day, Rawlins telegraphed to Ord. "The 28th U. S. C. T. is very much needed here just now. It may be two weeks before they can be relieved, but as soon as they can be relieved, they will be sent to join there Div." Copies, DLC-USG, V, 45, 71, 107; DNA, RG 108, Letters Sent. *O.R.*, I, xlii, part 3, 1011.

On Dec. 16, 4:15 P.M., Rawlins telegraphed to Meade. "~~If~~ In the heavy firing this afternoon is there anything indicative of any movement on the part of the Enemy   If so please communicate to these Head Qrs or to Genl Ord for his information   In a despatch from Gen Ord last night & in a communication today he fears for his Bermuda front & asks that the twenty Eighth (28) U S C T on fatigue duty here or some other regiment be sent to report to Gen Ferrero at Bermuda   That the withdrawal of troops for Genl Weitzels Expedition has left him so weak on the north of the river that he cannot detach from there without great danger   In case of attack it was Gen Grants desire that you assume command of all the forces & if it becomes necessary to do so the order will be made here" Telegram received (at 4:20 P.M.), DNA, RG 94, War Records Office, Army of the Potomac; copies, *ibid.*, RG 108, Letters Sent; DLC-USG, V, 45, 71, 107; (2) Meade Papers, PHi. Printed as sent at 4:20 P.M. in *O.R.*, I, xlii, part 3, 1015. At 4:45 P.M. (sent at 5:00 P.M.), Meade telegraphed to Rawlins. "Your despatch of 4.20 just received—There is nothing to indicate a movement, on the part of the enemy—They opened this P. M on the 9th corps front with a heavy gun to which our batteries have been replying.—This would have been reported, if I did not presume you would construe my silence ~~into~~ as indicative that all was right" ALS (telegram sent), DNA, RG 94, War Records Office, Army of the Potomac; telegram received (at 5:00 P.M.), *ibid.*, RG 108, Letters Received. *O.R.*, I, xlii, part 3, 1016. At 4:30 P.M. (sent at 5:00 P.M.), Meade telegraphed to Rawlins. "If there is any cause for concern for Bermuda Hundred —Brig Genl. Benham ~~comdr~~ command might be sent there from the lines in front of City Point—He ought to be able to take over some 2000 men." ALS (undated telegram sent), DNA, RG 94, War Records Office, Army of the Potomac; telegram received (at 5:00 P.M.), *ibid.*, RG 108, Letters Received. *O.R.*, I, xlii, part 3, 1015. On the same day, Rawlins telegraphed to Ord. "If you think there is any serious cause for concern on your Bermuda front about one thousand men from Gen Benhams command can be sent there temporarilly" Telegram received (at 5:50 P.M.), DNA, RG 94, War Records Office, Army of the Potomac; copies, *ibid.*, RG 108, Letters Sent; DLC-USG, V, 45, 71, 107. Printed as sent at 5:50 P.M. in *O.R.*, I, xlii, part 3, 1021. On the same day, Ord telegraphed to Rawlins. "On account of ~~important~~ interests there—and the force being so much less than I supposed—I do deem it important to have ~~an~~ the force which you propose Sent there as soon as may be—" ALS (telegram sent), DNA, RG 107, Telegrams Collected (Unbound); telegram received, *ibid.*, RG 108, Letters Received. *O.R.*, I, xlii, part 3, 1021. On the same day, Lt. Col. Ely S. Parker issued Special Orders No. 151. "Brig. Gen'l. H. W. Benham Comd'g. Defences at City Point will without delay detach from his Command one thousand men under their proper Officers, with directions to report to Gen'l. Ferrero, Comd'g. Bermuda Hundred Defences, for temporary duty." Copies, DLC-USG, V, 57, 62, 63, 64. *O.R.*, I, xlii, part 3, 1019.

On Dec. 17, 11:15 A.M. (sent at 11:30 A.M.), Meade telegraphed to Rawlins. "There is nothing of importance to communicate—A deserter from Mahone's Division came in yesterday—from his report the Division has returned to its old position in reserve—This accounts for the whole of Hills corps ~~and~~ proves its return to the lines around Petersburgh.—I have just received a telegram from Maj-Genl. Ord—announcing the passage of troops by rail towards Petersburgh— I infer from this Genl. Ord no longer anticipates offensive movements on his lines.—Have you any idea when the Lt. Genl. may be expected back?—" ALS (telegram sent), DNA, RG 94, War Records Office, Army of the Potomac; telegram received, *ibid.*, RG 108, Letters Received. *O.R.*, I, xlii, part 3, 1024. On the same day (Saturday), 11:40 A.M., Rawlins telegraphed to Meade. "Gen Grant telegraphs from Washington that he will be absent until Monday Next." Telegram received (at 11:45 A.M.), DNA, RG 94, War Records Office, Army of the Potomac; copies, *ibid.*, RG 108, Letters Sent; DLC-USG, V, 45, 71, 107. *O.R.*, I, xlii, part 3, 1024. On the same day, Brig. Gen. John W. Turner telegraphed to Rawlins. "A Deserter just in says he was in Richmond yesterday and saw a waggon train of 75 or 100 waggons passing through the city—heard a man say it ~~came~~ was Earlys waggons" ALS (telegram sent), DNA, RG 107, Telegrams Collected (Unbound); telegram received (at 2:40 P.M.), *ibid.*, RG 108, Letters Received. *O.R.*, I, xlii, part 3, 1032.

On Dec. 18, 2:15 P.M., Ord telegraphed to Rawlins. "Corps—Division and Brigade commanders are complaining bitterly that they cant get shoes—or clothing for their men tho repeatedly applied for at city point—I have several hundred men barefoot or supplied by Sutlers—is there no immediate remedy—" ALS (telegram sent), DNA, RG 107, Telegrams Collected (Unbound); telegram received, *ibid.*, RG 108, Letters Received. *O.R.*, I, xlii, part 3, 1037.

1. On Dec. 15, 2:00 P.M., Rawlins telegraphed to USG. "The following despatch just received" Telegram received, DNA, RG 107, Telegrams Collected (Bound). Rawlins transmitted a telegram of the same day from Ord to Rawlins conveying news from the *Richmond Examiner* of the U.S. capture of Bristol, Tenn. ALS (telegram sent), *ibid.*, Telegrams Collected (Unbound). On the same day, Rawlins telegraphed to USG transmitting a telegram from Gen. Robert E. Lee to C.S.A. Secretary of War James A. Seddon reporting U.S. movements. Telegram received (at 6:30 P.M.), *ibid.*, Telegrams Collected (Bound). Printed as sent at 4:20 P.M., received at 7:00 P.M., in *O.R.*, I, xlii, part 3, 1007.

On Dec. 16, 1:30 P.M., Rawlins telegraphed to USG. "Capt Babcoc[k] of the secret service sends the following information" Telegram received (at 2:15 P.M.), DNA, RG 107, Telegrams Collected (Bound); copy, *ibid.*, Telegrams Received in Cipher. *O.R.*, I, xlii, part 3, 1015. The enclosure is *ibid.*

On Dec. 18, 9:00 A.M., Rawlins telegraphed to USG. "The following despatch just received." Telegram received (at 11:00 A.M.), DNA, RG 107, Telegrams Collected (Bound); copy, *ibid.*, Telegrams Received in Cipher. The enclosed telegram from John C. Babcock to Capt. John McEntee is in *O.R.*, I, xlii, part 3, 1025.

To Maj. Gen. Henry W. Halleck

Washington. City, Dec. 15th 1864.

MAJ GENL. HALLECK.
CHIEF OF STAFF OF THE ARMY,
GENERAL:

Please communicate with Sherman and direct him to send no troops from his Army to Va. until plan of Campaign is fully agreed upon. My last instructions to Sherman contemplated his sending troops to operate against Richmond retaining all his artillery, cavalry and Inft'y sufficient to hold our base on the Atlantic secured by his campaign, and to compel the enemy to retain there at least the force he now has against us. Also that Artillery can be sent from here. to supply his wants

U. S. GRANT.
Lt Genl.

Copy, DNA, RG 108, Letters Received. *O.R.*, I, xliv, 715.

On Dec. 15, 1864, 11:10 A.M., Maj. Gen. Henry W. Halleck telegraphed to USG, City Point. "You are aware that a large amount of supplies were collected at Pensacola for Genl Sherman, & that canby held troops there and at Mobile to open communications with him if necessary. Should not Genl canby now be instructed to use these troops & supplies for other purposes? Will Genl

Sherman, after taking Savannah, base himself [on] that place & operate against [C]harleston, Branchville or Augusta? [I] do not know what instructions have been given him on this subject; but if he is to base himself on the coast, recruits, convalescents, &c., as well as future supplies, should be sent there for his army." ALS (telegram sent), DNA, RG 107, Telegrams Collected (Bound); telegram received, *ibid.*; (at 1:00 P.M.) *ibid.*, RG 108, Letters Received. *O.R.*, I, xliv, 715. USG probably responded to the question while in Washington. See *ibid.*, I, xli, part 4, 869. On Dec. 15, Brig. Gen. John A. Rawlins telegraphed to Halleck. "Lieut Genl Grant left last evening for Washington and will probably reach there this afternoon" Telegram received (at 3:15 P.M.), DNA, RG 107, Telegrams Collected (Bound); copies, *ibid.*, RG 108, Letters Sent; DLC-USG, V, 45, 71, 107. *O.R.*, I, xlii, part 3, 1007.

To Maj. Gen. George H. Thomas

(Cipher)   *Washington City,*
                                        Dec. 15th *1864* [*11:30* P.M.]

MAJ. GN. THOMAS, NASHVILLE TEN

I was just on my way to Nashville but receiving a dispatch from Van Duzer[1] detailing your splendid success of to-day I shall go no further.[2] Push the enemy now and give him ~~now~~ no rest until he is entirely destroyed. Your Army will cheerfully suffer many privations to break up Hoods Army and render it useless for future operations. Do not stop for trains or supplies but take them from the country as the enemy has done. Much is now expected.

U. S. GRANT
Lt. Gn

ALS (telegram sent), DNA, RG 107, Telegrams Collected (Bound); copies, *ibid.*, RG 108, Letters Sent; *ibid.*, RG 393, Dept. of the Cumberland, Telegrams Received; DLC-USG, V, 45, 71, 107; DLC-John M. Schofield. *O.R.*, I, xlv, part 2, 195. On Dec. 15, 1864, midnight, USG telegraphed to Maj. Gen. George H. Thomas. "Your dispatch of this evening just received. I congratulate you and the Army under your command for [to]-days operations and feel a conviction that to-morrow will ~~be~~ add more fruits to your victory." ALS (telegram sent), DNA, RG 107, Telegrams Collected (Bound); copies, *ibid.*, RG 108, Letters Sent; *ibid.*, RG 393, Dept. of the Cumberland, Telegrams Received; *ibid.*, 16th Army Corps, Letters Received; DLC-USG, V, 45, 71, 107; DLC-John M. Schofield. Printed as sent at 11:45 P.M. in *O.R.*, I, xlv, part 1, 50; *ibid.*, I, xlv, part 2, 195. See *ibid.*, p. 194. At 11:30 P.M. (Friday), USG telegraphed to Brig. Gen. John A. Rawlins. "I send you dispatch just received from Nashville. I shall not now go there. Will remain absent however until about Monday." ALS (telegram sent), DNA, RG 107, Telegrams Collected (Bound); copies, *ibid.*,

RG 108, Letters Sent; DLC-USG, V, 45, 73, 107. Printed as sent at 11:50 P.M. in *O.R.*, I, xlii, part 3, 1008; *ibid.*, I, xlv, part 2, 195. On Dec. 16, 6:00 P.M., Thomas telegraphed to President Abraham Lincoln, Secretary of War Edwin M. Stanton, and USG. "This Army thanks you for your approbation of its conduct yesterday and to assure you that it is not misplaced—I have the honor to report that the enemy has been pressed at all points to day in his line of retreat to the Brentwood Hills—Brig Gen Hatch of Wilsons corps of cavalry on the right turned the enemies left and captured a large number of prisoners number not yet reported—Maj Gen Schofield corps next on the left of cavalry carried several hills, captured many prisoners, and six pieces of Artillery—Brevet Maj Gen Smith next on left of Maj Gen Schofield carried the salient point of enemys line with McMillan's Brigade of McArthurs Division, capturing sixteen pieces of Artillery, two Brigadier Generals and about two thousand prisoners—Brig Gen Garrards Division of Smiths command, next on the left, and McArthur's Division carried the enemys entrenchments, capturing all the Artillery and troops of the enemy on the line   Brig Gen Woods troops ~~of~~ on Franklin pike took up the assault carrying the enemys entrenchments, in his retreat captured eight pieces of Artillery something over six hundred prisoners and drove the enemy within one mile of the Brentwood Hill Pass—Maj Gen Steedman commanding detachments of the different armies of the Military Division of Mississippi most nobly supported Gen Woods left and bore a most honorable part in the ~~situation~~ operations of the day   I have ordered the pursuit to be continued in the morning at daylight, although the troops are very much fatigued—The utmost enthusiasm prevails. I must not forget to report the operations of Brig Gen Johnson in successfully driving the enemy with the co-operation of the gunboats under Lieut Comdr Fitch from their established batteries on the Cumberland River, below the city of Nashville, and of the success of Brig Genl Croxtons Brigade in covering and returning our right and rear—The operations of yesterday and to day although I have no report of the number of prisoners captured by Johnson's and Croxton's commands, I know they have made a large number,   I am glad to be able to state that the numbers of prisoners captured yesterday greatly exceeds the number reported by telegraph last evening   The woods, fields and entrenchments are strewn with the enemys small arms, abandoned in their retreat,   In conclusion I am happy to state all this has been effected with but a very small loss to us— Our loss probably does not exceed three hundred & very few killed—"   Telegrams received (2—on Dec. 17, 5:30 A.M.), DNA, RG 107, Telegrams Collected (Bound); (marked as sent on Dec. 16, 8:00 P.M., received on Dec. 17, 2:40 P.M., sent to Rawlins) *ibid.*, RG 108, Letters Received; copies, DLC-John M. Schofield; Seward Papers, NRU. Printed as addressed also to Governor Andrew Johnson in *O.R.*, I, xlv, part 2, 210–11; *O.R.* (Navy), I, xxvi, 669–70.

1. On Dec. 15, Capt. John C. Van Duzer telegraphed to Maj. Thomas T. Eckert. "General Thomas with the forces under his Command attacked Hoods Army in front of Nashville at 9 oclock this morning & although the battle is not yet decided the whole action today was splendidly successful,   Our line advanced on the right 5 miles   The Enemy were driven from the River, from his Entrenchments from the Range of Hills on which his left rested & forced back upon his right and centre and the centre pushed back from one to three miles with the loss of 17 guns & about 1500 prisoners & his whole line of earth works except about a mile on his extreme right where no serious attempt was made to dislodge him. our casualties are ~~reported~~ light. Hoods whole army except the Cavalry &

a small force near Murfreesboro were Engaged." Telegram received, DNA, RG 108, Letters Received. On Dec. 16, Rawlins telegraphed to Maj. Gen. George G. Meade and to Maj. Gen. Edward O. C. Ord transmitting this telegram. Telegram received, *ibid.*, RG 94, War Records Office, Dept. of Va. and N. C., Army of the James, Unentered Papers; *ibid.*, Army of the Potomac; copy, *ibid.* On the same day, Rawlins telegraphed to USG. "No change in the ~~evening~~ enemy's position since you left—The following dispatch has been received from Genl Meade" Telegram received (at 10:40 A.M.), *ibid.*, RG 107, Telegrams Collected (Bound). Rawlins enclosed a copy of a telegram of 10:00 A.M. (sent at 10:15 A.M.) from Meade to Rawlins. "Your despatch announcing Genl. Thomas' Success has been received with great satisfaction, as the situation of affairs at Nashville were such as to afford cause for anxiety—I had every confidence in the judgement & high soldierly qualities of Genl. Thomas and am truly rejoiced to hear of his brilliant success.—" ALS (telegram sent), *ibid.*, RG 94, War Records Office, Army of the Potomac; telegram received (at 10:15 A.M.), *ibid.*, RG 108, Letters Received. *O.R.*, I, xlii, part 3, 1015; *ibid.*, I, xlv, part 2, 212–13. At 5:00 P.M., Rawlins telegraphed to USG. "If you have any further news of Genl Thomas success will you please send it as it inspires the army here with great enthusiasm." Telegram received (at 5:30 P.M.), DNA, RG 107, Telegrams Collected (Bound); copy, *ibid.*, Telegrams Received in Cipher. *O.R.*, I, xlv, part 2, 212. At 10:30 P.M., Stanton telegraphed to Rawlins. "The Western telegraph lines are working very badly on account of rain storms prevailing. The following unofficial despatches have been received. 'Nashville Dec 16th/64   Just returned from the battle field. Battle severe & terrific. Our forces victorious. 'Nashville 2-15 P. m. Hood has fallen back and is apparently doing his best to get away while Thomas is pressing him with great vigor frequently Capturing guns & men. Every thing so far is perfectly successful and prospect fair to crush Hood's army'" Telegram received (at 11:15 P.M.), DNA, RG 108, Letters Received. On the same day, Rawlins transmitted this telegram to Meade and all corps commanders. Telegram received, *ibid.*, RG 107, Telegrams Collected (Unbound); *ibid.*, RG 94, War Records Office, Dept. of Va. and N. C., Army of the James, Unentered Papers; copies, *ibid.*, Army of the Potomac; *ibid.*, RG 393, 2nd Army Corps, Telegrams Received. Also on Dec. 16, Rawlins telegraphed to USG transmitting war news from the *Richmond Dispatch* and *Richmond Examiner*. Telegram received (at 4:10 P.M.), *ibid.*, RG 107, Telegrams Collected (Bound). *O.R.*, I, xlv, part 2, 211–12. On Dec. 17, 6:00 P.M., Meade telegraphed to Rawlins. "I have ordered a salute of one hundred guns to be fired to morrow at Sunrise in honor of Maj. Genl. Thomas brilliant victory.—" ALS (telegram sent), DNA, RG 94, War Records Office, Army of the Potomac. At 6:30 P.M., Rawlins transmitted this telegram to USG. Telegram received (at 6:45 P.M.), *ibid.*, RG 107, Telegrams Collected (Bound); *ibid.*, RG 108, Letters Received. At 8:00 P.M., Thomas telegraphed to USG. "We have pressed the enemy today beyond Franklin, capturing his hospitals containing over fifteen hundred (1500) wounded and about one hundred & fifty (150) of our wounded in addition to the above—Genl. Knipe comdg a Division of Cavalry drove the enemy's rear guard through Franklin today capturing about two hundred fifty (250) prisoners & five (5) battle flags with very little loss on our side. Citizens of Franklin represent Hood's Army as p completely demoralized. In addition to the Captures of yesterday reported in my despatch of last night, I have the honor to report the capture of Gen. Rucker and about two hundred & fifty (250) prisoners of the enemy's cavalry in a fight that occurred about eight oclock last night between

Gen. Rucker & Gen. Hatch of our Cavalry   The enemy has been pressed today both in front & on both flanks   Brig Gen. Johnson succeeded in striking him on the flank just beyond Franklin capturing quite a number of prisoners number not yet reported. My Cavalry is pressing him closely though and I am very much in hopes of getting many more prisoners tomorrow. Luckily but little damage has been done the railroad and I expect to have trains close up to my army tomorrow night. I have just heard from Genl. Stoneman at Kingsport under date of thirteenth inst.   he left Knoxville on the tenth overtook Duke's formerly Morgans command on the twelfth and during the night drove him across the north fork of holston river   next morning crossed the river attacked captured & killed nearly the whole command taking the entire wagon train   Col. R. C. Morgan a brother of John Morgan is with many other officers, a prisoner—Duke's command is considered completely destroyed. The fighting was done by Gillem's command & the thirtieth Kentucky of Gen. Burbridges command. Stoneman in motion for Bristol where he hopes to intercept Vaughn a part of captured train was that lost by Gillam on retreat from Bulls gap—I now consider the cumberland perfectly safe from Nashville down and have directed the Chief Qr. Mr. to commence shipping stores up it immediately   as there also a fair prospect for another rise in the Tennessee river I have requested Admiral Lee to send some Iron Clads & gun boats up that river to destroy Hoods pontoon bridge if possible & cut off his retreat"   Telegram received, *ibid.* *O.R.*, I, xlv, part 2, 228–29.

2. Also on Dec. 17, 10:00 A.M., Stanton telegraphed to USG, Burlington, N. J. "Thomas ~~was~~ victorious yesterday. Hoods army broken driven back to the Brentwood hills, many prisoners and cannon taken   pursuit to be renewed today. our loss not over three hundred. Sherman took Fort McAllister Wednesday. If you start ~~now~~ soon there is yet time for your report to be made as promised. Details will be sent you soon as possible but the telegraph works badly. Despatches from Foster & ~~Sherman~~ are being received and a Messenger with sealed despatches from Sherman ~~is~~ has reached Fortress Monroe on his way up." ALS (telegram sent), DNA, RG 107, Telegrams Collected (Bound); telegram received (marked as sent at 11:00 A.M.), *ibid.*, RG 108, Letters Received. *O.R.*, I, xlv, part 2, 228. At 1:30 P.M., USG telegraphed to Stanton. "I leave here at 8. P. M today for City Point Via Washington"   Telegram received (at 3:30 P.M.), DNA, RG 107, Telegrams Collected (Bound); copies, *ibid.*, Telegrams Received in Cipher; *ibid.*, RG 108, Letters Sent; DLC-USG, V, 45, 71, 107.

To Maj. Gen. John A. Logan

From Burlington Dec. 17 4 30 P M *186*[4]
MAJ GN LOGAN LOUISVILLE KY,

The news from Thomas so far is in the highest degree gratifying. You need not go further. Before starting to join Sherman report in Washington.

U S. GRANT
Lt. Gen.

ALS (telegram sent), IHi; telegram received, DLC-John A. Logan. Entered in
USG's letterbooks dated Dec. 19, 1864, and so printed in *O.R.*, I, xlv, part 2,
265. On Dec. 17, 10:00 A.M., Maj. Gen. John A. Logan, Louisville, telegraphed
to USG. "have just arrived, weather bad, is raing since yesterday morning.
people here all jubilant over Genl Thomas success—Confidence seems to be restored. I will remain here to hear from you   all Things going right. it would
seem best that I return soon to Join my Command with Sherman" ALS (telegram sent), DLC-John A. Logan; telegram received (at 2:30 P.M.), DNA,
RG 107, Telegrams Collected (Bound); *ibid.*, RG 108, Letters Received. *O.R.*,
I, xlv, part 2, 230.
  On Dec. 13, Lt. Col. Theodore S. Bowers had issued Special Orders No.
149. "Maj. Gen'l. John A. Logan, will proceed immediately to Nashville Tenn.,
reporting by telegraph to the Lieutenant General Commanding, his arrival at
Louisville Ky. and also his arival at Nashville, Tenn." DS (facsimile), Mrs. John
A. Logan, *Reminiscences of a Soldier's Wife* (New York, 1913), p. 186. *O.R.*,
I, xlv, part 2, 171.

To Edwin M. Stanton

Washington City,
Dec. 18th *1864*

HON E M STANTON
    In my opinion no General Order should be issued which would
authorize ~~irresponsible persons~~ subordinate Military Commanders
to invade a foreign country, with which we are at peace, at their
discretion. If such officers should pursue Marauders fitted out in
Canada, to depridate upon our frontier, it should be the act of the
officer himself to be justified or condemned afterwards upon the
merits of the case. In all instances where to much delay will not
ensue they should wait for the authority of the Comd.g Gn. of the
Dept. at least, and ~~if~~ then his action should be reported, through
the proper channel, to the President at once.
                                              U. S. GRANT
                                              Lt. Gn.

ADfS, CSmH; ES, DNA, RG 94, Letters Received, 634E 1864. *O.R.*, I, xlii, part
3, 1033–34; *ibid.*, I, xliii, part 2, 800. Written on a letter of Dec. 17, 1864, from
Maj. Gen. John A. Dix, New York City, to Secretary of War Edwin M. Stanton.
"I have just received your letter of the 15th inst., advising me that the President
does not approve that part of my General Order No 97, 'which instructs all military commanders on the frontier in certain cases therein specified to cross the
boundary between the United States and Canada and directs pursuit into neutral

territory.' I shall immediately revoke the portion of the order thus disapproved. I beg leave most respectfully to represent that the revocation of this direction to military commanders on the frontier removes all hope of capturing marauders, who cross the boundary line for the purpose of committing depredations on our side. When St. Albans was attacked, the banks robbed, and several of the citizens shot, one of them mortally, a telegraphic despatch was immediately sent to me and was promptly answered by me; and yet so rapid were the movements of the marauders that before my order reached the pursuers the guilty parties had been arrested and delivered up, with the stolen property amounting to several hundred thousand dollars, to the Canadian authorities. When it is considered that St. Albans is several miles within the boundary line, it will be perceived that the pursuit of marauders will be wholly unavailing from points directly on the frontier if authority to pursue is to be waited for. When I issued Order No 97 I had satisfactory information from Toronto that a predatory expedition had been organized against Ogdensburg, separated from Canada by the River St. Lawrence less than a mile in width. If the local commander, in case of an attack on the place, is required to telegraph for orders to me, it is quite manifest that the marauders will be beyond his reach before he will receive my answer. There are strong manifestations of a purpose on the part of our citizens on the frontier to take the pursuit and capture of marauders into their own hands, and a desire to prevent these unauthorised acts of individuals was one of my motives in giving the authority in question to the local commanders. I do not state these considerations with the expectation of inducing the President to review his decision, which has no doubt been well considered, but that he may understand my reasons for giving a direction, which has incurred his disapproval." LS, DNA, RG 94, Letters Received, 634E 1864. *O.R.*, I, xliii, part 2, 799–800.

To Maj. Gen. William T. Sherman

Confidential   *Washington, D. C.*, Dec. 18th *1864*
MY DEAR GENERAL,

I have just received and read, I need not tell you with how much gratification, your letter to Gen. Halleck.[1] I congratulate you, and the brave officers and men under your command, on the sucsessful termination of your most brilliant campaign. I never had a doubt of the result. When apprehentions for your safety were expressed by the President I assured him with the Army you had, and you in command of it, there was no danger but you would *strike* bottom on Salt Water some place. That I would not feel the same security, in fact would not have entrusted the expedition to any other living commander.

It has been very hard work to get Thomas to attack Hood. I

gave him the most peremptory orders and had started to go there myself before he got off. He has done magnificently however since he started. Up to last night 5000 prisoners and 49 pieces of Captured Artillery, besides many wagons and innumerable small Arms, had been received in Nashville. This is exclusive of the enemy's loss at Franklin which amounted to Thirteen (13) General officers killed, wounded and captured. The enemy probably lost 5000 men at Franklin, and 10,000 in the last three days operations. B̶ Breckenridge is said to be making for Murphreesboro'. If so he is in a most excellent place.—Stoneman has nearly wiped out John Morgan's old command and five days ago entered Bristol. I did think the best thing to do was to bring the greater part of your Army here and wipe out Lee. The turn affairs t̶h̶i̶n̶g̶s̶ now seem to be taking has shaken me in that opinion. I doubt whether you may not accomplish more towards that result where you are than if brought here; especially as I am informed since my arrival in the City that it would take about two months to get you here with all the other calls there is for ocean transportation.

I want to get your views about what ought to be done and what can be done. If you capture the garrison of Savannah it certainly will compel Lee to detach from Richmond or give us nearly the whole South. My own opinion is that Lee is averse to going out of Va. and if the cause of the South is lost he wants Richmond to be the last place surrendered. If he has such views it may be well to indulge him until we get everything else in our hands.

Congratulating you and the Army again upon the splendid results of your campaign, the like of which is not read of in past history, I subscribe myself, more than ever, if possible,

Your Friend
U. S. GRANT
Lt. Gn.

To MAJ. GN. W. T. SHERMAN,
COMD.G MIL. DIV. OF THE MISS.

ALS, DLC-William T. Sherman. *O.R.*, I, xliv, 740–41. On Dec. 19, 1864, 3:30 P.M., Maj. Gen. Henry W. Halleck telegraphed to USG. "The steamer Louise, about to leave here for Hilton-Head has orders to touch at Fort-Monroe for despatches. As this vessel will probably reach Sherman several days before Major

Anderson from New-York, I suggest the propriety of sending a copy of your despatch of yesterday by her. Could you not telegraph it to Fort-Monroe in cipher?" ALS (telegram sent), DNA, RG 107, Telegrams Collected (Bound); telegram received, *ibid.*; *ibid.*, RG 108, Letters Received. Printed as sent at 3:50 P.M. in *O.R.*, I, xliv, 754. In addition to the letter written by USG, a copy prepared by Lt. Col. Theodore S. Bowers is in DLC-William T. Sherman. On Dec. 24, Maj. Gen. William T. Sherman, Savannah, wrote to USG. "Your letter of Decr. 18th is just received. I feel very much gratified at receiving the handsome commendation you pay my army. I will in General Orders convey to the officers and men the substance of your note. I am also gratified that you have modified your former orders, as I feared that the transportation of them by sea would very much disturb the unity and morale of my army, now so perfect. The occupation of Savannah, which I have heretofore reported, completes the first part of our game, and fulfils a great part of your instructions: and I am now engaged in dismantling the rebel forts which bear upon the sea and channels, and transferring the heavy ordnance and ammunition to Fort Pulaski, where they can be more easily guarded than if left in the city. ~~Th~~ The rebel inner lines, with some modifications, are well adapted to our purposes and with slight modifications can be held by a comparatively small force: and in about ten days I expect to be ready to sally forth again. I feel no doubt whatever as to our future plans. I have thought them over so long and so well, that they appear as clear as daylight. I left Augusta untouched on purpose: because now the enemy will be in doubt as to my objective point after crossing the Savannah River, whether it be Augusta or Charleston, and will naturally divide his forces. I will then move either on Branchville or Columbia, on any curved line that gives me the best supplies, breaking up in my course as much Railroad as possible. Then, ignoring Charleston and Augusta both, occupy Columbia and Camden: pausing there long enough to observe the effect, I would strike for the Charleston and Wilmington R. Road, somewhere between the Santee and the Cape Fear River, and if possible, communicate with the fleet under Admiral Dahlgren, whom I find a most agreeable gentleman, in every way accommodating himself to our wishes and plans. Then I would favor Wilmington, in the belief that Porter and Butler will fail in their present undertaking. Charleston is now a mere desolated wreck, and is hardly worthy the time it would take to starve it out. Still I am aware that historically and politically much importance is attached to the place,—and it may be that apart from its military importance, both you and the Administration would prefer I should give it more attention,—and it would be well for you to give me some general idea on that subject, as otherwise I would treat it, as I have expressed, as a point of little importance after all its Railroads leading into the interior are destroyed or occupied by us. But on the hypothesis of ignoring Charleston and Taking Wilmington I would then favor a movement direct on Raleigh. The game is then up with Lee, unless he comes out of Richmond, avoids you, and fights me: in which event, I should reckon on your being on his heels. Now that Hood is used up by Thomas, I feel disposed to bring the matter to an issue just as quick as possible. I feel confident that I can break up the whole R. Rd system of South Carolina and N. Carolina, and be on the Roanoke, either at Raleigh or Weldon, by the time the Spring fairly opens. And if you feel confident that you can whip Lee outside of his intrenchments, I feel equally confident that I can handle him in the open country. One reason why I would ignore Charleston is this:—that I believe they will reduce the garrison to a small force, with plenty of provisions, and I know that the Neck, back of Charleston, can be made impregnable to assault,—and we will hardly have time for siege operations. I will have to leave in Savannah a garrison, and if Thomas can spare them, would like to have all detachments, convalescents, &c, belonging to these four Corps, sent forward at once. I don't want to cripple Thomas, because I regard his operations as all-important, and I have ordered him to pursue Hood down into Alabama, trusting to the country for supplies. I reviewed one of my Corps today, and shall continue to review the whole army. I don't like to boast, but believe this Army has a confidence in itself that makes it almost irresistible. I wish you would run down and see us: it would have a good effect, and would show to both armies that they were acting on a common plan. The weather is now cool and pleasant, and the general health very good." LS, DNA, RG 108, Letters Received. *O.R.*, I, xliv, 797–98.

On Dec. 14, Maj. Gen. John G. Foster, Hilton Head, S. C., wrote to USG. "I have the honor to inform you that I have just returned from meeting Gen. Sherman, whom I met at Fort McAllister, at daylight this morning. Fort McAllister was taken by assault at half past four, last evening, by Hazen's Division of the 15th Corps. The garrison, numbering 250 men, were all made prisoners, and the armament of 21 guns, with stores, ammunition, &c fell into our hands. This important capture opens the Great Ogeechee River to supplies of all kinds, which can be safely landed immediately in the rear of Gen. Sherman's army. This army now holds Savannah closely besieged, having driven in the enemy from all his advanced positions, until the left wing rests on the Savannah River, 3½ miles above the City, and the right on the Ogeechee River. Gen. Slocum, on the left wing, holds Argyle Id, and has a captured steamer in use on the river at that point. A second captured steamer was burnt. The Central R.R. is thoroughly destroyed, also the Savannah & Charleston R. R. from the Savannah River to within 3½ miles of the City. The Gulf road is also destroyed for a long distance, and the bridge over the Ogeechee burned. Gen. Sherman is perfectly sure of capturing Savannah, and I am now forwarding a siege battery of 30 p'd'r Parrotts to be placed in position. In two days he will summon the City to surrender, and, if not yielded, will open his batteries. To prevent the escape of Hardee and the garrison, Gen. Sherman intends to throw one division across the Savannah River at Argyle Id. to hold the river bank opposite the City. I am, also, to hold the railroad and stage road in my present position between the Coosawhatchie and Tulifinny rivers. Admiral Dahlgren is to demonstrate against the water defenses of Savannah, to keep the garrisons in those works. Everything now seems extremely favorable to the entire success of Gen. Sherman's expectations. His army is in splendid condition, having lived, on its march, on the turkies, chickens, sweet potatoes, and other good things of the richest part of Georgia. The opposition to his march has been feeble. I am supplying everything needed, and aiding in every way within my power. I will send another dispatch as soon as Savannah falls." LS, DNA, RG 108, Letters Received. *O.R.*, I, xliv, 713. On Dec. 17, 2:30 P.M., Brig. Gen. John A. Rawlins telegraphed to USG transmitting the contents of this letter. Telegram received, DNA, RG 107, Telegrams Collected (Bound); copy, *ibid.*, Telegrams Received in Cipher. On Dec. 14, 1:40 P.M., Maj. Gen. Edward O. C. Ord telegraphed to USG. "A Richmond papers of to day says— 'Up to yesterday morning no fighting had taken place between Shermans Army and the Confederate troops in the defence of Savannah' . . . 'An official despatch of yesterday mentions that Sherman had developed his Army near the town'

~~another paper~~ the Whig—Says—'So far as we can learn Shermans Army has invested Savannah.—beyond the usual Skirmishing no fight had taken place—' A press telegram dated yesterday (13th) from Augusta Says—In the fight at Coosahatchee friday—General Gartrell was badly wounded in the Side by a shell —notwithstanding his severe wound he remained on the field until the fight closed'—None of the papers contain particulars of this Coosahatchee one Says 'No information of any conflict at that point since the 31st has been recieved at the war Department'—" ALS (telegram sent), *ibid.*, Telegrams Collected (Unbound); telegram received (at 2:45 P.M.), *ibid.*, Telegrams Collected (Bound); (at 2:05 P.M.) *ibid.*, RG 108, Letters Received. Printed as sent at 2:50 P.M. in *O.R.*, I, xliv, 714–15. USG had endorsed the telegram received. "Forward to Sec. of War." AES, DNA, RG 108, Letters Received. On Dec. 17, Rawlins telegraphed to USG. "[T]he Richmond papers of today contain the following— From Georgia Shermans movements &c The Augusta Register ~~received~~ record this morning says that it was stated in that city on the 13th that the federals have possession of the savannah albany and Gulf Rail Road It is also said that they captured a passenger train on the same: among the persons taken was R R Cuyler Esq the President of the Road It is also reported that the Yankees have possession of the Charleston and Savannah Rail Road Bridge over the Savannah River The Charleston mercury of the Day before says that meantime sherman has been pressing [s]teadily towards the city our forces had fallen back to the Junction of the Geo. Central & Charleston & Savannah R R about three (3) miles from the city at this important point which commands both roads Gen Hardee took his stand It was confidentially reported yesterday & we think that Shermans forces were in Hardees front & that a demand for the surrender of the City having been refused heavy fighting ensued & was going on yesterday of the results however if any no news whatever has reached us we may hear some thing today The Community of Savannah seen firm & quiet For the present the trains will cease to run through between the two (2) cities Gen Gartell states that for several days he observed frequent signals between the federal forces towards Port Royal & Shermans forces in the direction of Sisters Ferry on the Savannah R R The impression of south was that sherman was crossing at the ferry & would coopera[te] with Fosters forces in opening the way to Port Royal.'—The despatch speaking of the rai[d] into Sw Va says that—'Information was recd here yesterday that the main body had left the Rail Road a[t] Glade Spring and started towards the salt works six (6) miles distant and that the smaller party previously mentioned had passed Marion & were advancing on Wytheville which is fifty five miles this side of abingdon The object of this party is doubtless to break up the R R & thereby prevent reinforcements from being sent from the East to our troops at the Salt works They will of course destroy as much property as possible along their Route'—" Telegram received (at 5:50 P.M.), *ibid.*, RG 107, Telegrams Collected (Bound). *O.R.*, I, xliv, 736.

On Dec. 19, noon, Bvt. Maj. Gen. Montgomery C. Meigs telegraphed to USG. "Hilton Head, some days since, called for at least six light draft steamers to ply between the ocean fleet of transports and supply vessels and Gen. Sherman's army on the Ogeechee. I ordered the steamers to be selected from among those in the Chesapeake waters as the quickest mode of supplying this necessity. I am told that yesterday verbal orders, by your authority, were given, forbidding the detachment of the steamers. What shall be done? The forage and supply vessels rendezvoused at Port Royal cannot ascend Ogeechee." LS (telegram sent), DNA, RG 107, Telegrams Collected (Unbound); telegram received, *ibid.*, RG 108, Letters Received. *O.R.*, I, xliv, 755. At 3:30 P.M., USG telegraphed to Meigs. "My order against sending vessels to Savannah was given with the understanding that vessels were being sent to move Shermans Army. I soon learned the facts and directed Gen. Ingalls to go on. ~~with~~" ALS (telegram sent), CSmH; telegram received (at 4:00 P.M.), DNA, RG 92, Consolidated Correspondence, Grant; *ibid.*, RG 107, Telegrams Collected (Bound). *O.R.*, I, xliv, 755.

1. See *ibid.*, pp. 701–2. See also telegram to Edwin M. Stanton, Dec. 20, 1864.

To Maj. Gen. George H. Thomas

Washington City,
December 18th *1864*

MAJOR GENERAL THOMAS
NASHVILLE, TENN.

The armies operating against Richmond have fired two hundred guns in honor of your great victory. Sherman has fully established his base on Ossabaw Sound with Savannah fully invested. I hope to be able to fire a salute to-morrow in honor of the fall of Savannah. In all your operations we hear nothing of Forrest; Great precaution should be taken to prevent him crossing the Cumberland or Tennessee below Eastport. After Hood is driven as far as it is possible to follow him, you want to re-occupy Decatur and all other abandoned points.

U. S. GRANT
Lt. Gen.

Telegram received, DNA, RG 107, Telegrams Collected (Bound); copies, *ibid.*, RG 108, Letters Sent; *ibid.*, RG 393, Dept. of the Cumberland, Telegrams Received; DLC-USG, V, 45, 71, 107. Printed as sent at 12:20 P.M. in *O.R.*, I, xlv, part 2, 248. On Dec. 18, 1864, 11:00 P.M., Maj. Gen. George H. Thomas telegraphed to USG. "Yours of 12 20 P M to day received—I have already given orders to have Decatur occupied and also to throw a strong column on south side of the Tennessee towards Tuscumbia for the purpose of capturing Hoods depot there if possible and gaining possession of his pontoon bridge. I have also requested Admiral Lee to go up the Tennessee with a fleet of gunboats which he has promised to do, and his vessels are no doubt already on the way—Gen Wilson informed me to day that prisoners taken yesterday told him that Forrest Jackson and another division left Murfreesboro on Thursday for Columbia direct, and that Buford with another division left Murfreesboro the same day, and marched continuously until he reached Spring Hill where he assumed duties of rear guard to Rebel Army—I hope you may be able to fire a salute to morrow in honor of the capture of Savannah—" Telegram received, DNA, RG 107, Telegrams Collected (Bound); (on Dec. 19) *ibid.*, RG 108, Letters Received; copies, *ibid.*, RG 107, Telegrams Received in Cipher; *ibid.*, RG 393, Dept. of the Cumberland, Telegrams Sent. *O.R.*, I, xlv, part 2, 249.

To Helen Lynde Dent

[*Dec. 18, 1864*]

I have written to Julia to come here and bring Jess and Fred. with her. She probably will be starting soon. The Spring will soon open after which I cannot expect to see much of them before next winter unless the War should close earlyer.

My love to your children and kisses for them. Remember me to Mr. Dent, Aunt Fanny & Lewis Sheets.

Yours Truly
U. S. GRANT

ALS, John D. Burt, Redwood City, Calif. Written on the second sheet of a letter of Dec. 18, 1864, from Lt. Col. Frederick T. Dent, Washington, D. C., to his wife. "We arrived here this morning after a delightfull run had a splendid car all alone to ourselves and a handsome lunch we may go on today cant tell yet think however we will. I have just learned that Norman has been sent to Fort Delaware Brig Gen Shoepf is in command The authority to visit that place will have to be obtained from General Cadwallader comdg the Department write a letter to him requesting a pass tell him who you are and you will get it when you get to the Fort Send your card to Gen Shoepf—Love to all my darlings In haste" ALS, *ibid.*

To Maj. Gen. George G. Meade

City Point Va. Dec. 19th/64 [6:00 P.M.]

MAJ. GN. MEADE,

Senator Chandler and other gentlemen of the Committee on the Conduct of the War are here and will be out to see you in the 10 O'clock train. They will want to question yourself, Gns Potter

& Wilcox, Col. Loraine, Inspt. 9th Corps, Maj. Van Buren and Lt. Col. Pleasants ~~9th~~ 48 Pa.[1] Please notify these Officers to be present when the Committee arrives.

U. S. GRANT

Lt. Gen.

ALS (telegram sent), CSmH; telegram received (at 6:56 P.M.), DNA, RG 393, Army of the Potomac, Telegrams Received.

On Dec. 19, 1864, 11:25 A.M., Maj. Gen. George G. Meade telegraphed to Brig. Gen. John A. Rawlins. "Maj. Gen. Humphreys reports the Enemy made a slight demonstration on his picket line at 2.30 a m this day resulting in the loss of one killed one (1) wounded & 3 missing   the line was immediately reestablished & quiet soon restored   nothing else has occurred along the lines. Have you any Idea about what time the Lt. Gen may be expected to arrive today" Telegram received, *ibid.*, RG 108, Letters Received; copy, Meade Papers, PHi. *O.R.*, I, xlii, part 3, 1038. On the same day, Rawlins telegraphed to Meade. "The Lt Gen left Washington yesterday at 3 P M & he should be here before 3 today" Telegram received (at 11:40 A.M.), DNA, RG 94, War Records Office, Army of the Potomac. *O.R.*, I, xlii, part 3, 1039.

1. Testimony on the battle of the Crater given by Meade, Bvt. Maj. Gen. Robert B. Potter, Bvt. Maj. Gen. Orlando B. Willcox, Lt. Col. Charles G. Loring, asst. inspector gen., 9th Army Corps, Bvt. Lt. Col. James L. Van Buren, former aide to Maj. Gen. Ambrose E. Burnside, and Lt. Col. Henry Pleasants, 48th Pa., is in *Report of the Joint Committee on the Conduct of the War at the Second Session Thirty-eighth Congress* (Washington, 1865), I (Battle of Petersburg). All testified on Dec. 20, except Pleasants, who testified on Jan. 13, 1865, in Washington.

To Maj. Gen. William T. Sherman

———

City Point, Va., Dec. 19th 1864

MAJ. GEN. W. T. SHERMAN,
COM'D'G MIL. DIV OF THE MISS.
GENERAL;

Whilst North I met a number of our officers, who had just been paroled from Columbia S. C. They informed me that they understood before leaving that our prisoners who were in the line of your march had generally been removed to Florida. If this is the case Foster might send an expedition to rescue them.

Jeff Davis is said to be very sick, In fact deserters report his death. The people had a rumor that he took poison in a fit of despondensy over the military situation. Of course I credit no part of this, except that Davis is very sick, and do not suppose his reflections on Military matters soothe him any—

Yours Truly—

U. S. GRANT Lt Gen

Copies, DLC-USG, V, 45, 71, 107; DNA, RG 108, Letters Sent. *O.R.*, I, xliv, 754. On Dec. 26, 1864, Maj. Gen. William T. Sherman twice wrote to USG, the second time at 1:00 P.M. "Your letter of the 19th inst: is received. I have already written you fully since arriving here, in answer to your previous letters. I am very glad Jeff Davis is in the condition reported to you, and hope that before this time he is dead and out of the way—From my intercourse with the people of Georgia, I think it would give great satisfaction to them generally to know that this was so. Still I shall of course go on with my preparations without reference to anything of the kind and as though the Southern Confederacy possessed all the vitality which they boast of." Copy, DNA, RG 393, Military Div. of the Miss., Letters Sent in the Field. *O.R.*, I, xliv, 810. "In my letter to you of this morning, I omitted to answer your inquiry in relation to our prisoners held by the rebels. I have reason to know that they were hurried down from Millen to Savannah, and from here, on our approach, were sent down the 'Gulf Railroad' to its ~~Th~~ termination at Thomasville, and have since been taken, back to the old place at Andersonville. I have had my cavalry down to the Altamaha, some 50 miles down the Gulf Road, and do not think this is the point from whence they could be reached. But if an expedition were sent up the Apalachicola River and the Apalachicola Arsenal taken, I think they could be rescued from that direction." LS, DNA, RG 108, Letters Received. *O.R.*, I, xliv, 810.

To Maj. Gen. William T. Sherman

City Point, Va, Dec. 19th *1864.*

MAJ. GEN. W. T. SHERMAN,
COMD.G MIL. DIV. OF THE MISS.
GENERAL,

The bearer of this, Mr. W. R. Bergholz, is a Civil Engineer by profession and for some years a resident of Columbia S. C. There is probably no gentleman in the South better acquainted with the roads, fortifications and feelings of the people from Charleston to Richmond than Mr. B. He is at this time a refugee from his home and all his property without any expectations of returning to it until he can do so under the protection of the Stars & Stripes.

I had good reason for believing in the sincerity of Mr. Bergholz

Union proclivities before I ever saw him. An interview confirmed this opinion. I now send Mr. Bergholz to report to you believing he can be of great service to you, particularly so long as you remain in the South. You can attach him as an Asst. Eng. or in such capacity as you think best. Whilst he is retained in service he will have to be paid by the Quartermasters Dept. on orders from you or me, and I would suggest the pay of Capt. of Engineers be allowed.

> Very respectfully
> your obt. svt.
> U. S. GRANT
> Lt. Gen.

ALS, DLC-Orlando M. Poe. Maj. Gen. William T. Sherman added an undated endorsement to Capt. Orlando M. Poe. "You may employ the Bearer of this Mr Bergholz in the capacity stated, or if you have not the authority I will order the Qr Mr to take up his name as employed—but it is better you should employ, and use him." AES, *ibid.*

On Dec. 24, 1864, Maj. Gen. John A. Dix, New York City, telegraphed to USG. "I have a man believed to be a Confederate agent and is to be tried next week. Bergholtz is here & his testimony is indispensable to a conviction. Can I detain Bergholtz a few days?" Telegram received, DNA, RG 108, Letters Received; copy, *ibid.*, RG 393, Dept. of the East, Telegrams Sent. At 4:00 P.M., USG telegraphed to Dix. "Detain Mr. Bergholz to give testamony in the case alluded to in your dispatch." ALS (telegram sent), Kohns Collection, NN; telegram received, DNA, RG 107, Union Provost Marshals' File of Papers Relating to Individual Civilians.

Testimony

CITY POINT, VA., *December* 20, 1864.

Lieutenant General U. S. GRANT sworn and examined.

By Mr. Chandler:

Question. Will you give the committee such information as you may deem important in regard to the action before Petersburg, on the 30th of July last?

Answer. As you are aware, I made a feint on the north side of the James river, which I intended to convert into an attack if everything should prove favorable. By that movement the attention of the enemy was called to that side of the river, causing them to concentrate there. They were so well fortified there that an advance on that side could not be made without great sacrifice of life.

General Burnside had, prior to this, made a mine in front of the 9th corps, which I would not allow to be exploded until such time as it could be used advantageously. Finding that the principal part of the enemy's forces had been drawn to the north side of the James, I telegraphed to General Meade that then was the time to charge the mine and explode it, and directed him to make preparations to assault. My despatch gave no details at all how this was to be done. I left that to him, knowing him, as I did, to be fully capable of determining when and what ought to be done.

He prepared an order for assault, which was submitted to and approved by me. I think now it was all that we could have done; I think he could not have done better.

I was over on the north side of the river when these arrangements were made. I came back to the south side of the river before the explosion took place, and remained with General Meade until probably a half or three-quarters of an hour after the springing of the mine. I then rode down to the front; that is, I rode down as far as I could on horseback, and then went through to the front on foot. I there found that we had lost the opportunity which had been given us.

I am satisfied that if the troops had been properly commanded, and been led in accordance with General Meade's order, we would have captured Petersburg with all the artillery and a good portion of its support, without the loss of 500 men. There was a full half hour, I think, when there was no fire against our men, and they could have marched past the enemy's intrenchments just as they could in the open country.

But that opportunity was lost in consequence of the division commanders not going with their men, but allowing them to go into the enemy's intrenchments and spread themselves there, without going on further, thus giving the enemy time to collect and organize against them. I think I can say nothing more on that point.

I blame myself a little for one thing. General Meade, as I stated, on my telegraphic despatch from the north side of the James river, made his orders most perfectly. I do not think that now, knowing all the facts, I could improve upon his order.

But I was informed of this fact: that General Burnside, who was fully alive to the importance of this thing, trusted to the pulling of straws which division should lead. It happened to fall on what I thought was the worst commander in his corps. I knew that fact before the mine was exploded, but did nothing in regard to it. That is the only thing I blame myself for. I knew the man was the one that I considered the poorest division commander that General Burnside had—I mean General Ledlie.[1]

By Mr. Loan:

Question. There has been a great deal of controversy in regard to the sufficiency of the *debouchment* prepared by General Burnside for the egress of his troops after the explosion of the mine?

Answer. That I could not swear to exactly. I went beyond his *debouchment*, but did not think to note it. But I am satisfied that he did not make the *debouchment* that he was ordered to make. I know that as well as I know anything that I cannot exactly swear to. I went beyond it myself, and on my return to the rear ordered the troops back.

Question. I suppose the success of this enterprise was dependent in a great measure upon the surprise of the enemy, caused by the explosion of the mine, and prompt movements afterwards to avail yourself of the distraction occasioned by it?

Answer. It all depended upon that.

Question. Was there not some danger of apprising the enemy of the contemplated movement by undertaking to level the parapets and remove the abatis and other obstructions in front of our line?

Answer. Not at all. That could be done entirely under cover of the night. After dark we could take down any of our parapets and remove our abatis without their noticing it.

Question. So far as you are advised in the matter, was not a part of the disaster owing to the slow movement of our troops in passing over the ground?

Answer. I think if I had been a corps commander, and had had that in charge, I would have been down there, and would have seen that it was done right; or, if I had been the commander of the division that had to take the lead, I think I would have gone in with my division. We have a great many officers here who would have done the same thing.

Question. Did the slowness of the movement tend to promote the disaster?

Answer. I do not think that that alone had any effect at all.

Question. What, then, do you think was the cause of the disaster?

Answer. I think the cause of the disaster was simply the leaving the passage of orders from one to another down to an inefficient man. I blame his seniors also for not seeing that he did his duty, all the way up to myself.

Question. You think that the opportunity for success passed by owing to the confusion of the troops in consequence of the inefficiency of that division commander?

Answer. Yes, sir. As I understand it, the troops marched right into the breach caused by the explosion without there being a single division commander there. They had no person to direct them to go further, although the division commanders were directed in the most positive terms to march to what is called Cemetery hill, which would have given us everything.

Question. Speaking of those orders, was it judicious to direct the main advancing column to proceed directly to Cemetery hill without any regard to the enemy on their right and left?

Answer. Cemetery hill commanded the rear of their intrenched line; it commanded everything.

Question. The troops had to pass over considerable ground to reach Cemetery hill?

Answer. Only 300 or 400 yards.

Question. Then to accomplish that object, you do not think it would have been necessary to have taken possession of the enemy's batteries and intrenchments on the right and left of the crater of the mine?

Answer. Not at all. If they had marched through to the crest of that ridge they would then have taken everything in rear. I do not think there would have been any opposition at all to our troops had that been done. I think we would have cut off entirely those of the enemy to our right, while those on the left would have tried to make their escape across the Appomattox.

Question. There has been something said in regard to the changing of General Burnside's plan of putting his division of colored troops in the advance.

Answer. General Burnside wanted to put his colored division in front, and I believe if he had done so it would have been a success. Still I agreed with General Meade in his objection to that plan. General Meade said that if we put the colored troops in front (we had only that one division) and it should prove a failure, it would then be said, and very properly, that we were shoving those people ahead to get killed because we did not care anything about them. But that could not be said if we put white troops in front. That is the only point he changed, to my knowledge, after he had given his orders to General Burnside. It was then that General Burnside left his three division commanders to toss coppers or draw straws which should and which should not go in front.

By Mr. Julian:

Question. That change was made the evening before the assault, was it not?

Answer. I cannot say whether it was the evening before the explosion or twenty-four hours earlier.

Question. Was General Burnside's plan submitted to you for consideration?

Answer. He had no plan; he had merely to execute an order.

Question. He desired to use his colored troops for the advance?

Answer. Yes, sir; and that part was changed, I thought then very properly, and I think so yet; for we had but one division of colored troops in the whole army about Petersburg at that time, and I do not think it would have been proper to put them in front, for nothing but success would have justified it.

Report of the Joint Committee on the Conduct of the War at the Second Session Thirty-eighth Congress (Washington, 1865), I, 109–12 (Battle of Petersburg). See telegram to Maj. Gen. George G. Meade, Feb. 9, 1865.

On Dec. 20, 1864, 4:00 P.M., Maj. Gen. George G. Meade telegraphed to USG. "The Honl. Mr. Chandler desires me to ask you to have Maj. Genl. Ord &

Brig. Genl. Ferero at City Point by Eight o'clock this evening as the Comee desire to examine them." ALS (telegram sent), DNA, RG 393, Army of the Potomac, Telegrams Received; copies, *ibid.*, Letters Sent; Meade Papers, PHi.

On Jan. 9, 1865, Col. William A. Nichols, AGO, wrote to USG. "At the request of the Joint Committee of Congress on the condut of the war I transmit herewith for your revision a copy of your testimony before that committee." Copy, DNA, RG 94, Letters Sent. On Jan. 19, Col. James A. Hardie wrote to USG. "I am directed by the Secretary of War to enclose to you a copy of a communication addressed to this Department by the Honorable B. F. Wade, Chairman of the Committee on the Conduct of the War, and to say that it is desired that the request of the Committee, for the return of the testimony in relation to the battle before Petersburg, July 30, 1864, may be complied with at your earliest convenience." LS, *ibid.*, RG 108, Letters Received. Hardie enclosed a letter of Jan. 16 from U.S. Senator Benjamin F. Wade of Ohio to Secretary of War Edwin M. Stanton. "I am instructed by the Committee on the Conduct of the War to request that you will communicate with General Grant, and inform him that the Committee desire to obtain the testimony in relation to the battle before Petersburg, July 30. 1864, which was sent down to the Army of the Potomac for revision. . . ." Copy, *ibid.*

On Jan. 24, USG telegraphed to Maj. Gen. John G. Parke. "The Committee on the conduct of the War desire the return of the testimony in relation to the battle before Petersburg July 30th '64 which was sent down for revision to the following named officers: Genls O. B. Wilox; G. K. Warren; R. B. Potter Lt Cols C. G. Loring J. L. Vanburen J. C. Duane & Maj Gen H. J. Hunt. Please ascertain from the above named officers whether they have returned their testimony and report the result to me—" Telegram received (at 2:00 P.M.), *ibid.*, RG 393, Army of the Potomac, Miscellaneous Letters Received; copy, Meade Papers, PHi.

1. James H. Ledlie, born in 1832 in Utica, N. Y., a civil engineer before the Civil War, was appointed maj., 3rd N. Y. Art., as of May 22, 1861, and promoted to col. as of Dec. 23. Appointed brig. gen. as of Dec. 24, 1862, but not confirmed, he was reappointed as of Oct. 27, 1863. As commander of the 1st Div., 9th Army Corps, he was responsible for the initial assault at the battle of the Crater.

To Edwin M. Stanton

(Cipher)   City Point, Va, Dec. 20th 1864 [*10:30* A.M.]
HON. E. M. STANTON, WASHINGTON

I think Thomas has won the Major Gen.cy but I would wait a few days before giving it to see the extent of damages done Hood. Good for the draft ordered! It is to be hoped that we will have no use for more men than we have now but the number must be kept up. Rebel Congress is now in secret session and it is believed they are maturing a Negro conscript act. These people will all come to us if they can but they may be so guarded as to find it difficult to do.

U. S. GRANT

Lt. Gen.

ALS (telegram sent), Elkins Collection, Free Library of Philadelphia, Philadelphia, Pa.; telegram received (at 11:00 A.M.), DNA, RG 107, Telegrams Collected (Bound). *O.R.*, I, xlv, part 2, 283.

On Dec. 19, 1864, 3:30 P.M., USG telegraphed to Secretary of War Edwin M. Stanton. "On reflection I think it would have a good effect to allow Shermans letter to Genl Halleck, except such parts as refer to future movements, to be published. It is refreshing to see a commander, after a campaign of more than seven (7) months duration, ready for still further operations, and without wanting any outfit or rest" Telegram received (at 4:00 P.M.), DNA, RG 107, Telegrams Collected (Bound); copies, *ibid.*, Telegrams Received in Cipher; *ibid.*, RG 108, Letters Sent; DLC-USG, V, 45, 71, 107. *O.R.*, I, xliv, 754; *ibid.*, I, xlv, part 2, 264. At 8:00 P.M., Stanton telegraphed to USG. "You will see by todays papers [t]hat that Shermans despatch omittng such portions as seemed ~~im~~proper to be left out has already been published. One or two paragraphs more might have done good ~~howev~~ but being doubtful on the point they were skipped. The weather & rains will probably stop further pursuit of Hood but he will have a good time getting to some safe place. What about the Major Generalship has it been won? ~~Edwin M Stan~~ I have directed a new draft for Three hundred thousand men, and will put on two hundred more by the first of March if there appears then to be a necessity." ALS (telegram sent), DNA, RG 107, Telegrams Collected (Bound); telegram received (on Dec. 20), *ibid.*, RG 108, Letters Received. *O.R.*, I, xlv, part 2, 265.

On Dec. 23, 6:00 P.M., USG telegraphed to Stanton. "I think it would be appropriate now to confer on Gen. Thomas the vacant Major Generalcy in the regular Army. He seems to be pushing Hood with energy and I doubt not but he will completely destr[oy] that Army." ALS (telegram sent), New Hampshire Historical Society, Concord, N. H.; telegram received, DNA, RG 107, Telegrams Collected (Bound). *O.R.*, I, xlv, part 2, 318.

To Maj. Gen. Henry W. Halleck

(Cipher)   City Point, Va, Dec. 20th *1864*. [*12:30* P.M.]
MAJ. GEN. HALLECK, WASHINGTON,

I wish you would order one of the Inspector Gens. to report to me for special duty. I want to get in an official form some facts that I have learned in regard to arbitrary arrests and punishments by the Commander of the Dept. of N. C. & Va.

U. S. GRANT

Lt. Gn.

ALS (telegram sent), CSmH; telegram received (at 2:30 P.M.), DNA, RG 107, Telegrams Collected (Bound). *O.R.*, I, xlii, part 3, 1044. On Dec. 20, 1864, 4:35 P.M., Maj. Gen. Henry W. Halleck telegraphed to USG. "I think Col Schriver, now with Genl Meade, the very best man in the army for the purpose indicated. He is polite & at the same time thorough. If he will not answer I would suggest Acting Inspr Genl, Genl Ketchum, if the Secty of war can spare him. I will await your answer." ALS (telegram sent), DNA, RG 107, Telegrams Collected (Bound); telegram received, *ibid.; ibid.*, RG 108, Letters Received. *O.R.*, I, xlii, part 3, 1044.

On Dec. 22, Lt. Col. Theodore S. Bowers issued Special Orders No. 154. "Col. E. Schriver, Ass't. Insp'. Gen'l. U. S. A. will proceed without delay to Norfolk and Fort Monroe and inspect the prisons and places, where prisoners are held in confinement, at those places, and also at the places where persons are held in confinement in the Army of the James in the field, and ascertain the charges on which prisoners are held, how long and by whose authority they are so held and whether with, or without trial. He will specially and thoroughly investigate the case of Chaplain Henry N. Hudson of the 1st Reg't. New York Engineers, who is alleged to have been confined at Norfolk from some time in Septbr. until about, the 11th day of November 1864 and the manner of his confinement. Col. Schriver will make full and complete reports of his inspection and investigation under this order to the Lieut. Gen'l. Comd'g." Copies, DLC-USG, V, 57, 62, 63, 64. For the arrest of Chaplain Henry N. Hudson, largely for writing an unflattering account of Maj. Gen. Benjamin F. Butler for the *New-York Evening Post*, see Benjamin F. Butler, *Butler's Book* (Boston, 1892), pp. 833–36; *Private and Official Correspondence of Gen. Benjamin F. Butler . . .* (n.p., 1917), V, 160–67, 486–90; [Hudson], *A Chaplain's Campaign with Gen. Butler* (New York, 1865). On Jan. 14, 1865, Butler wrote to USG. "Chaplain Henry Hudson having forwarded his resignation after having been charged with high offences and misdemeanors, I have not thought proper to accept the same, but forward his resignation with a copy of the charges which I beg leave to present against him, and which could not be earlier tried because, being the prosecutor, I had no means of ordering the Court. I respectfully ask that these charges may be tried either by Court Martial, by yourself, or by the Sec'y of War. I take leave to send duplicate copies of the charges and resignation to the Chief of the Bureau of Military Justice." *Private and Official Correspondence of Gen. Benjamin F. Butler . . .*, V, 486.

On Feb. 2, USG wrote two endorsements. "Respy. forwarded to the Sec of War, and the acceptance of Chaplain Hudsons resignation recommended. These papers were forwarded to me by Maj Gen Butler from Fort Monroe after he was relieved from duty, and after an inspection, or inquiry was made in the case of Chaplain Hudson by B B Gen E. Schriver, Insp Gen U. S A. under my orders (which report of inspection is herewith forwarded)   By reference to the statement of Chaplain Hudson, enclosed in said report of inspection, it will be seen that at the date of said tender of resignation there were no charges preferred against him, but that he was on duty with his regiment, having been released from arrest (close) by Genl Butler's order, after a confinement in the Provost Guard prison from the 15th Sept until the 11th day of November. The reason recited in said order relieving him from such arrest for his long continued arrest was 'because of the impossibility of convening a Court Martial to try him, because of movements in the field' when in fact within the month immediately prior to that date a Court Martial was in session at Gen Butlers Headquarters in the field, convened by his own order—General Butler now (January 14) says 'he could not be earlier tried because he (Gen Butler) being the prosecutor, had no means of ordering the Court' It was General Butlers bounden duty, especially when the harsh manner in which he dealt with the accused is taken into consideration, to have made out and forwarded the charges against him to the proper authorities within the time required by law, but which he neglected to do. By further reference to the Inspector Generals report, and the date of charges in the case it will be seen that from the arrest and confinement of Chaplain Hudson until the prefering of the charges, a period of three months and 18 days intervened, fifty three days of which he was in close arrest. It is in consideration of all these facts and without excusing Chaplain Hudson for his disobedience of orders that I recommend the acceptance of his resignation." "Respy. forwarded to the Secretary of War, in connection with communication of Maj Gen Butler, enclosing charges against Chaplain Hudson forwardd this day" Copies, DLC-USG, V, 58.

On Jan. 16, Bowers telegraphed to Hudson, Northampton, Mass. "Please send to these Headquarters immediately on receipt of this communication the original copy of Gen, Butlers note to Mr. Nash containing order telegraphed to Gen, Terry for your release" Copies, *ibid.*, V, 46, 71, 107; DNA, RG 108, Letters Sent.

On Jan. 11, Bowers had issued Special Orders No. 9. "Major General E. O. C. Ord, commanding Department of Va. & N C, will, with competent officers of his own selection, at once relieve from duty and return to their respective commands, all officers on duty as Provost Marshals, or Assistant Provost Marshals within the Department and Army of the James, excepting those on duty with Corps, Divisions and Brigades in the field. He will also cause an immediate inspection to be made of all prisons and places where persons are confined in said Department and Army, and the case of each person confined in such prisons carefully investigated and inquired into. He will promptly discharge all persons found to be improperly confined in any of the prisons under such restrictions as he may deem proper. He will report the execution of this order to these Headquarters." Copies, DLC-USG, V, 57, 63, 64, 65. *O.R.*, I, xlvi, part 2, 94.

To Maj. Gen. Edward R. S. Canby

Head Quarters, Armies of the United States
City Point Va Dec 20. 1864

Maj. Genl E. R. S. Canby
Com'd'g. Trans. Miss. Div
General

When I went to Point in 1863 I was appraised of the fact that the children of the late Senator Douglass owned a Plantation some miles back from Greenville Miss. upon which there was one hundred and fifty bales of Cotton. I knew that Mr Douglass had left his family somewhat straightened in circumstances and thought his eminent services and particularly the course he took at the breaking out of the rebellion, entitled his family to all the aid that could be consistently given by the military. Greenville was a point to which the enemy used to come at that time and with their Artillery annoy our navigation of the river. To drive these troops away I sent Genl Steele with his Division, and being fully acquainted at that time with the location of Mrs Douglass plantation and the name of the overseer in charge of it I directed Steele to visit it and to move the Cotton back to Greenville and ship it to Cairo for the benefit of the children. Steele visited the plantation but to find the Cotton burned. His instructions were if the enemy burned the Cotton, he was then to take an equal amount from any disloyal owners and ship it in lieu of that destroyed. The enemy retired in front of General Steels forces and burned all cotton in their way, hence his failure to do what was expected.

I now write this to show you the action I took at the time and to suggest to you the propriety of saving from the first rebel cotton captured, one hundred and fifty bales for the benefit of Mr D's children. I am satisfied such a proceeding would be justified and approved of by the country and the administration. If the administration did not approve, they could take possession of the cotton as they would be advised of its shipment.

I hope you will give this matter attention   It will be restoring to the orphan children of one of our greatest statesmen, but a part of what they have been deprived by this rebellion and it would give to the widow the means of educating them in a manner befitting the station they are entitled to

Yours Truly

U. S. GRANT

Lt. Genl.

Copy, DNA, RG 366, Seventh Special Agency, Correspondence of H. A. Risley. On Jan. 12, 1865, Maj. Gen. Edward R. S. Canby wrote to USG. "I have the the honor to acknowledge the receipt of your letter of the 20th. Ulto. It will give me very great pleasure to carry out your suggestions with the first capture that may be made. I am afraid however that every bale of cotton within the Rebel lines from Wilmington to the Rio Grande is now covered by permits and that all that may be captured hereafter will have *loyal* owners. It is astonishing to find how much of the staple has long been 'owned or controlled' by persons within our lines. If I suceed I will consign it it to the Quartermaster in New York for the purpose you indicate and will advise you of the shipment." ALS, *ibid.*, RG 108, Letters Received. See letter to Maj. Gen. Frederick Steele, April 11, 1863; R. H. Thompson, "A Law Suit of Historical Interest," in Dunbar Rowland, ed., *Courts, Judges, and Lawyers of Mississippi 1798–1935* (Jackson, Miss., 1935), p. 332.

To Maj. Gen. Edward O. C. Ord

City Point, Va, Dec. 20th 1864 [*12:15* P.M.]

MAJ. GN. ORD.

On the 22d the French Consul in Richmond, or some one in his stead, will present himself on our picket line with a number of French subjects wishing to leave the South. Have them received at once and conveyed, with their baggage, on board any steamer that may be laying at Aiken's Landing at the time. I will send a steamer specially to convey them to Fortress Monroe where the French Vessel now is.

U. S. GRANT
Lt. Gn.

ALS (telegram sent), CSmH; telegram received, DNA, RG 393, Army of the Potomac, Telegrams Received.

On Dec. 20, 1864, USG wrote to Alfred Paul, French consul at Richmond. "Your communication of yesterday to Gen'l. Butler is this moment received by me. Instructions will be given at once to receive you, or any other person you may choose to send in your stead, and all foreign subjects accompanying the moment they present themselves at our picket lines. I will have a Steamer at Aiken's Landing to convey all persons so presenting themselves immediately to the French Steamer, which I believe is now at Fortress Monroe. Your communication to the Comd'r. of the French vessel alluded to will be forwarded by the first boat going to Fortress Monroe." Copies, DLC-USG, V, 45, 71, 107; DNA, RG 108, Letters Sent.

To Jesse Root Grant

Headquarters Armies of the U. S.
City Point Va. Dec. 20. 1864,

DEAR FATHER—

Sherman has now demonstrated his great Capacity as a Soldier by his unequalled campaign through Georgia. I know him well as

one of the greatest purest and best of men. He is poor and always
will be, but he is great and magnanimous—an Ohian, and I think
entitled to their greatest esteem and even benevolence. Now what
I Started to write about is this, I am not acquainted sufficiently in
Cincinnati to select the right person to write to, to inaugurate a
Subscription to present Mrs Sherman a comfortable furnished
house—Cincinnati will always be proud of Sherman as a citizen of
that city and Ohio may well be proud of him. If you can get this
thing up, put down for me $500, and for Genl R. Ingalls $250
more. I have been the recipient of many favors from the public &
will be but too happy if I can call their attention to one of our
nobles, greatest best men. I hope you will see some of the leading
Union men of Cincinnati all of whom you are acquainted with, and
have this thing put on foot without noise or parade. Sherman
would not approve of what I am doing in this matter, but still he
would feel Complimented & would appreciate such recognition of
his Services

affectionately
U. S. GRANT Lt Gn

Copy, DLC-William T. Sherman.

To Julia Dent Grant

City Point Va. Dec. 20th *1864.*

DEAR JULIA,
 I am not very well to-day though nothing special is the matter.
It has been a gloomy wet day and I have remained in bed all day
eating neither breakfast or dinner and have not smoked a cigar. I
can not get medecine to act on my [hemroid]. I have taken ten
pills and three Sedleits powders with but little effect. Whilst the
weather continues as it is but little can be done here. Better weather
and the fall of Richmond may be hoped for however this Winter.
 Love and Kisses for you and the children

ULYS.

ALS, DLC-USG.

To Edwin M. Stanton

From City Point Dec 21 *1864.* [*2:00* P.M.]

HON E. M. STANTON

About the first of the month I heard that E. A. Pollard was at Liberty at Fort Monroe, awaiting to be sent south   I forbid his being so sent, and ordered him to be placed in close confinement[1] and suppose he is in confinement. How he got to Fort Monroe and why he was allowed to telegraph from there I do not know   I will execute your orders in the case and furnish you all the information I can ascertain

U S GRANT
Lt Genl

Telegram received (at 2:40 P.M.), DNA, RG 107, Telegrams Collected (Bound); copies, *ibid.*, RG 108, Letters Sent; DLC-USG, V, 45, 71, 107. On Dec. 21, 1864, 12:50 P.M., Secretary of War Edwin M. Stanton telegraphed to USG. "E A Pollard a reporter and Editor of a Richmond paper is at Fortress-Monroe and this morning forwarded a telegram to Ben Wood. Is he there by your authority   If not no effort should be spared to ascertain how he came there and have him arrested and tried as a spy and the person who authorised or aided him to get within our lines and forts also punished" ALS (telegram sent), DNA, RG 107, Telegrams Collected (Bound); telegram received (at 1:00 P.M.), *ibid.*, RG 108, Letters Received. On the same day, Maj. Thomas T. Eckert telegraphed to USG. "The Secy of War directs me to say that he has ascertained that Pollard is a prisoner of War" Telegram received, *ibid.* On Dec. 22, USG telegraphed to Stanton. "Capt Conrad Provost Marshal at Fort Monroe ~~wishes~~ makes the following statement in relation to pallards 'A E Pollard come to this post several weeks ago from Brooklyn under an order from some officer of the Navy—He came for the purpose of being exchanged as a prisoner of war He went to Genl Butlers Hd Qrs at the front with one (1) of Genl Butlers staff but was ordered back to this post He has been allowed the liberty of the fort I have had him placed in close confinement in Compliance with your orders'" Telegram received (at 5:00 P.M.), *ibid.*, RG 107, Telegrams Collected (Bound); copies, *ibid.*, RG 108, Letters Sent; DLC-USG, V, 45, 73, 107.

1. See telegram to Maj. Gen. Benjamin F. Butler, Dec. 2, 1864.

To Maj. Gen. George H. Thomas

(Cipher)   City Point, Va, Dec. 22d *1864*. [*11:00* P.M.]
Maj. Gen. Thomas, Nashville Tenn.

You have the congratulations of the public for the energy with
which you ~~seem to be~~ are pushing Hood. I hope you will succeed
in reaching his pontoon bridge at Tuscumbia before he gets there.
Should you do so it looks to me that Hood is cut off. If you succeed
in destroying Hood's Army there ~~is~~ will be but one Army left to the
so called Confederacy capable of doing us harm. I will take care of
that and try to draw the sting from it so that in the Spring we shall
have easy sailing. You now have a big oportunity which I know
you are availing yourself of. Let us push and do all we can before
~~before~~ the enemy can derive benefit either from the rasing of Negro
troops or the concentration of white troops now in the field.

U. S. Grant
Lt. Gen.

ALS (telegram sent), OClWHi; telegram received (at 11:30 P.M.), DNA, RG
107, Telegrams Collected (Bound). *O.R.*, I, xlv, part 2, 307. On Dec. 24, 1864,
8:00 A.M., Maj. Gen. George H. Thomas telegraphed to USG. "Your telegram
of 22 is just recd. I am now, and shall continue to push Hood as rapidly as the
state of the weather and roads will permit. I am really very hopeful that either
Gen Steedman or Admiral Lee will reach the Tenn. in time to destroy Hoods
ponton bridge, in which event I shall certainly be able to capture or destroy
almost the entire army now with Hood" Telegram received (at 10:30 P.M.),
DNA, RG 107, Telegrams Collected (Bound); *ibid.*, RG 108, Letters Received;
copies, *ibid.*, RG 107, Telegrams Received in Cipher; *ibid.*, RG 393, Dept. of
the Cumberland, Telegrams Sent. *O.R.*, I, xlv, part 2, 329.

To Mary M. Bergholz

City Point, Va. Dec. 22d *1864*.

Mrs. M. M. Bergholz,
My Dear Madam,

I sent your husband a pass to Savannah, Ga, and a letter directed to Gen. Sherman providing for his employment. I am de-

sirous to know whether he has gone. It was plain to me that Col. Bilbour did not want Mr. Bergholz to leave him. My advice is that your husband keeps as clear as possible of a set of men who I think are planing something out of which they expect to realize large fortunes but ~~which is~~ in a way not reputable to lovers of their country. They will fail to in their design. I am against all enterprise which propose to help the enemy. The North Carolina Cotton speculation is one eminently of that sort. I write to you in this matter because Mr. Bergholz, if he accepts the employment which I proposed, will have left New York before this will reach there. If he has listened to proposals which I believe has been made to him urge him not to concider them for one moment. The little interview I had with your husband convinced me that he ~~was~~ is an honest, true and able man. If he is lead astray in this matter he will be ruined for life.

I shall be most happy to hear from you in reply to this, and always glad to hear from you when you have a spare moment. Your last letter in which you feared intrusion was no intrusion but afforded me great pleasure to know that you recollected your stopage at City Point with so much pleasure. I shall be most glad when I can see you again and when I can be of service to you and yours. —Write to me on receipt of this.

Respectfully &c.

U. S. GRANT

ALS, DLC-USG, I, B. USG addressed the envelope to Mrs. Bergholz at "37 Irving Place, Cor. E. 16th st." in New York City. AD, *ibid*.

To Julia Dent Grant

———

City Point, Va. Dec. 22d *1864*.

DEAR JULIA,

I have just received your first letter since I left Burlington. It is a dear kind letter, full of ambition of what you expect of me. I have not a doubt but all will be accomplished you expect. Be of good cheer. Have you let Fred & Buck start down here? They will spend their Christmass holiday as pleasantly with me as they can do elswhere.

Since my return I have felt more like a spell of sickness than any time since the begining of the war. I hope however a day or two will bring me out all well. Yesterday and to-day I have laid in bed and taken pills and Sedleitz Powders enough to work a tonic. I hope they will bring [me out]. It would not do for me to get sick at this time when there is so much to do and when we have it in our hands to do so much towards the suppression of the rebellion.

Love and Kisses for you and the children. Good night.

ULYS.

ALS, DLC-USG.

To H. H. Hunter et al.

City Point, Va, Dec. 22d *1864*.

H. H. HUNTER,
D. TALLMADGE,
JOHN T. BROSES,
DEAR SIRS:

I have just this moment received your printed letter in relation to your proposed movement in acknowledgement of one of Ohios greatest sons. I wrote only yesterday to my father[1] who resides in Covington Ky. on the same subject and asked him to inaugerate a subscription to present Mrs. Sherman with a furnished house in the city of Cincinnati. Gen. Sherman is eminently entitled to this mark of concideration and I directed my father to head the subscription with Five hundred dollars for me and half that amount from Gen. Ingalls, Chief Quartermaster of this Army, who is equally alive with myself to the eminent services of Gen. Sherman.[2] What ever direction this interprise in favor of Gn. Sherman may take you may set me down for the amount named.

I can not say a word too highly in praise of Gen. Sherman's services from the begining of the rebellion to the present day and will therefore abstain from flattery of him. Suffice it to say the Worlds history gives us record of his superiors and of but few equals. I am truly glad for the movement you have set on foot and of the opportunity of adding my mite in testemonial of so good and great a man.

Yours Truly

U. S. GRANT

Lt. Gn.

ALS, DLC-William T. Sherman. On Jan. 10, 1865, Jesse Root Grant wrote a letter in support of the project to purchase a home for Maj. Gen. William T. Sherman, indicating USG's strong support. Undated clipping from *Cincinnati Commercial. Ibid.* On Jan. 23, John D. Caldwell, secretary of the Cincinnati committee for the testimonial, wrote to USG. "I have had frequent interviews with your father relative to securing a people's gift to that victorious General, William T. Sherman, of Ohio, [con]sisting of a house and lot in Cincinnati or subur[bs.] My correspondence with the friends of General Sherman, at Lancaster, induced them to change the testimonial from a farm in Fairfield County to a fund of $100,000. The subscription papers I have in circulation in Hamilton County contain an expression of our wish that the testimonial shall result in selection of Cincinnati as the residence of Mrs. Sherman, who has only girls to be educated, and who frankly wrote to your father that her wish is to live in Cincinnati. I have a further wish to secure for the West if possible, at least for Ohio, ample provision as a 'Home of Invalids,' for the crippled, sick and penniless soldiers, who, when the war is closed, will need a hearty cheer at a fireside he may claim as his own, and where honorably he may retire to recuperate, or if unable to go again into active life, to lie down to die with a sense of gratification that loyal people have cared for him. How this is to be done, I can't say. I prefer voluntary supervision to State control. I would like to have your views. I have hit upon a plan of evoking the energies and applying the aid of women in preserving the history of the soldier. I send you some pamphlets on this subject; also, some Sherman subscription papers." *Ibid.* On March 10, the committee presented $10,000 to Sherman. *Ibid.*

1. See letter to Jesse Root Grant, Dec. 20, 1864.
2. Both USG and Brig. Gen. Rufus Ingalls signed their names and pledged the money on an undated printed form headed "Ohio Testimonial to Gen'l Sherman." ADS, Iowa Masonic Library, Cedar Rapids, Iowa. The form includes acknowledgment of payment.

To Edwin M. Stanton

From City Point Va Dec. 23rd noon *1864.*
Hon Edwin M. Stanton
Secy of War.

The following despatch just [r]eceived received—The sending of troops to Breckinridge accounts for Rhodes presence in in front of Custer—

U. S. Grant
Lt Genl.

"A Telegraph operator just from Richmond, and the office,[1] states as follows.

'Bragg telegraphed very often from Wilmington to Jeff Davis for reinforcements. U. S. fleet appeared off Wilmington 16th and 17th. On the 21st Genl Whitney[2] telegraphed to Jeff Davis that Fort Fisher was captured on the night of 20th—Beauregard telegraphed the capture of Savannah by unconditional surrender took place on the morning of the 20th. News received in Richmond night of 20th, not made public—Forces in Savannah officially reported to be fifteen to eighteen thousand (15 @ 18.000) men with Hardee in command. Before this news Beauregard telegraphed often that Savannah could not hold out much longer. Savannah River had been ~~obs~~ obstructed.

Some of Early's troops were sent to Breckenridge, some south to Petersburg or below. Breckenridge believed to have repulsed federals near Saltville—

News received from Hood that he is badly whipped, received partly by telegraph part by courier—

Jeff Davis very sick, unable to leav[e] his house, desease affection of throat & bronchia.

Principal means of supplies to Richmo[nd] by Danville road. About one hundred and fifty cars were at Greenville loaded with supplies—Burkeville Junctio[n] if occupied or broken up would starve the city out. No troops along line of Danville road except at bridges, in all very small amount—

Lee's Head Quarters at Dunn's Hil[l] often in Richmond. Gil-

mer³ Chief Engine[er] of Defences—Ten days ago only three
hundred and eighty thousand (380.000) rations of meat in Richmond—Beauregard telegraphed that after the fall of Savannah the
river would be a base for Sherman to operate on Augusta and
Charleston'

(signed) E. O. C ORD
Maj Genl"⁴

Telegram received (at 3:20 P.M.), DNA, RG 107, Telegrams Collected
(Bound); copy, *ibid.*, Telegrams Received in Cipher.

On Dec. 21, 1864, Maj. Gen. Edward O. C. Ord telegraphed to USG. "A
deserter from 18th Georgia—in this morning heard from the Doctor of the Regt
who got it from the Lieut just from Richmond—who heard it from a member of
the Cabinet night before last that Savannah had surrendered on the 16th, Genl
Hardee having telegraphed he could not hold it—was directed to Evacuate—
The deserter is an intelegent man and says He believes the statement—" ALS
(telegram sent), *ibid.*, Telegrams Collected (Unbound); telegram received (at
12:15 P.M.), *ibid.*, RG 108, Letters Received. At 4:45 P.M., USG telegraphed
to Maj. Gen. Henry W. Halleck. "The following dispatch just received . . . Hd
Qrs A of J Dec 21 *1864* LT GEN. GRANT Richmond papers just in says 'An
official despatch from Wilmington dated yesterday at 10 a m. says the advance
of the enemys fleet arrived off that point during last night. Over 30 steamers are
now assembling & more are following' Despatch from Dublin late last night
states that fighting had been going on near Mt Airy for two days. The salt works
were supposed to be safe thus far E O C ORD Maj Gen" Telegram sent and
received (at 4:35 P.M.), *ibid.*, RG 107, Telegrams Collected (Unbound). *O.R.*,
I, xlii, part 3, 1050. Ord's telegram: ALS (telegram sent), DNA, RG 107,
Telegrams Collected (Unbound); telegram received (on Dec. 22, 1:45 P.M.),
ibid., Telegrams Collected (Bound).

On Dec. 22, Ord telegraphed to USG. "The Richmond Examiner of to day
says that—'It was currently reported yesterday that two Divisions of the Enemy's
Cavalry had crossed the Blue Ridge and were moving towards Madison Court
House.' Later that 'Sheridan's Infantry had come up the Valley to a point between Harrisonburg and New Market. His advance is supposed to be intended
as a diversion in favor of the cavalry movement on this side of the mountains.
Early has marched out to meet him. The mounted force which has crossed the
mountains is four thousand in numbers and have four peices of artillery. They
were yesterday in Madison County.' The Enquirer says—'Some thirty five vessels
have appeared off New Inlet below Wilmington, and among them are recognised
the Colorado and Wa~~shbash~~, and it is inferable that this point is the object of the
great expedition which recently left Fortress Monroe under Butler and Porter.
An official report from Genl. Bragg in yesterday, states that owing to the severe
state of the weather the enemy of New Inlet have been unable to make any
demonstration. He states that he is fully ~~able~~ able to hold the City of Wilmington.' " ALS (telegram sent), *ibid.*, Telegrams Collected (Unbound); telegram
received (at 5:00 P.M.), *ibid.*, Telegrams Collected (Bound); (incomplete) *ibid.*,
RG 108, Letters Received. *O.R.*, I, xlii, part 3, 1055–56. USG endorsed this

telegram for transmission to Secretary of War Edwin M. Stanton. "Just received and respectfully forwarded." AES, DNA, RG 108, Letters Received. *O.R.*, I, xlii, part 3, 1056. Also on Dec. 22, USG telegraphed to Stanton. "Todays Richmond 'Despatch' contains the following—'In[f]ormation was received here on yesterday that a column of Sheridans forces estimated at Eight thousand men had crossed the Blue Ridge at Chester Gap and were moving towards Gordonsville. Another report puts the force of this column at five thousand Infantry and cavalry and four pieces of Artillery—They are said to have reached Madison [C.] H. at 5 o'clock on Tuesday Evening, since then nothing has been heard from them. Their object is believed to be to cut the Central RailRoad at Gordonsville. We however for reasons that it is not necessary to mention feel little apprehension for the safety of that point. The telegraph wire between Gordonsville and Trevillians nine miles this side was cut in several places yesterday morning— This was no doubt the work of the Enemys scouts. The Country in this neighborhood is densely wood and favorable to the operations of scouts. From Southwestern Virginia. We have no further news of Stoneman's operations in Southwestern Virginia There has been no confirmation of the report that Breckenridge had beaten the raiders near Glade Spring though the intelligence received on Tuesday relative to the fight at that place may be correct. Nothing in contradiction [o]f it has been heard. From the nature [o]f the case it is difficult to get any authentic information from points beyond Dublin station. An unofficial despatch from Lynchburg yesterday states that the damage done to the Lead works by the enemy was slight and will be speedily repaired. Sev Several days since a raiding party came up from Pensacola and cut the Mobile and Great Northern Rl Rd at Pollards 72 miles Northeast of Mobile and then retired—We are still without advices from Hood except through the Northern papers, such extracts from which will be found in another column. If half they tell be true Hood is in a bad fix indeed, perhaps the worst piece of their news is the reported death of Genl Forrest. Official information has been recd. here that a column of five thousand of the Enemy are on the Mobile and Ohio R. R north of its crossing of the Mississippi R. R.' It continues that 'nothing was heard from Wilmington on yesterday. From Savannah we have nothing'" Telegram received, DNA, RG 107, Telegrams Collected (Bound).

On Dec. 23, 8:30 P.M., Ord telegraphed to USG. "a file Richmond papers were sent thro Quarter master Bermuda—to you to day at one—they contain nothing—of interest—except—telegraphd from Wilmington Decr 22d viz The Federal Fleets have drawn off shore from the shore—only the masts of the colorado and the wabash are visible—It is uncertain whether they have sought Ports or gone south—high winds and very rough Sea—Genl Leventhorpe the enemies Gunboats and Barges below poplar point on the Roanoak river, on tuesday evening the fight continued (3)—three hours—the enemy were repulsed with severe loss—they resumed the attack on yesterday and landed some sharp shooters their main fleet of Gunboats and transports lies below in attacking force— The advanced guard of attacking force moving against gordonsville supposed to consist of a thousand or 15 hundred cavalry—reached Madison court house 15 miles from Gordonsville on Wedenesday the main body comprising infantry and cavalry were reported to be coming up—during yesterday the cavalry advanced three or four miles in the direction of gordonsville—and at last accounts our troops were skirmishing with them—It is reported that Rosser has driven the enemy back down the Valley—" ALS (telegram sent), *ibid.*, Telegrams Collected (Unbound). *O.R.*, I, xlii, part 3, 1066–67.

On Dec. 26, 2:10 P.M., Ord telegraphed to USG. "Richmond Whig of to day says—'Telegraphic—Wilmington Decr 24th—Seventy vessels of of the enemies fleet reported off Ft Fisher this morning—No demonstrations of landing yet—weather mild—A yankee gun boat grounded last night near Fort Fisher and was blown up by the enemy—Second despatch.' " ALS (telegram sent), DNA, RG 107, Telegrams Collected (Unbound). *O.R.*, I, xlii, part 3, 1080.

1. George E. Baker. *Ibid.*, p. 1067.
2. Maj. Gen. William H. C. Whiting, Dept. of N. C.
3. Maj. Gen. Jeremy F. Gilmer, chief engineer.
4. ALS (telegram sent at noon), DNA, RG 107, Telegrams Collected (Unbound); telegram received, *ibid.*, RG 108, Letters Received. On Dec. 23, USG transmitted this telegram to Maj. Gen. George G. Meade and all corps commanders. Copies (2), *ibid.*, RG 94, War Records Office, Army of the Potomac; *ibid.*, RG 393, 2nd Army Corps, Miscellaneous Records; *ibid.*, 9th Army Corps, 3rd Brigade, Letters Received.

To Robert Ould

December 24 1864

JUDGE R. OULD,
AGENT OF EXCHANGE
SIR!

I am informed that there is quite a number of Federal prisoners in Richmond who are suffering for want of proper clothing. I would respectfully request the authority to send for their benefit a few hundred blankets and ask that a commissioned officer from among the prisoners be allowed to receive and distribute them. If my request in this matter can be acceded to, I will be pleased to learn at what point and at what time they will be received, and the name of the officer designated to receive the clothing.

Very Respectfully
Your Obt Serv't
U S GRANT
Lieutenant General.

Copies, DLC-USG, V, 45, 71, 107; DNA, RG 94, Letters Received, 55A 1865; *ibid.*, RG 108, Letters Sent; USG 3. *O.R.*, II, vii, 1264. See letter to Robert Ould, Dec. 28, 1864.

To Edwin M. Stanton

(Cipher)   City Point, Va, Dec. 24th *1864*. [*9:00* P.M.]
HON. E. M. STANTON, SEC. OF WAR, WASHINGTON

I would much prefer seeing the three hundred thousand men called for go in to fill up old organizations than to see them come out as new regiments. It will be much more economical and the men will be much more effective under tried officers and along side of disciplined soldiers. Unless there will be great saving of time in getting men into the field by accepting regiments I would not recommend receiving new organizations.

U. S. GRANT
Lt. Gn.

ALS (telegram sent), CSmH; telegram received (at 10:00 P.M.), DNA, RG 107, Telegrams Collected (Bound). *O.R.*, I, xlii, part 3, 1068. On Dec. 24, 1864, Maj. Thomas M. Vincent, AGO, telegraphed to USG, Maj. Gen. George G. Meade, and Maj. Gen. George H. Thomas. "Applications are made by Governors of states to raise new regiments of Volunteers, under the recent call for three hundred Thousand (300,000) men. Although it is easier to raise the men by new regiments, the desire of the Department has been, so far as practicable, to secure recruits for old regiments and thus keep up their organ[i]z[a]tion. Before any authorizations, to raise new regiments are given, the Secretary of Wa[r] desires your views on the subject. Please reply fully by Telegram." Telegram sent, DNA, RG 107, Telegrams Collected (Unbound); telegram received, *ibid.*, RG 108, Letters Received; (at 7:10 P.M.) *ibid.*, RG 393, Army of the Potomac, Letters Received.

To Maj. Gen. Philip H. Sheridan

From City Point Dec 24 *1864*.

MAJ GENL SHERIDAN WINCHESTER

The Richmond papers of today has the following. Dec 23d   On the twentieth Genl Early reported one Division of the enemys Cavalry under Custer coming up the Valley and two divisions under Torbertt moving through Chester Gap with four pieces of artillery and thirty wagons. On the twenty second Rosser attacked Custers Division nine miles from Harrisonburg and drove it back

capturing forty prisoners. This morning Torbert attacked Lomax[1]
near Gordonsville and was repulsed and seriously punished. He is
retreating and Lomax is preparing to follow   Signed R E Lee
U S Grant Lt. Genl

Telegram received (at 4:00 P.M.), DNA, RG 107, Telegrams Collected (Unbound); *ibid.*, Telegrams Collected (Bound); copies, *ibid.*, RG 108, Letters Sent;
DLC-USG, V, 45, 71, 107. On Dec. 24, 1864, Maj. Gen. Philip H. Sheridan
telegraphed to Brig. Gen. John A. Rawlins. "I have no information from Genl
Torbert—Genl Custer has sent in his report of affair at Lacy springs near Harrisonburg, between Chapmans brigade of his Div. and Paynes brigade of Rosser
Cavly He repulsed & drove them and there was no necessity for his return except the bad weather, and total absence of forage. Genl Custer reports his loss—
2 killed 22 wounded 20 prisoners—The Enemys loss killed and wounded 100
and 27 prisoners—The fight occurred before day light—Genl Custer had (230)
two hundred and thirty of his men frost bitten in [the expedition.]" Telegram
sent, DNA, RG 107, Telegrams Collected (Unbound); telegram received (at
11:50 P.M.), *ibid. O.R.*, I, xliii, part 1, 39; *ibid.*, I, xliii, part 2, 825.

    At 3:23 P.M., Brig. Gen. John W. Turner had telegraphed to Rawlins
transmitting the information that USG later transmitted to Sheridan, and also
additional news. ". . . from Savannah It was reported on yesterday that savannah had been evacuated & that Sherman had taken possession. We could obtain
no Information of this report from War Office from Wilmington Dec 23 twenty
six (26) vessels of the Federal Fleet reappeared this morning there has been
no change since last dispatch." ALS (incomplete telegram sent), DNA, RG 107,
Telegrams Collected (Unbound); telegram received, *ibid.*, RG 108, Letters Received. On the same day, USG transmitted this telegram to Secretary of War
Edwin M. Stanton. Telegram received (at 4:00 P.M.), *ibid.*, RG 107, Telegrams Collected (Bound).

    On Dec. 20, 10:30 A.M., Sheridan had telegraphed to USG. "Information
from Genl Custer last night is to the effect that Rodes Div has gone to Richmond
and he thinks part of Hortons [*Wharton's*].—Rosser went back towards Lynchburg and it is said intended to go in the direction Withville I have ordered
Custer up the Vally to the James R and across to Lynchburg. I have Ordered
Torbert to Hedge in close to the Blue Ridge so as to avoid the Head Water of
the Rapid ann and to strike the road at Chalottes ville and follow up to Lynchburg
Communicate with Custer and uniting with him. Nothing but the Extremely bad
weather will prevent good results. No Artilly was taken and no Wagons—" ALS
(telegram sent), *ibid.*, Telegrams Collected (Unbound); telegram received (at
11:00 A.M.), *ibid.*, Telegrams Collected (Bound); *ibid.*, RG 108, Letters Received. *O.R.*, I, xliii, part 2, 809–10. On Dec. 21, 1:00 P.M., Sheridan telegraphed to Rawlins. "I heard from Genl Custer at Harrisonburg. he is in fine
spirits and says he will he hopes spend his Christmas in Lynchburg—I heard
from Genl. Torbert last night he was then near sperryville—The weather is so
very bad, rain, snow & sleet—that I feel a great deal of anxiety about the horses
—There is about 8000 Eight thousand men on this raid, no Artillery or wagons."
Telegram sent, DNA, RG 107, Telegrams Collected (Unbound); telegram
received (marked as sent at 1:30 P.M., received at 3:30 P.M., addressed to

USG), *ibid.*, Telegrams Collected (Bound). Printed as sent at 1:30 P.M. in *O.R.*, I, xliii, part 1, 38; *ibid.*, I, xliii, part 2, 816. On Dec. 22, 8:30 P.M., Sheridan telegraphed to Rawlins. "Genl. Custer reports that, at or near Harrisonburg he encountered Rosser' Division of Cavly. supported by Rodes Division of Infantry—The Cavly. & Infy: having marched from Waynesboro to meet him; and after a slight fight before daylight, he was obliged to come back—He captured (2) two battle flags, and (33) thirty three prisoners—He has not yet reported to me the particulars—The fight was between Chapmans brigade of Custers Div. and Paynes brigade of Rossers Cavly. Payne charged Chapmans Camp, ~~but~~ but Chapman was ready for him—Genl: Custer reports that Rossers Div: and Rodes Division ~~being at~~ came from Waynesboro—I have not heard from Torbert but sent this evening, to apprise him of the condition of affairs with Custer—If Custers information is correct: it will for a while, help Torbert—The weather here is intensely Cold, the ground covered with Snow—I am very anxious about Torbert, but think he will be able to take care of himself—Custers men and animals suffered much—" Telegram sent, DNA, RG 107, Telegrams Collected (Unbound); telegram received (marked as addressed to USG), *ibid.*, Telegrams Collected (Bound). Printed as addressed to USG and received on Dec. 23 in *O.R.*, I, xliii, part 1, 38; *ibid.*, I, xliii, part 2, 821. On Dec. 23, 1:30 P.M., Sheridan telegraphed to Rawlins. "Should you get any more news of Genl: Torbert in the Richmond papers of today, please telegraph me; I am very anxious about him, the weather has been so cold and stormy since he left: that his trip will, I fear be an embarrassing one.—" Telegram sent, DNA, RG 107, Telegrams Collected (Unbound); telegram received (at 1:50 P.M.), *ibid.*; *ibid.*, RG 108, Letters Received. *O.R.*, I, xliii, part 2, 824.

On Dec. 25, Sheridan telegraphed to USG, sending a copy to Maj. Gen. Henry W. Halleck. "Do you wish me to send the transportation of the 1st Div. Army of West Va. and the Provisional Division to City Point?" Copies (2), DLC-Philip H. Sheridan. On Dec. 26, Rawlins telegraphed to Sheridan. "Send forward the transportation of the troops referred to in your despatch as fast as convenient" Telegrams received (2), DNA, RG 107, Telegrams Collected (Unbound); copies, *ibid.*, RG 108, Letters Sent; DLC-USG, V, 45, 71, 107. An almost identical message dated Dec. 27 from USG to Sheridan is a telegram received, DNA, RG 107, Telegrams Collected (Unbound); *ibid.*, Telegrams Collected (Bound).

On Dec. 26, 11:00 P.M., Sheridan telegraphed to USG. "I have the honor to transmit the following report just recd Genl Torbert. 6 oclock A. M. Dec 26th 64 To MAJ GENL SHERIDAN. General. I have the honor to report that on thursday the 22d I reached the Rapid Ann. River at Liberty Mills, having driven Jacksons Brigade of Cavly: from Madison C. House—at Liberty Mills Jackson made a junction with McCausland with (2) two pieces of artillery—I drove them across the river but they had the bridge mined and it blew up as my men got to it. It was impossible to force a crossing in front so I made a detour on both flanks of (5) five or (6) six miles—which turned them out of their position, and we captured their Artillery ((2) two pieces) and several prisoners. This move took till (8) eight or (9) nine oclock at night. Next morning I pushed on towards Gordonsville and I found them strongly posted in the Gap, and I could not drive them out with 2000 two thousand men and I ~~made~~ was making a movement to turn the position when Infantry commenced to file into their breast

works, and I commenced to with draw and am now (10) ten miles south of
Warrenton, and may be on the Little River Tnpike to night—I will try and come
through Ashbys Gap. my men & horses suffered almost beyond description with
cold and bad weather—I captured ~~about~~ one herd of cattle going south about 200
—head—I recd your dispatches (2) concerning Custer. I heard nothing of matters in the vally, before I got your dispatches: and expected more trouble in my
rear: but thus far have not been troubled—Yours &c   Signed A. T. A. TORBERT
Bvt Maj Genl Chf of Cavly"   Telegram sent, *ibid.*, Telegrams Collected (Unbound); telegram received (on Dec. 27, 8:30 A.M.), *ibid.*, Telegrams Collected
(Bound). *O.R.*, I, xliii, part 1, 39; *ibid.*, I, xliii, part 2, 829. On Dec. 28, Sheridan
telegraphed to USG. "Genl: Torbert has just returned: in a more detailed report
he says, the great difficulty which he had, was the cold bad weather and the ice
on the roads—He brings in (2) two pieces of Artillery, captured at Liberty
Mills: thirty (30) prisoners, and (1000) one thousand head of stock—He reports
that Infy: came from Richmond to Gordonsville—that Rodes Div: was at Fisherville, between Stanton and Waynesboro, and did advance in the direction of
Harrisonburg when Custer was in that vicinity—Other information which I have
recd is to the effect, that Gordons Div: or apartof it, moved out in the direction
of Wytheville—West Va—This latter information comes from Rebel sources—"
ALS (telegram sent), DNA, RG 107, Telegrams Collected (Unbound); telegram received (at 12:20 P.M.), *ibid.* Printed as received at 12:35 P.M. in *O.R.*,
I, xliii, part 1, 39; *ibid.*, I, xliii, part 2, 833. On Dec. 28, 9:30 P.M., Sheridan
telegraphed to Rawlins. "The wagons of the (2) two divisions, last sent from
here will start for City Point to morrow morning—also the Ambulances—The
pressure is so hard on me to send more troops to Western Virginia—that I have
consented to send the other small Division of Genl: Crooks Command ~~westward~~,
to cover the RailRoad westward from Martinsburg—Genl: Crook thinks that
small Guerrillas parties will operate during the winter in the little vallies, all of
—which ~~all~~ run perpendicular to the railroad; and will give constant annoyance.
This will leave the (2) two Divs. of the 19th Corps intact; sofar as any military
operations, on the part of the Enemy of an an agressive character. I think they
are at an end in this valley for a long time to come—and it would be best perhaps
to send another Division off—The only argument against this, is, the insecurity
which it might create along this extended, and sensitive line; from Alexandria to
the Ohio River.—and when there are so many troublesome interests—Some loyal,
and some disloyal, some interested in Coal oil specution some in the Baltimore &
Ohio R. R. and some in the Canal—Sofar as the military situation is concerned;
it is my impression, that another Division could bespared—" ALS (telegram
sent), DNA, RG 107, Telegrams Collected (Unbound); telegram received (at
11:45 P.M.—addressed to USG), *ibid.*, Telegrams Collected (Bound); (on Dec.
29, 1:00 A.M.—addressed to USG) *ibid.*, RG 108, Letters Received. Printed as
addressed to USG in *O.R.*, I, xliii, part 2, 833. On Dec. 30, 3:00 P.M., USG
telegraphed to Sheridan. "You need not send more troops here until directed."
ALS (telegram sent), Columbia University, New York, N. Y.; copies, DLC-USG,
V, 45, 71, 107; DNA, RG 108, Letters Sent. *O.R.*, I, xliii, part 2, 840.

  1. Lunsford L. Lomax, born in 1835 at Newport, R. I., USMA 1856, resigned from the U.S. Army as of April 25, 1861. Early in the Civil War he
served as staff officer, then col., 11th Va. Cav. Appointed brig. gen. as of July
23, 1863, and maj. gen. as of Aug. 10, 1864, he commanded the cav. corps of
Lt. Gen. Jubal A. Early.

To Julia Dent Grant

City Point, Va, Dec. 24th *1864*.

DEAR JULIA,

Your dispatch to Fred. expressing your fears for *our Freddy* was received and answered the moment it come to hand. Gen. Augur will not let his children leave Washington if there is any danger and Fred will not start without them. I think you need give yourself no fear.—I am getting quite well. To-day is the first time I have been out to dinner for three days. I know how much there is dependent on me and will prove myself equal to the task. I believe determination can do a great deal to sustain one and I have that quality certainly to its fullest extent.

The Richmond papers of to-day are very blue over the situation of Military affairs. They say all they can to encourage their people of course but still show a very great weakness in the South. To add to their calamities they have had a great fire in Richmond, burning up all their forage, which they attribute to the work of an incindriary. Every thing seems to be working well and I have great hope this will be the last Winter of the War.—Kisses for you and the children.

ULYS.

ALS, DLC-USG.

To Edwin M. Stanton

(Cipher)   City Point, Va, Dec. 25th 1864 [*8:00* P.M.]
HON. E. M. STANTON, SEC. OF WAR, WASHINGTON
I have just received Gen. Foster's dispatch[1] announcing the capture of Savannah with Artillery, munitions of War, rail-road cars and cotton. I wish Hardee's fifteen to eighteen thousand of a garrison could have been added to the other captures. It is a good thing the way it stands and the country may well rejoice over it.

U. S. GRANT
Lt. Gn.

ALS (telegram sent), Wayde Chrismer, Bel Air, Md.; telegram received (at 9:30 P.M.), DNA, RG 107, Telegrams Collected (Bound). *O.R.*, I, xliv, 806. On Dec. 26, 1864, 1:00 P.M., Secretary of War Edwin M. Stanton telegraphed to USG. "I wish you a merry Christmas if not too late, and thank you for the Savannah News. It is a sore disappointment that it Hardies men force enable to get off his fifteen thousand from Shermans Sixty thousand. It looks like protracting the war while their armies continue to escape. I hope you will give immediate instructions to seize and hold the cotton. All sorts of schemes will be got up to hold it under sham titles of British & other private claimants. They should all be disregarded. And it ought not be be turned over to any Treasury agent but held by Military authority until a special order of the Department is given for the transfer. Thomas has been nominated for Major General." ALS (telegram sent), DNA, RG 107, Telegrams Collected (Bound); telegram received, *ibid.*, RG 108, Letters Received. Variant text in *O.R.*, I, xliv, 809.

1. On Dec. 22, 7:00 P.M., Maj. Gen. John G. Foster, steamer *Golden Gate*, Savannah River, telegraphed to USG and Maj. Gen. Henry W. Halleck. "I have the honor to report that I have just returned from Gen Shermans Head Quarters in Savannah I send maj Gray of my staff as bearer of despatches from Gen Sherman to you and also a message to the President The City of Savannah was occupied on the morning of the twenty first (21) Gen Hardie anticipating the contemplated assault escaped with the main body of his Infantry & light artillery on the afternoon & night of the twentieth (20) by crossing the River to the Union causeway oppesite the city. The Rebel Iron clads were blown up & the navy yard burned all the rest of the city is intact & contains twenty thousand (20,000) citizens quiet & well disposed The captures include eight hundred (800) prisoners one hundred and fifty (150) guns thirteen (13) Locomotives in good order one hundred and ninety (190) cars a large supply of ammunition and material of war Three (3) steamers and thirty two thousand (32000) bales of cotton safely stored in Warehouses. all these valuable fruits of an almost bloodless victory have been, 'Like Atlanta fairly won' I opened communication with the city with my steamers today taking up what torpedoes we could see and passing safely over others. arrangements are made to clear the channel of all obstructions" Telegrams received (2—on Dec. 25), DNA, RG 107, Telegrams Collected (Bound); (2) *ibid.*, RG 108, Letters Received; DLC-Robert T. Lincoln; copies, DNA, RG 393, Army of the Potomac, Telegrams Received; *ibid.*, 19th Army Corps, Miscellaneous Letters; *ibid.*, Dept. of the South, Letters Sent. Printed as received on Dec. 25, 7:00 P.M., in *O.R.*, I, xliv, 786. On Dec. 25, USG telegraphed to Maj. Gen. George G. Meade transmitting Foster's telegram. "The following despatch just received. You will please fire a salute in honor of this victory tomorrow morning" Copies (2), Meade Papers, PHi. At 9:00 P.M., Meade telegraphed to USG. "I tender you my hearty congratulations on the fall of Savanna—I have ordered a salute 100 guns to be fired at 7. a m tomorrow in honor of the event.—" ALS (telegram sent), DNA, RG 94, War Records Office, Army of the Potomac; telegram received, *ibid.*, RG 108, Letters Received. Printed as received at 9:15 P.M. in *O.R.*, I, xlii, part 3, 1073. On the same day, USG telegraphed to Meade and all corps commanders transmitting the text of a telegram of Dec. 22 from Maj. Gen. William T. Sherman, Savannah, to President Abraham Lincoln. "I beg to present you as a Christmas gift the city of Savannah with one hundred & fifty heavy guns & plenty of ammunition & also

about twenty five thousand (25.000) bales of Cotton." Telegram received, DNA, RG 94, War Records Office, Army of the Potomac; copy, *ibid.*, RG 393, 9th Army Corps, 3rd Brigade, Telegrams Received.

To Gustavus V. Fox

(Cipher)   City Point, Va, Dec. 25th 1864 [*8:30* P.M.]
G. V. Fox, Asst. sec. of the Navy,
Washington D. C.

Richmond papers are not published on Sunday and they announce that none will be published to-morrow. I have not therefore later news from Wilmington than you are possessed of and can not learn any thing through that source before Teusday.

U. S. Grant
Lt. Gen.

ALS (telegram sent), CSmH; telegram received (marked as sent at 8:00 P.M., received at 9:30 P.M.), DNA, RG 45, Miscellaneous Telegrams Received; *ibid.*, RG 107, Telegrams Collected (Bound). On Dec. 25, 1864, Asst. Secretary of the Navy Gustavus V. Fox telegraphed to USG. "Have you any paper to day to learn Wilmington news." Copy, *ibid.*, RG 45, Miscellaneous Letters Sent.

On Dec. 20, 11:10 A.M., Fox had telegraphed to USG. "I hope you will use every exertion to get us a Richmond paper as we shall hear first through that source concerning the joint expedition." Copy, *ibid. O.R.* (Navy), I, xi, 203. At 1:00 P.M., USG telegraphed to Fox. "We get the Richmond papers daily, a file of which is generally sent the Secretary of War   Yesterdays papers contain no notice of the Wilmington Expedition"   Telegram received (at 2:30 P.M.), DNA, RG 45, Miscellaneous Telegrams Received; *ibid.*, RG 107, Telegrams Collected (Bound); copies, *ibid.*, Telegrams Received in Cipher; *ibid.*, RG 108, Letters Sent; DLC-USG, V, 45, 71, 107. *O.R.* (Navy), I, xi, 203. At 9:30 A.M., Maj. Gen. Benjamin F. Butler, off Beaufort, N. C., telegraphed to USG. "Have done nothing   been waiting for Navy and Weather   Have sent full report by Mail"   ALS (telegram sent), DNA, RG 107, Telegrams Collected (Unbound); telegram received (on Dec. 27), *ibid.*, Telegrams Collected (Bound); (misdated Dec. 27) *ibid.*, RG 108, Letters Received. *O.R.*, I, xlii, part 3, 1048. On the same day, Butler wrote to USG reporting at length, and on Jan. 1, 1865, USG endorsed this report: "Respectfully forwarded." *Ibid.*, pp. 1048–49; *ibid.*, I, xlii, part 1, 964–65.

On Dec. 27, 1864, Tuesday, Fox telegraphed to USG. "The Explosion of the Gun boat spoken of by Richmond papers would seem to indicate operations commenced   parties from Roanoke Island say they have had the strongest gales ever known   Can you be at Fort Monroe or Norfolk Thursday forenoon without inconvenience?" Telegram received, DNA, RG 108, Letters Received; copy, *ibid.*, RG 45, Miscellaneous Letters Sent. *O.R.* (Navy), I, xi, 379. At midnight, USG

telegraphed to Fox. "I will meet you Thursday morning at Fortress Monroe."
ALS (telegram sent), Kohns Collection, NN; telegram received (on Dec. 28,
11:30 A.M.), DNA, RG 107, Telegrams Collected (Bound); DLC-Gist Blair.

To Maj. Gen. George G. Meade

City Point, Va, Dec. 25th 186[4]

MAJ. GEN. MEADE,

W. E. Alley is here with his family. He seems to have had an
order to report at your Head Quarters preparitory to being sent out
of the lines with his family. His expressed desire is to be allowed to
go North himself and seek employment leaving his family here
until he has the means of supporting them. Is there an objection to
this being granted?

U. S. GRANT
Lt. Gn.

ALS (telegram sent), CSmH; copies, DLC-USG, V, 45, 71, 107; DNA, RG
108, Letters Sent; (2) Meade Papers, PHi. On Dec. 25, 1864, 7:00 P.M., Maj.
Gen. George G. Meade telegraphed to USG. "Mr. Alley, was permitted to come
within my lines, upon the express understanding that he desired to take the oath
of allegiance & accompany his family North—This statement was acquiesced in
& confirmed by Mrs. Alley—After allowing them a reasonable time to make
arrangements I directed they should be sent North—I should object to either Mr.
& Mrs. Alley remaining within my lines for reasons I can not well give here.—"
ALS (telegram sent), DNA, RG 94, War Records Office, Army of the Potomac;
copies, *ibid.*, RG 393, Army of the Potomac, Letters Sent; Meade Papers, PHi.
See *O.R.*, I, xlii, part 3, 995.

To Maj. Gen. Henry W. Halleck

City Point, Va, Dec. 26th *1864.*

MAJ. GEN. H. W. HALLECK,
CHIEF OF STAFF OF THE ARMY,
GENERAL,

I am just in receipt of a letter from Gen. G. B. McClellen saying
that he purposes visiting Europe soon, with his family, and that

Mrs. McClellen desires to see her father before starting and requests a leave of absence for Col. Marcy that this desire may be gratified. I do not know the special duty Col. Marcy may be on at this time and do not therefore wish to order the leave granted lest is may interfere with important duties. If not inconsistent with public service however I wish this leave to be granted from Washington. Col. Marcy I believe is in Memphis Tenn. at this time.

> Very respectfully
> your obt. svt.
> U. S. GRANT
> Lt. Gen.

ALS, IHi. *O.R.*, I, xlii, part 3, 1077. On Dec. 29, 1864, Maj. Gen. Henry W. Halleck wrote to USG. "Your letter of the 26th in regard to a leave of absence for Col Marcy has been submitted to the Secty of War, who directs me to say that any application of Col Marcy, made in accordance with Army Regulations will recieve his immediate attention." ALS, DNA, RG 108, Letters Received. On Jan. 1, 1865, 5:30 P.M., USG telegraphed to Secretary of War Edwin M. Stanton. "I regret that leave of absence was not granted to Col. Marcy. Gen. ~~wro~~ McClellen wrote to me that he would sail for Europe in Jan.y and that his wife was very anxious to see her father before starting He had written to Col. Marcy to make the application but it would take so much time for his letter to reach and the application to come to Washington and back that he ventured to write to expedite the matter." ALS (telegram sent—misdated 1864), CSmH; copies, DLC-USG, V, 46, 71, 107; DNA, RG 108, Letters Sent.

To Julia Dent Grant

City Point, Va, Dec. 26th *1864.*

DEAR JULIA,

Freddy reached here yesterday all well. I telegraphed you immediately on his arrival but you may not have received the despatch. I had just ordered my horse to take a ride when he and Will Smith made their appearance at the head of the steps coming up the river bank. I at once sent for another horse and took Fred. with me. He has gone to-day with Capt. Hudson and two or three other officers to Gen. Meade's Hd Qrs. To-morrow he and his Uncle Fred go up to see Gen. Ord by special invitation. Altogether I think he will have a good time of it while he stays here. I will start him back promptly on New Years day so that he shall loose no time at, or from, school.

I do not know whether the PayMasters will have any money to pay at the end of this month so I will write to Russell Jones to send you all he has of mine. It must amount to several hundred dollars besides the gold.

All well here now. The good news received from Sherman is worth a greatdeal at this time. The rebels are very despondent and say, some of them, their cause is already lost. Love and kisses for you and the children.

ULYS.

ALS, DLC-USG.

To Maj. Gen. William T. Sherman

———

City Point, Va, Dec. 27th *1864.*

MAJ. GEN. W. T. SHERMAN,
COMD.G MIL. DIV. OF THE MISS.
GENERAL

Before writing you definite instructions for the next campaign, I wanted to receive your answer to my letter written from Washington.[1] Your confidance in being able to march up and join this Army pleases me and I believe it can be done. The effect of such a campaign will be to disorganize the South and prevent the organization of new Armies from their broken fragments. Hood is now retreating with his Army broken and demoralized. His loss in men has probably not been far from 20.000 besides deserters. If time is given the fragments may be collected together and many of the deserters reassembled. If we can we should act to prevent this. Your spare Army, as it were, moving as proposed will do this.

In addition to holding Savannah it looks to me that an intrenched camp ought to be held on the rail-road between Savannah and Charleston? Your movement towards Branchville will probably enable Foster to reach this with his own force. This will give us a position in the South from which we can threaten the interior without marching over long narrow causeways, easily defended, as we have hertofore been compelled to do. Could not such a camp be established about Pocotaligo or Coosawatchie?

I have thought that Hood being so completely wiped out for present harm I might bring A. J. Smith here with from ten to fifteen thousand. With this increase I could hold my lines and move out with a greater force than Lee has. It would compell Lee to retain all his present force in the defences of Richmond or abandon them entirely. This latter contingency is probably the only danger to the easy success of your expedition. In the event you should meet Lee's Army you would be compelled to beat it or find the sea-coast.

Of course I shall not let Lee's army escape if I can help it and will not let it go without following to the best of my ability.

Without waiting further directions then you may make preparation to start on your Northern expedition without delay. Break up the rail-roads in South & North Carolina and join the Armies operating against Richmond as soon as you can.

I will leave out all suggestions about the route you should take knowing that your information, gained daily in the progress of events, will be better than any that can be obtained now.

It may not be possible for you to march to the rear of Petersburg but failing in this you could strike either of the Sea coast ports in North Carolina held by us. From there you could take shipping. It would be decidedly preferable however if you could march the whole distance.

From the best information I have you will find no difficulty in supplying your Army until you cross the Roanoke. From there here is but a few days march and supplies could be collected south of the river to bring you through. I shall establish communication with you there, by Steamboat and gunboat. By this means your wants can be partially supplied.

I shall hope to hear from you soon and to hear you plan and about the time of starting.

Please instruct Foster to hold on to all the property captured in Savannah and especially the Cotton. Do not turn it over to citizens or Treasury Agents without orders of the War Department.[2]

> Very respectfully
> your obt. svt.
> U. S. GRANT
> Lt. Gn.

ALS, DLC-William T. Sherman. *O.R.*, I, xliv, 820–21. On Dec. 22, 1864, Maj. Gen. William T. Sherman wrote to USG. "I take great satisfaction in reporting that we are in possession of Savannah and all its forts. At first I proposed to extend across the river above the city from Slocum's left but the Enemy had a Gunboat & Ram heavily armed that would have made the step extra hazardous, also the submerged ricefields on the North East bank were impracticable. I then went to Hilton Head to arrange with Genl Foster to reinforce his movement from Broad River, but before I had completed the move, Hardee got his garrison across and off on the Union Plank Road, our troops entered at daylight yesterday, took about 8.00 prisoners, over 100 guns, some of the heaviest calibre and a perfect string of Forts from Savannah around to McAllister, also 12.000, bales of cotton, 190. cars. 13 locomotives, 3 steamboats and an immense supply of shells, shot and all kinds of ammunition There is a complete Arsenal here and much valuable machinery. The citizens mostly remain and the city is very quiet. The river below is much obstructed, but I parted with Admiral Dahlgren yesterday at 4. P. M. and he will at once get about removing them and opening a way. The enemy blew up an iron clad 'Savannah' a good Ram and three tenders, (small Steamers). As yet we have made but partial Inventory, but the above falls far short of our conquests. I have not a particle of doubt but that we have secured 150 fine guns with plenty of ammunition. I have now completed my first step and should like to go on to you, via Columbia and Raleigh, but will prepare to embark as soon as vessels come. Col Babcock will have told you all and you know better than any one else how much better troops arrive by a land march than when carried by transports. I will turn over to Foster Savannah, and all its outposts with say one Division of Infantry Kilpatrick's Cavalry and plenty of Artillery. Hardee has of course moved into South Carolina, but I do not believe his Georgia Troops, Militia and Fance (?) companies will work in South Carolina. His force is reported by citizens at from 15. to 20.000. The capture of Savannah with the incidental use of the River gives us a magnificent position in this quarter, and you can hold Lee, and if Thomas can continue as he did on the 18th, I can go on and smash South Carolina all to pieces, and also break up roads as far as the Roanoke. But as I before remarked, I will not look to coming to you as soon as transportation come. We are all well and confident as ever." Copies, DNA, RG 94, War Records Office, Union Battle Reports; *ibid.*, RG 393, Military Div. of the Miss., Letters Sent in the Field. On Dec. 26, USG wrote to Sherman. "Your very interesting letter of the 22d inst. brought by the hand of Maj. Gray, of Gn. Foster's Staff, is just at hand. As the Maj. starts back at once I can do no more at present than simply acknowledge its receipt. The capture of Savannah with all its immense stores must tell upon the people of the South. All well here," ALS, DLC-William T. Sherman. *O.R.*, I, xliv, 809–10. On Dec. 31, 3:00 P.M., Sherman wrote a letter not clearly addressed, but obviously intended for USG. "A

mail leaves at 5 P M for Hilton Head and New York. I have written a short official letter to Genl Halleck amounting to nothing simply because I suppose you
want to hear from me at every opportunity. I have already reviewed my 4 corps
and wind up in a day or two with Kilpatricks Cavalry which I keep out about 9
miles. There is no doubt of it, but this Army is in fine condition and impatient to
go ahead. I would like to have Foster reinforced, if possible, so that I will not have
to leave him a Division to hold Savannah. I will have all the heavy work done,
such as moving the captured artillery to Hilton Head where it can be more
safely guarded, and building the redoubts in the New Line for the defense of
Savannah. This will be close in for we dont care if the Enemy does shell the
town. 5000 men will be plenty and white troops will be best as the People are
dreadfully alarmed lest we garrison the place with Negros. Now no matter what
the Negro soldiers are, you know that people have prejudices which must be regarded. Prejudice like Religion cannot be discussed. As soon as I can accumulate enough provisions & forage to fill my wagons I will be ready for S Carolina,
and if you want me to take Charleston I think I can do it for I know the place
well. I was stationed there from 42 to 46, and used to hunt a good deal all along
the Cooper River. The direction to approach Charleston is from the North West,
down the peninsula between Ashley & Cooper, as also that ending on the Bay at
Mount Pleasant. You had better notify Genl Meigs to send at once enough provisions for 65000 men and 40000 horses & mules for 60 days, instead of the
daily allowance for you know I must work on the *surplus* & not on the daily
receipts. We have pretty well eaten up all the Rice & Rice Straw for 50 miles. By
making a wide circuit by Barnwell, Orangeburg, Columbia and Santee, I can
reach the neighborhood of Georgetown and get a *re* supply. I do not issue Rations
to the people, but order the Mayor to look to the People, and have give him the
rough Rice to be sold & exchanged into flour & meat. Thus the expense will fall
on the holders of this Rough Rice, which I treat as Prize of war, inasmuch as
Hardee refused to surrender & thereby escaped with with his Garrison. I take it
for granted that we will have to fight in South Carolina, though I believe G. W.
Smith with his Georgia Militia has returned to Georgia, by way of Augusta
saying he would be d——d if *he* would fight for South Carolina. The People here
seem to be well content as they have reason to be for our troops have behaved
magnificenly You would think it Sunday, so quiet is Every thing in the city day
& night. All recognize in my army a different body of men than I they have ever
seen before. I hope you will push Thomas up. Keep him going south anywhere.
Let him make a track down into Alabama, or if you think better he can again
come to Chattanooga and as far down as the Etowah, to which point I preserved
the iron rails ready to be used again. I am fully aware of your friendly feelings
toward me, and you may always depend on me as your steadfast supporter. Your
wish is Law & Gospel to me and such is the feeling that pervades my army. I
have an idea you will come to see me before I start" ALS, DNA, RG 108, Letters Received. *O.R.*, I, xliv, 841. On Jan. 2, 1865, Sherman wrote to USG. "I
have received by the hands of General Barnard your note of 26th and letter of
27th December. I herewith inclose to you a copy of a *projet* which I have this
morning, in strict confidence, discussed with my immediate Commanders. I shall
need, however, larger supplies of stores, especially grain. I will inclose to you
with this, letters from Gen. Easton, Q. M., and Col. Beckwith, C. S., setting
forth what will be required and trust you will forward them with your sanction
so that the necessary steps may be taken at once to enable me to carry out this

plan on time. I wrote you very fully on the 24th, and have nothing to add to that. Every thing here is quiet, and if I can get the necessary supplies in my wagons I shall be ready to start at the time indicated in my *projet*. But until those supplies are in hand I can do nothing: after they are, I shall be ready to move with great rapidity. I have heard of the affair at Cape Fear. It has turned out as you will remember I expected. I have furnished Gen. Easton a copy of the dispatch from the Sec'y of War. He will retain possession of all cotton here and ship it as fast as vessels can be had to New York. I shall immediately send the 17th Corps over to Port Royal—by boats to be furnished by Admiral Dahlgren and Gen. Foster, without interfering with Gen. Easton's vessels,—to make a lodgment on the Railroad at Pocataligo. Gen. Barnard will remain with me a few days, and I shall send this by a staff officer who can return on one of the vessels of the supply fleet. I suppose that now that Gen. Butler has got through, you can spare them to us. My Report of recent operations is nearly ready, and will be sent on in a day or two, as soon as some further subordinate Reports come in. . . . *Projet* for January (extremely confidential)   Right wing move men and artillery by transports to head of Broad River and Beaufort—get Port Royal Ferry and mass the wing at or in the neighborhood of Pocataligo. Left wing and cavalry work slowly across the causeway towards Hardeeville to open a road by which wagons can reach their corps about Broad River: also by a rapid movement of the left secure Sister's Ferry and out as far as the Augusta road (Robertsville)   In the meantime all guns, shot, shells, cotton &c to be got to a safe place, easy to guard, and provisions and wagons got ready for another *swath*, aiming to have our army in hand about the head of Broad River,—say Pocataligo, Robertsville & Coosawhatchie by the 15th Jan.'y. 2d—Move with loaded wagons by the roads leading in the direction of Columbia which afford the best chance of forage and provisions—Howard to be at Pocataligo 15th January, and Slocum to be at Robertsville and Kilpatrick at or near Coosawhatchie about same date. Gen. Foster's troops to occupy Savannah, and Gunboats to protect the rivers, as soon as Howard gets Pocataligo"   LS, DNA, RG 108, Letters Received. *O.R.*, I, xlvii, part 2, 6–7. On the same day, Bvt. Maj. Gen. John G. Barnard wrote to USG. "I found the 'California' which had brought Maj. Gray, at Fort Monroe & sailed in her a few hours after my arrival (Tuesday evening Dec 27)   I had a tedious voyage with a gale of wind dead ahead the whole way—reached Hilton Head at 9 P. M yesterday & arrived here last evening at 4. P. M.   Gen. Sherman sends dispatches today & a literal execution of your orders would require—or at least justify me—to return by the same steamer   But Gen Sherman prefers that I should stay long enough to see things for myself & for us to have some talk, and I believe it would meet the spirit of your orders to do so. I shall therefore remain for the Arago which leaves Hilton Head next Monday (the 9th)   I have already had an opportunity to meet Gens. Slocum, Howard and numerous other officers of rank and am very much pleased with the spirit & feeling which seems to pervade with all. Every day the magnitude of results of Shermans great march, combined with Hood's discmfiture impresses itself more & more upon me. I think we shall see 'daylight' this coming spring. At the time I left City Point I was about reviewing my examinations of the 'Fort Clifton' lines in view of an enterprise upon them. I feel however as if matters were approaching a *certain* result with such strides that it is inexpedient to run risks and perhaps lose men on uncertainties   Still circumstances might occur which would render such an enterprise expedient. If Maj. Michie get his pile bridge done in a week or ten days we shall have some 50 more available boats for such an operation. I presume

I shall reach City Point on the 12th." ALS, DNA, RG 108, Letters Received. *O.R.*, I, xlvii, part 2, 7–8. Also on Jan. 2, Bvt. Brig. Gen. Langdon C. Easton, Savannah, wrote to Bvt. Maj. Gen. Montgomery C. Meigs requesting grain for animals and subsistence for men for sixty days. *Ibid.*, p. 8. On Jan. 5, USG endorsed "Approved" on a copy of this letter. Copy, DNA, RG 108, Letters Received.

On Dec. 26, 1864, Maj. Gen. John G. Foster, Hilton Head, S. C., wrote to USG. "I have the honor to enclose a copy of my usual report, by each steamer, to General Halleck, by the hands of Captain Dunn of your Staff. Captain Dunn bears full dispatches from Gen'l Sherman and will be able to you fully the highly encouraging character of the situation in this Department. General Sherman is in excellent spirits, and his troops in splendid condition. His army, with the present morale and condition, is, in my humble opinion, more than a match for any army the Rebels can concentrate against it on this continent. Should it please you to give this Department a visit, you will, it is needless to assure you, receive the most cordial welcome." Copy, *ibid.*, RG 393, Dept. of the South, Letters Sent. *O.R.*, I, xliv, 816. On Dec. 29, Lt. Col. Frederick T. Dent telegraphed to USG. "Lieut Dunn of your staff left this place at nine (9) o'clock with despatches for you from Gen Sherman." Telegram received (press), DNA, RG 107, Telegrams Collected (Bound). On Dec. 24, Sherman wrote to Maj. Gen. Henry W. Halleck. *O.R.*, I, xliv, 798–800. USG endorsed this letter. "This letter was brought by Lieutenant Dunn, of my staff, with the request that I would open and read it, as it contained one or two points which his letter addressed to me does not contain." *Ibid.*, p. 800.

1. See letter to Maj. Gen. William T. Sherman, Dec. 18, 1864.
2. On Dec. 27, 1:00 P.M., Secretary of War Edwin M. Stanton telegraphed to USG. "Is there any objection th on Military grounds to the President removing the Blockade of Savannah by Proclamation and opening it to public trade except Contraband of War." ALS (telegram sent), DNA, RG 107, Telegrams Collected (Bound); telegram received, *ibid.*, RG 108, Letters Received. *O.R.*, I, xliv, 820. At 3:30 P.M., USG telegraphed to Stanton. "I think it would be better to defer the removal of the blockade of Savannah by proclaimation until Military operations in that quarter are ended." ALS (telegram sent), CSmH; telegram received (at 4:00 P.M.), DNA, RG 107, Telegrams Collected (Bound); Seward Papers, NRU. *O.R.*, I, xliv, 820. On Dec. 28, Stanton wrote to Secretary of State William H. Seward. "I have the honor in reply to your note in respect to opening the Port of Savanna, to enclose a telegram of General Grant who has been consulted on the point. General Halleck concurs with General Grant, and in my opinion it is better for the present to defer any action" ALS, Seward Papers, NRU.

To Col. Ralph C. Webster

City Pt
Dec 27 [*1864*]

COL WEBSTER

Lieut Porter of my staff left here yesterday on the River Queen with despatches for Gen Butler off Wilmington   I have heard

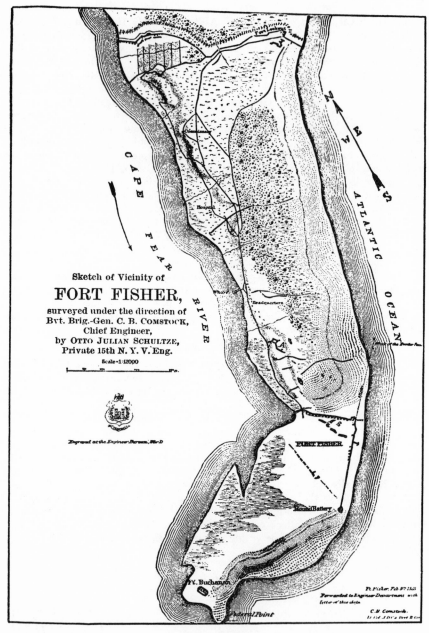

Fort Fisher

From **Memoirs** (*revised ed.; New York, 1909*), *II, between pp. 262–63*

from the fleet off that place & of the troops effecting a landing   you will communicate this to him & say that it is not necessary for him to go farther & that he will return to this place without delay

U S Grant
Lieut Gen

Telegram received (press), DNA, RG 107, Telegrams Collected (Bound); copies, *ibid.*, RG 108, Letters Sent; DLC-USG, V, 45, 71, 107. *O.R.*, I, xlii, part 3, 1080. On Dec. 27, 1864, 4:20 p.m., Col. Ralph C. Webster, q. m., telegraphed to USG. "Despatch received. Lieut Porter will return to City Point on first Boat in the morning" ALS (telegram sent), DNA, RG 107, Telegrams Collected (Bound). See telegram to Bvt. Maj. Gen. Montgomery C. Meigs, Feb. 3, 1865.

On Dec. 26, Brig. Gen. John A. Rawlins wrote to Maj. Gen. Benjamin F. Butler. "If the Expedition against Wilmington under Major General Weitzel, has not, when this reaches you, effected a landing, You will order its immediate return to the point from which it started in front of Richmond. So much time has, and will have elapsed, since the enemy became apprised of its destenation, that there is every reason to believe he has, or will have made ample preparations to defeat its object." Copy, DLC-USG, V, 71. Cancellation marks may indicate that this letter was never sent. On Dec. 27, 2:10 p.m., Maj. Gen. Edward O. C. Ord telegraphed to USG. "Richmond Whig of to-day says: Wilmington, *December 24.* Seventy vessels of the enemy's fleet reported off Fort Fisher this morning. No demonstrations of landing yet. Weather mild. A Yankee gun-boat grounded last night near Fort Fisher and was blown up by the enemy." *O.R.*, I, xlii, part 3, 1080. On the same day, USG telegraphed to Secretary of War Edwin M. Stanton. "Richmond papers of today announce the landing of our troops near Fort Fisher—I will get the papers in the course of an hour and send you full Extracts" Telegram received (at 4:00 p.m.), DNA, RG 107, Telegrams Collected (Bound). *O.R.*, I, xlii, part 3, 1080. On the same day, USG telegraphed to Stanton. "The following items are found in todays Richmond papers—'An official despatch from Genl Beauregard dated December 25th and received yesterday states that Genl Hardee reports that a force of the Enemy Infantry Artillery and Cavalry has moved from Savannah towards the Altamaha River: Gen'l Hardee has made proper disposition to check the column—The object of this column is probably to destroy the Savannah Albany & Gulf Rail Road—Its depots. etc. No report has been received from General Hood since the 28th of November. Wilmington N. C. Dec 25th   The Enemy's fleet over fifty vessels including two monitors several armed vessels and many heavily armed frigates and sloops of war made a furious attack on fort Fisher about one oclock yesterday and kept up an average fire of thirty shots per minute until night. Our loss is twenty three 23 wounded. The attack was renewed at ten oclock this morning The attack has been very furious and continues. No report of casualties today. Colonel Lamb who is in command of the fort replied to the enemy's fire slowly and deliberately   The Enemy under cover of the heavy fire landed about three 3 brigades two and a half miles above fort Fisher. They were immediately engaged by a smaller force—The Enemy held his ground at night—Second despatch!— Wilmington N. C. Dec 26th   The Enemy's Infantry attacked fort Fisher last night   they were repulsed with considerable loss. There was heavy rain and wind through the night. Prisoners report the twenty fourth corps of the Yankee

Army present under Butler. Wilmington! From our Wilmington telegrams it will be seen that the Yankee fleet attacked fort Fisher about one oclock P. M on Saturday & bombarded it heavily till night fall renewing the bombardment at ten oclock a m on Sunday and continuing it throughout the day that under cover of the fire of the fleet the Enemy landed an Infantry force about fort Fisher which attacked the fort on Sunday night & were repulsed—Fort Fisher is situated on a sand spit of the right bank of the Cape Fear River at its mouth twenty miles below Wilmington. The Enemy we presume reached their position above the fort not by passing up the river when they would have been obliged to run the gauntlet of the guns both of Fisher & Fort Caswell on the left bank but, by landing on the beach west of the mouth of the Cape Fear River—The Enemy's having effected a lodgement above the Fort is a serious matter. It will cost double the force to dislodge him that would have prevented his landing—The Raid on on Pollard!—Mobile Dec 19th. 1864. The Yanke raiders from Pensacola to Pollard destroyed all public and some private buildings, damaged the Road inconsiderably and the bridge over the Escambia was partly destroyed—Captain Henry Pope Qr Master was captured—A few negroes were stolen. Yesterday our forces pursued them. A portion of their supplies and transportation were captured— The road was strewn with their dead. There was an Infantry force of another raiding party near Goods Mills and Pensacola—Sunday its advance was met by our cavalry and driven back several miles. Captain Semmes arrived here yesterday from Europe via Matamoras' " Telegrams received (2—at 5:15 P.M.), DNA, RG 107, Telegrams Collected (Bound). At 8:00 P.M., Butler telegraphed to USG. "I have just returned from the expedition—We had a storm from Monday until Friday which was the earliest hour I could get out of Beaufort where I had put in for coal—most of the transport fleet having got out of coal and water— Without waiting for my return Admiral Porter exploded the torpedo at one (1) oclock on Friday Morning and commenced his attack at twelve fifty five (12-55) in the afternoon twelve (12) hours afterwards—He continued the bombardment of the fort until night—I arrived in the evening and commenced landing on the beach the next morning Got a portion of the troops on shore about two (2) oclock—Wietzal moved down upon the works capturing three hundred (300) men and ten (10) commissioned officers He brought his picket line within fifty yards of the work where he was opened upon by canister and musketry—He found seventeen (17) guns bearing upon the beach which was only wide enough for an assault of a thousand men in line—the guns protected by traverses and but one (1) dismounted notwithstanding the fire of the fleet had been opened upon them for five (5) hours—In the mean while the surf had so arisen as to render further landing nearly impracticable—After a thorough reconnoisance of the work finding it utterly impracticable for a land assault and that at least two (2) brigades of Hokes Division from before Richmond had arrived there and that the rest was on the road I withdrew the forces and ordered a reembarkation and had got on board all of the troops with the exception of about three hundred (300) when the surf was so high as to prevent either getting on or off the shore —I lay by until morning and took measures for their relief as soon as the sea might go down—They were under cover of the gunboats and I have no doubt they are all safely off—Our loss when I left was but twelve (12) wounded ten (10) of whom were by the shells of the Navy on our picket line near the fort— I will be up in the morning—" LS (telegram sent), *ibid.*, Telegrams Collected

(Unbound); telegram received (marked as sent at 9:30 P.M.), *ibid.*, Telegrams Collected (Bound); (at 10:00 P.M.) *ibid.*, RG 108, Letters Received. *O.R.*, I, xlii, part 1, 965–66; *ibid.*, I, xlii, part 3, 1085–86.

Addressee Unknown

City Point, Va, Dec. 27th *1864*.

DEAR SIR:

Your letter of the 20th in reply to one from me to your brother is received. I am under many obligations to you for the trouble you have taken in looking up a horse for me. I have no doubt but the mare you speak of would suit me and the price named would be quite low enough for a horse to drive with the one I have which I am told cost 2700 when Greenbacks were worth nearly double what they now are. It would suit me better however to have a horse two or three months later than to have one now which I could not use nor would not make arrangements to use before Spring. I do not therefore know exactly what to say in the matter. I believe you may say to let other parties take the mare. Give my kindest regards to your brother when he returns.

Yours truly
U. S. GRANT

ALS, MiD. The name of W. P. Trowbridge, written as docketing, then cancelled, may indicate the addressee. William P. Trowbridge, USMA 1848, brother of USG's friend from Detroit, Charles A. Trowbridge (*PUSG*, 9, 588), resigned in 1856 and became a prominent engineer in New York City and New Haven, Conn.

To Abraham Lincoln

(Cipher) City Point, Va, Dec. 28th 1864 [*8:30* P.M.]
A. LINCOLN, PRESIDENT.

The Wilmington expeditoin has proven a gross and culpipable failure. Many of the troops are now back here. Delays and free talk

of the object of the expedition enabled the enemy to move troops
~~there~~ to Wilmington to defeat it. After the expedition sailed from
Ft. Monroe three days of fine weather was squandered during
which ~~nothing~~ the enemy was without a force to protect himself.
Who is to blame I hope will be known.

U. S. GRANT
Lt. Gn.

ALS (telegram sent), CSmH; telegram received (at 9:35 P.M.), DLC-Robert T.
Lincoln. *O.R.*, I, xlii, part 3, 1087. A facsimile of the telegram sent in Stan. V.
Henkels, Catalogue No. 1194, June 8, 1917, following p. 32, apparently a manifold copy, has the time sent noted at the top (not in USG's hand), and the un-
corrected word "culpipable." On Dec. 28, 1864, 5:30 P.M., President Abraham
Lincoln telegraphed to USG. "If there be no objection, please tell me what you
now understand of the Wilmington expedition, present & prospective." ALS
(telegram sent), DNA, RG 107, Telegrams Collected (Bound); telegram received, *ibid.*, RG 108, Letters Received. *O.R.*, I, xlii, part 3, 1087. Lincoln,
Works, VIII, 187.

To Robert Ould

City Point Va. Dec. 28th 1864

JUDGE RO. OULD,
AGT. OF. EX.,
SIR

Immediately on receipt of yours of yesterday in relation to cotton being on board Steamer at Mobile, waiting notice of readiness
on the part of the United States Authorities to receive it, I telegraphed to the Sec. of War as follows. "Judge Ould informs me
that One thousand bales of Cotton were on shipboard at Mobile on
the 25th waiting a declairation of readiness on the part of the Federal Authorities to receive the same. I supposed ~~such~~ the Commanding officer at Mobile had been notified long ago to receive the
Cotton when offered and that it had been received in New York
before this. Will you please have the notice given ~~at once~~ now."[1]

I think there has been blundering elsewhere than at Wash-

ington. All the correspondence between Gen. Lee, you and myself
has been promptly forwarded there, and I have, never received
notice of disapproval of any part of my course. Immediately on
notifying you that your request to ship one thousand bales of cotton
from Mobile was acceded to, I telegraphed or wrote, to Washington asking notice to be sent to the Federal Commander in
Mobile Bay of this agreement, and to instruct him to notify, under
flag of truce, the Commanding Officer in Mobile his readiness to
receive the Cotton whenever the letter was ready to deliver it.

Resplly
your obt. Servt.
U. S. GRANT
Lt. General

Copies, DLC-USG, V, 45, 71, 107; DNA, RG 94, Letters Received, 55A 1865;
ibid., RG 108, Letters Sent. *O.R.*, II, vii, 1290. On Dec. 27, 1864, C.S.A. Agent
of Exchange Robert Ould wrote to USG. "I have received information from Mobile, of the date of the 25th inst. that the thousand bales of cotton were on board
of a steamer at that place, waiting for a declaration of readiness on the part of
the Federal authorities to receive the same. Before the receipt of that information,
I was strongly in hopes that the cotton was on its way to New York. If in any
manner you can hasten the time of its reception on board a Federal vessel, I will
be obliged to you." LS, DNA, RG 108, Letters Received. *O.R.*, II, vii, 1281. On
Dec. 30, USG wrote to Secretary of War Edwin M. Stanton. "I have the honor
to transmit herewith copies of correspondence between Judge Ould and myself
upon the matter of supplying blankets to our prisoners at and in the vicinity of
Richmond, also letters relating to the general supplying of prisoners for both
sides, and the shipment of Confederate Cotton from Mobile" LS, DNA, RG 94,
Letters Received, 55A 1865. *O.R.*, II, vii, 1296. The enclosures are listed *ibid.*
On Dec. 29, Maj. Gen. Henry W. Halleck endorsed to USG a copy of his letter
of Nov. 19 to Maj. Gen. Gordon Granger authorizing him to receive the cotton.
AES, DNA, RG 108, Letters Received. *O.R.*, II, vii, 1141. The enclosure is
ibid., pp. 1140–41.

1. Text taken from USG to Stanton, Dec. 28, 8:30 P.M. ALS (telegram
sent), CSmH; telegram received (at 9:35 P.M.), DNA, RG 107, Telegrams Collected (Bound). *O.R.*, II, vii, 1286. On Dec. 29, noon, Stanton telegraphed to
USG. "The General Halleck informs me that the necessary notice & orders in
respect to the cotton were forwarded sometime ago in duplicate to Generals
Canby and Granger. They are repeated today." ALS (telegram sent—misdated
Dec. 28), DNA, RG 107, Telegrams Collected (Bound); telegram received,
ibid., RG 108, Letters Received. *O.R.*, II, vii, 1292. On Dec. 30, USG endorsed
a copy of this telegram to Ould. Copies, DLC-USG, V, 71, 107; DNA, RG 94,
Letters Received, 55A 1865. *O.R.*, II, vii, 1292.

To Robert Ould

City Point, Va., Dec. 28th 1864

JUDGE RO OULD,
AGT. OF EXCHANGE,
SIR;

Your communication of the 27th inst. acknowledging receipt of Brig Gen. Wm N. R Beall's letter is recieved.[1] I think no better plan than that proposed by you for the distribution of contrubutions for prisoners of war, can be divised.

Viz: "The reception of supplies and their subsequent distribution among the prisoners on both sides, shall be certified by a committe of officers confined in the prisons so supplied. Such a parole will be given by such offices as will enable them to carry out this agreement with due facility. They will report through the proper officer their proceedings to their Governments."

As I understand it, under this arrangement but one officer of each party will be necessary as a General Agent to receive all supplies. This General Agent will consign such supplies to some one named officer at each prison to be supplied, and see that they reacher such officer. The consignee, with two other officers to be selected by him, will constitute a committe to attend to the distribution for that particular prison, and will forward a certified Statement of the amount recieved and distributed, to the respective Governments, through their proper General Agents

Respectfully
Your Obt. Servant
U. S GRANT
Lt. General

Copies, DLC-USG, V, 45, 71, 107; DNA, RG 94, Letters Received, 55A 1865; *ibid.*, RG 108, Letters Sent. *O.R.*, II, vii, 1290. On Dec. 27, 1864, C.S.A. Agent of Exchange Robert Ould wrote to USG. "Your note of the 24th inst. has been received. You can send as many blankets for the benefit of the Federal prisoners in Richmond as you may think proper. If you choose, you may send others for those confined at other places. The blankets will be received at Boulware's wharf (otherwise named the 'Graveyard') on James River. In order to give you sufficient time, I would suggest next Saturday, the 31st inst. at one O'clock P. M. as the day and hour when the articles will be received. The four officers highest in rank (not in Hospital) now at the Libby are Lt. Col. Hutchins 1st N. H. Cav. Major W. N. Owens 1st Ken. Cav. Capt. J. M. Wallace 3d Del. and Capt. J. M. Watson 2d N. Y. Mounted Rifles. You can select either one of them as the consignee. I will deliver the blankets to him, taking his receipts in duplicate one of which I will forward to you. He and as many assistants as he may need will be given such a parole as will enable them to discharge their duty effectively. Every reasonable and proper effort will be made by the Confederate authorities to secure such a distribution as you may desire. By using the word 'blankets,' I do not wish to be understood as limiting the supplies to that article." LS, DNA, RG 108, Letters Received. *O.R.*, II, vii, 1281. On Dec. 28, USG wrote to Ould. "I will cause one thousand blankets to be conveyed on the 31st to the point indicated by your communication of the 27th inst. The blankets will be consigned to the care of Lt. Col. Hutchins 1st. N. H. Cavalry, for distribution among Prisoners of War (Federal) confined in Richmond and vicinity" Copies, DLC-USG, V, 45, 71, 107; DNA, RG 94, Letters Received, 55A 1864; *ibid.*, RG 108, Letters Sent; USG 3. *O.R.*, II, vii, 1289–90.

Also on Dec. 28, Lt. Col. Theodore S. Bowers issued Special Orders No. 159. "Maj. Gen. B. F. Butler, Com'd'g Army of the James, will send forward and deliver to Judge Ro. Ould, Agent of Exchange, C. S. A., at Boulwares Wharf on the James River, at 1 o'clock P. M., Saturday Dec. 31st, 1864, One Thousand Army Blankets, consigned to Lieut Col Hutchins, 1st New-Hampshire Cavalry, for distribution to Federal Prisoners of War confined at Richmond and vicinity." ADS, DNA, RG 94, Letters Received, 55A 1865. *O.R.*, II, vii, 1291. On the same day, Brig. Gen. John A. Rawlins wrote to Maj. Gen. Benjamin F. Butler. "Please instruct Lieut Col Hutchins, 1st N. H. Cavalry, Consignee of blankets for Federal prisoners at Richmond to be sent through Judge Ould on the 31st inst, to distribute said blankets among such of our prisoners at Richmond as may be without blankets, at the rate of one to each officer and enlisted man. Such of them as are already supplied with that number will not be furnished additional ones. Should he have any on hand after supplying our prisoners at and in the vicinity of Richmond, he will procure them to be sent and distributed in like manner among our prisoners at the nearest point to Richmond where we may have any." Copies, DLC-USG, V, 45, 71, 107; DNA, RG 94, Letters Received, 55A 1865; *ibid.*, RG 108, Letters Sent; USG 3. *O.R.*, II, vii, 1291.

On Jan. 6, 1865, Ould endorsed to USG receipts for 1500 blankets distributed to U.S. prisoners in Richmond. ES, DNA, RG 108, Letters Received. Shortly thereafter, USG endorsed copies of these receipts to Secretary of War Edwin M. Stanton. Copy, DLC-USG, V, 58. See *O.R.*, II, viii, 71–73.

1. William N. R. Beall, born in Ky., USMA 1848, resigned from the U.S. Army as of Aug. 20, 1861. Captured at Port Hudson as a C.S.A. brig. gen. in July, 1863, he was imprisoned until Dec. 6, 1864, when released from Fort Warren, Mass., to participate in prisoner relief. *Ibid.*, II, vii, 1199–1200. See *ibid.*, pp. 1194–95, 1227, 1279–80. On Dec. 27, Ould wrote to USG. "I have received Brig Gen. Wm. N. R. Beall's letter and your indorsement thereon. If you will refer to my letter of the 11th of November last, addressed to yourself, you will find this paragraph, to wit: 'The reception of supplies and their subsequent distribution amongst the prisoners on both sides, shall be certified by a committee of officers confined in the prisons so supplied. Such a parole will be

given to such officers as will enable them to carry out this agreement with due facility. They will report through the proper agents, their proceedings to their respective governments.' When I framed the foregoing paragraph, my idea was that a Committee of three from each prison on both sides would be selected and paroled to atte[nd] to the distribution at the prison to which the Committee belonged. That seemed to me to be the best plan. If it was carried out, there would be on each side three times as many persons selected as there were prisons. I now again respectfully suggest that this plan be adopted. If you desire that six or more Federal officers sha[ll] be paroled to attend to the *reception* of such supplies as you may send, it will be done, although I do not see the necessity for any such number. It will take more to attend to the *distribution*. As many will be paroled for the latter purpose as you desire. I take it for granted that when supplies are sent, they will be consigned to some one named party. He will give duplicate receipts for the same, one of which will be forwarded to your government. If it does not correspond to the invoice, some irregularity will have intermediately taken place, which can be detected and corrected. The consignee and two others (to be named by him if you choose) will attend to the distribution at the particular prison and will forward a certificate of that fact to their Government. It seems to me that this plan is simple and will be effective. If you will suggest any other, or any addition to the foregoing, which will more effectually carry out the views of both parties for the speedy and certain relief of prisoners on both sides, it will be cheerfully adopted by our side. You may rest assured that the Confederate authorities will consent to any measure that will best secure the end proposed. If this plan is adopted, it would be well to have at least three officers at each prison on both sides" LS, DNA, RG 108, Letters Received. *O.R.*, II, vii, 1281–82.

On Feb. 7, 1865, USG endorsed a letter of Jan. 26 from Beall to Ould. "Respy transmitted to Judge Ould, Agent of Exchange, C. S. A. The three communications alluded to were not forwarded for the reason that the subject matter to which they related was acted upon here, and it was not deemed necessary to trouble you with them" Copy, DLC-USG, V, 58.

To Maj. Gen. Henry W. Halleck

(Cipher)   City Point, Va, Dec. 23st [29] 1864 [*10:30* P.M.]
MAJ. GEN. HALLECK, WASHINGTON

By all means stop the purchase of horses in the East and curtail it in the West. Now that Hood is disposed of there will be less necessity for cavalry there than heretofore.

U. S. GRANT
Lt. Gen.

ALS (telegram sent), CSmH; telegram received (at 11:00 P.M.), DNA, RG 107, Telegrams Collected (Bound). *O.R.*, I, xlii, part 3, 1091. On Dec. 29, 1864, 12:30 P.M., Maj. Gen. Henry W. Halleck telegraphed to USG. "There are now in this depôt over two thousand serviceable artillery horses, & over one thousand cavalry horses for issue. There are over ten thousand other cavalry horses which will probably be fit for issue within sixty days, and about a thousand which will answer for teams & ambulances. There are also some two thousand in hospital a part of which will be sold. There are also a considerable number in northern depôts which are kept there for convenience of forage. All approved requisitions from Sheridan's army, the Potomac & the James have been filled. Sherman is abundantly supplied. The difficulty of procuring forage in the north & east is already creating serious apprehensions of a failure of supply before spring. Under these circumstances the cavalry Bureau & Quarter Mr. Genl strongly urge that purchases at the north & East be discontinued till spring. Those at the west & Northwest for Thomas & Canby's forces must go on. Moreover, the Qr Mr. Genl has fifty millions of unpaid requisitions in the Treasury Dept, and unless the greatest economy is practiced the demands of government creditors cannot be met. If you have no objections the War Dept will stop the purchases as requested by the Qr. Mr. Genl." ALS (telegram sent), DNA, RG 107, Telegrams Collected (Bound); telegram received, *ibid.*; *ibid.*, RG 108, Letters Received. *O.R.*, I, xlii, part 3, 1090–91. See letter to Maj. Gen. Henry W. Halleck, Jan. 6, 1865.

On Jan. 3, 1865, 7:45 P.M., Lt. Col. Theodore S. Bowers telegraphed to Maj. Gen. Benjamin F. Butler and Maj. Gen. John G. Parke. "Put all team animals of your army on half rations & all cavalry horses on three quarters rations of forages until further orders" Telegram received, DLC-Benjamin F. Butler; DNA, RG 94, War Records Office, Army of the Potomac; copies, *ibid.*, RG 108, Letters Sent; DLC-USG, V, 46, 71, 107; Meade Papers, PHi. *O.R.*, I, xlvi, part 2, 19. At 8:30 P.M., Parke telegraphed to Bowers. "Your despatch directing a reduction of the forage ration has been received." Copies, DNA, RG 94, War Records Office, Army of the Potomac; *ibid.*, RG 393, Army of the Potomac, Letters Sent. *O.R.*, I, xlvi, part 2, 19. On Jan. 13, USG telegraphed to Maj. Gen. George G. Meade and Maj. Gen. Edward O. C. Ord. "Cavalry and Artillery horses may now be given full forage." ALS (telegram sent), Kohns Collection, NN; telegram received (at 10:15 A.M.), DNA, RG 94, War Records Office, Army of the Potomac; (at 11:30 A.M.) *ibid.*, RG 107, Telegrams Collected (Unbound); *ibid.*, RG 393, 24th Army Corps, Telegrams Received; (dated only Jan.) Ord Papers, CU-B. *O.R.*, I, xlvi, part 2, 113. On Jan. 18, USG telegraphed to Meade and Ord. "Full rations of grain and half rations of hay may now be issued to all animals." ALS (telegram sent), Kohns Collection, NN; telegram received (torn), DNA, RG 393, Army of the Potomac, Miscellaneous Letters Received; *ibid.*, Dept. of Va. and N. C., Telegrams Received.

To Edwin M. Stanton

From City Point Va Dec 30th 12. m *1864.*

HON EDWIN M. STANTON
SECY OF WAR.

I have ordered the Chief Quarter master to reassemble at Fort Monroe all the transports used by Genl Butler and additional ones sufficient to carry fifteen hundred men—eight thousand in all—and to have them fueled and watered to their fullest capacity for carrying troops: He thinks it can be done by Monday[1] morning—Not a person here knows the object of this but myself, Chief of Staff and Cipher Operator, who has to know it of course—It will not be known to another—

When all is ready I will send the troops and Commander selected to Fort Monroe and out to sea with sealed instructions, not to be opened until they pass the heads—

I would advise that Admiral Porter simply be directed to hold on as he is until he receives further orders from the Department: you will understand why I would say no more—

I am in hopes, by secrecy, the enemy may be lulled into such security as to induce him to send his Wilmington forces against Sherman or bring them back here, by the time we are ready to start. There will be no delay on the part of the troops

U. S. GRANT Lt Genl

Telegram received (at 7:00 P.M.), DNA, RG 107, Telegrams Collected (Bound); copies, *ibid.*, Telegrams Received in Cipher; *ibid.*, RG 108, Letters Sent; DLC-USG, V, 45, 71, 107. *O.R.*, I, xlii, part 3, 1098–99. On Dec. 30, 1864, 9:00 P.M., Secretary of War Edwin M. Stanton telegraphed to USG. "Your despatch of twelve noon today, just received, and I am rejoiced at its indications. No living man shall know any thing upon the subject from me except the Secretary of the Navy. I would suggest an express from you to Porter to let him know at the earliest ~~date~~ possible moment what to expect before he leaves." ALS (telegram sent), DNA, RG 107, Telegrams Collected (Bound); telegram received, *ibid.*, RG 108, Letters Received. *O.R.*, I, xlii, part 3, 1099. At 11:00 P.M., USG telegraphed to Stanton. "I will write and dispatch to Porter to go off to-night." ALS (telegram sent), Kohns Collection, NN; telegram received (at 11:45 P.M.), DNA, RG 107, Telegrams Collected (Bound). *O.R.*, I, xlii, part 3, 1100.

On Dec. 28, 3:30 P.M., Stanton telegraphed to USG. "The Navy Department has received two despatches which I have ordered to be sent to you. Fultons despatch indicates that Porter intends to continue the operations against Fort Fisher and hopes for success. Mr Fox goes down this evening to Fortress Monroe to consult with you about sending additional ~~force~~ land troops—" ALS (telegram sent), DNA, RG 107, Telegrams Collected (Bound); telegram received, *ibid.*, RG 108, Letters Received. *O.R.*, I, xlii, part 3, 1087. On Dec. 29, 12:10 P.M., USG, Fort Monroe, telegraphed to Maj. Thomas T. Eckert. "When did Sect Fox leave Washington." Copy, DNA, RG 94, War Records Office, Miscellaneous War Records. At 1:30 P.M., USG telegraphed to Asst. Secretary of the Navy Gustavus V. Fox. "I return to City Point immediately [h]aving learned that you have not yet [l]eft Washington" Telegram received (at 2:15 P.M.),

ibid., RG 45, Miscellaneous Telegrams Received. *O.R.*, I, li, part 1, 1197; *O.R.*
(Navy), I, xi, 388. On the same day, Fox telegraphed to USG. "I waited for
Porter's dispatches. Mr. Blair will explain. He reached Fort Monroe at 6 P. M.,
having left yesterday at 2 P. M. Mr. Welles has sent you a telegram in cipher,
which could not be sent until dispatches arrived. Porter will continue his fire but
it is hopeless alone." Copy, DNA, RG 45, Confidential Letters Sent. *O.R.* (Navy),
I, xi, 388. At 9:30 P.M., Secretary of the Navy Gideon Welles telegraphed to
USG. "The substance of dispatches and reports from Rear Admiral Porter, off
Wilmington, is briefly this; The ships can approach nearer to the enemy's works
than was anticipated. Their fire can keep the enemy away from their guns. A
landing can easily be effected upon the beach north of Fort Fisher, not only of
troops but all their supplies and artillery. This force can have its flanks protected by gunboats. The Navy can assist in the siege of Ft. Fisher precisely as
it covered the operations which resulted in the capture of Ft. Wagner. The winter season is the most favorable for operations against Ft. Fisher. The largest
naval force ever assembled is ready to lend its co-operation. Rear Admiral Porter
will remain off Ft. Fisher continuing a moderate fire to prevent new works from
being erected, and the ironclads have proved that they can maintain themselves
in spite of bad weather. Under all these circumstances I invite you to such a military co-operation as will ensure the fall of Ft. Fisher, the importance of which
has already received your careful consideration. This telegram is made at the
suggestion of the President and in hopes that you will be able, at this time, to give
the troops which heretofore were required elsewhere. If it cannot be done the
fleet will have to disperse whence it cannot again be brought to this coast." LS
(telegram sent), DNA, RG 107, Telegrams Collected (Bound); telegram received (on Dec. 30—marked as sent by Stanton), *ibid.*, RG 108, Letters Received. Printed as sent by Welles in *O.R.*, I, xlii, part 3, 1091; *O.R.* (Navy), I,
xi, 391–92. On Dec. 30, 10:30 A.M., USG telegraphed to Stanton. "Your telegram of 9.30 last evening just received—I will answer fully in a few hours—
Troops have all returned and transports dispursed" Telegrams received (2—
at 11:50 A.M. and 7:00 P.M.), DNA, RG 107, Telegrams Collected (Bound);
copies, *ibid.*, RG 108, Letters Sent; DLC-USG, V, 45, 71, 107. *O.R.*, I, xlii,
part 3, 1098. See following telegram.

1. Jan. 2, 1865.

To Edwin M. Stanton

(Cipher)   City Point, Va. Dec. 30th 1864 [2:00 P.M.]
HON. E. M. STANTON, SEC. OF WAR,

The accompanying dispatch was received over your signature
and answered. Subsequently a dispatch from operator was received
stating that it should have been signed G. Wells, Sec. of the Navy.
It is all right however for I do not propose to correspond with the
Navy Dept about Military operations except through you. My first

dispatch gives all that I would advise should be said to the Sec. of
the Navy for the present.

U. S. ~~GRANT~~

~~Lt. Gn.~~

I will say to Mr. Welles that I will advise with you about
further operations against Wilmington and he can get his information from you.

U. S. GRANT.

Lt. Gn.

ALS (facsimile telegram sent), Louis A. Coolidge, *Ulysses S. Grant* (Boston
and New York, 1922), between pp. 188–89; telegram received (at 7:00 P.M.),
DNA, RG 107, Telegrams Collected (Bound). *O.R.*, I, xlii, part 3, 1099. See
preceding telegram. On Dec. 30, 1864, 2:00 P.M., USG telegraphed to Secretary of the Navy Gideon Welles. "Your despatch 9.30 P. M 29th received—I
will advise fully with the Secretary of War about what you propose. Please call
on him for information" Telegram received (at 7:00 P.M.), DNA, RG 45, Miscellaneous Telegrams Received; *ibid.*, RG 107, Telegrams Collected (Bound);
copies (2), *ibid.*, Telegrams Received in Cipher; *ibid.*, RG 108, Letters Sent;
DLC-USG, V, 45, 71, 107. *O.R.*, I, xlii, part 3, 1100; *O.R.* (Navy), I, xi, 392.
     At 10:00 P.M. and 11:00 P.M., Secretary of War Edwin M. Stanton tele-
graphed to USG. "Ingalls requisition upon Meigs for the return of the transportation will of course set him and all the thousand and one guessers at work to nose
out the object—You cannot count upon any secrecy in the Navy. Newspaper
reporters have the run of that Department. Might it not throw them off to give
out here confidentially that the troops are going to Sherman to enable him to
march through the interior and garrison important points or else to attack Mobile. ~~Major Casey was detail~~" LS (telegram sent), DNA, RG 107, Telegrams
Collected (Bound); telegram received (on Dec. 31, 12:30 A.M.), *ibid.*, RG 108,
Letters Received. *O.R.*, I, xlii, part 3, 1099. "Major Casey a very intelligent officer of ~~the~~ Engineers ~~Department~~ was detailed to observe and report on the Torpedo Explosion. He seems a wide awake man and to have used his time ~~very~~
profitably in ~~noticing~~ acquiring information of the localities. If you have not seen
him he may be useful to you. Shall I send him to see you" ALS (telegram sent),
DNA, RG 107, Telegrams Collected (Bound); telegram received (on Dec. 31,
12:30 P.M.), *ibid.*, RG 108, Letters Received. *O.R.*, I, xlii, part 3, 1100.

To Maj. Gen. Henry W. Halleck

(Cipher)   City Point, Va, Dec. ~~23~~ 30th/64 1 a. m.
MAJ. GEN. HALLECK, WASHINGTON.

     My understanding was that Fort ~~Gibson~~ Smith and other posts
in Arkansas West of Little Rock were ordered abandoned solely

because Gen. Steele had failed to supply them in season. The
Statement of Gen. Steele brought by Capt. [*William Willard*]
Smith of your Staff shews that Fort Smith at least is supplied
and can be suppled by the Ark. River. I would order Fort Smith
held on to and all the other posts that can be suppled.

U. S. GRANT
Lt. Gen.

ALS (telegram sent), CSmH; telegram received (at 9:00 A.M.), DNA, RG
107, Telegrams Collected (Bound); DLC-Robert T. Lincoln. *O.R.*, I, xli, part 4,
962. On Dec. 28, 1864, Maj. Gen. Henry W. Halleck wrote to USG. "I enclose
herewith, by direction of the President, some papers in connexion with the orders
for the evacuation of Fort Smith, Ark. and its dependencies. I have not read
them, but presume they come from civilians interested in the maintenance &
supply of those posts. It is suggested that even if Forts Gibson & Smith are
abandoned for the winter, Fayettesville might be retained & supplied from Missouri. It is understood that the last train of supplies sent from Fort Scott has
been ~~supplied~~ captured by the enemy. It is understood here that no other trains
can be sent through during the winter. The President wishes you to examine
these papers and see of any modification of Genl Canby's order should be made.
I presume it has been executed by this time, or will be before despatches can
reach there. Please telegraph any orders you may decide upon." ALS, DNA, RG
108, Letters Received. *O.R.*, I, xli, part 4, 946.

To Maj. Gen. Henry W. Halleck

(Cipher)   City Point, Va Dec. 30th *1864*. [*11:00* P.M.]
MAJ. GEN. HALLECK, WASHINGTON.

I have no idea of keeping idle troops any place. But before taking troops away from Thomas it will be advisable to see whether
Hood halts his Army at Corinth. I do not think he will but think he
is much more likely to be thrown in front of Sherman. If so it will
be just where we want him to go. Let Thomas collect ~~his troops
that are out at Tuscumbia and Eastport as fast as possible and have
them ready to be shipped where ordered.~~ all troops not essential to
hold his communications at Eastport, if he chooses a part of them
at Tuscumbia, and be in readiness for their removal where they
can be used.

U. S. GRANT
Lt. Gn.

ALS (telegram sent), PHi; telegram received (at 11:45 P.M.), DNA, RG 107, Telegrams Collected (Bound). *O.R.*, I, xlv, part 2, 420. On Dec. 30, 1864, 1:30 P.M., Maj. Gen. Henry W. Halleck telegraphed to USG. "I think from the tone of Genl Thomas' telegram of last night that there is very little hope of his doing much further injury to Hood's army by pursuing it. You will percieve that he is disposed to postpone further operations till spring. This seems to me entirely wrong. In our present financial condition we cannot afford this delay. I therefore respectfully suggest whether Schofield and A. J. Smith with say twenty thousand men, should not be sent by water to Pascagoula to assist Canby in taking Mobile and then using it as a base against Selma & Montgomery. This would prevent any of Hood's force from being sent against Sherman, and the capture of Selma would be almost as disastrous to the enemy as that of Atlanta. Thomas with the remainder of his forces could certainly maintain the line of the Tennessee to Chatanooga. If Schofield should be sent, the two Depts, (Tenn & Ky.) should be united under Thomas. If Thomas was as active as Sherman I would say, march directly from Decatur to Taledega, Montgomery & Selma, living upon the country & anticipating Hood, should he move by Meridian. But I think Thomas entirely too slow to live on the country. He, however, will make the best possible defence. It is said that the rebels have a very large amount of supplies at Selma & Montgomery. If these can be captured & the Rail Roads destroyed, their western armies cannot get ammunition & ordnance stores. The reason for not suggesting that Schofield move from Vicksburg by Meridian is that the country is mostly stript of supplies & at this season very difficult of passage, while that from Mobile is less swampy, & moreover the operating army could be supplied by steamers on the Alabama river." ALS (telegram sent), DNA, RG 107, Telegrams Collected (Bound); telegram received, *ibid.*; *ibid.*, RG 108, Letters Received. *O.R.*, I, xlv, part 2, 419–20.

On Dec. 27, Maj. Gen. John M. Schofield, Columbia, Tenn., wrote to USG. "*Unofficial* . . . My eCorps was sent back to Tenn. by Genl. Sherman, instead of remaining with him on his march through Georgia, according to his original design, for two reasons, Viz:—1st Because Genl. Thomas was not regarded strong enough after it became evident that Hood designed to invade Tennessee, And—2d In order that I might fill up my Corps, from the new troops then arriving in Tennessee. These reasons now no longer exist. By uniting my troops to Stanley's we were able to hold Hood in check at Columbia, and Franklin until Genl. Thomas could concentrate at Nashville, and also to give Hood his death-blow at Franklin—Subsequent operations have shown how little fight was then left in his Army, and have taken that little out of it.—He now has not more than Fifteen thousand Infantry, about Ten thousand of whom, only, are armed, and they greatly demoralized. With time to reorganize and recruit he could not probably raise his force to more than half the strength he had at Franklin. Genl. Thomas has assigned several new regiments to my command, and I hope soon to make them effective, by distributing them in Old Brigades. I will have from Fifteen thousand to Eighteen thousand effective men—two-thirds of whom are the Veterans of the campaign in East Tennessee and Georgia.—A small force it is true, yet one which would at least be an appreciable addition to your Army in Virginia, or elsewhere, where decisive work is to be done. It may not be practicable now for me to join Genl. Sherman, but it would not be difficult to transfer my Command to Virginia.—I am aware that Genl. Thomas contemplates a 'Spring Campaign' into Alabama or Mississippi, with the Tennessee River as a base, and believe he considers my command a necessary part of the operating force. Without reference to the latter point, permit me to express the opinion that such a campaign would not be an economical or advantageous use of so many troops. If aggressive operations are to be continued in the Gulf States, it appears to me it would be much better to take Mobile and operate from that point, thus striking vital points (if there are any such), of rebel territory, by much shorter lines. But it appears to me that Lee's Army is virtually all that is left of the rebellion.—If we can concentrate force enough to destroy that we will destroy with it the rebel Government, and the occupation of the whole South will then be but a matter of a few weeks time. Excuse, General, the liberty I have taken in expressing my views thus freely and unsolicited. I have no other motive than a desire for the Nation's good, and a personal wish to serve where my little command can do the most. The change I suggest would of course deprive me of my ~~of~~ Department Command—But this would be a small loss to me or to the service. The present arrangement is an unsatisfactory one at best.—Nominally I command both a Department, and an Army in the field; but in fact, I do neither." ALS, DNA, RG 108, Letters Received; ADf, DLC-John M. Schofield. *O.R.*, I, xlv, part 2, 377–78.

To Maj. Gen. Henry W. Halleck

City Point, Va. Dec. 30th 1864

MAJ. GEN. H. W. HALLECK,
CHIEF OF STAFF OF THE ARMY
GENERAL,

The papers brought by Capt. Smith, of your Staff, reached me about One a. m. this morning, and were examined partially as soon as received and directions thereupon telegraphed to you. The papers will be more fully examined to day and if further suggestions are thought necessary they will be sent by Mail or telegraph according to the urgency.

The papers will be returned to-morrow

Very respectfully
U. S. GRANT
Lt Gn.

ALS, IHi.

To Rear Admiral David D. Porter

City Point, Dec, 30th 1864

DEAR ADMIRAL

Please hold on where you are for a few days, and I will endeavor to be back again with an increased force and without the former Commander. It is desirable the enemy should be lulled into all the security possible, in hopes he will send back here or against Sherman the reinforcements sent to defend Wilmington. At the same time it will be necessary to observe that that the enemy does not entrench further and if he attempts it, to prevent it. I will suggest whether it may not be made to appear that the ordinary Blockading Squadron is doing this. You however understand this matter much better than I do.

I cannot say what day our troops will be down. Your dispatch to the Secy of the Navy which informed me that you were still off Wilmington and still thought the capture of that place practicable was only rec'd to day I took immediate steps to have transports collected and am assured they will be ready with the coal and water on board by noon of the 2d of Jany There will be delay in embarking and sending off the troops.

There is not a soul here except my Chief of Staff Asst. Adj't. Genl. and myself know of this intended renewal of our effort against Wilmington. In Washington but two persons know of it and I am assured will not. The Commander of the expedition will probably be Maj. Genl. Terry. He will not know of it until he gets out to sea. He will go with sealed orders. It will not be necessary for me to let troops or Commander know even that they are going any place until the Steamers intended to carry them reach Fortress Monroe as I will have all rations, and other stores, loaded before hand.

The same troops that were with the first expedition reinforced by a Brigade will be sent now. If they effect a lodgment they can at least fortify and maintain themselves until reinforcements can be sent.

Please answer by bearer and designate where you will have the fleet congregate

> Very Respectfully
> Your ob't s'v't
> U. S. GRANT
> Lt. Genl.

REAR ADMIRAL PORTER
COMDG N'TH ATLANTIC BLOCKADING SQUADRON

Copies, DLC-USG, V, 45, 71, 107; DLC-William T. Sherman; DNA, RG 108, Letters Sent. *O.R.*, I, xlii, part 3, 1100–1; *O.R.* (Navy), I, xi, 394. On Jan. 1, 1865, Rear Admiral David D. Porter, Beaufort, N. C., wrote to USG. "I have just received yours of Dec. 30th. I shall be all ready; and thank god we are not to leave here with so easy a victory at hand. Thank you for so promptly trying to rectify the blunder so lately committed. I knew you would do it. I sent to General Sherman for troops, knowing he must be in Savannah. I would like the troops to rendezvous here. They should have provisions to last them on shore in case we are driven off by gales, but I can cover any number of of troops if it blows ever so hard. I held on here through all and the heaviest gales ever seen here. They seem to blow that I might show the commanders that we could ride it out at anchor. The rebels have no entrenchments nor will any they make avail them. We destroyed all their abattis, and made a beautiful bridge for the troops to cross on. They think they have whipt us. I made the ships go off as if they were crippled—some in tow. We lost one man killed! you may judge what a simple business it was. I will work night and day to be ready. We will have Wilmington in a week, weather permitting. Please impress the commander with the importance of consulting with me freely, as regards weather and landing." LS, CSmH. *O.R.*, I, xlvi, part 2, 5; *O.R.* (Navy), I, xi, 401–2.

To Maj. Gen. Benjamin F. Butler

City Point. Va. Dec. 30. [*1864*]

MAJ. GEN. B. F. BUTLER
COM'D'G ARMY OF THE JAMES

An investigation of the transportation matter complained of in your dispatch, shows that in the exchange of troops each command took its Regimental transportation and no more. Supply trains were neither sent or received.—Gen Ferriro tooke with him 9 Regiments and 32 teams. The Army of the Potomac received 6 Regiments and 12 ~~wagons~~. Teams. The difference betwen the two commands

was about 700. which would leave the Army of the James a gainer
in the transaction of 7 wagons, ~~and has nothing to complain of~~

U. S. GRANT

Lt. Gn.

LS (telegram sent), CSmH; telegram received, DLC-Benjamin F. Butler. On
Dec. 30, 1864, noon, Maj. Gen. Benjamin F. Butler telegraphed to USG. "When
General Ferraro's division of colored troops came from the Army of the Potomac
as is reported me by General Wietzal thier wagon train was kept by that army—
That leaves the third (3d) Division of my colored corps without wagons   Please
order the wagon train here which belongs to that Division—I do not exactly
understand why such action was taken—It certainly could not have been with
General Meades or Ingalls knowledge   The result in practice is that the 3d Division of the 25th Corps is without rations having no wagons to haul them—This
difficulty has not been experianced before because of the absence of the Expedi-
tionary Corps—" LS (telegram sent), DNA, RG 107, Telegrams Collected
(Unbound); telegram received, *ibid.*, RG 108, Letters Received. See *O.R.*, I,
xlii, part 3, 1102.

On the same day, USG telegraphed to Butler. "Please direct all the launches
used in your expedition against Wilmington to be sent to Fortress Monroe without delay." ALS (telegram sent), NHi; telegram received (misdated Dec. 31),
DLC-Benjamin F. Butler. On Dec. 31, Butler telegraphed to USG. "The
Launches will be Sent to the Chief Quarter Master at Ft Monroe"   Telegram
received (at 11:30 A.M.), DNA, RG 108, Letters Received; copies, *ibid.*, RG
107, Telegrams Collected (Unbound); *ibid.*, RG 393, Dept. of Va. and N. C.,
Telegrams Sent (Press). On Dec. 30, USG telegraphed to Butler. "I would give
no furlough except in extreme cases. Our veterans have had their furloughs and
the balance have either been but a short time in service or have but a short time
to remain." Telegram received, *ibid.*, RG 107, Telegrams Collected (Unbound);
copies, *ibid.*, RG 108, Letters Sent; DLC-USG, V, 45, 71, 107. On Jan. 9, 1865,
11:00 A.M., Maj. Gen. Edward O. C. Ord telegraphed to Brig. Gen. John A.
Rawlins. "Genl Butler has authorised Corps Commanders to grant furloughs to
one tenth their Commands—is it desirable to do so now—" ALS (telegram
sent), DNA, RG 107, Telegrams Collected (Unbound); telegram received,
ibid., RG 108, Letters Received. Rawlins replied by transmitting a copy of
USG's Dec. 30, 1864, telegram to Butler. Telegram received (at 11:45 A.M.),
ibid., RG 393, Dept. of Va. and N. C., Telegrams Received; copies, *ibid.*, RG
108, Letters Sent; DLC-USG, V, 46, 71, 107.

On Dec. 30, noon, Butler telegraphed to USG. "I am ready now to clear out
Dutch Gap—I think it best that we should get the channel opened as soon as
possible—I will proceed ~~now~~ if you see no objection" LS (telegram sent), DNA,
RG 107, Telegrams Collected (Unbound); telegram received, *ibid.*, RG 108,
Letters Received. On the same day, USG telegraphed to Butler. "I see no objection. On the contrary think it advisable to push it." Telegram received (at 3:45
P.M.), DLC-Benjamin F. Butler; copies, DLC-USG, V, 45, 71, 107; DNA, RG
108, Letters Sent. On Dec. 31, noon, Butler telegraphed to USG. "We propose
to explode the heading of Dutch Gap at 11. A M Tomorrow   I should be happy
to see yourself and friends. ~~if you choose to~~ at head Qrs   We must be near the
time because of the tide" ALS (telegram sent), *ibid.*, RG 107, Telegrams Col-

lected (Unbound); telegram received (misdated Jan. 1, 1865), *ibid.*, RG 108, Letters Received. *O.R.*, I, xlii, part 3, 1112. On Dec. 31, 1864, USG telegraphed to Butler. "Do not wait for me in your explosion. I doubt my ability to be up in the morning." ALS (telegram sent), Kohns Collection, NN; telegram received, DNA, RG 107, Telegrams Collected (Unbound). *O.R.*, I, xlii, part 3, 1112. On the same day, USG telegraphed to Butler and to Maj. Gen. John G. Parke. "To the end that our men may spend a quiet New Years day direct that there be no firing to-morrow except in reply to guns from the enemy. The usual vigilence however is to be preserved." ALS (telegram sent), CSmH; telegram received, DNA, RG 94, War Records Office, Army of the Potomac; *ibid.*, Engineering Branch; *ibid.*, RG 107, Telegrams Collected (Unbound); (2) *ibid.*, RG 393, Army of the Potomac, Telegrams Received. Printed as sent at 11:10 A.M. in *O.R.*, I, xlii, part 3, 1110. On the same day, Parke telegraphed to USG transmitting a telegram of 10:30 A.M. from Maj. Gen. Horatio G. Wright. "The Enemy made an attack upon the picket line on my front this morning at about 5 oclock on the left of the 1st Div & right of the 3d & succeeded in Killing 2 men & wounding 3. 37 men are reported missing the line was very soon established as before & all has been quiet since" Telegram received, DNA, RG 108, Letters Received. *O.R.*, I, xlii, part 3, 1106.

On Jan. 17, 1865, 12:53 P.M., Ord telegraphed to USG. "Shall I disconue work on Dutch Gap? The Commodore of the River flotilla has stated to me that he would not attempt to go through the canal if completed until the Batteries now commanding it and the river above are captured ~~on both banks of James River, as far up as he might be required to go~~—of course the canal is E. O. C. ~~Ord—Maj Genl~~—The freshet has washed in a quantity of earth from the Banks and the amount of labor to clear out the canal is reported by the Engineer to be still very large—and the labor very dangerous—" ALS (telegram sent), DNA, RG 107, Telegrams Collected (Unbound); telegram received, *ibid.*, RG 108, Letters Received. *O.R.*, I, xlvi, part 2, 164. On the same day, Lt. Col. Theodore S. Bowers telegraphed to Ord. "You may stop work on the Dutch Gap canal." Telegram received (at 5:30 P.M.), Ord Papers, CU-B; copies, DLC-USG, V, 46, 71, 107; DNA, RG 108, Letters Sent. *O.R.*, I, xlvi, part 2, 164.

To Edwin M. Stanton

(Cipher)   City Point, Va. Dec. 31st 1864 [*11:00* A.M.]
HON. E. M. STANTON, SEC. OF WAR, WASHINGTON

The chief Com.y goes from here this morning to Fortress Monroe to provision the steames collecting there and I had given directions his guess as to object was that steamers were going after Shermans Army to bring them here. He has not yet received any orders and does not even know that steamers are being collected. I will instruct him to say confidentially that he thinks we are either sending for Sherman or that we are going to reinforce him inclining to the latter opinion.

U. S. GRANT
Lt. Gn.

ALS (telegram sent), PPRF; telegram received (on Jan. 1, 1865, 10:00 A.M.), DNA, RG 107, Telegrams Collected (Bound). *O.R.*, I, xlii, part 3, 1106. See telegram to Gustavus V. Fox, Jan. 2, 1865.

To Edwin M. Stanton

———

City Point, Va. Dec. 31st 1864

HON. E. M. STANTON,
SEC. OF WAR,
SIR:

In all the promotions given by brevet, and especially in the Staff Departments, about the most meritorious among the Quartermasters has been overlooked. I mean Brig. Gen. Robt. Allen. Being absent from commanders making recommendations he has not been thought of.

It is not necessary for me to say any thing about the services or merits of General Allen as they are as well known at the Dept. as by any one else. I would therefore respectfully recommend that he be promoted to the rank of Brigadier General, by Brevet, in the Regular Army, giving as many Brevets as are required to bring him up from his present rank in the Army to that to which he is recommended. As Gen. Allen is the Senior Quartermaster of those Breveted, or proposed to be Breveted, I would further recommend that such date be given to his promotion as will continue him the senior.

I have the honor to be
Very respectfully
your obt. svt.
U. S. GRANT
Lt. Gn.

ALS, DNA, RG 94, ACP, 278 1875. See telegram to Maj. Gen. Henry W. Halleck, Feb. 27, 1865.

On Dec. 20, 1864, Brig. Gen. Robert Allen, Louisville, wrote to USG. "I notice that a long list of Brevets have been made running very liberally into my Department, and that one of your friends has been left out in the cold. My friend Ingalls, I presume, is, a Brevet Major General. I am very glad of that, but I have self appreciation enough to think my claims to that destinction are quite equal to his, but let that pass My object in writing is to ask your kind offices in favor of Col. W. Myers. He has been passed over in making the Brevets and there is no officer in the Department ~~in the Department~~ that has *earned* promotion, if he has not. He has managed the Depot at St Louis, which is second to none, in the Army, with signal ability and eminent success. The Army does not contain a more faithful energetic and honest Public Servant, I will feel myself greatly obliged if you will recommend him for a brevet, not only because he merits it, but because others less worthy have received it" ALS, DNA, RG 108, Letters Received. No action followed.

To Col. Edward D. Townsend

City Point Va. Dec 31st 1864.

GEN. E. D. TOWNSEND,
ASSISTANT ADJUTANT GENERAL
WASHINGTON D. C.
GENERAL:

Your communication of date 28th inst. inclosing copy of letter of George H. Stuart Esq. Chairman Christian Commission is received. I have no objection to the parties named, or a similar number of other good men going south for the purpose indicated. I am inclined to think that much reliable information of the real condition of our prisoners could thus be obtained. It might lead to the amelioration of their condition and would at least have a most beneficial effect upon the public mind.

Of course if the Confederate Authorities consented to these agents visiting our prisoners they might require in return the privilege of sending an equal number to visit their prisoners in our hands. If so I see no objection to their sending men of good Christian Character for that purpose.

Very Respectfully
Your Obt. Sevt.
U. S. GRANT
Lieut. General.

LS, DNA, RG 94, Letters Received, 1325A 1864. *O.R.*, II, vii, 1300–1. On Dec.
28, 1864, Col. Edward D. Townsend, AGO, wrote to USG. "I enclose herewith
a copy of a letter from George H. Stuart, Esqre., Chairman of the U. S. Christian
Commission, in reply to the communication from this office of the 7th instant, a
copy of which was transmitted to you at its date. The Secretary of War does not
consent that *any* letter shall be addressed by Mr. Stuart to Jefferson Davis, and
Mr. Stuart has been so informed. The Secretary desires to know whether there
be any objection to the gentlemen named by Mr. Stuart to be sent by the Commission to visit southern prisons." LS, DNA, RG 108, Letters Received. *O.R.*,
II, vii, 1287. The enclosure is *ibid.*, pp. 1257–58.

To Maj. Gen. Henry W. Halleck

City Point, Va. Dec 31st 1864

MAJ. GEN. H. W. HALLECK
CHF. OF STAFF OF THE ARMY
WASHINGTON D. C.
GENERAL:

The letter of Brig. Gen. H. E. Paine,[1] U. S. Vols. to the Secy of
War, of date the 15th inst., enclosing one of the same date to same
address, from Brig Gen. W. R N. Beall, C. S. A. together with
your answer, referred to me, is received and read.[2]

The arrangement for the distribution of supplies concluded
between myself and Judge Ould is, that a Committe of Commissioned officers at each particular prison on both sides shall receive
and distribute the supplies for that prison.

I accepted the condition that all Committes recieving and distributing supplies to prisoners should be Commissioned Officers
gladly. It gives this duty to more responsible parties, and their reports, which are provided for, will enable the Government and the
friends of prisoners to know that articles were properly disposed of

When there are less than three Commissioned officers at any
one prison enough will have to be transferred to give this number,
to carry out the agreement. I have to request, therefore, that such
transfers be made

Very Resplly
Your Obt Svt
U. S. GRANT
Lt General

Copies, DLC-USG, V, 45, 71, 107; DNA, RG 108, Letters Sent. *O.R.*, II, vii, 1299.

1. Halbert E. Paine, born in Ohio in 1826, practiced law in Milwaukee, Wis., in partnership with Carl Schurz before the Civil War. Appointed col., 4th Wis. Cav., as of July 2, 1861, and brig. gen. as of March 13, 1863, his field service ended after he lost a leg as a result of a wound received at Port Hudson on May 27. On Nov. 21, 1864, he was assigned to superintend the sale of C.S.A. cotton in New York City for the benefit of prisoners held by the U.S. *Ibid.*, pp. 1148–49. On Jan. 28, 1865, Paine, New York City, wrote to Maj. Gen. Henry W. Halleck reporting a request from Brig. Gen. William N. R. Beall to distribute to prisoners contributions from friends within U.S. lines. *Ibid.*, II, viii, 139–40. On Feb. 7, USG endorsed this letter. "Respy returned. No stipulation has been entered into between Judge Ould and myself authorizing contributions to confederate prisoners of of war from friends within our lines, nor would I consent to such an arrangement" Copy, DLC-USG, V, 58. *O.R.*, II, viii, 140.

2. See *ibid.*, II, vii, 1226–27, 1248–49, 1277–79.

To Edwin M. Stanton

City Point, Va. Jan.y 1st 1865

Hon. E. M. Stanton,
Sec. of War,
Sir:

Herewith I submit a statement hastily drawn up by Lt. Col. Comstock, of my staff, who was with the expedition which moved against Fort Fisher.[1] It gives his views of the situation, and no one had a better opportunity of seeing than he had and no one is more capable of judging. The fact is, there are but two ways of taking Fort Fisher, operating from the water. One is to surprise them whilst there is but a small garrison defending the place. The other is, for the Navy to run a portion of their fFleet into Cape Fear River whilst the enemy's batteries are kept down by the fire from the balance. Troops can then land and hold the point until the troops in the Fort surrender. With Cape Fear River in the hands of the enemy they have the same command over the sandspit on which Cape Fort Fisher is built that we have. In the three days of good weather which elapsed after the Army had reached the scene of action, before the Navy appeared, our troops had the chance of capturing Fort Fisher whilst it had an insufficient garrison to hold it. The del[ay] gave the enemy time to accumulate a force

Every preparation is now going on to get troops back to the Mouth of Cape Fear River as soon as possible. The enemy may by that time have withdrawn Hoke's Division which went from here to Wilmington. If not, Admiral Porter will have to run a portion of his Fleet by the batteries, as suggested before, or there will be no earthly use of landing troops.

The failure before was the result of delay, by the Navy, I do not say unavoidable for I know nothing of the cause. Now the work to be done is likely to require a much greater risk on their part than if this delay had not occured[.] I know Admiral Porter to be possessed of as fine judgement as any other officer and capable of taking as great risks. It will be necessary however that he should know and appreciate the situation in all its bearings and be ready to act according to the imergency. I will write to him fully, or send a copy of this, and also send the same Staff Officer who accompanied the expedition before who will lay the whole thing before him.

It seems to me proper that these views should be laid before Admiral Porter by the sec. of the Navy also,

> I have the honor to be
> Very respectfully
> U. S. GRANT
> Lt. Gen.

ALS, DLC-Edwin M. Stanton. *O.R.*, I, xlvi, part 2, 3.

On Dec. 29, 1864, Maj. Gen. Benjamin F. Butler wrote to USG. "I do my self the honor to forword you the enclosed slip from the Philadelphia Press under date of December 15th by which you will see by the description of the vessels, every officer being stated and the accuracy of the entire plan of attack which if it had been carried out by running by Fort Fisher as proposed would have ensured success must have all been communicated from the fleet—" L (unsigned), DNA, RG 108, Letters Received. The enclosed clipping from the *Philadelphia Press*, Dec. 20, contained a report from Hampton Roads, Dec. 15. Also on Dec. 29, Butler telegraphed to USG transmitting a telegram from Brig. Gen. Charles K. Graham. Telegram received (at 3:00 P.M.), *ibid.* See *O.R.*, I, xlii, part 3, 1098.

1. LS, DNA, RG 108, Letters Received; ADfS, DLC-Cyrus B. Comstock. *O.R.*, I, xlvi, part 2, 4–5. See *ibid.*, I, xlii, part 3, 1113. On Dec. 31, Brig. Gen. Truman Seymour wrote to Lt. Col. Cyrus B. Comstock. "About Wilmington! In October 1863, with Captain Reese. U. S. Engineers, I made a careful examina-

tion of the works at the mouth of Cape Fear River. The Federal Point defences, even then, were apparently too strong to be attacked with sufficient chances of success. The occupation of Oak Island, with Fort Caswell, involved the closing of only one Entrance—and the Fort was protected by a work, the counterpart of Fort Wagner, the experience upon which was quite sufficient to show that some force, or seige operations or both, would be required here. On Smiths Island however there was then nothing to prevent immediate and successful occupation. Opposite Fort Caswell a few laborers were *just commencing* the construction of a work of some magnitude. At the North Extremity (Zeek's Island) there was a small battery of three or four guns looking upon the channel—*and it was open in the rear*. The possession of Smiths Island would prevent blockade-running. From three to five thousand men would be ample—they could easily land at the Eastern Extremity of the Island—and the seizure of the Zeeks Island [b]attery was the only point upon which there could be any doubt. This project was duly forwarded to Major General Halleck, through his Chief of Staff, Brig-Genl Cullum—and that was the end of it. The troops that might well have been devoted to this all-important operation were soon after sent to Florida. Smiths Island is just as important now as it was then. If no works have been constructed that would prevent our landing at the S. E. extremity—and particularly if the Zeeks Island work has not been materially changed—this project is yet feasible. Perhaps a small force (comparitively) neatly landed at night, might carry the Fort opposite Caswell by a Coup-de-main: if it failed, then a seige operation upon it, with assistance from Vessels, should soon compel it to fall—since it cannot be as easily reinforced or supplied as Fort Fisher. And if Zeeks Island (*not* an island, actually) were not successfully surprised, the presence of a few heavy rifles *not far from it* would go far to stop blockade-running by that entrance. I should like to try the Experiment. Wilmington *must be* blockaded. It is not impossible that the value of Smiths Island may have been underrated as a means of effecting it. . . . Note the shelter to be had under Smiths Island against N. or N. E. storms!" ALS, DLC-Cyrus B. Comstock.

To Edwin M. Stanton

[*Jan. 1–3, 1865*]

Respy. returned to the Sec of War, with the request that the name of M G. W. S. Rosecrans, U. S V. be submitted to the President for dismissal from service, in violation of G. O. 151, A G O. series 1862 in permitting the publication of Maj Gen Pleasanton's report —and sub-reports of officers under him of operation against the rebel Geneal Price in October last; and that M G. Pleasanton be reprimanded for the pulication of said reports on authority he should have known to be insufficient, and using disrespectful language in speaking of Genl Curtis command in ~~the~~ his communica-

tion in answer to General Roscrans' request as to what had become
of the unaccounted for tenth gun. Also, that Brig Gen Jno McNeil
be reprimanded for using disrespectful language towards Maj Gen
Pleasanton in his communication to Hon J. B. Henderson, U. S
Senator, of date Dec. 13d 1864, and for seeking redress of griev-
ances through other than the regular military channels, instead
of applying to the proper military authorities in the manner prescribed by Army Regulations and orders.

U. S GRANT,
Lieutenant General

Copy, DLC-USG, V, 58. On Dec. 29, 1864, Maj. Gen. Henry W. Halleck wrote
to USG. "I enclose herewith Brig Genl Mc Neil's Protest against certain Statements of Major Genl Peasenton's Report, published in the St Louis papers, also
papers containing that Report and also one by Col Philips. As these Reports &
others have been published without authority and in direct violation of Army
Regulations & orders, and especially of your General Orders, I think such conduct
deserves & requires to be officially noticed & punished. I submit the matter for
your instructions. Please return these papers for file, and also the Protest of Genl
Curtis, which was forwarded to you some days ago, as the Secty of War wishes
to see it, and no copy was retained." ALS, DNA, RG 108, Letters Sent (Press).
On Nov. 10, 1st Lt. George T. Robinson, chief engineer, Dept. of Kansas,
wrote a lengthy report concerning the quarrel between Maj. Gen. Samuel R.
Curtis and Maj. Gen. William S. Rosecrans. O.R., I, xli, part 1, 546–50. On Dec.
11, Halleck endorsed this report. "Respectfully forwarde[d] to Lt Genl Grant"
AES, DNA, RG 108, Letters Received. O.R., I, xli, part 1, 550.

To Maj. Gen. Henry W. Halleck

City Point Va.
3.30 P. M Jan 1. 1865.

MAJOR GEN HALLECK.
CHF OF STAFF.

I sent instructions to Gen. Sherman which advised that Gen
Foster organize all the colored troops he could for his Dept.

Negroes here would return white troops to their Regts, but you
may direct Gen. Meigs to send orders to Capt Strang[1] to return

without them. Please also instruct Sherman and Foster to retain
all negroes south until the return of warm weather.

U S GRANT
Lt Gen

Telegram received (at 5:00 P.M.), DNA, RG 107, Telegrams Collected
(Bound); copies, *ibid.*, Telegrams Received in Cipher; *ibid.*, RG 108, Letters
Sent; DLC-USG, V, 46, 71, 107. *O.R.*, I, xlvii, part 2, 3. On Dec. 31, 1864, 3:00
P.M., Maj. Gen. Henry W. Halleck telegraphed to USG. "I learn from a letter of
Genl Foster that all able-bodied negroes brought in by Sherman are to be shipped
to City Point. Permit me to suggest that they be armed, organized and used in
the Dept of the South, during the winter. Our experience is that negroes brought
north during the cold weather from a warm climate are almost useless; moreover, they suffer very much from cold. To send them north at the present time
would create a panic among them & prevent others from coming in from the
interior of the country. Rebel papers are already harping on this point in order
to frighten their slaves. The Secty of War & Genl Meigs concur in these views."
ALS (telegram sent), DNA, RG 107, Telegrams Collected (Bound); telegram
received, *ibid.*; (on Jan. 1, 1865) *ibid.*, RG 108, Letters Received. *O.R.*, I, xlii,
part 3, 1105–6; *ibid.*, I, xliv, 840.
    On Dec. 14, Brig. Gen. John A. Rawlins had written to Maj. Gen. William
T. Sherman. "In order to conduct efficiently the business and perform the work
in the QuarterMasters Dep't. of the Armies operating against Richmond, and to
return all the enlisted men now serving in said Department, it is necessary to
obtain the services of a large number of negroes. You will therefore please send
to this point all the able bodied negroes you can spare from those now with your
Army. All the negro women and children can also be sent up and colonized at
some point on the James river, where they can be protected and easily subsisted.
If you have not sufficient means of transportation to move them up, by sending
word here, the QuarterMasters Department will promptly furnish it" LS, DNA,
RG 393, Military Div. of the Miss., Letters Received.

    1. Capt. Edward J. Strang, q. m. as of April 13, 1863.

To Maj. Gen. Henry W. Halleck

———

City Point, Va, Jan.y 1st 18645

MAJ. GEN. H. W. HALLECK,
CHIEF OF STAFF OF THE ARMY,
GENERAL,

    Herewith I return you the papers addressed to the President of
the United States petitioning to have the terretoritory of Arkansas

and the Indian Country ordered to be evacuated by Gen. Canby still held. My understanding was that Gen. Canby only ordered the abandenment of the territory West of Little Rock because General Steele failed to supply the Garrisons in that country whilst it was possible. It seems from Gen. Steele's statement that there is no difficulty about supplying ~~Little~~ Fort Smith. As I telegraphed on receipt of the papers that post at least should be held. No one of them should be abandened where troops can be maintained until the roads get so that fresh supplies can be thrown in.

I presume the orders have gone to Gen. Reynolds and Gen. Canby to hold on to Fort Smith and such of the other posts ordered to be abandened as he can? I think it advisable to give him the additiona[l] order to resume possession of such of them as he may find it necessary to abandon for the Winter at the earliest practicable moment of supplying them in the Spring.

Very respectfully
Your obt. svt.
U. S. GRANT
Lt. Gen.

ALS, IHi. *O.R.*, I, xlviii, part 1, 391.

On Jan. 11, 1865, 3:07 P.M., Maj. Gen. Henry W. Halleck telegraphed to USG. "Senator Pomeroy & the Agent of [O]verland Mail Route have just requested me to call your attention to the inadequate protection given by Genl Curtis against Indians, and also to the project submitted by Genl Conner. Genl Canby telegraphs that a steamship was sent to Mobile on the 16th ultimo for the cotton, and that the delay has resulted from the neglect of the rebel authorities to furnish the cotton. The expense of demurrage is very heavy, and Genl Granger proposes to send the steamship back without the cotton, unless it is delivered very soon. Perhaps Mr Ould should be notified of this." ALS (telegram sent), DNA, RG 107, Telegrams Collected (Bound); telegram received, *ibid.*; *ibid.*, Telegrams Collected (Unbound); *ibid.*, RG 108, Letters Received. *O.R.*, I, xlviii, part 1, 486–87. See letter to Robert Ould, Jan. 12, 1865. On Jan. 21, USG, Washington, telegraphed to Brig. Gen. John A. Rawlins. "Send to Gen. Halleck the reports of Gen. Curtis & Gen. Conner on the subject of requirements for protection of Overland Mail routes." ALS (telegram sent), DNA, RG 107, Telegrams Collected (Bound). *O.R.*, I, xlviii, part 1, 599.

On Jan. 12, Postmaster Gen. William Dennison wrote to USG. "I beg to introduce to you George K. Otis Esq. General Superintendent of the Overland Mail Line, who visits you at my request to consult with you with reference to the depredations committed by the Indians of the plains, and as to the disposition of the U. S. troops for the protection of the mails and citizens on the route. Mr Otis

is thoroughly conversant with the route and the district of country through which
it passes, and I commend the suggestions which he has to offer to your immediate consideration. Permit me to say that the threatening movements of the
Indians, and the destruction of property, is putting the mail service in such imminent peril as to compel the temporary suspension of the service west of Denver,
and the transportation of mails by sea for the Pacific Coast for which I have
given orders this morning, at the instance of the Special Agent of this Department now at Fort Kearney." Copy, DNA, RG 28, Letters Sent by the Postmaster Gen.

To Julia Dent Grant

City Point, Va Jan 1st *18645*.

DEAR JULIA,

Happy New Year to you. Fred. starts home this morning and
will tell you I am quite well. I must commence taking quinine however. Every one on the Staff have been sick, Col. Badeau and Col.
Porter so much so that they had to be sent home.

I inclose you two strips of paper which I want you to read
and preserve. Sherman's letter shows how noble a man he is. How
few there are who when rising to popular favor as he now is would
stop to say a word in defence of the only one between himself and
the highest in command. I am glad to say that I appreciated Sherman from the first feeling him to be what he has proven to the world
he is. Good buy.

ULYS.

Kisses for you and the children.

U.

ALS, DLC-USG.
    On Jan. 1, 1865, Secretary of War Edwin M. Stanton telegraphed to USG.
"With the compliments of the Season I wish you a happy New Year." ALS (telegram sent), DNA, RG 107, Telegrams Collected (Bound). On Jan. 2, Stanton
telegraphed a similar message to Julia Dent Grant. ALS (telegram sent), *ibid.*;
telegram received, USG 3.

To William W. Smith

Head Quarters, Armies of the United States,
City Point, Va. Jany. 1st 1864 [*1865*]

DEAR SMITH,

Your letter of the 29th Ult. saying the sale of *Oil Lands*, one eighth of which is in my name, will be greatly accelerated in Phila. by having my concent to the sales is received. I have a perfect abhorence of having any interest in anything which might prove speculative at the expense of a confiding public,   I do not think the Company you represent, or are one of, feel any doubt about the lands you actually have possession of containing rich deposites of oil. If I knew w[ha]t I believe in the matter I would not hesitate about lending my name. As it is however I would pre[fer] giving no special assent in the matter, leaving those who understand more about it than I do to work it out.

I will say in conclusion that no amount of wealth would be any inducement for me to hold an interest in any fictitious corporation, or one which it was expected to make money out of at the expense of purchasers of shares.

Yours Truly
U. S. GRANT
Lt. Gen.

Copy (photostat), DLC-USG, I, D.

To Edwin M. Stanton

(Cipher)   City Point Va. Jan. 2d 1865 [*3:00* P.M.]

~~MAJ. GEN. H. W. HALLECK~~, HON. E M STANTON SECRETAY OF WAR WASHINGTON,[1]

Gen. Sheridan proposed sending another Division of troops here but I suspended his action.[2] Let him get them to Baltimore now as soon as possible, and all the Infantry on vessels that can go to Wilmington ready for orders. Should I send his troops there I

will send him with them. I can not go myself so long as Butler
would be left here in command. ~~I have never stated~~ I will state that
the former expedition was put under Weitzel by order and I never
dreamed of Butler going until ~~he passe~~ he stopped here on on his
way down the river. The operations taking place within the Geo-
graphical limits of his Dept. I did not like to order him back.

U. S. GRANT
Lt. Gn

ALS (telegram sent), CSmH; telegram received (at 4:30 P.M.), DNA, RG 107,
Telegrams Collected (Bound). *O.R.*, I, xlvi, part 2, 9–10.

    1. Addressed by Brig. Gen. John A. Rawlins.
    2. See telegram to Maj. Gen. Philip H. Sheridan, Dec. 24, 1864. On Jan. 2,
1865, 10:00 P.M., Maj. Gen. Philip H. Sheridan, Winchester, Va., telegraphed
to Maj. Gen. Henry W. Halleck, sending a copy to USG. "I can have a division
of infantry in readiness to embark by rail at 10 o'clock tomorrow if transportation can be furnished I will try and have the transportation at Stevenson Depot
at that time. Troops are encamped at the depot & I will not give the order to get
ready until I know iat what hour the transportation will be ready" Telegram
received, DNA, RG 108, Letters Received. *O.R.*, I, xlvi, part 2, 16.

To Edwin M. Stanton

(Cipher)   City Point, Va, Jan.y 2d 1864 [*1865, 11:00* P.M.]
HON. E. M. STANTON, SEC. OF WAR, WASHINGTON
I do not know how many men Gen. Sheridan will send, probably
4,000 My idea was that he could send them easyer to Baltimore
than Washington and by having the Infantry loaded on Sea going
transports they could be sent direct to Wilmington if a lodgement
is effected. We will probably reach Porters Fleet next Friday.[1]
Transports however are not all ~~here yet~~. At Ft. Monroe yet.

U. S. GRANT
Lt. Gen.

AL (telegram sent), CSmH; telegram received, DNA, RG 107, Telegrams Collected (Bound). *O.R.*, I, xlvi, part 2, 10. The signature appears to have been
added in another hand resembling that of USG.
    On Jan. 2, 1865, 1:00 P.M., USG telegraphed to Secretary of War Edwin
M. Stanton. "Can you get the Navy Dept to send twenty (20) large launches,
like those formerly furnished the Army, to the Qr. Mr. at Fortress Monroe at

once?" Telegram received (at 1:40 P.M.), DNA, RG 107, Telegrams Collected (Bound); copies, *ibid.*, Telegrams Received in Cipher; *ibid.*, RG 108, Letters Sent; DLC-USG, V, 46, 71, 107. *O.R.*, I, xlvi, part 2, 9. Asst. Secretary of the Navy Gustavus V. Fox endorsed this telegram. "Telegraphed Jan. 2d to Commandants of Portsmouth, Boston, New York, Phila Norfolk and Washington, to know how many Launches and 1st Cutters with oars, they have available for instant service—To reply immediately" ES, DNA, RG 107, Telegrams Collected (Bound). *O.R.*, I, xlvi, part 2, 9. See following telegram.

At 9:00 P.M., Stanton telegraphed to USG. "There are no transports at Baltimore. A number are collecting at Fort Monroe—Enquiry made as to transports available at New York will know to morrow Do you wish any sent from New York to Baltimore & if so for how many men." LS (telegram sent), DNA, RG 107, Telegrams Collected (Bound); telegram received, *ibid.*, RG 108, Letters Received. *O.R.*, I, xlvi, part 2, 10.

    1. Jan. 6.

To Gustavus V. Fox

City Point Va
Jany 2d 1865 10 p m

HON G. V. FOX
ASST SECY NAVY

    It was today I said troops were to be assembled at Fort Monroe. The whole number required are not there yet, Admiral Porter should coal and fill up at once and be ready, The troops will probably be off Fort Fisher by Friday[1] next. I think the fleet will be able to furnish boat enough, if they cannot be got conveniently elsewhere.

U. S. GRANT
Lt Genl

Telegrams received (2), DNA, RG 107, Telegrams Collected (Bound); copies, *ibid.*, Telegrams Received in Cipher; *ibid.*, RG 108, Letters Sent; DLC-USG, V, 46, 71, 107. Printed as received at 11:00 P.M. in *O.R.*, I, xlvi, part 2, 10; *O.R.* (Navy), I, xi, 403. In USG's letterbooks, the first sentence reads "vessels" in place of "troops." On Jan. 2, 1865, 8:00 P.M., Asst. Secretary of the Navy Gustavus V. Fox telegraphed to USG. "I have telegraphed to all the Navy Yards for boats; I am afraid we cannot have many on hand. There are only two at this Yard which will leave immediately. Perhaps the Qr Mr at NewYork better be directed to go into the market and purchase all he can find. Such sized boats are scarce. Please write fully to Adml Porter as early as possible; I notified him yesterday of the fact only knowing no more. He must coal and fill up with ammunitions and provisions is the reason I ask you to write to him; I wrote him that your force would leave today but if it is not so he should know it" Telegram received, DNA, RG 108, Letters Received; copies, *ibid.*, RG 45, Confidential Letters Sent; DLC-Gideon Welles. *O.R.*, I, xlvi, part 2, 10–11; *O.R.* (Navy), I, xi, 403.

Also on Jan. 2, USG telegraphed to Lt. Col. Michael R. Morgan, commissary, Fort Monroe. "Report by telegraph the moment the vessels will be provisioned" Telegram received, DNA, RG 107, Telegrams Collected (Bound); copies, *ibid.*, RG 108, Letters Sent; DLC-USG, V, 46, 71, 107. *O.R.*, I, xlvi, part 2, 11. At 8:00 P.M., Morgan telegraphed to Brig. Gen. John A. Rawlins. "*All the Vessels have not yet arrived—those now here have been all provisioned.*" ALS (telegram sent), DNA, RG 107, Telegrams Collected (Unbound). *O.R.*, I, xlvi, part 2, 11.

On Jan. 2, Lt. Col. Theodore S. Bowers issued Special Orders No. 2. "Eight thousand infantry, and two batteries of artillery, without horses, will be got in immediate readiness to embark on transports, with orders to report to Maj Gen. W. T. Sherman, at Savannah, Ga. ~~12~~ . . . They will be provided with four days cooked rations in haversacks. ~~23~~ . . . The troops and artillery of the late expedition against Wilmington having experienced in embarking and debarking, will be selected; and to make up the balance of the eight thousand, good and tried soldiers of the 2d Brigade, 1st Division, 24th Army Corps be taken. 4 . . . Brevet Maj. Gen A H Terry, U S V., is assigned to the command of these forces. 5 Every practicable precaution will be observed to prevent information of any movement of troops, getting to the enemy." Copies, DLC-USG, V, 57, 63, 64, 65. *O.R.*, I, xlvi, part 2, 11.

On Jan. 3, Rawlins telegraphed twice to Morgan, the second time at 10:30 A.M. "You will put rations on such Boats as the Quarter Masters Dept furnish you" Telegram received, DNA, RG 107, Telegrams Collected (Bound). "Please state the number of vessels, and number of men they will transport, that have up to this time reported and been provisioned at Fort Monroe under your recent orders." Copies, DLC-USG, V, 46, 71, 107; DNA, RG 108, Letters Sent. *O.R.*, I, xlvi, part 2, 21. At 11:30 A.M. and 1:00 P.M., Morgan telegraphed to Rawlins. "The Steamer Illinois keeps things back—She will not be coaled until tomorrow morning Four extra steamers have been sent here to report to the QuarterMaster—Three of these are coaled—No one knows what they are here for—I suggest one of them, the 'Atlantic' to take the place of the 'Illinois.' " ALS (telegram sent), DNA, RG 107, Telegrams Collected (Unbound). *O.R.*, I, xlvi, part 2, 21–22. "There have an abundance of vessels reported but from want of dock accomodation coaling is a slow operation—Coaling is the hitch—There are nine (9) vessels ready for sea—They will carry four thousand, four hundred and seventy five ~~men~~ (4475) men—I have decided to take everything that is fit and is coaled—By doing this we will get through, I hope, by ten (10) o'clock tonight —Will report when through—" ALS (telegram sent), DNA, RG 107, Telegrams Collected (Unbound); telegram received, *ibid. O.R.*, I, xlvi, part 2, 22. At 2:00 P.M., Rawlins telegraphed to Morgan. "The extra vessels you speak of as having reported to the Quartermaster, are evidently intended to make up the Fleet you are rationing, and Capt. Howell a. q. m. has been directed to so instruct the Q. M. at Ft. Monroe. Ration them same as others and soon as possible. If any vessel is so large it cannot get up here, the troops it is to carry will be sent to Fort Monroe in river transports." Copies, DLC-USG, V, 46, 71, 107; DNA,

RG 108, Letters Sent. *O.R.*, I, xlvi, part 2, 22. At 5:30 P.M. and 6:30 P.M., Morgan telegraphed to Rawlins. "Since my last four vessels have been made ready for sea—They will carry Two thousand one hundred and fifty (2150) men—The Atlantic fourteen hundred (1400) men can not go up to City Point— She is not rationed now but she will be tonight and ready for sea in the morning —Gen. Ingalls has asked for the spare transportation to be sent to Balto. It has been so ordered—" "By Summing up you will see that the Atlantic alone is unprovisioned—I may then say that all is ready, as the Atlantic can not go up to City Point and before troops come to her she will be ready—" ALS (telegrams sent), DNA, RG 107, Telegrams Collected (Unbound); telegrams received, *ibid*. *O.R.*, I, xlvi, part 2, 22.

On Jan. 3, Capt. John M. Berrien, commandant, Navy Yard, Norfolk, telegraphed to USG. "I am directed by the Hon. Secretary of the Navy to turn over to you all the Launches and large boats we have. Please direct me in the premises" ALS (telegram sent), DNA, RG 107, Telegrams Collected (Unbound); telegram received, *ibid.*; *ibid.*, RG 94, War Records Office, Army of the Potomac. *O.R.*, I, xlvi, part 2, 21. At 7:20 P.M., USG telegraphed to Berrien. "Please send the launches & large boats to Col. Webster Qr. Mr. at Fortress Monroe by tomorrow noon." ALS (telegram sent), Kohns Collection, NN; copies, DLC-USG, V, 46, 71, 107; DNA, RG 108, Letters Sent. *O.R.*, I, xlvi, part 2, 21.

1. Jan. 6.

To Maj. Gen. Henry W. Halleck

City Point Va.
7 P. M. Jan. 2. 18645.

MAJ. GEN H. W. HALLECK.
CHF OF STAFF.

Inform Gen. Thomas th[at] he will require no new outfit of teams,   His troops will either operate in a country which will supply them, or withdraw (the surplus ones,) where it is not desirable to transport wagons & mules. There has always been an unnecessary accumulation of teams in the Dept. of the Cumberland, along the line of the R. R. where every supply but fuel was brought on the cars'. The Dept. of the Ohio also had a large number of wagons & mules owing to having attempted to supply themselves through Cumberland Gap.

U S GRANT
Lt Gen

Telegram received (at 9:00 P.M.), DNA, RG 107, Telegrams Collected (Bound); copies, *ibid.*, Telegrams Received in Cipher; *ibid.*, RG 108, Letters Sent; DLC-USG, V, 46, 71, 107. *O.R.*, I, xlv, part 2, 481. See *ibid.*, pp. 441–42, 495.

On Jan. 2, 1865, 8:00 P.M., Maj. Gen. George H. Thomas telegraphed to USG. "Reports recd. today seem to confirm my reports that Hood has gone to Corinth with his army but I can scarcely believe he will attempt to halt at Corinth with the R R broken in his rear & besides this I have recd a telegram from Steedman dated Cortland Dec 31 in which he states that citizens and deserters inform him that there is no force of the enemy either at Florence or Tuscumbia It was also reported to him that the enemys ponton train had left LaGrange on the mornig of the 30th for Russellville with orders to go to Columbus Miss. He had sent his cavalry force in pursuit hoping to be able to overtake it on the road & destroy it" Telegram received, DNA, RG 108, Letters Received. Printed as addressed to Maj. Gen. Henry W. Halleck in *O.R.*, I, xlv, part 2, 482. The absence of other copies of this telegram addressed to USG suggests that Thomas never intended to send it directly to USG, that an error was made in preparing a copy for USG.

To Maj. Gen. Benjamin F. Butler

City Point, Va. Jan. 2d *1864.* [*1865, 10:15* A.M.]

MAJ. GEN. BUTLER,

F. P. Blair, Sr. left here yesterday to return home thinking no reply would be made to his letter. I forwarded Mr. Seddens letter and I think Mr. B. may be looked for back again by Friday next. You may say so if any enquiries are made by ᵾ rebel authorities.

U. S. GRANT
Lt. Gen.

ALS (telegram sent), CSmH; telegram received, DLC-Benjamin F. Butler. On Jan. 1, 1865, 7:30 P.M., Maj. Gen. Benjamin F. Butler telegraphed to USG. "At the moment I have recieved a letter from James A. Seddon Esqr claimig to be Confederate Secretary of War to Francis P. Blair Esq of the District of Colum-baia which I forward at once." ALS (telegram sent), DNA, RG 107, Telegrams Collected (Unbound); telegram received, *ibid.*, RG 108, Letters Received.

On Dec. 28, 1864, President Abraham Lincoln issued a pass to Francis P. Blair, Sr., to go to Richmond to negotiate with President Jefferson Davis. Lincoln, *Works*, VIII, 188–89; Edward Chase Kirkland, *The Peacemakers of 1864* (New York, 1927), pp. 197–98. On Dec. 30, USG telegraphed to Butler. "A sealed letter to Mr Davis will leave here in a few minutes please have an officer at Aikens Landing to receive & pass it through Outer Lines & into the hands of a Commissioned Confederate Officer without ~~fail~~ delay" Telegram received,

DLC-Benjamin F. Butler; copies, DLC-USG, V, 45, 71, 107; DNA, RG 108, Letters Sent. On the same day, USG telegraphed to Capt. Charles E. Mitchell, ordnance boat *Baltimore.* "Mr Blair will not be down until tomorrow. He desires me to ask you to wait for him." Telegram received (press), *ibid.,* RG 107, Telegrams Collected (Bound). On Dec. 31, 11:15 A.M., USG telegraphed to Col. Ralph C. Webster, q. m., Fort Monroe. "Please ask Capt. Mitchel of Θ Navy Ordnance boat Baltimore to hold on for Mr. Blair. He will not be able to go down to-night." ALS (telegram sent), CSmH; telegram received (press), DNA, RG 107, Telegrams Collected (Bound). On Jan. 1, 1865, USG telegraphed to Webster. "Please say to Capt Mitchell Navy Ordnance boat that Mr. Blair leaves here at 2.30 p. m. for Fortress Monroe. Please to fire up by the time he gets there." ALS (telegram sent), MHi; telegram received (press), DNA, RG 107, Telegrams Collected (Bound). *O.R.,* I, xlvi, part 2, 5. On the same day, Webster telegraphed to USG. "The Baltimore left here last, evening but I cannot learn in which direction. If she can be found I will hold her as directed." ALS (telegram sent), DNA, RG 107, Telegrams Collected (Unbound).

On Jan. 4, Asst. Secretary of the Navy Gustavus V. Fox wrote to USG. "Confidential . . . To day we recd dispatches from Porter dated the 29. ult—stating that the enemy are removing the guns from Fort Fisher preparatory to changing the arrangement of their defences—The Phila Inquirer of to day has all the information contd in the documents that have just come from Richmond *through Genl Butler's Hd Qrs*—I think, last summer, after my visit to you with Genl Gilmore that you were under the impression that one of us gave publicity to the object of our visit—I trusted to time to enable you to discover all the leaks in the vicinity of your Hd Qrs. Mr Blair Sr, alone, will leave Washington Saturday and arrive off City Point about noon in the screw stmr Don, Capt Parker, comg the Potomac Flotilla—As he goes by consent of the Prest at the request of Mr Davis I ask, from Mr. Blair, that you will make arrangements to get him through comfortably as early as practicable, and as secretly. I have suggested to him to lay to off City Point and let an officer go on shore from the vessel and receive your directions as to the best method of going through. The Don can go up as far as desired and remain until Mr Blair returns and I will direct Capt Parker to report to you and receive any directions you may give—Please acknowledge the receipt of this letter by telegraph. I got the Prest to put into the old capitol the man who caused to be published the Wilmington expedition—Yesterday the Balt. Am. sent me word that they had information that another expedition was fitting out—I sent them word that the Govt would deal very summarily with the first party who published it—To night Mr Go Bright the agent of the associated Press informed me that he had such news from Hampton Roads but had suppressed it— . . . The Country will [*not*] forgive us for another failure at Wilmington, and I have so informed Porter." ALS, *ibid.,* RG 108, Letters Received. *O.R.,* I, xlvi, part 2, 29; *O.R.* (Navy), I, xi, 409. On Jan. 8, 10:00 A.M., USG telegraphed to Fox. "Your letter of the 4th just received. Your request will be attended to." ALS (telegram sent), Kohns Collection, NN; telegrams received (2—at 5:00 P.M.), DNA, RG 107, Telegrams Collected (Bound). Printed as received at 4:50 P.M. in *O.R.,* I, xlvi, part 2, 67.

To Maj. Gen. John G. Parke

City Point, Va, Jan. 2d 1864 [*1865*]

MAJ. GEN. PARKE, COMD.G A. P.

Gen. Lee has made application for the recovery of the body of Capt. R. B. Davis who was killed on the 1st of Oct. near the Peebles House. He understands that the grave is marked with a headboard giving the name of Capt. Davis and probably his regt. the ~~4th~~ 40th Va. Please have it disinterred and sent into the rebel lines at the most convenient point for you to deliver it. Inform me as early as you can the time and place where you will deliver it. I want to answer Gen. Lee's letter by 12 m. to-morrow.

U. S. GRANT
Lt. Gn

ALS (telegram sent), CSmH; copies, DLC-USG, V, 46, 71, 107; DNA, RG 108, Letters Sent; Meade Papers, PHi. On Jan. 3, 1865, Maj. Gen. John G. Parke twice telegraphed to USG, first at 10:00 A.M. "Your Tel. in reference to disinterring the body of Capt. R. B. Davis, 40th. Va. Regt. was rec'd. last ev'g. Enquiry was immediately made of the several Commanders that were ~~located in~~ engaged near the Peeble's House on the 1st. of Oct., & also of those that have been camped in that vicinity since that date. As yet I have not been able to learn any-thing in reference to the location of the grave. The Pro: Mar. of the 9th. Corps, had charge of ~~the~~ removing the bodies of offrs. & men of the 9th. Corps who fell in that vicinity. He does not remember having seen the grave of Capt. Davis. He goes out today & will make diligent search for it. Every effort will be made to ~~recover~~ discover the grave. As soon as I learn any thing positive will notify you, stating time & place of delivery" ALS (telegram sent), DNA, RG 393, Army of the Potomac, Miscellaneous Letters Received; copy, *ibid.*, Letters Sent. "It has just been reported that the Chaplain of the 198th. Pa. Vols. has identified the grave where Capt. Davis of the Rebel Army is buried—I will direct that all preparations be made for disinterring the body—and have it sent through the lines on the Squirrel Level Road, at about noon on Thursday the 5th:" ALS (telegram sent), *ibid.*, Miscellaneous Letters Received; telegram received, *ibid.*, RG 108, Letters Received. See letter to Gen. Robert E. Lee, Jan. 3, 1865.

To Richard J. Oglesby

HEADQ'RS ARMIES OF THE UNITED STATES,
CITY POINT, Va., Jan. 2, 1865.

DEAR GOVERNOR—Now that you are about taking your place as commander-in-chief of all the militia of the state of Illinois, and

will have to select your staff, permit me to put in one good word in
behalf of a most capable and worthy officer. I refer to Col. John S.
Loomis. He has served faithfully and efficiently in the office of the
adjutant general of the state from the first organization of state
troops in this rebellion. I was about headquarters at Springfield
when the first troops were being raised, and I tell you in all candor,
that but for J. S. Loomis Illinois would to-day have no record of
what she then did. I give him my most hearty indorsement for the
position of adjutant general of the state.

Hoping you every success in your present responsible position,
and that you will not be kept so busy but what you will still get a
chance to talk, I subscribe myself,

Your friend,   U. S. GRANT, Lieut. Gen.

Chicago Times, Jan. 12, 1865. The reporter, writing from Springfield, Jan. 11,
provided some background. "The following letter was inclosed to Gov. Oglesby
by Gen. Grant, in a letter to the former chaplain of his old regiment, Rev. J. L.
Crane, pastor of the M. E. church in this city. It arrived too late to influence the
appointment indicated, . . ." *Ibid.* See letter to Richard J. Oglesby, Feb. 2, 1865.

To Gen. Robert E. Lee

City Point, Va., Jany. 3d 1865

GEN. R. E. LEE.
COM'D'G ARMY N. VA.
GENERAL

Your note of the 31st of Dec. in relation to the recovery of the
body of Capt R. B. Davis was received yesterday.[1] I at once gave
directions for the disinterment and delivery of the body at your lines
and directed that I should be notified at the earliest moment the
time and place of this delivery. I enclose you the reply received
from Gen. Parke.[2] "Search will be made and if the body of Capt.
Davis can be found it will be delivered to his friends at the earliest
practicable moment."

Very Respectfully
Your obt Servt
U. S. GRANT
Lt. Gen'l

Copies, DLC-USG, V, 46, 71, 107; DNA, RG 108, Letters Sent. On Jan. 3, 1865, USG wrote to Gen. Robert E. Lee. "I am glad to be able to inform you that the grave of Capt. Davis has been identified. The body will be disinterred and delivered to persons sent to recieve it about noon of the 5th instant. It will be sent through our lines on the Squirrel level." Copies, *ibid*.

1. On Dec. 31, 1864, Lee wrote to USG. "The friends of the late Captain Robert B Davis, 40th Va Regt, who was killed near Peeble's house on the 1st Oct: are very desirous to recover his remains. They state that they have seen in Northern papers that the grave of the deceased is designated by a head-board, showing his name and rank. As I presume you would not be willing to permit a party to enter your lines for the purpose of disinterring the body, should you see proper to comply with the wishes of the family of the deceased, and cause the remains to be removed, I will receive them at such point as you may designate. It will be a great gratification to the afflicted family of Captain Davis." LS, PPRF.
2. See telegram to Maj. Gen. John G. Parke, Jan. 2, 1865.

To Robert Ould

City Point, Va. Jany 3d 1865

JUDGE RO. OULD.
AGENT OF EXCHANGE
SIR;

Herewith I have the honor to enclose official Copy of General Orders No. 299,[1] from the War Department of date December 7th 1864. You will see that it contemplates the paroleing of two officers for the purpose of receiving and distributing supplies. I am not aware that any other officer than Gen. Beall has been paroled by the Federal Authorities, as General Agent for the receipt and distribution of supplies to Confederate prisoners in our hands. I will however state that should *they* parole two, I have no doubt that the same number will be paroled on our part. I will be glad to send through the lines supplies of Clothing and provisions so soon as notified when and where they will be received.

I have the honor to be
Very Respectfully
Your Obt. Svt.
U. S GRANT
Lt. Genl.

Copies, DLC-USG, V, 46, 71, 107; DNA, RG 108, Letters Sent. *O.R.*, II, viii, 14. On Jan. 8, 1865, C.S.A. Agent of Exchange Robert Ould wrote to USG. "Your note of the 3d Inst. was received yesterday. General Hays and Colonel Wild [*Weld*] will be given as you suggest such parole as will enable them 'to receive and distribute to the United States prisoners of war such articles of clothing and other necessaries as may be issued by the Government or contributed from other sources.' I will be ready at any time you may designate, to receive any supplies which you may send, at Boulware's wharf on James River, and at Charleston Harbor. Those which are sent to James River will be distributed amongst the prisoners at Richmond, Danville and Salisbury, and those received at Charleston will be forwarded to the other points where your prisoners are confined. There are about twenty thousand prisoners at the three places just named and twenty five thousand further South. I will be obliged to you, if you will give Major General Trimble a parole similar to that given to General Beall, in order that he may assist the latter in the discharge of his duties. You can notify me through the lines when you will have the supplies at Boulware's wharf, stating as nearly as you can the amount. I will thank you to give me a notice of a week or ten days as to supplies sent to Charleston." LS, DNA, RG 108, Letters Received. *O.R.*, II, viii, 45–46. On Jan. 10, USG endorsed this letter. "Respectfully forwarded to the Secretary of War. It will be seen from the within letter that the Confederate authorities have paroled Gen. Hays and Col. Wild, the officers designated in General Orders No. 299, as Agents, &c. I have therefore to request that if Gen. Trimble is objected to, some other Confederate officer be paroled at once, and that I be furnished with the name of the officer so paroled." ES, DNA, RG 108, Letters Received. *O.R.*, II, viii, 46. On Jan. 12, 4:35 P.M., Maj. Gen. Henry W. Halleck telegraphed to USG. "The Secty of War (now absent) formerly refused to parole Genl Trimble; and probably would do so again. Perhaps it would be well to ask Mr. Ould to name some one else, or to permit Genl Beall to do so." ALS (telegram sent), DNA, RG 107, Telegrams Collected (Bound); telegram received, *ibid.*; *ibid.*, RG 108, Letters Sent. *O.R.*, II, viii, 56. On the same day, USG wrote to Ould. "I am informed that a parole is refused Genl. Trimble because he is personally objectionable to the Federal Government. Will you therefore be pleased to name some one else or permit Gen. Beale to do so." Copies, DLC-USG, V, 46, 71, 107; DNA, RG 108, Letters Sent.

On Jan. 3, 2:00 P.M., Halleck telegraphed to USG. "I learn from the Qr.-Mr. & Com Genls that there are supplies at Fort-Monroe & in the James which can be sent to our prisoners in accordance with Genl Orders No. 299, Dec 7th, 1864; but that no special requisitions had been made for that purpose. It was understood that as soon as you perfected the arrangements with Mr. Ould, [som]e one would be designated by yourself or Genl Butler, to deliver supplies to Genl Hays or Col Wild [w]ithin the enemy's lines. In order to properly settle the accounts it would be best that all the issues should be on a special requisitions naming the object. The Secty of War is anxious that supplies be forwarded as promptly as possible. It is not known here whether any of the officers named in Order 299 have been accepted by the enemy." ALS (telegram sent), *ibid.*, RG 107, Telegrams Collected (Bound); telegram received, *ibid.*; (at 2:20 P.M.) *ibid.*, RG 108, Letters Received. *O.R.*, II, viii, 13. At 3:00 P.M., USG telegraphed to Halleck. "Special Orders *298* & *299* have not been received here" Telegram received (at 3:45 P.M.), DNA, RG 107, Telegrams Collected (Bound); copies, *ibid.*, RG 94, Letters Received, 4A 1865; *ibid.*, RG 107, Telegrams Re-

ceived in Cipher; *ibid.*, RG 108, Letters Sent; DLC-USG, V, 46, 71, 107. USG's
letterbooks refer to "General Orders."

Also on Jan. 3, Halleck wrote to USG. "In compliance with the instructions
of the Secty of War to transmit to you all papers in regard to supply of prisoners
of War, I enclose herewith certain papers recieved from Genl Paine. The Secty
War refused permission to purchase on credit before the arrival of the cotton, on
the ground that such a proceeding would give to the Rebel Govt and agents an
acknowledged credit in our markets. The furnishing supplies from friends should
be governed by what the Rebels do in regard to our prisoners. The transfer of
com. officers to camps where there are none has been ordered. The release on
parole of other officers to assist Genl Beall is deemed objectionable on account
of the facilities it would afford to communicate between the different camps and
arrange plans of escapes, But if the enemy should allow Genl Hays an assistant,
probably the Secty would permit one to Genl Beall. Since commencing this letter
I learn that Genl Beall's course of conduct in New York has been so conspicuous
& offensive that the Secty of War has ordered his sign to be taken down. Genl
Paine has also been directed to suspend his parole & take him in custody till the
cotton arrives. The selection of Genl Beall was unfortunate, for he seems disposed to make all the trouble he can. His parole will be renewed the moment the
cotton reaches New York." ALS, DNA, RG 108, Letters Received. *O.R.*, II, viii,
13–14. The enclosures are *ibid.*, II, vii, 1287–89. On the same day, Col. John
C. Kelton endorsed to USG a letter of Dec. 30, 1864, from C.S.A. Brig. Gen.
William N. R. Beall to Ould. AES, DNA, RG 108, Letters Received. *O.R.*, II,
vii, 1297.

1. *Ibid.*, p. 1198.

To Edwin M. Stanton

(Cipher)   City Point, Va. Jan. 3d 1865. [*5:30* P.M.]
HON. E. M. STANTON, SEC. OF WAR, WASHINGTON,

The expedition against Wilmington will commence their embarkation to-morrow morning and if the weather will permit going
to sea will be with Admiral Porter on Friday.[1] Here there is not the
slightes suspicion where troops are going.

The orders to the officer commanding ~~officer~~ enjoin secrecy
and designate Savannah and to report to Sherman as their destination.

U. S. GRANT
Lt. Gen.

ALS (telegram sent), CSmH; telegram received (at 7:00 P.M.), DNA, RG 107,
Telegrams Collected (Bound). *O.R.*, I, xlvi, part 2, 18.

1. Jan. 6, 1865.

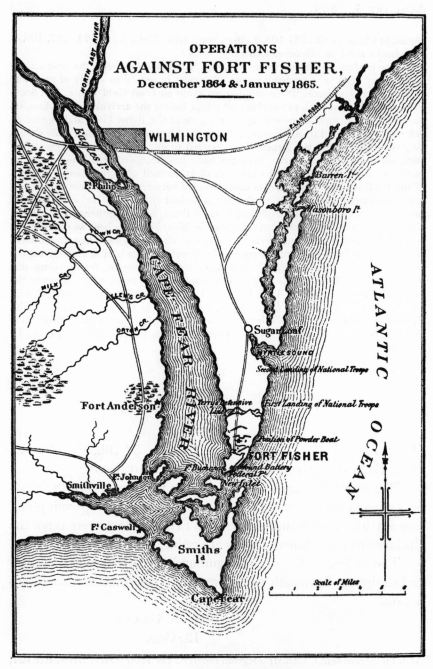

Operations against Fort Fisher

From Adam Badeau, **Military History of Ulysses S. Grant**
(*New York, 1868–81*), *III*

To Edwin M. Stanton

From City Point Jan 3d *18645.*

HON E M STANTON
SEC WAR
The Richmond Enquirer of to day says—
"The Danville railroad is the great connecting line between
Richmond and the sources of supply for the army now defending
this City. unless that road can be properly managed can have a
head and directory at least competent to supply trains with wood
and water as well as to repair leaky Engines and above all without honest and earnest men at the termini of the road it will [b]e
but a few weeks before this City will be besieged not by the enemy
only but by the stupidity of the management [o]f this road. At a
late important juncture of military affairs this road was so incom-
petently managed that a great disaster was imminent and only
prevented by the interposition of Providence and not by the enterprise & management of the Danville Road. During a recent serious
scarcity of rations a train of Cars nine (9) in number came into
Richmond with two Cars for Government and seven for individuals. Rumor is busy with a thousand reports of bribery and
corruption and the military authorities are loud in complaints
against this road. The Whig represents the people of Richmond
suffering for want of fuel and urges that the Government shall
furnish wood as it does food. Hard wood is one hundred dollars
per Cord"

U S GRANT
Lt Genl

Telegram received (at 7:00 P.M.), DNA, RG 107, Telegrams Collected
(Bound). *O.R.*, I, xlvi, part 2, 18–19.

To Rear Admiral David D. Porter

City Point Jany 3d 1865

DEAR ADMIRAL

I send Maj, Genl, A. H. Terry with the same troops General Butler had, with one picked Brigade added to renew the attempt on Fort Fisher, In addition to this I have ordered General Sheridan to send a Division of Infantry to Baltimore to be put on sea going transports, so that they can go also if their services are found necessary, This will augment Genl, Terry's force from four to five thousand men, These troops will be at Fort Monroe if the transportation can be obtained, (there is but little doubt it can) ready to sail at an hours notice,

Genl, Terry will show you the instructions he is acting under, My views are that Fort Fisher can be taken, from the water front, only in two way's, One is to surprise the enemy when they have an insufficient force their The other is to for the Navy to run into Cape Fear River with vessels enough to contend against anything the enemy may have there, If the landing can be effected before this is done, well and good, But if the enemy are in very strong force, a landing may not be practicable until we have possssion of the river,

Gen, Terry will consult with you fully, and will be governed by your suggestions as far as his responsibility for the safety of his command will admit of,

Hoping you all sorts of good weather and success, I remain

Yours Truly
U. S. GRANT
Lt, Genl,

ADMIRAL D. D. PORTER
COM'DG N, AT BLOCK-SQUADRON

Copies, DLC-USG, V, 46, 72, 107; DNA, RG 108, Letters Sent. *O.R.*, I, xlvi, part 2, 19–20; *O.R.* (Navy), I, xi, 404–5.

To Bvt. Maj. Gen. Alfred H. Terry

———

City Point Jany. 3d 1865

MAJ. GEN. A. H. TERRY
COMDG EXPEDITION
GENERAL,

The expedition entrusted to your command has been fitted out to renew the attempt to capture Fort Fisher, North Carolina and Wilmington ultimately if the fort falls, You will, then proceed with as little delay as possible to the Naval Fleet lying off Cape Fear River, and report the arrival of yourself and command to Rear Admiral D. D. Porter Commanding North Atlantic Blockading Squadron, It is exceedingly desirable that the most complete understanding should exist between yourself and the Naval Commander, I suggest therefore that you consult with Admiral Porter freely, and get from him the part to be performed by each branch of the public service, so that there may be unity of action, It would be well to have the whole programme laid down in writing I have served with Admiral Porter, and know that you can rely on his judgment, and his nerve to undertake what he proposes, I would therefore defer to him as much as is consistent with your own responsibilities,

The first object to be attained is to get a firm position on the spit of land on which Fort Fisher is built, from which you can operate against that Fort, You want to look to the practicability of receiving your supplies, and to defending yourself against superior forces sent against you by any of the avenues left open to the enemy, if such a position can be obtained the seige of Fort Fisher will not be abandoned until it's reduction is accomplished or another plan of campaign is ordered from these Hd Qrs.

My own views are that if you effect a landing the Navy ought to run a portion of their fleet into Cape Fear River, whilst the ballance of it operates on the outside, Land forces cannot invest Fort Fisher or cut it off from supplies or reenforcements, whilst the ~~enemy~~ river is in posession of the enemy,

A seige train will be loaded on vessels ~~will be~~ and sent to Fort Monroe in readiness to be sent to you if required, All other supplies can be drawn from Beaufort as you need them,

Keep the fleet of vessels with you until your position is assured, When you find they can be spared, order the back, or such of them as you can spare to Fort Monroe to report for orders,

In case of failure to effect a landing, bring your command back to Beaufort and report to these HeadQuarters for further instructions, You will not debark at Beaufort until so directed

General Sheridan has been ordered to send a Division of troops to Baltimore and place them on sea going vessels, These troops will be brought to Fort Monroe and kept there on the vessels until you are heard from, Should you require them they will be sent to you,

> Very Resp'y
> Your ob't sv't
> U. S. GRANT
> Lt. Genl.

Copies, DLC-USG, V, 46, 72, 107; DNA, RG 108, Letters Sent. *O.R.*, I, xxxiv, part 1, 41–42; *ibid.*, I, xxxvi, part 1, 45; *ibid.*, I, xxxviii, part 1, 34; *ibid.*, I, xlvi, part 2, 25; *O.R.* (Navy), I, xi, 404.

On Jan. 2, 1865, USG telegraphed to Maj. Gen. Benjamin F. Butler. "Please send Maj. Gen. Terry to City Point to see me this morning." ALS (telegram sent), Kohns Collection, NN; copies, DLC-USG, V, 46, 71, 107; DNA, RG 108, Letters Sent. *O.R.*, I, xlvi, part 2, 15. On the same day, Butler telegraphed to USG. "Maj Gen Terry has been ordered to report to you. With your leave if you are to be home this afternoon I will come over & see you—" LS (telegram sent), DNA, RG 107, Telegrams Collected (Unbound). On the same day, USG telegraphed to Butler. "I will be at home all day. When you was in New York I promised Gen Weitzel a leave of absence from the first of the year for thirty days. Does he desire to go? If so he had better start at once." Telegram received, DLC-Benjamin F. Butler; copies, DLC-USG, V, 46, 71, 107; DNA, RG 108, Letters Sent. *O.R.*, I, xlvi, part 2, 15. On Jan. 3, 10:00 A.M., Butler telegraphed to USG. "Have seen my chief qrmr at FtMonroe, whom I ordered here for consultation on another matter. I think the boats will not be ready at FtMonroe till tomorrow mornng. Is that so understood by you? Shall we move at once" Telegram received, DNA, RG 108, Letters Received. *O.R.*, I, xlvi, part 2, 24. At 6:00 P.M., USG wrote to Butler. "Order Col. Dodge to report to Maj. Gen. Terry to accompany his Command as Quarter Master, and remain with it until he is relieved by Gen. Terry, when he will return to the Army of the James—" Copies, DLC-USG, V, 46, 71, 107; DNA, RG 108, Letters Sent. *O.R.*, I, xlvi, part 2, 24.

To William Dennison

City Point, Va., January 4th 1865

HON. W. DENNISON,
POST MASTER GENERAL,
SIR:

I have the honor to acknowledge the receipt of your communication in relation to the expediency of establishing a Money Post Office at City Point, and asking my wishes upon the subject.

In reply I have simply to say that I fully approve the system and believe that it will be highly advantageous to the soldier in the transmission of his money to his family or relations. Any appointment of a post Master for this office that you may make will be satisfactory to me—

Resplly &c
U S GRANT
Lt. Gen'l

Copies, DLC-USG, V, 46, 71, 107; DNA, RG 108, Letters Sent. On Dec. 28, 1864, Postmaster Gen. William Dennison wrote to USG. "A communication with respect to the expediency of establishing a Money Order Post Office at City Point, was sent from this Department on the 31st of October, 1864, to A. H. Markland, Esqr, Special Agent, and by him referred to your Headquarters in order that your views on the subject might be ascertained. In reply thereto a letter was addressed to Mr. Markland on the 17th ultimo by Col. T. S. Bowers, Assistant Adjutant General, stating 'that the Lieutenant General deems it inexpedient to establish a money-order office at City Point at present.' Mr. Parker, the Special Agent in charge of the Post-Office at City Point, to-day informs this Department that Col. Bowers recently expressed, with your assent, a desire that the money-order business might now be put into operation at that Office; I have therefore thought proper to address you on this subject in order that I might be fully informed as to your wishes which I shall endeavor to carry out as far as possible. In this connection I beg to suggest for your consideration that under existing law the appointment of a Postmaster at City Point will be necessary before that postoffice can be made a money-order office. I should be unwilling to appoint to that position any person who had not been designated by yourself. I transmit herewith a pamphlet giving a detailed statement of the Money Order System, and a list of money-order offices . . . P. S.—I would add that the Money Order System is especially advantageous to the Soldier in affording him a cheap and secure agency for the transmission of his money to his family or relations, thereby inducing him to form habits of prudence and economy." LS, *ibid.*, Letters Received.

To Edwin M. Stanton

———

From City Point Va Jan 4 *1864*5.

HON E M STANTON

The Richmond papers of today contain the following des-patches "From Genl Beauregard" The following official des-patch from Gen Beauregard was received yesterday by the War Dept "Charleston S C Jany 2d." The federal raiders are reported to have returned from the Mobile and Ohio rail road going west-ward they left Forty (40) wounded Gen Gholsim[1] badly wounded The damage to the Road will be repaired in about ten (10) days (signed) G. T. BEAUREGARD "From Genl Hardee" The sudjoined dispatch from General Hardee received yesterday afternoon by the Secretary of War, gives us the latest news from South Carolina. "Charleston Jany 2d. The enemy are landing in force on the south carolina side of the Savannah River & are driving in our pickets towards Hardeesville signed W. J. HARDEE An official report of the damage done to the Salt Works states that the ~~fighting~~ piping cisterns etc are uninjured. The sheds are all de-stroyed there are seven hundred and eighty eight ([7]88) Kettles broken and twelve hundred & eighty (1280) good Kettles remain-ing. The total amount of salt at the works is ninety two thousand (92000) bushels damaged slightly by the fire. The wells are not seriously damaged

U. S GRANT
Lt Genl

Telegram received (at 7:00 P.M.), DNA, RG 107, Telegrams Collected (Bound).

1. Samuel J. Gholson, judge of the U.S. District Court of Miss. for twenty-two years, appointed C.S.A. brig. gen. as of May 6, 1864, was wounded at an engagement at Egypt, Miss., on Dec. 28. See *O.R.*, I, xlv, part 2, 753.

To Edwin M. Stanton

City Point, Va. Jan. 4th *1864*5.

HON. E. M. STANTON,
SEC. OF WAR,
SIR:

I am constrained to request the removal of Maj. Gen. B. F. Butler from the command of the Department of N. C. & Va. I do this with reluctance but the good of the service requires it. In my absence Gen. Butler necessarily commands, and there is a lack of confidence felt in his Military ability, making him an unsafe commander for a large Army. His administration of the affairs of his Department is also objectionable.

> Very respectfully
> your obt. svt.
> U. S. GRANT
> Lt. Gen.

ALS, DNA, RG 94, Letters Received, 1369A 1865. *O.R.*, I, xlvi, part 2, 29. On Jan. 6, 1865, 1:00 P.M., USG telegraphed to President Abraham Lincoln. "I wrote a letter to the Secretary of War, which was mailed yesterday; asking to have General Butler removed from command. Learning that the Secy of War left Washington yesterday I telegraph you asking that prompt action may be taken in the matter" Telegram received (at 9:50 P.M.), DLC-Robert T. Lincoln; DNA, RG 107, Telegrams Collected (Bound); copies, *ibid.*, Telegrams Received in Cipher; *ibid.*, RG 94, Letters Received, 1369A 1865; *ibid.*, RG 108, Letters Sent; DLC-USG, V, 46, 71, 107; DLC-Benjamin F. Butler. *O.R.*, I, xlvi, part 2, 52. On Jan. 7, 11:00 A.M., Maj. Gen. Henry W. Halleck telegraphed to USG. "I send you by telegraph Genl. Order No. 1, relieving Genl Butler from his command. It will not be entered on the files or published here till you have it delivered to him. Please answer by telegraph the [d]ate that Genl Butler is [r]elieved." ALS (telegram sent), DNA, RG 107, Telegrams Collected (Bound); telegram received, *ibid.*; *ibid.*, RG 108, Letters Received. *O.R.*, I, xlvi, part 2, 60. Halleck enclosed a copy of General Orders No. 1, War Dept., Jan. 7. "I. By direction of the President of the United States Major Genl B. F. Butler is relieved from the command of the Department of North Carolina and Virginia. Lt General Grant will designate an officer to take this command temporarily   II. Major Genl Butler on being relieved will repair to Lowell, Mass. and report by letter to the Adjt General of the Army." ADf, DNA, RG 94, Letters Received, 49W 1865; *ibid.*, RG 107, Telegrams Collected (Bound); telegram received, *ibid.*; *ibid.*, RG 108, Letters Received. *O.R.*, I, xlvi, part 2, 60. On the same day, Lt. Col. Theodore S. Bowers issued Special Orders No. 5. "In pursuance of Gen. Orders No 1, War Department, Adjutant Generals Office, Washington D C,

Jan. 7 1865, Maj. Gen. E. O. C. Ord, U S Vols., will relieve Maj. Gen B. F. Butler in the command of the Department of Virginia and NorthCarolina, temporarily. Maj. Gen. B. F. Butler will turn over to Maj. Gen. E. O C. Ord, the records and orders of the Department, and all public money in his possession, or subject to his order, collected by virtue of rules and regulations which he may have established. The Department Staff will report to Maj. Gen. Ord for duty." Copies, DLC-USG, V, 57, 63, 64, 65; DLC-Andrew Johnson; DNA, RG 94, Letters Received, 1369A 1865; *ibid.*, RG 107, Telegrams Received in Cipher. *O.R.*, I, xlvi, part 2, 61. On Jan. 8, 10:30 A.M., USG telegraphed to Halleck transmitting a copy of Special Orders No. 5. "Genera[l] Ord[er] No 1, from the Adjutant Generals Office together with the following order from this Head Quarters has been deliver[ed] to Gen Butler and he may [be] regarded as relieved from duty from this date." Telegram received (at 5:00 P.M.), DNA, RG 107, Telegrams Collected (Bound); copies, *ibid.*, Telegrams Received in Cipher; *ibid.*, RG 94, Letters Received, 1369A 1865; *ibid.*, RG 108, Letters Sent; DLC-USG, V, 46, 71, 107. *O.R.*, I, xlvi, part 2, 67.

On Jan. 11, 10:35 P.M., Maj. Gen. Edward O. C. Ord telegraphed to USG. "Genl Butler sends up 700 of his parting order printed   I told him before he left there was no objection to his taking leave in an order—but it contains these words—'I have refused to order the sacrifice of such soldiers and am relieved from your command—The wasted blood of my men does not stain my garments —For my action I am responsible to god and my country'—shall I send this out —" ALS (telegram sent), DNA, RG 108, Letters Received; telegram received (at 10:40 P.M.), *ibid. O.R.*, I, xlvi, part 2, 98. At 10:45 P.M., Bowers telegraphed to Ord. "Gen Grant directs me to say to you, that Gen Butlers parting orders may be sent out." Telegram received, Ord Papers, CU-B; copies, DLC-USG, V, 46, 71, 107; DNA, RG 108, Letters Sent. *O.R.*, I, xlvi, part 2, 98. Butler's orders are *ibid.*, pp. 70–71, and Butler sent USG an autographed copy. AES, DNA, RG 108, Letters Received. On Jan. 13, Butler wrote to Brig. Gen. John A. Rawlins. "Private. . . . You know that I like to see a thing well done, if done at all, and I must say my enemies about your headquarters are very bungling in their malice and will bring the general into remark. Take the article in the Herald by Cadwallader, and it will appear to have been dictated at headquarters, where I know the general had nothing to do with it. It was not telegraphed, and to have reached Tuesday's Herald must have left in the mail-boat at 10 a. m., when the order for my removal was not served on me till 12 m. of the same day, Sunday. Unless the orders of the general are disclosed before they are made public, how could the 'news of General Butler's removal excite much comment; but as far as I can learn but little or no animadversion.' It could not have been known beyond General Grant's personal staff, and whatever may have been the feelings of some of those gentlemen toward myself, I should not expect much, if any, animadversion with them. Again, Cadwallader could never have written this sentence: [']It has been General Butler's misfortune to appoint too many of (these) selfish and irresponsible persons to official positions of trust and responsibility. Their indiscretions have cost him dearly, &c.['] Now, as I appointed Cadwallader himself as a lieutenant in the U. S. Volunteers, as I supposed and believed at the wish of General Grant, for the selfish reason on Cadwallader's part that he wished to escape the draft which would take him away from general headquarters as a reporter, and as he is wholly 'irresponsible,' and as not only I but General Grant is 'suffering from his indiscretion,' although he had this piece

of news in advance of anybody else, I do not believe he would wish to communicate it to the Herald. Now, wasn't the fellow who got up this dispatch a bungler?
Again, to put the removal on the ground that I was the last of the 'civilian generals' brings an issue between the regulars and volunteers, and I assure you that
the person who penned that does not love the general, or else is as stupid as a
quartermaster who would let the horses of a whole army starve for want of forage
when there is plenty in the country, if he had a little energy to get it, because
the Regular Army do not like the general. They did not before the war, and his
great success since has not increased their love, and his day of trial is coming,
and therefore they seek to throw off those of the volunteers who would be his
friends, and it is of no consequence to him whether the injury proceeds from their
enmity or incapacity. Now, my dear Rawlins, look after those stupid fellows a
little, or they will do mischief to their chief. They have already circulated a story
that General Grant has always been opposed to me, and that I have been thrust
upon him for political reasons, so, if possible, to get a personal issue between me
and the general. It will be his fault if that issue comes, not mine; it will be my
misfortune, and the work of his subordinates. The navy waits at Beaufort again,
and the army waits for them." *O.R.*, I, xlvi, part 2, 120–21.

To Maj. Gen. Henry W. Halleck

City Point Va
7.30 P. m Jan 4. [*1865*]

MAJOR GEN H. W. HALLECK.
CHIEF OF STAFF

I hear nothing either through rebel papers or direct from
Granger's movement from Pascagoula.

I would like to have Gen. Canby operate against Mobile this
winter with such force as he can collect from his own command
but I will not send any troops to him from Middle Tennessee. If
Hood goes south from Corinth order A. J. Smith & two Divisions
besides to Baltimore Md to be thrown where they may be wanted
on arrival.

U S GRANT
Lt Gen

Telegram received (at 8:40 P.M.), DNA, RG 107, Telegrams Collected
(Bound); copies, *ibid.*, Telegrams Received in Cipher; *ibid.*, RG 108, Letters
Sent; DLC-USG, V, 46, 71, 107. *O.R.*, I, xlv, part 2, 506; *ibid.*, I, xlviii, part
1, 408.

To Rear Admiral David D. Porter

City Point Jany 4th 18645

DEAR ADMIRAL

Your letter brought by the hands of Lt. Porter is received, The instructions to Genl, Terry were given before its receipt but you will see that Gen, Terry has not only been instructed to consult with but to be guided by your counsel as far as is consistent with his responsibilities,

In my letter of instructions and also in my letter to you written at the same time, I state that a Division of troops numbering from four to five thousand ~~troops~~ men will be in readiness at Fort Monroe to sail to you at an hour's notice, In addition to this if it becomes necessary to our success, I will send all the men that can be used,

Very Truly Yours
U. S. GRANT
Lt, Genl,

REAR ADMIRAL D. D. PORTER
COMDG N'TH AT-BL-SQR

Copies, DLC-USG, V, 46, 72, 107; DNA, RG 108, Letters Sent. *O.R.*, I, xlvi, part 2, 29–30. On Jan. 3, 1865, Rear Admiral David D. Porter, "Flag Ship 'Malvern,'" Beaufort, N. C., wrote to USG. "I hold it to be a good rule never to send a boy on a man's errand, and we must now calculate that the rebels having ascertained their weakness, will take measures to strengthen themselves. The great thing was to effect a landing, which being done everything else was easy— the troops could have fortified themselves where they landed against one hundred thousand men, covered as they were by over 80 heavy guns on the gun boats, strung all along the beach. There is no use fretting over the past—we must endeavor to avoid mistakes in the future, and if any expedition fails now to take the works, which were comparatively weak ten days ago, the sagacity of the leaders of the late expedition will be applauded. The failure to assault the works so battered, and the people so demoralized by the dreadful bombardment, will set the rebels to work making themselves much stronger, and this is what I wish to draw your attention to. We cannot stop their work without bringing the whole squadron into play, and firing away all our ammunition before the time comes for work. It is no joke getting in coal and ammunition lying outside. The ships can only carry ten hours firing. Now I propose (if it is possible) that you send every man you can spare here—with entrenching tools, and 15 thirty pounders— the last party had not even a spade. An army can entrench themselves at Masonboro and stay as long as they like, if a typhoon blows the ships to sea. I have received a letter from sherman—he wants me to time my operations by his, which I think a good plan—we will make a sure thing of it—but the troops and the Navy must be ready to strike at a moment's notice, and when the enemy least expects us. we will have the report spread that the troops are to cooperate with sherman in the attack on Charleston. I hope sherman will be allowed to carry out his plans—he will have Wilmington in less than a month, and Charleston will fall like a ripe pear. I expect you understand all this better than I do. I have made arrangements to keep communication open with Sherman from the time he starts. Capt Breese will give you all the latest news." LS, DNA, RG 108, Letters Received. *O.R.*, I, xlvi, part 2, 20; *O.R.* (Navy), I, xi, 405–6.

On Jan. 14, Porter, "Off Fort Fisher," wrote to USG. "The forces under General Terry were landed yesterday without accident or opposition and their supplies followed immediately—To day I hope to finish landing the Guns which will be all left to do—Genl' Terry is throwing up a breastwork across the neck of land from Battery Anderson to the River Battery Anderson is called by us Flag Pond Battery—I find Genl' Terry most agreable and efficient but I think from the way he is going to work that he would like to have more men—This however is a mere matter of opinion of mine which you may take for what it is worth Genl' Terry has said nothing about wanting more men and I judge is one of those who would not ask for reinforcement unless it should be absolutely necessay—Yesterday afternoon after landing the Troops I went with a portion of the Fleet to attack the Fort—Our fire completely silenced them as usual The Iron clads fired nearly all day yesterday and the Fort bears many scars but I cannot tell how much harm was done—We suffered no loss whatever— . . . I think small arm ammunition is wanted as some was wet in landing Provisions also—We cannot average more than two days a week in which any thing can be landed safely—" LS, DNA, RG 108, Letters Received. *O.R.*, I, xlvi, part 2, 128–29; *O.R.* (Navy), I, xi, 432.

To Bvt. Maj. Gen. Alfred H. Terry

City Point Jany 4th 186[5]

MAJ. GEN. A. H. TERRY
COMDG EX-AGAINST FORT FISHER
GENERAL

A letter received from Admiral Porter since th your former instructions were delivered asks that the transport fleet may be assembled at Beaufort N. C. As the collection of so many vessels loaded with troops at that point would be likely to advertise to the enemy the object of the obj expedition, I think it will be desirable for you to run in with your own vessels and consult with Admiral Porter, leaving the remainder of the vessels outside, As you go without the Naval Brigade you will require the assistance of the

Navy both in men, and boats, to aid you in landing troops and supplies, I have not a doubt but it will afford the Naval Commander
pleasure to furnish these, but it ~~will want~~ is a subject you will want
to have understood before, leaving Beaufort, On your arrival off
Fort Fisher especially if a landing is effected you may find yourself
deficient in many things you will want, Such of them as Beaufort
will supply send there directly for, For the balance send to Fort
Monroe, communicating from that point directly with these Headquarters by telegraph,

    During the operations of the expedition placed in your com-
mand you will, in all official matters communicate directly with
these Headquarters, unless otherwise ordered,

Very Respectfully
Your obt, svt
U. S. GRANT
Lt, Genl,

Copies, DLC-USG, V, 46, 72, 107; DNA, RG 108, Letters Sent. *O.R.*, I, xlvi,
part 2, 35.

    On Jan. 4, 1865, Lt. Col. Cyrus B. Comstock twice telegraphed to Bvt. Maj.
Gen. Alfred H. Terry. "The hospital steamers fitted up are at Savannah. You
will have to make the best arrangements you can, using in emergency the cabins
of the transports which take the troops. You should supply yourself with the
Napoleon ammunition needed—say, 300 rounds per gun." *Ibid.* "The Lt. Gen.
desires me to ask how many steamers have gone down & how many are now at
Bermuda. What ~~part~~ fraction of your force is aboard." ALS (telegram sent),
DNA, RG 94, War Records Office, Miscellaneous War Records. *O.R.*, I, xlvi,
part 2, 35. At 7:20 P.M., Terry, Bermuda Hundred, telegraphed to Comstock.
"One brigade of Genl Ames division has gone down on river steamers to be
transhipped on the Atlantic The remainder of his division is now embarking.
The batteries are also embarking. Eleven boats have reported, the first of them
came about two hours since. ~~The embarkation of Ame's division will be com-
pleted in an hour & a half.~~" ALS (telegram sent), DNA, RG 107, Telegrams
Collected (Unbound). On Jan. 5, Lt. Col. Theodore S. Bowers issued Special
Orders No. 5. "Lieut. Col. C. B. Comstock, Aid-de-Camp, will report to Maj Gen.
A. H. Terry. as Chief Engineer of the Expedition under his command." ADS,
DLC-Cyrus B. Comstock; copies (designated Special Orders No. 3, Jan. 4),
DLC-USG, V, 57, 63, 64, 65. Dated Jan. 4 in *O.R.*, I, xlvi, part 2, 30. Reports
of Jan. 8, 9, and 11 from Comstock to Brig. Gen. John A. Rawlins are *ibid.*, pp.
69, 79–80, 93.

    On Jan. 10, Terry, "Steam Ship McClellan Beaufort No. Ca." wrote to
Rawlins. "I have the honor to report that the fleet of transports containing the
troops under my command sailed from Fort Monroe on Friday the 6th inst. at
4 o'Cl'k A. M. Owing to the extremely heavy weather experienced none of the
vessels arrived off this port until Sunday morning the 8th; during that day they

all with the exception of the Steamer Tonawanda, which has on board a portion
of General Ames Division, were collected at the appointed rendezvous twenty
miles off the harbor. The Tonawanda has not yet reported. I came into the harbor with my own vessel, waited upon Admiral Porter, notified him of the approach of the land forces, and said to him that they would be ready to proceed to
their destination at any time when he should be ready. The Admiral informed
me that the weather was such as to preclude the possibility of making a landing
and that in his judgment some time would elapse before there would be a favorable opportunity. That opportunity has not yet occurred, but I have given him
fully to understand that the land forces are and will be ready to move at any and
at all times. This delay may cause us some inconvenience as regards coal, as the
vessels lying off the land are of course consuming fuel and there is scarcely any
here belonging to either the army or the navy. Before I left Fort Monroe I directed Col. Dodge, Chief Quarter Master, to make arrangements to have two
coal schooners follow us immediately, and since our arrival here I have instructed
him to send for enough additional coal to re-supply all the vessels. Fortunately
I found here a schooner which was loaded with commissary stores for the former
expedition: she has on board two hundred thousand rations so that there will be
no embarrassment on that score. Water is being procured from the Newport
River for the supply of those ships which have no condensers. Four of the transports received damage in the gale, which has compelled them to come in here to
refit; they are all however fully repaired or will be so to day. From the present
appearance of the weather we shall be able to proceed to-morrow or next day."
LS, NHi. *O.R.*, I, xlvi, part 2, 89–90.

On Jan. 13, Terry, "Before Wilmington," twice telegraphed to Rawlins.
"We arrived here last night and disembarked today, getting the infantry on
shore at 3 P M: Our ammunition is landed and most of the stores. We hold a
line across the point from the Flag Pond battery, but it is not a good one and
probably will have to be changed during the night: As soon as the line is determined upon I shall fortify it. Tomorrow I intend to move down troops under
cover of the navy fire and determine whither an assault is advisable: prisoners
and deserters report that Hokes Div. is here, or that three brigades are here. A
portion of the ammunition in the mens boxes was spoiled in getting through the
surf: Please send me Three hundred Thousand (300.000) rounds of calibre
fifty eight (58) I think that fifty wagons and teams should also be sent down;
They will be useful in any event" "After consultation with Col. Comstock and
in view of what I think is the ascertained fact; that the whole, or nearly the
whole of Hokes force is still here I think that it would be advisable to send the
balance of the troops which Gen. Grant spoke of sending forward. It seems indispensable to hold strongly the line towards Wilmington; and for this purpose
at least four (4) of my brigades are necessary, leaving only two brigades for
operations against the fort. In case an assault should be tried and be unsuccessful
the losses which would be incurred would leave an entirely insufficient force for
further operations. I suggest that these which should be sent in vessels capable
of standing a storm at their anchors here and should be provisioned coaled and
watered for at least fifteen days so that in case the weather should prevent the
landing of supplies for more troops than we now have, they could remain on
the vessels . . . P. S. Please send me twenty (20) Paulins to cover stores and
ammunition" Telegrams received (sent via Fort Monroe, Jan. 15, 7:00 P.M.,
received at 11:00 P.M.), DNA, RG 107, Telegrams Collected (Bound); (on
Jan. 16) *ibid.*, RG 108, Letters Received; copies (2—one of the second), *ibid.*,

RG 107, Telegrams Collected (Unbound); (the first) *ibid.*, Telegrams Received in Cipher; DLC-Edwin M. Stanton. *O.R.*, I, xlvi, part 2, 122.

On Jan. 16, 4:00 P.M., USG telegraphed to Maj. Gen. Henry W. Halleck. "The following has been received from Genl. Terry. Orders have been given for Everything required." Telegram received (at 5:00 P.M.), DNA, RG 107, Telegrams Collected (Bound); copy (marked as received at 5:30 P.M.), *ibid.*, Telegrams Received in Cipher. Correspondence concerning sending supplies and reinforcements to Terry is in *O.R.*, I, xlvi, part 2, 145, 151–52, 163–64, 165.

On Jan. 16, 10:30 A.M., Capt. Henry C. Robinett, Fort Monroe, telegraphed to Bowers. "Steamer Caliafornia leaves here 12. o'clock. Capt's of transports returned from Expedition to Wil. report all forces safely and nicely landed ~~and~~ on Friday last; and skirmishing going on about Ft Fisher. They Supposed it already in our possesion. Of course none of troops that left here last are included." ALS (telegram sent), DNA, RG 107, Telegrams Collected (Unbound); telegrams received (2—at 12:10 P.M.), *ibid.*, Telegrams Collected (Bound). A copy, *ibid.*, Telegrams Collected (Unbound), is dated Jan. 15, and the telegram is printed with that date in *O.R.*, I, xlvi, part 2, 141.

On Jan. 15, Terry, "On Federal Point," telegraphed to Rawlins. "I have the honor to report that Fort Fisher was carried by assault this afternoon and evening by General Ames Division (the second) and the 2nd Brigade of the First Division of the 24th Army Corps, gallantly aided by a battalion of marines and seamen from the Navy. The assault was preceded by a heavy bombardment from the fleet and was made at 3.30 P. M. when the First Brigade (Curtis') of Ames Division effected a lodgment upon the parapet but full possession of the work was not obtained until 10. P. M. The behavior of ~~the troops~~ both officers and men, was most admirable. All the works south of Fort Fisher are now occupied by our troops. We have not less than twelve hundred prisoners including General Whiting & Col. Lamb the commandant of the Fort. I regret to say that our loss is severe especially in officers. I am not yet able to form an estimate of the number of casualties—" LS (telegram sent), DNA, RG 107, Telegrams Collected (Unbound); telegram received (sent via Fort Monroe, Jan. 17, received at 9:10 A.M.), *ibid.*, Telegrams Collected (Bound). *O.R.*, I, xlvi, part 2, 140. On Jan. 17, USG telegraphed to Secretary of War Edwin M. Stanton transmitting the telegram printed above. "The following official dispatch from Brevet Maj Genl A H Terry Comdg the land forces operating against Fort Fisher announcing its capture by the united valor of the army and navy is Just received. I have ordered a Salute of one hundred guns to be fired by each army here in honor of their great triumph" Telegram received (at 10:45 A.M.), DNA, RG 107, Telegrams Collected (Bound); copies, *ibid.*, RG 108, Letters Sent; DLC-USG, V, 46, 71, 107. *O.R.*, I, xlvi, part 2, 158. USG's letterbooks indicate that Rawlins also transmitted Terry's telegram to Maj. Gen. George G. Meade and Maj. Gen. Edward O. C. Ord. Copies, DLC-USG, V, 46, 71, 107; DNA, RG 108, Letters Sent. Recipient copies indicate that Rawlins telegraphed to Meade and Ord at 8:45 A.M. "The following dispatch just received—In honor of this Signal victory you will fire a salute of 100 guns" Telegram received, Ord Papers, CU-B; DNA, RG 94, War Records Office, Army of the Potomac; *ibid.*, RG 393, Army of the Potomac, Miscellaneous Letters Received; *ibid.*, 24th Army Corps, Telegrams Received; copies, *ibid.*, 9th Army Corps, 2nd Div., Telegrams Received; (2) Meade Papers, PHi. *O.R.*, I, xlvi, part 2, 159. Enclosed was a telegram from Comstock to Rawlins, Jan. 16, 2:00 A.M. "After a careful reconnaissance on the 14th it was decided to risk an assault on Ft. Fisher. Paines division with Col Abbots brigade to hold our line already strong, across the peninsula & facing Wilmington, against Hoke, while Ames divisn ~~to~~ should assault on the West end of the ~~work~~ land front ~~while~~ and four hundred marines & sixteen hundred sailors ~~assaulted~~ on the east end. After three hours of heavy navy fire the assault was made at 3 P. M. on the 15th. Curtis brigade led & as soon as it got on the ~~north~~ west end of the land front was followed by Penny-backers & later by Bells. After desperate fighting gaining foot by foot ~~at~~ & severe loss, at 5 P. M. we had possession of about half the land front. Abbots brigade was then taken from our line facing Wilmington & put into ~~the wo~~ Ft. Fisher & on ~~again~~ pushing it forward at 10. P. M. it took the rest of the work with little resistance, the garrison falling back to the extreme point of the peninsula where they were followed & captured—among others Gen. Whiting & Col Lamb both wounded. I think we have ~~nearly or~~ quite 1000 prisoners. I hope our own loss may not exceed 500 but it is impossible to judge in the night. Among the wounded are the commanders of the three leading brigades, Gen. Curtis being wounded not severely but Cols. Pennybacker & Bell dangerously. The ~~fort~~ land front was a formidable one, the parapet in places 15 or 20 feet high but the men went at it nobly, under a severe musketry fire. The ~~navy~~ marines & sailors went up gallantly but the musketry fire from the east end of the land front was so severe that they did not succeed in entering the work. The navy fire on the work, judging from the holes must have been terrific. Many of the guns were injured, how many there were on the point I cannot say—perhaps 30 or 40." ALS (tele-gram sent), DNA, RG 107, Telegrams Collected (Unbound); copies, *ibid.*, RG 94, War Records Office, Army of the Potomac; *ibid.*, RG 107, Telegrams Col-lected (Bound); *ibid.*, RG 393, 9th Army Corps, 2nd Div., Telegrams Received; *ibid.*, Army of the Potomac, Miscellaneous Letters Received; *ibid.*, 2nd Army Corps, Telegrams Received; *ibid.*, 24th Army Corps, Telegrams Received; Ord Papers, CU-B; DLC-Edwin M. Stanton; Meade Papers, PHi. *O.R.*, I, xlvi, part 1, 405–6. On Jan. 17, 9:45 A.M., Meade telegraphed to Rawlins. "A salute of one hundred guns will be fired this day at 12. M, in honor of the brilliant & glorious capture of Fort Fisher; which I deem to be one of the most important events that could ~~that~~ have occurred at this time, & on which I most heartily congratulate the Lt. Genl. Comd." ALS (telegram sent), DNA, RG 94, War Records Office, Army of the Potomac; telegram received, *ibid.*, RG 108, Letters Received. *O.R.*, I, xlvi, part 2, 159. Also on Jan. 17, Lt. Col. Horace Porter, Fort Monroe, trans-mitted a copy of Comstock's telegram to Asst. Secretary of War Charles A. Dana. ALS (telegram sent), DNA, RG 107, Telegrams Collected (Unbound); tele-gram received, *ibid.*, Telegrams Collected (Bound).

On Jan. 16, Comstock twice wrote to Rawlins, first at 3:00 A.M. "Thank God, we have Ft. Fisher. How, the telegrams will tell. Curtis brigade which led, behaved spledidly & he should have the full star, as I hope Terry will get two. Our ~~troops~~ leading three brigades were badly disorganized by the assault, but even if ~~they~~ the rebs had held strongly after dark I think we should have got the work tonight, though they say it was being reinforced, I haven't talked with Gn Terry yet but think we can now push Hoke into Wilmington & perhaps cap-ture it though it is reported strongly fortified. The force about Wilmington is reported all the way from 6 to 13000 men. I woudnt be surprised if the rebs had 1800 men in Ft Fisher when we assaulted. Send the division from Crook." "I was too sleepy this morning when writing & had too little time to give details of last nights work & will try to do it now, and first for the best sketch I can make yet, . . . On the land front at the ~~beginning of the Navy fire~~ (originally) there were ~~from 12 to 15~~ 16 guns—heavy, on the sea front about the same. At the capture we found perhaps 6 of the guns on the land front & 12 on the sea front, still serviceable. There were small guns at various points of the work   The parapet on the land front & from it as far as f, on the sea front averages about 15 feet high above the very slight ditch in front, which is no obstacle & having the palisades in front of it. The traverses rise from ~~8~~ 5 to 10 feet higher than the parapet & run back into the work thirty or forty feet, the earth being being excavated at their inner ends so as there to make some of them 25 feet high. To get earth for these enormous traverse bomb proofs on the land front the ground has been dug away in rear of the land front ~~I~~in some places six feet deep for a hundred feet square thus giving cover from fire in all directions. The land front to us looked like this, ~~to us~~ before getting in. . . . Gn Terry & I went up to within about 400 yards of the right or west end of the land front & concluded that was the best place to try an assault,   We could not see a swampy stream close up to the work which was quite an obstacle. The morning of the 15th our skirmishers were pushed to within 300 yards of the fort at this end where they soon covered themselves. When the assault was made the navy fired over, & Curtis' brigade rushed first from the rifle pits where they first came up (see fig 1) over 300 yds of open, to this skirmish line. Next they rushed for the fort covering at first ~~about~~ in line about half the front but under the musketry fire from the centre & left of the force closing to the right, & after a little hesitation went through the gaps made by navy fire in palisades at a, swarmed up the parapet to the traverse at b & there fought 20 minutes over the parapet. Pennybackers brigade was then ordered up & succeeded in passing to the right of the work driving the enemy from behind the stockade running from the parapet to Cape Fear river & getting into one of the excavations behind b. Meantime the men at b had gone to c & so on; Bells brigade was sent in & the enemy were finally driven back to d after three hours obstinate fighting. Meanwhile as the progress had got to be slow & things looked doubtful Abbots brigade was ordered from the Wilmington line although Hoke was then demonstrating against it, & the sailors & marines who had gone up handsomely but back in a great hurry, were sent to take Abbots place. Abbot's first brigade got in about dark—Gn Terrys H. Q. were about 500 yds from the work—The brigade was sent up to finish the work by a night assault but we heard for an hour nothing of it. Impatient at last we went into the work, found the three leading brigades largely in bomb proofs or under cover, much broken up, & that it was prepared to intrench & hold on till morning. After examination the order to try to carry the other traverses one by one was made peremptory & at 9½ P. M. the men after loss of time were got in motion, the enemy were already leaving, made little resistance were followed without fight to ~~Federal pt~~ Ft. Buchanan where they surrendered. Whiting had three balls in his leg & wanted it distinctly understood, he had been brought there against his consent, & found fault with those 'above' for doing nothing, probably referring to Hokes failing to make a serious attack. Instead of 1000 we already have nearly 1900 well prisoners & some hundreds of wounded & the rebel ordnance officer says there are 72 guns in the work. Their force was nearly equal to our assaulting column (3000 men). If I had known just how things were I should not have dared to advise an assault—the work was stronger than it looked, & I dont quite see yet how the devil we succeeded—it must be the same good luck that has given us five days of splendid weather when all the old sea dogs said it couldnt possibly last more than three. That reminds me of Ammen who isn't a croaker & who wishes to be remembered to the general. Gen. Terry has just come in from the Malvern where he has been to see the Sec. of War & says the Secy. is wild with delight—has breveted or promoted all the brigade & division commandrs in the assault & some staff officers & given me two brevets making Brig. Gn. in the regular army. I should have been satisfied with one & suspect the Senate will see it in the same light. Gen Terry gave me more credit than was deserved, for while a staff officer can give his opinion, the responsibility is entirely on the commander. Terry has his two stars. We all think we have done a big thing in getting into the infernal place, & it looks ugly enough now as you look at it from the outside. Our loss is about 660, the navy think theirs two or three hundred. We are getting our wounded & prisons off & ~~today~~ tomorrow will have supples in Cape Fear river into which the Navy are feeling their way. . . . P. S. We are not quite certain whether Wilmington or the other (Ft. Caswell) entrance should be the next thing, the admiral seems to favor the last. It will probably depend on what the Navy finds across the river. Meanwhile we are freeing ourselves of wounded & prisons as fast as possible. Thinking it might be important that Sherman should know at once of the fall of Ft. Fisher as by delay the news might not be able to follow, I took the liberty of sending ~~yesterday~~ today a dispatch boat with the news to Hilton Head, to Foster & Sherman." ALS, *ibid.*, RG 108, Letters from Comstock.

To Julia Dent Grant

City Point, Va, Jan. 4th *1864*5.

DEAR JULIA,

I received your two despatches one Wishing me a "Happy New Year," the other announcing the present of a furnished house in Phila. I think you had as well arrange to move into your new house at once and get Missy and Jess. at good schools. Leave the boys where they are. They have been changed from one school to another often enough. Fred may keep Little Rebel with him at least until other dispositions are made. As soon as I can I will run up and see you in your new house.

I presume before this you have received $500 00. which I directed Capt. Leet to send you and also some money from Jones. I have not heard from Jones however myself and it may be he has no money of mine except the gold. That you will get but I want you to keep it. It may be that going into a new house you will want many things the house is not provided with. If so write to me about how much you will want and I will get the money. The house being furnished it is likely $1000 00 will fit you up elegantly. I can get that for you easily. Recollect now that you want to save out of your $500 00 per month enough to buy you a carriage. I will then give you Egypt and another good horse to go with him.

Love and kisses for you and the children.

ULYS.

ALS, DLC-USG.

To George H. Stuart et al.

City Point, Va. Jan.y 4th *18645.*

M'SSRS GEO. H. STUART, A. E. BORIE, WM C. KENT,
E. C. KNIGHT, DAVIS PEARSON, GEO. W. WHITNEY AND
JAS. GRAHAM, COMMITTEE,
GENTLEMEN

Through you the Loyal Citizens of Philadelphia have seen fit to present me with a house, lot and furnature, in your beautiful city. The letter notifying me of this is just received.

It is with feelings of gratitude and pride that I accept this substantial testimonial of the esteem of your Loyal citizens. Gratitude, because it is evidence of a deep set determination on the part of a large number of citizens that this war shall go on until the Union is restored. Pride, that my humble efforts in so great a cause should attract such a token from a city of strangers to me.

I will not predict a day when we will have peace again, with a Union restored. But that that day will come is as sure as the rising of to-morrow's Sun. I have never doubted this in the darkest days of this dark and terrible rebellion.

Until this happy day of peace does come my family will occupy and enjoy your magnificent present. But until that I do not expect, nor desire, to see much of the enjoyments of a home fireside.

I have the honor to be
with great respect
Your obt. svt.
U. S. GRANT
Lt. Gen. U. S. A.

ALS, DLC-George H. Stuart. On Dec. 23, 1864, the members of the committee
prepared a printed letter. "Learning some time since that LIEUTENANT GENERAL
GRANT was desirous of securing a house in Philadelphia, a number of gentlemen have formed the project of purchasing and furnishing a residence in this
city, and presenting it to the general, as a home for himself and family, in order
to show the very high consideration with which his military abilities are regarded. Feeling that this mark of personal esteem, proposed to be shown to the
Commander of our Armies, will commend itself at once to you, we annex a list
of the subscriptions already received, and would be happy to add your name to
the number, should you desire to aid in the matter. We are desirous of having
the whole completed by New Year's Day, and in the mean time, you can communicate, at your convenience, with any member of the Committee. On account
of the largely increased value of Real Estate, an amount larger than was at first
deemed necessary, will be required." War Library and Museum, Military Order
of the Loyal Legion, Philadelphia, Pa. On a second sheet, the committee listed
forty-seven subscribers who had pledged amounts between $1000 and $250 to
the fund. A final list of subscribers and an account of expenses is *ibid*. On Jan.
2, 1865, the committee, probably through George H. Stuart, wrote to USG.
"Having accidentally learned accidentally that Mrs. Grant was looking for, and
unable to obtain a house in this city, which you have Concluded to make your
place of residence, it affords us great pleasure to present to yourself and family,
a house furnished and ready, in our City of Homes, Philadelphia. As citizens of
the United States we beg your acceptance of this gift as a slight testimonial of
the gratitude we feel, in common with all loyal citizens, for the eminent services
you have rendered to the nation, during its present struggle for the suppression of
the Rebellion, and as a token of our appreciation of the your distinguished military ability, patriotism, and moral worth, which has given to our country so
much of its present security, and made its prospects for future happiness &
prosperity so bright and cheerful. As citizens of Philada, feeling that it would
be a high honor to have you for a fellow townsman, we present it as a token of
the welcome which our entire city extends to your family, whilst you are still
fighting the battles of the nation, as also and which we wish to most heartily
extend to yourself, when the war shall be over. In requesting your acceptance of
the title deed herewith present[ed], let us Express the hope that through the instrumentality of yourself, and other tried and trusted heroes, the time may soon
come when the blessings of Union and peace, founded on the principles of justice
and freedom, shall crown the efforts now so nobly made That our Country may
come forth from the terrible ordeal, stronger, better, purer, and freeer is our
hearty sincere earnest wish, and to this End, we pray that God may long spare
your useful valuable valuable [li]fe and continue your invaluable services for our
national prosperity and peace." ADf, DLC-George H. Stuart.

On Jan. 6, USG wrote to Stuart in his capacity as chairman of the Christian
Commission. "The beautiful ring which I hope was the means of contributing
largely to the humane and charitable Commission of which you are an honored
member, and which the contributors saw fit to present me with is received. As
surmised by you I have but little use for such orniments for myself but appreciate
the compliment none the less. I have every reason for feeling very gratiful to the
citizens of Philadelphia for repeated marks of concideration and shall always be
glad of an oppertunity for showing it." ALS, *ibid*.

To Edwin M. Stanton

(Cipher)   City Point, Va, Jan. 5th 1865 [*11:00* A.M.]
HON. E. M. STANTON, SEC. OF WAR.

I will start in a few minuets for Fortress Monroe to see the fleet
sail from there and to complete instructions if anything further
should be required. It will get to sea this afternoon.

When the troops sent by Sheridan are embarked please order
them to rendezvous at Ft. Monroe and report by telegraph to me
for further orders.

U. S. GRANT
Lt. Gen

ALS (telegram sent), CSmH; telegram received, DNA, RG 107, Telegrams
Collected (Bound). *O.R.*, I, xlvi, part 2, 38. On Jan. 5, 1865, 12:30 P.M., Sec-
retary of War Edwin M. Stanton telegraphed to USG. "Your ~~Instructions~~ in-
structions will be given to Sheridan. I expect to leave here this afternoon for
Fortress Monroe and thence to Savannah with Collecter Draper" ALS (telegram
sent), DNA, RG 107, Telegrams Collected (Bound); telegram received, *ibid.*,
RG 108, Letters Received. *O.R.*, I, xlvi, part 2, 38.
     At 12:20 P.M., USG telegraphed to Brig. Gen. Israel Vogdes, Portsmouth,
Va. "I will be in Norfolk this evening." *Ibid.*, p. 46. Also on Jan. 5, Lt. Col. Cyrus
B. Comstock twice telegraphed to Bvt. Maj. Gen. Alfred H. Terry. "If conven-
ient the general would like to have you come over here & go with him down to
Ft Monroe leaving a staff-officer to take care of the balance of the embarcation."
"The general would like to have you stop here as you go down. Can you tell about
what hour it will be? Will your Qr Mr be able to furnish me a tent?" ALS
(telegrams sent), DNA, RG 107, Telegrams Collected (Unbound).
     At 8:00 P.M., Asst. Secretary of the Navy Gustavus V. Fox telegraphed to
USG. "Can you not possibly go down the coast for a few days. I think we have
a fine sea steamer at Norfolk and I will accompany you: It seems to be worth a
few hours of the directing mind" Telegram received, *ibid.*, Telegrams Collected
(Bound); *ibid.*, RG 108, Letters Received; copy, *ibid.*, RG 45, Miscellaneous
Letters Sent. *O.R.*, I, xlvi, part 2, 39; *O.R.* (Navy), I, xi, 411. On Jan. 6, 10:00
A.M., USG telegraphed to Fox. "It will hardly be possible for me to leave here
for a few days; If I can go however I will let you know" Telegram received (at
11:00 A.M.), DNA, RG 45, Miscellaneous Telegrams Received; (2) *ibid.*, RG
107, Telegrams Collected (Bound); copies, *ibid.*, Telegrams Received in Cipher;
ibid., RG 108, Letters Sent; DLC-USG, V, 46, 71, 107. *O.R.*, I, xlvi, part 2, 52.
     On Jan. 7, Fox telegraphed to USG. "I go north tomorrow night on account
of the death of an Uncle Shall return Thursday morning. I shall not go if you
call for me before I start." Copy, DNA, RG 45, Miscellaneous Letters Sent. On
Jan. 9, 2:30 P.M., USG telegraphed to Fox. "I cannot leave here at this time. I
must be here to take advantage of any great reduction of the enemy's forces."

ALS (telegram sent), CSmH; telegrams received (2—at 3:50 P.M.), DNA, RG 107, Telegrams Collected (Bound). *O.R.*, I, xlvi, part 2, 74.

To Maj. Gen. Henry W. Halleck

(Cipher)   Fortress Monroe Va
                                            Jan.y 5th 1865

MAJ. GEN ~~MEIGS~~, HALLECK WASHINGTON

Please have everything called for by Sherman forwarded without delay. He cannot move until the forage and subsistence called for is received. A Special Messenger from Sherman has just left here with his requisitions.

U. S. GRANT
Lt. Gn

ALS (telegram sent), PPRF; telegram received (marked as sent at 8:00 P.M., received at 9:00 P.M.), DNA, RG 107, Telegrams Collected (Bound); (marked as sent at 7:00 P.M.) *ibid.*, Telegrams Collected (Unbound). Printed as sent at 8:00 A.M. in *O.R.*, I, xlvii, part 2, 16. See letter to Maj. Gen. William T. Sherman, Dec. 27, 1864.

To Edwin M. Stanton

(Cipher)   City Point, Va, Jan. 6th 1865 [*5:30* P.M.]
HON. E. M. STANTON, SEC. OF WAR, FORTRESS MONROE, VA,

I am just in receipt of a letter from Sherman asking me to reinforce Foster so that he will not be compelled to leave a Division of his Army there.[1] Please say to Sherman that I will send the Division now embarking at Baltimore. They probably will reach him two days after you do. I wrote to Sherman some time ago to direct Foster to organize Negro troops to do Garrison duty. ~~He answers that no matter how good Colored troops are there is a prejudice against them in Savannah and that the best kind of feeling exists now and had better be kept up. This is the idea conveyed in his letter. It would be well to say~~

Please say to Sherman that if Foster will go to work and organize Colored troops they can garrison the Forts and islands leaving all of his white troops for Savannah and the camp at Pocotaligo enabling the Division which I now send to return in the Spring if necessary.

U. S. GRANT
Lt. Gen

ALS (telegram sent), CSmH; copies, DLC-USG, V, 46, 71, 107; DNA, RG 108, Letters Sent. *O.R.*, I, xlvii, part 2, 18. On Jan. 5, 1865, 2:50 P.M., Secretary of War Edwin M. Stanton telegraphed to USG, Fort Monroe. "I think it would be useful if you would write to Sherman urging him to give facilities to the organization of Colored troops. He does not seem to appreciate the importance of this measure and ~~is in fact~~ appears indifferent if not hostile" ALS (telegram sent), DNA, RG 107, Telegrams Collected (Bound); telegram received (marked as sent at 3:00 P.M.), *ibid.*, RG 108, Letters Received. *O.R.*, I, xlvii, part 2, 16.

On Jan. 6, 5:00 P.M., Stanton, Fort Monroe, telegraphed to USG. "Mrs Foster wants the General to be sent to Baltimore for an operation on his leg. I am in favor of gratifying her Is there any good man that can be assigned to that command. If there is I will relieve him while there and make the appointment" ALS (telegram sent), DNA, RG 107, Telegrams Collected (Unbound); telegram received, *ibid.*; *ibid.*, RG 108, Letters Received. *O.R.*, I, xlvii, part 2, 18. At 8:30 P.M., USG telegraphed to Stanton. "Gen, Logan, or Ord, either will be good men to relieve Foster." Copies, DLC-USG, V, 46, 71, 107; DNA, RG 108, Letters Sent. *O.R.*, I, xlvii, part 2, 18.

1. See letter to Maj. Gen. William T. Sherman, Dec. 27, 1864.

To Bvt. Maj. Gen. Montgomery C. Meigs

(Cipher)   City Point, Va, Jan. 6th 1865 [*11:30* A.M.]
MAJ. GEN. MEIGS, Q. M. GEN. WASHINGTON D. C.

I wish you would push grain and such Commissary stores as may be turned over to your Dept. for transportation to Sherman with the least possible delay. His movements depend on the receipt of these articles. After about the 15th inst. it is desirable that a large quantity of grain and Comy. stores for Sherman's Army be shipped on schooners with a few propellers that could tow them in case of necessity. They should report to Admiral Porter who will watch S's movements and send supplies wherever needed.

U. S. GRANT
Lt. Gen.

ALS (telegram sent), CSmH; telegram received (at 1:40 P.M.), DNA, RG 92, Correspondence Relating to Various Subjects; (2) *ibid.*, RG 107, Telegrams Collected (Bound). *O.R.*, I, xlvii, part 2, 19.

To Maj. Gen. Henry W. Halleck

City Point, Va, Jan. 6th *1864*5.

MAJ. GEN. H. W. HALLECK,
CHIEF OF STAFF OF THE ARMY,
GENERAL,

On mature reflection I am of the opinion the purchase of horses should be renewed in the East, and that all the horses that can be got elswhere between this and Spring ought to be purchased. If we can start out in the Spring with a reserve of twenty or thirty thousand spare Cavalry horses they will be worth as much to us as that number of veteran troops. The resources of the South, in that respect, are now about exhausted. If we can keep the enemy's Cavalry on the move we will soon wear them out and be able to ride over their whole country comparitively unmolested.

I would say let purchases be resumed and collect all the Cavalry horses possible between this and next April.

Very respectfully
your obt. svt.
U. S. GRANT
Lt. Gen

ALS, IHi. *O.R.*, I, xlvi, part 2, 53. On Jan. 8, 1865, Maj. Gen. Henry W. Halleck wrote to USG. "Your letter of the 6th in regard to cavalry horses has been shown to Mr. Dana and he agrees with me that action should be postponed till the Secty of War & Genl Meigs return. I fear that there will be very serious difficulties in foraging the animals we now have to supply from the north & east. The crop of hay is very short; in some places not one third of the usual mowings. Our official reports state that nearly all the hay along the Rail Road lines has already been cleaned out. Farmers were obliged to send their produce to market early in order to raise money to pay heavy local taxes for bounties to volunteers. Many have also sold their teams. The rivers and canals are closed by ice, and the country roads in New York & the New England states have been very bad. Many of the rail roads have more than they can do with passengers & private freight. All these causes combined have affected, & will, during the winter, still more seriously affect our supply of forage. Without the greatest care and energy we shall not be able to feed the animals we have on hand. You complain of a want of forage on the James. We are much of the time here on half rations. Sherman's army at Savannah complained, although we sent much more forage there than you directed. In fine, there is a scarcity of forage every where at the north. Private gentlemen and omnibus & city R. R. companies say that they can scarcely procure enough in market for their private animals. Under these circumstances due precaution should be taken not to purchase cavalry horses till they are absolutely required. Otherwise large numbers will actually starve or be of little or no use. In respect to the west and south west, the difficulty of foraging is not so great, and purchases can be continued, at least for a time. All cavalry horses purchased there have been sent to Genl Thomas' command to the entire exclusion of Genl Canby's Division. The issue of cavalry horses to the troops in Ky. & Tenn. from Oct. 1st to Dec 31st has been 28,189, in addition to siezures in the field. Within this period of three months our loss in killed, starved and broken-down has probably been not less than 10,000, and Genl Wilson asks that that number be supplied *immediately*, by impressing, if necessary, horses in Ill. Ind. & Ohio! At this rate of accumulating and destroying horses, it will soon be impossible to supply either forage or horses in the west. Letters from Genl Thomas' army state that his very large cavalry force has been actually injurious to the movements of that army, by blocking up the roads with its supply trains." LS, DNA, RG 108, Letters Received. *O.R.*, I, xlvi, part 2, 68.

To Edwin M. Stanton

(Cipher)   City Point, Va, Jan. 7th 1865
HON. E. M. STANTON, FORTRESS MONROE, VA,

Please say to Gen. Sherman that I do not regard the capture of Charleston as of any Military importance. He can pass it by unless in doing so he leaves a force in his rear which it will be dangerous to have there. It will be left entirely to his own discretion whether Charleston shall be taken now.

U. S. GRANT
Lt. Gen.

ALS (facsimile telegram sent), Paul C. Richards, Catalogue No. 148 [1981], p. 28; copies, DLC-USG, V, 46, 71, 107; DNA, RG 108, Letters Sent. *O.R.*, I, xlvii, part 2, 21. On Jan. 6, 1865, 3:00 P.M., Secretary of War Edwin M. Stanton, "Revenue Cutter Northerner," Fort Monroe, telegraphed to USG. "I arrived here an hour ago en route for Savanna via Hilton Head. ~~Have you any comm~~ and shall remain until tomorrow morning. Have you any word you wish to send? or any military news. Meigs. Townsend & Barnes are with me." ALS (telegram sent), DNA, RG 107, Telegrams Collected (Unbound); telegram received, *ibid.*; *ibid.*, RG 108, Letters Received. *O.R.*, I, xlvii, part 2, 18. On Jan. 7, 12:15 P.M., Stanton, "Steamer Nevada off Fortress Monroe," telegraphed to USG. "Have just received your telegram of this date and will communicate your views

to General Sherman. Will be off in half an hour. With good wishes for you."
ALS (telegram sent), DNA, RG 107, Telegrams Collected (Unbound); telegram received, *ibid.; ibid.*, RG 108, Letters Received. *O.R.*, I, xlvii, part 2, 21.

To Edwin M. Stanton

H'd Qrs Armies of the U. S.

City Point, Va., Jany 7th/65

Respectfully forwarded—To avoid publicity of the time of sailing
and destination of the expedition against Fort Fisher, my orders
to Gen. Butler to prepare it were given verbally, and the instructions to the Commanding Officer of the expepedition were made by
him and submitted to me. I append to the report a copy of Gen
Butlers instructions to Gen. Weitzel, together with copies of my
written dispatches and instructions to Gen. Butler relating to the
expedition,

It will be perceived that it was never contemplated that Gen.
Butler should accompany the expedition, but that Maj. Gen. G.
Weitzel was specially named as the Commander of it. My hopes of
success rested entirely on our ability to capture Fort Fisher, (and
I had even a hope of getting Wilmington) before the enemy could
get troops there to oppose us. I knew that the enemy had taken
nearly the entire garrison of Wilmington and its dependencies to
oppose Sherman. I am inclined to ascribe the delay, which has cost
us so dearly, to an experiment. I refer to the explosion of Gunpowder in the open air.

My dispatches to Gen. Butler, will show his report to be in
error where he states that he returned, after having effected a landing in obedience to my instructions. On the contrary these instructions contemplated no withdrawal, or no failure after a landing
was made.

U. S. GRANT.

Lieut. Genl.

ES, DNA, RG 94, General Information Index. *O.R.*, I, xlii, part 1, 970. Originally written on a lengthy letter of Jan. 3, 1865, from Maj. Gen. Benjamin F.
Butler to USG reporting the Fort Fisher expedition. *Ibid.*, pp. 966–70.

On Jan. 6, 10:00 A.M., USG telegraphed to Brig. Gen. George F. Shepley. "Last night I lost, some place, from my overcoat pocket, a large package of papers containing Gen. Butler's report of the Wilmington Expedition. The only two places I had my coat off was at the theatre and at the hotel kept by Mr. Phillips. Will you be good enough to have enquiries made at both places and telegh me the result." Telegram received, DNA, RG 94, Generals' Papers and Books, Grant; *ibid.*, RG 107, Telegrams Collected (Unbound). On the same day, Shepley, Norfolk, telegraphed to USG. "An Official document from Hd Qrs. Army of the James, addressed to you, has been picked up here, and is in my possession. What will you have done with it?" LS (telegram sent), *ibid.*; telegram received, *ibid.* On the same day, USG telegraphed to Shepley. "Send a staff officer with the document picked up addressed to me, to Fortress Monroe, to take the first steamer bound for City Point. Let him deliver it to me in person." Telegram received, *ibid.*; *ibid.*, RG 393, Dept. of Va. and N. C., Telegrams Received. On the same day, Shepley telegraphed to USG. "Lieut. DePeyster of my staff has started for City Point with the document you desire." Telegrams received (2), *ibid.*, RG 107, Telegrams Collected (Unbound). On Jan. 7, USG wrote to Secretary of War Edwin M. Stanton. "Herewith I have the honor to forward Maj. Gen. B. F. Butler's, and subordinate reports of the expedition against Fort Fisher N. C. As the report of Rear Admiral Porter has been published in the papers I would respectfully request that Gen. Butler's report, with all the papers accompanying it be also given to the public—" Copies, DLC-USG, V, 46, 71, 107; DNA, RG 108, Letters Sent. *O.R.*, I, xlii, part 1, 966.

On Jan. 8, 10:00 P.M., USG telegraphed to Capt. George K. Leet. "Send back Maj Gen Butlers report of the Wilmington Expedition to me, I wish to change the endorsement, If you have already delivered it to the Secretary of War, please call for it in my name and return it," Telegrams received (2—on Jan. 9, 4:00 A.M.), DNA, RG 107, Telegrams Collected (Bound); copies, *ibid.*, Telegrams Received in Cipher; *ibid.*, RG 108, Letters Sent; DLC-USG, V, 46, 71, 107. *O.R.*, I, xlvi, part 2, 68. On Jan. 9, 11:30 A.M., Leet telegraphed to USG. "Gen. Butlers Report of the Wilmington Expedition will be returned by todays mail" ALS (telegram sent), DNA, RG 107, Telegrams Collected (Bound); telegram received, *ibid. O.R.*, I, xlvi, part 2, 75.

On Jan. 11, 10:45 A.M., Butler telegraphed to USG. "I have asked the President for permission to publish my report of the Wilmington affair. He answers that no report has ever been received at the War Department. You told me you had forwarded it. Has it been lost again? If so, I have a copy—" ALS (telegram sent), DNA, RG 107, Telegrams Collected (Unbound); telegram received (at 11:00 A.M.), *ibid.*, RG 108, Letters Received. *O.R.*, I, xlvi, part 2, 97. See Lincoln, *Works*, VIII, 207. On the same day, Brig. Gen. John A. Rawlins telegraphed to Butler. "Gen'l. Grant telegraphed to Capt Leet to return your report, to enable him to revise his endorsement on it. It will arrive here probably to day and will be returned by Special Messenger to morrow. He has requested its publication." Copies, DLC-USG, V, 46, 71, 107; DNA, RG 108, Letters Sent. *O.R.*, I, xlvi, part 2, 98. The endorsement dated Jan. 7 printed above is probably USG's revision and no copy of the original endorsement has been found.

On Jan. 20, 4:00 P.M., Rawlins telegraphed to USG, Washington. "The following is a copy of a private note received by todays mail from Gen Weitzel enclosing a copy from the papers of your instructions for the first Wilmington Expedition of date Dec 6th 1864. Thinking it might possibly be of service to you while at Washington, I forward it. . . . 'Cincinnati O. Jany 16th 1865 *Private* BR GEN RAWLINS Chief of Staff Dr Sir: I find in this mornings papers the enclosed. I ask it as a favor of you to say to Genl Grant that I was surprised & astonished when I saw it; that Genl Butler never showed it to me, or spoke of it to me, & that his instructions to me did not cover the requirements of this document and that he said to me when I reported an assault impracticable that he would do nothing more than to withdraw—If I had ever seen a copy of the enclosed instructions I would have acted accordingly. . . . G. WEITZEL Maj Genl' " Telegram received (at 8:30 P.M.), DNA, RG 107, Telegrams Collected (Bound); *ibid.*, RG 108, Letters Received; copies, *ibid.*, RG 107, Telegrams Received in Cipher; *ibid.*, RG 108, Letters Sent; DLC-USG, V, 46, 72, 107. *O.R.*, I, xlvi, part 2, 184.

On Jan. 15, Rawlins wrote to Lt. Col. Cyrus B. Comstock. "You will please forward by Capt, Robinette Aid-de-Camp, the statements of Lieut, Geo, W Ross and the other officers and men, made to you, (and which you read to the Lieutenant General) concerning the condition of Fort Fisher, during the attacks on it, on the 25th day of December 1864, In the event you have not these statements with you, or that they are where they cannot be got at, you will please procure the statements anew and send them together with any similar information you may be able to obtain, Capt Robinette will return as soon as you deliver to him such dispatches on this subject as you may have to forward" Copies, DLC-USG, V, 46, 71, 108; DNA, RG 108, Letters Sent. *O.R.*, I, xlii, part 1, 975. On Jan. 17, Comstock wrote to Rawlins transmitting the reports. *Ibid.*, pp. 975–77. On Feb. 2, USG endorsed these documents. "Respy forwarded to the secretary of war with the request that these papers be filed with Maj Gen Butlers' report of the expedition against Fort Fisher, N. C. as statements appended to said report by me. I should have appended them when I forwarded the report, but Lt Col Comstock, ADC to whom they were made was absent on the second expedition against the Fort and had them with him. These statements of the officers and men named were reduced to writing immediately after the return of the unsuccessful expedition against Fort Fisher, and were handed to Col. Comstock abut the 2d day of Januay 1865. Gen Butler before ordering the re-embarkation and return of the expedition he assumed to command, might have had within information, and it was his duty before giving such orders to have known the result of the reconnaissance, which could have been most satisfactorily learned from those most in advance." Copy, DLC-USG, V, 58. *O.R.*, I, xlii, part 1, 977.

To Charles A. Dana

City Point Va.
Jany 7th 1865.

HON C. A. DANA
ASST SECY OF WAR.

Todays Richmond papers contain the following items.

"Mobile Jany 5th A raid reported advancing south towards

Smithfield twenty miles North of Aberdeen—the destruction of property is unknown—It is also reported that Genl Hoods Army has crossed the Tennessee river and is moving on Tupelo—It will probably be the future base of operations—The Fort Gaines prisoners are expected to arrive in this city today from Western North Carolina."

"We learn—says the Raleigh 'Confederate' of the 3rd inst—that on the 2nd of December a fight took place at Shoemakers Gap between Captain N. Prices Rosses & Gartrells Companies and some deserters, tories & robbers: They attacked our forces from Ambush but were speedily routed & severely chastised. They lost 14 killed, 4 wounded & 4 were taken prisoners. We lost none in killed or wounded—The woods were fired during the engagement which caused the discharge of a considerable number of guns which had been thrown away by the enemy—Capt Price was in command of the battalion and distinguished himself by coolness and bravery as did his entire command—." The Columbia "Carolinian" says Genl D. H. Hill passed down the Railroad yesterday under orders to report to Genl Beauregard at Charleston

"Confederate Yankees!

The 'Rebel' notices the arrival at Selma on 20th ult of a detachment of four or five hundred galvanized yankees under the charge of Captains Clarke & Rice & Adjutant Seymour of the 10th Tennessee on their way to the front. They are, says the 'Rebel', strong able bodied soldiers mostly foreigners embracing almost every European nationality with only a slight mixture of genuine Yankees. Capt Clarke informs us that almost any number could have been obtained but that only those were accepted who had no families in the North and few ties to attach them to that section —They will be distributed through the Irish Regiments of the Army of Tennessee and fill up their depleted ranks." Nothing from Sherman

U S Grant Lt Genl

Telegram received (on Jan. 8, 1865, 8:50 A.M.), DNA, RG 107, Telegrams Collected (Bound); *ibid.*, Telegrams Collected (Unbound).

To Maj. Gen. Henry W. Halleck

City Point
Jany 7th 1865 8. P. M.

MAJ GEN H. W. HALLECK
CHIEF OF STAFF.

Please order Gen Thomas if he is assured of the departure of Hood South from Corinth to send Schofield here with his corps with as little delay as possible—I would recommend at the same time that the Department of the Cumberland and the Ohio be united in one Department—Schofields corps might be assembled at Annapolis Md—Its transportation ~~could~~ can be left at Louisville Ky until further orders

U. S. GRANT
Lt Genl

Telegram received (on Jan. 8, 1865, 9:30 A.M.), DNA, RG 107, Telegrams Collected (Bound); copies, *ibid.*, Telegrams Received in Cipher; *ibid.*, RG 108, Letters Sent; DLC-USG, V, 46, 71, 107; (2) DLC-John M. Schofield. *O.R.*, I, xlv, part 2, 529. See *ibid.*, p. 540.

On Jan. 9, 6:00 P.M., USG telegraphed to Maj. Gen. Henry W. Halleck. "Were orders sent to Genl Thomas to send Schofields Corps to Annapolis as soon as Hood was known to have gone south of Corinth? When started it would be advisable to have the troops transported on boats, if navigation is not closed, to Wheeling and Parkersburg, one half to come over the Baltimore and Ohio Road the other ~~half~~ over the Pennsylvania Central" Telegram received (at 7:20 P.M.), DNA, RG 107, Telegrams Collected (Bound); copies, *ibid.*, Telegrams Received in Cipher; *ibid.*, RG 108, Letters Sent; DLC-USG, V, 46, 71, 107; (2) DLC-John M. Schofield. *O.R.*, I, xlv, part 2, 553; *ibid.*, I, xlvi, part 2, 74. At 9:20 P.M., Halleck telegraphed to USG. "Your orders about Schofield's corps were immediately transmitted. As soon as an answer is recieved transportation, by the most expeditious routes, will be ordered. I fear the corps is much scattered. You said nothing in your orders about the artillery." ALS (telegram sent), DNA, RG 107, Telegrams Collected (Bound); telegram received, *ibid.*; (marked as sent at 10:30 P.M., received on Jan. 10) *ibid.*, RG 108, Letters Received. *O.R.*, I, xlv, part 2, 554; *ibid.*, I, xlvi, part 2, 75.

On Jan. 10, 1:00 P.M., Asst. Secretary of War Charles A. Dana telegraphed to USG. "I will at once send Col. Parsons to ~~Louisville North~~ West to take charge of the transportation of Schofield's corps. No doubt it will be best to move the whole body by boats from Eastport to Parkersburg if the navigation allows and thence [b]y B & O railroad to Annapolis. When Hooker's force went to ~~Ch~~ Tennessee all were moved over that road with great promptness & success. A capital advantage of that line is that it avoid[s] all large towns. If the Ohio river should be frozen they can be moved by rail from Cairo, Evansville or Jeffersonville to Parkersburg or Bellair according to circumstances. ~~C. A. Dana~~ Your order says nothing about artillery I think that had better be left behind. If the men are needed, they can come, and find new batteries & horses here." ALS (telegram sent), DNA, RG 107, Telegrams Collected (Bound); telegram received (on Jan. 12), *ibid.*, RG 108, Letters Received. *O.R.*, I, xlv, part 2, 560. On Jan. 12, 11:00 A.M., USG telegraphed to Halleck. "You may direct the batteries of Schofields Corps be left behind. I think however it may be advisable for him to bring two companies of Artillerests to each Division to be fitted up here if necessary." ALS (telegram sent), Mitten Collection, InHi; telegram received (at 12:25 P.M.), DNA, RG 107, Telegrams Collected (Bound). *O.R.*, I, xlv, part 2, 573; *ibid.*, I, xlvi, part 2, 105.

On Jan. 16, 12:30 P.M., Halleck telegraphed to USG. "There are no accommodations whatever for additional troops at Annapolis, and if Genl Schofield's corps is to stop there any time they must suffer greatly in this weather. Here and at Alexandria we can give shelter to all without additional expense. I would therefore suggest that they be brought here till transports are ready for them either at Annapolis or Alexandria." ALS (telegram sent), DNA, RG 107, Telegrams Collected (Bound); telegram received, *ibid.*; (marked as sent at 1:30 P.M.) *ibid.*, RG 108, Letters Received. *O.R.*, I, xlv, part 2, 596. At 3:30 P.M., USG telegraphed to Halleck. "Annapolis was named as the destination of Schofield's Corps for the reason that it was most favorable for embarkation & it was supposed by the time it reached there, present operations of the armies would develop the point most important to send it. If you deem it best, however, you may change its destination to Alexandria." Telegram received (at 5:00 P.M.), DNA, RG 107, Telegrams Collected (Bound); copies, *ibid.*, Telegrams Received in Cipher; *ibid.*, RG 108, Letters Sent; DLC-USG, V, 46, 71, 107; DLC-John M. Schofield. *O.R.*, I, xlv, part 2, 596.

On Jan. 17, 2:30 P.M., Halleck telegraphed to USG. "I presumed that your order in regard to Schofield's corps was intended to supercede that in relation to Genl A. J. Smith's command, & that the latter was to remain with Genl Thomas. Was I right?" ALS (telegram sent), DNA, RG 107, Telegrams Collected (Bound); telegram received, *ibid.*; *ibid.*, RG 108, Letters Received. *O.R.*, I, xlv, part 2, 601. On the same day, USG telegraphed to Halleck. "Your understanding of my orders, as expressed in your dispatch of 2.30 to-day is correct." Telegram received (at 6:10 P.M.), DNA, RG 107, Telegrams Collected (Bound); copies, *ibid.*, RG 108, Letters Sent; DLC-USG, V, 46, 71, 107. *O.R.*, I, xlv, part 2, 602.

To Maj. Gen. Lewis Wallace

(Cipher)   City Point, Va, Jan. 7th 1865 [*10:00* P.M.]
MAJ. GEN. WALLACE, BALTIMORE MD.

Vessels were sent from Ft. Monroe to Baltimore on the 3d inst. to bring down a Div. of Sheridans Army. A dispatch from Sheridan of this afternoon says the troops have been compelled to go into camp for want of transportation.[1] Enquiry shows the trans-

ports to be there. Please require your quartermaster to see that the
troops are embarked and got off without delay.

U. S. GRANT
Lt. Gen.

ALS (telegram sent), deCoppet Collection, NjP; telegram received, DNA, RG
107, Telegrams Collected (Unbound); *ibid.*, RG 393, Middle Dept., Telegrams
Sent (Press). *O.R.*, I, xlvi, part 2, 65–66. On Jan. 8, 1865, 2:00 P.M., Maj. Gen.
Lewis Wallace, Baltimore, telegraphed to USG. "I know nothing of the movement of the troops from Gen Sheridan, except what the depot quartermaster,
informed on Friday night, that a division had arrived, but there was no troops
ready, whereupon I provided camp ground. The quartermaster now informs me
that transportation for 3000 is here. Remainder of vessels expected hourly from
New York, having left on 5th and 7th. Transportation sent from Old Point was
not sufficient. Gen Grover, who is in command, informs me he will embark the
troops and depart as each vessel is ready without waiting for all, and with all
possible haste. I will render him all the aid I can" AL (telegram sent), DNA,
RG 107, Telegrams Collected (Unbound); LS, *ibid.*, RG 393, Middle Dept.,
Telegrams Sent (Press); telegram received, *ibid.*, RG 107, Telegrams Collected
(Unbound); (on Jan. 9, 2:00 P.M.) *ibid.*, RG 108, Letters Received. *O.R.*, I,
xlvi, part 2, 73. On the same day, Wallace wrote to USG an expanded version of
the same message, explaining that difficulties with the telegraph compelled him
to send the letter by boat. LS, DNA, RG 393, Middle Dept., Letters Sent
(Press). On Jan. 11, 2:30 P.M., Wallace telegraphed to USG. "Transportation
for eight hundred (800) Men of Grovers command still lacking—The Oriental
hourly expected. I have hurried the Quarter Masters and all parties and if there
were any ocean going steamers here would seize them but we know of none this
side of Fort Monroe if there are any there" ALS (telegram sent), *ibid.*, RG
107, Telegrams Collected (Unbound); telegram received, *ibid.*; (on Jan. 12)
ibid., RG 108, Letters Received. *O.R.*, I, xlvi, part 2, 103.
    At 5:50 P.M., Lt. Col. Theodore S. Bowers telegraphed to Wallace. "You
are authorized and directed to retain the eleventh (11th) Indiana Regt at Balto
as a part of your command" Telegram received, DNA, RG 107, Telegrams
Collected (Unbound); copies, *ibid.*, RG 108, Letters Sent; DLC-USG, V, 46, 71,
107. *O.R.*, I, xlvi, part 2, 104. On the same day, 1st Lt. William M. Dunn, Jr.,
telegraphed to Wallace. "Genl Grant has consented to ke let you keep the 11
Ind. You and I are responsible for the filling up of it." Telegrams received (2),
DNA, RG 107, Telegrams Collected (Unbound). See *O.R.*, I, xlvi, part 2, 183.

    1. On Jan. 7, 12:30 P.M., Maj. Gen. Philip H. Sheridan, Winchester, Va.,
telegraphed to Secretary of War Edwin M. Stanton reporting that the transports
for his troops were not ready at Baltimore. Telegram received, DNA, RG 108,
Letters Received. *O.R.*, I, xlvi, part 2, 64. At 5:30 P.M. and 9:00 P.M., USG
telegraphed to Sheridan. "Hold the trains of Grover's Division for further orders.
Transports were reported to have ⨎ left Ft. Monroe two or three days ago for
Baltimore to carry at least four thousand men" Telegram received (on Jan. 8,
9:15 A.M.), DNA, RG 107, Telegrams Collected (Bound); *ibid.*, Telegrams
Collected (Unbound); copies, *ibid.*, Telegrams Received in Cipher; *ibid.*, RG
108, Letters Sent; DLC-USG, V, 46, 71, 107. *O.R.*, I, xlvi, part 2, 64. "on inquiry I find that steamers sufficient to carry about 5000 men should have been

in Baltimore last Thursday night. the quartermaster is now making inquries
to find where these vessels are." Telegram received, DNA, RG 107, Telegrams
Collected (Unbound); copies, *ibid.*, Telegrams Received in Cipher; *ibid.*, RG
108, Letters Sent; DLC-USG, V, 46, 71, 107. Printed as received on Jan. 8,
9:10 A.M., in *O.R.*, I, xlvi, part 2, 64. On Jan. 8, 1:00 P.M., Sheridan telegraphed to USG. "*Confidential.* . . . ~~Grovers~~ Grovers Division left Stevensons
Depôt at 12, o'clock on the ~~6th~~ sixth, and arrived in Baltimore that night. I sent
the troops on a dispatch from the Sect. of war, 'that the transports would be in
Baltimore.' Genl Grover on his arrival in Baltimore telegraphed that he had to
go into camp, as transportation was not on hand, and would not be, until this
evening January 8th. This gives the Bounty Brokers a chance to work on the men
—and I am afraid will cause desertion." Telegram sent, DNA, RG 107, Telegrams Collected (Unbound); telegrams received (2), *ibid.*; (on Jan. 9) *ibid.*,
RG 108, Letters Received. *O.R.*, I, xlvi, part 2, 72. On Jan. 11, 1:30 P.M., Sheridan telegraphed to USG. "I am afraid the delay of 'Grovers Div:' at Baltimore
will be annoying to you, I can not account for it, as I supposed from the telegram
of the 'Honr Sect of War,' that every thing would be in readiness—Genl Grover
telegraphs me, that he is only partly off—and that it is all on account of the
transportation—I rsply forward a copy of the telegram on which the troops were
sent to Baltimore— . . . The weather is very bad here ~~at~~ I have nothing new to
report." Telegram sent, DNA, RG 107, Telegrams Collected (Unbound); telegrams received (2—marked as sent on Jan. 10, 2:30 P.M.), *ibid.*; (at 2:00
P.M.) *ibid.*, Telegrams Collected (Bound); (marked as sent on Jan. 10, received
on Jan. 12) *ibid.*, RG 108, Letters Received. Printed as sent on Jan. 10 in *O.R.*,
I, xlvi, part 2, 91.

On Jan. 7, Lt. Col. Ely S. Parker wrote to Lt. Col. Michael R. Morgan.
"You will immediately proceed to Fort Monroe and load such sea-going vessels,
as may arrive at that point, with fifteen days rations of provisions and to see that
such vessels are supplied with fuel and water. You will also provision each vessel
with ten days extra rations of hard bread, if the quantity on hand at Fort Monroe
will permit, but if there be not a sufficient quantity, then you will supply as many
days extra rations of hard bread to each vessel as the quantity on hand will allow.
You will report by telegraph to these Headquarters the number of vessels you
may provision and the amount" Copies, DLC-USG, V, 46, 71, 107; DNA, RG
108, Letters Sent. *O.R.*, I, xlvi, part 2, 61. On Jan. 12, USG telegraphed to
Morgan. "Has any of the vessels loaded with troops from Baltimore made their
appearance yet?" ALS (telegram sent), Kohns Collection, NN; copies, DLC-
USG, V, 46, 71, 107; DNA, RG 108, Letters Sent. *O.R.*, I, xlvi, part 2, 105. On
the same day, Morgan telegraphed to USG. "Yes, Two—See dispatch in cipher—" ALS (telegram sent), DNA, RG 107, Telegrams Collected (Unbound).
At 1:00 P.M., Morgan telegraphed to Brig. Gen. John A. Rawlins. "About fifteen hundred men have arrived with fifteen gallons of water to a man—By direction of Gen. Grant, I ordered them ashore at Newport News while rations are
being put on board, and water replenished—Have I done rightly?" ALS (telegram sent), *ibid.*; telegram received, *ibid. O.R.*, I, xlvi, part 2, 105. At 4:00
P.M., Rawlins telegraphed to Morgan. "All troops arriving at Fort Monroe from
Gen'l. Sheridan's Army, will proceed as fast as the vessels can get on coal, water
and rations to Savannah, Ga. and report to Maj. Gen. Sherman for orders, and
in the event Gen. Sherman should have departed from there, they will report to
Maj. Gen'l. J. G. Foster for orders. Each vessel transporting these troops will
start the moment it is ready, and a copy of this order will be furnished by you to

the Officer in Command of troops on board of each of said vessels, and also to the Commanding Officer of the whole of said troops. The greatest promptitude possible in their departure is required." Copies, DLC-USG, V, 46, 71, 107; DNA, RG 108, Letters Sent. *O.R.*, I, xlvi, part 2, 106. On the same day, Morgan wrote to Rawlins. "Two steamers, the 'Ariel' 973 men and the 'Sedgwick' 496 men, have arrived—The troops were rationed up to tomorrow night—They have water at the rate of a gallon per man for fifteen days—I will have issued some salt-water soap—I am not certain about the coal but will be, and now believe they have on board from thirteen to fifteen t̶o̶ days coal—The division commander is not here but gave the first brigade orders to keep on hand four days rations and to stay on board ship until they got different orders from him or higher authority—'By direction' of Gen. Grant I directed them to go on shore as per inclosed copy of order—Col. Washburn informed me that the̶y̶ division was waiting for transportation and I concluded they would not be all o̶n̶ s̶h̶o̶r̶e̶ here for two days at the earliest—In the mean while t̶h̶e̶y̶ w̶i̶l̶l̶ these transports will be rationed and filled up with water, the troops will be on board again h̶a̶v̶i̶n̶g̶ with cooked rations for three days, I will suggest; and will have stretched their legs— If the division Commander comes in the mean while he can do as he pleases— . . . P. S—The Baltic went up yesterday to Annapolis, ready for sea—She ought to take a brigade on board." ALS, DNA, RG 108, Letters Received. *O.R.*, I, xlvi, part 2, 106. The enclosure is *ibid.*, pp. 106–7.

On Jan. 13, noon, 2:30 P.M., and 8:00 P.M., Morgan telegraphed to Rawlins. "The 'Sedgwick' five hundred and one men, 'Ariel' nine hundred and seventy three men and 'Ashland' two hundred and seventy men have sailed in perfect order—" ALS (telegram sent), DNA, RG 107, Telegrams Collected (Unbound); telegram received, *ibid.* "The Steamer Victor with three hundred and seventy five (375) men has sailed—All right—Plenty of Hard Bread—" "Steamer Illinois goes to sea at 11 o'clock with Twelve hundred and Eighty seven (1287) men—All right—" ALS (telegrams sent), *ibid.* At 7:00 P.M., Morgan wrote to Rawlins. "I am making out, but very tired at such slow work— We have given them all fifteen days Rations and ten days *extra* of Hard Bread— Plenty of coal & water—The men off the 'Ariel' & 'Sedgwick' cooked, last night, three days pork, had a bath in the James this morning and were off to sea before 12 o'clock—t̶h̶i̶s̶ m̶o̶r̶n̶i̶n̶g̶—That Col. Washburn was tip-top—Brig-Gen—Somebody has just left me with his orders—It is a moon-light night and they should be out before eleven o'clock—This makes 3406 men, more or less—Grover has not yet arrived—Everybody here does well, Commissaries and—quartermasters— I hope to go up Sunday That Brigadier alluded to above is in command of the troops on board the Illinois. . . . Gen. Butler is here yet—" ALS, *ibid.*, RG 108, Letters Received. *O.R.*, I, xlvi, part 2, 114.

On Jan. 14, Morgan telegraphed to Rawlins. "Nothing has arrived to-day, and the end is not yet—" ALS (telegram sent), DNA, RG 107, Telegrams Collected (Unbound).

On Jan. 15, 1:20 P.M., 4:00 P.M., and 10:30 P.M., Morgan telegraphed to Rawlins. "I have finished my work—" ALS (telegram sent), *ibid.* "Steamer 'Oriental' seven hundred & seventy eight (778) men has sailed—The 'Suwo Nada' nine hundred & thirty (930) men will start in half an hour—This makes six vessels, 5109 men, all as ordered—" ALS (telegram sent), *ibid.*; telegram received, *ibid.* "If in summing up today I said six vessels I was wrong, I should have said seven—" ALS (telegram sent), *ibid.*

On Jan. 14, 11:15 P.M., Bvt. Maj. Gen. Cuvier Grover telegraphed to

Rawlins. "Have arrived with the last of my Division, ~~and report for orde~~ excepting the 11th Indiana vols which was left at Baltimore by orders from your Hd
Qrs—I report for orders pursuant to instructions from Hd Qrs Middle Mil Division" ALS (telegram sent), *ibid.*

To Maj. Gen. Irvin McDowell

City Point, Va, Jan. 8th *18645.*

MAJ. GEN. I. McDOWELL,
COMD.G DEPT. OF THE PACIFIC,
GENERAL,

It is known that Dr. Gwinn, former United States Senator from
Cal. has gone to Mexico and taken service under the Maxamillian
Government. It is understood also that he has been appointed Gov-
erner General of Sonora. The Dr. is a rebel of the most virulent
order. His being formerly a resident of California, and now getting
to that State in Mexico bordering on the State of his former residence, portends no good to us. May it not be his design to entice
into Sonora the dissatisfied spirits of California, and if the opportunity occurs, organize them and invade the State?—I write, without having discussed this question with any one, to put you on your
guard against what I believe may prove a great danger.—Watch
this matter closely and should you find these apprehensions well
founded, prepare to meet them. You will find no difficulty in raising
any number of Volunteers that may be necessary in California to
repel an invasion of the state. Especially will this be the case where
the invasion comes from a country with which we are at peace.

In an event like the one alluded to I would not rest satisfied
with simply driving the invaders on to Mexican soil, but would
pursue ~~them~~ him until overtaken, and would retain possession of
the territory from which the invader started until indemnity for the
past, and security for the future, satisfactory to the Government,
was insured.

This letter, which may have to be regarded as instructions for
your guidance, is written entirely without knowledge of what the
President would advise in case of an invasion of our territory from

that of Mexico, but with a conviction that it is right and just. The case supposed is a very different one from those that have occured starting from Canada. In the latter case rebels have fitted out for the invasion of our Northern frontier, upon Canadian soil, secretly, and without the knowledge of Canadian authorities. In the threatened invasion it will be the act of officials of the usurpers of the Government of Mexico, and, in my judgement, would justify direct assistance on our part to re-establish the legitimate government over that country.

This letter is intended as *private* until the exigency contemplated calls for action on your part, when it will be regarded as instructions for your guidance in the absence of more recent orders.

> Very respectfully
> your obt. svt.
> U. S. GRANT
> Lt. Gen

ALS, California Historical Society, San Francisco, Calif. *O.R.*, I, l, part 2, 1118. An account of the abortive efforts to form a colony in Sonora is in Lately Thomas, *Between Two Empires: The Life Story of California's First Senator, William McKendree Gwin* (Boston, 1969), pp. 286–352. On March 12, 1865, Maj. Gen. Irvin McDowell, San Francisco, wrote to USG. "I was exceedingly gratified by the receipt of your letter of the 8th of January cautioning me concerning the movements of Doctor Gwin, and giving contingent instructions with reference to any hostile movements he may cause to be undertaken against the United States from the Mexican State of Sonora. I have taken the deepest interest in this Mexican question ever since England and Spain withdrew from the invasion of Mexico, and it became evident the french were continuing it for other than the ostensible object for which it was set on foot. Since coming here I have received from Mr. Seward some notes from Paris showing for what purpose it was understood, there, Dr. Gwin was sent to Mexico! The war in the east has forced, and is forcing numbers of persons inimical to us into my Department and the fortunate result of the last election and the little hope the dissunionists have of a future here, is making them turn their attention to Mexico as a place of refuge. I beleive this is the case also with those from the South Western States and Texas, as I hear of persons coming over from Texas into Chihuahua and thence to Sonora! It was not long since the Democratic Press of this city stated that there were two persons here as agents of Dr. Gwin, and invited people desirous of going to Mexico, to apply to them for information I required each to state whether this was, or not true! One, in effect admitted it was, and the other—Mr. Ridge denied it, and called on me in person to account for his presence in this country! He said he was an Englishman representing British capitalists, and being largely interested in Mexico was deeply concerned in whatever related to that country, and in this way came to know Dr. Gwin both in ~~that~~ Paris and in

Mexico and had freely conferred with him in both places. Mr. Ridge's object in coming to Mexico was to obtain a concession to light the city with gas, and one to build a Rail Road to the Pacific. He showed me letters confirming his statements. He is a remarkably intelligent man of fine presence, and he impressed me favorably as being straightforward and truthful. He said it was a question, when he was in Paris, how Maximillian was to support his court, government and Army, and at the same time repay Napoleon the expenses incurred by France in the invasion and conquest of the country! The latter decided the former must have the revenue from the customs, and he would look to be re-imbursed from the resources of the northern States, which Dr. Gwin had represented as great. Napoleon asked the Dr. if those resources could soon be rendered available. The latter answered that by drawing there Anglo Saxon and Celtic emigration from every and any quarter a revenue of millions might be had in a short time. The Doctor was asked to undertake the enterprise, which he consented to do, and was now carrying it on! I think if the french wanted only a Superintending Mining Engineer or administrator of finances they would have sent a frenchman, for their conceit of themselves as miners and administrative agents is great. And if they wanted a mere director of Anglo American Emigration and *wanted an American* they would have been apt to choose one from that section of the country known to have the greatest enterprise and largest population! It therefore seems to me that it is precisely because of Dr. Gwin's known connection with the rebels and secessionists, and especially with those from this state that caused him to be chosen as being the person best suited to attract an emigration of our enemies and to plant upon our frontiers a people hostile to our institutions our influence and our progress. Such a suppositi[o]n is in direct accordance with the principles announced by Napoleon in his letter to General Forey in which he speaks of staying the progress and influence of the UnitedStates over the continent! The desire of putting a negative on the U. S. is no doubt combined with the intent to affect something positive for France by obtaining—as he did Savoy and Niece, as his recompense for interfering in Italy—a province for himself from Mexico. I have looked upon the whole scheme of Dr. Gwin as hostile to us, and upon him as an enemy, and shall therefore do whatever I can that will tend to thwart it and him! Before the receipt of your letter I had ordered that no one should embark for Mexico without a permit, and that this permit should only be given to loyal persons going on some legitimate business. And, that no agent of Dr. Gwin should be suffered to remain in this Department. I have assigned an excellent officer Brig. Genl. Mason—to the command in Arizona and have provided him with a sufficient force to watch the frontier. This country is alive to this whole question and the people would respond instantly to any call upon them to meet an aggression upon our Mexican frontier! I am assembling a Small reserve of two or three regiments at this place as a nucleus for a force to provide for any contingency. I feel strong enough on land for all enimies either domestic or foreign, but in view of possible, may I not say probable, hostilities to the south of us, I beg to call attention to the state of our fleet on this coast. I do not pretend to speak of my own knowledge, or with any precision even from what has been told me, yet enough has been said to warrant my feeling that on the ocean we are by no means in a desirable condition. The only vessel in this port is a double-ender gun boat, and a small vessel as revenue cutter, with a monitor for harbor defence. From the statements of Naval officers, who speak as if they knew, the whole fleet on the coast is quite inferior to that of those who may become their antagonists! The desert south of Ft. Yuma makes it desirable that in any operations we may have to undertake in Sonora we should have possession of the port of Guymas, if not of Mazatlan. On account of the great saving in cost of transportation. I have just sent supplies for southern Arizona to Guymas to be sent up through northern Sonora, provided the Juares Govenor of Sonora—Peschiera —now in command will give them safe conduct. I am in hopes the capture of Charleston and Wilmington may release sufficient naval force to enable the Department to reenforce the fleet in these waters so that we may hold the Gulf of California. In all that I have done I have acted with every circumspection so as to give no pretext to foreign nations for making reclamations upon the Government. The measures taken have been announced as military precautions, and affect only our own citizens. That amid the overwhelming cares incident to your present duty this distant field should have engaged your personal attention is very gratifying, and it is no less so that I should—before your letter was received, —have, in the main, acted in accordance with the views you have done me the honor to express to me—" ALS, DNA, RG 108, Letters Received; ADf, ICN. *O.R.*, I, l, part 2, 1158–60. McDowell enclosed a copy of his General Orders No. 5. *Ibid.*, p. 1133.

To Bvt. Brig. Gen. Henry L. Abbot

City Point Jany 8th 1865

BRV'T, BRIG, GENL, H. L. ABBOTT
COMMANDING SEIGE ARTILLERY
GENERAL

As soon as you can get under weigh with the troops and train heretofore directed to be put on Ship board proceed to Beaufort N. C. and report to Brv't Maj, Gen, A. H. Terry for further orders. If on arrival at Beaufort you find Gen, Terry has left there you will proceed to where he has been directed off New Inlet to Cape Fear River N. C.

If you learn before arrival at Beaufort that Gen, Terry has sailed from their it will not be necessary for you to put into that port, but you will proceed immediately to report to him wherever he may be All further orders and directions you will receive from Maj, Gen, Terry Comdg expedition against Fort Fisher,

Very Respectfully
Your ob't sv't
U. S. GRANT
Lt Genl,

Copies, DLC-USG, V, 46, 72, 107; DNA, RG 108, Letters Sent. *O.R.*, I, xlvi, part 2, 72.

On Jan. 5, 1865, members of USG's staff ordered Bvt. Brig. Gen. Henry L. Abbot to hd. qrs., where he was placed in charge of the siege equipment for the Fort Fisher expedition. *Ibid.*, pp. 44–45. At 10:30 P.M., USG telegraphed to Brig. Gen. Alexander B. Dyer, chief of ordnance. "Please have fifteen (15) Cohorn Mortars at with implements complete at Fort Monroe at the earliest moment, and notify me how soon to expect them there" Telegram received (at 10:55 P.M.), DNA, RG 107, Telegrams Collected (Bound); copies, *ibid.*, Telegrams Received in Cipher; *ibid.*, RG 108, Letters Sent; DLC-USG, V, 46, 71, 107. *O.R.*, I, xlvi, part 2, 39. On Jan. 6, Dyer telegraphed to USG. "Mortars by Special Messenger from Springfield Armory—Beds & implements from Washington Arsenal—" ALS (telegram sent), DNA, RG 107, Telegrams Collected (Unbound); copy, *ibid.*, RG 156, Letters Sent. On Jan. 16, Col. William Maynadier, act. chief of ordnance, telegraphed to USG. "The Cohorn Mortars asked for by your telegram of the 5th instant were at Fort Monroe on the 11th instant" LS (telegram sent), *ibid.*, RG 107, Telegrams Collected (Unbound); copy, RG 156, Letters Sent. *O.R.*, I, xlvi, part 2, 146. On Jan. 6, Lt. Col. Theodore S. Bowers issued Special Orders No. 4. "Brig. Gen Benham, will detach from his command one full company of engineers for duty with Brevet Brig. General Abbott, commanding seige-train; and order the Commanding Officer of the company detached to report in person and without delay to Brevet Brig Gen Abbott for instructions and orders as to tools, outfit &c required." Copies, DLC-USG, V, 57, 63, 64, 65. *O.R.*, I, xlvi, part 2, 54. On Jan. 8, USG's staff provided a crew for the launches accompanying Abbot's expedition. *Ibid.*, pp. 71–72.

To Francis P. Blair, Sr.

City Point, Va, Jan. 8th *1865.*

F. P. BLAIR, SR.
DEAR SIR:

In the morning immediately after Breakfast I will send an officer with you to Aikins Landing with written instructions regarding your passage through our lines. I will telegraph Gen. Ord to-night to have an Ambulance at the landing by 10 a. m. in charge of an officer authorized to bear a "Flag of Truce" but without saying anything of the object of the truce.[1] The letter which will accompany you will direct that you be taken directly through our lines and that no mention be made of your going.

I should be pleased to have you stay with us to-night if your vessel arrives in time and it suits your convenience.

> I have the honor to be
> Very respectfully
> your obt. svt.
> U. S. GRANT
> Lt. Gn.

ALS, Blair Lee Papers, NjP.

1. On Jan. 8, 1865, USG telegraphed to Maj. Gen. Edward O. C. Ord. "Please send an ambulance to Aikens Ldg by ten a. m tomorrow in charge of a staff officer authorized to bear a Flag of truce. He will wait at the Landg for written instructions from me." Telegram received, DNA, RG 393, Dept. of Va. and N. C., Telegrams Received.

To Charles A. Dana

> City Point Va
> Jany 9th 1865

HON. C. A. DANA
ASST SECY OF WAR.

The Richmond papers of today have the following items—

"Destructive fire at Charlotte S. C!!

Confederate Warehouse and Depots burned!—Vast amount of Stores consumed!

Charlotte Jany 7th

A terrible conflagration occurred here this morning about 3' O'clock originating in the Paymasters Office and adjoining the Charlotte and Columbia R. R. Depot sheds which together with the adjoining warehouses were burned to the ground—A vast amount of stores was consumed—Two men are supposed to have been burned—

From South Carolina!!

Charleston Jany 6th   The Enemy in unknown force crossed New River on the road to Grahamville this morning—Our forces burnt the bridge across New River—The main body of the Enemy is still believed to be in the neighborhood—Genl Wheeler is watching his movements which are not yet fully developed—Grahamville is 70 miles from Charleston and 34 miles from Savannah on the Charleston and Savannah R. R.—

From Alabama! The Fort Gaines Prisoners exchanged! etc— Mobile Jany 6th   The Ft Gaines prisoners reached this city last evening—Major Carcel the Assistant Commissioner of exchange has issued an order declaring them exchange—

A special telegram to the "Advertiser" from Senatobia 5th says that scouts report troops were leaving Memphis going down the river—

The battle of Nashville!! The official report!

The following official dispatch was received at the War Department saturday night—

Macon Jany 7th.

To GENL S. COOPER
A AND I GENL

General Hood reports from Spring Hill Dec 27th 1864 that on the morning of the 15th inst, in front of Nashville the enemy attacked both flanks of his army—They were repulsed on the right with heavy loss but towards evening they drove in his Infantry outposts on the f left flank.—Early on the 16th the Enemy made a general attack on his entire line—All their assaults were handsomely repulsed with heavy loss until 3.30 P. M when a portion of our line to the left of Centre suddenly gave way causing our lines to give way at all points, our troops retreating rapidly—Fifty pieces of Artillery and several Ordnance wagons were lost by us on that day. Our loss in killed and wounded small, in prisoners not ascertained. Major Genl Ed Johnson—Brig Genls L. B. Smith and H. R. Jackson captured

(signed) G. T. BEAUREGARD Genl"—

Virginia and Tennessee Road!!

From the Lynchburg "Republican" we learn that a large number of hands have been employed on the Tennessee Railroad to repair the damages caused by the late raid of Stoneman—The work will be pushed forward with all the accustomed energy of Col Owen and Major Godwin and it is hoped the repairs will be completed within the next six weeks or two months—The Salt works! A gentleman just from Saltville informs the Lynchburg "Virginian" that the works can be put in operation again in two weeks. The damage done by the Enemy was not of a serious character—

Gen D. H. Hill has reported ~~the~~ to Beauregard at Charleston. Genl Prices death is contradicted. The report of Genl. Forrests assassination is also contradicted—

Another attack upon Wilmington is anticipated!!"

The "Examiner" says that it is now well ascertained that Sher~~mans~~ is advancing with a large portion of his army in the direction of Charleston, but whether he will attempt the capture of that city or move towards Branchville cannot be ascertained until he reaches the Combahee river and that if the Charleston and Branchville R. R. can be kept intact Sherman's purposes will probably be thwarted"

U. S. GRANT
Lt Genl

Telegram received (at 6:40 P.M.), DNA, RG 107, Telegrams Collected (Bound).

To Maj. Gen. Henry W. Halleck

(Cipher)   City Point, Va, Jan. 9th 18645. [8:30 P.M.]
MAJ. GEN. HALLECK, WASHINGTON

The subject of forage is growing ~~to be~~ into a serious matter. For the last week animals have been on half rations and at that no supplies are accumulated. Forage is issued as it arrives and at no time for the last five days has there been two days supply ahead. The Q. M. here has represented this matter fully and urged the necessity of getting forward supplies in time to have avoided this state of affairs. I am inclined to believe Col. Brown[1] entirely incompetant for his responsible position. I wish you would call the

attention of the Act. Q. M. Gn. to this matter and require him to
see that a full supply of grain & hay is immediately forwarded and
that it is hereafter kept up.

U. S. Grant

Lt. Gn.

ALS (telegram sent), CSmH; telegram received (marked as sent at 9:00 P.M.,
received at 9:30 P.M.), DNA, RG 107, Telegrams Collected (Bound). *O.R.*,
I, xlvi, part 2, 74. On Jan. 10, 1865, 1:30 P.M., Maj. Gen. Henry W. Halleck
telegraphed to USG. "Your telegram about forage has been transmitted to Genl
Thomas. I think the difficulty is less the fault of Col Brown than the absolute
scarcity in the northern & eastern states, and the difficulty of transportation now
that the canals & rivers are frozen up. I will get what facts I can and write to
you." ALS (telegram sent), DNA, RG 107, Telegrams Collected (Bound);
telegram received, *ibid.*; (on Jan. 12) *ibid.*, RG 108, Letters Received. *O.R.*, I,
xlvi, part 2, 82.

1. S. Lockwood Brown, appointed q. m. and capt. as of Oct. 31, 1861, and
assigned as col. as of Aug. 2, 1864, defended himself against USG's charges. See
ibid., pp. 115–17. See also *ibid.*, pp. 39–40, 82, 207, 298.

To Maj. Gen. Edward O. C. Ord

(Cipher)   City Point, Va, Jan.y 9th 1865 [3:00 P.M.]
Maj. Gen. Ord.

I want you to have a thorough examination made of your Bermuda front and report whether in your judgement we can go
through by a surprise and by massing. I could give you an additional Corps to hold what you got and would give up all North of
the James except two or three important points if it could be done.

U. S. Grant

Lt. Gn.

ALS (telegram sent), CSmH; telegram received (at 3:30 P.M.), Ord Papers,
CU-B. Printed as sent at 3:30 P.M. in *O.R.*, I, xlvi, part 2, 79. On Jan. 9, 1865,
4:20 P.M., Maj. Gen. Edward O. C. Ord telegraphed to USG. "Cipher dispatch
received; will be attended to." *Ibid.* On Jan. 11, 6:00 P.M., Ord telegraphed to
USG. "have made the examination of Bermuda front—a north Carolina Brigade
has taken the place of Corses—(which came to the north of the James—there
appears a reserve force near where the Petersburg RRoad crosses deep creek, I
will call in person to morrow and give other details" ALS (telegram sent),
DNA, RG 108, Letters Received; telegram received, *ibid. O.R.*, I, xlvi, part 2, 98.

To Charles A. Dana

City Point Va
Jany 10th 1865

HON C. A. DANA
ASST SECY OF WAR.

The following items are found in todays Richmond papers—

Charlotte Jany 9th—The fire which occurred here Saturday morning was the result of accident—The Paymasters office in which the fire originated and the government warehouses including the Quarter Masters and Commissary's office and a portion of the North Carolina and Charlotte & South Carolina Depot buildings were burned. The loss was at first estimated as high as twenty millions of dollars in present currency but has since been greatly reduced by the quantity of grain sugar, etc saved from the ruins—"

From South Carolina!!

Charleston Jany 8th. A dispatch from Grahams dated 12. P. M says No news from the enemy this morning—A gentleman just from Savannah reports that Sherman has sent the 17th Army Corps round to Beaufort to cooperate with Fosters troops, between Pocotaligo and Coosawatchie—

From Charleston!!

Charleston Jany 9th—Nothing received from below today—A dispatch from Macon reports the enemy one or two thousand strong with wagons & Artillery on the Ocohee river moving in the direction of South-western Georgia—

Genl Joseph E Johnston!!

Genl Johnston was in Columbia S C. on the 13th Inst—

Supplies and the RailRoads!!

A fire has occurred in a government store house at Charlotte in North Carolina—It contained forty thousand (40.000) bushels of corn only ten thousand bushels of which was saved and that in a parched condition, also some sugar, no meat—This is the loss: by what means it was caused, whether by the agency of a yankee incendiary or simple negligence of a guard is not yet ascertained—

The public is much more engaged with the general facts that vast accumulations of supplies are made in that quarter which are not forward to the army with the diligence required by the present condition of affairs—The fault is evidently in the Rail Road between Richmond and Greensboro and the blame has generally been laid on the Richmond and Danville company—

Latest from the South & Southwest!!

The following dispatch has been received at the War Dept from Macon Georgia—'Genl Hood reports from Tupelo Jany 6th 1865, that Thomas appeared to be moving up the Tennessee river until 9. o'clock A. M on the 5th—Scouts report six gunboats and sixty transports had passed Savannah going towards Eastport loaded with troops and supplies   (signed) G. T. BEAUREGARD Maj Genl'

U. S. GRANT

Lt Genl

Telegram received (on Jan. 11, 1865, 9:30 A.M.), DNA, RG 107, Telegrams Collected (Bound); *ibid.*, Telegrams Collected (Unbound). *O.R.*, I, xlvii, part 2, 32. A telegram of Jan. 10 from Maj. Gen. Edward O. C. Ord to USG transmitted another newspaper account of the fire in Charlotte, N. C. ALS (telegram sent), DNA, RG 107, Telegrams Collected (Unbound).

To Charles W. Ford

City Point, Va, Jan. 10th *1865.*

DEAR FORD,

I understand there are back taxes on Mr. Dent's place (now including two places belonging to me) amounting to some $1,400 00 which if not paid this month the land will be sold. If I send money there to settle this it will be the last of it. Now I want to ask you to do me a favor. Select some eliable man to attend to the matter for me. Let the land be sold for the taxes and buy it in for me and call on you for the means to pay for it. I will send you a draft for $1500 00 as soon as I can procure it and before the money will be required. If this should not prove enough please advance for me and I will pay at once. My only reason for wishing to buy in the land instead of paying off the incumbrance is this. I am not able, and under the circumstances not willing, to loose the money. These taxes were due before I owned any of the land and it is not my debt. John Dent paid off an incumbrance of $4000 00, and ~~taxes~~, interest, on the whole tract and now owns the whole with the exception of what I have. He made me buy over and pay him the cash for forty acres which Mr. Dent had previously given to Mrs. Grant though it had not been deeded to her. Another forty acres I bought and paid for. Mr. Dent many years ago signified the way his land was to be divided. Now all but the little I have goes to one for a paltry sum. You can understand that I would naturally want to make him pay his own taxes.

Yours Truly
U. S. GRANT

ALS, USG 3.

To J. Russell Jones

City Point, Va, Jan 10th *1865*.

DEAR JONES,

I have just learned that Mr. Dent's farm, near St. Louis, is about being sold for taxes. Mr. D. is my father-in-law. Sixty acres of the tract was given to Mrs. Grant and eighty acres more of it I have purchased since the war began, not knowing there was any back taxes due. I have written to Chas Ford, U. S. Express Agt. St. Louis, a particular friend of mine, to attend to this for me. Now as I invest as fast as I save a dollar, and a little faster because I keep myself in debt all the time, I never have $1500 00. What I now want to ask is this favor; that you borrow from Corwith, or some one, on my 5-20 bonds the sum of $1500 00 on four months time. Get a draft for that amount in favor of Chas Ford, U. S. Ex Co. St. Louis, and send it to him advising me of the fact.

I wrote to you last month asking you to send what means I might have with you to Mrs. Grant. I received no answer from

which I infer you did not get my letter. I wanted to send the gold
as a New Years present, and any other funds because I was hard up.

Please let me know if you can make this arrangement for me.

Yours Truly

U. S. GRANT

ALS, ICarbS.

To Julia Dent Grant

City Point, Va, Jan. 11th *1865.*

DEAR JULIA,

I have just rec'd a letter from Jones saying he had sent you
$475 00   This however includes the gold which I do not want you
to spend. If it is necessary for you to have more money I will try
to send it. I have received a letter from Jim. Casey saying that
$1400 00 ba[ck] taxes are due on your fathers place and unless
paid this month the place will be sold. Now I cannot afford to send
$1400 there and get no return for it. I know if I pay up the taxes
it will be the last I shall ever see of the money. Looking to my own
interest in the matter I wrote to Ford to attend to the matter for me
and to let the farm be sold for taxes and him to buy it in in my
name. I at the same time arranged for borrowing the money to
send to him. A tax title amounts to no title atall but it is good until
the money paid is refunded. If I can I will force John to make Nelly
and Emma deeds to their land and probably to Fred. also.

I receive all your letters. Some of them are rather cross.—Love
and kisses for you and the children.

ULYS.

ALS, DLC-USG.
On Jan. 17, 1865, Capt. George K. Leet telegraphed to USG. "The following received at Eight oclock this evening—'Phila. Jan. 17th. I will leave Phila.
One fifteen P. M. train today. Will reach Washington about seven oclock—Have
missed the boat at Balto. Please let the General know the above MRS. U. S.
GRANT' Phila train is in but I cannot find Mrs. Grant. Think she has stopped
at Baltimore. Will telegraph [*to*] ascertain" ALS (telegram sent), DNA, RG
107, Telegrams Collected (Unbound).

To Robert Ould

In the Field Jany 12th 1865.

Judge Ro. Ould.
Agent of Exchange, C. S. A.

I have the honor to inform you that Gen. Canby telegraphs to Washington that a steam ship was sent to Mobile on the sixteenth (16th) ultimo for the cotton, and that the delay has resulted from the neglect of those who were to furnish the cotton. The expense for demurrage is very heavy, and Gen. Granger proposes to send the steam ship north without the cotton, unless it is delivered very soon.

Please advise me of any information you may have upon this matter and whether you have taken the necessary steps to expedite the shipping of it.

I am very respectfully
Your Ob't. Serv't.
U. S. Grant.
Lieut. Gen'l.

Copies, DLC-USG, V, 46, 71, 107; DNA, RG 108, Letters Sent. *O.R.*, II, viii, 57. See telegram to Maj. Gen. Henry W. Halleck, Jan. 15, 1865. On Jan. 14, 1865, Robert Ould wrote to USG. "Your communication of the 12th inst has been received. There seems to be some extraordinary mistake somewhere, about the cotton to be shipped from Mobile. I have already acquainted you with the substance of the telegraph from Mobile, of the date of the 25th of Dec. last. I have now before me a letter from the Agent of the Confederate States, having charge of the matter, dated Mobile, Dec. 23d 1864, from which I extract the following paragraph, to wit: 'The cotton has been furnished and is all ready, on board the lighter, awaiting reply from the Federal Commander to a communication from Gen'l. Maury, notifying him that it is ready to be delivered.' This, you perceive, is utterly inconsistent with Gen'l. Canby's telegraph of the 16th Ulto. I hope that we shall soon arrive at the truth of the matter." Copies, DNA, RG 109, Ould Letterbook; Ould Letterbook, Archives Div., Virginia State Library, Richmond, Va. *O.R.*, II, viii, 70.

On Jan. 16, 11:15 a.m., Maj. Gen. Henry W. Halleck telegraphed to USG. "The transport for the cotton reached Mobile Bay on the 16th of December and General Granger immediately notified Genl Maury that he was ready to recieve it. Col Sautelle, who reached New-Orleans Jany 4th says that the vessel was still waiting when he left Mobile, but no reply had been recieved from Genl Maury. Genl Canby says that the delay is entirely due to the rebel authorities in Mobile."

ALS (telegram sent), DNA, RG 107, Telegrams Collected (Bound); telegram received, *ibid.*; (marked as sent at 10:30 A.M.) *ibid.*, RG 108, Letters Received. *O.R.*, II, viii, 78.

To Maj. Gen. George G. Meade

By Telegraph from City Pt 8 P M
Dated Jany 14 18645.

To MAJ GEN MEADE

Four (4) or five (5) men of the Veteran Corps who have just reached here in charge of recruits are believed to be guilty of great outrages to the recruits   With your permission I desire to have them tried by the Court Martial now in session here   The testimony has been sifted & the trial will only consume a couple of days

U S GRANT
Lt Genl

Telegram received, DNA, RG 393, Army of the Potomac, Miscellaneous Letters Received; copies, *ibid.*, RG 108, Letters Sent; DLC-USG, V, 46, 71, 107; (2) Meade Papers, PHi. On Jan. 14, 1865, 8:30 P.M., Maj. Gen. George G. Meade telegraphed to USG. "I will direct the Judge Advocate of the Court at City Point to try the men of the Veteran Reserve Corps referred to by you." Copies (2—one misdated Jan. 11), *ibid.*; DNA, RG 393, Army of the Potomac, Letters Sent.

On Dec. 30, 1864, Special Orders No. 354, Army of the Potomac, announced the staff officers accompanying Meade to Philadelphia and assigned Maj. Gen. John G. Parke to temporary command of the Army of the Potomac. *O.R.*, I, xlii, part 3, 1104. On Jan. 6, 1865, Friday, USG telegraphed to Meade, Philadelphia. "I wish you to return so as to take the boat from Washington or Baltimore by Monday at furthest." Copies, DLC-USG, V, 46, 71, 107; DNA, RG 108, Letters Sent. *O.R.*, I, xlvi, part 2, 53. On Jan. 10, Brig. Gen. John A. Rawlins telegraphed to Parke. "Genl Meade left Fort Monroe for this point at 10.30 A. M. of today." ALS (telegram sent), DNA, RG 107, Telegrams Collected (Unbound). See *O.R.*, I, xlvi, part 2, 82. On the same day, Meade wrote to his wife. "I reached City Point at 6 P. M. to-day. I found the cause of my recall to be as I expected. General Grant had received information of Lee's sending off two divisions of troops, and was, and is, under the impression that it is the commencement of the evacuation of Richmond. Should this prove to be the case, or should Lee materially weaken his force, we will take the initiative, and for this contingency I was required." George Meade, *The Life and Letters of George Gordon Meade* (New York, 1913), II, 255.

On Jan. 15, 9:00 A.M., Meade telegraphed to USG. "If you will be at home today I will ~~come~~ go down to City Point—" ALS (telegram sent), DNA, RG 94, War Records Office, Army of the Potomac; copy, *ibid.*, RG 393, Army of the

Potomac, Letters Sent. *O.R.*, I, xlvi, part 2, 134. On the same day, Lt. Col. Theodore S. Bowers telegraphed to Meade. "Gen Grant will not be at his HeadQuarters until late this evening" Telegram received (at 10:35 A.M.), DNA, RG
94, War Records Office, Army of the Potomac. *O.R.*, I, xlvi, part 2, 134. On Jan.
16, 9:00 A.M., Meade telegraphed to Bowers. "Will the lieutenant-general be at
home to-day?" *Ibid.*, p. 145. On the same day, Bowers telegraphed to Meade.
"Gen Grant will not be at home before tomorrow" Telegram received (at
10:15 A.M.), DNA, RG 94, War Records Office, Army of the Potomac. *O.R.*, I,
xlvi, part 2, 146. On Jan. 18, 9:30 A.M., Meade telegraphed to Rawlins. "I
desire to see the Lt. Genl. comd. & would therefore be glad to know whether he
has returned & will be at his Hd Qrs this morning.—" ALS (telegram sent),
DNA, RG 94, War Records Office, Army of the Potomac.

To Abraham Lincoln

City Point Va
2 P M Jan 15. 1865

HIS EXCELLENCY THE PRESIDENT U. S.

I send you by telegraph message from Davis & other dispatches
from Richmond Whig,[1] concerning the arrest of Ex Senator Foote,[2]
which is all the information I have on the subject, Any further information that I obtain will be sent you,[3] what is likely to be
done with him is difficult to conjecture, I suppose they will at
furthest do nothing more than imprison him,

U S GRANT
Lt Gen

Telegram received (at 9:00 P.M.), DLC-Robert T. Lincoln; DNA, RG 107,
Telegrams Collected (Bound); copies, *ibid.*, Telegrams Received in Cipher;
ibid., RG 108, Letters Sent; DLC-USG, V, 46, 71, 107. *O.R.*, I, xlvi, part 2, 133.
On Jan. 14, 1865, President Abraham Lincoln telegraphed to USG. "You have
perhaps seen in the papers that Ex. Senator Foote, with his family, attempted to
escape from Richmond to Washington, and that he was pursued and ~~carried~~
taken back. His wife and child are now here, Please give me the earliest information you may receive concerning him—what is likely to be done with him &c."
ALS (telegram sent), DNA, RG 107, Telegrams Collected (Bound); telegram
received (marked as sent at 6:00 P.M.), *ibid.*, RG 108, Letters Received. *O.R.*,
I, xlvi, part 2, 126. Lincoln, *Works*, VIII, 216.

1. Telegram received (at 1:40 P.M.), DNA, RG 107, Telegrams Collected
(Bound). *O.R.*, I, xlvi, part 2, 133–34.

2. Henry S. Foote, born in Va. in 1800, practiced law in Miss., where he was elected U.S. Senator (1847–52) and governor (1852–54). Elected to the C.S.A. Congress, he maintained a bitter feud with Jefferson Davis until he resigned to undertake a peace mission. H. S. Foote, *War of the Rebellion* (New York, 1866), pp. 374–415; *O.R.*, I, xlvi, part 2, *passim*; *ibid.*, II, viii, *passim*.

3. On Jan. 16, 1865, USG telegraphed to Lincoln. "The following is obtained from todays Richmond Dispatch—'Hon H. S. Foote of Tennessee is still at Fredericksburgh   The House of representatives not having yet decided what action they will take in his case. Persons who came down from Fredericksburgh yesterday state that Mr Foote was very indignant that he should have been arrested and demanded to be brought to Richmond immediately and when this was refused him he wrote to Judge Halyburton petitioning for a writ of habeas corpus'" Telegram received (at 6:10 P.M.), DLC-Robert T. Lincoln; DNA, RG 107, Telegrams Collected (Bound).

To Maj. Gen. Henry W. Halleck

City Point Va
Jany 15th 1865

MAJ GEN H W. HALLECK
CHIEF OF STAFF.

Under the arrangement for the release and exchange of prisoners of war set forth in the letter of which the following is a copy Judge Ould has notified Col Mulford Ass't Agent of Exchange that orders have gone out for the release of all prisoners coming within said agreement held by their side,   You will therefore please direct all prisoners that come within said agreement held by us to be released and sent to Ft Monroe there to be detained subject to the orders of Col Mulford

U S GRANT Lt Genl

Letter   "City Pt Va
Jany 13th 1865

COL JNO E MULFORD
ASST AGENT OF EXCHANGE
COL

The letter of Judge R Ould Agent of Exchange C. S. of date 'Richmond Sept 12th 1864'[1] in answer to yours of the 10th of same month, accepting the propositions made by him under ~~the~~ date of August 22nd 1864[2] that 'All prisoners of War on each side be released from confinement, close or irons, as the case may be, and either placed in the condition of other prisoners of war or sent to their respective homes for equivalent;' has been duly referred to me for my consideration and action and I am of the opinion that the proposition as made by Judge Ould and accepted by the Government through you is just and equally fair and beneficial to both sides. You will therefore communicate to Judge Ould without delay that our Govt. stands by its's acceptance of his proposition hereintofore referred to without excepting from its operations any of the cases proposed by Gen. Butler and referred to in his (Judge Ould's) letter of Sept. 12th, that the parties for whose release said agreement was made shall all be mutually delivered, the party having the excess to receive proper equivalents & that you are authorized to carry the agreement into immediate effect on our side

very Respy

Signed U. S Grant Lt Gen"

Telegram received (at 12:20 p.m.), DNA, RG 107, Telegrams Collected (Bound); copies, *ibid.*, RG 108, Letters Sent; DLC-USG, V, 46, 71, 107; USG 3. *O.R.*, II, viii, 63, 74. The letter to Lt. Col. John E. Mulford is also entered separately in USG's letterbooks. On Jan. 15, 1865, noon, USG telegraphed to the commanding officer, Point Lookout, Md. "Col. Mulford Agent of Ex. will call on you for officers and men to meet a new arrangement we have made—Let him have what he calls for—" Telegram received, DNA, RG 107, Telegrams Collected (Unbound); *ibid.*, RG 393, Middle Military Div., Telegrams Received; copies, *ibid.*, RG 108, Letters Sent; DLC-USG, V, 46, 71, 107; USG 3. At 3:00 p.m., Maj. Gen. Henry W. Halleck telegraphed to USG. "Does your order to send prisoners to Fort Monroe include the five hundred officers sent to Morris Island to be exposed to enemy's fire the same as our officers confined in the City of Charleston?" ALS (telegram sent), DNA, RG 107, Telegrams Collected (Bound); telegram received, *ibid.*; *ibid.*, Telegrams Collected (Unbound); *ibid.*, RG 108, Letters Received. *O.R.*, II, viii, 74. On Jan. 16, USG telegraphed to Halleck. "My order to Send prisoners to Ft. Monroe does not include the 500 sent to Morris Island." Telegram received (at 6:10 p.m.), DNA, RG 107, Telegrams Collected (Bound); copies, *ibid.*, RG 108, Letters Sent; DLC-USG, V, 46, 71, 107. *O.R.*, II, viii, 811.

1. *Ibid.*, II, vii, 807.
2. *Ibid.*, pp. 667–68.

To Maj. Gen. Henry W. Halleck

City Point Va
12 m. Jan. 15. 1865

MAJ. GEN. H. W. HALLECK,
CHF OF STAFF,

I have just received a communication from Judge R. Ould, Confederate Agt of Exchange under date of 14th inst.[1] in which he says "I have already acquainted you with the substance of the telegrams from Mobile of the date of the 25th of Dec. last. I have now before me a letter from the Agent of the Confederate States having charge of the matter, dated Mobile Dec. 23d 1864, from which I extract the following paragraph, towit: 'the cotton has been furnished & is already on board the lighter awaiting reply from the Federal commander to a communication from Gen. Maury notifying him that it is ready to be delivered' "

Please communicate the above to Genl. Canby with directions to inquire into the matter and take immediate steps to have the vessels that are to transport the cotton report at once in Mobile Harbor to receive it, and the proper parties in Mobile notified of the fact. I much fear unless something is done in this matter soon we will be denied permission to send through Supplies for our prisoners, for whose benefit especially the arrangement for serving prisoners was entered into by us.

U. S. GRANT
Lt. Gen.

Telegram received (at 4:30 P.M.), DNA, RG 107, Telegrams Collected (Bound); copies, *ibid.*, Telegrams Received in Cipher; *ibid.*, RG 108, Letters Sent; DLC-USG, V, 46, 71, 107. *O.R.*, II, viii, 74.

On Jan. 15, 1865, USG telegraphed to Maj. Gen. Henry W. Halleck. "Judge Ould Confederate Agent of Exchange in an intrview with Col Mulford yesterday requested that Genl Vance should be paroled as Genl Bealls Assistant— Please have Vance so paroled" Telegram received (at 10:50 A.M.), DNA, RG 107, Telegrams Collected (Bound); copies, *ibid.*, RG 108, Letters Sent; *ibid.*, RG 249, Letters Received; DLC-USG, V, 46, 72, 107. *O.R.*, II, viii, 73. See *ibid.*, p. 74. On Jan. 17, Robert Ould wrote to USG. "Brig. Gen'l. Vance and any other Officer whom Gen'l. Beall may select as his assistant, will be acceptable to the Confederate Authorities." Copies, DNA, RG 109, Ould Letterbook; Ould

Letterbook, Archives Div., Virginia State Library, Richmond, Va. *O.R.*, II, viii, 83. On Jan. 23, USG telegraphed to Halleck transmitting this letter. Telegram received (at 3:30 P.M.), DNA, RG 107, Telegrams Collected (Bound); copies, *ibid.*, Telegrams Received in Cipher; *ibid.*, RG 108, Letters Sent; DLC-USG, V, 46, 72, 108. *O.R.*, II, viii, 113.

On Feb. 10, Ould wrote to USG. "The Confederate Authorities desire to send from Mobile an additional supply of fifteen hundred bales of cotton, to be disposed of by our Agents in New York, for the benefit of our prisoners. The cotton will be ready for delivery at an early day. I will thank you to instruct your military authorities near Mobile, to notify Maj. Gen'l. Maury of the time when they will be ready to receive it." Copy, DNA, RG 109, Ould Letterbook. *O.R.*, II, viii, 202–3.

1. See letter to Robert Ould, Jan. 12, 1865.

To Abraham Lincoln

City Point [*Jan.*] 17 [*1865*]

A. LINCOLN—PRESIDENT

From the Richmond papers of today I learn that on, yesterday Judge Haliburton of the Confederate Court of the Eastern Dist of Virginia issued a writ of Habeas Corpus on the petition of Gov Foote returnable on thursday next   it is supposed by the Papers however that this matter was settled yesterday by the confederate House of Representatives declaring that they are of opinion that the good of the country would not be subserved by the forced attendance of said member upon the sessions of this House but that under all the circumstances of the case it is expedient that the Mily authorities discharge him from custody   It is presumed that Mr Foote has already been placed at liberty

U S GRANT

Telegram received (at 6:10 P.M.), Seward Papers, NRU; DNA, RG 107, Telegrams Collected (Bound); copies, *ibid.*, RG 108, Letters Sent; DLC-USG, V, 46, 71, 107. *O.R.*, I, xlvi, part 2, 158. See telegram to Abraham Lincoln, Jan. 15, 1865.

On Jan. 17, 1865, 3:00 P.M., Maj. Gen. Edward O. C. Ord telegraphed to USG. "~~in the Sentinel~~ In to days Sentinel's report of proceedings of Rebel House of Reps yesterday—is a warm debate upon an article of the Sentinel, stigmatising as treason—the proposition before the house in secret session to open negociations for peace—A motion to allow resolutions to come up, which pronounced the sentinel article false was lost—Vote 32 ayes 36 noes—Smith of Alabama regarded this vote as endorsing the Sentinels article and left to go home—After wards they took a vote on a Resolution that no privelige had been violated in arresting Foote, one of their members—and that he be left to the care of the military— lost vote 36 noes-35 ayes—I think these proceedings important enough to tele- graph to ~~Washington~~ President—Barksdale quelled the storm by stating by au- thority that the Sentinel was not Mr Davis organ" ALS (telegram sent), DNA, RG 107, Telegrams Collected (Unbound). *O.R.*, I, xlvi, part 2, 163.

To Edwin M. Stanton

By Telegraph from City Point. 12.45. a. m.

Dated Jan 18 18~~64~~5.

To Hon Edwin M Stanton Secy War

Your dispatch of ten (10) O'clock last Evening[1] has just reached me. Owing to the time that has elapsed I am confident but that you have left   If I cannot come myself leaving here by sun up I will send Gen Rawlins & will run to Washington to see you in a day or two.

U. S. Grant.

Lt Genl

Telegram received, DLC-Edwin M. Stanton; copies, DLC-USG, V, 46, 72, 107; DNA, RG 108, Letters Sent. *O.R.*, I, xlvi, part 2, 168. On Jan. 18, 1865, 3:00 A.M., Secretary of War Edwin M. Stanton, Fort Monroe, telegraphed to USG. "Your telegram just received. There is an urgent necessity for me to be in Wash- ington and as you ~~cannot~~ could not reach here starting at sun up before twelve or one oclock I shall go on to Washington hoping to see you there very soon. ~~Nothing had been heard~~ Sherman was anxiously expecting the troops that were to sail from Baltimore but nothing had been heard from them. General Terry wanted the residue of his own division to be sent him. Your reccommendation of General Terry for ~~Major General~~ Brigadier in the regular service will be carried out. While at Fort Fisher I gave him an appointment of full Major General and would have also given the Brigadiership but General Townsend thought there is no vacancy. I am sure there is. ~~and that Thomas'~~ It was understood at Savannah that Beauregard had gone West to bring down Hoods forces to operate against Sherman." ALS (telegram sent), DNA, RG 107, Telegrams Collected (Un- bound); telegram received (marked as sent at 4:05 A.M.), *ibid.*, RG 108, Let- ters Received. *O.R.*, I, xlvi, part 2, 168–69. On Jan. 17, USG had telegraphed to Stanton. "As a substantial recognition of the bravery of both officers and men in the Capture of Fort Fisher & the important service thereby rendered their Country, I do most respectfully recommend Brevet Maj Gen Alfred H. Terry, U. S. Vols, their Commanding Officer for appointment as Brigadier General in the regular Army." Telegram received, DLC-Edwin M. Stanton; (at 2:10 P.M.)

DNA, RG 107, Telegrams Collected (Bound); copies, *ibid.*, RG 108, Letters Sent; DLC-USG, V, 46, 71, 107. *O.R.*, I, xlvi, part 2, 158.

Also on Jan. 17, USG telegraphed to Stanton. "The following is from the Richmond Whig. The other papers publish the same dispatch. 'Fall of Fort Fisher. The Unwelcome news of the fall of Fort Fisher commanding the entrance to Cape Fear River, was received this morning, and occasioned in this Community a sensation of profound regret. The Capture of this Fort is equivalent to the Closure of the Harbor of Wilmington by the enemy's fleet—It is situated about eighteen miles below the City but was the Main defence of the entrance to the River, and its fall therefore, will prevent in future, the arrival or departure of Blockade Runners. How far this reverse may prove injurious to our Cause remains to be seen, but at present we regard it rather as an unfortunate than disastrous event. The following is the official report "Head Qr's N. Virginia Jan. 16th HON. J. A. SEDDON General Bragg reports that the enemy bombarded Fort Fisher furiously all day yesterday. At four P. M. their infantry advanced to the Assault, a heavy demonstration at the same hour being made against their rear by our troops—At half past six P. M. General Whiting reported that their attack had failed, and the garrison was being strengthened with fresh troops. About ten P. M. the Fort was Captured with most of its garrison. No further particulars at the time known (signed) R. E LEE" The Capture of Beverly. The following official Telegram was received at the War Department, last night. "HeadQrs. Jan. 15th 1865 HON. J. A. SEDDON. Gen'l. Early reports that Gen'l. Rosser at the head of three hundred men surprised, and Captured the garrison at Beverly Randolph County, on the eleventh instant—Killing and wounding a Considerable number and taking five hundred and eighty prisoners —His loss slight. (signed) R E LEE" The same paper states that the Hon. Pierre Soule had arrived in Mexico on a mission for the Confederate states. Street rumors in Richmond say that Seddon has been removed, and Gen'l. Breckinridge, made Sec'y. of War. Other Changes are talked about but nothing official—The Confederate House of Representatives declared by resolution, yesterday in the case of Gov. Foote, that under all the circumstances of the case, it is expedient that the Military Authorities discharge him from Custody, and it is presumed that he has been placed at liberty.'" Telegram received, DLC-Edwin M. Stanton; (2—at 5:05 P.M.) DNA, RG 107, Telegrams Collected (Bound).

On Jan. 18, 4:00 A.M., Stanton telegraphed to USG. "The Hospital Steamer R S Spalding a fast Sailer on which I came up will return to Fort Fisher at twelve oclock today. If you have any despatches or messenger to send to General Terry she will afford the best and soonest opportunity. She is at Fortress Monroe. and I am just starting for Washington." ALS (telegram sent), *ibid.*, Telegrams Collected (Unbound); telegram received (at 8:45 A.M.), *ibid.*, RG 108, Letters Received. *O.R.*, I, xlvi, part 2, 169. At 9:30 A.M., USG telegraphed to Stanton. "I was just starting to Ft Monroe to meet you when your dispatch was received announcing that you were about starting for Washington. Your dispatch of 10 a. m. the 17th did not reach me until about One this morning and was immediately replied to." ALS (telegram sent), MdAN; telegram received (at 10:50 A.M.), DNA, RG 107, Telegrams Collected (Bound). *O.R.*, I, xlvi, part 2, 169. At 7:00 P.M., USG telegraphed to Stanton. "The confirmation of Gen Thomas and Gen Sheridan to the rank of Major General in the Regular Army makes two vacancies. I hope Genl Terry will get one of these." Telegram received (at 8:00

P.M.), DNA, RG 107, Telegrams Collected (Bound); copies, *ibid.*, Telegrams Received in Cipher; *ibid.*, RG 108, Letters Sent; DLC-USG, V, 46, 72, 107. *O.R.*, I, xlvi, part 2, 170.

1. On Jan. 17, 10:00 P.M., Stanton, Fort Monroe, telegraphed to USG. "I have just arrived from Savannah having stopped six hours yesterday at Fort Fisher. My telegram to the President a copy of which goes with this gives ~~what~~ I the particulars learned from Admiral Porter & General Terry also the movements of General Shermans force. I staid with Sherman four days, ~~I~~ and would be glad to see you so as to communicate some other matters that cannot be safely written but am ~~sick~~ too unwell to go to City Point if you can come here. At General Shermans request North Carolina was put in the Department of the South and added to his command. General Townsend will send you a copy of the order. Please let me know if ~~you can come~~ I shall wait here to see you." ALS (telegram sent), CSmH; telegram received, DNA, RG 108, Letters Received. *O.R.*, I, xlvi, part 2, 157. The enclosure is *ibid.*, pp. 155–57.

To Edwin M. Stanton

(Cipher)   City Point, Va, Jan. 18th 1865 [*1:30* P.M.]
HON. E. M. STANTON, SEC. OF WAR, WASHINGTON,

Can not the troops now in the Dept. of Va. ~~be a~~ and comprising the 24th & 25th Corps be named as a grand Army Corps or given some name to entitle the Commanding officer the Staff of a Corps Comd.r. I understand the Auditor is rejecting the account of Dept. Staff officers where the Dept. has not a Corps organization.

U. S. GRANT
Lt. Gen.

ALS (telegram sent), CSmH; telegram received (at 2:55 P.M.), DNA, RG 107, Telegrams Collected (Bound). *O.R.*, I, xlvi, part 2, 169.

On Jan. 13, 1865, 10:30 A.M., Maj. Gen. Edward O. C. Ord telegraphed to USG. "I shall be glad if you can send Gibbon to the Twenty-fourth at once." *Ibid.*, p. 122. On the same day, USG telegraphed to Maj. Gen. George G. Meade. "Please relieve Gen Gibbon and order him to report to me as soon as possible for Assignment to the 24th A C" Telegram received (at 9:45 P.M.), DNA, RG 94, War Records Office, Army of the Potomac; copies (2), Meade Papers, PHi. *O.R.*, I, xlvi, part 2, 113. At 10:30 P.M., Meade telegraphed to USG. "Genl. Gibbon has been ordered to report to you at once—I am truly glad you have been able to give him a corps.—" ALS (telegram sent), DNA, RG 94, War Records Office, Army of the Potomac; copies, *ibid.*, RG 393, Army of the Potomac, Letters Sent; (2) Meade Papers, PHi. *O.R.*, I, xlvi, part 2, 113. See *ibid.*, p. 126.

To Maj. Gen. Henry W. Halleck

City Point Va
9 P M Jan. 18th 1865

MAJ GEN H W HALLECK
CHF OF STAFF

I now understand that Beauregard has gone west to gather up what can be saved from Hoods Army to bring against Sherman. If this be the case Selma and Montgomery will be easily reached. I do not believe though that Thomas will ever get there from the north. He is too ponderous in his preparations and equipments to move through a country rapidly enough to live off it. West of the Mississippi, we do not want to do more than defend what we now hold, but I do want Genl Canby to make a winter campaign, either from Mobile Bay, or from some point in Florida. You might order all the cavalry horses now in the west to Gen Canby and direct him to make an independent campaign, looking to the capture of Mobile, first, if the job does not promise too long a one, and Montgomery and Selma, and the destruction of all roads, machine shops and stores, the main object—

Thomas can do without horses for some time. A portion of his troops could be sent by water to Gen Canby. If Thomas does[1] move in co-operation, probably the best route for him to take would be by way of Chattanooga, repairing the road to Rome and starting from there, These I give as views—What I would order, is, that Gen Canby be furnished cavalry horses and be directed to prepare to commence a campaign, and that Thomas be telegraphed to see what he could do—and when, and get his views upon the choice of routes, looking upon Selma as his objective point, Thomas must make a campaign, or spare his surplus troops,

U. S. GRANT
Lt Genl

Telegram received (at 11:00 P.M.), DNA, RG 107, Telegrams Collected (Bound); copies, *ibid.*, Telegrams Received in Cipher; *ibid.*, RG 108, Letters Sent; DLC-USG, V, 46, 72, 107. *O.R.*, I, xlv, part 2, 609–10. On Jan. 18, 1865, 11:00 A.M., Maj. Gen. Henry W. Halleck telegraphed to USG. "I learn from

Genl Canby that if Genl Thomas proposes to move on Selma, or some othe point towards the Gulf, he (Canby) can cooperate with a force of from fifteen or twenty thousand men. To do this efficiently he will require remounts for a part of his cavalry. You will remember that since about the first of October *all* cavalry horses purchased in the west & northwest have been sent to Genl Thomas, to the entire exclusion of Missouri, Arkansas, Mississippi & Louisiana. Consequently these departments must now have a large number of dismounted cavalry. The question now arises whether we shall continue to send all cavalry horses to Genl Thomas, or whether Genl Canby's command should recieve its due proportion. This must be decided, in a measure, by your plan of ulterior operations in that part of the country. Whatever that may be, it is obviously important that there should be a concert of action between Canby & Thomas, for the former cannot safely reduce his garrisons on the Miss. River to operate against the interior of Alabama, unless the latter assists at the same time by pursuing Hood or keeping him away from Memphis, Vicksburg, Natches, &c. Canby seems very anxious to make a campaign this winter, while the weather is favorable, if a plan can be determined on, & he can be certain of the cooperation of Thomas. I feel confident that Selma & Montgomery can be taken this winter if Thomas & Canby's forces can either unite or cooperate. Genl Sherman writes me that abundant supplies will be found in all the interior of Alabama." ALS (telegram sent), DNA, RG 107, Telegrams Collected (Bound); telegram received (marked as sent at 4:30 P.M.), *ibid.*; (marked as sent at 4:00 P.M.) *ibid.*, RG 108, Letters Received. Printed as sent at 4:30 P.M. in *O.R.*, I, xlv, part 2, 609. See *ibid.*, p. 614. At 9:30 P.M., USG telegraphed to Halleck. "It will not do for Canby to rely on either Granger or Hurlbut as first in command of an important campaign—" Telegram received (at 11:00 P.M.), DNA, RG 107, Telegrams Collected (Bound); copies, *ibid.*, Telegrams Received in Cipher; *ibid.*, RG 108, Letters Sent; DLC-USG, V, 46, 72, 107. *O.R.*, I, xlviii, part 1, 573.

1. "not" inserted in USG's letterbooks.

To Robert Ould

City Point Jany 19th 1865

COL, ROBT, OULD
AGENT OF EXCHANGE
SIR.

Enclosed I send you the names of a number of gentlemen who have been selected by the United States Christian Commission, to go South for the purpose of visiting such prisons as they may be permitted to visit containing Federal Prisoners of War, and to see for the body of which they are members, and for the public generally their condition and circumstances,   Three of these gentlemen, are now here waiting your action,   I would state, any priviledge you will grant in this matter will be extended to an equal number of gentlemen sent from the South for the same purpose Should this favor be granted it will probably serve to satisfy the friends of prisoners both North and South, of the exageration of the reports of suffering so rife in both sections

I would respectfully ask a reply to this at your earliest convenience

Very Respectfully
U. S. GRANT Lt. Gen

Copies, DLC-USG, V, 46, 72, 107; DNA, RG 108, Letters Sent. *O.R.*, II, viii, 89. Apparently enclosed was a copy of a letter of Jan. 19, 1865, from Brig. Gen. John A. Rawlins to Lt. Col. John E. Mulford. "The Right Rev—Alfred Lee D. D. of Delaware   Rev—Bishop E E Janes D. D of New York, and H. G. Jones Esq of Philadelphia, are appointed by the U. S. Christian Commission to visit our prisoners held by the Confederate States Authorities,   If these gentlemen are permitted to pass through the lines South on their Mission, alike number of gentlemen from the Confederate States will be allowed the priviledge of of visiting their prisoners in the North,   the letter herewith addressed to Judge Ould contains an application for the necessary authority for them to proceed on their Mission,   You will therefore please forward it at the earliest possible moment, and should the authority asked for be granted afford these gentlemen every means in your power to facilitate their getting through"   Copies, DLC-USG, V, 46, 72, 107; DNA, RG 108, Letters Sent. *O.R.*, II, viii, 89. On Jan. 24, C.S.A. Agent of Exchange Robert Ould wrote to USG. "Your communication of the 19th inst, enclosing 'the names of a number of gentlemen who have been selected by the United States Christian Commission, to go South for the purpose of visiting' our prisons, has been received. You further state that any privilege granted in the matter would be extended to an equal number of gentlemen sent by us for similar purposes, and that such action might probably serve to satisfy the friends of prisoners both North and South of the exaggerations of the reports of suffering so rife in both sections. On the 24th of January 1864, in a letter to Major Gen. Hitchcock, C[o]mmissioner of Exchange, I proposed that a proper number of Surgeons, to be selected by their own Government, should be permitted to attend prisoners on each side respectively, for the purpose of taking charge of their health and comfort, receiving and distributing contributions, and making report of any matters relating to the welfare of the parties under their care. Although just one year has elapsed since the date of that communication, no answer has been returned. I have no doubt but that the persons referred to in your letter are very respectable gentlemen, yet they are certainly not as well suited to minister to the wants of prisoners as accredited officers whose routine of duty makes them peculiarly fitted to relieve the sick and wounded. I therefore respectfully suggest that your application be so changed as to embrace my offer, so long treated with silence. I am quite confident that all the interests of humanity will be promoted by the modification. It is true that your prisoners are suffering. It is one of the calamities and necessities of the war, made so not by our choice. We have done every thing we can consistently with the duty we owe to ourselves. We intend to do the same in the future. But that great suffering must ensue if your prisoners remain in our hands, is very certain. For that reason I propose that all of them be delivered to you in exchange man for man and officer for officer according to grade, for those of ours whom you hold. Will not the cause of humanity be far more promoted by such a course, than even if as you suggest the friends of prisoners both North and South are satisfied of the exaggeration of the reports of suffering so rife in both sections. If however prisoners are to remain in confinement at least let us mutually send to their relief and comfort stationary agents whose official duty requires them to devote all their time and labor to their sacred mission. For the reasons stated, I decline the proposed visit of the gentlemen to whom you refer. In doing so, I shall be glad to hear from you whether either of the alternatives presented, meets with your favor." LS, DLC-George H. Stuart. *O.R.*, II, viii, 122–23.

On Oct. 31, 1864, George H. Stuart, U.S. Christian Commission, had written to Secretary of War Edwin M. Stanton asking permission to attempt to send delegates to prisoners in C.S.A. custody. LS, DNA, RG 94, Letters Received, 2259S 1864. *O.R.*, II, vii, 1074. On Nov. 29, USG endorsed this letter. "Respectfully returned. I see no impropriety in granting permission to the Commission to send a certain number of good christian men to make the attempt within proposed, and if successful I know of no special reason why proper christian agents from the South, should not permitted to visit and administer to rebel prisoners in our hands" ES, DNA, RG 94, Letters Received, 2259S 1864. *O.R.*, II, vii, 1075.

On Jan. 14, 1865, Stuart wrote to USG. "The gentlemen whose names were referred to you by the Secretary of War and who were approved of by you as a delegation to visit the Union prisoners in the hands of the rebels, are desirous of reporting at your Head Quarters at the earliest practicable date. They may not be all able to go down to City Point together, but the present design is to start from Philadelphia on Wednesday morning early, which will allow them to report at City Point on Thursday afternoon. On that day will you be in the army? and upon receipt of this will you be kind *enough to telegraph me* that I may make the final arrangements—or, if necessary, make any change. We are anxious, not to change any of your arrangements, but simply to know how we best should direct our own movements in the matter." LS, DNA, RG 108, Letters Received. On Jan. 19, 12:30 P.M., USG telegraphed to Stuart. "Your letter of fourteenth (14) just received & read. when the gentlemen you speak of arrived they will be sent through the lines if no objection is made on the other side" Telegram received, *ibid.*, RG 107, Telegrams Collected (Unbound); copies, *ibid.*, RG 108, Letters Sent; DLC-USG, V, 46, 72, 107.

To Edwin M. Stanton

(Cipher)   City Point, Va, Jan. 19th *18645*. [*1:00* P.M.]
HON. E. M. STANTON, WASHINGTON.

Col. Comstock in a dispatch of the 17th from Fort Fisher says;
The enemy have this morning been blowing up works near Fort

Caswell and it is not improbable that when the Navy get down they will find it evacuated. They are moving cautiously. Our prisoners are 1900. Guns uninjured and all reported 72.

U. S. Grant

Lt. Gen.

ALS (telegram sent), ICHi; telegram received (at 2:25 P.M.), DNA, RG 107, Telegrams Collected (Bound). *O.R.*, I, xlvi, part 2, 176. On Jan. 17, 1865, 9:30 A.M., Bvt. Brig. Gen. Cyrus B. Comstock, "Near Fort Fisher," telegraphed to USG. "Capt Lockwood has Gen Terrys strong approval of and application to accompany a gallant officer Capt Lawrence who is severely wounded and needs great care, to his home. Can telegraphic authority be sent to Capt H. C. Lockwood A. de C. at Ft Monroe on receipt of this, to accompany Capt Lawrence to Newport R. I. and then rejoin his command   The enemy have this morning been blowing up works near Ft Caswell ~~and all reported 72~~ and it is not impossible that when the navy get down they will find it evacuated. They are moving cautiously. Our prisoners are 1900—guns uninjured and all reported 72" Telegram received, DNA, RG 107, Telegrams Collected (Unbound); (on Jan. 19) *ibid.*, RG 108, Letters Received. *O.R.*, I, xlvi, part 2, 166–67. On the same day, Comstock wrote to USG. "I asked for permission for Capt Lockwood to ~~Capt~~ accompany Capt Lawrence A. A. D. C. on Gen Ames Staff to his home. I have seen Capt. Lawrence many times since we have been here, he is a most brave & gallant gentleman. At the assault of Ft. Fisher he was with the leading brigade & was the first man through the palisade, had turned to take a guidon to take to the top of the parapet when a shell exploded near him wounding him severely in the throat & taking off his left arm & afterward he got a bullet through the other arm. I know of no reward too high for an officer who will lead troops forward in that way & think he should at once be breveted at least as high as Lt. Col. for the most distinguished gallantry. If this cannot be done he should have a captaincy or majority in the volunteer staff, or still better in the regular service. Never a man in the world deserved it more." ALS, DNA, RG 108, Letters Sent by Cyrus B. Comstock. On Jan. 18, Comstock wrote to Brig. Gen. John A. Rawlins. "There is one thing which I am not sure I have mentioned in my previous letters. On the morning of the 16th about 8 a. m. a magazine in Ft. Fisher exploded killing & wounding nearly ~~200~~ 130 men, the majority being killed. So far as can now be ascertained it arose from gross carelessness on the part of the commander of the brigade garrisoning the work, who was mortally wounded, in allowing men with lighted torches to pass in & out of it though previously cautioned of the danger. As I thought yesterday, Ft. Caswell & probably all the works around Smithville have been abandoned. Ft Caswell was blown up & the Navy from below now have possession of it. No vessel from here has yet been down, the greatest caution being shown in the movemts of the naval vessels, & therefore slowness. I had supposed before this time some of the batteries up the river would have been tried by them, but no vessel has been above Ft. Fisher in the river. The number of guns of all kinds & there are a good many kinds, Gen Abbott already reports as at least 845. & perhaps more. Of these ~~I think 20~~ 18 ~~& perhaps more~~ are injured   There is one very highly finished 150 pounder Armstrong gun. It is very highly finished, the barrel showing the weldings just as a stub & twist shot gun does, the carriage being of mahogany. As no Ordnance Dept. would spend so much money on finish, I think it must have been a present from English sympathise[rs.] Gen. Terry is very anxious to send it to West Point as a trophy; as we make no Armstrong ammunition & have no such guns in our service & it is not needed here—he will send it to old Pt. & would like to have ~~you~~ the general send it to West Point. There is another queer gun here—a brass cylinder about three feet long & a foot in diameter bored full of holes so as to make 120 barrels, all to fire at a time. This should also go to West Pt & I think Gen. Terry will send them both, to Old Pt. I wish you would have Duane send his photographer down here to take a few photographs of Ft Fisher. It is the only way to give a good idea of it & three days would be enough. Jan 19. I have detained Capt Robinett a day in order to be able if possible to give something definite in reference to the state of affairs. Reconnaissances pushed out today along the whole of the rebel front show that he holds a line runing from Sugar loaf hill on the Cape Fear across to the Sound. This line is reported strong through out its length and with abbatis on our left. Sixty prisoners were captured on our extreme right on Masonboro Sound belonging to Kirklands brigade, they agree in stating that the whole of Hokes division with a brigade of he reserves is in our front, Kirkland Hagood & Colquitt occupying the line. A straight line would be a mile & a quarter long & a part of it is covered by a swamp reported impracticable. I ran up in a steamer today about two miles above the Navy till I drew the fire of Ft Anderson a heavy work opposite Sugar loaf & could see clearly four or five hundred yards of their line nearest Cape fear river. It is of the same character as the lines around Petersburg & a land attack would have if as the prisoners state, three brigades are holding a mile & a quarter, about the same chances of success in an attack as there. Gen Terry has been down today to Smithville where the Admiral is lying, to see if he wont move up, but the Admiral says now all the important work is done, he dont want to lose any vessels by torpedoes in this river & says it will take ten or twelve days to move up to Wilmington—indeed I think he said something to Gen. Terry about letting Sherman take it. I dont know exactly what Gen. Terrys ideas are but I dont think the possession of Wilmington of sufficient importance to lose 500 men in attacking rifle pits, with no certainty of success. If the Navy will move up gradually it will be easy to go on, though our force would be about 6000 men. I think Sherman will need all the men that can be spared & so do not think now, any renforcemts should be sent to us, as one big army in this quarter is worth a dozen small ones. Sherman is anxious about New Berne & wrote on the 17 inst to Ad. Porter asking to have as many gun boats kept there as were necessary. I wrote to you about NewBerne from Beaufort, afterward, I saw Gen. Palmer who told me Hokes attack last winte[r] was repulsed with 3500 men, that he could now raise about 2500 men & with the gun boats felt tolerably safe, but would be sure with the gunboats & 3500 men. The Admiral has ordered some gunboats from Plymouth to that Point. Would it be well to send 1000 men to him? Sherman was at Savannah on the 17th & expected to start in a day or two. Capt. Bresse came across one of Gen. Whitings boat crew who was very communicative & who Breese thinks was honest. He says he heard Whiting say that Gen. Lee telegraphed him, that he must hold Ft Fisher at all hazards or he should be forced to evacuate Richmond. I give it for what it is worth. Bragg, prisons say is in our immediate front—Whiting abuses him for not attacking us during the assalt of Ft. Fisher. At the works at & near Ft. Caswell & Smithville the navy have already found, Breese told me today, 77 guns, at Ft. Fisher the number now is 85, making 162 guns in all, most of them heavy ones, Ft. Caswell was badly injured by the explosion of its magazines—I go down tomorrow to see what state it is in, as I suppose it will have to be held permantly. Our estimate of Hokes force is 4000 men, & 1000 additional of the N. C. Reserves. To attack him in an intrnched line here, or around Wilmington with 6000 to his 5000 seems hardly advisable. Unless the Navy then can move up the river with us, I doubt if Gen Terry will move without reenfrcemts. I enclose with this a statement as to the force in Ft Fisher when Butler was before it . . . P S. A number of torpedoes have been taken out of the river, & on the land front a short distance in front of the palisads, 22 have been dug up. Fortunately we ~~either~~ did not move over them, going to the right where it was marshy." ALS, *ibid.*

On Jan. 19, 2:00 P.M., Bvt. Maj. Gen. Edward Ferrero telegraphed to USG. "A Deserter has just come into our lines He left his Regt at 9 a m today & states that it was reported that Willmington has fallen with thirty three million 33 000 000 dollars of cotton That the Rebels had fired it on leaving & that our men arrived in time to extinguish the flames" ALS (telegram sent), *ibid.*, RG 107, Telegrams Collected (Unbound). At 3:30 P.M., USG telegraphed to Secretary of War Edwin M. Stanton transmitting this telegram, but sending it as written by Maj. Gen. Edward O. C. Ord at 3:00 P.M. Telegram received (at 5:00 P.M.), *ibid.*, Telegrams Collected (Bound); copy, *ibid.*, Telegrams Received in Cipher. *O.R.*, I, xlvi, part 2, 180.

On Jan. 21, Maj. Gen. John Gibbon telegraphed to Rawlins. "The report of the fall of Wilmington and the capture of cotton is repeated to-day by deserters, who say that the news will be in to-day's papers." *Ibid.*, p. 194.

For reports of Maj. Gen. Alfred H. Terry and Comstock of operations at Fort Fisher, see *ibid.*, I, xlvi, part 1, 394–401, 406–9; *ibid.*, I, xlvi, part 2, 197–98, 275.

To Gustavus V. Fox

(Cipher)   City Point, Va, Jan. 19th 1865 [*9:30* A.M.]
HON. G. V. FOX ASST. SEC. OF THE NAVY WASHINGTON,

It will be impossible for Mr. Blair to go through directly to Richmond. When he arrives however he will be sent through as comfortably and as expeditiously as possible.

U. S. GRANT
Lt. Gen.

ALS (telegram sent), CSmH; telegrams received (2—at 2:40 P.M.), DNA, RG 107, Telegrams Collected (Bound); Blair Lee Papers, NjP. *O.R.*, I, xlvi, part 2, 177. On Jan. 17, 1865, 8:10 P.M., Asst. Secretary of the Navy Gustavus V. Fox telegraphed to USG. "Mr F. P Blair Senior will go immediately to Richmond. Will you be good enough to telegraph me when he can go through, by water if possible, so there shall be no delay. He is too old to endure the fatigue of a land march and delay I congratulate you upon the Federal Point affair" Telegram received, DNA, RG 107, Telegrams Collected (Bound); (marked as sent on Jan. 18, 8:30 P.M.) *ibid.*, RG 108, Letters Received; copy, *ibid.*, RG 45, Mis-

cellaneous Letters Sent. *O.R.*, I, xlvi, part 2, 158; *O.R.* (Navy), I, xi, 605. On
Jan. 19, 5:00 P.M., USG telegraphed to Fox. "The Flag of Truce Steamer is
now in James River. If Mr. Blair arrives during its stay I can send him through
to Richmond promptly and comfortably." ALS (telegram sent), CSmH; telegram received (at 6:00 P.M.), DNA, RG 107, Telegrams Collected (Bound);
Blair Lee Papers, NjP. *O.R.*, I, xlvi, part 2, 177. At 7:30 P.M., Fox telegraphed
to USG. "He will leave at Eleven A M tomorrow and ought to reach you Sunday
P M early Please detain the boat" Telegram received, DNA, RG 107, Telegrams Collected (Bound); copy, *ibid.*, RG 45, Miscellaneous Letters Sent. *O.R.*,
I, xlvi, part 2, 177; *O.R.* (Navy), I, xi, 614. On Jan. 20, 6:00 P.M., USG, Fort
Monroe, telegraphed to Maj. Gen. Edward O. C. Ord. "Please notify Col. Mul-
ford on Steamer New York to remain at Varina until Mr. Blair arrives and is
passed through the lines." ALS (telegram sent), DNA, RG 107, Telegrams
Collected (Bound); telegram received, *ibid.*, Telegrams Collected (Unbound).
See following telegram. On the same day, Lt. Col. John E. Mulford, Varina, Va.,
telegraphed to USG. "Your despatch relating to Mr Blair recd—Will ~~attend~~
carry out your instructions—." ALS (telegram sent), DNA, RG 107, Telegrams
Collected (Unbound). On Jan. 21, Brig. Gen. John A. Rawlins telegraphed to
Mulford. "Mr F. P. Blair is desirous of getting through to Richmond without
unnecessary detention, Please use every exertion possible to facilitate his desires"
Copies, DLC-USG, V, 46, 72, 107; DNA, RG 108, Letters Sent. On Jan. 22,
10:05 A.M., Mulford telegraphed to Rawlins. "Mr Blair arrived here last night
I have all arrangmts made to land him in Richmnd this P M." ALS (telegram
sent), *ibid.*, RG 107, Telegrams Collected (Unbound).

To Maj. Gen. George G. Meade and
Maj. Gen. Edward O. C. Ord

(Cipher)   City Point, Va, Jan.y 20th 1864~~5~~. [*11:00* A.M.]
MAJ. GENS. ORD & MEADE,

    I leave at 12 for Washington. Will remain there but a few
hours. During my absence be prepared to take the offensive if it
should be found that the enemy are drawing off any conciderable
portion of their troops, an event not impossible though which is not
likely within the limits of my absence.

U. S. GRANT
Lt. Gen.

ALS (telegram sent), PPRF; telegram received, Ord Papers, CU-B. *O.R.*, I,
xlvi, part 2, 184.
    On Jan. 20, 1865, 10:30 A.M., USG telegraphed to Secretary of War Edwin
M. Stanton. "I will leave for Washington at noon today—Will you please order
Genl Sheridan up to the city to meet me there tomorrow?" Telegram received
(at 11:00 A.M.), DNA, RG 107, Telegrams Collected (Bound); copies (marked
as sent at 11:30 A.M.), *ibid.*, RG 108, Letters Sent; DLC-USG, V, 46, (marked

as sent at 10:30 A.M.) 72, 107. *O.R.*, I, xlvi, part 2, 183. On the same day, USG telegraphed to Maj. Thomas T. Eckert. "Please telegraph me at Fortress Monroe, whether it is likely the ice will obstruct my getting to Washington to morrow morning If so I will go to Annapolis and have a train of cars meet me there at 7 A. M." Copies, DLC-USG, V, 46, 72, 107; DNA, RG 108, Letters Sent. At 6:00 P.M., USG, Fort Monroe, telegraphed to Stanton. "Please have the Q. M. notified to have a car at Annapolis for me at 7 a. m. in the morning to take me to Washington." ALS (telegram sent), *ibid.*, RG 107, Telegrams Collected (Unbound); telegram received (at 6:30 P.M.), *ibid.*, Telegrams Collected (Bound). *O.R.*, I, xlvi, part 2, 183. On the sheet containing this telegram and one to Maj. Gen. Edward O. C. Ord (see preceding telegram), USG wrote in the margin. "If there is no Cipher operator send these dispatches through plain." AE, DNA, RG 107, Telegrams Collected (Unbound).

To Abraham Lincoln

Annapolis Junction Md.
Jan.y 21st 1865

A. LINCOLN PRESIDENT,
SIR;

Your favor of this date in relation to your son serving in some Military capacity is received. I will be most happy to have him in my Military family in the manner you propose. The nominal rank given him is immaterial but I would suggest that of Capt. as I have three Staff officers now, of conciderable service, in no higher grade. Indeed I have one officer with only the rank of Lieut. who has been in the service from the begining of the war.[1] This however will make no difference and I would still say give the rank of Capt.— Please excuse my writing on a half sheet. I had no resource but to take the blank half of your letter.

Very respectfully
your obt. svt,
U. S. GRANT
Lt. Gen

ALS, DLC-Robert T. Lincoln. On Jan. 19, 1865, President Abraham Lincoln wrote to USG. "Please read and answer this letter as though I was not President, but only a friend. My son, now in his twenty second year, having graduated at Harvard, wishes to see something of the war before it ends. I do not wish to put him in the ranks, nor yet to give him a commission, to which those who have already served long, are better entitled, and better qualified to hold. Could he, without embarrassment to you, or detriment to the service, go into your Military family with some nominal rank, I, and not the public, furnishing his necessary means? If no, say so without the least hesitation, because I am as anxious, and as deeply interested, that you shall not be encumbered as you can be yourself—" ALS (facsimile), Sotheby Parke Bernet Sale, Nov. 14, 1978, No. 501; DfS, DLC-Robert T. Lincoln. Lincoln, *Works*, VIII, 223. Robert T. Lincoln was appointed capt. and adjt. as of Feb. 11. According to Horace Porter, Lincoln and USG had already discussed the matter before exchanging correspondence. *Campaigning with Grant* (New York, 1897), p. 388. On Jan. 22, Robert T. Lincoln wrote to USG. "I have been informed by my father this morning, of your kindness in allowing me to become one of your Staff, and I desire to express to you both his and my own hearty thanks for it. As I have been living at Cambridge for nearly five years, and left there with the expectation of returning, it will be necessary for me to go back and arrange my affairs before going to City Point; and as I also very much desire to be present at the Inauguration, unless I can in any way be useful before, I would request your kind indulgence until after that time, when I will have the honor to report to you in person—." ALS, OClWHi.

On April 21, Capt. Lincoln wrote to Brig. Gen. Lorenzo Thomas tendering his resignation. ALS, IHi. On April 30, USG endorsed this letter. "In approving the resignation of Capt. Lincoln it affords me pleasure to testify to the uniform good conduct of this young officer and to say that by his course in the performance of his duties, and in his social intercourse, he has won the esteem and lasting friendship of all with whom he has come in contact." AES, *ibid.*

1. See letter to Edwin M. Stanton, Feb. 3, 1865.

To Edwin M. Stanton

Washington D. C. Jany 21st 1865

HON, E, M, STANTON
SECY OF WAR
SIR.

On Maj, Genl, Lewis Wallace leaving the Middle Department on orders given him[1] please assign Maj, Genl, A, E, Burnside to the temporary command of that Dept,[2]

Very Respy
Your obt svt
U, S, GRANT
Lieut, Genl,

Copies, DLC-USG, V, 46, 72, 107; DNA, RG 108, Letters Sent. *O.R.*, I, xlvi, part 2, 190.

1. On Jan. 14, 1865, Maj. Gen. Lewis Wallace wrote to USG. "I had a visit yesterday from a Mr. S. S. Brown, formerly a schoolmate of mine in Indiana,

now a Texas refugee, residing near Monterey, Mexico. Feeling assured of his reliability, but without giving him any idea of what was in contemplation, I drew from him a great deal of information about transactions in Matamoras; which, at my suggestion, he summed up in the enclosed note. You will not fail, I know, to appreciate his first sentence, wherein he discribes the use the rebels are making of that city. There was one point in his conversation to which he reverted several times, and which was suggestive of a new idea; it was that, if overtures were now made to them, he believed the rebel soldiery in Western Texas, particularly those at Brownsville, would gladly unite with us, and cross the river *under the Juarez flag.* This belief he based upon the great disheartenment that prevailed all through the region & West of the Mississippi. Altogether, his remarks upon this point made a strong impression upon me. Recurring to my past letters—The greater conveniency of the route by the way of Brasos is self-apparent. Before deciding, anything, I submit to you, therefore, if it is not best to let me go, and take a look at it, and see exactly what obstacles are in way, and how they may be removed, if at all. The adoption of the Juarez Flag on the bank of the Rio Grande, as the basis of a compromise, would stagger the rebellion, next to the giving in of the State of Georgia. It is worth a trial anyhow. While Blair and Singleton are in Richmond, let me from Brasos, upon my own authority, invite the commandant of Brownsville to an interview on the old battle field of Palo Alto. If the man's a soldier, I'll wager you a month's pay that I win, and that Blair & Co. lose. You know how to get me there—an order to make an inspection of affairs on the Rio Grande will do. Such information as Brown's will, I think, fully justify examination. If it be found true, you may be position, on report of the facts, to send me troops to smother the Brownsville-Matamoras trade. Then it will be my own fault, if I don't get, the arms through. Such an inspection ought not to consume more than a month. If you say so, McCook, who is now here, can take care of my department, until results are had. If you send me, I will at least put you in possession of the 'situation' in that region, and test fully the virtue of the rebel commandant at Brownsville. If I win him to my views, all the bad luck will be to Maximilian. The hand writing of my friend Brown is so execrable that, to save you trouble, I have illustrated it with pencil ~~illustrations~~. interlineations. Finally, General, if you think me persistent in the Mexican idea, please ascribe it to yourself. 'Hold on,' is the lesson you are constantly teaching us. Had Butler served under you as some of the rest of us have, *he wouldn't have left Ft. Fisher.*" ALS, DNA, RG 108, Letters Received. *O.R.,* I, xlviii, part 1, 512. The enclosure is *ibid.,* pp. 512–13. On Jan. 21, Lt. Col. Theodore S. Bowers telegraphed to Lt. Col. Ely S. Parker. "Please make order in case of Maj. Gen. Lewis Wallace. The papers are on the table." ALS (telegram sent), DNA, RG 107, Telegrams Collected (Bound). *O.R.,* I, xlvi, part 2, 191. On Jan. 22, Parker issued Special Orders No. 16. "Maj Gen Lew. Wallace U. S. Vols will proceed, via the Rio Grande, to Western Texas, and inspect the condition of military affairs in that vicinity and on the Rio Grande—Military Authorities will afford him every means in their power to facilitate him in the execution of this order." ADS, Wallace Papers, InHi. *O.R.,* I, xlvi, part 2, 201. On Jan. 26, Wallace telegraphed to USG. "Please direct that Lieut Colonel Catlin—Inspector General this Department accompany me." ALS (telegram sent), DNA, RG 107, Telegrams Collected (Unbound); *ibid.,* RG 393, Middle Dept. and 8th Army Corps, Telegrams Sent (Press). At 3:00 P.M., USG telegraphed to Wallace. "You are authorized to take Lt. Col. Catlin with you." ALS (telegram sent), OClWHi; telegram received, RPB; (press) DNA, RG 107,

Telegrams Collected (Bound). On Jan. 27 (Friday), 1:00 P.M., Wallace telegraphed to USG. "I will be ready to leave here on Monday next. Is it your desire
that I turn ~~ov~~ the Department over to General McCook during my absence?"
ALS (telegram sent), *ibid.*, Telegrams Collected (Unbound); *ibid.*, RG 393,
Middle Dept., Telegrams Sent (Press); telegram received, *ibid.*, RG 108, Letters Received. *O.R.*, I, xlvi, part 2, 279. See *ibid.*, pp. 307–8.

On Feb. 22, Wallace, New Orleans, wrote to USG. "After unavoidable
delays, such as failures of connections, I at last Reached this City, and now
wait only for a vessel to carry me to Brazos. Arrived there, it will take but few
days to obtain all the facts necessary for a Report on the Relations, Military and
Commercial, of Matamoras and Brownsville. From Reliable information already
at hand, I am justified in saying now, that the statements of Mr S. S. Brown
forwarded you from Baltimore, are in nowise Exaggerated. Matamoras is, to all
intents and purposes, a Rebel port, free at that, and you can Readily imagine
the uses they put it to. There is never a day that there are not from Seventy five
to One hundred & fifty vessels off Bagdad, discharging & Recieving Cargoes. I
would have postponed writing to you, however, had it not been for a Report in
official circles to the Effect that our Consul at Matamoras has been ordered off
by Mejia. That personage (the Consul) will doubtless Communicate the particulars to Mr Seward; and I therefore Refrain from Sending a version of the affair,
but venture to suggest that it might be well Enough not to notice it until I can
be heard from. In an unauthorized way I will Endeavor to possess myself of the
facts. Should they turn out serious, I am sure you will discern the policy of
waiting until it Can be seen whether the Mexican Republic Cannot be put in
position to fight its own and our battles, without involving us, an Eventuality
Exactly co-incident with Mr Sewards views. As to the prospects of such an
Eventuality, without going into details, I will say generally but positively, that
I have now an arrangement so complete that it will hardly be necessary for the
Government to loan me a Gun, not Even a Pistol. This arrangement depends
Entirely upon your giving me Command of ~~the~~ Texas as a Military Department,
*with orders to Report directly to yo*self, and upon your sending me a division
of Infantry, and a brigade of Cavalry with the Ordinary Complement of Guns.
The main body of these forces acting on the defensive, and posted at San Patricio,
the lowest ford on the Nueces River, will Completely sever communication between the Rio Grande and Middle and Eastern Texas. You served, if I am not
mistaken, on the Rio Grande line, but I am not sure that you have a present
Recollection of the topography of the Nueces Region. I will therefore venture to
speak with some particularity of San Patricio. It is about twenty miles North
west of Corpus Christi. The Road Connecting the two points is on the Right bank
of the River, and always good. The west bank of the River is verry bluffy. The
channel is deep but narrow. The East bank is low & level, and Can be overlooked from the opposite bluffs fifteen or twenty miles. At San Patricio: is a
ford, which is, so to speak, a great funnel, through which everything going &
Coming from Matamoras, Rio Grande City (near Camargo) and Laredo (old
Ft McIntosh) must pass; and of necessity, for the desert belt called *Mustang
Prairie* makes the Region between the Rio Grande and the Nueces ordinarily impossible for travel, Except by way of the few traces marked by springs. Of these
traces there are but three at all useful to the Rebels, because they are the only
ones that strike the Rio Grande in a south westerly direction; One beginning at
Laredo, Another at Ringgold City, and the third at Brownsville, all of which
unite about twenty five miles from & West of San Patricio ford. This Rough

description will Enable you to see that, if your object is simply to sever Connection or communication between Mexico and Texas, it is only necessary to fortify San Patricio. This done, small garrisons can safely hold Brownsville, Rio Grande City & Laredo, thus putting our Government in position to let Maximillian verry severely alone, *until I get my arrangements perfected*. My purpose is to see, before the position of San Patricio is occupied, whether I can make accommodations with the Rebels. If the intelligence at hand is true, sucess in this part of the Enterprise is quite promising. My propositions will be based on Cotton, which, together with the fading prospects of the Confederacy, has brought the Rebels to a low point of demoralization. The way to a private interview with Kirby Smith is clear; and I shall act in it as if already appointed to the Command of the *Department of Texas*. Conditions will, of course, be subject to approval, and forwarded to you instantly. If accommodations are impossible, and if, in consequence, it becomes necessary to occupy toSan Patricio, then, behind that position, and under its Cover, I shall initiate the organization of the Territory or new *state of Rio Grande*, without which it will be difficult to find plausible pretexts for the assemblage of men and materials Essential to ulterior operations. Permit me to hope, however, that you will not delay creating the Department, and dispatching the troops. In selecting troops, please send me Western men; You Know how Easily southern people affilliate with them; and if the thing is at all possible, it would give me additional Confidence to have my old Regiment, the 11th Indiana, and the 8th Illinois Cavalry, (Col. Clendenin's,) ordered to Report to me. I would also like the Regiment of Texans now serving in this Department. They Know the Region of Western Texas perfectly. While passing through Indianapolis, I suceeded in getting four hundred drilled conscripts for the 11th Indiana, so that it will now be Respectably strong in numbers." LS, DNA, RG 108, Letters Received; ADf (incomplete), Wallace Papers, InHi. *O.R.*, I, xlviii, part 1, 937–38.

On March 14, Wallace, Brazos Santiago, Tex., wrote to USG. "Upon my arrival at New Orleans I was fortunate Enough to meet Mr Charles Worthington, Collector of Port of Brazos. Mr Worthington, beside being a citizen of Texas, well Known particularly in the western part, is shrewd, discreet, & trustworthy, & intimately acquainted with such controlling Rebels at Brownsville as Brig Genl J. E. Slaughter, Commanding the West Dist of Texas, Hd Qrs at Brownsville, and Col J. S. Ford, Commanding a Regiment in Slaughters District. For the purpose of sounding Genl Slaughter, I sent Mr Worthington from this post to Matamoras. He managed his charge with shrewdness & sucess —His Report is subjoined. Obtaining an interview with Genl Slaughter he found that gentleman disposed to talk freely about the situation, and about a settlement of difficulties. He then proposed that the General should meet me under a flag of truce. The proposal was accepted, and Point Isabel named as the place of conference, and 12½ o clock P. M, Wednesday the 9th instant as the time. To Cover the Real object of the meeting, at General Slaughters instance, the Rendition of criminals was specified as the subject of Conference. In this Connection I call your attention to General Slaughters note in Reply to Mr Worthingtons, On the 9th inst a 'Norther' sprung up, making it impossible on the part of both of us to fulfill the Engagement. On the following morning, I sent a letter under flag of truce to Genl Slaughter, a copy of which is Enclosed, in which I approved Mr Worthingtons proposal, stated why I could not cross to Point Isabel, and asked a Renewal of the arrangement. The officer to whom my letter was delivered for transmission, at the same time forwarded one to me from Genl Slaughter, a

glance at which will satify you, I think, that that gentleman is as anxious in
the business as I am myself. In fact General, I am minute in my narrative Expressly to show you why I feel assured that the Rebels authorities in this part of
the world are Really verry desirous of a speedy peace, at least so far as concerns
themselves. On the 11th instant, the signals agreed on announced Genl Slaughters arrival at Point Isabel. I at once went over to meet him carrying along supplies and tents. The Generals party Consisted of his staff and Col Ford and mine
of Lt Col. Woolley, Lt Col Catlin, Maj Ross of my staff & Mr Worthington. The
conference lasted until the next day in the afternoon. On both sides there was an
Effort to make it agreeable. If you at any time hear, in the way of complaint,
that I have been hob-nobbing and sleeping with the Rebels in this Region, please
understand the matter & take care of me. Verry Early in the interview, I made
up my mind that both General Slaughter & Col Ford were not only willing but
anxious to find some ground upon which they could honorably get from under
what they admited to be a failing Confederacy. In justice to them I will add
that both went into the Rebellion Reluctantly. I will say further that Genl Slaughter placed his disposition to bring about an accommodation upon grounds of
humanity, and an unwillingness to see his state invaded & Ruined, and the war
decline into guerrilla murders. He and Ford insisted that they Could procrasti-
nate the final Result indefinitely, but at the same time frankly admitted that, if
that were done, the North would ultimately conquer the South as a desert. When
I urged that, in the present situation of the war West of the Mississippi, they
could not Reason~~ly~~ably hope for assistance from Richmond and their Eastern
armies: that they were practically isolated: that, as a Consequence, their highest
present obligations were to their Trans-Mississippi Army, and Citizens, whose
honor and Welfare they were charged with & alone bound to Regard: they agreed
with me without hesitation, and asked me to give them such propositions as
would cover those objects, and at the same time be likely to prove acceptable to
our government. It was delicate business but I did my best. How I suceeded
you will find by Reference to a copy of the propositions themselves which I have
the honor of transmitting herewith. Permit me to say that they were hurriedly
drawn, yet drawn with an Eye special to President Lincolns proclamations, and
to what I interpret as a prevalent sentiment of the Northern people. I was careful
not to assume authorization, or to commit the government in any manner: the
propositions are only offerred as a basis of settlement, as an invitation to further
and formal negotiations. They are addressed to the *Confederate Military authorities* as the only ones now Existing in the Trans-Mississippi Region, who on their
side have any power, and upon whom all Responsibility is at present Resting. To
satisfy military pride, the propositions assume the settlement to be voluntary on
the part of the Rebels. To save military honor, they are drawn with an intent to
cover all classes of persons, whose welfare & security are supposed to be in the
Keeping of the said authorities. To soldiers & citizens, they offer the alternatives, if you wish to Remain in the United States, to become citizens, you must
take the oath of all~~i~~egiance; if you do not desire to become citizens again, you
are at liberty to go abroad with your property. To get their Consent to consider
their confiscation of property of Union men void, it is proposed that the United
States shall not undertake *f~~au~~rther* to Execute the confiscation laws of the Federal
Congress. So far as we are concerned, you will observe, this would operate pros-
pectively, not Retrospectively: in other words, Confiscations by our courts had
to this time would Remain in force. Fortunately, it is well Known that in the
Trans-Mississippi states, while there have been many siezures & occupations of

the property of Rebels, there have been but few, if any, final Confiscations by judicial decrees. In Reference to slave property, both Genl Slaughter and Col Ford admitted that as a value it had ceased to be of great importance. The only Condition they talked about Respecting it was that, as its abolition was inevitable, the interests of the Negro, as well as the necessities of the people of these states, Required the adoption of a system of gradual Emancipation. I had no difficulty, Consequently, in getting them to accept for the present a general Reference of the subject to our Congress. This Referrence, you will please observe, involves, not a question about abolition, but simply such questions as, whether the abolition shall be gradual or immediate, and whether it shall be with or without Compensation. It may be well for me to Remark here that no doubt the Rebel authorities will interpret the permission proposed to be given those of their people who may choose to go abroad to make preparations for departure, to include the Right to sell their slaves or take them away out of the Country. I submit it to our authorities whether such an interpretation may not be granted. Practically the grand Result will not be Effected. They Cannot carry a slave to a foreign country where his freedom will not be assured: neither will a sale now Retard the inevitable liberation: Emancipation will be as certain to find the property in the hands in of one man as in those of another. Is the Concession of any actual materiality? It only Remains for me to inform you that Genl Slaughter & Col Ford Recieved the propositions & undertook to forward them immediately to Genl Walker Commanding the state of Texas, and to Genl Kirby Smith. Col Ford is to take them in person, and as he is politically the most influential Confederate soldier in Texas, that fact gives me additional confidance. He will go first to Galveston, where according to the understanding I am in a few days to follow him. Secrecy is, for the present as much Required on their part as on my own. Looking forward to an interview with Genl Kirby Smith, I intend asking Genl Canby to send me Genl Davis, of Texas, Commanding a brigade in our army. Smith and Davis have been life long friends. at present, General, I see nothing Else important to send you. Except that our Consul Mr Atchinson [*Etchison*], whom Mejia is said to have outraged, is a humbug, a drunkard, and a fool. His official conduct was unworthy our government. He has mutilated the books of his consulate. He charged our own citizens unwarrantable fees; and I am assured on Excellent authority that it can be Established that he has in his pockets several thousand dollars in Gold not his own. Even his washerwoman was left unpaid. Certainly there is nothing in the affair justifying attention. Mr Wood our Commercial Agent, has, since Atchinsons departure, Reached Matamoros and been Kindly Recieved by Maxamillians officials. As to the Rebel trade by way of Matamoras and Brownsville I think it is only sufficient to say that I can stand on my boat and count a least one hundred vessels, of all Kinds, lying off Bagdad. Neither the port of New Orleans, nor that of Baltimore can present today such a promise of Commercial activity." LS, DNA, RG 108, Letters Received; ADfS, Wallace Papers, InHi. *O.R.*, I, xlviii, part 1, 1276–79. On March 28, Maj. Gen. John A. Dix, New York City, wrote to USG. "I have just received the accompanying despatches from the 'Military Division of West Mississippi,' and inferring from the letter addressed to me that they are of more than ordinary importance, I send Capt. Thos. Lord, one of my Aides, by steamer direct, to your Head Quarters, to deliver them to you.—I shall thus anticipate the ordinary mail and passenger communication through Baltimore, by more than 24 hours." ALS, DNA, RG 108, Letters Received. *O.R.*, I, xlviii, part 1, 1276. On March 14, Wallace wrote to USG. "Confidential. . . . In a confidential way I will say that both

Slaughter and Ford, with whom I had the interview which forms the subject of my general despatch of this date, entered heartily into the Mexican project. It is understood between us that the pacification of Texas is the preliminary step to a crossing of the Rio Grande. In the propositions made to them, a copy of which has been forwarded you, not a word is said about the arms now in the hands of the Confederates. *We expect to get their use.* Neither can they see any reason why that portion of the cotton now in Texas, and belonging to the Confederate Government, should not be diverted to the same purpose. Of this latter, however, I was not sanguine—Mr. Lincoln's cotton agents will say something on that point. In course of the conversation, I drew from Ford that he feared Kirby Smith would be in the way of a settlement, because there was a growing suspicion that he (Smith) was carrying on negotiations with Maxmilian. The suspicion was founded upon ~~certain~~ some newspaper articles of late appearance, favoring imperial annexation, which, it was well understood, had been written by certain gentlemen on Smith's staff. In answer to a question, Ford assured me that if such a sale was attempted, he would instantly bring about a counter-revolution. Gen. Slaughter was of opinion that the best way for officers in his situation to get honorably back into the Union was to cross the river, conquer two or three sStates from the French, and ultimately annex them, with all their inhabitants, to the United States. In short, I think they anticipate such a step as an immediate consequence of peace. Of all these things, however, I will keep you posted." ALS, DNA, RG 108, Letters Received. *O.R.,* I, xlviii, part 1, 1166–67.

On April 18, Wallace, Baltimore, wrote to USG. "In continuation of my report, dated 'Brasos Santiago, March 14th, I have the honor to submit the following. It occurred to me that it would be a point gained, if I could prevail on Col. Ford to accompany me to Galveston. Accordingly, I sent Gen. Slaughter the letter, dated 'Brasos Santiago, March 17 1865,' and recieved a reply from Col. Ford himself, dated March 19. Copies are enclosed. The absence of Gen. Slaughter, devolving the command at Brownsville upon the Colonel, made it impossible for the latter to comply with my request. That he wished to go, I have no doubt. His letter fairly commits him. When Gen. Davis joined me, in the hope that slaughter had returned to Brownsville, or had, at least, been heard from, I again addressed Col. Ford. This last communication was of the 24th, March. See the accompanying copy, together with that of his reply, dated of the 26th. Unfortunately, Gen. S. had neither ~~been~~ returned nor been heard from. I arrived off Galveston on the evening of the 29 March, and on the 30th communicated with Brig. Gen. J. M. Hawes, comg defenses of the city, through whom I sent a letter to Maj. Gen. J. G. Walker, then in command of the *District of Texas.* Copies are enclosed. At the sametime mine of the 30th to Walker was delivered for transmission, his of the 25th was recieved by me, and of that, also, I furnish a copy. As you will see, Gen. Walker belongs to the 'radicals', from whom nothing is to be hoped. Though little Known, he has the reputation of being a good soldier. Unlike Slaughter and Ford, he is not a citizen of Texas, and hence has not the same interest in her welfare. He admits he is tired of the war, yet relies on 300.000 veterans whom he yet claims. A Galveston paper of the 30th announced that Gen. Magruder was daily expected at Houston to relieve him of his command, a fact rather demonstrative of what I had elsewhere heard: viz. that he (Walker) was not in full accord with Gen. E. Kirby Smith. After reading his letter, I took a view of Galveston, and when I saw behind the town the masts of several blockade runners, loading and unloading, I thought the reason of the stand he had assumed was quite plain—*there was too much money being made.*

It was apparent that it was useless to wait longer; and as the doing so might compromise the dignity of our Government, I sailed to New Orleans, intending to put the business, when I arrived there, in the hands of Maj. Gen. Hurlburt. Before leaving, however, I sent Gen. Walker a short note, of which a copy is enclosed, dated April 2nd. How much he made off me, I leave you to judge. At New Orleans, I called upon Gen. Hurlburt, explained the affair to him, stated my belief that Walker would not carry out the intention of Slaughter, Ford, and myself, by forwarding the propositions to Gen. Smith, and suggested that direct communication be opened with that officer. Gen. H. acceded to the suggestion, and agreed with me that the matter had at least gone far enough to induce Smith to 'define his position.' I also suggested that Mr. Worthington should be again sent to Matamoras, for the purpose of carrying to Slaughter and Ford the result of my visit to Galveston, and to sound them with a view to ascertaining if they were disposed to act independently of Walker and Smith. Mr. Worthington was of opinion that they could be prevailed upon to take that course, if they were assured of sufficient support. Remembering the anxiety those Gentlemen had shown in the conference at Point Isabel, I was of the same opinion. Gen. Hurlburt thought such a result was worth the effort, and accepted the suggestion. If Worthington was able to carry out with him the news of the fall of Richmond, the Surrender of Lee, and the flight of Jeff. Davis, I am confident he will succeed. So the business stands unconcluded, and I am not yet out of hope. Of one thing I am sure—the Texas rebels are without heart or confidence, and divided amongst themselves. The soldiers and subordinates are anxious to make peace, and it is almost certain that Kirby Smith will come to terms now, *provided he is not too far committed to Maximilian*. Another point I am sure of. If Davis and Smith attempt coalition with or annexation to the new empire of Mexico, they will be resisted by the rebel soldiers themselves. In view of such a contingency, it would be well enough, I think, to give the commanding officer at Brasos appropriate directions. By Mr. Worthington I sent Slaughter and Ford the letter, which concludes the correspondence, dated 'New Orleans, April 6, 1865,' of which I send you a copy." ALS, DNA, RG 108, Letters Received; ADfS, Wallace Papers, InHi. *O.R.*, I, xlviii, part 2, 457–58. On April 19, Wallace wrote to USG. "Circumstances have doubtless made it impossible for you to send me the notice to accompany you as ~~wer~~ you were Kind enough to suggest the morning of your passage through this city. The formal report of the result of my negotiations in Texas, with correspondence, is being copied. I think it better briefly to sum it up for your immediate information. I went to Galveston, according to the arrangement agreed upon with Slaughter and Ford. A Gen. Walker, comg the Dept. of Texas, there declined an interview upon the basis proposed, upon which I proceeded to NewOrleans, and arranged with Gen. Hurburt to ~~send~~ open communication with Kirby Smith upon the subject. Gen. H. and myself concluded that the affair had gone far enough at least to make Smith 'show his hand' I also arranged in New Orleans for Mr. Worthington to return to Matamoras, and sound Slaughter and Ford, to ascertain if they were willing to act independently of Smith—a result ~~quite likely~~ not at all improbable. So the matter stands. That an arrangement with Kirby Smith is practicable *now*, I dont doubt at all. [Ten thousand men landed on ~~g~~Galveston Island will insure it absolutely.] I feel sure he will surrender without a shot fired. I will forward the regular report, if you desire it, or bring it on with me, when I hear from you." ADfS (brackets in original), Wallace Papers, InHi. *O.R.*, I, xlviii, part 2, 122.

On May 16, Wallace wrote to USG. "Inclosed please find the conclusion of my report concerning the Point Isabel interview. Since writing it, Gen. E. Kirby Smith, according to report has refused to surrender, and urged his soldiers to hold out, as they have means to maintain themselves *until assisted from abroad.* Please revert to the confidential letter I sent you from Brasos, giving the substance of what Colonel Ford told me about Gen. Smith's *suspected negotiations with Maximilian.* That, in my opinion, is the key to Smith's strange conduct. Reasoning from Ford's statement, I cannot do otherwise than believe that there is a secret arrangement existing between the Mexican Imperialists and the Texan Confederates, contemplating ultimate annexation of Texas and mutual support, or the support without the annexation. Probably you have sufficient data upon which to form a detirminate opinion the subject. You will pardon me, I am sure, for calling your attention to the point made." ALS, DNA, RG 108, Letters Received; ADfS, Wallace Papers, InHi. *O.R.,* I, xlviii, part 2, 457. Wallace enclosed his letter of April 18 to USG and other correspondence. *Ibid.,* pp. 37, 458–63.

2. On Feb. 2, Parker wrote to Maj. Gen. Ambrose E. Burnside, Providence, R. I. "The Lieut General Comd'g. directs me to say to you, that he has received your dispatch of this date, asking for permission to see him at City Point on Sunday next, and answered it by telegraph in the negative. He further directs me to say, that he asked to have you put in temporary command of the Middle Department during the absence of Maj. Gen. Lew. Wallace, and supposed it had been so ordered, but from the caption of your dispatch, infers it has not, and that such being the state of the case, he has at present no command to which he can assign you, or duty on which to order you without making changes it is not desirable should be made—" ALS, DNA, RG 94, Generals' Papers and Books, Burnside. *O.R.,* I, xlvi, part 2, 353.

To Edwin M. Stanton

———

Washington D. C. Jan 21st *1865*

HON. E. M. STANTON
SEC. OF WAR,
SIR:

I have authorized Col. Mulford, Agt. of Exchange, to reniew negociations for the exchange of all prisoners now held by either party. The first interview between our Agt. and Col. Ould, Rebel Agt. has already been had. No doubt but a fare agreement that an arrangement will be entered into. Indeed on the strength of that interview an exc[han]g, limited one, is now going on near Richmond.

Yours Truly
U. S. GRANT
Lt. Gn.

We are sending supplies to our prisoners at least weekly. They are received by officers of our own selection, released Federal prisoners, who distribute them as directed.

U. S. G.

ALS, DLC-Edwin M. Stanton. *O.R.*, II, viii, 98.

To Maj. Gen. William T. Sherman

———

Washington, D. C., Jan.y 21st *18645*

MAJ. GEN. W. T. SHERMAN,
COMD.G MIL. DIV. OF THE MISS.
GENERAL,

Your letters brought by Gen. Barnard were rec'd at City Point and read with interest. Not having them with me however I cannot say that in this I will be able to satisfy you on all points of recommendation. As I arrived here at 1 p. m and must leave at 6 p. m. having in the mean time spent over three hours with the Secretary and Gen. Halleck, I must be brief.

Before your last request to have Thomas make a campaign into the heart of Alabama I had ordered Schofield to Annapolis Md with his Corps. The advance 6000 will reach the Sea board by the 23d, the remainder following as rapidly as rail-road transportation can be procured from Cincinnati. The Corps numbers over 21000 men. I was induced to do this because I did not believe Thomas could possibly be got off before Spring. His pursuit of Hood indicated a sluggishness that satisfied me that he would never do to conduct one of your campaigns.

The command of the advance of the pursuit was left to subordinates whilst Thomas followed far behind. When Hood had crossed the Tennessee and those in pursuit had reached it Thomas had not much more than half crossed the state, from which he returned to Nashville to take steamer for EastPort. He is possessed of excellet judgement, great coolness and honesty, but he is not good on a pursuit. He also reported his troops fagged and that it was necessary to equip up. This report, and a determination to give the enemy no rest, determined me to use his surplus troops elswhere.

Thomas is still left with a sufficient force, surplus, to go to Selma under an energetic leader. He has been telegraphed to to know whether he could go, and if so by which of several routes he would select. No reply is yet received. Canby has been ordered to act offensively from the Sea coast to the interior, towards Montgomery & Selma. Thomas forces will move from the North at an early day or some of his troops will be sent to Canby. Without further reinforcement ~~he~~ Canby will have a moving column of 20.000 men.

Fort Fisher, you are aware, has been captured. We have a force there of 8.000 effective, ~~a~~At New Bern about half that number. It is rumored through deserters that Wilmington also has fallen. I am inclined to believe the rumor because on the 17th we know the enemy were blowing up their works about Fort Caswell and that on the 18th Terry moved on Wilmington.

If Wilmington is captured Schofield will go there. If it is not he will be sent to New Bern. In either event all the surplus forces at the two points will move to the interior, towards Goldsboro, in cooperation with your movements. From either point rail-road communication can be run out, there being here abundance of rolling stock suited to the gage of those roads.

There has been about 16000 men sent from Lee's Army South. Of these you will have 14000 against you if Wilmington is not held by the enemy, casualties at Fort Fisher having ovetaken about 2,000.

All these troops are subject to your orders as you come in communication with them. They will be so instructed. From about Richmond I will watch Lee closely and if he detaches much more, or attempts to evacuate, will pitch in. In the mean time should you be brought to a halt any where I can send two Corps of 30.000 effective men to your support, from the troops about Richmond.

To resume: Canby is ordered to operate to the interior from the Gulf. A. J. Smith may go from the North but I think it doubt-

ful. A force of 28 or 30.000 will co-operate with you from New
Bern or Wilmington or both. You can call for reinforcements.

This will be handed to you by Capt. Hudson, of my staff, who
will return with any message you may have for me. If there is any
thing I can do for you in the way of having supplies on shipboard
at any point on the Sea coast, ready for you, let me know it.

Yours Truly

U. S. GRANT

Lt. Gn.

ALS, DLC-William T. Sherman. Printed as received on Jan. 29, 1865, in *O.R.*,
I, xlvii, part 2, 101–2. On Jan. 16, Maj. Gen. William T. Sherman, Savannah,
twice wrote to USG. "I have written you less than I had designed but I have had
visits from many including General Barnard and Mr Stanton who will tell you
all matters of interest. General Barnard staid over one steamer at my request to
Study the relation of the parts of this Coast, and will explain things clearly. I
dont want to assume the control of Matters here further than to give uniformity
of action, though it was well to place the Dept of the South subject to my command.—This Monday is the day for Howard to put his Right wing at Pocotaligo
and fortify. He was across Port Royal with the 17th Corps and out some 4 miles
when I last heard—the 18th Corps is now passig from Thunder bolt to Port
Royal—the 20th Corps is across the Union Causeway, and Davis and Kilpatrick
will move up to Sisters Ferry, and I will get all my army on hand on a line from
Sisters Ferry to Pocataligo. I have not heard frm you since Col Ewing went up,
but suppose the route I indicate will be the best. I now take it some if not all of
Hoods Army will be worked over this way and Thomas should be pressed down
to Selma. If Thomas would prefer to watch Tennessee, order him to send a small
force from Chattanooga down toward Rome, and detach Schofield with 35000
men including Wilson to Selma, via Tuscaloosa and to return via Talladega &
Rome. That Circuit would be easy to make and would tear out the heart of Alabama, and prevent the farmers planting corn, because all rails would be burned,
horses & mules taken, and corn eaten up. I would risk that march with just
enough wagons to carry the command across Sand Mountain. I think the farmers
of Georgia are organizing against Jeff Davis, but dont build any Castles on that
hope." "Since my letter of this mornig, I have official Reports, from Genl Howard
comd Right Wing. He crossed from Beaufort Island on Saturday the 14th by
Port Royal Ferry to the main land with the 17th Corps Gen Blair and marched
for Pocotaligo. They encountered the enemy near Gardner's [*Garden's*] Corner
but soon outflanked thim and followed dislodging him from positon to positon
till he took refuge in a strong fort at Pocotaligo. This is described as a well constructed enclosed work, pierced for 24 guns, and the approaches covered by the
peculiar Salt Marsh points that guard this Coast. Night overtook the Command
there and Sunday mornig the enemy was gone. Howard expresses great satisfaction thereat as it was Sunday and it saved him an assault which might have cost
him some valuable lives. As it was he lost Lt Chandler of Gen Leggetts staff
killed and Capt Kellogg of Gen Giles A Smiths staff wounded He writes that
eight or ten will cover his loss He reports three Guns captured at Gardners

Corners. We are therefore now in possession of good high ground on the Rail Road at Pocataligo with a good road back 25 miles to Beaufort. I will order Howard to feign towards Charleston, but proceed to get my army & trains across, and can start North the momt I can get my wagons loaded. The weather at Sea has been so stormy that vessels are behind and it has been touch & go to get daily food. I have ordered Slocum to push a Division up to Hardeeville and Purysburgh and think I can use the Savannah River up to that point. We are hard at work cuordurying the Road across the rice-field by the Union Causeway The Secretary told me I would surely receive 4000 men from Baltim to garrison Savannah. They are not heard of here yet." ALS, DNA, RG 108, Letters Received. *O.R.*, I, xlvii, part 2, 58–60.

On Jan. 24, Maj. Lewis M. Dayton, Beaufort, S. C., telegraphed to USG. "I was directed this morning by Gen. Sherman to write you by Steamer Arago he reached here yesterday from Savannah and went this morning to Pocotologo to look to matters in person and purposes tomorrow to secure Salkehatchie bridge as a demonstration and also to then reconnoitre until Gen Slocum gets out to high ground from Wheelers [*Sister's*] ferry. The storm has been severe and continuous for several days delaying movements by bad roads but now it is clear; The roads are improving rapidly and it bids fair for good weather I may hear from the General during the night and will despatch you further" Telegram received (on Jan. 29), DNA, RG 107, Telegrams Collected (Bound); *ibid.*, RG 108, Letters Received. *O.R.*, I, xlvii, part 2, 122.

On Jan. 29, Sherman, Pocotaligo, S. C., wrote to USG. "Capt Hudson has this moment arrived with your letter of Jan 21, which I have read with interest. The capture of Fort Fisher has a most important bearing on my campaign and I rejoice in it for many reasons, because of its intrinsic importance and because it gives me another point of security on the seaboard. I hope General Terry will follow it up by the capture of Wilmington although I did not look for it from Admiral Porters despatch to me. I rejoiced that Terry was not a WestPointer, that he belonged to your army, and that he had the Same troops with which Butler feared to make the attempt—Porter is in high glee. Admiral Dahlgren, whose fleet is reinforced by some new iron clad wants to make an assault a-la-Fisher on FMoultrie but I withold my consent for the reason that the capture of all Sullivans Island is not conclusive as to Charleston. The capture of all of James Island would be, but all pronounce that impossible at this time. Therefore I am moving as hitherto designed for the Railroad west of Branchville, then swing across to Orangeburg, which will interpose my army between Charleston and the Interior. Contemperaneous with this Foster will demonstrate up the Edisto, and afterward make a lodgmt at Bulls Bay, and occupy the Common Road which leads from Mountpleasant towards Georgetown. When I get to Columbia I think I shall move straight for Goldsboro via Fayetteville. By this circuit I cut all Roads and devastate the land; and the forces along the coast commanded by Foster will follow my movemt taking any thing the enemy lets go, or so occupies his attention that he cannot detach all his forces against me. I feel sure of getting Wilmington & may be Charleston: and being at Goldsboro, with its railroad finished back to Morehead City & Wilmington, I can easily take Raleigh, when it seems that Lee must come out of his trenches or allow his army to be absolutely invested. If Schofield comes to Beaufort he should be pushed out to Kingston on the Neuse, & may be Goldsboro, or rather a point on the Wilmington Road south of Goldsboro. It is not necessary to storm Goldsboro, because it is in a desolate region of no importance in itself; and if its Garrison is forced to draw supplies from its north it will be eating up the same stores on which Lee ~~supplies~~ depends for his command. I have no doubt Hood will bring his army to Augusta, and Canby and Thomas should penetrate Alabama as far as possible, to keep employed at least a part of Hoods Army: or what would accomplish the same thing Thomas might reoccupy the Rail roads from Chattanooga forward to the Etowah, viz Rome, Kingston & Allatoona thereby threatening Georgia. I know that the Georgia troops are disaffected. At Savannah I met delegations frm the several counties to the South West, that manifested a decidedly hostile spirit to the Confederate Cause. I nursed it along as far as possible and instructed Grover to keep it up. My Left Wing must now be at Sisters Ferry crossing the Savannah River to the East bank   Slocum has orders to be at Robertville tomorrow prepared to move on Barnwell. Howard is here all ready to start for the Augusta Railroad at Midway. We find the enemy on the East side of the Salkehatchie and cavalry in our front, but all give ground on our approach, and seem to be merely watching us. If I start on Tuesday, in one week I will be near Orangeburg, having broken up the Augusta Road from the Edisto westward twenty or twenty five miles. I will be sure that every Rail is twisted. Should I encounter too much opposition near Orangeburg then I will for a time neglect that Branch, ~~but~~ and rapidly move on Columbia and fill up the triangle formed by the Congaree & Wateree, tributaries of the santee, breaking up that great center of the Carolina Road. Up to that point I feel full confidence, but from there I may have to maneuver some, and will be guided by the questions of weather and supplies. You remember I had fine weather all february for my Meridian trip, and my memory of the weather at Charleston is that February is usually a fine month. Before the March storms come, I should be within striking distance of the Coast. The months of April & May will be the best for operations from Goldsboro, to Raleigh and the Roanoke. You may rest assured that I will keep my troops well in hand, and if I get worsted will aim to make the enemy pay so dearly that you will have less to do. I know this trip is necessary to the war. *It must be made* sooner or later, and I am on time and in the right position for it. My army is large enough for the purpose, and I ask no reinforcemt but simply wish the utmost activity at all other points, so that concentration against me may not be universal. I expect Davis will move Heaven & Earth to catch me, for success to my column, is fatal to his dream of Empire. Richmond is not more vital to his cause than Columbia and the heart of South Carolina. If Thomas will not move on Selma, order him to occupy Rome, Kingston and Allatoona, and again threaten Georgia in the direction of Athens. I think the Poor White trash of the South are falling out of their Ranks, by sickness, desertion and every other available means; but there is a large class of vindictive southerners who will fight to the last. The squabbles in Richmond, the howls in Charleston, and the disintegration elswhere, are all good omens to us, but we must not relax one iota, but on the contrary pile up our Efforts. I would ere this have been off, but we had terrific Rains which caught me in motion, and nearly drowned some of my columns in the Rice fields of the savannah, swept away one Causeway which had been carefully cuorduroyed, and made the Swamps hereabout mere lakes of slimy mud, but the weather is now good and I have my army on terra firma. Supplies too came for a long time by daily driblets instead of in bulk, but this is now all remedied, and I hope to start on Tuesday. I will issue instructions to Foster, based on the reinforcmt of North Carolina, and if Schofield comes you had better relieve Foster who cannot take the Field & needs an operation on his leg, and let Schofield take command, with HeadQrs at Beaufort N. C. & orders to secure if possible Goldsboro, with rail road connections back to to Beaufort & Wilmington. If Lee lets us get that position he is gone up.—I will start with my Atlanta army about 60000, supplied as before and depending on the country for all in excess of 30 days. I will have less cattle on the hoof, but I hear of hogs, cows & calves in Barnwell & the Columbia Districts. Even here we found some forage. Of course the Enemy will carry off & destroy some forage, but I will burn the houses where the People burn forage, and they will get tired of that. I must risk Hood, & trust to you to hold Lee, or be on his heels if he comes south. I can observe that the Enemy has some respect for my men, for they gave up Poca-taligo quick, when they heard that the attacking force belonged to me. I will try and keep up that feeling which is a real Power. . . . I leave my chief Qr Mr & commissary behind to follow coastwise" ALS, PPRF. *O.R.*, I, xlvii, part 2, 154–56.

To Edwin M. Stanton

(Cipher)   City Point, Va, Dec. [*Jan.*] 23d *18645*. [*10:00* P.M.]
HON. E. M. STANTON, SEC. OF WAR, WASHINGTON
One of my staff has just returned from Ft. Fisher with Dispatches from Gn. Terry from which I extract the following   On the 16th the Enemy blew up Forts Caswell & Campbell and abandoned them and the works on Smiths Island, those at Smithville and on Rives [*Reeves'*] Point. ~~and~~ tThese places were occupied by the Navy. The whole number of guns captured amounts to 162. A large number of small arms also fell into our hands besides quan-tities of Ordnance & Commissary stores. Our Casualties proves smaller than at first reported. They foot up thus. 12 Officers & 107 men killed 45 Officers & 495 men wounded.[1]

U. S. GRANT
Lt. Gen.

ALS (telegram sent), CSmH; telegram received (on Jan. 24, 1865, 11:25 A.M.), DNA, RG 107, Telegrams Collected (Bound). *O.R.*, I, xlvi, part 2, 205.

1. See *ibid.*, I, xlvi, part 1, 401–2.

To Maj. Gen. Henry W. Halleck

(Cipher)   City Point, Va, Jan.y 23d *18645*. [*2:00* P.M.]
MAJ. GEN. HALLECK, WASHINGTON,

Please have all transports collected for the transportation of Schofield's command coaled and watered and rations loaded. The troops should start with five days issued and from ~~200~~ two to two hundred and fifty thousand rations stored in the hold of the vessels. This will give a supply that ~~woul~~ will last ~~on~~ until ~~supple~~ more could be got to them. As soon as transports for a Division are ready they might be sent to Fortress Monroe to report by telegraph for orders.

U. S. GRANT
Lt. Gn.

ALS (telegram sent), Dr. Victor Turner, Newark, Ohio; telegram received (at 3:30 P.M.), DNA, RG 107, Telegrams Collected (Bound). *O.R.*, I, xlvii, part 2, 115–16.

On Jan. 23, 1865, 5:00 P.M., USG telegraphed to Maj. Gen. Henry W. Halleck. "Unless otherwise directed the first Division of Schofields command that can be got on transports may be sent to Fort Fisher. Let them report from Ft. Monroe however as they pass." ALS (telegram sent), OClWHi; telegram received (at 7:00 P.M.), DNA, RG 107, Telegrams Collected (Bound). At 3:50 P.M., Halleck telegraphed to USG. "Some time since orders were sent to Genl Thomas to forward to Savannah via New York all fractions of regiments, & c. belonging to the corps under Genl Sherman. Genl Meagher telegraphs to day from Pittsburg that he has seven thousand men & wants transports ready in New York; but Genl VanVleit says that he cannot furnish them if he sends transports here to meet Schofield's corps. To which shall the transports be given first? If Meagher's command stop in New York, it is feared that very many will desert, & there are no quarters for them on Governor's Island. Please reply immediately." ALS (telegram sent), *ibid.*; telegram received, *ibid.*; (marked as sent at 3:30 P.M.) *ibid.*, RG 108, Letters Received. *O.R.*, I, xlvii, part 2, 116. At 7:00 P.M., USG telegraphed to Halleck. "Order Maher to Alexandria. We will send Schofields Corps first and add this detachment to it until such time as it can be got to Sherman. It is to late now for it to reach Sherman from Pocotaligo." ALS (telegram sent), PPRF; telegram received (at 7:00 P.M.), DNA, RG 107, Telegrams Collected (Bound). Printed as received at 7:30 P.M. in *O.R.*, I, xlvii, part 2, 116.

To Jesse Root Grant

City Point, Va, Jan 23d *1865*.

DEAR FATHER,

Enclosed I send you $100 00 out of which direct Uncle Samuel to keep $80 00 and send the other $20 00 to Aunt Polly as a present from Julia.

In one of your previous letters you asked me if there was an objection to appointing a person who has not been in the service to one of the Staff Corps? There is an objection except to the Pay Dept.

I should feel very sorry to see the Sherman movement fail. He is one of the best as well as one of the ablest men in this country.

I received a letter from Belville Simpson to-day asking if I could put him in some place if he enlisted to save him from the ordinary duties of a soldier. If he enlists I will do what I can. But tell him not to enter the service with such an understanding. I have kept John[1] in about the only such position I have and sometime since ordered him from Nashville here to take it again at my Hd Qrs. Why he has not come I do not know.—Julia will be very glad to have mother pay her a visit. Only to-day she was saying that as soon as she got in her new house she intended writing to you and her asking you if you would not come on and visit her. Remember me to all at home.

Yours Truly

U. S. GRANT

ALS, NHi.

1. John Simpson, born in 1840 in Bethel County, Ohio (son of USG's uncle Samuel Simpson), enlisted in the 5th Ohio Cav. as of Sept. 27, 1862. On May 18, 1865, Brig. Gen. John A. Rawlins wrote to Brig. Gen. Lorenzo Thomas. "Private John Simpson Co, "A" 5th Ohio Cavalry who comes within the provision's of Genl, Orders No, 83 A. G. O. current series for Muster-out is on detached service at Maj, Gen, W. T. Sherman's Headquarters, at Alexandria Va, and his Co, & Regt, is in North Carolina,   You will please issue an order authorising and directing any Commissary or Asst, Commissary of Muster's of Genl, Shermans Army to Muster him out of service" Copies, DLC-USG, V, 46, 76, 108; DNA, RG 108, Letters Sent. See letter to Jesse Root Grant, March 19, 1865. John Simpson's younger brother was named Robert B(elville).

To Elihu B. Washburne

———

City Point, Va, Dec. [*Jan.*] 23d *1865*.

HON. E. B. WASHBURN,
DEAR SIR:

I have several letters from you which I must answer as soon as I can get a day to write, which I hope will be within a day or two. Now however I write on another matter.

I see some objections are raised to Meades confirmation as Major General in the Regular Army. What the objections are I do not know and can not therefore address myself to them. I am very sorry this should be so. Gen. Meade is one of our truest men and ablest officers. He has been constantly with that Army confronting the strongest, best appointed and most confidant Army in the South. He therefore has not had the same opportunity of wining laurels so distinctively marked as have fallen to the lot of other Generals. But I defy any one to name a commander who could do more than he has done with the same chances. I am satisfied with a full knowledge of the man, what he has done, and the circumstances attending all his Military acts, all objections would be removed. I wrote a letter to M̶r̶. Senator Wilson to-day in his behalf which I hope will have some weight. If you can put in a word with some of the other Senators, particularly those who oppose his confirmation, and are willing to do it, I will feel much obliged.

Yours Truly
U. S. GRANT

ALS, IHi. USG's error in recording the month is repeated in copies of this letter dated Dec. 23, 1864, in CtY and Meade Papers, PHi. The latter, however, has been corrected to Jan. 23, 1865.

On Feb. 2, USG telegraphed to Maj. Gen. George G. Meade. "I am happy to state to you that I am just in receipt of a dispatch from Washington announcing your confirmation as Major General in the Regular Army by a heavy majority." ALS (telegram sent), CSmH; telegram received (at 10:35 A.M.), Meade Papers, PHi. *O.R.*, I, xlvi, part 2, 353. At 11:15 A.M., Meade telegraphed to USG. "Many thanks for your kind telegram—Be assured I shall ever most gratefully remember your kindness on this and other occasions—" ALS (telegram sent), DNA, RG 94, War Records Office, Army of the Potomac; copies, *ibid.*, RG 393, Army of the Potomac, Letters Sent; Meade Papers, PHi. *O.R.*, I, xlvi, part 2,

353. See George Meade, *The Life and Letters of George Gordon Meade* (New York, 1913), II, 223–24, 244–60 *passim*.

To Henry Wilson

———

City Point Va Jany 23rd *18645*.

HON H. WILSON
CH. COM. MIL. AFFAIRS
SIR,

I see that Gens Thomas and Sheridan have been confirmed as Major Generals in the Regular Army, whilst no mention is made of Gen Meade's confirmation to the same rank. From this I infer objections have been raised. This I regret.

Gen Meade was appointed at my solicitation after a campaign the most protracted, and covering more severely contested battles, than any of which we have any account in history—

I have been with Gen Meade during the whole campaign, and not only made the recommendation upon a conviction that this recognition of his services was fully won, but that he was eminently qualified for the command such rank would entitle him to—

I know Gen Meade well. What the objections raised to his confirmation are, I do not know. Did I know, I would address myself directly to these objections—

Hoping that your Honorable Body will consider this case favorably, I subscribe myself

With Great Respect
Your Obt. Svt.
U. S. GRANT
Lt. Gen

Copies, Meade Papers, PHi; DLC-USG, V, 46, 72, 108; DNA, RG 108, Letters Sent. *O.R.*, I, xlvi, part 2, 206.

PONTOON BRIDGE ON THE JAMES RIVER ABOVE JONES'LANDING, FROM THE NORTH SIDE. 68 BOATS

O.R. Atlas, *plate CXXV, no. 11.*

U.S. forces sank vessels as obstructions in the James River to blockade C.S.A. naval forces upriver. Photograph attributed to Mathew B. Brady. *Courtesy National Archives.*

To Edwin M. Stanton

City Point Va
4 30 P. M. Jan 24 1865

HON. EDWIN M. STANTON
SECRETARY OF WAR.

I respectfully request that the Hon. Secretary of the Navy re-move Capt Parker U. S. N. from command of the James river flotilla tonight, by telegraph. With three days notice of his danger, and a large fleet at his command, when I sent a Staff officer to him this morning before daylight on hearing that the rebel rams were coming down the river, and that two of them had passed the ob-structions, he had but one, that a wooden one and the torpedo boat above the pontoon bridge at Aikens Landing.

On my arrival here yesterday from Washington I requested him to get to the front every boat he had in the river within reach, This he should had done two days before without notice. The rebels have suffered severely in today's operations, but with a no doubt gallant set of commanders for the vessels they have been allowed to contribute but little to this result,   One rebel Gunboat was blown up by a shell from Battery Parsons, one other sunk, & the third disabled, the fourth, the Virginia was hit a great many times but I do not know that she was injured. It is the judgment of officers who were present that had the Monitor been in her place on learning that the Virginia and Fredericksburg were aground both those vessels would have been destroyed before they could have been got off; as it is only the weaker vessel of the two was disabled. The rebels still have five Gunboats above us.

U S GRANT Lt Gen

Telegram received (at 6:00 P.M.), DNA, RG 107, Telegrams Collected (Bound); copies, *ibid.*, Telegrams Received in Cipher; *ibid.*, RG 108, Letters Sent; DLC-USG, V, 46, 72, 108. *O.R.*, I, xlvi, part 2, 218–19. On Jan. 24, 1865, 9:10 P.M., Secretary of War Edwin M. Stanton telegraphed to USG. "Admiral Faragut is ordered to City Point and will start for Annapolis as soon as an extra train can be had. In the meantime Parker has been removed and Radford ordered to take command of the fleet" ALS (telegram sent), DNA, RG 107, Telegrams Collected (Bound); telegram received, *ibid.*, RG 108, Letters Received. *O.R.*, I, xlvi, part 2, 219. The telegram received included a postscript. "Secy Fox is in the office at Washington—" On the same day, Commodore William Radford telegraphed to USG. "I will leave at early daylight & go up the James river as far as I can, The Saugus left for Washington this morning Telegraph there to turn her back No vessel could overtake from me" Copies, DNA, RG 45, Miscellaneous Letters Received; (press) *ibid*., RG 107, Telegrams Collected (Bound). On the same day, USG transmitted this telegram to Secretary of the Navy Gideon Welles. "The following is forwarded for your information." Telegrams received, *ibid*.

On Jan. 21, 7:00 P.M., Brig. Gen. John A. Rawlins had telegraphed to USG. "We have information today from Col Sharp that on tuesday last an order was issued in Richmond that the rebel fleet should go down the river, either pass or attack our Iron Clads and attempt the destruction of City Pt. It was known in Richmond that we had two monitors up the river, but it was supposed that their vessels would be strong enough for the attempt, it being claimed that now, in the absence of the larger part of our Iron fleet was the opportunity for they own that upon the return of our Iron Clads theirs would be permanently shut up in the upper part of the James river, and that even if the movement resulted in the loss of their vessels, it could be no worse than what would eventually be the case and might inflict incalculable damage to us. There is no doubt that the order was given on tuesday, but why it was not carried out was not explained" Telegram received, *ibid*.; copy, *ibid*., Telegrams Received in Cipher. *O.R.*, I, xlvi, part 2, 190–91. As printed, the telegram includes a postscript. "(Substance of this was sent to Captain Parker. He was advised to take the necessary precautionary measures.)" *Ibid*., p. 191. Letterbook copies of the telegram from Rawlins to USG (misdated Jan. 22) include the postscript as a marginal note. Copies, DLC-USG, V, 46, 72, 108; DNA, RG 108, Letters Sent. On Jan. 22, Commander William A. Parker, U.S. Monitor *Onondaga*, Aiken's Landing, wrote to Rawlins. "I have the honor to acknowledge the receipt of your communication of the 21st Inst conveying the information that an order was issued on Tuesday last, that the Rebel Fleet should come down the River; either pass or attack the Monitors, and attempt the destruction of City Point. I thank you very much for this information; and I shall exercise more than usual vigilance to defeat any plan the rebels may have in contemplation on the River In this connection I would beg leave to suggest that the Flag of truce boat be not allowed to come above the Pontoon Bridge to land prisoners, as I consider it highly objectionable for the Rebels to have a close view of our Monitors or our method of Drill or Exercise: Deep Bottom is a convenient place to land prisoners for exchange." LS, *ibid*., Letters Received. *O.R.*, I, xlvi, part 2, 200.

On Jan. 23, 5:40 P.M., 10:00 P.M., and 11:00 P.M., Maj. Gen. John Gibbon telegraphed to Rawlins. "The right of Genl. Ferrero's picket line which rests on the James just below the Howlett House Battery was attacked last night The attack was repulsed. A deserter reported to Genl. Ferrero that the object was to ascertain if the obstructions in the river had been carried away. Small boats were in readiness to cooperate in case the attack succeeded. The attempt was to have been made on Saturday night but the small boats were not ready. Eight guns and ten hats were picked up this morning at the point where the attack was made. Every caution has been taken to prevent a surprise" ALS (telegram sent), DNA, RG 107, Telegrams Collected (Unbound); telegram received, *ibid*., RG 108, Letters Received. *O.R.*, I, xlvi, part 2, 209. "General Kautz sends in a deserter from the Hampton Legion, Gary's brigade, who says the brigade

moved at 11 o'clock to-day with three days' rations. He does not know where
they went. I will ascertain shortly the meaning of the firing on the river." *Ibid.*
"The firing tonight is from Fort Brady, trying to hit three guns boats reported
by our pickets as having made their appearance in the bend of the river above,
It is a waste of ammunition, and I do not place much reliance on the report"
ALS (telegram sent), DNA, RG 108, Letters Received; telegram received, *ibid.*
O.R., I, xlvi, part 2, 210.

At 9:15 P.M., Bvt. Maj. Gen. Edward Ferrero, Bermuda Hundred, telegraphed to USG. "Artillery firing River Batteries—Slight firing on extreme right
of my Picket line—Expecting an attack but am prepared for it—" ALS (telegram sent), DNA, RG 107, Telegrams Collected (Unbound).

On the same day, 11:45 A.M., Maj. Gen. George G. Meade telegraphed to
Rawlins. "What news of the Lt. Genl—I did not expect when he left that he could
get back in 48 hours, but I should like to know when his return is anticipated."
ALS (telegram sent), *ibid.*, RG 94, War Records Office, Army of the Potomac.
O.R., I, xlvi, part 2, 206. On the same day, Rawlins twice telegraphed to Meade.
"We have no news of the Lt. Gen. having yet started from Washington" Tele-
gram received, DNA, RG 107, Telegrams Collected (Unbound). "General Grant
has arrived." *O.R.*, I, xlvi, part 2, 206.

To Gideon Welles

City Point, Va. Jan. 24th 1865 [*6:00* P.M.]
HON. G. WELLS, SEC. OF THE NAVY, WASHINGTN
I have been unable to get Capt. Parker, by requesting, to assemble
his Gunboats near the obstructions in James River. He seems help-
less. I have now sent orders directly to Commanders of Vessels and
respectfully request that you will sustain this course. Please direct
during present imergency my orders be obeyed.
                                   U. S. GRANT
                                   Lt. Gn.

ALS (telegram sent), IHi; telegrams received (2—at 7:30 P.M.), DNA, RG
107, Telegrams Collected (Bound). *O.R.*, I, xlvi, part 2, 223; *O.R.* (Navy), I,
xi, 635–36. On Jan. 24, 1865, 7:40 P.M. and 10:00 P.M., Secretary of the Navy
Gideon Welles telegraphed to Commander William A. Parker, first asking him
to report to the Navy Dept. and to USG, then removing him from command.
O.R., I, xlvi, part 2, 224.

On the same day, USG issued special orders for gunboat commanders. "All
Gun Boats now in the James River above City Point will immediately proceed to
the front above the Pontoon Bridge near Varina Landing. This order is impera-
tive, the orders of any Naval Commanders to the contrary notwithstanding By
Authority of the Secretary of the Navy" Copies, DLC-USG, V, 46, 72, 108.
O.R., I, xlvi, part 2, 225; *O.R.* (Navy), I, xi, 635.

Also on Jan. 24, Commodore Joseph Lanman, U.S.S. *Minnesota*, Hampton Roads, telegraphed to USG. "Will General Grant have the goodness to inform me if the 'Rams' have passed the obstructions, or if there is any probability of their doing so, Can the Navy at Hampton Roads be of any service to the General?" LS (telegram sent), DNA, RG 45, Area File; telegram received, *ibid.*, RG 108, Letters Received. *O.R.*, I, xlvi, part 2, 227. On the same day, USG telegraphed to Lanman. "Two Rebel Rams passed the obstructions before daylight this morning but went back again. Your vessels can be of service and I was in hopes some of them were on the way so as to arrive here during the night." ALS (telegram sent), OClWHi; telegram received (press), DNA, RG 94, Army of the James, Letters Sent. *O.R.*, I, xlvi, part 2, 227; *O.R.* (Navy), I, xi, 643. Lanman received this telegram at 10:00 P.M. *Ibid.*

On Feb. 5, Parker, Atlantic Hotel, Norfolk, wrote to USG. "I most humbly and earnestly beg that you will be pleased to allow me to return to duty on board the Onondaga. I acknowledge my transgressions, and implore your mercy in my case. I deeply regret that I ever gave you any cause of complaint, and promise in the future that your orders shall be punctually and implicitly obeyed. A request from you to the Navy Department would restore me to duty immediately. I beg for your forgiveness, general, and earnestly hope you will grant my request." *O.R.*, I, xlvi, part 2, 388. At 8:00 P.M., USG telegraphed to Welles. "I am in receipt of an earnest appeal from Capt. Parker U. S. N. to be restored to the command of the Onondaga. I have no objection to his return to that command so long as a senior commands the Division." ALS (facsimile telegram sent), Daniel F. Kelleher Co., Inc., 553rd Sale, March 11, 1982, II, 20; telegram received (at 9:00 P.M.), DNA, RG 107, Telegrams Collected (Bound). *O.R.*, I, xlvi, part 2, 389. A court-martial subsequently convicted Parker, but Welles set aside the sentence of dismissal. *O.R.* (Navy), I, xi, 662–63.

To Gideon Welles

City Point, Va, Jan.y 24th *1864*5.

HON. G. WELLS,
SEC. OF THE NAVY,
SIR:

I would respectfully call your attention to the fact that the Rebels are now at work on a formidable Ram in the Roanoke River, at a place known as Rainbow Bluff. This ram they expect to complete within the next five or six weeks.

It is hardly necessary for me to call your attention to the disaster that would be caused by allowing this vessel to get in commission against anything we now have afloat in Albermarl Sound. I would respectfully suggest th[at] one of the Monitors now no longer of use with Admiral Porter be worked through Hatteras

Inle[t] and that, in addition, the Ram Albermarl be raised and repair[ed] for use.

> I have the honor to be
> Very respectful[ly]
> your obt. svt.
> U. S. GRANT
> Lt. Gen

ALS, DNA, RG 45, Miscellaneous Letters Received. *O.R.*, I, xlvi, part 2, 223; *O.R.* (Navy), I, xi, 721–22. On Jan. 31, 1865, Secretary of the Navy Gideon Welles wrote to USG. "The Department has received your letter of the 24th instant,—calling attention to the rebel ram building in Roanoke river and suggesting measures to provide against disaster from it,—and has transmitted a copy of it to Rear Admiral Porter." LS, DNA, RG 108, Letters Received. *O.R.*, I, xlvi, part 2, 313; *O.R.* (Navy), I, xi, 722. On Feb. 11, Rear Admiral David D. Porter, Cape Fear River, wrote to USG. "The Secretary of the Navy has referred your letter of the 24th January to me, in relation to the ram said to be building at Rainbow Bluff, as it is in my district. Ample precautions have been taken to meet any case of this kind, and more are in progress. No ram can get into the sounds if officers do their duty and carry out my orders. At New Berne there are torpedo-boats, also at Plymouth, which are the best defense against rams. The obstructions at New Berne, originally very strong, have given way in one place. The vessel sunk there has been moved by the force of the current. As these obstructions are under the charge of the military commander, I would suggest that the gap be filled up with crib-work and stone, which is stronger, and will stand better than sunken vessels. Torpedoes are ordered to be sunk in both rivers worked by galvanic batteries. The ram Albemarle is being raised, but could not be made available in four months, except to sink as an obstruction." *O.R.*, I, xlvi, part 2, 524; *O.R.* (Navy), I, xii, 15.

To Gustavus V. Fox

> City Point Va
> Jany 24th 1865 [*9:35* A.M.]

HON G. V. FOX
ASST SECY OF THE NAVY.

The Enemys Ironclads came down below the obstructions this morning and returned to the neighborhood of Howletts before daylight. Since their return there has been a heavy explosion about the obstructions. There are three (3) of these Ironclads in view and I am inclined to believe they will make an effort to get down here to destroy our stores—. Will you please order up the gunboats now

about Ft Monroe with orders that they shall not stop for night
or other cause until they reach the front now occupied by our
gunboats?

U S GRANT
Lt Genl

Telegram received, DNA, RG 45, Miscellaneous Letters Received; (3—at 9:25
A.M.) *ibid.*, RG 107, Telegrams Collected (Bound); copies, *ibid.*, RG 108, Letters Sent; DLC-USG, V, 46, 72, 108. *O.R.*, I, xlvi, part 2, 221; *O.R.* (Navy), I,
xi, 635. On Jan. 24, 1865, 9:30 A.M., USG had telegraphed to Asst. Secretary of
the Navy Gustavus V. Fox. "I would like to leave Fort Monroe tomorrow evening
or next day morning for Fort Fisher. Can you not go? I would also be pleased to
go on a naval vessel if it is convenient to spare one—Ocean transportation is now
all employed carrying troops" Telegrams received (2—at 11:00 A.M.), DNA,
RG 107, Telegrams Collected (Bound); copies (marked as received at 10:05
A.M.), *ibid.*, Telegrams Received in Cipher; *ibid.*, RG 108, Letters Sent; DLC-
USG, V, 46, 72, 108. Printed as received at 10:35 A.M. in *O.R.*, I, xlvi, part 2,
220. On the same day, Fox telegraphed to USG. "The 'Ironsides' and 'Atlanta'
have both started up James River The former on a draft of sixteen feet ought to
reach City Point, The latter is less. The 'Saugus' started from Norfolk for this
place but was sent for today. I do not understand where our torpedo Boat is. She
ought to dispose of all the rams if they come below the obstructions The 'Rhode
Island' one of the fastest and best ocean steamers will be at the Roads ready for
you thursday morning. I cannot tell until tomorrow whether I can get off. We
are frozen up here. will telegraph in the morning." Telegram received, DNA,
RG 108, Letters Received. *O.R.*, I, xlvi, part 2, 221; *O.R.* (Navy), I, xi, 641.
Lt. Col. Ely S. Parker added a postscript to the telegram received. "Capt Fox is
waiting for an answer So says Tel. opr"
    On the same day, Fox again telegraphed to USG. "I will send an order now
removing Com. Parker, The next in rank is, I think, Com'r Nichols A a fair
Officer. If you deem it unadvisable you can withhold the order. I will go with you
thursday unless I notify you to the contrary tomorrow. The Secy of War will
send me over to Annapolis in the evening—" Telegram received, DNA, RG
108, Letters Received. *O.R.*, I, xlvi, part 2, 221; *O.R.* (Navy), I, xi, 637. On the
same day, USG twice telegraphed to Fox. "If the weather holds dry I want to go
to Ft. Fisher as soon as possible so as to be here whenever the roads admit of
troops moving. If it should a rain a day or two would not make any difference; I
should particularly like you to go with me however," "Commander Nichols will
no doubt do. I will advise you as soon as I know it will be safe for me to leave. It
will not be earlier than thursday morning." Telegrams received (at 9:50 P.M.
and 10:00 P.M.), DNA, RG 45, Miscellaneous Letters Received; (press) *ibid.*,
RG 107, Telegrams Collected (Bound); copies, *ibid.*, RG 108, Letters Sent;
DLC-USG, V, 46, 72, 108. *O.R.*, I, xlvi, part 2, 221, 222; *O.R.* (Navy), I, xi,
638, 695.
    Also on Jan. 24, Tuesday, Fox twice telegraphed to USG, first at 1:00 P.M.
"Have telegraphed to Norfolk about a steamer Will send you word this evening
Thursday morning would be the time Have ordered several iron clads up the
James. We have a torpedo boat up there unless she is under repair" Telegram
received, DNA, RG 107, Telegrams Collected (Bound). *O.R.*, I, xlvi, part 2,

222. "The President just sent for me and suggested that Admiral Farragut should go down to James River and he leaves for Annapolis in an hour, Before that I had ordered Commo. Radford of the 'Ironsides' to go up and take Command in the James River, He will be there tomorrow afternoon, Capt Parker will be removed tonight if you desire it, The Saugus has been sent for to return at once to James River. The 'Atlanta' goes up at daylight & any and all wooden Boats at Norfolk, The 'Roanoke' Ironclad frigate stationed at Point Lookout has been ordered to Hampton Roads, The 'Rhode Island' is placed at your service at Hampton Roads and if you do not go for three or four days I think I can get off. I cannot ~~unless~~ understand why the torpedo Boat did not attack, Do you know any reason?" Telegram received, DNA, RG 108, Letters Received. *O.R.*, I, xlvi, part 2, 222; *O.R.* (Navy), I, xi, 637. On the same day, USG telegraphed to Fox. "I shall be truly glad to see Adml Farragut but in the present emergency he can be of no service nor can Capt Radford though let him come. There would be no difficulty about getting commanders of vessels where you want them." Telegram received (at 9:45 P.M.), DNA, RG 45, Miscellaneous Letters Received; (press) *ibid.*, RG 107, Telegrams Collected (Bound); copies, *ibid.*, RG 108, Letters Sent; DLC-USG, V, 46, 72, 108. *O.R.*, I, xlvi, part 2, 222; (received at 9:40 P.M.) *O.R.* (Navy), I, xi, 640. At 8:00 P.M., USG telegraphed to Fox. "Until all is secure here I cannot leave for Wilmington; it will be Thursday morning at the earliest before I can leave" Telegram received (at 8:10 P.M.), DNA, RG 45, Miscellaneous Letters Received; (2) *ibid.*, RG 107, Telegrams Collected (Bound); copies, *ibid.*, Telegrams Received in Cipher; *ibid.*, RG 108, Letters Sent; DLC-USG, V, 46, 72, 108. *O.R.*, I, xlvi, part 2, 223; *O.R.* (Navy), I, xi, 694.

On Jan. 25, 11:30 A.M. and 7:00 P.M., USG telegraphed to Fox. "The rebel fleet run up the river last night, or this morning, past our upper batteries thus shewing present danger to be at an end. I will leave here at 10 a. m. for Cape Fear River. Hope you will be able to go." "I will wait at Hampton Roads until Friday Morning for you. Shall not start from here until 10 p. m. to-morrow evening unless you say you cannot go." ALS (telegrams sent), OClWHi; telegrams received (the first marked as sent at 11:00 A.M., received at 1:00 P.M. and 8:00 P.M.), DNA, RG 45, Miscellaneous Letters Received; (2 of the first) *ibid.*, RG 107, Telegrams Collected (Bound). *O.R.*, I, xlvi, part 2, 255, 256. The first is printed as received at 12:40 P.M.

To Gustavus V. Fox

By Telegraph from City Pt
Dated [Jan.] 24 *1864.* [*1865*]

To Asst Sec Fox[1]

If the Rebel Rams do not get down to-night I think everything will be safe before to-morrow night. I expect but little assistance however in case of an attack from the Navy under Capt. Parker. I have been compelled to take the matter in my own hands to get vessels to the front ordering by direction of the Sec. of the Navy. I know no reason why the Torpedo boat did not attack. As I understand the rebel rams run our batteries to the obstructions and there leisurely removed and blew them up only opposed by a little Infantry from the shore. When I sent up before daylight Capt. Parker had Removed the Monitor to below the ~~obstructions~~ Pontoon bridge. To-night I understand he has hauled down the river leaving what obstructions still remains to be removed without opposition from him. I have sent an urgent appeal for him to go back. I have been busy all day getting up material to reniew the obstructions and Army officers are now at it.

U. S. GRANT
Lt. Gn

ALS (telegram sent), PPRF; telegram received (at 9:40 P.M.), DNA, RG 107, Telegrams Collected (Bound). *O.R.*, I, xlvi, part 2, 223; *O.R.* (Navy), I, xi, 635.

1. Heading not in USG's hand.

To Maj. Gen. Henry W. Halleck

(Cipher)   City Point, Va, Jan. 24th 1865 [*9:30* A.M.]
MAJ. GN. HALLECK, WASHINGTON

I shall probably leave here by noon to-morrow for Fort Fisher. All the troops of Schofields command may be forwarded directly to that point. ~~unl Maher's~~ Meagher's[1] command will go in the same way in the absence of further directions. If Schofield reaches Washington in time I would like to have him accompany me.

U. S. GRANT
Lt. Gen.

ALS (telegram sent), PPRF; telegram received (at 11:00 A.M.), DNA, RG 107, Telegrams Collected (Bound); DLC-John M. Schofield. *O.R.*, I, xlvi, part 2, 219; *ibid.*, I, xlvii, part 2, 121. On Jan. 24, 1865, noon, Maj. Gen. Henry W. Halleck telegraphed to USG. "If Genl Schofield does not arrive in time to join you, I will send him forward on the first transport." ALS (telegram sent), DNA, RG 107, Telegrams Collected (Bound); telegram received, *ibid. O.R.*, I, xlvi, part 2, 219; *ibid.*, I, xlvii, part 2, 121.

1. Not in USG's hand.

To Maj. Gen. Henry W. Halleck

———

(Cipher)   City Point, Va, Jan. 24th *18645*. [*1:30* P.M.]
MAJ. GEN. HALLECK, WASHINGTON,

About 3 a. m. this morning four of the enemy's gunboats come down the river passing our batteries North of the James, one or two of them passing below the obstructions. ~~in the river~~. For some reason they returned without passing far below. Two, the Virginia & Fredericksburg, grounded not far from the Howlett House and under ~~the b~~ one of our Land batteries. For several hours they were pownded from this battery but with what effect cannot be known. The Drury was blown up by a shot from Fort Parsons and one other gunboat disabled. The two boats that were aground are now off and have passed a short distance up the river.

The freshet which ~~has taken place~~ we have had in the last few days has displaced a portion of the obstructions in the river and made the passage easy. The Naval force here is not near adequate to the protection of the river should the enemy attempt to come down. I have telegraphed the Sec. of the Navy however for more vessels.

U. S. GRANT
Lt. Gn.

ALS (telegram sent), PPRF; telegram received (at 2:30 P.M.), DNA, RG 107, Telegrams Collected (Bound). *O.R.*, I, xlvi, part 2, 219–20.

To Maj. Gen. Henry W. Halleck

———

(Cipher)   City Point, Va. Jan. 24th *18645*. [*8:00* P.M.]
MAJ. GEN. HALLECK, WASHINGTON,

Please ask the Chief of Ordnance to send a competant Ordnance officer to report to Gen. Terry, at least temporarily. There is a great~~deel of~~ many Shells and other stores to pick up, and much of the ordnance that can be dispensed with. The varieties of ammunition for the guns in the different forts ~~its~~ numerous. The sec-

ond Division of Schofields command embarked may be sent to
Beaufort N. C.

U. S. GRANT
Lt. Gn.

ALS (telegram sent), CSmH; telegram received (at 10:20 P.M.), DNA, RG
107, Telegrams Collected (Bound). *O.R.*, I, xlvi, part 2, 220.

On Jan. 23, 1865, Lt. Col. Ely S. Parker issued Special Orders No. 17. "Maj,
Gen, John Gibbon Com'dg Army of the James will immediately forward to Maj,
Gen, Terry at Ft, Fisher, fifty, Six Mule teams and the Caisons, Wagons, and
Horses of batteries "E" 3d U, S, Artillery and the 16th N. Y. Ind'p't battery now
here, and one Company of Cavalry numbering at liast fifty men for duty as order-
lies and couriers," Copies, DLC-USG, V, 54, 57, 63, 65. *O.R.*, I, xlvi, part 2, 207.

On Jan. 24, USG telegraphed to Maj. Gen. John Gibbon. "Please direct
your Q. M. to send to Fort Fisher all the wagon train, with their proportion of
the supply train as fast as the Q. M. here will furnish transportation." ALS
(telegram sent), CSmH; telegram received, Ord Papers, CU-B. *O.R.*, I, xlvi, part
2, 239. On Jan. 25, USG telegraphed to Gibbon. "You will please send to Ft.
Fisher all of the ambulances ambulance teams & drivers belonging to the troops
now there calling upon the chief q. m. here for transportation" Telegram received, DNA, RG 94, War Records Office, Dept. of Va. and N. C.; copies, *ibid.*,
RG 108, Letters Sent; DLC-USG, V, 46, 72, 108.

To Maj. Gen. John Gibbon

———

By Telegraph from City Pt
Dated January 24 18645.

To MAJ GEN GIBBON

I have two Engineer officers, and the quartermaster up the river,
all morning making arrangements to effectually blockade the river.
All the heavily loaded vessels we have and some of the Gunboats
will be sunk if necessary to close the channel should the enemy
start down. I wish you would suggest to Capt Parker the placing
of some torpedoes up where the obstructions are immediately after
dark. If they lose tonight they will be too late and I think they are
as it is. Some Ironclads are ordered up from below.

U. S. GRANT
Lt Genl.

Telegram received (at 2:00 P.M.), Ord Papers, CU-B; copies, DLC-USG, V, 46,
72, 108; DNA, RG 108, Letters Sent. *O.R.*, I, xlvi, part 2, 236. On Jan. 24,

1865, 1:20 P.M., Maj. Gen. John Gibbon had telegraphed to USG. "The two rams have withdrawn to a point above the Howlett House Battery, and firing has now ceased there I would not be surprised if they made another attempt to come down probably tonight, and if our gun-boats act as they did before there will be nothing to stop them. I think torpedoes would be of more service than barges where the water is so deep" ALS (telegram sent), DNA, RG 107, Telegrams Collected (Unbound); telegram received, *ibid.*, RG 108, Letters Received. *O.R.*, I, xlvi, part 2, 236.

At 2:55 A.M., 3:20 A.M., 3:58 A.M., and 4:15 A.M., Gibbon telegraphed to Brig. Gen. John A. Rawlins. "The enemys gun boats have passed our obstructions opposite crows nest. It is not know how many but two are reported" "Genl. Ferrero telegraphs the enemy's gun boats have certainly passed the obstructions. The Comdg. officer at the canal reports three boats, two ironclads and a one wooden boat as having passed the upper end of the canal and that the wooden boat was coming back. I have telegraphed Genl. Ferrero to know what evidence he has of the passage of the obstructions, and sent an officer with some orderlies to Varina to report the facts." "The signal officer at crws nest reports that the enemys gun boats have not yet passed the obstructions they are at sleepy Hollow" "I shall know shortly from the Comdr of the Onondago if the enemy's boats have yet reached the obstructions They may be waiting for daylight to pass them. I have sent for two tugs from Bermuda Hundred to bring vessels up to the draw in the bridge at Varina with a view of sinking them there if it becomes necessary. but I will not sink them unless it becomes the only way to stop the gunboats" ALS (telegrams sent), DNA, RG 107, Telegrams Collected (Unbound); telegrams received, *ibid.*, RG 108, Letters Received. *O.R.*, I, xlvi, part 2, 232–33. The first is printed as sent at 3:00 A.M. The telegram received of the last is misdated Jan. 25 and printed again with that date *ibid.*, p. 259. On Jan. 24, USG telegraphed to Gibbon. "Your despatches received—every thing is astir and we are getting coal boats and barges ready to send up to use if necessary" Telegram received (at 4:35 A.M.), Ord Papers, CU-B; copies, DLC-USG, V, 46, 72, 108; DNA, RG 108, Letters Sent. Printed as sent at 4:35 A.M., received at 4:55 A.M., in *O.R.*, I, xlvi, part 2, 233. At 4:55 A.M., Gibbon telegraphed to Rawlins, then to USG. "Genl. Grant's despatch of 4.35 received. An intelligent officer should be sent up with the barges so as to exercise good judgement about where to sink them in case of necessity. I think the best place is the draw in the bridge at Varina, next to that Deep Bottom." ALS (telegram sent), DNA, RG 107, Telegrams Collected (Unbound). *O.R.*, I, xlvi, part 2, 233. "The signal officer at the Crows Nest tower reports as follows 'The Rebel Gun boats have been below our obstructions nearly as far as Battery Sawyer. They have now gone back and are no longer in sight' " ALS (incomplete telegram sent), DNA, RG 107, Telegrams Collected (Unbound); telegram received (at 5:25 A.M.—misdated Jan. 25), *ibid.*, RG 108, Letters Received. *O.R.*, I, xlvi, part 2, 234. At 5:30 A.M., USG telegraphed to Gibbon. "If the rebel GunBoats have gone back Above the obstructions and you have any schooner or other craft available now is the time to sink where the other obstructions are" Telegram received, Ord Papers, CU-B; copies, DLC-USG, V, 46, 72, 108; DNA, RG 108, Letters Sent. *O.R.*, I, xlvi, part 2, 234. At 7:00 A.M., 8:03 A.M., and 8:33 A.M., Gibbon telegraphed to USG. "I have sent your despatch to Capt Parker but have as yet received no answer. My Engineer officer is just in from the canal. The enemy's gun boats are lying some ~~distance~~ 2 miles below the upper end of the canal The Onondago dropped down to Jones' landing, but I hear is now on her way back" ALS (telegram sent), DNA, RG 107, Telegrams Collected (Unbound). *O.R.*, I, xlvi, part 2, 234. "One of my officers has just returned from the point of land below the canal—He crossed the canal and went within ¼ of a mile of three rebels guns boats built like the Atlanta which are ~~lay~~ lying directly under the Howlett House Battery. On his way back he witnessed an explosion at the obstructions, and the enemy have doubtless blown up the obstructions and will soon no doubt attempt to go down. All now depends on our gun boats, and means should be ready to place other obstructions. The Eng. officer reports 30 feet of water in the draw of the bridge at Varina and of course barges sunk there would do but little good." ALS (telegram sent), DNA, RG 107, Telegrams Collected (Unbound); telegram received, *ibid.*, RG 108, Letters Received. *O.R.*, I, xlvi, part 2, 234–35. "The Signal Officer on Crows nest tower reports that one of the rebel boats which came down this morning was blown up by a percussion Shell from Battery Parsons. It is possible this may have been the explosion I reported in my last despatch as having taken place at the obstructions" Telegram received (at 8:40 A.M.), DNA, RG 108, Letters Received. *O.R.*, I, xlvi, part 2, 235. On Jan. 24, Bvt. Maj. Gen. Alexander S. Webb twice telegraphed to Rawlins, first at 9:45 A.M. "If it is not contraband with you let us know the news from the seat of War on our right—There seems to be a difference of opinion up there." ALS (telegram sent), DNA, RG 94, War Records Office, Army of the Potomac. *O.R.*, I, xlvi, part 2, 228. "This is the way the Rebels report the position of the Gunboats. The following message was intercepted at 10-30 a m. 'Col B & A. B. The heavy firing heard last night was all except a few guns from Battery F in stewarts front on Terrys front at our left a good deal of picket firing towards the James. afterwards a gunboat near Dutch Gap opened & was answered by our batteries at Howlett's & Bishop's. The firing was brought on by an attempt of Terry on our left on saturday last to advance his picket line. 'From C.—~~to~~ no change on hand or noticed sgd Sergt R. at C—' '" Telegram received, DNA, RG 108, Letters Received. *O.R.*, I, xlvi, part 2, 229. At 10:00 A.M. and 10:55 A.M., Gibbon telegraphed to USG messages which USG transmitted to his corps commanders. "The following dispatch just received from Gen'l Ferrero, our shots strike the grounded boats every time, but they seem to shed them, They appear to be aground bow up stream easy range but we have not metal enough. If the Navy would ~~join~~ give us a lift we can destroy them all, one is blown up, one is disabled and two others aground. The Onandago just below the pontoon bridge." Telegrams received (2), DNA, RG 107, Telegrams Collected (Unbound); *ibid.*, RG 393, 9th Army Corps, Telegrams Received; copies, *ibid.*, 2nd Army Corps, Telegrams Received; Meade Collection, PHi. *O.R.*, I, xlvi, part 2, 228. "The signal towr report one of the rebel rams coming down the river to meet the Onondago which is on its way up" ALS (telegram sent), DNA, RG 107, Telegrams Collected (Unbound); telegrams received (4), *ibid.*, RG 108, Letters Received; copies, *ibid.*, RG 393, 5th Army Corps, 3rd Div., 3rd Brigade, Telegrams Received; Meade Papers, PHi. *O.R.*, I, xlvi, part 2, 235. On the same day, USG twice telegraphed to Gibbon. "I will send an Engineer officer this morning to obstruct the channel in the river. If the point for obstructions is fixed below Dutch Gap place batteries to command the river at the point selected." "I sent a dispatch to Capt. Parker before receiving yours asking him to go up with his Monitor and finish up the ~~job~~ Rebel Navy. I also send your dispatch to him as a further encouragement." ALS (telegrams sent), OClWHi; telegrams received, Ord Papers, CU-B. *O.R.*, I, xlvi, part 2, 234, 236.

Also on Jan. 24, Lt. Col. Edward W. Smith, adjt. for Gibbon, twice telegraphed to USG. "Officer reports from Dutch Gap that one monitor and two Gunboats have come up the River and are shelling the rebel Gunboats. The latter reply slowly,   One of ~~rebel~~ Gunboats is slowly moving up the River, has not yet come round the bend. Genl Gibbon has gone to the river"   "Genl Ferrero reports 12 10 P M that the rebel Gunboats which were aground have got off and are under the lea of Trents Reach"   Telegrams received (at noon and 12:20 P.M.), DNA, RG 108, Letters Received. *O.R.*, I, xlvi, part 2, 235. The second is printed as sent at 12:45 P.M.

On the same day, USG telegraphed to Gibbon. "Please ask Capt, Parker of the Navy why it is not practicable for him to place torpedoes where the rebel Gunboats pass the obstructions? and why it is not practicable for him to attack, when they pass with but two boats as was the case this evening? There ought to be quite a fleet of Gunboats at the front"   Copies, DLC-USG, V, 46, 72, 108; DNA, RG 108, Letters Sent. *O.R.*, I, xlvi, part 2, 237. At 4:55 P.M., Gibbon telegraphed to USG. "I do not hear from Capt. Parker and do not know whether he intends to place torpedos or not. I have heard nothing of the officer and barges sent up by you, and have myself made no other arrangement than to prepare to throw some vessels into the bridge draw, which from the depth of water can be of but little service. A movement is reported as taking place on our right for which we are all prepared"   ALS (telegram sent), DNA, RG 107, Telegrams Collected (Unbound); telegram received (at 5:00 P.M.), *ibid.*, RG 108, Letters Received. *O.R.*, I, xlvi, part 2, 237.

To Maj. Gen. John Gibbon

> By Telegraph from City Pt.
> Dated Jan 24 *1864.*[5]

To MAJ GEN GIBBON

The obstructions in the river will be laid tonight where they were before. I will send you immediately two, one hundred pound Parrotts to cover the obstructions.[1] They are now afloat. Where will you have them landed? Lest you should have no officer to superinted planting them I send an officer up with the guns to attend to it. You can send him back with the boat if you do not require him.

U. S. GRANT.
Lt Genl.

Telegram received, Ord Papers, CU-B; copies, DLC-USG, V, 46, 72, 108; DNA, RG 108, Letters Sent. *O.R.*, I, xlvi, part 2, 237. On Jan. 24, 1865, 5:05 P.M., Maj. Gen. John Gibbon telegraphed to USG. "There is no place on this side the river where guns can be placed to command the obstructions. One might go to Fort Brady to replace one disabled today and the other at the Crow-nest battery, but it will be a work of some days to get them into position. In both cases they would be landed at Varina, and I would recommend they be placed in position there first to aid in defence of the river at that point." ALS (telegram sent), DNA, RG 107, Telegrams Collected (Unbound); telegram received (at 5:10 P.M.), *ibid.*, RG 108, Letters Received. *O.R.*, I, xlvi, part 2, 237.

At 6:00 P.M., 8:00 P.M., 10:40 P.M., and 11:20 P.M., Gibbon telegraphed to USG. "I have barges already to chain together a fill up the draw in the bridge. It would be useless to sink them. Would it not be well to put these in position as soon as all the gun-boats are above. They could not then fall below the bridge. The Onondago now lies only a short distance above Aikens instead of being close below the obstructions where she could take advantage of any delay the enemy meets with there" ALS (telegram sent), DNA, RG 107, Telegrams Collected (Unbound); telegram received (at 7:35 P.M.), *ibid.*, RG 108, Letters Received. *O.R.*, I, xlvi, part 2, 238. "Gen Ferrero reports that a small Tug seen near the wreck of the enemys Gunboat drifted to the obstructions was boarded by our men and towed to Shore. It was injured by the explosion was partially filled with water and contains four (4) torpedoes" Telegram received (no time recorded), DNA, RG 108, Letters Received. *O.R.*, I, xlvi, part 2, 238. "Four men from the enemy's gun boat have arrived here. The Drury was blown up The Fredericksburg & Virginia are both aground. One of these men says he is a deserter from the Virginia, that the Fredericksburg got thro' the obstructions. Com. Mitchell is in command" "Genl. Kautz's scouting parties report that the Charles City road is strongly picketed, and there are extensive ~~biviae~~ bivoac fires in the vacinity of Whites Tavern This force is too far out to intend to attack us, and I think is there for the purpose of being on hand in case the rams should succeed in getting thro'. I therefore think the rams will make another attempt. I have ordered Genl Kautz to make a reconnoissance early in the morning, and if I find the enemy moves far enough down the Charles City road will move out a force to attack him" ALS (telegrams sent), DNA, RG 107, Telegrams Collected (Unbound); telegrams received, *ibid.*, RG 108, Letters Received. *O.R.*, I, xlvi, part 2, 236, 238–39. On Jan. 25, 9:30 A.M., Gibbon telegraphed to USG. "Genl. Kautz reports this morning that his scouting parties have been to Whites tavern, report the enemy's pickets in their usual place and no evidence of any force being there. He expresses the opinion that his former report was exagerated. He has other parties out & I expect to hear further from him. I have most of the 24th Corps ready to move out if it becomes favorable to do so" ALS (telegram sent), DNA, RG 107, Telegrams Collected (Bound); telegram received (at 10:55 A.M.), *ibid.*, RG 108, Letters Received. *O.R.*, I, xlvi, part 2, 259–60.

On Jan. 24, Lt. Col. Frederick T. Dent wrote to Gibbon. "Lt, Genl, Grant desires me to say to you that we have parties now endeavoring to place obstructions where the old ones were, that Gunboats and others will have to pass frequently during the night, the draw you propose to obstruct he therefore does not wish you to close it, unless you are well assured that the Reb. Rams have passed the old obstructions and are really coming down, he further desires me to say to you that he wishes you to urge upon Capt, Parker how important it is that his Monitor should be up close to, or even at the old line of obstructions and entreat him to so place the Onondaga that in the event of an attempt of the rams to come down he may engage them while they are in the act of passing these obstructions," Copies, DLC-USG, V, 46, 72, 108; DNA, RG 108, Letters Sent. *O.R.*, I, xlvi, part 2, 238.

1. On Jan. 24, Lt. Col. Ely S. Parker wrote to commanding officer, siege train, Broadway Landing. "Will send to City Point two (2) one hundred p'd'r, guns and men to work them   If he has ~~not~~ 4 one hundred pdrs, he will send them, and the men,   If he has not the men he will send report by bearer," Copies, DLC-USG, V, 46, 72, 108; DNA, RG 108, Letters Sent. See *O.R.*, I, xlvi, part 2, 230–31, for plans, later changed, to place the guns at City Point. On the same day, Bvt. Brig. Gen. Henry L. Abbot wrote and telegraphed to Brig. Gen. John A. Rawlins reporting his arrival at Broadway Landing from Fort Fisher with his siege train, also requesting a telegraph operator. *Ibid.*, pp. 241–42. See *ibid.*, p. 229. On Jan. 25, USG telegraphed to Maj. Gen. John G. Parke. "Please direct Mr Caldwell to establish a Telegraph office at Broadway Landing & put an operator there" Telegram received (at 8:00 P.M.), DNA, RG 393, Army of the Potomac, Miscellaneous Letters Received; copies, *ibid.*, RG 108, Letters Sent; DLC-USG, V, 46, 72, 108. See *O.R.*, I, xlvi, part 2, 260.

To Commander William A. Parker

City Point, Va, Jan.y 24th 1865

CAPT. PARKER, NAVY. CARE GEN. GIBBON.

What fleet have you collected or ordered to the front? You ought to have every gunboat you can get in the river up with you. Should the enemy attempt to come down the river it is your duty, in view of the large amount of stores here, to attack with all the vessels you have, using your vessels as rams as well as batteries, even at the expense of half the boats you have got. I will send vessels up the river under an Engineer officer who will place them in position for sinking to obstruct the Channel.

U. S. GRANT
Lt. Gen.

ALS, OClWHi. *O.R.*, I, xlvi, part 2, 224; *O.R.* (Navy), I, xi, 636. On Jan. 24, 1865, Commander William A. Parker, Jones' Landing, telegraphed to USG. "Despatch received—I am on my way to engage the rebel rams" ALS (telegram sent—undated), DNA, RG 107, Telegrams Collected (Unbound); telegram received, *ibid.*, RG 108, Letters Received. *O.R.*, I, xlvi, part 2, 225.

At 6:45 A.M., Lt. Col. Frederick T. Dent, "Onondago Upper Ponton Bridge," telegraphed to USG. "A picket officer is just in and reports, one of the Reb Rams passed below the obstructions at 4 oclock and has now gone back above them—" ALS (telegram sent), DNA, RG 107, Telegrams Collected (Unbound). *O.R.*, I, xlvi, part 2, 239. On the same day, Bvt. Maj. Gen. Edward Ferrero telegraphed to Dent. "The Rebel Boat was blown up by a Percussion Shell from Battery 'Parsons—There are two more Gun Boats below Howletts aground—Am firing at them now—" Telegram received, DNA, RG 107, Telegrams Collected (Unbound). On the same day, Ferrero telegraphed to Brig. Gen. John A. Raw-lins. " 'Glorious—' We have blown up one Ram disabled a small gunboat & have two (2) Rams aground & we are hitting them every shot. I am determined to blow them all out of water & feel confident to succeed—" Telegram received, *ibid.*, RG 108, Letters Received. *O.R.*, I, xlvi, part 2, 247. At 9:20 A.M., Dent, Jones' Landing, telegraphed to USG. "Ferrero telegraphs me that one rebel boat is blown up, one disabled, and two others aground. The Hunchback has gone up, and I have just seen Captain Parker. His iron-clad is disabled in her propeller, but at his request I have given him two tugs to tow him up. Ferrero says, with the assistance of the navy, he can destroy the whole fleet. I think things are working well now, and we stand a better chance of sinking or destroying all their boats than they have of even getting this far down the river." *Ibid.*, p. 239. On the same day, USG telegraphed to Dent. "If the Rebel gunboats are aground Capt. Parker should run up close to them with his Monitor and disable them. See if he will not do it." ALS (telegram sent), OClWHi; copies, DLC-USG, V, 46, 72, 108; DNA, RG 108, Letters Sent. *O.R.*, I, xlvi, part 2, 239. On the same day, Dent twice telegraphed to Ferrero. "How goes the fight three naval boats went up to your assistance" "All the naval boats have gone up to your assistance —give it to them from your battery" ALS (telegrams sent), DNA, RG 107, Telegrams Collected (Unbound). On the same day, Dent telegraphed three times to USG. "General Gibbon has given orders to have barges ready to fill the gap in the unfinished pile bridge and they are collecting them fast will not be sunk unless necessary—~~it is just reported that the reb~~" "The Onondago double tur-reted monitor is now on its way up towed by two tugs— . . . Fort Brady has opened I think some of their boats are trying to go back up the river" "I have just received the following from Gen Ferero 'The two boats that were aground have ~~moved~~ got off & moved under shelter of Trent Reach one disabled—I sunk two boats and disabled one the best I could do' " ALS (telegrams sent), *ibid.* The last is in *O.R.*, I, xlvi, part 2, 240.

To Commander William A. Parker

City Point, Va. Jan. 24th 1865

CAPT. PARKER, COMD.G NAVAL FLOTILLA JAMES RIVER,
VIA JONES LANDING.[1]

Please inform me what vessels you have at the front. At this juncture of affairs all the vessels you can controll should be got immediately to the front, or at least above the large amount of pub-lic stores accumulated for the subsistence of the Army and Navy. The delay of the last few days in preparing for a visit from the enemy, which I found on my return to this place yesterday had been expected, was providentially prevented from proving fatal to

us. It would be better to obstruct the channel of the river with
sunken Gunboats than that a rebel ram should reach City Point.

U. S. GRANT
Lt. Gn.

ALS, OClWHi. *O.R.*, I, xlvi, part 2, 225; *O.R.* (Navy), I, xi, 636. On Jan. 24,
1865, Commander William A. Parker twice telegraphed to USG, first from
Jones' Landing. "Your despatch of the 24th inst recd. The Names of the Vessels
at the front are as follows. Onodndaga—Massasoit—and Hunchback. below
Dutch Gap. Commodore Morris—at Turkey Bend. Eutaw at Deep Bottom, Daylight, New Market Road, Miami City Point. Genl Putnam, and Commo Barney—
at the Appomattox River—Several others are at the Norfolk Navy Yard under-
going repairs and expected to return in a few days. I will Endavor to get still
more vessels to the front as you request," Telegram received, DNA, RG 108,
Letters Received; copy (marked as sent from Aiken's Landing), *ibid.*, RG 94,
War Records Office, Army of the Potomac. *O.R.*, I, xlvi, part 2, 225; *O.R.*
(Navy), I, xi, 636. "I have to report that I have been relieved from the Com-
mand of the James River Division I will be at City Point tomorrow morning"
Telegram received (on Jan. 25, 10:15 A.M.), DNA, RG 108, Letters Received.
O.R., I, xlvi, part 2, 225; *O.R.* (Navy), I, xi, 638.

1. Three words not in USG's hand.

To Commanding Officer, Atlanta

City Point Jany 24th 1865

COMDG OFFICER
G. B. ATLANTIC
SIR

If it is possible for you to get over the bar at Harrisons Landing, please run up the river to the extrime point now occupied by
our Gunboats I enclose you copy of a dispatch from the Hon, Secy
of the Navy

The importance of having your vessel above is so great that I
request you will make the effort to cross the bar at the expense of
grounding your vessel Lest you may not have a good pilot for the
upper river I send one with the Steamer carrying this,

Very Respectfully
Your obt svt
U. S. GRANT
Lieut. Genl,

Copies, DLC-USG, V, 46, 72, 108; DNA, RG 108, Letters Sent. *O.R.*, I, xlvi, part 2, 226; *O.R.* (Navy), I, xi, 640. USG enclosed a copy of a telegram of Jan. 24, 1865, from Secretary of the Navy Gideon Welles to Capt. John M. Berrien, Norfolk, asking him to send all ironclads within his reach up James River. USG endorsed the telegram received. "Forward above to Capt Parker on Onondaga via Jones Landing." AES, DNA, RG 108, Letters Received. *O.R.*, I, xlvi, part 2, 226.

On Jan. 24, USG telegraphed to Berrien. "Please inform me what Iron Clads you can send up the River & how soon the first will start   They should run night and day until they reach their destination" Telegram received, DNA, RG 94, War Records Office, Army of the Potomac; copies, *ibid.*, RG 108, Letters Sent; DLC-USG, V, 46, 72, 108. *O.R.*, I, xlvi, part 2, 226; *O.R.* (Navy), I, xi, 639. On the same day, Berrien telegraphed to USG. "Telegram recd. The Atlanta will be sent at once & the Iron-sides will follow. Dictator not available" Telegram received, DNA, RG 108, Letters Received. *O.R.*, I, xlvi, part 2, 226; *O.R.* (Navy), I, xi, 639.

To Reuben E. Fenton

City Point, Va. Jan.y 24th *1864*5.

HIS EXCELLENCY R. E. FENTON
GOVERNOR OF NEW YORK,
SIR:

I am just in receipt of your letter of the 18th inst. enclosing to me the very complimentary resolutions passed by the two houses of your State Legislature, to the Armies which I have the honor to command. For the officers, and Armies, named in the resolutions, I return to the Legislature of the "Empire State," through you, theirs, and my, most hearty thanks for this greatful, though unexpected, mark of their confidence.

I am Governor, with great respect,
your obt. svt.
U. S. GRANT
Lt. Gen. U. S. A.

ALS, Madigan Collection, NN. On Jan. 18, 1865, Governor Reuben E. Fenton of N. Y. wrote to USG. "In compliance with the request made in Joint Resolutions passed by the Senate and Assembly of the State of New York, commendatory of the conduct and services of certain Officers in the Army and Navy of the United States, I take great pleasure in forwarding to you the enclosed Resolution referring to yourself and the brave officers and men composing the Armies of the Potomac and the James. I most sincerely join in the expression of thanks for these distinguished services, and with the loyal people of the nation, acknowledge my deep and heartfelt gratitude." LS, USG 3. A copy of the resolution is *ibid.*

To Elihu B. Washburne

City Point, Va Jan.y 24th *1865*.

HON. E. B. WASHBURN
DEAR SIR:

Your letter announcing the completion of the Medal was duly received and not answered because I expected to be in Washington about as early as a letter would get there. I did go but not as early by a day or two as I expected and then was in such haste that I saw no one out of the War, and my own, office. I can hardly say when I will be up again. Not for a week or two probably. I do not want the Medal here where there would be such danger of loosing it. You can therefore keep it where you deem best until I am ready to take charge of it.

Mrs. Grant is under many obligations to you for your kind offices in writing for the girl that used to live with her. She may be sent to Burlington N. J. We have had quite an exciting time here since 3 a. m. to-day. The heavy freshet we have been having the last few days has washed away some of our obstructions in the James. About that hour four of the enemy gunboats started down the river and one or two of them actually passed the obstructions. Providence seemed to be on our side. Our Navy certainly was not. Notwithst[an]ding several days notice had been given not a single pr[e]paration seemed to have been made to receive such a visit. Fortunately however two of the enemy's boats grounded near the Howlett House and those that had passed down turned back. Two of the enemy's boats were sunk and one disabled. The two aground were well pummeled for several hours and must both of them been injured though the report I get is: two sunk, one disabled. This was all done from land batteries. The Naval force left here is not adequate to the work with the obstructions removed. I hope however to have all right. We have all b[een] very busy since 5 a. [m.] and will ha[ve] all right before there is any letup.

U. S. GRANT

ALS, IHi.
On Dec. 9, 1864, U.S. Representative Elihu B. Washburne of Ill. tele-

graphed to USG. "Maj Genl. Jack Logan and myself leave for City-Point this afternoon in the Steamer Dictater   The medal not yet finished." ALS (telegram sent), DNA, RG 107, Telegrams Collected (Unbound). See Lincoln, *Works*, VIII, 105.

On Dec. 30, Secretary of War Edwin M. Stanton wrote to USG. "I transmit herewith a copy of the Joint Resolution of thanks to you when a Major General of the Army, passed by the Senate and House of Representatives, and approved by the President December 17, 1863. The Gold Medal voted you in the same Resolution would be presented at the same time if its preparation had been committed to the charge of the Department" LS (facsimile), [William H. Allen], *American Civil War Book and Grant Album . . .* (Boston and New York, 1894), p. [189]. *O.R.*, I, xlii, part 3, 1100.

On Feb. 1, 1865, Washburne telegraphed to USG. "Meade confirmed by a heavy vote. Please telegraph me when you will be here. I may have to go to Nor-folk on a committee of investigation, but do not want to leave till you come. ~~here~~" ALS (telegram sent), DNA, RG 107, Telegrams Collected (Unbound). An undated telegram, 10:30 A.M., from USG to Washburne was probably sent the same day. "Your dispatch received. It is impossible for me to say when I can go to Washington. Will ask Genl. Halleck or the Sec. of War to inform you in advance when I do go." Copy, *ibid.*, Telegrams Received in Cipher. On Feb. 6, Washburne telegraphed to USG. "I want to go to Norfolk and other places in vicinity, the last of this week, to investigate for Congress the question of trade with rebel States. If you are to be here, however, at that time, I will delay going, as I want to see you to present medal and also about that Galena matter. Please answer by telegraph" ALS (telegram sent), *ibid.*, Telegrams Collected (Unbound). On the same day, USG telegraphed to Washburne. "I expect to be here all this week" Telegram received (at 4:50 P.M.), DLC-Elihu B. Washburne; (press) DNA, RG 107, Telegrams Collected (Bound). On Feb. 10, 3:45 [P.M.], Stanton telegraphed to Washburne. "General & Mrs Grant are at Willards" ALS (telegram sent), *ibid.*; telegram received, DLC-Elihu B. Washburne. See speech, [*March 11, 1865*].

To Edwin M. Stanton

(Cipher)   City Point, Va, Jan.y 25th 1865 [*11:30* A.M.]
HON. E. M. STANTON, SEC. OF WAR, WASHINGTON

Present danger from the Rebel Navy in James River is at an end and I will take care that there shall be none in future. With a proper Naval commander, and the fleet there is at his disposal there should have been no cause for apprehension.—During the night the rebel gunboats run back up the river and were shelled from our batteries. One of them seemed very much disabled. Gen. Ferrero reports that one was blown up and one sunk. We know one was blown up by a shot from Battery Parsons but I am not entirely satisfied that another was sunk though it may be so.

U. S. GRANT

Lt. Gn

ALS (telegram sent), CSmH; telegram received (at 12:15 P.M.), DNA, RG 107, Telegrams Collected (Bound). *O.R.*, I, xlvi, part 2, 253.

On Jan. 25, 1865, Commodore William Radford, U.S.S. *New Ironsides*, telegraphed to USG. "I am underway and coming up the James River rapidly." LS (telegram sent), DNA, RG 107, Telegrams Collected (Bound); telegram received (at 1:30 P.M.), *ibid.*, RG 108, Letters Received. *O.R.*, I, xlvi, part 2, 256. On the same day, Lt. Commander Homer C. Blake, U.S.S. *Onondaga*, telegraphed and signaled to USG. "I have assumed, temporarily, command of the Division. As soon as the Tug is ready I am going up with the Onondaga, to meet the Rebel Ram at the Obstructions" Telegram received (at 1:00 P.M.), DNA, RG 45, Area File. "I have command of the Onondaga pro-tempore." Signal received (at 10:15 P.M.), *ibid.* On the same day, USG telegraphed to Blake. "I will send officers to-night to complete the obstructions in the river. Please give them assistance and protection from the Navy." ALS (telegram sent), OClWHi; copies, DLC-USG, V, 46, 72, 108; DNA, RG 108, Letters Sent. *O.R.*, I, xlvi, part 2, 256; *O.R.* (Navy), I, xi, 641. At 11:45 P.M., 2nd Lt. John W. French, Crow's Nest Tower, signaled to Brig. Gen. John A. Rawlins. "The schooners are properly sunk in the reach." ALS (signal sent), DNA, RG 107, Telegrams Collected (Unbound).

On Jan. 26, 4:25 [P.M.], Lt. Col. Frederick T. Dent, "General Ferero's Head Quarters," telegraphed to USG. "I have been to the Battery Parsons—the Reb Rams are at the ancorage line far above where the Reb flag of truce boat lands, all is quiet at the obstruction no reb boats anywhere about the naval vessels are at ~~ancor~~ anchor below the point below the obstructions—one 100 pounder will be in possition in Battery Spofford just in the ravine below the obstructions before night" ALS (telegram sent), *ibid.*

To Edwin M. Stanton

———

(Cipher)   City Point, Va, Jan. 25th 18645. [9:00 P.M.]
HON. E. M. STANTON, SEC. OF WAR, WASHINGTON.

If an order is published allowing prisoners in our hands to purchase food and clothing when they have the means of paying for them, a similar order will be made in favor of our men held in the south. I would respectfully recommend that such an order be made to take effect on the 1st Proximo and that a copy be telegraphed here to be sent through the lines so that we can get the benefit of it for our men at once.

> U. S. GRANT
> Lt. Gn

ALS (telegram sent), The Scriptorium, Beverly Hills, Calif.; telegram received (at 11:00 P.M.), DNA, RG 107, Telegrams Collected (Bound). *O.R.*, I, xlvi, part 2, 253–54.

To Maj. Gen. Henry W. Halleck

(Cipher)   City Point, Va, Jan.y 25th 1865 [*11:30* A.M.]
MAJ. GEN. HALLECK, WASHINGTON

I will leave here at 10 a. m. to-morrow for Cape Fear River and Hampton Roads in the evening. I go from Hampton on the "Rhode Island." I would like Gen. Schofield to go down with me but if he deems his presence with his troops necessary he need not go. How soon will the First Division get off?

> U. S. GRANT
> Lt. Gen.

ALS (telegram sent), OClWHi; telegram received (marked as sent at 11:00 A.M., received at 1:00 P.M.), DNA, RG 107, Telegrams Collected (Bound). *O.R.*, I, xlvi, part 2, 254. On Jan. 25, 1865, 10:45 A.M., Maj. Gen. Henry W. Halleck telegraphed to USG. "Genl Schofield has just arrived. Shall he go to Fort Monroe to join you, or shall he wait to accompany his first transports." ALS (telegram sent), DNA, RG 107, Telegrams Collected (Bound); telegram received, *ibid.*; *ibid.*, RG 108, Letters Received. *O.R.*, I, xlvi, part 2, 254.

On Jan. 24, 8:30 P.M., Halleck had telegraphed to USG. "Col Wise telegraphs from [N]ew York that ocean transports for Sixteen thousand men will be here by the end of this week" ALS (telegram sent), DNA, RG 107, Telegrams Collected (Bound); telegram received, *ibid.*; *ibid.*, RG 108, Letters Received. *O.R.*, I, xlvi, part 2, 220.

To Maj. Gen. Henry W. Halleck

City Point, Va, Jan.y 25th *18645*. [*11:30* A.M.]
MAJ. GEN. HALLECK, WASHINGTON,

When Canby is supplied, horses may be sent up the Tennessee as Gen. Thomas requests, and let him use all exertions to get off

during the first favorable weather we may have. It is a great pity
that our Cavalry could not have taken advantage of Hood & Forrest's forces being on furlough. They would have been in a country
where they could have fed off the enemy and where they could have
collected their own horses.

U. S. GRANT

Lt. Gen.

ALS (telegram sent), OClWHi; telegram received (at 3:00 P.M.), DNA, RG
107, Telegrams Collected (Bound). *O.R.*, I, xlix, part 1, 581. On Jan. 25, 1865,
10:30 P.M., Maj. Gen. Henry W. Halleck telegraphed to USG. "After reading
Genl Thomas' telegram of 7.30 last evening, please give me your instructions
before going south, if you wish to send troops to the Gulf, in order that I may
order transports. After conversing with Genl Schofield, I am satisfied that no
movement will be made from the Tennessee this winter." ALS (telegram sent),
DNA, RG 107, Telegrams Collected (Bound); telegram received, *ibid.*; *ibid.*,
RG 108, Letters Received. *O.R.*, I, xlix, part 1, 581. See *ibid.*, I, xlv, part 2,
627–28. On Jan. 26, 9:00 A.M., USG telegraphed to Halleck. "You may order
Gen. Thomas to send Smith's command to eCanby with all dispatch. I do not
think however it will do for Thomas to strip himself of Cavalry as close as he
proposes. If he will send one Division of three or four thousand it will be sufficient." ALS (telegram sent), OClWHi; telegram received (at 10:00 A.M.), DNA,
RG 107, Telegrams Collected (Bound). *O.R.*, I, xlix, part 1, 584.

On Feb. 8, 9:30 P.M., USG telegraphed to Halleck. "I think it will be well
to give A. J. Smith's Command a Corps organization. I would suggest for it the
12th Corps, or 26th as you think best." ALS (telegram sent), OClWHi; copies,
DLC-USG, V, 46, 73, 108; (marked as received at 10:20 P.M.) DNA, RG 107,
Telegrams Received in Cipher; *ibid.*, RG 108, Letters Sent. *O.R.*, I, xlix, part
1, 668.

To Maj. Gen. Henry W. Halleck

(Cipher)   City Point, Va, Jan.y 25th *18645*. [*2:00* P.M.]
MAJ. GN. HALLECK, WASHINGTON,

Please inform me if an Ordnance officer has been ordered from
Washington to Fort Fisher. If there has been none ordered I will
have to take one from here. An officer going should be provided
with a Gin and Sling Cart and all the appliances for handling
heavy guns. A regiment of Heavy Artillery ought to be sent to the

Cape Fear River to garrison the Forts. Please inform me if one can
be sent from Washington.

U. S. GRANT

Lt. Gen.

ALS (telegram sent), OClWHi; telegram received (at 5:00 P.M.), DNA, RG
107, Telegrams Collected (Bound). *O.R.*, I, xlvi, part 2, 254. On Jan. 25, 1865,
9:00 P.M., Maj. Gen. Henry W. Halleck telegraphed to USG. "Ordnance officer
ordered to-day to Fort Fisher. Gin &c will be sent by first transports. ~~Will~~ To
send an artillery regt from here will leave a part of our line without any garrisons. Abbotts regt. is heavy artillery. Will send another, if you so direct. Schofield
cannot reach Fort Monroe in time to join you. No transports have yet reached
Alexandria, but ar[e] hourly expected. Those at Baltimore are frozen in." ALS
(telegram sent), DNA, RG 107, Telegrams Collected (Bound); telegram received, *ibid.*; *ibid.*, RG 108, Letters Received. *O.R.*, I, xlvi, part 2, 254. See
telegram to Maj. Gen. Henry W. Halleck, Jan. 25, 1865, 10:30 P.M.

To Maj. Gen. Henry W. Halleck

———

City Point Va

9 30 P M Jany 25 1865

MAJ GEN H W HALLECK

CHF OF STAFF

Genl Reynolds dispatch of the 14th is received.[1]

It corresponds with what was my own views, but is very far at
variance from those expressed by Steele and others, whose statements were submitted some time since.

It will be well to get from Genl Reynolds his views of the line
that should be taken up and held next spring. His views will be
given entirely independent of what may be said by speculators, and
others interested in having this and that place occupied by troops

U S GRANT

Lt Genl

Telegram received (at 11:00 P.M.), DNA, RG 107, Telegrams Collected
(Bound); copies, *ibid.*, Telegrams Received in Cipher; *ibid.*, RG 108, Letters
Sent; DLC-USG, V, 46, 72, 108. *O.R.*, I, xlviii, part 1, 638. See *ibid.*, p. 649. On
Feb. 14, 1865, 7:00 P.M., USG telegraphed to Maj. Gen. Henry W. Halleck.
"If Gen, Reynolds has not already been authorized to change the Garrisons of
his Dept, as suggested in his dispatch of the 8th inst, it will be well to notify him

to carry out his own suggestions, as soon as he can," Copies, DLC-USG, V, 46, 73, 108; (marked as received at 7:10 P.M.) DNA, RG 107, Telegrams Received in Cipher; *ibid.*, RG 108, Letters Sent. *O.R.*, I, xlviii, part 1, 845. See *ibid.*, p. 776.

1. See *ibid.*, p. 515.

To Maj. Gen. Henry W. Halleck

(Cipher)   City Point, Va, Jan.y 25th 1865 [*10:30* P.M.]
MAJ. GEN. HALLECK, WASHINGTON,

I do not want to draw any troops from Washington that cannot be well spared. I will garrison the Forts on Cape Fear with Heavy Artillerists from here.

I will not leave Hampton roads until Friday[1] mornings. It is probable that Asst. Sec. of the Navy will accompany me. If so Schofield can leave Washingto[n] with him to-morrow evening. Answer if I shall wait for them.

U. S. GRANT
Lt. Gn.

ALS (telegram sent), PPRF; telegram received (at 11:00 P.M.), DNA, RG 107, Telegrams Collected (Bound). *O.R.*, I, xlvi, part 2, 255.

1. Jan. 27, 1865.

To Maj. Gen. John Gibbon

City Point, Va, Jan.y 25th 1865
MAJ. GN. GIBBON,

Five One hundred pound Parrott guns were sent last night to be planted on the south side of the river at places previously prepared for them. Gen. Abbott had the matter in charge. There is one more of these guns here which Gen. Abbott will be directed to send to Fort Brady.

If the enemy have not yet left your right I think it will be well to attack them.

U. S. GRANT
Lt. Gn.

ALS (telegram sent), OClWHi; telegram received (at 10:40 A.M.), Ord Papers, CU-B. *O.R.*, I, xlvi, part 2, 259. On Jan. 25, 1865, 10:30 A.M., Maj. Gen. John Gibbon telegraphed to Brig. Gen. John A. Rawlins. "Please state whether the 2 one hundred pounders mentioned by Gen Grant yesterday were sent, one of them is required to replace a ~~one~~ gun disabled yesterday in Fort Brady" ALS (telegram sent), DNA, RG 107, Telegrams Collected (Unbound); telegram received (at 10:15 A.M.), *ibid.*, RG 108, Letters Received. *O.R.*, I, xlvi, part 2, 259.

At 9:50 A.M., Maj. Gen. John G. Parke had telegraphed to Rawlins. "Can you give us any information about the heavy firing last night or the gun-boats?" *Ibid.*, p. 255. Rawlins replied: "We cannot." *Ibid.* At 10:20 A.M., Gibbon telegraphed to USG. "The enemy's gun-boats ran past Fort Brady about 3 a. m. and passed up the river. One is reported as a good deal crippled. Five vessels are reported to have gone up" ALS (telegram sent), DNA, RG 107, Telegrams Collected (Unbound); telegram received, *ibid.*, RG 108, Letters Received. *O.R.*, I, xlvi, part 2, 255. Rawlins drafted a telegram to Parke at the foot of the telegram received. "The above dispach explains the heavy firing this morning" ADfS, DNA, RG 108, Letters Received; telegram received, *ibid.*, RG 393, 9th Army Corps, Telegrams Received. *O.R.*, I, xlvi, part 2, 255. The telegram was transmitted to all corps commanders.

At 9:30 P.M., USG telegraphed to Gibbon. "In placing torpedoes in the river, place none above Cox Landing at present," Copies, DLC-USG, V, 46, 72, 108; DNA, RG 108, Letters Sent. *O.R.*, I, xlvi, part 2, 260. At 10:30 P.M., Gibbon telegraphed to USG. "Your cipher despatch is received. ~~The matter~~ Nothing has yet been done in the matter, and it will be arranged as you direct" ALS (telegram sent), DNA, RG 107, Telegrams Collected (Unbound); telegram received (marked as sent at 10:00 P.M., received at 10:30 P.M.), *ibid.*, RG 108, Letters Received. Printed as sent at 10:00 P.M. in *O.R.*, I, xlvi, part 2, 260.

To Maj. Gen. Edward O. C. Ord

(Cipher)   City Point, Va, Jan. 25th 1865 [*3:00* P.M.]
MAJ. GN. ORD, FT. MONROE, VA,

I shall leave here to-morrow to be absent several days. I wish you to return to your Hd Qrs, in the field so that in case of necessity you will be on hand to take charge of Armies operating from here. It will answer if you start up in the morning.

U. S. GRANT

Lt. Gn.

ALS (telegram sent), OClWHi; telegram received, Ord Papers, CU-B. *O.R.*, I, xlvi, part 2, 259.

To Maj. Gen. Henry W. Halleck

———

(Cipher)   City Point, Va, Jan.y 26th *18645*. [*1:00* P.M.]
MAJ. GEN. HALLECK, WASHINGTON,

Gen. Terry applies for a Paymaster to Pay off the staff officers of his command.[1] They have to purchase everything and many of them are without means. Gen. Tower[2] is wanted for the command of Norfolk. It will not require so much activity as intelligence and integrity. If Tower cannot be spared we can do very well here.[3]

U. S. GRANT

Lt. Gn

ALS (telegram sent), OClWHi; telegram received (at 1:30 P.M.), DNA, RG 107, Telegrams Collected (Bound). *O.R.*, I, xlvi, part 2, 267. On Jan. 26, 1865, noon, Maj. Gen. Henry W. Halleck had telegraphed to USG. "Asst Secty Fox & Genl Schofield will leave at 3 P. M. via Annapolis to join you at Fort Monroe. I asked Genl Thomas if he could spare Genl Tower but he has not answered. I doubt if he is able to do any active duty" ALS (telegram sent—misdated Jan. 25), DNA, RG 107, Telegrams Collected (Bound); telegram received, *ibid.*; *ibid.*, RG 108, Letters Received. *O.R.*, I, xlvi, part 2, 267.

1. On Jan. 28, Paymaster Amos Binney, Norfolk, telegraphed to USG. "A Paymaster with twenty thousand dollars leaves for Fort Fisher direct this morning—" ALS (telegram sent), DNA, RG 107, Telegrams Collected (Unbound).

2. Zealous B. Tower, born in 1819 in Cohasset, Mass., USMA 1841, served in the Corps of Engineers and in the Mexican War, and was appointed brig. gen. as of Nov. 23, 1861. So severely wounded at the second battle of Bull Run that he was disabled for nearly two years, he served as chief engineer of the defenses of Nashville from Sept., 1864, through the close of the war. On May 20, 1865, USG wrote to Secretary of War Edwin M. Stanton. "I would respectfully recommend the appointment, by brevet, of Brig. Gn. Z. B. Tower to the rank of Major Gen. of Vols. for past services. He has been recommended by Gen. Pope and Gen. Thomas both for full promotion, I understand, and as he was badly wounded in Gen. Pope's Campaign, thus being unable to take the field again, I would advise this recognition." ALS, *ibid.*, RG 94, ACP, 1537 ACP 1872. *O.R.*, I, xlix, part 2, 847.

3. See telegram to Maj. Gen. Edward O. C. Ord, Feb. 1, 1865.

To Maj. Gen. Winfield S. Hancock

City Point Jany 26th 1865

MAJ, GEN, W, S, HANCOCK
COMDG 1ST ARMY CORPS
GENERAL,

Lieut, Col, W. L. Duff Acting Inspector General on my Staff and from some time in 1862 up to my promotion to present grade, Chief of Artillery with me goes out of service, by limitation, on the 29th inst,   Knowing that he would like to remain in the Army I wrote to the Sec, of War without his (Duff's) knowledge recommending him for a Colonelcy in your Corps   If Col, Duff should get the appointment he can be of great service in raising troops in the State of Illinois where he is intimately acquainted, and has resided for many years,

I hope you will intercede to secure this appointment, so that Col, Duff can be, mustered in as Col, of the 1st Corps the day he is mustered out of the 2d Ill, Artillery

Very Respectfully
Your obt svt
U, S, GRANT
Lt, Genl,

Copies, DLC-USG, V, 46, 72, 108; DNA, RG 108, Letters Sent. On Jan. 24, 1865, USG wrote to Secretary of War Edwin M. Stanton. "I would respectfully recommend Lt, Col, W, L, Duff Act, Inspector Genl, on my Staff for the position of Col, in the new 1st Corps now being raised,   Col, Duff's term of service expires *now* within a few days leaving him within the rules established for Officering the new regiments,   He has served three years with the rank of Lieut, Colonel," Copies, *ibid.* See telegram to Brig. Gen. Lorenzo Thomas, Feb. 14, 1865.

To Maj. Gen. John G. Parke

City Point, Va. Jan 26th 1865

MAJ. GEN. PARKE, COMD.G A. P.

I shall leave here this evening to be absent several days. ~~Let none of the General officers~~   Give no leaves to Gen. Officers in my absence. I would prefer that Gen. Humphreys, who has a leave, should not avail him self of it at present.[1]

U. S. GRANT
Lt. Gn

ALS (telegram sent), OClWHi; telegram received (at 10:10 A.M.), DNA, RG 94, War Records Office, Army of the Potomac. *O.R.*, I, xlvi, part 2, 267. Also on Jan. 26, 1865, 7:00 P.M., USG telegraphed to Maj. Gen. John G. Parke. "I leave this evening to be absent for several days. In case of any active operations you will report to and receive orders from Gen. Ord." ALS (telegram sent), OClWHi; copies, DLC-USG, V, 46, 72, 108; DNA, RG 108, Letters Sent. On the same day, USG telegraphed to Maj. Gen. Edward O. C. Ord. "Maj Gen Parke has been notified of my intended absence & in case of active operations to report to you." Telegram received (at 7:00 P.M.), Ord Papers, CU-B; copies, DLC-USG, V, 46, 72, 108; DNA, RG 108, Letters Sent. *O.R.*, I, xlvi, part 2, 269.

On Jan. 27, Commodore Joseph Lanman, U.S.S. *Minnesota*, telegraphed to Secretary of the Navy Gideon Welles. "The Asst. Secy. of the Navy desired me to say that Lt. Genl. Grant and himself sailed by the Rhode Island at 10 A. M." LS (telegram sent), DNA, RG 45, Area File.

1. On Jan. 26, Lt. Col. Ely S. Parker twice telegraphed to Bvt. Brig. Gen. Henry L. Abbot, Broadway Landing, first revoking his leave, then reversing himself. Copies, DLC-USG, V, 46, 72, 108; DNA, RG 108, Letters Sent. *O.R.*, I, xlvi, part 2, 269.

To Brig. Gen. Innis N. Palmer

(Cipher)   City Point, Va, Jan. 26th 1865 [*10:30* A.M.]
BRIG. GEN. I. N. PALMER, NEW BERN N. C.

All asked for by you has been ordered. Not less than 6000 men will report to you. Prepare accordingly.

U. S. GRANT
Lt. Gen.

ALS (telegram sent), OClWHi; copies, DLC-USG, V, 46, 72, 108; DNA, RG 108, Letters Sent. *O.R.*, I, xlvi, part 2, 271.

On Jan. 20, 1865, Brig. Gen. Innis N. Palmer, Norfolk, telegraphed to Lt. Col. Theodore S. Bowers. "I have come from North Carolina for the purpose of seeing Gen Grant on important business. Is he at City Point? If not where can I communicate with him—I remain in Norfolk awaiting reply—" Telegram received, DNA, RG 107, Telegrams Collected (Unbound). On the same day, Lt. Col. Ely S. Parker telegraphed to Palmer. "Gen Grant will be in Washington tomorrow morning—Left here this P. M." ALS (telegram sent), *ibid.*; telegram received, *ibid.* On Jan. 21, USG, Washington, telegraphed to Palmer. "Wait at

Ft. Monroe until I get there. I will leave Annapolis at 5 a. m. to-morrow." ALS (telegram sent), *ibid.*, Telegrams Collected (Bound).

On Jan. 24, Palmer, Fort Monroe, wrote to USG. "I beg leave to call your attention to the following matters in relation to affairs in the *District of North Carolina.* General *Sherman*, who has recently assumed the command of the *Dept. of the South*, has been furnished by me with an account of all the troops, supplies of every kind, land and water transportation, Rail Road rolling stock, etc: etc:. In order to fully carry out the views of General Sherman it will be necessary to seize, and securely hold Kinston, and to complete the Rail Road from New Berne to that place. For this purpose I would require an additional force, temporarily, of say, 5000 men, and about 15 miles of rail road iron, and a few experienced rail road builders. I would request, also, to be furnished with a light draft steamer capable of carrying, say *800* men, or two companies of cavalry, or a battery of Artillery. There is no such steamer now in my District. The *'Escort'* is about the class of steamer needed, and she was under orders for New Berne when the change in the Department was made, when the order was countermanded. In order to clear out the Neuse River, and keep it open for small boats, I would require, temporarily, one or two light draft Army Gun Boats. My plan for seizing Kinston would be to cross the Neuse at a point some seven miles below the town, and for this I would require a Pontoon Bridge, say 200 yards long. I would call your attention to the fact that the rebels are pushing the work on the ram at *Edwards* Ferry, some fifty miles up the Roanoke River from Plymouth. I have sent a small expedition to endeavor to surprise, capture, and burn this ram, and I am hopeful, but not confident of success. The ram 'Albemarle', recently sunk by the Navy, is lying at the wharf at Plymouth, and she can easily be raised. If this is done she will be a match for anything the rebels can bring down. It is a matter of surprise to me that this has not been done before this. Unless we have something in the sounds to cope with the rebel rams, we must expect at no distant day to have some serious disaster, for one single ram, if properly managed can drive every one of our wooden vessels from the sSounds. It would require but little ingenuity to carry one of our iron clads or rams over the bar at Hatteras Inlet, and I cannot too strongly urge this matter upon your attention. If with all our iron-clads and rams we permit ourselves to be caught as we were at Plymouth last spring, it will be a lasting disgrace to us. I shall enclose for your information the last account of progress on the ram, from a deserter who came in here yesterday. I received similar accounts every few days, and they can be relied upon." LS, *ibid.*, RG 108, Letters Received; copy (dated Jan. 23), *ibid.*, RG 393, Dept. of Va. and N. C., Letters Sent. Dated Jan. 24 in *O.R.*, I, xlvi, part 2, 251–52. On the same day, USG wrote to Brig. Gen. Rufus Ingalls. "As rapidly as it can be sent, in addition to previous calls I want fifteen miles of R. R. iron sent from Norfolk or elsewhere to Beaufort N, C,   Men will also be required to lay the track from New Berne to Kinston,   The Steamer Escort or one of like draft and capacity will be wanted at Beaufort for permanent use"   Copies, DLC-USG, V, 46, 72, 108; DNA, RG 108, Letters Sent. *O.R.*, I, xlvii, part 2, 122. See *ibid.*, p. 279.

On Jan. 25 (via Fort Monroe, Jan. 26), Palmer, near Roanoke Island, N. C., telegraphed to USG. "Adml Porter has ordered all gun boats that can be spared from the sound to Newbern as he says that Nooke [*Hoke*] is going to attack that place. I do not know how the Admiral recieved the information. My scouts who are constantly out report nothing unusual in the direction of Kinston"   Telegram received, DNA, RG 108, Letters Received. *O.R.*, I, xlvi, part 2, 263. On Jan. 26, Palmer, New Berne, N. C., twice wrote to USG. "Yesterday I sent, from near Roanoke, a few lines informing you of rumors of an intended attack on this place. Since my arrival here I learn nothing to cause me to think that any immediate attack is intended. It was undoubtedly the intention to make a demonstration in this direction, but Wilmington now occupies all the attention of the enemy in this state. The bridges across the Roanoke at Weldon, Gaston, & Danville are all carried away, and the one from Weldon, or a large portion of it, with all the rail road iron upon it, is blocking up the Cashie river near our Post of Plymouth. It is said that the bridge at Kinston was taken up to save it from being carried off by freshet. It is also rumored that Kinston is to be evacuated. I shall soon learn all about this. This extraordinary freshet has somewhat interfered with my expedition to Edwards Ferry. The roads are almost impassable, and the river is still very high. A *surprise* just now is impossible, but the force is still up the Chowan, ready to strike when a favorable time shall arrive. Up to Tuesday last (the 24th) Wilmington was not captured, as I have an officer here who spent that day at Fort Fisher." "Major Goureaud of Gen. Foster's staff has brought me despatches from Gen. Sherman & Foster. As the Major also brought dispatches for you which are forwarded by Lieut. Pratt, I have no doubt you will be informed of the substance of Gen Sherman's instructions to me, which are generally to hold on here, watch well the Rail Road and keep it in order,—have every preparation made to secure his supplies from Morehead City when he gets into this state &c&c, and he was good enough to give me confidentially his plans for the future. You may rest assured General that I shall devote all my energies to these objects and I shall hope to be of no small aid, in which case I can have it to say that 'I too was of Sherman's Army'. I shall probably need some rail road builders, and some more workmen to enlarge the wharf at Morehead City, but of this I shall inform you as soon as I can ascertain precisely what I shall require." ALS, DNA, RG 108, Letters Received. *O.R.*, I, xlvi, part 2, 271–72.

On Jan. 29, Palmer telegraphed to USG, Morehead City, N. C. "I will come down immediately" ALS (telegram sent), DNA, RG 107, Telegrams Collected (Unbound).

To Abraham Lincoln

(Cipher)   City Point, Va. Jan. 31st *18645*. [*10:00* A.M.]
~~HON. E. M. STANTON, SEC. OF WAR~~, A. LINCOLN PRESIDENT
WASHINGTON
~~I have a communication~~ The following communication was received here last evening. Petersburg, Va, Jan. 30th 1865 LIEUT. GN. U. S. GRANT, SIR: We desire to pass your lines under safe conduct, and to proceed to Washington, to hold a conference with President Lincoln, upon the subject of the existing War, and with a view of ascertaining upon what terms it may be terminated, in

pursuance of the course indicated by him in his letter to Mr. F. P. Blair of 18th of Jan.y 1865[1] of which we presume you have a copy; and if not we wish to see you in person, if convenient, and to confer with you upon the subject. (Signed) Yours very respectfully, ALEXANDER STEPHENS, J. A. CAMPBELL, R. M. T. HUNTER. I have sent directions to receive these gentlemen and expect to have them at my quarters this evening awaiting your instructions.

U. S. GRANT
Lt. Gn.

ALS (telegram sent), OClWHi; telegram received, DLC-Robert T. Lincoln; (at 12:30 P.M.) DNA, RG 107, Telegrams Collected (Bound). Incomplete in *O.R.*, I, xlvi, part 2, 311. On Jan. 31, 1865, 1:30 P.M., President Abraham Lincoln telegraphed to USG. "A messenger is coming to you [o]n the business contained in your despatch—Detain the gentlemen in comfortable quarters until he arrives & then act upon the message he brings, as far as applicable, ~~they~~ it having been made up to pass through Gen. Ord's hands, & when the gentlemen were supposed to be beyond our lines." ALS (telegram sent), DNA, RG 107, Telegrams Collected (Bound); telegram received, *ibid.*, RG 108, Letters Received. *O.R.*, I, xlvi, part 2, 311. Lincoln, *Works*, VIII, 249–50. On Jan. 30, Secretary of War Edwin M. Stanton drafted a telegram to Maj. Gen. Edward O. C. Ord, then re-addressed it to USG. "The President desires that you will please procure for the bearer, Major Thomas T Eckart, an interview with Messrs Stevens Hunter and Campbell,—and if on his return to you he requests it—pass them through our lines to Fortress Monroe by such route and under such military precautions as you may deem prudent, giving them protection and comfortable quarters while there; and that you let none of this, have any effect upon your military movements or plans." ALS (telegram sent), Justin G. Turner, Los Angeles, Calif.; copy, DLC-Robert T. Lincoln. Printed as addressed to Ord in *O.R.*, I, xlvi, part 2, 302. For additional correspondence (Jan. 29–30) regarding the arrival of the C.S.A. commissioners, see *ibid.*, pp. 290–91, 292, 297, 301–2. Lincoln, *Works*, VIII, 276–77.

1. *Ibid.*, pp. 220–21.

To Alexander H. Stephens et al.

———

January 31st *1864*5.

HON. ALEXANDER H. STEPHENS, J. A CAMPBELL, AND
R. M. T HUNTER
GENTLEMEN!

Your communication of yesterday[1] requesting an interview with myself and a safe conduct to Washington and return, is received.

I will instruct the Commanding Officer of the forces near Peters-burg to receive you, notifying you at what point of the line and the time when and where conveyance will be ready for you.

Your letter to me has been telegraphed to Washington for in-structions. I have no doubt but that before you arrive at my Head-quarters an answer will be received directing me to comply with your request. Should a different reply be received I promise you a safe and immediate return within your own lines.

I am, very respectfully

U. S. Grant

Lieutenant General.

Copies, DLC-USG, V, 46, 72, 108; DNA, RG 108, Letters Sent; (certified by Lt. Col. Theodore S. Bowers) Justin G. Turner, Los Angeles, Calif. *O.R.*, I, xlvi, part 2, 312.

1. See preceding telegram.

To Edwin M. Stanton

(Cipher)   City Point, Va, Jan. 31st 1865 [*10:00* A.M.]
Hon. E. M. Stanton, Sec. of War, Washington,
Please inform Gn. Schofield that since my absence Mahone's Div. about 5.000 strong, has gone South. My opinion is however they will not stop at Wilmington. It is important ~~to get~~ that Schofield should move without any delay.

U. S. Grant

Lt. Gen

ALS (telegram sent), OClWHi; telegram received (at 10:25 A.M.), DNA, RG 107, Telegrams Collected (Bound); DLC-John M. Schofield. Printed (as entered in USG's letterbooks) as sent at 7:00 A.M. in *O.R.*, I, xlvi, part 2, 311; *ibid.*, I, xlvii, part 2, 179.
     Probably on Jan. 30, 1865, 4:35 P.M., USG telegraphed to Maj. Thomas T. Eckert. "Please ascertain from the sec. and answer quick if any of Gen. Schofield's troops have sailed." ALS (undated telegram sent), DNA, RG 107, Telegrams Collected (Bound). On the same day, 5:35 P.M., Secretary of War Edwin M. Stanton telegraphed to USG, Fort Monroe. "None of Schofields troops have sailed yet they are at Alexandria & river closed but moderating." ALS (telegram sent—dated Jan. 31), *ibid.*; telegram received (dated Jan. 30), *ibid.*, RG 108, Letters Received.

On Feb. 2, 11:00 A.M., USG telegraphed to Maj. Gen. John M. Schofield. "Mahone's Division which was reported to have gone south has returned to Petersburg. They did go south near or quite to Welden probably to meet a raid sent by Palmer to destroy the ram which is being built in the Roanoke." ALS (telegram sent), Robert S. Ruwitch, Northbrook, Ill.; telegram received (at 11:30 A.M.), DNA, RG 107, Telegrams Collected (Bound). *O.R.*, I, xlvii, part 2, 213.

To Edwin M. Stanton

(Cipher)   City Point, Va, Jan.y 31st/65 [*11:30* A.M.]
HON. E. M. STANTON, SEC. OF WAR, WASHINGTON
Please constitute N. C. a Dept. for present purposes, Maj. Gn. Schofield in command subject to Shermans orders. It is impossible for Foster to give orders from Hilton Head as well as I can from here. I will give Gn. Schofield all his orders and instructions until Sherman gets in reach of him.

U. S. GRANT
Lt. Gn

ALS (telegram sent), OClWHi; telegram received (at 1:20 P.M.), DNA, RG 107, Telegrams Collected (Bound). *O.R.*, I, xlvi, part 2, 312; *ibid.*, I, xlvii, part 2, 179. On Jan. 31, 1865, 4:30 P.M., Secretary of War Edwin M. Stanton telegraphed to USG. "The Department of North Carolina with Schofield Commander has been ordered as you requested" ALS (telegram sent), DNA, RG 107, Telegrams Collected (Bound); telegram received (marked as sent at 5:30 P.M.), *ibid.*, RG 108, Letters Received. *O.R.*, I, xlvi, part 2, 312; *ibid.*, I, xlvii, part 2, 179.

On Jan. 26, Maj. Gen. Alfred H. Terry wrote to Brig. Gen. John A. Rawlins. "I have the honor to report that I have received from Major General Foster Comdg the Department of the South a letter informing me that the State of North Carolina has been added to his command. He has also sent to me a confidential letter of instructions for my guidance. I enclose copies of both these letters. By the Lieutenant General's letter of instructions to me dated 'HdQus Armies of the United States City Point Va January 4th 1865', I was instructed during the operations of the expedition under my command in all official matters to communicate directly with Army Head Quarters unless otherwise ordered. I shall write to Major General Foster & inform him of the nature of my instructions, & also inform him that I have asked directions in regard to the matter from the Lt. General. I shall also say to him that until I receive such instructions I shall endeavour to conform to his views so far as they are applicable to the state of affairs here. I respectfully ask that I may be instructed as to what course I am to pursue & to what Head Quarters I am to report." Copy, DNA, RG 108, Letters Received. *O.R.*, I, xlvi, part 2, 270. The enclosures are *ibid.*, pp. 270–71.

To Edwin M. Stanton

City Point, Va, Jan.y 31st *18645*. [*7:30* P.M.]
HON. E. M. STANTON, SEC. OF WAR WASHN.

On my arrival here this morning I received a letter from Messrs Stevens Hunter & Campbell which I immediately telegraphed the contents of to the President and sent at the same time a staff officer to receive the gentlemen and conduct them to my quarters to await the action of the President. The gentlemen have arrived and since their arrival I have been put in possession of the telegraphic correspondence which had been going on for two days previous. Had I known of this correspondence in time these gentlemen would not have been received within our lines.

U. S. GRANT
Lt. Gn.

ALS (telegram sent), OClWHi; telegram received (at 8:30 P.M.), DNA, RG 107, Telegrams Collected (Bound). *O.R.*, I, xlvi, part 2, 311–12.

To Edwin M. Stanton

"Cipher"   City Point Va, Jany 31st 1865
HON, E, M, STANTON
SEC, OF WAR WASHINGTON

I am just in receipt of a letter from the late Lt, Col, Jas. H Stokes from which I learn he has not been reinstated, or the order dismissing him revoked, I understood after his explanation, which, taken in connection with what I know of his services, was eminentl[y] satisfactory to me, at least, that the order had been revoked, I believe grea[t] injustice has been done Col, Stokes an[d] hope it will be repaired as far as pos[s]ible, Representations by Mr, Osborne and Gen, Burnside were very strong against the Col, but his explanation is more convincing

U. S. GRANT
Lieut, Genl

Telegram, copies, DLC-USG, V, 46, 72, 108; DNA, RG 108, Letters Sent. See telegram to Edwin M. Stanton, Sept. 22, 1864.

To Maj. Gen. John G. Parke

City Point, Va. Jany 31st 1865. [7:00 P.M.]

MAJ GEN. PARKE

Make preparation so that if called on you can move at short notice with the Army of the Potomac provided with six days rations. In case of a flank move, the Garrison to hold the lines will be reduced to a minimum. Such portions of the 9th and 6th Corps as you may select will be left behind, say one division from each, and the Garrisons of the enclosed works or batteries, Written instructions will be sent in advance of any move.

U. S. GRANT
Lieut. General.

Telegram, copies, DLC-USG, V, 46, 73, 108; DNA, RG 108, Letters Sent. *O.R.*, I, xlvi, part 2, 314.

On Jan. 31, 1865, USG telegraphed to Maj. Gen. George G. Meade. "Please return immediately" Copies, DLC-USG, V, 46, 72, 108; DNA, RG 108, Letters Sent. *O.R.*, I, xlvi, part 2, 314.

At 11:00 A.M., Tuesday, USG telegraphed to Maj. Gen. Edward O. C. Ord. "Prepare your troops with Six days rations, four of them in Haversacks, from Thursday next, preparatory to moving with all available forces at that time. Instructions will be sent to you to-morrow." Copies, DLC-USG, V, 46, 73, 108; DNA, RG 108, Letters Sent; *ibid.*, RG 393, 24th Army Corps, Telegrams Received. *O.R.*, I, xlvi, part 2, 318. On the same day, Ord telegraphed to USG. "*All* my bridges are carried away by the ice—I have but Six days rations within reach ~~bridge tuesday in hands of troops~~ afloat bridges may be repaired by tomorrow Are you aware that by the Presidents order—I ~~have~~ sent word yesterday P M through Genl Parke, that the three Peace Commissioners—will be met at or where they now are—on Genl Parkes front—by a messenger from Washington—, I presume the negociations are to be conducted at City Point—Stephens Hunter and Campell—are Davis Commissioners—will this affect your order to move" ALS (telegram sent), DNA, RG 94, War Records Office, Miscellaneous War Records; telegram received (at 3:30 P.M.), *ibid.*, RG 108, Letters Received. *O.R.*, I, xlvi, part 2, 319.

To Maj. Gen. John M. Schofield

City Point, Va, Jan. 31st *18645*. [11:30 A.M.]

MAJ. GEN. SCHOFIELD, WASHINGTON.

There are about 5000 troops here beloning to Terry's command which will be forwarded as rapidly as possible. Mechanics

have already gone to Beaufort. They can be transfered to Fort
Fisher if you deem it advisable. A Pile driver will leave Annapolis
on Thursday[1] for Fort Fisher with a sufficient force to work it. The
Pontoon train left here on Sunday.

U. S. GRANT

Lt. Gn.

ALS (telegram sent), OClWHi; telegrams received (2—at 1:20 P.M.), DNA,
RG 107, Telegrams Collected (Bound); DLC-John M. Schofield. *O.R.*, I, xlvii,
part 2, 191.

   1. Feb. 2, 1865.

To Maj. Gen. John M. Schofield

City Point, Va., Jan 31 *18645*.

MAJ. GEN. J. M. SCHOFIELD.
COMDG. ARMY OF THE OHIO.
GENERAL!

   I have requested, by telegraph, that for present purposes, North
Carolina be erected into a Department and that you be placed in
command of it, subject to Maj. Gen. Sherman's orders. Of course
you will receive orders from me direct until such time as Gen.
Sherman gets within communicating distance of you. This obvi-
ates the necessity of my publishing the order which I informed
you would meet you at Fortress Monroe.—If the order referred to
should not be published from the Adjt Gen'ls Office, you will regard these instructions as your authority to assume command of
all the troops in N. C. dating all official communications "Headquarters Army of the Ohio".—Your Headquarters will be in the
field and with the portion of the Army where you feel yourself
most needed. In the first move you will go to Cape Fear River.

   Your movements are intended as coöperative with Sherman's
movement through the States of South and North Carolina. The
first point to be obtained is to secure Wilmington. Goldsboro' will
then be your objective point moving either from Wilmington or
New Bern, or both as you may deem best. Should you not be able
to reach Goldsboro' you will advance on the line, or lines, of rail-

way connecting that place with the seacoast as near to it as you can, building the road behind you.—The enterprise under you has two objects; the first is to give Gen. Sherman material aid, if needed, in his march North; the second to open a base of supplies for him on the line of his march. As soon therefore as you can determine which of the two points, Wilmington or New Bern, you can best use for throwing supplies from, to the interior, you will commence the accumulation of twenty days rations and forage for 60000 men and 20000 animals. You will get of these as many as you can house and protect to such point in the interior as you may be able to occupy.

I believe Gen'l Palmer has received some instructions directly from Gen. Sherman on the subject of securing supplies for his Army. You can learn what steps he has taken and be governed in your requisitions accordingly. A supply of ordnance stores will also be necessary.

Make all your requisitions upon the Chiefs of their respective departments, in the field, with me at City Point. Communicate with me by every opportunity and should you deem it necessary at any time send a special boat to Fortress Monroe from which point you can communicate by telegraph.

The supplies referred to in these instructions are exclusive of those required by your own command.

The movements of the enemy may justify you, or even make it your imperative duty, to cut loose from your base and strike for the interior to aid Sherman. In such case you will act on your own judgment without waiting for instructions. You will report however what you propose doing. The details for carrying out these instructions are necessarily left to you. I would urge however, if I did not know that you are already fully alive to the importance of it, prompt action. Sherman may be looked for in the neighborhood of Goldsboro' any time from the 22d to the 28th of February This limits your time very materially.

If rolling stock is not secured in the capture of Wilmington it can be supplied from Washington. A large force of railroad men has already been sent to Beaufort and other mechanics will go to

Fort Fisher in a day or two. On this point I have informed you by telegraph.

> Very respectfully
> Your obdt serv't
> U. S. GRANT
> Lieutenant General.

Copies, DLC-USG, V, 46, 72, 108; DNA, RG 108, Letters Sent; DLC-John M. Schofield; (certified by Lt. Col. Theodore S. Bowers, prepared for Maj. Gen. William T. Sherman) DLC-William T. Sherman. *O.R.*, I, xlvii, part 2, 189–90; (incomplete) *ibid.*, I, xxxiv, part 1, 43; *ibid.*, I, xxxvi, part 1, 46–47; *ibid.*, I, xxxviii, part 1, 35–36.

On Jan. 31, 1865, 1:20 P.M., Maj. Gen. John M. Schofield, Washington, D. C., telegraphed to USG. "I have received your dispatch of 10 a. m to the Secretary of War. Genl Rucker thinks it will be impossible to get out of the Potomac before Friday or Saturday, but will try to break the ice tomorrow. Genl Meagher's detachment about 5,500 strong is ordered to Anapolis where there will be transports enough for it. I propose to send all of Genl Meaghers troops to Newburn and take the 23d Corps to Cape Fear River. Meagher will probably get down first but will I presume not be strong enough for the move against Wilmington. Please inform me if you approve this arrangement." ALS (telegram sent), DNA, RG 107, Telegrams Collected (Unbound); telegrams received (2), *ibid.*, Telegrams Collected (Bound); *ibid.*, RG 108, Letters Received. *O.R.*, I, xlvii, part 2, 191. See telegram to Edwin M. Stanton, Jan. 31, 1865, 10:00 A.M. At 7:00 P.M., USG telegraphed to Schofield. "The arrangement you have made to send Gen. Maher'seagher command to New Bern is satisfactory." ALS (telegram sent), OClWHi; telegrams received (2—at 7:50 P.M.), DNA, RG 107, Telegrams Collected (Bound); DLC-John M. Schofield. *O.R.*, I, xlvii, part 2, 191. At 3:40 P.M., Maj. Gen. Henry W. Halleck telegraphed to USG. "The order placing Pope in Genl command in the west and putting Kansas under Genl Dodge has just been issued and telegraphed to Genl Pope. The legislature of Kansas has passed resolutions asking that more troops be sent to that state. They will be sent to you by mail. Troops from the west arrive [sl]owly. Genl Meagher's division is ordered to embark at Annapolis [It] will be slow work as the transports must be coaled & provisioned by lighters. The weather is rapidly moderating, & an effort will be made to-morrow to make a channel for the transports at Alexandria." ALS (telegram sent), DNA, RG 107, Telegrams Collected (Bound); telegram received, *ibid.*; (marked as sent at 3:30 P.M.) *ibid.*, RG 108, Letters Received. *O.R.*, I, xlvi, part 2, 313; *ibid.*, I, xlviii, part 1, 694.

At 3:00 P.M., USG had telegraphed to Halleck. "Please inform me when Gn. Schofield will leave Washington. I want to send his instructions to Ft. Monroe by a Staff Officer to deliver them as the General passes." ALS (telegram sent), OClWHi; telegram received (at 4:00 P.M.), DNA, RG 107, Telegrams Collected (Bound); DLC-John M. Schofield. *O.R.*, I, xlvi, part 2, 313. At 8:30 P.M., Halleck telegraphed to USG. "Genl Schofield will leave with first detachment from Alexandria. We shall attempt to open passage to-morrow. Will telegraph in time to have despatches reach Schofield at Fort Monroe." ALS (telegram sent), DNA, RG 107, Telegrams Collected (Bound); telegram received (marked as sent at 8:30 A.M.), *ibid.*; *ibid.*, RG 108, Letters Received. *O.R.*, I, xlvi, part 2, 313.

At 3:30 P.M., USG had telegraphed to Maj. Gen. Philip H. Sheridan. "Do you think it would be safe for you to spare a Div. of Cavalry to send to N. C.?" ALS (telegram sent), OClWHi; copies, DLC-USG, V, 46, 72, 108; DNA, RG 108, Letters Sent. *O.R.*, I, xlvi, part 2, 323. On Feb. 2, 1:00 P.M., Sheridan, Winchester, Va., telegraphed to USG. "The only fighting force that I now have here is cavalry; I believe that I could spare a division but it will increase the feeling of insecurity which the sending off of the infantry produced: Then Crook wants more cavalry. The indications now are that the enemy will get together a considerable force of cavalry in the spring I have now 10.000 cavalry in pretty good condition and in another month it will be in excellent condition. I would like to comply with your wishes and if the division is much needed it would perhaps be best to take a little risk I delayed one day in replying to your telegram as I was reviewing the cavalry & wished to see it before sending an answer" Telegram received, DNA, RG 108, Letters Received; copies, *ibid.*, RG 107, Telegrams Received in Cipher; (2) DLC-Philip H. Sheridan. *O.R.*, I, xlvi, part 2, 356.

On Feb. 2, 2:30 P.M., Schofield telegraphed to USG. "I expect to get off tomorrow with one division beside Genl Meaghers command. I will go with the advance and will stop at Fort Monroe for your orders. I will telegraph you when I start." ALS (telegram sent), DNA, RG 107, Telegrams Collected (Unbound); telegram received, *ibid.*, Telegrams Collected (Bound); *ibid.*, RG 108, Letters Received. *O.R.*, I, xlvii, part 2, 213. On Feb. 3, 11:45 P.M., Schofield telegraphed to USG. "I will start at six a. m. tomorrow, and hope to get through the ice by tomorrow evening." ALS (telegram sent), DNA, RG 107, Telegrams Collected (Unbound); telegram received, *ibid.* *O.R.*, I, xlvi, part 2, 361. On Feb. 5, Schofield, Fort Monroe, telegraphed to USG. "I have just arrived here with my advance. Have you any instructions for me?" Telegram received (at 7:05 P.M.), DNA, RG 108, Letters Received; copies, *ibid.*, RG 393, Dept. of N. C., Letters Sent; DLC-John M. Schofield. *O.R.*, I, xlvii, part 2, 315. On the same day, USG telegraphed to Schofield. "Your instructions were left with Col, Webster Quartermaster, I have no further instructions," Telegram received (press), DNA, RG 107, Telegrams Collected (Bound); copies, *ibid.*, RG 108, Letters Sent; DLC-USG, V, 46, 72, 108. *O.R.*, I, xlvii, part 2, 315.

To Maj. Gen. George H. Thomas

City Point, Va, Jan.y 31st *1864*5.

MAJ. GEN. G. H. THOMAS,
COMD.G ARMY OF THE CUM.D.
GENERAL.

With this I send you a letter just received from General Sherman.[1] At the time of writing it Gen. Sherman was not informed of of the depletion of your command by my orders. It will be impossible for you at present to move South, as he contemplated, with the force of Infantry indicated.

Gen. Sherman is advised before this of the changes made and that for the Winter you will be on the defensive. I think however an expedition from East Tennessee, under General Stoneman, might penetrate South Carolina well down towards Columbia, destroying the rail-road and Military resources of the country, thus visiting a portion of the state which will not be reached by Sherman's forces. He might also be able to return to East Tennessee by way of Salisbury N. C. thus releasing some of our prisoners of War, in rebel hands. Of the practicability of doing this Gen. Stoneman will have to be the judge making up his mind from information obtained whilst executing the first part of his instructions. Sherman's movements will attract the attention of all the force the enemy can collect thus facilitating the execution of this.

Three thousand Cavalry would be sufficient force to take. This probably can be raised in the old Dept. of the Ohio without taking any now under Gen. Wilson. It would require though the reorganization of the two regiments of Ky. Cavalry which Stoneman had in his very successful raid into S. W. Va.—It will also be necessary probably for you to send, in addition to the force now in East Tennessee, a small force Division of Infantry to enable Gen. Gelham[2] to hold the upper end of Holston Valley and the mountain passess in rear of Stoneman.

You may order such expedition. To save time I will send a copy of this to Gen. Stoneman so that he can begin his preparations, without loss of time, and can commence his correspondence with you as to these preparations.

As this expedition goes to destroy and not to fight battles, but to avoid them where practicable, particularly against anything like equal forces, or where a great object is not to be gained, it should go as light as possible. Stoneman's experiance in raiding will teach him in this matter better than he can be directed.

Let there be no delay in the preparations for this expedition and keep me advised of its progress.

> Very respectfully
> your obt. svt.
> U. S. GRANT
> Lt. Gn.

ALS, CSmH. *O.R.*, I, xlix, part 1, 616–17. On Feb. 9, 1865, Maj. Gen. George H. Thomas, Paducah, Ky., wrote to USG. "I have just received your letter of the 31st January at the hands of Col Dent & will proceed at once to organise the force for the expedition under Genl Stoneman and get it off with as little delay as possible. Col Merrill's Regiment of Cavalry was ordered to report to me last fall, but only a portion has yet arrived from St Louis. If I could get that Regiment at once I would add it to Stoneman's force. It is in a fine state of discipline and would be valuable to Stoneman as an aid to prevent straggling." ALS, MH. *O.R.*, I, xlix, part 1, 678. On Feb. 12, 8:00 P.M., Thomas, Nashville, telegraphed to USG. "Your communication at the hands of Lt. Col. Dent recd. Am making best progress possible to furnish force cavalry to Gen Stoneman; I need however about 1000 horses to fit him out and which when done will make his outfit as complete as has ever been furnished to any officer—Am hoping to get them immediately & when recd theire will be no further delay in Gen Stonemans starting out" Telegram received (at 11:45 P.M.), DNA, RG 107, Telegrams Collected (Bound); (on Feb. 13) *ibid.*, RG 108, Letters Received; copies, *ibid.*, RG 107, Telegrams Received in Cipher; *ibid.*, RG 393, Dept. of the Cumberland, Telegrams Sent. *O.R.*, I, xlix, part 1, 700.

1. See letter to Maj. Gen. William T. Sherman, Feb. 1, 1865.
2. Alvan C. Gillem, born in Tenn. in 1830, USMA 1851, was appointed col., 10th Tenn., as of May 13, 1862, and brig. gen. as of Aug. 17, 1863. After receiving a copy of USG's letter to Thomas, Maj. Gen. George Stoneman wrote Gillem to prepare "your fine body of Cossacks," officially known as the Cav. Div., District of East Tenn. *O.R.*, I, xlix, part 1, 663.

To Abraham Lincoln

From City Point Va Feb'y 1st 12 30 P. M *18645*.

HIS EXCELLENCY A. LINCOLN
PREST U. S.

Your despatch received; there will be no armistice in consequence of the presence of Mr Stephens and others within our lines.

The troops are kept in readiness to move at the shortest notice if occasion should justify it

U. S. Grant
Lieut Genl

Telegram received (at 2:30 P.M.), DLC-Robert T. Lincoln; (at 2:20 P.M.) DNA, RG 107, Telegrams Collected (Bound); copies, *ibid.*, RG 108, Letters Sent; DLC-USG, V, 46, 72, 108. *O.R.*, I, xlvi, part 2, 341.

On Feb. 1, 1865, 9:30 A.M., President Abraham Lincoln telegraphed to USG. "Let nothing which is transpiring, change, hinder, or delay your Military movements, or plans." ALS (telegram sent), DNA, RG 107, Telegrams Collected (Bound); telegram received, *ibid.*, RG 108, Letters Received. *O.R.*, I, xlvi, part 2, 341. Lincoln, *Works*, VIII, 252.

On the same day, Alexander H. Stephens, Robert M. T. Hunter, and John A. Campbell wrote to USG. "We desire to go to Washington City to confer informally with President Lincoln personally, in reference to the matters mentioned in his letter to F. P. Blair Esq. of the 18th Jan'y Ult without any personal compromise on any questions in the letter. We have the permission to do so from the Authorities in Richmond." LS, Justin G. Turner, Los Angeles, Calif.

To Edwin M. Stanton

City Point, Va, Feb.y 1st 1865 [*10:30* P.M.]
Hon. E. M. Stanton, Sec. of War, Washington
Now that the interview between Maj. Eckert,[1] anunder his written instructions, and Mr. Stevens & party, has ended I will state confidentially and but not officially to become a matter of record, that I am convinced, upon conversation with Messrs Stevens & Hunter that their intentions are good and their desire sincere to restore peace and Union. I have not felt myself at liberty to express even views of my own or even to account for my reticency. This has placed me in an alquerd position which I could have avoided by not seeing them in the first instance. I fear now their going back without any expression from any one in authority will have a bad influance. At the same time I recognize the difficulties in the way of receiving these informal commissioners at this time and do not know what to recommend. I am sorry however that Mr. Lincoln can not have an interview with the two named in this dispatch if

not all three now within our lines. Their letter to me was all that the Presidents instruction contemplated to secure their safe conduct if they had used the same language to Maj. Eckert.

U. S. GRANT
Lt. Gn

ALS (telegram sent), OClWHi; telegram received (on Feb. 2, 1865, 4:35 A.M.), DLC-Robert T. Lincoln; DNA, RG 107, Telegrams Collected (Bound). *O.R.*, I, xlvi, part 2, 342–43.

On Feb. 1, 11:30 P.M., Secretary of State William H. Seward telegraphed to USG. "I ~~drove~~ arrived here at 10 this evening—and shall remain ~~Here to meet here her~~ here to meet the persons from Richmond, Send Major Eckert here if he is with you" ALS (telegram sent), DNA, RG 107, Telegrams Collected (Unbound). *O.R.*, I, xlvi, part 2, 342.

On Feb. 2, 9:00 A.M., President Abraham Lincoln telegraphed to USG. "Say to the gentlemen I will meet them personally at Fortress-Monroe, as soon as I can get there—" ALS (telegram sent), DNA, RG 107, Telegrams Collected (Bound); copy, DLC-Robert T. Lincoln. *O.R.*, I, xlvi, part 2, 352. Lincoln, *Works*, VIII, 356. At 11:30 A.M., Maj. Thomas T. Eckert, Fort Monroe, telegraphed to USG. "I arrived here at 9 O'Clock this A. M. Mr Seward expresses his satisfaction of course pursued in reply to letters recd. yesterday He came here on strength of first letter you recd. on which you admitted them within your lines from that it was believed they would accept the terms, therefore started at once to save ~~time~~ delay Mr Seward desires me to say to you confidentially General, message just recd stating the President left Washington at 9 O'Clock this A. M. for FtMonroe" Telegram received, DNA, RG 108, Letters Received. *O.R.*, I, xlvi, part 2, 353.

At 9:00 A.M., USG telegraphed to Seward, Fort Monroe, sending a copy to Secretary of War Edwin M. Stanton. "The gentlemen here have accepted the proposed terms and will start for Fortress Monroe at 9.30 a. m." ALS (telegram sent), CSmH; telegram received (at 9:30 A.M.), DNA, RG 107, Telegrams Collected (Bound); DLC-Robert T. Lincoln. *O.R.*, I, xlvi, part 2, 352. At 2:00 P.M., Seward telegraphed to USG. "You state 'The Gentlemen here have accepted the proposed terms and will start for Fort Monroe at 9.30 A M,' Please telegraph me the form & words of their acceptance, ~~with as little~~ as soon as possible. ~~from~~" Copy, DNA, RG 107, Telegrams Collected (Unbound). On the same day, USG telegraphed to Seward. "I have sent the letter refered to ~~you~~ in your dispatch by the hands of a Staff Officer to be delivered to you. I retained no copy of it." ALS (telegram sent), Kohns Collection, NN; typescript telegram received (at 3:30 P.M.), Seward Papers, NRU.

On Feb. 3, Eckert telegraphed to USG. "The President directs me to say that Mr Stephens had some conversatio[n] with him on the subject of prisoners and [t]ha[t] he referred the matter to you, and desires that you confer with Mr Stephens on the subject. The interview has concluded & both parties ~~will~~ preparing ~~for~~ to return—~~fair probability;~~ leave about 4 ~~3~~ P M." ALS (telegram sent), DNA, RG 107, Telegrams Collected (Unbound); telegram received, *ibid.*, RG 108, Letters Received. *O.R.*, I, xlvi, part 2, 360. On the same day, USG telegraphed to Maj. Gen. George G. Meade. "Steven~~son~~ and party wil[l] return here to night and will be sent to you by the 10. a m Train Tomorro[w] to be past through the lines as they come. Please notify they commanding office[r] on the front of the enemy where they will go through of the fact so that [p]reparations may be made to receive them" Telegram received (at 3:00 P.M.—misaddressed to Stanton), DNA, RG 94, War Records Office, Miscellaneous War Records. *O.R.*, I, xlvi, part 2, 361. On the same day, USG telegraphed to Maj. Gen. Edward O. C. Ord. "Please send a spring wagon & an ambulance to Aikens Landing to be there at 8 a m tomo[rr]ow to take Mr Stephens & party through the lines, also notify the rebel authoties that they will be there" Telegram received, Ord Papers, CU-B; copies, DLC-USG, V, 46, 72, 108; DNA, RG 108, Letters Sent. *O.R.*, I, xlvi, part 2, 363.

On Feb. 8, 2:30 P.M., Lincoln telegraphed to USG. "I am called on by the House of Representatives to give an account of my interview with Messrs. Stephens, Hunter & Campbell; and it is very desireable to me to put in your despatch of Feb. 1st to ~~Mr. Stan~~ the Sec. of War, in which among other things you say 'I fear now their going back without any expression from any one in authority will have a bad influence' I think the despatch ~~dos~~ does you credit ~~so that~~ while I do not see that it can embarrass you. May I use it?" ALS (telegram sent), DNA, RG 107, Telegrams Collected (Bound); telegram received, *ibid.*, RG 108, Letters Received. *O.R.*, I, xlvi, part 2, 473. Lincoln, *Works*, VIII, 269. At 7:30 P.M., USG telegraphed to Lincoln. "By all means use my dispatch refered to in yours of this date if you desire to do so. It was marked confidential in contradistinction to official dispatches but not to prevent such use being made of it as you or the Sec. of War mike think proper." ALS (telegram sent), Lamon Papers, CSmH; telegram received (at 10:20 P.M.), DLC-Robert T. Lincoln; DNA, RG 107, Telegrams Collected (Bound). *O.R.*, I, xlvi, part 2, 474.

1. Thomas T. Eckert, born in Ohio in 1825, had experience as a telegrapher and telegraph co. executive before the Civil War. Appointed maj. and aide as of April 7, 1862, he served as asst. superintendent, U.S. Military Telegraph. On Jan. 30, 1865, President Abraham Lincoln sent Eckert to deliver a message to the C.S.A. commissioners. Lincoln, *Works*, VIII, 246, 277–78. See David Homer Bates, *Lincoln in the Telegraph Office* (New York, 1907), pp. 334–38.

To Maj. Gen. Edward O. C. Ord

(Cipher)   City Point, Va, Feb.y 1st *18645*. [*4:30* P.M.]
MAJ. GEN. ORD.

I think it will be advisable on relieving Gen. Shepley from command[1] in Norfolk to place Gen. Vogdes[2] in his place. He is next in rank in that command and is an old Brig. Gen. and as he is an old army officer ~~and~~ expecting to spend his days in the service an honest administration can better be expected from him than from an untried officer who does not expect to remain in the service. I do not order this selection but advise it and would recommend its being made early.

U. S. GRANT
Lt. Gn.

ALS (telegram sent), OClWHi; copies, DLC-USG, V, 46, 72, 108; DNA, RG 108, Letters Sent. *O.R.*, I, xlvi, part 2, 347–48. On Feb. 1, 1865, 6:00 P.M., Maj. Gen. Edward O. C. Ord telegraphed to USG. "Enquire of any officer of the army who has ever served with Gen. Vogdes, in the field or in garrison, his fitness for command; and I am sure you will change your mind: He would bring us into contempt" Telegram received, DNA, RG 108, Letters Received. *O.R.*, I, xlvi, part 2, 348. At 7:00 P.M., USG telegraphed to Ord. "Do not give Gen. Vogdes the command at Norfolk if you deem him unfit for it. You know him better than I do." ALS (telegram sent), OClWHi; copies, DLC-USG, V, 46, 72, 108; DNA, RG 108, Letters Sent. *O.R.*, I, xlvi, part 2, 348. On the same day, Ord telegraphed to USG. "I propose ordering at once Gen Vogdes to relieve Gen Gordon on the Commission. Gen Gordon to relieve Gen Shepley and the latter to report for duty when the Court of which he is president adjourns to Gen Weitzel if you approve." Telegram received (at 6:25 P.M.), DNA, RG 108, Letters Received. Printed as sent at 6:20 P.M. in *O.R.*, I, xlvi, part 2, 348. On the same day, Brig. Gen. John A. Rawlins telegraphed to Ord. "Your dispatch of 6:20 P. M rec'd. The changes you propose are approved." Telegram received (at 9:00 P.M.), Ord Papers, CU-B; copies, DLC-USG, V, 46, 72, 108; DNA, RG 108, Letters Sent. *O.R.*, I, xlvi, part 2, 348.

On the same day, Rawlins telegraphed to Ord. "Maj Gen Terry Comdg Ft Fisher says that there are here besides detachments of regiments & companies with him two regiments belonging to the division and brigade organizations with him. You will please send them forward as well as the detachments heretofore ordered to join their respective commands at Fort Fisher." Telegram received (at 6:50 P.M.), DNA, RG 94, War Records Office, Miscellaneous War Records. Printed as sent at 6:50 P.M. in *O.R.*, I, xlvi, part 2, 348–49. At 7:10 P.M., Ord telegraphed to Rawlins. "All regiments and detachments belonging to General Terry's command have been ordered to join him." *Ibid.*, p. 349.

1. On Jan. 18, 2:30 P.M., USG telegraphed to Maj. Gen. Henry W. Halleck. "If Gen. Tower can be spared from his present duties please order him to report to Gen. Ord for duty. He wants him to relieve Gen. Shepley in the command of the Dist. of Norfok." ALS (telegram sent), CSmH; telegram received (at 5:00 P.M.), DNA, RG 107, Telegrams Collected (Bound). *O.R.*, I, xlvi, part 2, 170. On Jan. 26, 10:30 A.M., USG telegraphed to Halleck. "Has Gen. Tower been ordered to report to Gen. Ord? If he has not been I will have Gen. Shepley relieved with some officer now here." ALS (telegram sent), OClWHi; telegram received (at 11:05 A.M.), DNA, RG 107, Telegrams Collected (Bound). *O.R.*, I, xlvi, part 2, 266. See telegram to Maj. Gen. Henry W. Halleck, Jan. 26, 1865.

2. Israel Vogdes of Pa., USMA 1837, asst. professor of mathematics at USMA (1837–43), stationed at Fort Pickens, Fla., when the Civil War began,

was appointed brig. gen. as of Nov. 29, 1862. Assigned to command the defenses of Norfolk and Portsmouth on April 27, 1864, he served there until March, 1865. See *Calendar*, March 7, 1865.

To Maj. Gen. William T. Sherman

City Point, Va, Feb.y [1] *1864*5.

Maj. Gen. W. T. Sherman,
Comd.g Mil. Div. of the Miss.
General.

Without much expectation of it reaching you in time to be of any service I have mailed to you copies of instruction[s] to Schofield and Thomas.[1] I had informed Schofield by telegraph of the departure of Mahones Division, South, from the Petersburg front. These troops marched down the Weldon road and as they apparently went without baggage it is doubtful whether they have not returned. I was absent from here when they left. Just returned yesterday morning from Cape Fear River. I went there to determine where Schofields Corps had better go to operate against Wilmington & Goldsboro   The instructions with this will inform you of the conclution arrived at. Schofield was with me and the plan of the movement against Wilmington fully determined before we started back, hence the absenc[e] of more detailed instructions to him. He will land one Divisio[n] at Smithville and move rapidly up the south side of the river and secure the W & C rail-roa[d] and with his Pontoon train cross onto the Island south of the City if he can. With the aid of the gunboats there is no doubt but this move will drive the enemy from their position eight miles East of the City either back to their inner line or away altogether. There will be a large force on the North bank of Cape Fear river ready to follow up and invest the garrison if they should go inside.

The rail-roads of N. C. are 4 ft. 8½ in. gauge. I have sent large parties of rail-road men there to build them up and have ordered stock to run them. We have abundance of it idle from the non use of the Va. roads.

I have taken every precaution to have supplies ready for you wherever you may turn up. I did this before when you left Atlanta and regret that they did not reach you promptly when you reached Saltwater. The fact is Foster, from physical disability is entirely unfit for his command. I would like to change him for a man that can get about and see for himself.

Alexander Stevens, R. M. T. Hunter & Judge Campbelle are now at my Hd Qrs. very desirous of going to Washing[ton] to see Mr. Lincoln, informally, on th[e] subject of peace. The Peace feeling within the rebel lines is gaining ground rapidly. This however should not relax our energies in the least, but should stimulate us to greater activity.

I have received your very kind letter in which you say you would decline, or are opposed, to promotion. No one would be more pleased at your advancement than I, and if you should be placed in my position and I put subordinate it would not change our personal relations in the least. I wo[uld] make the same exertions to support you that you have ever done to support me, and would do all in my power to make our cause win

Yours Truly. U. S. GRANT, Lt. Gn

ALS, DLC-William T. Sherman. *O.R.*, I, xlvii, part 2, 193–94. On Jan. 21, 1865, Maj. Gen. William T. Sherman, Savannah, wrote to USG. "In fulfillment of my projet General Howard moved the Seventeenth Corps, General Blair, from Thunderbolt to Beaufort, S. C., and on the 14th by a rapid movement secured the Port Royal Ferry and moved against Pocotaligo, which he gained on the 15th, the day appointed. By that course he secured the use of the ground in South Carolina up to the Salkehatchie (Saltkatcher), and General Slocum was ordered in like manner to get his wing up about Robertsville by the way of the Savannah River and the Union Causeway. The transfer of men, animals, and wagons by steamer is a very slow process, and on the 19th General Slocum had only two divisions of the Twentieth at Purysburg and Hardeeville with open communications with Howard. John E. Smith crossed by the Union Causeway, on which Slocum had put ten days' hard work, but the hard rains had raised the Savannah River so that the whole country was under water, and the corduroy road on the Union Causeway was carried away, cutting off one brigade of John E. Smith, one division of the Fifteenth Corps (Corse's), and all of the Fourteenth Corps, General Davis. All were ordered to move up the west bank of the Savannah to cross at Sister's Ferry, but the rains have so flooded the country that we have been brought to a standstill; but I will persevere and get the army as soon as possible up to the line from Sister's Ferry to Pocotaligo, where we will have terra firma to work on. Our supplies have come daily, that is, we have never had four days' forage ahead, but I will depend on enough coming to get me out to the neighborhood of Barnwell, where we will find some. General Grover's division now occupies Savannah, which I had refortified, and I have turned over everything to General Foster, so that nothing now hinders me but water. I rather think the heavy rains in January will give us good weather in February and March. You cannot do much in Virginia till April or May, and when I am at Goldsborough and move against Raleigh, Lee will be forced to divide his command or give up Richmond. I am rejoiced that Terry took Fisher, because it silences Butler, who was to you a dangerous man. His address to his troops on being relieved was a direct, mean, and malicious attack on you, and I amired the patience and skill by which you relieved yourself and the country of him. If you want some new and fresh men, able to handle large armies, I will offer you Charles R. Woods, Hazen, and Mower, all good and capable officers for an army of any size. Of course, I prefer to have them myself, but would give them up if you can do better by them. As soon as possible, if I were in your place, I would break up the Department of the James, make the Richmond army one; then when I get to Goldsborough you will have a force to watch Lee, and I can be directed to gradually close in, cutting all communications. In the meantime Thomas' army should not be reduced too much, but he should hold Chattanooga, Decatur, and Eastport, collect supplies, and in all February and March move on Tuscaloosa, Selma, Montgomery, and back to Rome, Ga., when he could be met from Chattanooga. I take it for granted that Beauregard will bring, as fast as he can, such part of Hood's army as can be moved over to Augusta to hit me in flank as I swing round Charleston. To cover the withdrawal Forrest will be left in Mississippi and West Tennessee, to divert attention by threatening the boats on the Mississippi and Tennessee Rivers. This should be disregarded and Thomas should break through the shell, expose the trick, and prevent the planting of corn this spring in Middle Alabama. The people of Georgia, like those of Mississippi, are worn out with care, but they are so afraid of their own leaders that they fear to organize for positive resistance. Their motives of 'honor' and 'fair play' are, that by abandoning the cause now they would be construed as 'mean' for leaving their commands in the scrape. I have met the overtures of the people frankly, and given them the best advice I knew how. I inclose copies of orders issued for the guidance of General Foster and other officers on this coast. These orders are made on conference with the Secretary of War. I have been told that Congress meditates a bill to make another lieutenant-general for me. I have written to John Sherman to stop it, if it is designed for me. It would be mischievous, for there are enough rascals who would try to sow differences between us, whereas you and I now are in perfect understanding. I would rather have you in command than anybody else, for you are fair, honest, and have at heart the same purpose that should animate all. I should emphatically decline any commission calculated to bring us into rivalry, and I ask you to advise all your friends in Congress to this effect, especially Mr. Washburne. I doubt if men in Congress fully realize that you and I are honest in our professions of want of ambition. I know I feel none, and to-day will gladly surrender my position and influence to any other who is better able to wield the power. The flurry attending my recent success will soon blow over, and give place to new developments. I inclose a letter of general instructions to General Thomas, which I beg you to revise and indorse or modify." *Ibid.*, pp. 102–4.

1. See letters to Maj. Gen. John M. Schofield and to Maj. Gen. George H. Thomas, Jan. 31, 1865.

To Edwin M. Stanton

(Cipher)   City Point, Va, Feb.y 2d *18645.* [*11:30* A.M.]
Hon. E. M. Stanton, Sec. of War Washington

I am endeavoring to make arrangements to exchange about 3000 prisoners per week. This is as fast, and possibly faster, than they can be delivered to us. Please have facilities given Lt. Col. Mulford to get rebel prisoners to comply with this arrangement. I would like disabled troops, troops from Mo. Ky. Tenn. Ark. & La. sent first as but few of these will be got in the ranks again and as we can count upon but little reinforcement from the prisoners we get.

                                                            U. S. Grant
                                                            Lt. Gn.

ALS (telegram sent), CSmH; telegram received (at 1:00 P.M.), DNA, RG 107, Telegrams Collected (Bound); *ibid.*, RG 249, Letters Received. *O.R.*, II, viii, 170. Two copies in DLC-Edwin M. Stanton include one misdated Feb. 21, 1865. On Feb. 3, Bvt. Brig. Gen. William Hoffman, commissary gen. of prisoners, telegraphed to USG. "Rebel prisoners of war belonging to regiments from Missouri, Kentucky, Tennessee, Arkansas, and Louisiana, and disabled prisoners are distributed through all the prison stations. Shall I collect them together at Point-Lookout preparatory to their being forwarded for exchange? It will be attended with some delay. Some deliveries must first be made from there to make room for them." ALS (telegram sent), DNA, RG 107, Telegrams Collected (Unbound); telegram received (at 12:30 P.M.), *ibid.*, RG 108, Letters Received. *O.R.*, II, viii, 173. On the same day, USG telegraphed to Hoffman. "The prisoners designated in your despatch may be collected at Point Lookout as far as there is room for them; in the mean time exchanges will be made from those prisoners convenient to reach—" Telegram received (at 4:00 P.M.), DNA, RG 107, Telegrams Collected (Bound); *ibid.*, RG 249, Letters Received; copies, *ibid.*, RG 107, Telegrams Received in Cipher; *ibid.*, RG 108, Letters Sent; DLC-USG, V, 46, 72, 108; USG 3. *O.R.*, II, viii, 173.

To Edwin M. Stanton

                                        City Point Va, Feby 2d 1865 [*9:30* P.M.]
Hon, E, M, Stanton
Sec, of War, Washington

I am in receipt of a letter from Gen, Sherman,[1] He expected to move from Pocotaligo on Teusday[2] last, He asks to have Foster

relieved and Schofield, succeed him, Head, Qrs, at Beaufort N, C.
He was not aware of N, C, being taken from Fosters command,
however I would favor the removal of Foster on the ground of
Phisical disability. We want a man who is not confined to his
Qaurters, Terry would suit me for that command, Now that
Schofield goes to N, C, two of his Division commanders rank Terry

U, S, GRANT
Lieut, Genl,

Telegram received (at 10:15 P.M.—faded), DNA, RG 107, Telegrams Collected
(Bound); copies, *ibid.*, Telegrams Received in Cipher; *ibid.*, RG 108, Letters
Sent; DLC-USG, V, 46, 72, 108. *O.R.*, I, xlvii, part 2, 204.

1. See letter to Maj. Gen. William T. Sherman, Feb. 1, 1865.
2. Jan. 31.

To Maj. Gen. Edward O. C. Ord

———

City-Point, Va. Feby 2nd 1865

MAJ GEN E. O. C ORD.
COMD'G ARMY OF THE JAMES
GENERAL:

By information received from Richmond I learn that on the
last occasion when your Cavalry went out they could have gone into
Richmond without opposition, if they had attempted it. From the
Nine Mile road into the City there is but little at present to resist
an advance   I wish you would have this matter investigated as far
as you can, without attracting the attention of the enemy to it, and
also get such information as you can of the condition of the roads
which would have to be traversed to get from your position by
the enemy's left, and on to the rail-roads running North from
Richmond.

If this weather continues for a few days. I think of making
such a move. You would be reinforced in that Case with one Corps
from the Army of the Potomac and a Second Corps would be held

in readiness to join you if any considerable force should be taken
from Petersburg to go against you.

>   Very Respectfully
>   Your Obt. Svt.
>   U. S. Grant.
>   Lieut. General.

Copies, DLC-USG, V, 46, 73, 108; DNA, RG 108, Letters Sent. *O.R.*, I, xlvi,
part 2, 356. On Feb. 3, 1865, Bvt. Maj. Gen. August V. Kautz wrote to Brig.
Gen. John W. Turner, chief of staff for Maj. Gen. Edward O. C. Ord, stating
that he doubted that the expedition could have entered Richmond but expressing
interest in probing, either by patrols or through spies, and asking for money to
pay the latter. *Ibid.*, pp. 363–64. On the same day, Ord endorsed this letter to
USG. *Ibid.*, p. 364. See letter to Edwin M. Stanton, Feb. 4, 1865.

To Lt. Col. John E. Mulford

>   City Point, Va, Feb.y 2d *1864*5.

Lt. Col. Mulford, Steamer New York,
Telegraph to Jones' Landing.

Inform Col. Hatch[1] who is now on his way to see you that all
Confederate Prisoners confined in cells or in irons have been ordered to Fortress Monroe subject to your orders for the purpose of
carrying out the proposition made by Col. Ould. Ask that a corresponding order may be made for Federal prisoners and that they
be brought to Richmond so that the exchange may be speedily
made. You may also make arrangements for exchanging 3000 prisoners per week, or as mayny as can be delivered on each side. I
think 3,000 probably is as many as can be delivered weekly until
arrangements better than now exist can be made for transporting
them. Let your arrangements look to an exchange, man for man,
until the party having the fewest prisoners is exhausted of all on
hand.

>   U. S. Grant
>   Lt. Gn.

ALS (telegram sent), CSmH; copies, DLC-USG, V, 46, 72, 108; DNA, RG 108,
Letters Sent; USG 3. *O.R.*, II, viii, 170. On Feb. 2, 1865, Lt. Col. John E. Mul-

ford, Varina, Va., telegraphed to USG. "Your despatch received. I have already forwarded Mr Ould a letter on the subject of hostages of which I send you a copy. The other matter I will arrange immediately & report to you the result." ALS (telegram sent), DNA, RG 107, Telegrams Collected (Unbound); telegram received (at 1:45 P.M.—marked as sent from Jones' Landing), *ibid.*, RG 108, Letters Received. *O.R.*, II, viii, 171.

On the same day, Lt. Col. Theodore S. Bowers wrote to Mulford. "Your telegram in relation to clothing for prisoners, is received 2.500 Blouses shirts and trousers will be sent you to morrow There are no blankets here now but a supply is expected in a fiew day's" Copies, DLC-USG, V, 46, 72, 108; DNA, RG 108, Letters Sent.

1. C.S.A. Lt. Col. William H. Hatch, asst. agent of exchange.

To Richard J. Oglesby

City Point, Va, Feb.y 2d *1864*5.

DEAR GOVERNOR,

Your letter of the 26th of Jan.y, is received. I did not know that Gen. Haynie was an applica[n]t for the office of Adj. Gn. of th[e] state or I would not have written a line to prejudice his chances of appointment. I have a high appreciations of Col. Loomis' services in the office, and especially at the begining of the War when he really seemed to be the only man in the office capable of keeping a record for future reference. But I have an equal appreciation of Gn. Haynie's services in the field, and of the stand he has taken on the side of the country.

Everything now points to an early termination of the rebellion. Our Armies, I think, are well disposed for irresistable action. Every week henceforth may be expected to chronicle events ~~having~~ full of importance. I cannot write of plans but they will be developed to the public as they transpire.

Wishing you a long life and a successful administration of State Affairs, I subscribe myself,

Truly Yours
U. S. GRANT
~~Lt.~~

ALS, Oglesby Papers, IHi.

To Edwin M. Stanton

————

City Point Va, Feby 3d 1865 [2:00 P.M.]

HON, E. M. STANTON
SEC, OF WAR WASHINGTON

I think it advisable to request the Navy to keep two or three Vessels patrolling between Cape Henry, and Cape Fear during the transit of Schofields troops   It is bearly possible for one of the Enemy's Privateers to get on that route and do us great injury,   If you agree with me will you please request this?

U. S. GRANT
Lieut, Genl,

Telegram, copies, DLC-USG, V, 46, 72, 108; DLC-John M. Schofield; DNA, RG 107, Telegrams Received in Cipher; *ibid.*, RG 108, Letters Sent. *O.R.*, I, xlvii, part 2, 284–85; *O.R.* (Navy), I, xii, 4.

To Edwin M. Stanton

————

City Point Va, Feby 3d 1865 [9:00 P.M.]

HON, E. M. STANTON
SEC, OF WAR WASHINGTON

In view of elections to be held in Tennessee, and important Legislation that is expected in that state,[1] I would submit whether it is not better that the whole state should be under one commander,   If you approve this I would suggest that West Ky. and West Tenn, be added to Gen, Thomas command and that Gen, Washburne be returned to the command of the latter,   Whilst Gen, Dana might do well in the field I do not think him the most suitable man for the command of a Dept,   Gen, Washburne has been ordered to report to Gen, Ord,[2]   But as that order probably only went out to day it can be changed if you approve,   If Gen, Banks is not to go back to the Dept, of the Gulf I would suggest some other Officer than Gen, Hurlbut for the command of that Dept,

If the change in Thomas command is made it would be advisable to add the state of Miss, to the Gulf Dept,

U. S. GRANT
Lieut Genl,

Telegram, copies, DLC-USG, V, 46, 72, 108; DNA, RG 108, Letters Sent; (addressed to Maj. Gen. Henry W. Halleck—received at 10:40 P.M.) *ibid.*, RG 107, Telegrams Received in Cipher. *O.R.*, I, xlviii, part 1, 727. On Feb. 4, 1865, 1:50 P.M., Halleck telegraphed to USG. "Order to Genl Washburne has been countermanded. I concur with you in regard to Genl Dana, but it would be still worse to add the posts on the Mississippi to Genl Banks' command. The latter is still under orders to return to his Dept, but I believe is now in Washington. It seems necessary that the troops on both sides of the river as high as Memphis should be under the same commander, as they must be used to prevent Kirby Smith from uniting with Hood, & therefore must operate sometimes on one bank & sometimes on the other. I have just recieved a communication from Genl Canby on this subject, & I will telegraph to Genl Thomas for his views. Probably the matter had better be left as it is, until we hear from Thomas." ALS (telegram sent), DNA, RG 107, Telegrams Collected (Bound); telegram received, *ibid.*; (marked as sent at 1:20 P.M.) *ibid.*, RG 108, Letters Received. *O.R.*, I, xlviii, part 1, 736–37. At 5:00 P.M., USG telegraphed to Halleck. "If Gen. Washburn is not placed in command of West Tenn. I want him to come on to take command at Norfolk. He is one of the best administrative Officers we have and will effectually stop supplies being sent through our lines to the enemy where ever he is. We want such a ~~com~~ man at each of the above places." ALS (telegram sent), OClWHi; copies, DLC-USG, V, 46, 72, 108; DNA, RG 107, Telegrams Received in Cipher; *ibid.*, RG 108, Letters Sent. Printed as received at 7:30 P.M. in *O.R.*, I, xlvi, part 2, 366; *ibid.*, I, xlviii, part 1, 737. See telegram to Maj. Gen. Edward O. C. Ord, Feb. 7, 1865.

On Feb. 20, U.S. Representative Elihu B. Washburne wrote to USG. "Becoming satisfied that your order in regard to Genl. Washburn going to Memphis had not been executed, I called at the War Dept. this morning to enquire about it. Genl. Townsend sent over to Hallack and found nothing had been done, and then H. sent off a *feeble* despatch of which a copy is enclosed, which is no order at all. I am willing that Genl. Hallack should punish me all he is able to, for my instrumentality in getting through the Lt. General Bill, but I protest against his visiting his ill will towards me on a faithful officer, who was in noway responsible for my action in that matter. Mrs. W. arrived here safely on Saturday night." ALS, DNA, RG 108, Letters Received. *O.R.*, I, xlix, part 1, 746–47. On Feb. 22, Lt. Col. Theodore S. Bowers issued Special Orders No. 36 assigning Maj. Gen. Cadwallader C. Washburn to command the District of West Tenn. Copies, DLC-USG, V, 57, 63, 64, 65. *O.R.*, I, xlix, part 1, 947.

1. A constitutional convention that first convened at Nashville on Jan. 9 proposed an amendment abolishing slavery, ratified by popular vote on Feb. 22. Thomas B. Alexander, *Political Reconstruction in Tennessee* (Nashville, 1950), pp. 18–36.

2. On Feb. 2, 11:00 A.M., USG telegraphed to Maj. Gen. Edward O. C.

Ord. "If you have not already put Gordon in Command at Norfolk I will order
C C Washburn there   he made the best Comdr for West Tennesse we have Ever
had"   Telegram received, Ord Papers, CU-B; DNA, RG 107, Telegrams Collected (Unbound); copies, *ibid.*, RG 108, Letters Sent; DLC-USG, V, 46, 72,
108. *O.R.*, I, xlvi, part 2, 356. At 9:30 P.M., USG telegraphed to Halleck.
"Please order Gen. Dana to relieve Maj. Gen. C. C. Washburn and order him to
report to Gn. Ord for duty. Gen. Tower need not be relieved from his present
duties. If already relieved he can be returned." ALS (telegram sent), CSmH;
telegram received (at 10:15 P.M.), DNA, RG 107, Telegrams Collected (Bound).
O.R., I, xlviii, part 1, 720.

To Edwin M. Stanton

City Point, Va. Feb.y 3d *1864*5.

HON. E. M. STANTON,
SEC. OF WAR,
SIR:

I would respectfully recommend the appointment of 1st Lieut.
Wm M. Dunn, 83d Indiana Infantry Vols, for the appointment of
2d Lieut. 4th U. S. Infantry.

Lieut. Dunn entered the Three months service at the breaking
out of the rebellion, as a private, and has continued in service ever
since. He is now, and has been since the fall of Vicksburg, been
serving on my Staff. He is now in his Twenty second year, a young
man of fine character and great soldierly ambition. His father, Col.
Dunn, Asst. Judge Advocate General, has been a warm supporter
of the Government through all its trials, so that this appointment,
good in itself, has been twice earned.

Hoping that it will be found consistent with established rules
to make this appointment, I subscribe myself,

Very respectfully
your obt. svt.
U. S. GRANT
Lt. Gen

ALS, DNA, RG 94, ACP, 2187 1871. No appointment followed.

To Bvt. Maj. Gen. Montgomery C. Meigs

(Cipher)   City Point, Va, Feb.y 3 *18645*. [*9:30* P.M.]
MAJ. GEN. MEIGS Q. M. GN. WASHINGTON

Gen. Ingalls will be in Washington to-morrow. He can answer your questions in regard to Col. Webster. Col. Dodge[1] will probably return to the Dept. of Va. so that it will not be necessary to put the Q. M. 24th Corps in as Chief in the Dept.

U. S. GRANT
Lt. Gn.

ALS (telegram sent), CSmH; telegram received (at 10:40 P.M.), DNA, RG 107, Telegrams Collected (Bound). *O.R.*, I, xlvi, part 2, 361. On Jan. 26, 1865, Maj. Gen. Edward O. C. Ord wrote to USG requesting that Lt. Col. John B. Howard replace Col. Ralph C. Webster as q. m., Dept. of Va. and N. C., and USG endorsed the letter on the same day. "Respy forwarded to the QMG with the request that Col Webster be assigned to duty outside of the Dept of Virginia" Copy, DLC-USG, V, 58. On Feb. 1, Bvt. Maj. Gen. Montgomery C. Meigs wrote to USG. "I have received a request from you that Colonel R. C. Webster, now Chief Quartermaster of the Dept. of Virginia, be assigned to duty outside of that Department, and I have nominated him to the Secretary of War as a member of a board for the examination of Quartermasters in the Department of the Cumberland. This, if approved, will not vacate his present rank and position, and before any action is taken which may look to such a result, I request to be informed whether there are any charges against Colonel Webster tending to show unfitness for his present position from any cause. He had the confidence and esteem of Colonel Biggs, who highly recommended him to me, and he, so far as my information goes, has shown fidelity and, at least, reasonable ability in the discharge of his duties. I see that Genl. Ord requests that the Chief Qr. Mr. of the 24th. Army Corps, may be appointed Chief Qr. Mr. of the Dept. of Virginia, in place of Colonel Webster. The law intends that these staff officers shall not be changed upon change of commanders without some good reason beyond the wishes of the local commander. If Colonel Webster has not failed in ability or worth he ought not to lose his rank and position. I do not think that he has been so connected with the late commander of the Department as to make it difficult for him to serve usefully under any new Commanding General. You will relieve me from embarrassment if you will inform me of any grounds for your request, which go to show that a change is necessary for the good of the service. I know that you would not lightly make such a request, and have therefore taken steps for his temporary assignment to duty elsewhere." LS, DNA, RG 92, Miscellaneous Letters Sent (Press).

1. George S. Dodge of Vt., appointed q. m. and capt. as of May 12, 1862, assigned as chief q. m. and col., Army of the James, had accompanied the Fort Fisher expedition.

To Maj. Gen. Henry W. Halleck

City Point, Va, Feb.y 3d *1864*5.

MAJ. GEN. HALLECK, WASHINGTON.

Gen. Thomas' dispatch of the ~~29th~~ 1st received.[1] I do not think it will be safe to deplete his Army of Five Divisions of Cavalry. Three or Four thousand will be sufficient for Canby and will leave Thomas with enough to meet Forrest if he should attempt to come North or to penetrate Alabama if Forrest should turn against Canby. Sherman is very desirous that Thomas should push a force down to Kingston and Rome this Winter repairing the road after him if he can do no more. I doubt whether he has the force to do this now that Smith is taken from him. It might be submitted to him however whether it can be done or not. I have sent a staff officer with instructions for Gen. Thomas to send Stoneman from Knoxville on a raid upon the roads in the North part of South Carolina. This however will take none, or but few, of his troops from Middle Tennessee

U. S. GRANT
Lt. Gen.

ALS (telegram sent), deCoppet Collection, NjP; copies, DLC-USG, V, 46, 72, 108; (marked as sent at 1:00 P.M., received at 2:10 P.M.) DNA, RG 107, Telegrams Received in Cipher; *ibid.*, RG 108, Letters Sent. Printed as received at 4:00 P.M. in *O.R.*, I, xlix, part 1, 636–37. On Feb. 4, 1865, 1:00 P.M., USG telegraphed to Maj. Gen. Henry W. Halleck. "Gen, Thomas may send all the troops ordered before forwarding transportation except such as can be carried along without delaying the movement, About half the transportation of the troops going to Canby should follow as rapidly as possible" Copies, DLC-USG, V, 46, 72, 108; (marked as received at 3:15 P.M.) DNA, RG 107, Telegrams Received in Cipher; *ibid.*, RG 108, Letters Sent. *O.R.*, I, xlix, part 1, 646.

1. See *ibid.*, pp. 623–24.

To Edwin M. Stanton

City Point Va, Feby 4th 1865 [*10:00* P.M.]

HON, E, M, STANTON

SEC, OF WAR, WASHINGTON

I have ordered the Cavalry to move down the Welden road to morrow for the purpose of breaking up the enemy's wagon train, as far as they can, which is being used to draw supplies from Bellefield to Petersburg, A Corps of Infantry goes as far as Stony Creek in support, I telegraph this so that you may know the object of the movement when you hear of it,

U. S. GRANT Lt. Genl.

Telegram, copies, DLC-USG, V, 46, 72, 108; (marked as received at 11:40 P.M.) DNA, RG 107, Telegrams Received in Cipher; *ibid.*, RG 108, Letters Sent. *O.R.*, I, xlvi, part 2, 366.

To Edwin M. Stanton

City Point Feby 4th 1865

HON, E, M, STANTON

SEC, OF WAR

SIR!

Two or three times each week, scouts are sent from here into Richmond, The only funds the Provost Marshal has for defraying their expences is United States Currency, These funds naturally would attract suspicion and have therefore to be converted for their use, If therefore you have any Rebel Currency I would respectfully request that from twenty to fifty thousand dollars be sent to Col, Geo, H, Sharpe Asst Provost Marshal General at City Point,

Very Respy Your obt svt

U, S, GRANT

Lt, Gen,

Copies, DLC-USG, V, 46, 72, 108; DNA, RG 108, Letters Sent. *O.R.*, I, xlvi, part 2, 366. See letter to Maj. Gen. Edward O. C. Ord, Feb. 2, 1865.

On Feb. 8, 1865, USG telegraphed to Maj. Gen. Edward O. C. Ord. "Please turn over to Col. George H. Sharpe asst. Pro. Mar. Gen. ten thousand (10000) dollars confederate money"   Telegram received, Ord Papers, CU-B.

To Edwin M. Stanton

Confidential   City Point, Va, Feb.y 4th *1864*5.
HON. E. M. STANTON,
SEC. OF WAR,
DEAR SIR:

The appearance of Mr. Stephens and party within our lines has had no influance on Military movements whatever. The swamps about Richmond and Petersburg are entirely impassable for Artillery if I wanted to move by either flank. But I do not want to do anything to force the enemy from Richmond until Schofield carries out his programme. He is to take Wilmington and then push out to Goldsboro', or as near it as he can go, and build up the road after him. He will then be in a position to assist Sherman if Lee should leave Richmond with any considerable force, and the two together will be strong enough for all the enemy have to put against them. Terry is being reinforced from here with the fragments of Divisions which were left behind when he started on his expedition. The number left in this way proves to be 5500 men. Schofield takes about 23000 effective men and Terry has already about 7500. Altogether this makes a formidable force.

I shall necessarily have to take the odium of apparent inactivity but if it results, as I expect it will, in the discomfiture of Lee's Army, I shall be entirely satisfied.

> Very respectfully
> your obt. svt.
> U. S. GRANT
> Lt. Gn.

ALS, DLC-Edwin M. Stanton. *O.R.*, I, xlvi, part 2, 365. On Feb. 4, 1865, President Abraham Lincoln drafted, and Secretary of War Edwin M. Stanton signed, a telegram to USG. "The President desires me to repeat that nothing transpired, or transpiring with the three gentleman from Richmond, ~~will~~ is to cause any change hindrance or delay, of your military plans or operations." LS (telegram

sent), Edward C. Stone Collection, Boston University Library, Boston, Mass.;
telegram received (marked as sent at 12:30 P.M.), DNA, RG 108, Letters Received; copy (marked as sent at 12:20 P.M.), DLC-Robert T. Lincoln. *O.R.*, I,
xlvi, part 2, 365. Lincoln, *Works*, VIII, 258.

On Feb. 7, USG telegraphed to Stanton transmitting documents printed in
the *Richmond Dispatch* concerning the C.S.A. commissioners. *O.R.*, I, xlvi, part
2, 446; (incomplete) *ibid.*, I, xlvii, part 2, 328.

To Maj. Gen. Henry W. Halleck

City Point Va, Feby 4th 1865 [*3:00* P.M.]

MAJ, GENL, HALLECK WASHINGTON

I respectfully request that Gen, Ord may be named as permanent Commander of the Dept, of Va,   If Hancock is to be returned
to the field I would name him for the Dept of the South,   Otherwise I would leave my recommendation of Gen, Terry made to the
Sec, of War in a dispatch of yesterday

U. S. GRANT
Lieut Genl.

Telegram, copies, DLC-USG, V, 46, 72, 108; (marked as received at 4:30 P.M.)
DNA, RG 107, Telegrams Received in Cipher; *ibid.*, RG 108, Letters Sent.
Printed as received at 6:00 P.M. in *O.R.*, I, xlvi, part 2, 366. See telegram to
Maj. Gen. Henry W. Halleck, Feb. 6, 1865.

On Feb. 4, 1865, 10:30 A.M., Maj. Gen. Edward O. C. Ord telegraphed to
Brig. Gen. John A. Rawlins. "Signal officer Cobb's Hill reports four extra trains
passing toward Petersburg, on the Petersburg and Richmond Railroad, after
dark last night; thought them heavily loaded. Trains returned toward Richmond
at 9 and 10.15 p. m." *O.R.*, I, xlvi, part 2, 383. On the same day, USG telegraphed to Ord. "You can go to Ft. Monroe to return to-morrow evening or
night." ALS (telegram sent), Kohns Collection, NN; telegram received, Ord
Papers, CU-B. *O.R.*, I, xlvi, part 2, 383.

To Maj. Gen. George G. Meade

(Cipher)   City Point, Va, Feb.y 4th *18645*. [*6:45* P.M.]

MAJ. GEN. MEADE,

I presume you are in receipt of my answer to your dispatch of
1.30 p. m. before this. Your arrangements are satisfactory. The

object to be attained are of importance. I will telegraph to Sec.
Stanton in advance shewing the object of the movement the publication of which, with the reports of operations, will satisfy the
public. When do your troops start out?

U. S. GRANT
Lt. Gen.

ALS (telegram sent), OClWHi; telegram received, DNA, RG 94, War Records
Office, Army of the Potomac. *O.R.*, I, xlvi, part 2, 368. See following letter. On
Feb. 4, 1865, 7:45 P.M., Maj. Gen. George G. Meade telegraphed to USG.
"Despatch of 7. P. M received—The orders are all issued—The cavalry will move
at 3. A M & the infantry at 7. A M. Contrabands have come in this P. M reporting the departure last thursday week of Butlers division of cavalry for No. Ca.—
this would leave only one division W. H. F. Lee's to oppose Gregg.—" ALS
(telegram sent), DNA, RG 94, War Records Office, Army of the Potomac; telegram received (at 8:15 P.M.), *ibid.*, RG 108, Letters Received. Printed as sent
at 8:15 P.M. in *O.R.*, I, xlvi, part 2, 368. At 8:30 P.M., USG telegraphed to
Meade. "If Gregg can possibly go to Bellefield he probably will be enabled to
destroy a large amount of stores accumulated there. The departure of one Division of the enemy's Cavalry will favor this." ALS (telegram sent), OClWHi;
telegram received, DNA, RG 94, War Records Office, Army of the Potomac;
ibid., RG 107, Telegrams Collected (Unbound). *O.R.*, I, xlvi, part 2, 368.
Meade endorsed this telegram to Bvt. Maj. Gen. David M. Gregg. *Ibid.*, p. 369.
At 9:30 P.M., Meade telegraphed to USG. "Orders have been sent to Gregg to
proceed to Bellfield provided he finds on reaching Dinwiddie C. H. any confirmation of the contraband's report, or obtains any reliable intelligence leading him
to believe he can affect anything there The depot is however undoubtedly at
Hicksford across the Meherrin and is guarded by artillery as it was when Warren
was there We also believe that W. H. F Lee's division of cav. is in that vicinity
—Gregg goes without artillery" Telegram received (at 10:15 P.M.), DNA, RG
108, Letters Received; copies (misdated Feb. 5), *ibid.*, RG 393, Army of the
Potomac, Letters Sent; Meade Papers, PHi. *O.R.*, I, xlvi, part 2, 369; (misdated
Feb. 5) *ibid.*, p. 390; *ibid.*, I, xlvi, part 1, 150.
    Also on Feb. 4, USG telegraphed to Meade. "will you be at your Head Qrs
tomorrow forenoon? If so I will go out & take Mrs Grant with me." Telegram
received, DNA, RG 94, War Records Office, Army of the Potomac. *O.R.*, I, xlvi,
part 2, 369. On the same day (sent at 11:20 P.M.), Meade telegraphed to USG.
"I propose going out with the troops on the Vaughan Road to morrow at 8 a. m.
In case I should not I will advise you and will then be most happy to see Mrs
Grant & yourself." Telegram sent, DNA, RG 94, War Records Office, Army of
the Potomac; copies, *ibid.*, RG 393, Army of the Potomac, Letters Sent; Meade
Papers, PHi. *O.R.*, I, xlvi, part 2, 369. On the same day, USG telegraphed to
Meade. "Do not return to your Hd Qrs on account of my proposed visit—any other
day will suit me as well for going out as tomorrow" Telegram received, DNA,
RG 94, War Records Office, Army of the Potomac. *O.R.*, I, xlvi, part 2, 369.

To Maj. Gen. George G. Meade

Confidential.   City Point, Va, Feby 4th 1865.
MAJ GEN. G. G. MEADE
COMD'G ARMY POTOMAC
GENERAL:

I would like to take advantage of the present good weather to destroy or capture as much as possible of the Enemy's wagon Train, which it is understood is being used in connection with the Weldon Railroad to partially supply the troops about Petersburg. You may get the Cavalry ready to do this as soon as possible—I think the Cavalry should start at 3 A. M. either to-morrow or the day following, carrying one and a-half-days forage and three days rations with them. They should take no wagons and but few ambulances. Let the 2nd Corps move at the same time, but independent of the Cavalry, as far south as Stoney Creek Station, to remain there until the Cavalry has done the enemy all the harm it can and returns to that point. The Infantry may take four days rations in haversacks and one and a half days forage for the Cavalry in wagons The Artillery taken along may be reduced to one battery to each Division or one Section from each Battery at your option. The 5th Corps should also be held in readiness to go to the support of the 2d Corps if the enemy should move out to attack. Probably it will be well to move the 5th Corps at the same time with the 2d Corps sending it by a road west of the one taken by the latter, and to go but about half way to Stoney Creek unless required to do so to meet movements of the enemy. They will go out prepared to remain four days.

> Very Respectfully.
> Your Obt. Servt.
> U. S. GRANT.
> Lieut Gen

Copies, DLC-USG, V, 46, 73, 108; DNA, RG 108, Letters Sent; (2) Meade Papers, PHi. *O.R.*, I, xlvi, part 2, 367. On Feb. 4, 1865, 1:45 P.M. (sent at 2:10 P.M.), Maj. Gen. George G. Meade telegraphed to USG. "Despatch per Capt Dunn received. The second corps has one division in the line—the relieving this

Division would take time & attract the attention of the enemy—I propose to send the 5th corps to stoney creek & ~~the~~ two divisions of the 2d. to Ream's Station, where they will be in position to support Warren, or return to our left flank if threatened—Please advise me if this meets your approbation." ALS (telegram sent), DNA, RG 94, War Records Office, Army of the Potomac; telegram received (at 3:00 P.M.), *ibid.*, RG 108, Letters Received. *O.R.*, I, xlvi, part 2, 367. See *ibid.*, pp. 370–71. At 3:30 P.M., USG telegraphed to Meade. "Your arrangement for moving troops is satisfactory. I mentioned the 2d Corps for the longest march merely because the last expedition was made by the 5th Corps." ALS (telegram sent), OClWHi; telegram received, DNA, RG 94, War Records Office, Army of the Potomac. *O.R.*, I, xlvi, part 2, 367. At 3:45 P.M. (sent at 4:30 P.M.), Meade telegraphed to USG. "I am awaiting a reply to my telegram of 1.45 before issuing any orders—I learn the enemy wagon on the Boydtown plank road crossing the Nottoway at Burchets bridge—I propose to send Warren to the crossing of stony creek by the Vaughn road, and Humphreys to the crossing of Hatchers run by the same road—This will be extending our positions in supporting distances nearly to Dinwiddie C. H.—The cavalry will strike the road at Dinwiddie & move up & down looking for the trains—We have as good a chance of striking these trains near Dinwiddie as near Bellefield, and the infantry will not have so far to march & should the enemy be disposed to come out & fight we shall be in good position to invite them—Please let me have your views & the movement will at once be ordered for tomorrow—I venture to make one suggestion—Are the objects to be attained commensurate with the disappointment which the public are sure to entertain, if you make any movement & return without some striking result.—" ALS (telegram sent), DNA, RG 94, War Records Office, Army of the Potomac; telegram received (at 5:45 P.M.), *ibid.*, RG 108, Letters Received. *O.R.*, I, xlvi, part 2, 367–68. See preceding telegram.

To Commander Daniel Ammen

HEAD-QUARTERS ARMIES OF THE UNITED STATES,
CITY POINT, Feb. 4th, 1865.

DEAR AMMEN,—

Your letter of the 16th of January is just received. You have no doubt seen by the papers that the very thing you so strongly hoped had already taken place. I mean, Butler had been removed at my request. The failure at Fort Fisher was not without important and valuable results.

I have long thought from the representations of army officers that the change you suggest in naval commander in South Atlantic[1] should also be made. I do not, however, feel myself authorized to suggest changes of naval commanders, so long as their duties are confined to blockading. When it comes to co-operation with the army in an attack, I do not hesitate.

Everything now seems to be progressing favorably. I am sending an additional force of about twenty-eight thousand effective men to Cape Fear River and New-Berne. These troops, or part of them, sailed this morning, and so far their destination does not seem to have been suspected even by our own people. Before the enemy are aware of it, I hope to have Wilmington, and, before they can prevent it, Goldsborough. This will make a formidable force to co-operate with Sherman. I shall also have the railroad in working order from Wilmington to New-Berne out as far as we occupy, and supplies thrown out for Sherman's use.

I have been a little negligent about answering your very welcome letters, but I am none the less glad to receive them. I will be very much pleased to hear from you whenever you can find time to write, and will answer when there is anything to say.

Yours truly,
U. S. GRANT.

You will see that Terry has been made a full major-general of volunteers and a brigadier-general in the regular army. I have also recommended him for the command now held by Foster.

Daniel Ammen, *The Old Navy and the New* (Philadelphia, 1891), pp. 532–33. In his letter to USG, Commander Daniel Ammen had stated that the U.S. Navy could silence the guns at Fort Fisher and cover a landing nearby. *Ibid.*, p. 533.

1. Rear Admiral John A. Dahlgren commanded the South Atlantic Blockading Squadron.

To Edwin M. Stanton

City Point, Va, Feb 5th 1865 [11:30 P.M.]

HON, E, M, STANTON
SECY OF WAR, WASHINGTON

Will you please say to the President, that Lieut, Markbreit has been released from prison and is now on his way North,[1] Arrangement's for Exchange of all prisoners of War is now complete and Exchanges will now go on rapidly,   All but two of those that were in close confinement in Richmond are now on the Steamer New York,   I am also in receipt of supplies of Clothing for our prisoners and the completion of arrangements for transportation and distribution[2]

U, S, GRANT

Lieut, Genl,

Telegram, copies, DLC-USG, V, 46, 72, 108; DNA, RG 108, Letters Sent. *O.R.*, II, viii, 182, 811.

1. 1st Lt. Leopold Markbreit, 28th Ohio, captured while serving on the staff of Brig. Gen. William W. Averell, had been held in a cell at Libby Prison, Richmond, in retaliation for treatment of prisoners at Johnson's Island, Ohio. *O.R.*, II, vii, 197, 211–12, 457, 983, 1190–91, 1231; *ibid.*, II, viii, 28–30. On Jan. 7, 1865, Maj. Gen. Ethan A. Hitchcock wrote to USG. "I have the honor to enclose, with this, by the direction of the President, certain papers numbered from 1 to 18 inclusive, in relation to several officers, including Lt. Markbreit. Among these papers there is one (no. 6) containing the copy of an endorsement by Mr. Ould proposing a certain measure, the character of which will be seen by reference to it. That proposition was submitted to the Sec'y of War, and was by him approved, which approval I communicated to Lt. Col. Mulford, Since which no official communication has been made to me on the subject. It is known however, that the arrangement did not take effect. Lt. Markbreit is step brother to Mr. Hassaurek, our minister to Equador, and Mr. Hassaurek is interested in his case. The President has directed me to place these papers in his hands, to be by him submitted to yourself; and I am further directed by His Excellency to advise you that it is his desire that you would examine the subject to which they refer, or, to use his own language, he desires you to *reconsider* the matter and give Such orders as in your judgment maybe Suitable and proper. . . . P. S—The papers enclosed with this belong to the War Office and to my own office, and I respectfully request their return by the hands of Mr. Hassaurek if convenient." Copy, DLC-Ethan A. Hitchcock. *O.R.*, II, viii, 34. See Lincoln, *Works*, VIII, 10, 263–64.

2. On Feb. 1, Brig. Gen. Joseph Hayes, Richmond, wrote to USG's hd. qrs. "I have the honor to report my arrival in this City from Danville on Thursday, the 26th ulto. Upon the following day, I received official information from Mr. Ould, Agent of Exchange, of my appointment as Agent to receive and distribute supplies for Union prisoners. Yesterday, the supplies, consisting of six hundred and fifty private packages and fifty bales of blankets were transferred to me. I have been paroled to attend to this business together with Lieut. L. Markbriet, 28th Ohio Vols., who will assist me. A suitable warehouse has been provided for storing the supplies, and I am assured by Mr. Ould that every facility for their transportation will be provided. I have this day issued two hundred and fifty blankets to the Federal prisoners in this City, and shall in a day or two, as soon as transportation can be obtained, send the balance to the prisoners at Danville

and Salisbury, who are in more pressing need. I have nominated three officers at each of those prisons to receive and distribute these supplies. A traveling agent will accompany them upon the road to ensure their safe delivery. In addition to the blankets, I think there are needed at least 2000 Complete suits of clothing (exclusive of overcoats which are unnessessary) to clothe our men that are absolutely naked, or nearly so. I would recommend that they be sent. I find myself in need of funds to defray the public expenses incident to my present position, and therefore would request that ($10000) Ten Thousand Dollars) in Confederate funds be sent me by next flag of truce." Copy, DNA, RG 108, Letters Received. *O.R.*, II, viii, 167. On Feb. 6, USG endorsed this letter. "Respy. forwarded to the secretary of war for his information. No action is required on any of the requisitions as they can all be attended to from here, and in the greater part have already been filled" Copy, DLC-USG, V, 58. *O.R.*, II, viii, 167.

On Jan. 23, Francis B. Hayes, Boston, had written to USG. "My brother, Brig. Genl. Joseph Hayes, who was captured before Petersburg several months since, lies immured in a rebel prison at Danville, Va. A letter was received from him dated Decr. 17th last. He had been in Hospital, but had then recovered from his severe illness. He is anxious to be again back in his country's service, and trusts that Government will insist upon his release by exchange. May I beg for the sake of this brave brother of mine, and for his aged & widowed mother, that yu will urge Governmt to insist upon his release? We all look to yu as our chief help & stay under Providence, and must ask yu to urge his exchange, & insist upon it, as far as is proper—My brother never has repined at his sufferings. He has blamed no one even for his capture. He has always been obedient to his superiors, and he is only anxious again to be at liberty to peril his life for his country. Yu have no more faithful officer, nor more devoted soldier than he is. May I not then earnestly entreat you to urge his immediate exchange, that he may be restored to his country & his devoted friends. That GOD may bless yu General in your noble efforts for your country, is the sincere prayer of . . ." ALS, DNA, RG 108, Miscellaneous Papers. On Jan. 27, Hayes again wrote to USG. "I wrote yu a few days since in regard to procuring the exchange of Genl. Joseph Hayes, my brother. Since writing yu I learn it is the desire of Governmt he should act as agent for distributing supplies among our prisoners, being under parole—If that is the wish of Governmt, I pray yu use his services as yu think best. His family would, I know, Express my brother's wish, dearest to his heart, to be of service to the country in this time of her peril. He would wish to be of service in any manner, in any condition, in any place yu thught best. He enterd the service from patriotic motives solely—being entirely independent in his circumstances, and he has first & only at heart the good of his country. He wished his liberty only to devote himself to his country. Will yu please, therfore, exercise your own judgment, uninfluenced by any thing I have heretofore written in behalf of his Mother or family, that my brother may serve the country either at the South or North, precisely as yu think he may be of the most use. This, I know, would be his earnest desire." ALS, *ibid.*

To Maj. Gen. Henry W. Halleck

———

City Point Va, Feby 5th 1865 [*10:30* P.M.]

MAJ, GEN, HALLECK
WASHINGTON

Gregg's Cavalry moved out this A, M, and went as far as Dind-widdle C, H,   He met but little opposition,   As far as he could learn, owing to the destruction of the Welden Bridge and bridge on Boydtown road but few stores were remaining at Bellefield and but few wagons were on the road,   He captured 18 wagons and fifty prisoners,   Warren moved at 7. A, M, to go as far as Stony Creek   He met with but little opposition and reports no casualties, He captured about 30 prisoners,   Humphrey's moved out on the Vaughn road to crossing of Hatchers Run,   He was attacked late in the afternoon but repulsed every attack,   What the casualities have been I do not know,

U, S, GRANT
Lieut, Genl,

Telegram, copies, DLC-USG, V, 46, 72, 108; (marked as received at midnight) DNA, RG 107, Telegrams Received in Cipher; *ibid.*, RG 108, Letters Sent. *O.R.*, I, xlvi, part 2, 388.

To Maj. Gen. John G. Foster

———

City Point, Va, Feb.y 5th *18645*.

MAJ. GEN. FOSTER,
COMD.G DEPT. OF THE SOUTH,
GENERAL,

You are authorized to exchange all rebel prisoners confined within the limits of your command for an equal number of our men held in the South. In making exchanges you will be governed by the Cartel agreed upon in Eighteen sixty two ~~(1862)~~ regulating equivolents where officers of equal rank cannot be exchanged. For any prisoners you may have in close confinement, or in Irons, either

by sentence or in retalliation for like punishment inflicted upon our
men, you must demand the same class of prisone[rs] in return

> Very respectfully
> your. obt. svt.
> U. S. GRANT
> Lt. Gn,

ALS, CSmH.
    On Feb. 14, 1865, Bvt. Brig. Gen. William Hoffman, commissary gen. of
prisoners, telegraphed to USG. "We have six hundred rebel officers at Fort Pulaski and there are as many of our officers held in the vicinity of Charleston. I
respectfully suggest that the rebel officers be delivered on condition that as many
of our officers be delivered to us at the same time" ALS (telegram sent), DNA,
RG 107, Telegrams Collected (Unbound); telegram received (at 12:30 P.M.),
ibid., RG 108, Letters Received. *O.R.*, II, viii, 218–19. On the same day, USG
telegraphed to Hoffman. "Your despatch in reference to exchange of prisoners of
war now at Fort Pulaski is received. On the fifth (5) inst I authorized Maj Gen
J G Foster Com'd'g Detachment of the South to effect the exchange of all prisoners of war within the limits of his Command. I have not yet heard from him on
the subject but presume he will carry out my instructions as promptly as possible." Telegram received (at 3:45 P.M.), DNA, RG 107, Telegrams Collected
(Bound); *ibid.*, RG 249, Letters Received; copies, *ibid.*, RG 108, Letters Sent;
DLC-USG, V, 46, 73, 108; USG 3. *O.R.*, II, viii, 219. On Feb. 9, Maj. Gen. John
G. Foster had relinquished command of the Dept. of the South to Maj. Gen.
Quincy A. Gillmore. *Ibid.*, I, xlvii, part 2, 369.
    On Feb. 22, 7:30 P.M., USG telegraphed to Maj. Gen. Henry W. Halleck.
"Please order Gen. Gilmore to send ~~use~~ here all rebel prisoners in his Dept. for
Exchange." ALS (telegram sent), OClWHi; telegram received (at 8:00 P.M.),
DLC-Edwin M. Stanton. *O.R.*, II, viii, 289. On Feb. 25, Gillmore wrote to USG.
"I have the honor to acknowledge the receipt of your letter of the 5th inst. addressed to Major General. Foster. giving authority to exchange all prisoners of
war now held by me in this Department. In consequence of the evacuation of
Charleston and the adjacent country, the exchange, at this point, will undoubtedly
be accompanied by many difficulties. I have sent two letters to the Officer Com'd'g
the Confederate forces near this Department, through the Commanding Officers
at Savannah and Charleston respectively, but as yet have received no reply. I
will inform you of the result—as soon as I hear from the, Confederate authorities." LS, DNA, RG 108, Letters Received. *O.R.*, II, viii, 309.

To Maj. Gen. George G. Meade

By Telegraph from Ci[t]y Point 7 15 [P.M.]
Dated Feby 5 1864.5

To GENL MEADE

Your despatch of 6 45 just recd. Bring Warren & Cavy back &
if you can follow the enemy do it If we can follow the enemy up
although it was not con[tem]plated before it may lead to getting
the south side road or a position from which it can be reached
Change original instructions to give all advantages you can take
of the enemys acts

U S GRANT
Lt Genl

Telegram received, DNA, RG 94, War Records Office, Army of the Potomac;
copies, *ibid.*, RG 108, Letters Sent; DLC-USG, V, 46, 72, 108; (2) Meade
Papers, PHi. *O.R.*, I, xlvi, part 2, 390. On Feb. 5, 1865, 2:30 P.M., "Crossing of
Hachers Run by Vaughan Road," and 6:45 P.M., "Vaughn Road & Hatchers
Run," Maj. Gen. George G. Meade telegraphed to USG. "Humphreys was in
position at this point & armstrongs Mill by ten (10) a m crossing at both places
with but little opposition taking 9 prisoners all of Pegrams Division he is now
getting in position & pushing out the Vaughan Road to communicate in the Gen
Warren reports at one P M he has crossed Most of his Infantry but has to build
a bridge 960 feet in length to cross artillery & trains will be over by 3 P. M
Nothing has been heard from Gregg here The reports of prisoners I am led to
believe the Enemy may attempt to interfere between Warren & Humphreys to
keep open these communications of 4 miles I have ordered up pParkes Reserve
Division & have directed the available troops in the City Point lines to replace
them with Parke Warren reports taking thirty (30) prisoners when crossing
the Run. I can hear nothing of the Enemys Cavalry & the prisoners here know
nothing of any troops Cavalry or Infantry going south." "The enemeny at 5.15
attacked Gen Humphreys right & have been engaging him till this moment, Gen
Humphreys has repulsed all their attacks—I have ordered up to his Support not
only a division from the 9th Corps but one from the 6th Corps—Gen Warren is
in position at Hayons [*Hargrave's*] about 3½ miles from here has met no
enemy—Gen Gregg reports that having occupied Dinwiddie Court House & hearing nothing of any trains or the enemy had returned to the crossing of Hatchers
run by the Malone road—I have Sent orders to Gen Gregg to return to Gen Warren & report to that officer unless you Send other off orders for him—I think the
enemy are trying to turn Humphreys right & cut our communications with our
line of works—Renoes [*Besides*] pegrams & Gordons Divisions deserters report
the movement to their right of Heth & Mahone. I shall leave Humphreys & Warren in their present positions with directions to support each other—I dont think
the Cavalry will do anything in the Way of destroying trains. I shall await your
instructions—It is estimated Humphreys losses in Wounded may amount to 300

—Please acknowledge at once—" Telegrams received (the first at 3:00 P.M.), DNA, RG 108, Letters Received; copies, *ibid.*, RG 393, Army of the Potomac, Letters Sent; (2) Meade Papers, PHi. Printed with the first sent at 3:00 P.M., the second at 7:10 P.M., in *O.R.*, I, xlvi, part 1, 149; *ibid.*, I, xlvi, part 2, 389.

At 8:00 P.M., "Crossing of Hatchers Run & Vaughn road," and 10:00 P.M., "Head Qurs A-P," Meade telegraphed to USG. "I have withdrawn Warren & the Cavalry to this Point directing two divisions to remain on the other side of the run One to cross to this side as a reserve for contingencies. Humphreys is instructed to await developements & to attack if advantageous & drive the enemy into their works. The enemy have a strong line of works facing through the Clement's house This house is the place where the shot fell near us on the last movement. That is to say since then the enemy have advanced their line unless we can carry this line we can hardly reach the Boydtown plank road, on south side Railroad without a flank movement immediately to the left. I presume it was to stop this they attacked Humphreys right" "I send a despatch from Gen Gregg recd on my arrival just now—aA Staff officer who carried my last despatch to Gen Warren reports that on leaving three squadrons of Greggs Cavy Came in to Warren saying the enemys Ca̵yvalry had attacked Greggs rear guard & Cut them off. I am a little apprehensive of the enemys Cavy interposing between Gregg & Warren & preventing the latter using the road he advanced on to withdraw his artillery & trains. I have however sent orders to Gregg to open this road if possible & escort back Warrens trains" Telegrams received (at 8:25 P.M. and 10:00 P.M.), DNA, RG 108, Letters Received; copies, *ibid.*, RG 393, Army of the Potomac, Letters Sent; (2) Meade Papers, PHi. Printed with the first sent at 8:22 P.M. in *O.R.*, I, xlvi, part 1, 150; *ibid.*, I, xlvi, part 2, 390–91. The enclosure is *ibid.*, p. 409. On the same day, USG telegraphed to Meade. "Please report to me the situation of our troops now and of the Enemys forces so far as you know it also state what you propose for the mornings movement I would not advise any withdrawal in the morning unless forced to do it we should either carry out the first design or else meet the enemy outside his entrenchments" Telegram received (at 10:25 P.M.), DNA, RG 94, War Records Office, Army of the Potomac; copies, *ibid.*, RG 108, Letters Sent; DLC-USG, V, 46, 72, 108; (2) Meade Papers, PHi. *O.R.*, I, xlvi, part 2, 391. At 10:30 P.M., Meade telegraphed to USG. "I moved out this morning on the vaughn road. The 2d Corps to the crossing of Hatchers Run on the road from Reams Station to Dinwiddie C H. The 5th Corps & on a road crossing Hatchers Run. Still lower down, The cavy Divn under Gen Gregg—Gen Gregg was ordered to move to Dinwiddie C H & move up & down the Boydton Road to intercept & capture the Enemys trains & was further ordered to determine whether or not he could in any way inflict damge upon the enemy—Gen Warren was to support Gen Gregg, Gen Humphreys to support Gen Warren, all other available troops of this army were to be held ready to move at short notice. The different commands reached their post in due season but it was found difficult to open communication between Gens Humphreys & Warren along the Vaughn road, Gen Gregg proceeded to Dinwiddie C H & moved up & down the Vaughan road & captured some 18 wagons & 50 prisoners including one colonel—Finding that the Boydton road was but little used since the destruction of the bridges on that road & on the Weldon RR he returned to Malones bridge on Hatchers Run. At 4 15 P M the enemy with what was reported to be Hills Corps & Gordons & Pegrams Division attacked Humphreys. They were hansomely repulsed with a loss to Humphreys of 300. Since this force had attacked Humphreys right consisting of but one (1) Divn entire & one Brig it became necessary to Send for men enough to hold our communications with our rear line—One Divn of the 9th & one Divn of the 6th Corps were therefore ordered to reinforce Humphreys. Warren with the cavy have been ordered to connect with his left & to report to him. In the morning if I find that this ~~force~~ force of the enemy is outside of his works, I shall attack & Drive him into them taking advantage of anything ~~disclosed~~ disclosed by the operation. During the day it is Estimated that we have taken 100 prisoners." Telegram received (at 10:30 P.M.), DNA, RG 108, Letters Received; copies, *ibid.*, RG 393, Army of the Potomac, Letters Sent; (2) Meade Papers, PHi. Printed as sent at 11:15 P.M. in *O.R.*, I, xlvi, part 1, 150–51; *ibid.*, I, xlvi, part 2, 391–92.

To Gen. Robert E. Lee

Feby 6th 1865

GEN, R, E LEE
COMDG ARMY N, VA,
GENERAL!

Your letter of the 4th inst in relation to Sergt W. M. Waterbury 3d N, C, Cavalry was received yesterday   I immediately set on foot inquiries as to the circumstances of his capture and present where abouts   I forward you the result of that inquiry,

Very Respectfully
Your obt svt
U. S. GRANT
Lieut, Genl,

Copies, DLC-USG, V, 46, 72, 108; DNA, RG 108, Letters Sent. On Feb. 4, 1865, Gen. Robert E. Lee wrote to USG. "It is reported that Sergt. W M Watterbury Co D 3rd Regt N Carolina Cavalry, a prisoner of war in the hands of your forces, has been condemned to be hanged on the 8th inst as a spy, by sentence of a Court Martial sitting at or near City Point. I know nothing of the truth of the report, but beg leave to make the following statement of facts received from Brig Gen Barringer to whose brigade Watterbury belongs. Watterbury was employed on outpost duty, in charge of a party, and was made prisoner in some affair of outposts in which he was engaged about two months since, and taken to City Point. Gen Barringer has learned that subsequently, he contrived to elude the guard, and to effect his escape from your lines, passed himself off as a Federal Cavalryman in search of a horse. He was suffered to proceed on this mission in company with a sentinel, whom he managed to make prisoner. While endeavoring to make his way out, the sentinel recovered his arms while Waterbury was asleep, and shot him through the lungs, leaving him for dead. He was found in this condition by some Federal soldiers and conveyed to the house of a

Dr Bryan, where contrary to expectation he recovered sufficiently to be removed to City Point, where he was tried and condemned, according to the report referred to. Brig Gen Barringer and Maj Gen W H F Lee, concur in asserting that Watterbury was simply engaged on outpost duty when captured, and was never used as a spy. The circumstances under which he was made prisoner, show that he did not enter your lines voluntarily, and if he subsequently assumed a disguise it would appear to have been done to effect his escape. Supposing that it is your desire to know the truth of the case, I have deemed it my duty to make the facts known to you, as they have been presented to me. You will probably be able to verify the statement, and prevent an innocent man from suffering, should it be substantiated. The manner of the capture of Watterbury in the first instance is doubtless accurately represented by his Comd.g officer. I do not know whence he derived the other circumstances." LS, NHi. On Feb. 5, USG telegraphed to the commanding officer, Point Lookout, Md. "Sergeant W M Watterbery Co D 3rd North Carolina Cavalry was forwarded from here to Point Lookout by Gen Patrick Pro Mar: Gen as a prisoner of war January 15th 1865—please inform me without delay, whether he is under charges or has been tried by a court Martial or whether he is treated ~~differently~~ different from other prisoners of war" Telegram received, DNA, RG 107, Telegrams Collected (Bound); *ibid.*, Telegrams Collected (Unbound); *ibid.*, RG 393, Middle Military Div., Letters Received; copies, *ibid.*, RG 108, Letters Sent; DLC-USG, V, 46, 72, 108. On Feb. 6, 9:00 A.M., Brig. Gen. James Barnes, Point Lookout, telegraphed to USG. "Your despatch received Half an hour since. Serg't Waterbury 3rd N C Cav a prisoner of war was received here on 16th of January. In consequence of a special letter relating to him from the Pro mar Genls office he was kept in close confinement ten 10 days. He was then placed in the General Camp and is there now on the same footing as other prisoners." ALS (telegram sent), DNA, RG 107, Telegrams Collected (Unbound).

To Edwin M. Stanton

City Point Va, Feby 6th 1865

Hon, E, M, Stanton
Sec, of War
Washington

In the affair of yesterday when the enemy attacked a part of the 2d Corps and were handsomely repulsed, leaving a part of their dead for us to bury, our losses were Three Officers and Eighteen men killed, Eleven Officers and Ninety two men wounded, and Twenty two men missing, In front of one Brig of Motts Div, he buried Thirty-one of the enemy and counted twenty-two graves besides some of which were large enough for five or six bodies each, Gen, Smythe[1] estimates the loss of the enemy in his front at two hundred, Our captures for the day were about One hundred men, half of these taken by the Cavalry and the rest by the 5th and 2d Corps, This afternoon, the 5th Corps advanced and drove the enemy back on to their Artillery, probably into their intrenchments, beyond Dabney's Mill, Here the enemy was reinforced and drove Warren back Our troops are still out and will not be returned to their old position unless driven to it by the difficulty of supplying them, The casualties for today I will report as soon as learned

U, S, GRANT
Lieut, Genl,

Telegram, copies, DLC-USG, V, 46, 72, 108; (marked as sent at midnight, received on Feb. 7, 1865, 2:20 A.M.) DNA, RG 107, Telegrams Received in Cipher; *ibid.*, RG 108, Letters Sent. *O.R.*, I, xlvi, part 2, 415.

1. Thomas A. Smyth, born in Ireland in 1832, emigrated to the U.S. in 1854, and was a coachmaker in Del. on the eve of the Civil War. Appointed maj., 1st Del., as of Oct. 17, 1861, and col. as of Feb. 7, 1863, he was appointed brig. gen. as of Oct. 1, 1864. He assumed command of the 2nd Div., 2nd Army Corps, on Jan. 14, 1865. *Ibid.*, p. 127. See also *ibid.*, p. 427.

To Edwin M. Stanton

———

CITY POINT, VA., *February 6, 1865.*

HON. E. M. STANTON:

The Richmond Dispatch to-day says that a rumor was current yesterday that Sherman had reached and was destroying the railroad at Midway, ten miles west of Branchville. The Whig, however, says that the rumor was without foundation, as the tenor of official dispatches received at the War Department last evening renders it certain that such was not the case. On Saturday[1] telegraphic communication was temporarily suspended with Augusta, but was resumed on yesterday. The Whig remarks that a repulse of Sherman, who is now apparently presumptuous on account of his unimpeded march through Georgia, would work wonders in bringing the North to its senses. The Confederate generals and the men under their commands on his front are commissioners to whose pacific exertions the country may well look with anxious and prayerful solicitude. The Enquirer reports that the salt-works are again in successful operation. C. C. Clay, jr.,[2] is reported having arrived in the Confederacy. The Peace Commissioners arrived in Richmond Saturday evening. The same evening a large war meeting was held, which was addressed by Henry A. Wise. Governor Smith issues a notice to-day to the citizens of Richmond, Va., and citizens of other States sojourning in Richmond, to meet this evening to respond to the answer made by President Lincoln to the Confederate deputies sent to confer with him on the subject of peace. It is expected that Stephens will be invited by the Confederate Congress to address them before leaving for Georgia, whither it is rumored he intends going to arouse the people of that State to renewed vigor in prosecuting the war. The general tone of all the Richmond papers to-day says that there is nothing left for the South to do but to fight it out.

U. S. GRANT,
Lieutenant-General.

O.R., I, xlvi, part 2, 414; (incomplete) *ibid.*, I, xlvii, part 2, 317–18.

On Feb. 5, 1865, Bvt. Brig. Gen. Cyrus B. Comstock, Fort Fisher, telegraphed to USG. "A despatch from one of Gen Fosters Staff to Schofield dated dated Feby 2d states that Sherman with his troops started Feby 1st to move rapidly into the interior of S. C. Other information is, that had previously been, at Pocotologo—None of Schofields troops have yet arrived. All quiet except that the navy occasionally shell Ft. Anderson. Loud cheering along the rebel lines was thought to by Gen Paine to indicate reinforcements. All quiet and weather warm" Telegram received (on Feb. 7, 10:00 A.M.), DNA, RG 108, Letters Received. Printed as received on Feb. 7, 9:30 A.M., in *O.R.*, I, xlvii, part 2, 306.

On Feb. 2, Maj. Gen. John G. Foster, Hilton Head, S. C., telegraphed to USG, sending a copy to Secretary of War Edwin M. Stanton. "I have recd. despatch from Sherman who was at a point four miles South of Hickory Springs last night (1st) He expected to be at Rivers bridge tonight (2d) and at a point midway between Branchville and Augusta tomorrow night—The roads were fair —Gen Hatch's Div. is demonstrating towards Combahee and feigning to attempt forcing a crossing—Gen E. E. Potter with with three regiments is demonstrating from Edisto Island towards Wellstown [*Willstown*]. In two days this force will be added to that on Folly Island to demonstrate against James Island—I shall keep things active & strive to aid Sherman in every way in my power" Telegram received (on Feb. 6, 6:00 P.M.), DNA, RG 107, Telegrams Collected (Bound); (on Feb. 6) *ibid.*, RG 108, Letters Received; copies, *ibid.*, RG 107, Telegrams Received in Cipher; *ibid.*, RG 393, Dept. of the South, Letters Sent. *O.R.*, I, xlvii, part 2, 210. On Feb. 4, Foster wrote (and telegraphed the same message) to USG, sending a copy to Maj. Gen. Henry W. Halleck.

"Maj. Gray of my Staff returned last night from Gen. Shermans HeadQuarters with the latest information. He left, Gen'l Sherman at a place called 'The Store,' at the cross roads near Duck Bridge, over Coosawhatchie River, 31½ miles from Pocotaligo Station, on the evening of Feb'y 2d. He had with him at that point Three Divisions of the 15th Corps, which Corps had moved out from Pocotaligo, on the 1st marching to Hickory Hill, 18 miles on that day, and 12 miles to 'The Store' on the second day. Gen Howard with the 17th Corps, was on the evening of the 2d, near Whippy Swamp, near the Salkehatchie River. He had also marched from near Pocolaligo on the 1st Inst. taking the right hand road lying near the Salkehatchie River. Gen. Slocum with the main body of the left wing, which had marched up the South bank of the Savannah river, has been at Sisters Ferry several days constructing a Pontoon Bridge across the river. Two Divisions of the 20th Corps which had crossed the river opposite Savannah, marched up the North bank and were at Robertsville. The crossing of the river at Sisters Ferry, has been found to be more difficult than was expected, on account of the long distance to be corduroyed on each side, and I learned at Savannah, this morning that Gen. Slocum will hardly be able to get his troops well over the river, ready for a start, before tomorrow (the 5th). This will delay Gen Sherman a little. Maj. Gray reports the roads fair, and all the wagons of the right wing up. There were no stragglers, and the troops found in the country, forage enough for the animals, and cattle and hogs for the army. The inhabitants generally with their slaves and moveables, had moved higher up the country; the troops burned all buildings and fences on the route. There was nothing but Cavalry encountered thus far; Gen Sherman intended breaking the Railroad near Midway, to the west of Branchville, and thought after that, he might find opposition in crossing the Edisto river. It is possible that the troops in his front may receive reinforcements from Hood. Gen Sherman wished me to press upon Gen Schofield, the necessity of his advance, which I have done." LS, DNA, RG 108, Letters Received; telegram received (on Feb. 8), *ibid. O.R.*, I, xlvii, part 2, 299–300.

1. Feb. 4.
2. Clement C. Clay, Jr., born in Ala. in 1816, U.S. Senator from Ala. (1853–61), served in the C.S.A. Congress, then went to Canada in 1864 to initiate peace negotiations with the U.S. and additionally to further the C.S.A. cause. On Feb. 2, 1865, Clay landed at Charleston, S. C. Ruth Ketring Nuermberger, *The Clays of Alabama: A Planter-Lawyer-Politician Family* (Lexington, Ky., 1958), p. 262.

To Edwin M. Stanton

———

Headqrs Armies of the U S
City Point, Va., Feb. 6 [*1865*]
Respectfully forwarded to the Sec. of War with the recommendation tha[t] if Lt. S. B. Davis has been sentenced to death, as a

"Spy," execution be stayed until such evidenc[e] as Judge Ould may have can be heard.

Arrangements can be made with the Rebel Agt. of Exchanges I think, to have no executions, on either side, of parties belonging to the other until proceedings are submit[ted] to the authorities on the side to which the prisoner belongs, and a sufficient time elapses for them to file their answer, if they have any, why there should be no execution

U. S. Grant
Lt. Gn

AES, DNA, RG 107, Letters Received from Bureaus. Written on a letter of Feb. 4, 1865, from C.S.A. Agent of Exchange Robert Ould to Lt. Col. John E. Mulford. "I beg leave to call your special attention to the case of Lt. S. B. Davis, who it appears is being tried before a Court Martial of which Lt. Col. Webber is President, Sitting in Cincinnati. He is charged with being a 'Spy.' Lt. Davis is an officer of the Confederate army, and was acting in obedience to orders. In no Sense of the term was he a spy. Will you please inform me what has been done in his case and convey to the Federal authorities the assurance that he is not a Spy, and that proof will be furnished to that effect?" ALS, *ibid. O.R.*, II, viii, 181. C.S.A. 1st Lt. Samuel B. Davis was arrested at Newark, Ohio, on Jan. 14 while returning from Canada, where he had carried papers to Lt. John Y. Beall concerning an attempt to capture the prison at Johnson's Island, Ohio. Davis argued unsuccessfully at his court-martial that he was a bearer of dispatches rather than a spy. Maj. Gen. Joseph Hooker commuted the death sentence, and Davis was ordered released from Fort Warren, Boston Harbor, on Dec. 20. See *O.R.*, II, viii, 132–33, 191–92, 204, 309, 736, 837; Lincoln, *Works*, VIII, 291–92; Lewis H. Bond, *The Capture and Trial of a Confederate Spy Sent to Ohio by Jefferson Davis* (Cincinnati, 1887); [Samuel B. Davis], *Escape of a Confederate Officer from Prison. . . .* (Norfolk, Va., 1892).

On Feb. 12, Gen. Robert E. Lee wrote to USG. "The accompanying communication addressed to Hon. Chas. A. Dana Asst. Secty of War, Washington D. C. in relation to Lt. S. B. Davis an officer of the Army of the C. S., condemned to die on the 17th of this month by sentence of a United States military Court, has been sent to me with the request that I would transmit it through your lines. I very respectfully request that you will forward it to Washington as addressed." ALS (faded), Scheide Library, Princeton, N. J. See *O.R.*, II, viii, 261–62.

On Feb. 13, USG wrote to Ould. "Your communication in relation to Lieut Davis condemned to death as a 'spy' was received and forwarded to the Sec. of War with the recommendation that his execution be suspended until you could have time to forward evidence in his behalf. I send you now the action taken in his case, which you will perceive was taken prior to the receipt of your letter." Copies, DLC-USG, V, 46, 72, 108; DNA, RG 108, Letters Sent. *O.R.*, II, viii, 216–17.

To Maj. Gen. Henry W. Halleck

Cipher   City Point, Va. Feb.y 6th 1865 [7:00 P.M.]
MAJ. GEN. HALLECK, WASHINGTON

I think Gen. Dix will be an excellent selection for the command in Ky. I am glad to see Burbridge is about being removed from there. I should have much more faith in Terry than Gilmore for the command of the Dept. of the South and his administration would be much more economical. However we will do the best we can.

U. S. GRANT
Lt. Gen.

ALS (telegram sent), CSmH; copies, DLC-USG, V, 46, 72, 108; (marked as received at 7:20 P.M.) DNA, RG 107, Telegrams Received in Cipher; *ibid.*, RG 108, Letters Received. Printed as received at 8:00 P.M. in *O.R.*, I, xlvi, part 2, 415. On Feb. 6, 1865, 2:34 P.M., Maj. Gen. Henry W. Halleck telegraphed to USG. "Genl Ord is assigned as requested. Before your telegram to the Secty, Genl Gillmore had been sent South to relieve Genl Foster. I think his familiarity with that part of the coast & the defences of Charleston render him most suitable for that command. There must be a change in Kentucky & Genl Dix is proposed for the place. What do you think? As soon as we get Genl Thomas views about Dept lines, the matter must be acted on. Genl Dix seems to be best suited for the political complexion of affairs in Kentucky, though too old for active military operations." ALS (telegram sent), DNA, RG 107, Telegrams Collected (Bound); telegram received, *ibid.*; (marked as sent at 2:30 P.M.) *ibid.*, RG 108, Letters Received. *O.R.*, I, xlvi, part 2, 415; (incomplete) *ibid.*, I, xlvii, part 2, 318. See telegram to Maj. Gen. Henry W. Halleck, Feb. 4, 1865.

On Feb. 13, Maj. Gen. Quincy A. Gillmore, Hilton Head, S. C., wrote to USG. "I have the honor to report that I assumed command of this Department on the evening of the 9th Instant. I started the same night to set on foot a demonstration which Gen'l Sherman had ordered to be made on the 8th at Bulls Bay, S. C., but which Gen'l Foster delayed, because Gen'l Sherman's advance had been somewhat retarded by bad roads. Before the troops were ready to embark from Folly Island, where they had been rendezvoused, I ascertained that my presence was required at Hilton Head, and therefore left Brig. Gen. Potter to take charge of the demonstration, in co-operation with a suitable force from the Navy. I have since learned that the landing would probably be effected yesterday. Gen'l Potter's orders were to seize the principal roads leading to the interior, throw up works, and give the affair the appearance of a permanent lodgment, for the purpose of cooperating with Gen'l Sherman. Gen'l Potter has but Thirteen hundred (1300) men and I can spare him no more. Genl Hatch with Thirty-five hundred (3500) men is north of the Combahee River. He has destroyed several miles of the Railroad north of Pocotaligo, including some important Trustle

Bridges. I will at once, push him forward as Gen'l Sherman directs, towards the
Edisto River, if it be a possible thing to do so. I shall visit him tomorrow. A
package of dispatches from your HeadQuarters, for General Sherman, was turned
over to me by Gen Foster, to be forwarded. They are now in Gen. Hatch's possession, who has directions to send them, if it can be done with safety, otherwise
their contents will be communicated, verbally, to two or three trusty scouts, who
will try and find their way to Gen'l Sherman's HeadQuarters. Gen Hatch may
not be able to spare a suitable ~~person~~ escort for such a purpose." LS, DNA, RG
108, Letters Received. *O.R.*, I, xlvii, part 2, 411–12. On the same day, Gillmore
telegraphed to USG. "The enclosed dispatch contains the latest information from
Gen. Shermans Army; His instructions in regard to Bull's Bay are now being carried out Gen. Hatch is north of the Combahee River, & will push forward. I
shall visit him tomorrow, and remain with him some days, if necessary.—" LS
(telegram sent—marked as received on Feb. 17, 4:30 P.M.), DNA, RG 108,
Letters Received; telegram received, *ibid.*; (on Feb. 17, 5:00 P.M.) *ibid.*, RG
107, Telegrams Collected (Bound). *O.R.*, I, xlvii, part 2, 411. The enclosure is
ibid., p. 338. On Feb. 17, Gillmore telegraphed to USG. "I send you by mail
Charleston newspapers of the 8. 9. 10 & 11th which give the latest news from
Sherman. They state that he crossed the South Fork of the Edisto at Binmakers
bridge on the ninth. I have possession of the Charleston and Savannah RR as far
as the Edisto. The enemy are on the line of the Edisto at Jacksonboro and
Willstown. Gen Hatchs division captured six guns on the 15th The road has
been so thoroughly destroyed that there is no use of keeping up the entrenched
camp at Pocotolago Station I can make much better use of the troops elsewhere
and ask authority to use my discretion in the matter. The place can at any time
be occupied in a few hours. I have no despatches from Bulls Bay later than the
12th. Gen Potter expected to land there on the 13th. I shall go up there tomorrow." Telegram received (on Feb. 21, 10:00 A.M.), DNA, RG 107, Telegrams
Collected (Bound); *ibid.*, RG 108, Letters Received; copies, *ibid.*, RG 107, Telegrams Received in Cipher; *ibid.*, RG 393, Dept. of the South, Letters Sent. *O.R.*,
I, xlvii, part 2, 463.

On Feb. 14, Maj. Gen. John G. Foster, Norfolk, telegraphed to USG. "I
have the honor to report that I left Hilton Head on the 11th inst on the steamship
Arago, and arrived in Hampton Roads last night,—having experienced a North
Easterly gale off Hatteras. Gen Gillmore relieved me of the command of the Department of the South on the 9th inst. The military news that I bring is not
important—A report had reached Hilton Head as I was leaving that Gen Sherman
had taken Branchville, but I could not trace it to any reliable source—The rebels
had fallen back from the Combahee river, and Gen Hatch had orders to follow &
destroy the railroad—He had crossed the Combahee, advancing towards the
Ashepoo river. Brig Gen E E Potter, with a small brigade had demonstrated from
Edisto Island towards Willstown, but found the enemy in force. On the 8th, 9th,
& 10th, he demonstrated supported by Gen Scheimmelfennig, on James Island,
but found the enemy still in force there—The force then had orders to proceed
to Bulls Bay, and hold the roads by which the enemy might escape from Mount
Pleasant. I am to leave for Baltimore tonight to obtain surgical relief from my
present disability—" ALS (telegram sent), DNA, RG 107, Telegrams Collected (Unbound); telegram received, *ibid.*; (at 1:30 P.M.) *ibid.*, Telegrams
Collected (Bound); *ibid.*, RG 108, Letters Received. *O.R.*, I, xlvii, part 2, 423.

To Maj. Gen. George G. Meade

————

By Telegraph from City Point
Dated Feby 6th *1864*5. [*2:50* P.M.]

To MAJ GENL MEADE

I would not recommend making any attack against intreched
lines but I think it will be well to hold out to Hatchers Ru[n.] It
will give us a better chance for covering future movements & when
we do start we will entirely a[ban]don all extension beyond our
present lines. Please i[n]for[m] me about what our casualties have
been & what you think have been those of the enemy

U S GRANT
Lt Genl

Telegram received (at 3:00 P.M.), DNA, RG 94, War Records Office, Army of
the Potomac; copies, *ibid.*, RG 108, Letters Sent; DLC-USG, V, 46, 72, 108; (2)
Meade Papers, PHi. *O.R.*, I, xlvi, part 2, 417.

On Feb. 6, 1865, Maj. Gen. George G. Meade twice telegraphed to USG,
first at 1:00 A.M. "I have just recd intilligence that my aide Capt Jay taking
orders to Gen Gregg met the enemy in force where the malone road leaves the
Halifax Road. Jay was fired on & is missing but his Escort Escaped. This is
~~undauphes~~ undoubtedly the enemys cavy come up from Stoney Creek They are
now in Greggs rear on the ~~hall~~ h rood he took & only 1½ miles from him if he
is at malones bridge. I have sent this information to warren with directions to
make every effort to communicate it to Gregg & have ~~his~~ instructed Warren to
send a Division to ~~send~~ cover our rear between him & the vaughn road. I am in
hopes warrens artillery & trains ordered back on the rood he took will get ~~it~~ in
safely" "Major Jay has returned & it now is certain that he was Captured by our
own men—None of the enemys Cavy in vicinity of Malones Crossing" Telegrams
received (at 1:00 A.M. and 5:30 A.M.), DNA, RG 108, Letters Received; copies,
ibid., RG 393, Army of the Potomac, Letters Sent; (2) Meade Papers, PHi.
Printed as sent at 1:15 A.M. and 5:30 A.M. in *O.R.*, I, xlvi, part 1, 151, 152;
ibid., I, xlvi, part 2, 416. At 7:15 A.M., Meade telegraphed to USG. "Maj Genls
Warren & Humphreys have both tlegraphed me this morning & ~~announce~~ inform
me of their being in position their right well supported near Fort Cummings &
two Div of the 5th Corps over Hatcher's Run forming their left Greggs Cavly is
now with Warren. Trains all came up the Vaughan Road. I have telegraphed for
them to move out at once to determine whether or not Hill A Ps or any portion
of the enemy's force is now outside of their line of works In case any should be
found they are to be driven in Heth charged in two Lines & was badly repulsed.
. . . ~~Deserters report that~~ subsequently the whole of Hill's Corps participated in
the attack. The above is the report of deserters." Telegram sent, DNA, RG 94,
War Records Office, Army of the Potomac; telegram received, *ibid.*, RG 108,
Letters Received. *O.R.*, I, xlvi, part 2, 417. At 1:00 P.M., Meade, "Hatchers

run," telegraphed to USG. "Humphreys reconnaissances shew the enemy to have retired within his main line of works leaving his dead on the field now being buried by us—Warren across Hatchers run is now moving out to feel the enemy— Deserters say their line now passes thru' Dabneys Mill to Gravelly run & it is probable Warren will find them in this line—If they are outside, he will attack —If however they are not so found, your instructions will be required as I have accomplished, all originally designed, or now practicable—The condition of the roads very bad & want of trains & supplies ~~preeludedes~~ preclude, any extended movement to the left—It remains therefore either to entrench, where we are, or to withdraw—If these partial movements are contemplated it would probably be well to extend our entrenched line to Hatchers run, as this would then be the point of departure and we would be nearer to threaten the enemys line of communications on the Boydtown plank road—At the same time the enemy would without doubt extend their line over lapping us, as they have done each time we extended   Your views & orders are desired.—" ALS (telegram sent), DNA, RG 107, Telegrams Collected (Unbound); telegram received (at 2:25 P.M.), *ibid.*, RG 108, Letters Received. *O.R.*, I, xlvi, part 2, 417.

At 8:40 P.M., Meade, "Hatchers Run," telegraphed to USG. "Major Gen Warren advanced about 2 P. M. on the Dabneys Mill & Vaughen road, both columns, Had a spirited contest with the enemy & steadily drove before him till about 6.30 P M when the column on the Mill road having forced the enemy beyond Dabneys Mill and until they opened on them with artillery fire endicating he was in his line of Works where being reinforced Warrens troops were in turn compelled to retire in considerable confusion   The enemy was however checked before reaching the position occupied this morning and Warrens troops rallied in this position—The column on the Vaughn road was recalled when others were forced back—The troops are now being formed in the lines occupied this morning—The fighting has been determined principally in dense woods & the losses considerable particularly with column compelled to retire—I am not able at present to give an estimate of them" Telegram received, DNA, RG 108, Letters Received; copies, *ibid.*, RG 393, Army of the Potomac, Letters Sent; (2) Meade Papers, PHi. Printed as written at 7:30 P.M., sent via Aiken House, 8:40 P.M., in *O.R.*, I, xlvi, part 1, 152; *ibid.*, I, xlvi, part 2, 418. At 8:40 P.M., Meade telegraphed to USG transmitting a report of casualties of Maj. Gen. Andrew A. Humphreys. Telegram received (at 11:05 P.M.), DNA, RG 108, Letters Received; copies (incomplete), *ibid.*, RG 393, Army of the Potomac, Letters Sent; Meade Papers, PHi. The enclosure is in *O.R.*, I, xlvi, part 2, 427.

To Edwin M. Stanton

(Cipher)   City Point, Va, Feb.y 6~~7~~th 186~~4~~5. [*10:00* A.M.]
HON. E. M. STANTON, SEC. OF WAR, WASHINGTON.

A Mr. Laws is here with a steamer partially loaded with sugar and coffee and a permit from the Treasury Dept. to go through into Va. & N. C. and to bring out 10.000 bales of cotton. I have

positively refused to adopt this mode of feeding the southern Army
unless it is on the direct order of the President. It is a humiliating
fact that speculators have represented the location of cotton at different points in the south, and obtain permits to bring it out, covering more than the entire amount of the staple in all the cotton
growing states. I take this to be so from what I know and from
statements contained in a letter recently received from Gen. Canby.
It is our interest now to stop all supplies going in to the south
between Charleston and the James River. Cotton only comes out,
on private account, except in payment for absolute necessaries ~~to~~
for the support of the War.

U. S. GRANT
Lt. Gn.

ALS (telegram sent), deCoppet Collection, NjP; copies, DLC-USG, V, 46, 72,
108; (marked as received at 11:30 A.M.) DNA, RG 107, Telegrams Received
in Cipher; *ibid.*, RG 108, Letters Sent. *O.R.*, I, xlvi, part 2, 445. On Feb. 7,
1865, 3:40 P.M., Secretary of War Edwin M. Stanton telegraphed to USG. "The
President directs that You will regard all [t]rade permits licenses or privileges of
every Kind by whomsoever signed and by whomsoever held as subject to your authority and approval as Commander of the United-States forces in the field, and
~~whenever you when~~ such permits as you deem ~~inconsisten~~ prejudicial to the Military service by feeding or supporting the rebel armies or persons in hostility to
the Government you may disregard and annul, and if necessary to the public
safety, seize the property of the traders. In short the President [ord]ers that you
'as being responsible for military results must be allowed to be judge and mater
on the subject of trade with the enemy' " ALS (telegram sent), DNA, RG 107,
Telegrams Collected (Bound); telegram received, *ibid.*, RG 108, Letters Received. Printed as sent at 3:00 P.M. in *O.R.*, I, xlvi, part 2, 445.
    In a communication dated only "Feb.," President Abraham Lincoln wrote
to USG. "Some time ago you telegraphed that you had stopped a Mr. Laws from
passing our lines with a boat and cargo, and I directed you to be informed that
you must be allowed to do as you pleased in such matters. To-night Mr. Laws
calls on me, and I have told him, and now tell you that the matter, as to his
passing the lines is under your control absolutely; and that he can have any relaxation you choose to give him & none other." ADfS, DLC-Robert T. Lincoln;
copy, DLC-John G. Nicolay. Lincoln, *Works*, VIII, 267–68. No evidence exists
that Lincoln sent or that USG received this communication.
    On Feb. 8, USG twice telegraphed to Brig. Gen. George F. Shepley, Nor-
folk. "A Mr Laws has been here seeking authority to go through to the Chowan.
He has a Steamer at Norfolk loaded with goods for the use of people in Rebellion
& expected to bring back Cotton. You will please see that neither he, his boat or
cargo can go through." "Please have the Boat taken to Norfolk by Mr Laws examined & report her contents   Do not take the invoices or bills approved by the
Treasury but report from actual examination" Telegrams received (two ver-
sions of the first), DNA, RG 107, Telegrams Collected (Unbound); copies,

ibid., RG 108, Letters Sent; DLC-USG, V, 46, 73, 108. On Feb. 11, Brig. Gen. George H. Gordon telegraphed to USG. "I have the honor to report the cargo of the Steamer 'Emma Dunn' owned by Mr Laws, to consist of Two Hundred & three (203) Sacks of Coffee, and Two Hundred & Eighty Two (282) barrels Brown Sugar ~~comparing~~ corresponding with the Manifest. After a careful examination of the Cargo nothing else was found." LS (telegram sent), DNA, RG 107, Telegrams Collected (Unbound); telegram received, *ibid.*

On Feb. 18, Lt. Col. Orrin L. Mann, 39th Ill., provost marshal, District of Eastern Va., Norfolk, telegraphed to USG. "Mr. *David O. Laws* of Baltimore ~~who~~ has information which I regard reliable that a member of his family is seriously ill. He wishes to go home few days. Himself boat and cargo were stoped here by your order. Have no doubt he will return. The General Commanding District *approves*." ALS (telegram sent), *ibid.*; telegram received, *ibid.* On the same day, Lt. Col. Theodore S. Bowers telegraphed to Mann. "Gen. Grant did not order the detention of Mr. Laws at Norfolk. he directed that neither he nor his boat should be permitted to go South—Laws is at liberty to go North at will and to take his boat & cargo with him if he wishes—The only order in his case is that he shall not go South or send boats there—" Telegram received, *ibid.*

To Bvt. Brig. Gen. William Hoffman

(Cipher)   City Point, Va Feb.y 7th/65 [*11:30* A.M.]
~~MAJ. GN.~~ COL. W. HOFFMAN, WASHINGTON

The prisoners you have at Fort Delaware may be forwarded direct to City Point. The proportion of officers is not material. Six per cent of the whole number of prisoners will answer. I think Pryor[1] and a Sergeant Waterbury now at Point Lookout I think should not be exchanged so long as we hold a prisoner.

U. S. GRANT
Lt. Gn.

ALS (telegram sent), CSmH; telegram received (at 1:30 P.M.), DNA, RG 107, Telegrams Collected (Bound); *ibid.*, RG 249, Letters Received; DLC-Robert T. Lincoln. *O.R.*, II, viii, 191. On Feb. 7, 1865, Bvt. Brig. Gen. William Hoffman telegraphed to USG. "One thousand prisoners at Fort Delaware are ready to be forwarded. May they be sent direct from there to City-Point. What proportion of officers do you wish." ALS (telegram sent), DNA, RG 107, Telegrams Collected (Unbound); telegram received, *ibid.*, RG 108, Letters Received. *O.R.*, II, viii, 191.

On Feb. 6, Hoffman had telegraphed to USG. "Will the prisoners who are to be forwarded for exchange be released on parole before exchange. In that case they will be required to sign paroles before being forwarded which will cause some delay" ALS (telegram sent), DNA, RG 107, Telegrams Collected (Unbound); telegram received (at 10:37 A.M.), *ibid.*, RG 108, Letters Received. At

11:00 A.M., USG telegraphed to Hoffman. "All exchanged prisoners are paroled before exchange. Flag of truce boats will be at Point Lookout on the 9th to take about 2.000 prisoners." Telegram received (at noon), *ibid.*, RG 107, Telegrams Collected (Bound); *ibid.*, RG 249, Letters Received; copies, *ibid.*, RG 108, Letters Sent; DLC-USG, V, 46, 72, 108; USG 3. *O.R.*, II, viii, 188. At 11:00 A.M., Hoffman telegraphed to USG. "Five hundred prisoners are ready to be forwarded from City-Point, and five hundred per day will be ready till three thousand are forwarded. Meanwhile others will be collected there from Western stations" ALS (telegram sent), DNA, RG 107, Telegrams Collected (Unbound); telegram received, *ibid.*, RG 108, Letters Received.

Also on Feb. 6, Brig. Gen. John A. Rawlins telegraphed to Maj. Gen. Edward O. C. Ord. "Your dispatch in relation to releasing certain Prisoners of war on taking the oath of allegiance is received—They cannot be released before being exchanged for prisoners of ours—They should be among the first forwarded for exchange if they desire it and be made acquainted with special orders No 3 current series relating to deserters from the enemy & informed that if they came voluntarily into our lines they will be permitted to remain unmolested under the provisions of said order" Telegram received, Ord Papers, CU-B; copies, DLC-USG, V, 46, 72, 108; DNA, RG 108, Letters Sent. *O.R.*, II, viii, 187.

1. Roger A. Pryor, born in 1828 in Va., a lawyer, newspaper editor, U.S. Representative from Va. (1859–61), and a leading secessionist, served as col., 3rd Va., and was appointed brig. gen. as of April 16, 1862. Dissatisfied with failure to obtain a suitable command, Pryor resigned his commission on Aug. 26, 1863, enlisted as a private, 3rd Va. Cav., and was captured while exchanging newspapers. See telegram to Maj. Gen. George G. Meade, Nov. 30, 1864.

To Maj. Gen. Henry W. Halleck

City Point Va, Feby 7th 1865 [*noon*]

MAJ, GENL, H, W, HALLECKE
WASHINGTON

I will be in Washington Thursday[1] or Friday next,   Please notify the Com- on the Conduct of the War,   I will be obliged to you also if you will notify Mr, Washburne,

U. S. GRANT
Lt, Genl

Telegram, copies, DLC-USG, V, 46, 73, 108; (marked as received at 1:00 P.M.) DNA, RG 107, Telegrams Received in Cipher; *ibid.*, RG 108, Letters Sent; DLC-Elihu B. Washburne. Printed as received at 1:30 P.M. in *O.R.*, I, xlvi, part 2, 447. On Feb. 7, 1865, 1:30 P.M., USG telegraphed to Maj. Gen. George G. Meade. "I will go to Washington to-morrow, or as soon as you notify me the troops now out, are in the new position they are to occupy. I was summoned some

two weeks since to appear before the Committee on the Conduct of the War."
ALS (telegram sent), Goodspeed's Book Shop, Inc., Boston, Mass.; telegram
received, DNA, RG 94, War Records Office, Army of the Potomac; (2) *ibid.*,
RG 107, Telegrams Collected (Unbound). *O.R.*, I, xlvi, part 2, 448.

On Jan. 25, 2:00 P.M., USG had telegraphed to Secretary of War Edwin
M. Stanton. "It will be impossible for me to respond to the call of the Committee
on the conduct of the War at present. I will go however when I can. In the mean-
time if the Committee will summons Gen. Rawlins Chief of staff they will be
able to learn from him about all I could tell them." Telegram received (at 6:00
P.M.), DNA, RG 107, Telegrams Collected (Bound); copies, *ibid.*, Telegrams
Received in Cipher; *ibid.*, RG 108, Letters Sent; DLC-USG, V, 46, 72, 108.
O.R., I, xlvi, part 2, 253. See *ibid.*, p. 185.

1. Feb. 9.

To Maj. Gen. George G. Meade

City Point, Va, Feb.y 7th/65 [*3:00* A.M.]

MAJ. GEN. MEADE,

The idea I intended to convey was that we should hold permanently out to Hatcher's Run fortifying as you think best, but destroying no works already made. Then when we come to make a
general move against the enemy we would hold our present line
and abandon all the new works outside of them. You have been
o~~f~~ver the ground where our troops now are and I have not. Take
up such line for permanent occupation as you think will best secure our purposes. ~~My~~ I thought likely we should hold from our
present left to Armstrongs Mill. The Cavalry could then picket
down Hatcher's Run and cover our rear easier than at present. In
view of the bad weather the troops had better be got back into the
position you intend them to occupy. It will be advisable to send this
order to Warren at once so as to avoid any further attack unless
promising great advantages to us.

U. S. GRANT
Lt. Gn.

ALS (telegram sent), PPRF; telegram received (at 11:30 A.M.), DNA, RG 94,
War Records Office, Army of the Potomac. Printed as sent at 11:30 A.M. in
O.R., I, xlvi, part 2, 447–48. On Feb. 7, 1865, 10:15 A.M., Maj. Gen. George G.
Meade telegraphed to USG. "Warren reports at 7.30 a m every thing quiet in

his front. The character of the Weather today and the ignorance I am under of the exact moral condition of Warren Corps & his losses from stragglers has restrained me from giving him positive orders to attack but I have directed him to push out strong reconnoissances & left to his judgement based on the result of these reconnoissances & his knowledge of the state of his command whether to attack or not From all I can learn unofficially the desaster Yesterday arose from the enemy suddenly towards the close of the day withdrawing from the column on the Vaughn road & concentrating on the column ~~on~~ at Dabneys Mill which when one part of the line was broken the whole retired in disorder, Warren had one whole Division Wheatons 6th Corps not engaged 1 Brigade reached the mill just as the line had given way but were unable owing to the confusion & the dense woods to do any thing towards remedying the evil, In reference to holding Hatchers run my Idea was to hold it permanently by a strong line which a small force could hold if we moved further to the left. If it is designed only to hold it temporarily & to abandon, the object I had in View would not be attained, We have now a line of breastworks all the way but my suggestion was to a permanent line with redoubts—" Telegram received (at 10:55 A.M.), DNA, RG 108, Letters Received; copies, *ibid.*, RG 393, Army of the Potomac, Letters Sent; (2) Meade Papers, PHi. Printed as sent at 10:50 A.M. in *O.R.*, I, xlvi, part 1, 152–53; *ibid.*, I, xlvi, part 2, 447.

At 2:45 P.M. and 5:15 P.M., Meade telegraphed to USG. "Cipher despatch recd. I will notify you as soon as the troops are in position but I hardly think it will be by tomorrow as I have some works to erect before I can unmass the forces on the left. As soon as your despatch of 11 30 A M was recd. I forwarded it to Gen Warren directing him to cease offensive operations unless some very important advantage has to be gained. At 12 20 before my despatch had reached him he reported Crawford having carried the enemys line of skirmish rifle pits, and that a prisoner reported them in line of battle near Dabneys mill where they were yesterday. I expect soon to hear my despatch has reached him; I was desirous for the morale of the command that the offensive should be taken. Warren has sent in the return of one Div. and I hope from it that the losses yesterday will be much less than was at first supposed Large numbers of stragglers have come in during the night and this morning—A deserter reports Rhodes old Div. as having been moved from the north of the Appomattox to enemys rear. Has Gen Ord. heard anything of this" "I have just received a dispatch from Maj Gen Warren announcing he had recovered most of the ground he occupied yesterday & had again drawn the fire of the artillery in the Enemys works as this accomplishes all I expected him to do I have directed him to withdraw to Hatchers Run & shall hold the line from H. [*Fort*] Sampson to Armstrongs, Mill with the 2d Corps and post the 5th Corps from the Vaughan Road ~~Coming~~ crossing back towards the Halifax Road prepared to meet a flank movement of the Enemy or to support any point threatened in front" Telegrams received (at 4:30 P.M. and 5:25 P.M.), DNA, RG 108, Letters Received; copies, *ibid.*, RG 393, Army of the Potomac, Letters Sent; (2) Meade Papers, PHi. Printed as sent at 4:00 P.M. and 5:22 P.M. in *O.R.*, I, xlvi, part 1, 153–54; *ibid.*, I, xlvi, part 2, 448.

To Maj. Gen. Edward O. C. Ord

City Point Va Feby 7th 1865

MAJ. GN. ORD.

You probably had better assign a temporary commander to the District of Norfolk. It is by no means certain that Washburn will be here. I ordered him here but the day following I asked to have him put in command of West Tenn. The first order was suspended until bounderies of Western Depts. are rearranged. It may or may not be that Washburn will come East.

U. S. GRANT
Lt. Gn.

ALS (telegram sent), Burrows Sloan, Jr., Princeton, N. J.; telegram received (at 10:15 A.M.), Ord Papers, CU-B. *O.R.*, I, xlvi, part 2, 467. See telegram to Maj. Gen. Henry W. Halleck, Feb. 4, 1865.

On Feb. 6, 1865, Maj. Gen. Edward O. C. Ord twice telegraphed to USG, the second time at 11:50 P.M. "The Signal Officer on CrowNest tower states that an orderly from the Commander of the picket reports at 7.30 P. M. that the Rams are moving down the river very rapidly &c Signed L. B. NORTON—Capt. Ch S. C." ALS (telegram sent), RG 45, Area File; telegram received, *ibid.*, RG 108, Letters Received. *O.R.*, I, xlvi, part 2, 440. "General Heckman reports as follows: My staff officer has returned. He reports one of the enemy's wooden patrol boats as having passed the grave-yard. He could learn nothing of their rams or any of their other boats." *Ibid.*

On Feb. 7, Ord telegraphed to USG. "The enemys Flag of Truce boat with prisoners for exchange now comes below Ft Brady. They learn all about it and vicinity. I think they should land their boat above the fort on a sort of neutral grounds. Shall I so order it through Col Mulford" Telegram received, DNA, RG 108, Letters Received. *O.R.*, I, xlvi, part 2, 466. On the same day, USG telegraphed to Ord. "The 'Flag of Truce' boat running down below Fort Brady gives no opportunities to the enemy to learn about our lines that they would not have by landing further up the river & transporting their returned prisoners through our lines on shore. I would quite as lieave the enemy would come down to the obstructions as any other way." Telegram received (at 10:03 P.M.), Ord Papers, CU-B; copies, DLC-USG, V, 46, 72, 108; DNA, RG 108, Letters Sent. *O.R.*, I, xlvi, part 2, 466.

Also on Feb. 7, Ord twice telegraphed to Brig. Gen. John A. Rawlins, the second time at 12:15 P.M. "The following despatch just received from Gen Graham. the expedetion boat to Pagan creek resulted in the capture of a torpedo boat with torpedo weighing 75 pounds & taking prisoner Ensign Herris of the Confederate Navy who destroyed the schooner in Warwick River last fall & the tug boat Lizzie Freeman off Pagan creek in December signed CHAS. H. GRAHAM Gen. Vodges reports Feb'y 4th. The land force sent to Pagan creek have returned

& report having made a careful reconnoisance of the creek and vicinity without finding any torpedoes or indication that there are any in preparation the party that intended operating in that vicinity had returned to Richmond some time since" Telegram received (at 9:50 A.M.), DNA, RG 108, Letters Received. See *O.R.*, I, xlvi, part 2, 384, 467. "The following dispatch was received ~~last night~~—yesterday Cols Spear has just returned from a reconnoissance with two hundred men—He went as far as the 'White Oak' Swamp, on the other side of which was a picket post of eight men, one of whom he captured The picket post belonged to the 7th S. C. Regiment Gearys Brigade No sign of the enemy on this side of the Swamp, and no change in the position or strength of Geary's command could be ascertained Col Spear went out by 'Riddles Shop' the same route pursued by Col. Evans' on the 27th Ult. I have a number of individual Scouts out—two came back reporting that they could not get through 'White Oak Swamp' on account of the enemys pickets They could give no information of the enemy—One represented himself as a deserter and found a man who wanted to show him the way to 'Long Bridge,' and help him on, saying seven deserters had crossed there the day before—Col Spear has four other prisoners, two of them Soldiers and the others Claiming to be Citizens (Signed) A V KAUTZ B. M. G." ALS (telegram sent), DNA, RG 108, Letters Received; telegram received (marked as sent at 12:10 P.M.), *ibid. O.R.*, I, xlvi, part 2, 466.

To Edwin M. Stanton

City Point Va, Feby 8th 1865 [*12:30* P.M.]

HON, E, M, STANTON
SEC, OF WAR, WASHINGTON

I have not yet got the full report of casualities in the 5th Corps Gen, Warren however pushed forward yesterday to the most advanced position occupied by him the day before, His casualities so far as heard ~~from~~ were much fewer than was expected, The number of prisoners delivered at City Point is two hundred & seven

U, S, GRANT
Lt, Gen,

Telegram, copies, DLC-USG, V, 46, 73, 108; (marked as received at 2:40 P.M.) DNA, RG 107, Telegrams Received in Cipher; *ibid.*, RG 108, Letters Sent. *O.R.*, I, xlvi, part 2, 474.

To Edwin M. Stanton

(Cipher)   City Point, Va, Feb.y 8th *18645*. [5:00 P.M.]
HON. E. M. STANTON, SEC. OF WAR, WASHINGTON

In the movements of the last few days the Cavalry picked up the following poster.

"Attention Farmers"
Communication having been interrupted by the recent rains Gen Lees Army is now almost without rations, He therefore Calls upon the Citizens to sell or loan as much Corn Meal & Molasses as they Can spare He will pay market price for the same or return it in kind as soon as practicable, persons having any of Such supplies to spare will please apply to

(signed) W. H. MANN
Agt. for Maj. Fannhill [*Tannahill*]
U. S. GRANT
Lt. Gn.

ALS (telegram sent), CSmH; copies, DLC-USG, V, 46, 73, 108; (marked as received at 10:20 P.M.) DNA, RG 107, Telegrams Received in Cipher; *ibid.*, RG 108, Letters Sent. *O.R.*, I, xlvi, part 2, 474. The text of the poster, not in USG's hand, appeared on a second sheet for insertion in the telegram sent.

On Feb. 8, 1865, USG telegraphed to Secretary of War Edwin M. Stanton transmitting information from southern newspapers. *Ibid.*, pp. 474–75. At 12:30 P.M., USG telegraphed to Maj. Gen. Henry W. Halleck transmitting a report from Col. George H. Sharpe to Lt. Col. Theodore S. Bowers conveying information from agents in Richmond. Copy (marked as received at 6:00 P.M.), DNA, RG 107, Telegrams Received in Cipher. Printed as received at 7:40 P.M. in *O.R.*, I, xlvi, part 2, 475.

To Maj. Gen. George G. Meade

By Telegraph from City Point
Dated Feb 8th *18645*.

To MAJ GENL MEADE
Rhodes Division was the only one left in the valley. If it has come to your front I have no information of the fact. If you ascertain certainly it is there let me know so that I can inform Sheridan of the

fact. Let me know about the result of warrens two advances. I sent no dispatch yesterday to Washington

U S GRANT
Lt Genl

Telegram received (at 11:00 A.M.), DNA, RG 107, Telegrams Collected (Unbound); copies (2), Meade Papers, PHi. *O.R.*, I, xlvi, part 2, 476. Entered as sent on Feb. 7, 1865, in USG's letterbooks.

On Feb. 8, 12:30 P.M., Maj. Gen. George G. Meade telegraphed to USG. "Yesterday Maj Gen Warren again advanced from his position on the right bank of Hatchers Run & encountering the Enemy carried the line of rifle pits occupied by the Enemys skirmish line & continued the advance till the fire of the artillery in the Enemys work near Dabneys Mill was drawn & till he (Warren) had passed over most of the ground he had occupied the day before   this operation was performed during the prevelance of a violent Hail storm   the resistence offered by the Enemy outside his works was not however so great as the day before   having accomplishd all that was practicable & the Enemy declining battle outside his works I directed the withdrawal of the troops to Hatchers Run which was effected soon after night fall   I forward Maj Gen Warrens Report just received. The casualties of the 3 days operations will not now as far as I can judge in the absence of official returns exceed 1500 which is about double the number of wounded brought to the Rear   The prisoners will exceed 200   the Cavalry on the 5th captured 25 wagons instead of 18 as previously reported. I am now preparing an entreched line from Ft Cummings our left to Armstrongs Mill   this line will be held by the 2d corps & the 5th will be moved to defend our left & rear   the Cavalry & the reserves of the 6th corps have been returned to their former positions   The reserves of the 9th will be returned so soon as the condition of the new line justifies" Telegram received (at 1:35 P.M.), DNA, RG 108, Letters Received; copies, *ibid.*, RG 393, Army of the Potomac, Letters Sent; (2) Meade Papers, PHi. Printed as sent at 1:25 P.M. in *O.R.*, I, xlvi, part 1, 154; *ibid.*, I, xlvi, part 2, 476. The enclosure is *ibid.*, p. 787. At 1:00 P.M., Meade telegraphed to USG. "The above is all the information we have about Rhodes old Division—It would appear from it, if reliable, that this Division has been here since the 17th of January—" ALS (telegram sent), DNA, RG 393, Army of the Potomac, Miscellaneous Letters Received; telegram received (at 2:10 P.M.), *ibid.*, RG 108, Letters Received. *O.R.*, I, xlvi, part 2, 476. The enclosure is *ibid.*, pp. 476–77. At 4:00 P.M., Meade telegraphed to USG. "Official returns of Casualties received show 5th Corps 1400 2d Corps 140 Cavalry 150 in all—1690 which includes over 600 missing of whom the greater portion will turn up being stragglers—I send a notice found by Gregg posted up in Dinwiddie CH. If the enemy does not attack us today I think you can leave with security tomorrow" Telegram received (at 4:20 P.M.), DNA, RG 108, Letters Received; copies, *ibid.*, RG 393, Army of the Potomac, Letters Sent; Meade Papers, PHi. Printed as sent at 4:20 P.M. in *O.R.*, I, xlvi, part 1, 154; *ibid.*, I, xlvi, part 2, 477. For the enclosure, see preceding telegram. On the same day, USG telegraphed to Meade transmitting information about the battle of Hatcher's Run from the *Richmond Whig*. Telegram received (at 4:45 P.M.), DNA, RG 94, War Records Office, Army of the Potomac; copies (2), Meade Papers, PHi. Printed as sent at 4:45 P.M. in *O.R.*, I, xlvi, part 2, 477.

To Maj. Gen. John M. Schofield

Head Quarters Armies of the U. S.
City Point, Va.
February 8th 1865—10 P. M.

MAJOR-GENERAL SCHOFIELD,
FORT FISHER, N. C.

For the last three days there have been many troops arriving in Richmond, from the valley or Southwestern Virginia. This is evidently a movement to get troops to send South, and to enable the enemy to hold Wilmington also.

I have not a doubt but that the quicker you can bring your troops against Wilmington, the smaller the force you will have to contend against.

U. S. GRANT,
Lieut-Gen'l.

Telegram received (at 10:00 P.M.), DNA, RG 94, Army of the James, Telegrams Sent (Press); copies, *ibid.*, RG 108, Letters Sent; *ibid.*, RG 393, Dept. of N. C., Telegrams Received; DLC-USG, V, 46, 73, 108; DLC-John M. Schofield. *O.R.*, I, xlvii, part 2, 355. On Feb. 8, 1865, USG telegraphed to q. m., Fort Monroe. "You will send the above dispatch aboard the first transport going to Cape Fear River and place it in the hands of a commissioned officer to be delivered to Gn. Schofield. Transports must now be passing hourly but not touching at Ft. Monroe. You can send this in a tug to go until they meet one." ALS (undated telegram sent), Kohns Collection, NN; telegram received, DNA, RG 94, Army of the James, Telegrams Sent (Press). *O.R.*, I, xlvii, part 2, 355.

On the same day, Maj. Gen. John M. Schofield, Federal Point, N. C., telegraphed to USG. "I arrived here this morning with one division. Have had very rough weather and been much delayed by it. I hope to get the troops all landed by tomorrow night and send the transports back for the other divisions. There is no apparent change in the situation since you were here. I propose to commence operations at once without waiting for the other troops as time is important. I think I can take Fort Anderson and possibly Wilmington with the force I now have." ALS (telegram sent via Fort Monroe, Feb. 11, 5:00 P.M.), DNA, RG 107, Telegrams Collected (Unbound); telegram received (on Feb. 11, 6:00 P.M.), *ibid.*, Telegrams Collected (Bound); *ibid.*, RG 108, Letters Received. *O.R.*, I, xlvii, part 2, 355–56.

To Maj. Gen. Philip H. Sheridan

(Cipher)   City Point, Va, Feb.y 8th 1865 [*noon*]
MAJ. GEN. SHERIDAN, WINCHESTER VA,

There has been conciderable movement of troops from the Valley or elsewhere over the Va. Central road. Field Artillery has been coming in for three days past. Rhodes Division was reported in front of Meade yesterday. We learn from Richmond that 2000 Infantry passed through there, going south, last Saturday.[1] Wickham's[2] Brigade of Cavalry has arrived here and Butler's[3] gone from here South. We have extended our lines over four miles more to our left. This brings us no nearer the South side road but will enable us to secure good crossings of Hatchers' run when we do move. I believe there is no enemy now to prevent you reaching the Va. Central road, and possibly the Canal, when the weather will permit you to move.

U. S. GRANT
Lt. Gn.

ALS (telegram sent), IHi; telegram received (at 3:00 P.M.), DNA, RG 107, Telegrams Collected (Bound); *ibid.*, Telegrams Collected (Unbound). *O.R.*, I, xlvi, part 2, 495. On Feb. 8, 1865, 8:30 P.M., Maj. Gen. Philip H. Sheridan telegraphed to USG. "Your despatch of to day recd   I feel very certain of being able to break the Central Rail Road, and the Canal, as soon as the weather will permit—At present we have (12) twelve inches of Snow on the ground; and have had Snow on the ground, since the (10th) tenth of last December, with extremely cold weather. All the late expeditions to break up Guerrilla bands have had many men frost bitten—The following is my latest information as to the movements of the enemy—This information I have had through different sources for the last ten (10) days. Two (2) Divisions of the Troops from the valley were encamped on the road from Petersburg to Richmond—the other Division was in the trenches having taken the place of a Div: sent south—said to be Kershaw—Whartons Division from (3000 to 4000) three to four thousand strong, was on the Rail Road near Fisherville—between Stanton and Waynesboro—Lomax' Cavly: moved from the east side of Blue Ridge, to the valley, and thence to Warm Springs—his Cavly: is now south from Warm Springs, Scattered through the numerous little vallies in the vicinity of Parisburg [*Pearisburg*]—Rosser sent Wickhams Brigade to the east side of Blue Ridge—his own (Rossers) brigade was (6) six miles west of Stanton— Paynes brigade was near Lexington   Two (2) Horse Batteries were disbanded, and the pieces sent to Waynesboro ~~or Stanton~~ or Richmond—There was considerable artillery in the upper valley in the vicinity of Lynchburg, this artillery belonged to the Infy: Div sent by Early to Richmond—as these Div: I know did not take their Batteries with them—It has been reported to me within a day, or two, that one (1) brigade of Whartons Div: had left for Dublin station, probably it went to Richmond—The foregoing information was obtained from a man that I sent to Richmond—also from my scouts sent to Staunton—Since then I have sent down to burn the bridge at Lynchburg—There has been a report here, and it has undoubtedly reached the rebels, that there was to be a big Cavly: raid sent out from this point—This report was brought here from Washington where it originated—it may have caused this movement of Arty: by the Rebels—" Telegram sent, DNA, RG 107, Telegrams Collected (Unbound); telegram received (at 10:30 P.M.), *ibid.*, Telegrams Collected (Bound); *ibid.*, RG 108, Letters Received. *O.R.*, I, xlvi, part 2, 496.

On Feb. 12, Sheridan telegraphed to USG. "The weather here still continues very bad—the deep snow is still on the ground, and very cold—It is utterly impossible to do anything here in such weather—I never have experienced a colder or worse winter—I can not learn as yet, that any troops have left here for Richmond—Echols Brig: went to the narrows, on New River, about (20) twenty miles from Dublin Depôt—I do not know what this move means, except it is to collect provisions from about ~~Par~~ Parisburg—" Telegram sent, DNA, RG 107, Telegrams Collected (Unbound); telegram received, *ibid.*; (at 10:00 P.M.) *ibid.*, Telegrams Collected (Bound); (on Feb. 13) *ibid.*, RG 108, Letters Received. *O.R.*, I, xlvi, part 2, 545.

On Feb. 13, 10:30 A.M., USG telegraphed to Sheridan. "I do not care about your moving until the weather and roads are such as to give assurances of overcoming all obsticles except those interposed by the enemy." ALS (telegram sent), IHi; telegram received (at 11:30 A.M.), DNA, RG 107, Telegrams Collected (Bound); *ibid.*, Telegrams Collected (Unbound). *O.R.*, I, xlvi, part 2, 553.

1. Feb. 4.
2. Williams C. Wickham, born in Richmond, Va., in 1820, a lawyer and planter, was a Unionist in 1861 but entered C.S.A. service as capt., Hanover Dragoons. Appointed brig. gen. as of Sept. 1, 1863, he resigned as of Oct. 5, 1864, to take his seat in the C.S.A. Congress. The cav. brigade in Maj. Gen. Fitzhugh Lee's div. retained Wickham's name.
3. Matthew C. Butler, born in Greenville, S. C., in 1836, studied law and was elected to the S. C. legislature on the eve of the Civil War. Entering the war as capt., Hampton Legion, he was appointed brig. gen. as of Sept. 1, 1863, and maj. gen. as of Sept. 19, 1864. On Jan. 19, 1865, Butler's cav. div. was ordered from Va. to S. C. *O.R.*, I, xlvi, part 2, 1101.

To Maj. Gen. Henry W. Halleck

(Cipher)   City Point, Va, Feb.y 9th 1865 [*11:30* A.M.]
~~Hon~~ MAJ. GN. HALLECK, WASHINGTON,

I start in a few minuets for Washington. If there is any difficulty to be apprehended from ice please telegraph me to Fortress
Monroe.

U. S. GRANT
Lt. Gn.

ALS (telegram sent), Kohns Collection, NN; copies, DLC-USG, V, 46, 73, 108;
(marked as received at 11:45 A.M.) DNA, RG 107, Telegrams Received in Cipher; *ibid.*, RG 108, Letters Sent. *O.R.*, I, xlvi, part 2, 497. On Feb. 9, 1865,
12:45 P.M., Maj. Gen. Henry W. Halleck telegraphed to USG. "Genl Rucker
thinks you will have difficulty with ice in the Potomac. If you come by Annapolis,
you had better telegraph to Capt Blodget, as trains are very irregular." ALS
(telegram sent), DNA, RG 107, Telegrams Collected (Bound); telegram received, *ibid.*; *ibid.*, Telegrams Collected (Unbound); (at 1:00 P.M.) *ibid.*, RG
108, Letters Received. *O.R.*, I, xlvi, part 2, 497. On the same day, Brig. Gen.
Rufus Ingalls telegraphed to Brig. Gen. John A. Rawlins. "Gen Rucker reports
heavy ice in the Potomac again. Probably you had better go by way of Annapolis.
If you do so telegraph to Capt Blodgett there to have ambulance & cars in readiness." Telegram received, DNA, RG 108, Letters Received. *O.R.*, I, xlvi, part
2, 498.

At 11:00 A.M., USG telegraphed to Maj. Gen. George G. Meade and Maj.
Gen. Edward O. C. Ord. "I will leave here at twelve 12 noon for Washington to
remain absent four 4 or five 5 days unless sooner recalled. Please inform Col.
Bowers of all movements or changes so that he may keep me advised—" Telegram received, Ord Papers, CU-B; DNA, RG 94, War Records Office, Miscellaneous War Records; *ibid.*, RG 107, Telegrams Collected (Unbound); copies,
ibid., RG 108, Letters Sent; DLC-USG, V, 46, 73, 108. *O.R.*, I, xlvi, part 2, 498.
Telegrams sent by Lt. Col. Theodore S. Bowers to USG in Washington, Feb.
9–12, are *ibid.*, pp. 499, 513, 524–25, 539; *ibid.*, I, xlvii, part 2, 372–73, 385.

To Maj. Gen. Edward R. S. Canby

City Point Va, Feby 9th 1865

MAJ, GEN, CANBY
COM'DG MIL, DIV. W, MISS
GENERAL!

I have ordered Genl, Grierson to report to you to take Chief
Command of your Cavalry operating from Mobile Bay.[1] I do not

mean to fasten on you Commanders against your judgment or wishes, But you applied for Averill, I supposed for that service, I have no faith in him and can not point to a single sucess of his except in his reports, Grierson on the contrary has been a most successful Cavalry Commander He set the first example in making long raids by going through from Memphis to Baton Rouge, His raid this winter on to the Mobile and Ohio rail road was most important in its results and most successfully executed, I do not think I could have sent you a better man than Grierson to Command your Cavalry on an expedition to the interior of Alabama, Unless you go yourself I am afraid your other troops will not be so well commanded, What is wanted is a Commander who will not be afraid to cut loose from his base of supplies and who will make the best use of the resources of the Country, An Army the size of the one you will have can always get to some place where they can be supplied, if they should fail to reach the point started for,

> Very Respectfully
> Your obt svt
> U, S, GRANT
> Lt, Genl,

Copies, DLC-USG, V, 46, 73, 108; DNA, RG 108, Letters Sent; Grierson Papers, IHi. *O.R.*, I, xlviii, part 1, 786. On Feb. 11, 1865, 1:00 P.M., Maj. Gen. Edward R. S. Canby telegraphed to USG. "Your telegram of the first just recd The troops and supplies are being concentrated as rapidly as possible. The supply of grain is ample for the present and there will be no difficulty if the requisitions already made are filled. The Q. M. Gen. was asked some time since to send a part of the hay required by sea. I telegraph to him today to repeat the recommendation" Telegrams received (2—received on Feb. 17 and on Feb. 18, noon), DNA, RG 107, Telegrams Collected (Bound); (on Feb. 17) *ibid.*, RG 108, Letters Received; copies (2), *ibid.*, RG 107, Telegrams Received in Cipher. *O.R.*, I, xlix, part 1, 699. Canby was responding to a telegram sent by Maj. Gen. Henry W. Halleck. *Ibid.*, pp. 626–27.

On March 5, Canby wrote to USG. "*Confidential.* . . . I have the honor to acknowledge the receipt of your communication of the 9th ultimo. I have no personal knowledge of Gen. Averill. My application for him was based on the reputation he had with the officers of his regiment, (3d Cavalry,) as an active and enterprising officer. I am, however, greatly pleased with the change you have made, in sending General Grierson. I have made applications for General Gillmore and General W. F. Smith. The first had been assigned to another command, and the second application has been declined. The object in making these appli-

cations, was to have some one near, in whom the Department and yourself had
confidence, who could take the general conduct of the campaign, and carry out
the plan of operations, in case of any accident to myself. I have no other choice in
this respect. Steele, I think, is deficient in the qualities of organization and preparation. The same objection, I believe, applies to A. J. Smith, in a smaller degree,
but I have not known him so long and so well as Steele. Granger possesses these
to a greater extent than the others, but is deficient in other respects. Of the three
I incline to Smith, but any one in whom you have sufficient confidence to place
in that position, would be acceptable to me. Osterhous has just reported, and has
impressed me favorably, but I do not yet know him well, except by reputation.
The Department of the Gulf will need an energetic commander with positive
qualities of administration. Gen. Hurlbut has succeeded very well, but is anxious
to leave the service, and his resignation will be forwarded with the recommendation, that it shall not take effect, until his successor has been designated, and has
arrived. I have no one now that can replace him." LS, DNA, RG 108, Letters
Received. *O.R.*, I, xlviii, part 1, 1092.

1. On Oct. 5, 1864, Brig. Gen. Benjamin H. Grierson, Memphis, drafted a
lengthy letter to USG complaining about lack of opportunity to use his talents as
cav. commander. ADf, Grierson Papers, IHi. There is no evidence that this letter
was sent to USG. On Jan. 17, 1865, Maj. Gen. Henry W. Halleck forwarded to
USG a request by Grierson for authority to organize cav. regts. into a div., and
between Jan. 25 and 27, USG endorsed this letter. "Respy. returned. It is desirable that we should have in Tennessee a force of Cavalry, in one body, to cope
with anything the enemy can attempt a northern movement with, or that can
take the offensive against the enemy if desirable. I have great confidence in General Grierson as a commander, but I do not think it advisable to divide the cavalry under General Thomas" Copy, DLC-USG, V, 58. On Feb. 8, Lt. Col.
Theodore S. Bowers wrote to Grierson. "Lieutenant General Grant directs me to
acknowledge the receipt by him of your letter of date Feby 6. 1865, and to forward to you herewith Special Orders No 29." ALS, Grierson Papers, IHi. Special
Orders No. 29, Armies of the U.S., was enclosed. "Brig Gen. B. H. Grierson,
U. S. Vols., will report in person without delay to these Headquarters for orders."
DS, *ibid. O.R.*, I, xlviii, part 1, 772. On Feb. 9, 10:00 A.M., USG telegraphed to
Halleck. "I have ordered Gen. Grierson to Canby to Command his Cavalry. I
think he could not have known Averell or he would not have applied for him."
ALS (telegram sent), CSmH; copies, DLC-USG, V, 46, 73, 108; (incomplete)
DNA, RG 94, Letters Received, 153A 1865; (marked as received at 11:00 A.M.)
ibid., RG 107, Telegrams Received in Cipher; *ibid.*, RG 108, Letters Sent. *O.R.*,
I, xlviii, part 1, 786. On the same day, Brig. Gen. John A. Rawlins telegraphed
to Grierson. "Proceed at once to Washn where you will see Gen Grant & receive
orders—" Telegram received, Grierson Papers, IHi; (press) DNA, RG 107,
Telegrams Collected (Bound); copies, *ibid.*, RG 108, Letters Sent; DLC-USG,
V, 46, 73, 108. *O.R.*, I, xlix, part 1, 679. See *ibid.*, I, xlviii, part 1, 823.

To Maj. Gen. George G. Meade

———

By Telegraph from City Point 10 A M
Dated Feby 9th *18645.*

To MAJ GEN MEADE

The committee on the conduct of the war have published the result of their investigation of the mine explosion Their opinions are not sustained by Knowledge of the facts nor by my evidence nor yours either do I suppose. Gen Burnsides evidence apparently has been their guide & to draw it mildly he has forgotten some of the facts. I think in justification to yourself who seems to be the only party censured, Burnside should be brought before a Court Martial and let the proceedings of the Court go before the public along with the report of the Congressional Committee

U S GRANT Lt Gen

Telegram received, DNA, RG 94, War Records Office, Army of the Potomac; *ibid.,* RG 107, Telegrams Collected (Unbound); copies, *ibid.,* RG 108, Letters Sent; DLC-USG, V, 46, 73, 108; (2) Meade Papers, PHi. *O.R.,* I, xlvi, part 2, 497–98. On Feb. 9, 1865, 11:15 A.M., Maj. Gen. George G. Meade telegraphed to USG. "I think the report of the Comee on the conduct of the War when the truth comes to be put before the country will prove a greater failure even than the Mine.—If I can get the proceedings of the Court of Inquiry published I am willing to abide by the judgement of the public One of my friends in the Senate promised to call for it, but I asked him not to do so till I could ascertain it would be agreeable to the War Dept—My return direct to this place prevented me from seeing Mr. Stanton upon this point—If you are going to Washington you might mention the Subject You are aware I preferred Charges against Burnside but they did not include his neglect of duty about the mine because that was then in the hands of the court of Inquiry.—Are you going to Washn today?—" ALS (telegram sent), DNA, RG 94, War Records Office, Army of the Potomac; telegram received, *ibid.,* RG 108, Letters Received. *O.R.,* I, xlvi, part 2, 498. On the same day, Lt. Col. Theodore S. Bowers telegraphed to Meade. "Gen Grants started at 11 30 a m your cipher dispatch of 11.15 will reach him at Fort Monroe" Telegram received (at 1:45 P.M.), DNA, RG 94, War Records Office, Army of the Potomac. *O.R.,* I, xlvi, part 2, 498. See *ibid.,* pp. 548, 554.

To Maj. Gen. George G. Meade

Cipher

Washington City,
Feb.y 10th *1865* [*2:00* P.M.]

MAJ. GEN. MEADE, CITY POINT, VA.

Order to Baltimore some of your old, reliable and reduced regiments, so that the whole number of men sent will number from ten to twelve hundred, to go North to take charge of camps of drafted men. We want the most reliable men and officers for this duty. There is a regiment of regulars here, numbering about seven hundred men for duty, mostly new men, that will be sent to you. Telegraph to Gen Halleck the regiments you select.[1]

U. S. GRANT
Lt. Gn.

ALS (telegram sent), DNA, RG 107, Telegrams Collected (Bound); telegram sent (misdated), *ibid.*; telegram received, *ibid.*, RG 94, War Records Office, Army of the Potomac. *O.R.*, I, xlvi, part 2, 513.

1. See *ibid.*, pp. 513–14, 540.

Testimony

WASHINGTON, *February* 11, 1865.
Lieutenant General U. S. GRANT sworn and examined.

By the chairman:

Question. We have been instructed by the Senate to inquire into the cause or causes of the failure of the expedition against Fort Fisher, North Carolina, in December last. Will you state, in your own way, what you know upon that subject, so far as you may deem it proper to state it?

Answer. I cannot give the dates without the records. For a long time back the navy has been very anxious to have the port of Wilmington closed as an avenue of supplies for the rebels; and some two or three months before the expedition started, I agreed with the navy to send a military force down there to co-operate with the navy. There was no time fixed, for it would take them some little time to collect their fleet. While preparations were being made the whole affair was so thoroughly advertised to the country and to the south that they were fully prepared for us, and I kept putting it off. At that time I collected all the information I could about Cape Fear river, the strength of the enemy's works, the garrison they had, together with all the maps, charts, and other information, which I turned over to General Weitzel. I had detailed General Weitzel as the commander of the expedition, a fact which General Butler understood. It was so thoroughly advertised to the enemy and to the country that I kept putting off the expedition. A short time before the expedition actually started the gunpowder plot was got up— the powder-boat. It seemed to be a favorite scheme with General Butler. He had been to see me several months before, and wanted to blow up Charleston with a vessel loaded with a thousand tons of powder. I did not favor it, because I did not believe it would have any effect. About the time the expedition did start General Butler got up this idea of a powder-vessel, and sent me a statement of the casualties that had occurred in some place in England from the explosion of a large quantity of gunpowder, and wanted to know what I thought about it. I turned the matter over to Colonel Comstock, of my staff, who made a report upon the subject of the effect that the explosion of 300 or 400 tons of powder out at sea would do no damage. That was my opinion. It was referred to the chief engineer, General Delafield, and he thought it would have about the same effect on the fort that firing feathers from muskets would have on the enemy. I believe that is the way he expressed his opinion upon the subject. However, it was submitted to Admiral Porter and the Navy Department, and, I believe, was favored by them. I was then asked if I would allow them to have 2,500 men to hold the point of land upon which Fort Fisher is built, in case they could take the fort by that means. I told them that I would certainly spare them that number of men at any time; and they went to work getting up the powder-boat. In the mean time, while preparations were being made for this, General Sherman began to get on so far through Georgia that the enemy, in order to raise a force to put against him, pretty nearly abandoned Fort Fisher and Wilmington. This information I obtained from southern papers and other sources. I saw that Bragg had gone, and the statement was that he had taken about 8,000 men from there. I knew that was about the force he had; and from the information which I had, they had very few of their old regular troops there, as they called them, but mostly senior and junior reserves, men too old or too young to come in under the conscript law. I thought then was the time for the expedition to move. I accordingly ordered General Butler to get off 6,500 men under General Weitzel. General Weitzel had been named for that purpose two or three months before. The expedition was got off with commendable promptness from his army on James river. When they all sailed down, General Butler also went down the river, stopping at my headquarters Then was the first that I ever dreamed of his going with the expedition. He knew that it was not intended that he should go. But all my orders and instructions were sent through him as the commander of the department from which the troops intended for the expedition were taken, and also as commander of the department in which they were to operate. Military courtesy requires that orders should go in that way. But I never dreamed of his going until he passed by my headquarters on his way down to Fortress Monroe. After he had got there, finding that the expedition was delayed, I sent him a despatch, which I have sent in as one of the papers accompanying his report, urging him to go ahead with or without his powder-boat; not to let that detain him. My calculations for success were based as much upon finding the enemy's troops still away as upon anything else. I never had any faith in the powder-boat doing anything. I did not know but it might probably have some effect, but I did not believe it would.

Question. The expectation was to surprise the fort?

Answer. Yes, sir. And my instructions were very clear, that if they effected a landing there above Fort Fisher, that in itself was to be considered a success; and if the fort did not fall immediately upon their landing, then they were to intrench themselves and remain there and co-operate with the navy until the fort did fall. In my instructions I provided for a bold dash for the capture of Wilmington, in case Fort Fisher did fall immediately upon the landing of the troops. If it did not fall, then they were to intrench, enter upon a siege of the place, and remain there until it did fall. And the capture of Wilmington would thus become a matter for future consideration. General Butler came away from Fort Fisher in violation of the instructions which I gave him. From his own official report it is evident that he forgot his instructions in that particular; his report shows that.

Question. Was it ever contemplated that the fleet should endeavor to run by the fort?

Answer. My instructions for the first expedition contemplated nothing of the kind, though I rather thought they might do it; but when the second expedition went down, in my instructions to General Terry, I said that the enemy being so much better prepared than before, in consequence of our having once attempted and failed, the navy ought to take greater risks than they were called upon to do in the first instance, and, if necessary, attempt to run by; but since the fort has been taken I have been down there, and I know now that it would have been impossible for the navy to have run by the fort. The nature of the channel was such that they could not run by until the fort was taken.

Question. What would have rendered it impossible for the navy to run by the fort before it was taken—the depth of water in the channel?

Answer. To begin with, there is not so great depth of water in the channel as the charts show. Then the channel is a winding one, with reefs extending into it, compelling vessels to keep near shore. Lightest draught vessels only could get in, and these would require the assistance of good pilots.

Question. How do the blockade runners get in? they run in at night I understand.

Answer. They draw less water than our gunboats do, and, besides, they have to run no risk of the fort firing upon them; still some of the blockade runners get wrecked trying to get in. Our gunboats have to go in on high tide.

Question. Was it your opinion that General Weitzel's report to General Butler was not correct, and that they should have assaulted the fort?

Answer. I have not censured any person for not assaulting the fort, for they were not ordered by me to assault it; but General Curtis,[1] who commanded the troops that got nearest to the fort, and one or two other officers who were there, voluntarily came forward and made statements, which I have forwarded here and asked to have attached to the report, in which they give it as their opinion that the fort could have been carried by assault; that at the very time they were called back they were up so near that they virtually had the fort; that if they had not been called back, in an hour or two more they would have taken the fort.

Question. What progress had they made?

Answer. They had actually got up so close to it that some of the men could look into the rear of the fort. Those statements are here with the Secretary of War. General Curtis, Lieutenant Ross,[2] and some other officers made statements to that effect.

Question. How many men had they there at the time?

Answer. General Curtis commanded a brigade; but there were only a few men who got up that close to the fort; a few men from the skirmish line.

Question. Was not that fort considered a very formidable work?

Answer. It is a very formidable work to carry by assault; but when four or five shells a second are exploding in any work the men are inclined to keep under shelter.

Question. At the time General Curtis and his men were there the fort was, of course, in better condition than after the second bombardment?

Answer. It was probably in better condition the second time than when it was first attacked, because the first assault gave them the opportunity to ascertain the weak points of the fort, and they had time to strengthen it. I have no doubt that when the second bombardment commenced the fort was in a better condition that when the first bombardment commenced; and when the assault was made the garrison was double as large as General Butler himself stated it to have been when he was there. He told me that, from all the evidence he could obtain from deserters and prisoners, he supposed they had about 1,200 men when he was there. When we finally took the fort we killed, wounded, and captured about 2,500 of the enemy.

Question. General Weitzel says that the first bombardment did not injure the fort for defensible purposes. Admiral Porter says that the second bombardment knocked the fort into a pulp.

Answer. At the second bombardment there were some guns dismounted in the fort, it may be most of them, as would have been the case at the time of the first bombardment had it been continued. General Weitzel was not ordered by me to assault the fort, but to intrench there, and continue there, under the protection of the navy, until the fort did fall.

By Mr. Gooch:

Question. Did General Butler find the condition of things contemplated in his instructions in relation to the landing and intrenching upon the land there?

Answer. General Weitzel and the other officers who were there could answer that question positively from their own knowledge; but there is no question that General Butler could have remained there, in obedience to my instructions; but I do not think he was guided by them; I do not think he paid any particular attention to them. I will state, in regard to the second expedition, that I ordered General Butler to get up the same expedition that went first with him, together with enough additional men to make the force 8,000 men, to go under General Terry, with orders to report to General Sherman at Savannah. I then gave my instructions to General Terry himself; but General Terry did not know where he was going, supposing, of course, that he was going to Savannah, till he got down to City Point on his way out. I changed that portion of my instructions which ordered General Butler to send additional forces, to be black and white troops, sufficient to make the number 8,000; and directed him to send, in addition to the forces that went the first time, one brigade of General Terry's own division, num-

bering about 1,500 men, so that the second expedition did actually
go with about 8,000 men.

Question. General Terry had the assistance of marines and
sailors on the second expedition, had he not?

Answer. Yes, sir; General Butler did not wait for that.

Question. Was there any obstacle in the way of making a full
landing at the time of the first expedition, so far as you know?

Answer. I do not think there could have been, from the fact
that General Butler landed a portion of his troops, and then reembarked them some hours afterwards. The time spent in re-
embarking could have been spent in debarking.

Question. With the force that General Butler had, could he
have held that position and carried out your instructions?

Answer. There is no question about that, so far as the mere
holding of the place is concerned, with the navy there to cover
them. They could have intrenched themselves in a few hours so as
to be able to remain there.

By Mr. Odell:

Question. They did stay there all night, did they not?

Answer. A few remained there all night; and then if there were
not men enough already there, I had plenty more I could have sent
down there afterwards.

By the chairman:

Question. Have you any means of knowing what force the
enemy had about there within a day's march?

Answer. I knew that one division had left Lee's front to go
there, and that made me extremely anxious to hear that General
Butler had got possession of Fort Fisher, and also Wilmington, if
possible, before the enemy got down there. Whether that division
did reach Fort Fisher or Wilmington, in whole or in part, before
General Butler left, I am not prepared to say. I think the navy was
under the impression that it did not get there for two days afterwards. But that is a matter for them to testify to; I cannot say
about it.

When I met General Terry down there I went with him down
to Fortress Monroe to see him off. I then told him that I should go

immediately back to City Point and have a siege train loaded on board vessels, and send it down to Fortress Monroe, so that if, after he had effected a landing, he should find it necessary to go into a siege, he could send up for it, as it would be subject to his orders, and it would go right down to him. Before it started I said that as it would already be on shipboard it might as well go down to Beaufort. And, finally, after he had started some days I sent it on to the fleet, near Cape Fear river. That was a force really in excess of the 8,000 men; they never had use for the siege train, but three pieces were taken on shore, and three companies of men, as I understand. The rest were sent back without going ashore at all.

Question. You spoke of troops landing there and being covered by the navy. Is not that rather a dangerous coast for a fleet to lay off?

Answer. They have been there all the time.

Question. They have been there during calm weather. But were they not prevented at one time from going there by the storm?

Answer. I am not sailor enough to say whether or not they could have remained there then. But they have since landed and remained there; a force not much larger than General Butler had. With all the casualties in taking that place, the force there is about the size of the force General Butler had. After sending off the sick, wounded, and disabled men, the force is now about what General Butler had, and it has remained there ever since, navy and all.

Question. You do not know particularly about the exposed condition of the coast and the danger to shipping there?

Answer. No sir. There may be times when a fleet could not lay off there. But if the troops were fortified strongly there they could defend themselves.

Question. Was there any culpable delay in the progress of that expedition, so far as you know; and if so, what was it, and who is to blame about it?

Answer. I have no means of knowing further than General Butler's own report. There was a delay that worried me excessively, because I wanted to take advantage of the absence of Bragg and his forces. And I telegraphed to General Butler, as I have already stated, to go with or without his powder-boat. But General Butler was evidently determined not to go without it, for he said, in his despatch to me, that it would soon be loaded. And after they had got started, I should think there was a delay of more than a week, perhaps ten days, after they left Fortress Monroe before the troops were landed.

Question. Did you understand that any portion of that delay was on account of boisterous weather?

Answer. Yes, sir. But I understood from General Butler himself, and also from Colonel Comstock, of my staff, that they went down there and lay there for three days of beautiful weather, but the navy did not get there, and when the navy did get there the transports had so nearly exhausted their supplies of coal and water that they had to run back to Beaufort and get a new supply. And there they had some boisterous weather.

By Mr. Odell:

Question. Did the delay resulting from the failure of the army and navy to get together make any difference when they did come to make the attack?

Answer. That depends upon whether or not the division of troops that left Lee's front really got down there before our troops landed. General Butler maintains that at least two brigades of them were there. I do not know how that was. If the enemy got no re-enforcements there the delay made no difference.

Question. Do you know a reporter by the name of Cadwallader connected with your army?

Answer. I do.

Question. Did you direct that he should be appointed an officer in order to save him from the draft?

Answer. Never.

Question. Do you know anything about his appointment?

Answer. I do not know anything about it except what I have since heard from the man himself. The man has no more connexion with me than any other reporter who behaves himself. He was absolutely drafted, and went off to obey the draft, and he states that when he got to New York he found that $800 had been paid for a substitute for him, and that substitute was in the army, and he returned. I heard him say that after he had returned, and had a substitute in the army, General Butler had appointed him a second lieutenant in a colored regiment, and that that was the first that he knew about it.

Question. Do you know anything about Chaplain Hudson.[3]

Answer. I had that case investigated, but I cannot give the exact result of the investigation. The man was confined for fifty-odd days in what is called the bull-pen, near General Butler's headquarters, I understand—put in with deserters and all sorts of prisoners. The investigation shows that he was there that length of time without charges and without trial, though during a good part of the time he was there General Butler had a court-martial sitting right at his headquarters and could have tried him.

By the chairman:

Question. How long ago was that?

Answer. He was confined there during the fall, in the months of September, October, and November. He was released while General Butler was in New York city, at the time of the election. He was released on the 9th of November, I think.

Question. When did the case come to your knowledge?

Answer. I received a letter from a lady here in this city telling me about the case. I immediately ordered Chaplain Hudson to report to me, and then I had his case investigated. The man had been all this time in confinement without my knowledge.

Question. Without any charges?

Answer. Never had any charges preferred against him until after General Butler was relieved.

Question. What was alleged against him?

Answer. Absence without leave, I believe; and there may be other charges. All the papers in the case are now in this city. No officer has a right to confine a commissioned officer in a prison or guard-house except for mutiny, or for some offence where it would not be safe to trust the man at large. A commissioned officer, for ordinary breaches of military discipline, is put under arrest. This was only a case of that sort, for which he should not have been confined at all, except in his own tent, under arrest. When this case came to my knowledge I immediately ordered an examination made of all the prisoners about Norfolk, Fort Monroe, and Portsmouth, to see if there were any more such cases.

By Mr. Odell:

Question. What was the result of your examination?

Answer. The result was to find a great many persons in prison without charges. Some had been there for a great length of time.

Question. In the bull-pen?

Answer. "Bull-pen" is merely the name given by the men themselves to a guard-house or prison. When prisoners are first brought in they are put there until they can be sent off to other prisons or guard-houses, or can be tried and disposed of. It is a place in charge of the provost guard.

Question. Were there men placed there by order of General Butler?

Answer. They were placed there by his provost marshals and officers. In many instances there was nothing at all to show by whom they were put there. I have not only ordered an examination to be made of all the prisoners there, but I intend sending inspectors to make an examination of prisons in all the other departments, with authority to correct all such abuses that they may find.

By the chairman:

Question. I am glad of that. There are too many cases of that kind, not only in the army down there, but here and elsewhere.

Answer. It may be so without my knowing it or even being able to correct it entirely.

Question. It is stated, upon what authority I do not know, that you are charged entirely with the exchange of prisoners.

Answer. That is correct; and what is more, I have effected an arrangement for the exchange of prisoners, man for man and officer for officer, or his equivalent, according to the old cartel, until one or the other party has exhausted the number they now hold. I get a great number of letters daily from friends of prisoners in the south, every one of which I cause to be answered, telling them that this arrangement has been made, and that I suppose exchanges can be made at the rate of 3,000 per week. The fact is, that I do not believe the south can deliver our prisoners to us as fast as that, on account of want of transportation on their part. But just as fast as they can deliver our prisoners to us I will receive them, and deliver their prisoners to them.

Question. There is no impediment in the way?

Answer. No, sir; I will take the prisoners as fast as they can deliver them. And I would add, that after I have caused the letters to be answered, I refer the letters to Colonel Mulford, the commissioner of exchanges, so that he may effect special exchanges in those cases wherever he can do so. The Salisbury prisoners will be coming right on. I myself saw Colonel Hatch, the assistant commissioner of exchanges on the part of the south, and he told me that the Salisbury and Danville prisoners would be coming on at once. He said that he could bring them on at the rate of 5,000 or 6,000 a week. But I do not believe he can do that. Their roads are now taxed to their utmost capacity for military purposes, and are becoming less and less efficient every day. Many of the bridges are now down. I merely fixed, as a matter of judgment, that 3,000 a week will be as fast as they can deliver them.

Question. The fact is, that there is no impediment now in the way except the lack of transportation?

Answer. That is all. There is no impediment on our side. I could deliver and receive every one of them in a very short time if they will deliver those they hold. We have lost some two weeks lately on account of ice in the river.

Question. It has been said that we refused to exchange prisoners because we found ours starved, diseased, and unserviceable when we received them, and did not like to exchange sound men for such men?

Answer. There never has been any such reason as that. That has been a reason for making exchanges. I will confess that if our men who are prisoners in the south were really well taken care of, suffering nothing except a little privation of liberty, then, in a military point of view, it would not be good policy for us to exchange, because every man they get back is forced right into the army at once, while that is not the case with our prisoners when we receive them. In fact, the half of our returned prisoners will never go into the army again, and none of them will until after they have had a furlough of thirty or sixty days. Still, the fact of their suffering as they do is a reason for making this exchange as rapidly as possible.

Question. And never has been a reason for not making the exchange?

Answer. It never has. Exchanges having been suspended by reason of disagreement on the part of agents of exchange on both sides before I came in command of the armies of the United States, and it then being near the opening of the spring campaign, I did not deem it advisable or just to the men who had to fight our battles to re-enforce the enemy with thirty or forty thousand disciplined troops at that time. An immediate resumption of exchanges would have had that effect without giving us corresponding benefits. The suffering said to exist among our prisoners south was a powerful argument against the course pursued, and I so felt it.

Report of the Joint Committee on the Conduct of the War at the Second Session Thirty-eighth Congress (Washington, 1865), II, 51–56 (Fort Fisher Expedition); III, 76–77 (Miscellaneous).

Part of USG's testimony concerning prisoners, possibly all that he actually said, appeared almost immediately in newspapers. *New York Tribune*, Feb. 13, 1865. On Feb. 13, 1:00 P.M., USG telegraphed to Secretary of War Edwin M. Stanton. "Will you please ask Hon. B. Wade, Ch. Com. on Conduct of the War, to send me my evidence before them for revision. I wish to add to my answer to their question on the subject of exchanges." ALS (telegram sent), CSmH; copies, DLC-USG, V, 46, 73, 108; (marked as received at 2:00 P.M.) DNA, RG 107, Telegrams Received in Cipher; *ibid.*, RG 108, Letters Sent. On Feb. 16, Col. Edward D. Townsend, AGO, wrote to USG. "At the request of the Committee of Congress on the Conduct of the War I transmit to you for revision a copy of your testimony before that Committee" Copy, *ibid.*, RG 94, Letters Sent.

1. N. Martin Curtis, born in N. Y. in 1835, entered the Civil War as capt., 16th N. Y., and served as col., 142nd N. Y., before promotion to bvt. brig. gen. as of Oct. 28, 1864. His report of the first Fort Fisher expedition is in *O.R.*, I, xlii, part 1, 982–84. His conduct in the capture of Fort Fisher resulted in an appointment as brig. gen. as of Jan. 15, 1865.

2. 1st Lt. George W. Ross, 117th N. Y., aide to Curtis. *Ibid.*, p. 976.

3. See telegram to Maj. Gen. Henry W. Halleck, Dec. 20, 1864.

To John W. Garrett

WAR DEPARTMENT,
Washington City, February 11, 1865—3.10 p. m.
J. W. GARRETT,
President of Baltimore and Ohio Railroad, Baltimore:
I wish to leave here at 10 this evening. Besides my own party
there will be a committee of Congress going with me; probably a
party of fifteen in all. If more convenient for you to send a car at a
later hour it will answer my purpose. Please answer.
U. S. GRANT,
Lieutenant-General.

O.R., I, xlvi, part 2, 524.
On Feb. 12, 1865, 3:30 P.M., USG, Fort Monroe, telegraphed to Lt. Col.
Theodore S. Bowers. "Just arrived will leave here for City Pt. at 4 P. M." Tele-
gram sent, DNA, RG 107, Telegrams Collected (Unbound).

Concerning Charles H. Ray

Trade will be subject to the approval of the Dept. Commanders
so far as left for the military to control. I see less objection to Whis-
key being introduced into the South than to any other one article.
Dr. Ray has asked my opinion particularly as to the propriety of
taking this article up White river, the Yazoo and the St. Francis.
Gen Dana will have to be referred to in matter of trade on the
Yazoo, and Gen Reynolds when permits are desired on the other
two streams.
U. S. GRANT
Lt. Genl.
Washington D. C.
Feby 11th 1865.

Copies, DLC-Robert T. Lincoln; DNA, RG 109, Union Provost Marshals' File
of Papers Relating to Individual Civilians. Written on a message from President
Abraham Lincoln to USG dated Feb., 1865. "Dr. Ray whom you know will talk
to you about a certain matter about which I would like your opinion informally
expressed." Copies, *ibid.* Lincoln, *Works*, VIII, 288. See *ibid.*, p. 299.

To Brig. Gen. George H. Gordon

Head Qrs. Armies of the U. States
Fortress Monroe, Va, Feb.y 12th 1865

BRIG. GEN. GORDON,
COMD.G DIST. OF NORFOLK, VA.
GENERAL,

The "Committee on Commerce" visit Norfolk for the purpose of investigating the trade heretofore carried on from there with rebellious states. You will please give every facility for conducting these investigations. When the Committee wish to return to Washington you will please direct the Quartermaster to provide them, and all connected with them, transportation to Baltimore.

Very respectfully
Your obt. svt.
U. S. GRANT
Lt. Gn.

ALS, ICarbS. George H. Gordon, born in Charlestown, Mass., in 1823, USMA 1846, resigned from the U.S. Army in 1854, attended Harvard Law School (1855–56), then practiced law in Boston. Appointed col., 2nd Mass., in May, 1861, Gordon served in the Shenandoah Valley, was appointed brig. gen. as of June 9, 1862, then served in several theaters of war. On Sept. 27, 1864, Gordon visited USG at City Point and received assurances of an assignment to USG's army. Gordon, *A War Diary of Events in the War of the Great Rebellion: 1863– 1865* (Boston, 1882), pp. 350–52. On Oct. 1, Lt. Col. Ely S. Parker issued Special Orders No. 101. "Brig. Gen. Geo. H. Gordon U. S. Vol's. will report without delay to Maj. Gen. B. F. Butler, Commdg. Dep't. of Va. and N. C. for assignment." DS, DNA, RG 94, War Records Office, Army of the Potomac. *O.R.*, I, xlii, part 3, 32.

On Feb. 14, 1865, USG telegraphed to U.S. Representative Elihu B. Washburne. "Will you remain in Norfolk tomorrow If so I think of Going down tonight—" Telegram received (dated "14," docketed Feb. 14), DNA, RG 107, Telegrams Collected (Unbound).

To Maj. Gen. Henry W. Halleck

City Point Va, Feby 13th 1865 [12:30 P.M.]

MAJ, GEN, HALLECK

WASHINGTON

I wish every effort would be made to pay the Army up to the 31st of Dec, 1864, There is much dissatisfaction felt by Officer's and men who have families partially or wholly dependent upon their pay for a support on account of delay in receiving their due's, Will you please submit this matter to the Secretaries of War and the Treasury?

U. S. GRANT
Lieut, Gen,

Telegram, copies, DLC-USG, V, 46, 73, 108; (marked as received at 12:45 P.M.) DNA, RG 107, Telegrams Received in Cipher; *ibid.*, RG 108, Letters Sent. Printed as received at 1:00 P.M. in *O.R.*, I, xlvi, part 2, 547–48. On Feb. 15, 1865, Maj. Gen. Henry W. Halleck wrote to USG. "Confidential . . . In reply to your telegram in regard to the payment of the troops before Richmond, I would remark that these troops have been paid generally to a later period than those in the West and South. Some are unpaid for seven or eight months. The fault is not in the Pay Department, but a want of money in the Treasury. There will be a change of the head in a few days, but whether that will help us any remains to be seen. Officers and members of Congress have suggested that the money be given to the Pay Dep't. in preference to the Quartermaster's, Commissary's and other supply Departments. You will readily perceive by doing this we would necessarily cut off the supplies of our army. I understand that the Qr. Mr. Dep't. is already some $180,000,000 in debt, and that until a part of this at least is paid, it will be almost impossible to purchase and transport supplies. The manu-facturers cannot furnish cloth, or the shoemakers make shoes, or the railroads transport troops and supplies, much longer, unless paid a part, at least, of their claims. Some of the western roads cannot pay their employées and threaten to stop running their trains, if they cannot be paid what the government owes them. Serious difficulties also exist with the New York Central, Hudson River, Harlem and other roads. What is here said of the Qr. Mr.'s Dep't also applies to the Commissary, Medical, Ordnance and other Departments. If we pay the troops to the exclusion of the other creditors of the government, supplies must stop and our armies be left without food, clothing, and ammunition. We must equalize and distribute the government indebtedness in such a way as to keep the wheels going. I give you these views as the result of various consultations with the heads of departments. What we want is some more great victories to give more con-fidence in our currency and to convince financial men that the war is near its close. In money matters, these are the darkest days we have yet had during the war. But I hope that relief is not very distant" LS, DNA, RG 108, Letters Re-ceived. *O.R.*, I, xlvi, part 2, 561–62.

On Feb. 13, Halleck wrote to USG. "As the time is approaching for organizing the cavalry for the spring campaign, I forward the following items in regard to its condition and wants, collected by the Cavalry Bureau, to January 1st, 1865. Cavalrymen present for duty, 105.434. Cavalrymen present and absent, 160.237. Cavalry horses, serviceable, 77.847. Cavalry horses, unserviceable, 9.659. Cavalry horses purchased during the year 154.400. The number *expended* has been much greater than this, as the cavalry force has been less than the previous year; and moreover a considerable number of team and captured horses have been issued to the cavalry, and also recuperated animals. The expenditure of cavalry horses during the year has probably been little less than 180.000. The waste or loss of cavalry equipments during the year is estimated as follows: Carbines expended 93.394. Pistols expended 71.000. Sabres expended 90.000. Horse equitments expended 150.000. Expense of cavalry in horses, pay, forage, rations, clothing, ordnance, equipments and transportation $125.000.000. *One hundred and twenty five millions of dollars* is certainly a pretty large sum for keeping up our cavalry force for one year! In regard to particular commands, there are in the armies of the Potomac and the James about 10.000 mounted men, and in the Middle Division under Genl Sheridan about 12.000, which can be kept efficient by issues from here, except in case of extraordinary causalities. Genl. Sherman has with him in the field about 6.500 men, which, since he left Atlanta, he has kept mounted by captures from the enemy. In the Dept. of the Ohio, (now Kentucky), there were issued to Genl. Burbridge for his Saltville expedition 6.000 horses. On his return, 4.000 were reported lost or unserviceable. When Hood commenced his march against Nashville, Genl. Thomas' immediate command had only about 5.000 effective cavalry, but between the 1st of October and 31st of December, all horses purchased in the west were sent to his chief of cavalry, the issues amounting to 23.000, and including those sent to Genl. Burbridge during the same period, 29.000, in three months, to Genl. Thomas' entire command. As Genls. Wilson and Burbridge have made requisitions since that period for 14.000 additional horses, it is presumed that about the same number were lost or disabled during that period of three months. As soon as Genl. Thomas determined to make no further advance during the winter, and Genl. Canby was directed to assume active operations in the field, orders were given to resume issues to his (Canby's) command, in preference to all others. In Genl. Canby's entire Division there were about 30.000 effective cavalrymen, of which only about one half were mounted. As, however, his cavalry force was so disproportionate to his infantry, his requisitions are for only 6.000 horses, which will soon be filled. Major Genl. Dodge has made a requisition for 1.000 horses to be sent to Fort Leavenworth, to remount some regiments to be sent against the Indians on the Overland Mail Route. Orders have been given to fill this, as soon as Genl. Canby receives his six thousand horses. It is proper to remark that inspection reports for the end of December showed a cavalry force in the Dept. of Kansas of 4.581 men present for duty, and 4,386 serviceable horses. Major Genl. Thomas has made a requisition for 3.000 cavalry horses to be sent to General Stoneman in East Tennessee. This requisition will be filled next after those of Genls. Dodge and Canby. No issues of cavalry horses have been made to the Dept. of Arkansas for several months, and ~~more than~~ about one half of the cavalry there are entirely dismounted. In regard to the enormous surplus of cavalry in the western and south-western armies, as compared with infantry, I would remark that it has resulted in a great measure from the repeated requisitions of Genls. Rosecrans,

Banks, and others for increase of mounted forces, and their mounting infantry as cavalry. They were repeatedly informed that so large a cavalry force could not be supported, and experience has placed this question beyond a doubt. Moreover, no general can command and efficiently employ, in our broken and wooded country, a body of cavalry of more than 10.000 or 12.000 men. In regard to the Dept. of North Carolina, which is nearly destitute of cavalry, I would respectfully suggest that some regiments or a brigade be sent there from Genl. Sheridan's command. The mounted infantry and militia in Kentucky and Tennessee have destroyed a vast number of horses, without rendering very efficient service in the field. The same remark is partly applicable to the mounted militia in Missouri. The terms of service of many of these will soon expire. There was with Genl. Thomas' army on the 1st of January about 19.000 mounted men, about 16.000 of which were near Eastport. A part of Knipe's division was then dismounted at Louisville; it has since been remounted and sent to Genl. Canby. This will leave Genl. Thomas about 15.000. Genl. Wilson wants 10.000 additional remounts for the spring campaign. It is certain that so large a number of remounts cannot be supplied to that army, even if we make no further issues to other cavalry troops supplied from the west. Neither will it be possible, in my opinion, for such a cavalry force to be subsisted in any operations against Selma or Montgomery. Like all extravagant undertakings, its very magnitude will defeat it, the horses will starve, the equipments be lost, and the men left on foot along the road. Moreover, I learn from the Qr. Mr. Genl. that he is now some $180.000.000. in debt, and that, unless more money is soon raised, it will be very difficult to purchase supplies for the army. Under these circumstances, I desire your instructions in regard to the number of cavalry to be fitted out for Genl. Thomas' expedition, and whether horses shall be furnished to him in preference to all other commands in the west and southwest; bearing in mind that it will not be possible to furnish horses, forage and transportation to anything like the whole cavalry force in those Depts. and Divisions. It is also proper to determine when the purchase of remounts shall be resumed for Sheridan and the armies of the Potomac and the James. Considering that the Qr. Mr. Dept. cannot now supply forage to the animals we have on hand, I would not advise purchases to be commenced before the middle of March, and I doubt whether navigation will be sufficiently opened by that time to enable us to bring forward horses and supplies. The railroads of the north cannot do this." LS (partly in tabular form), DNA, RG 108, Letters Received. *O.R.*, I, xlvi, part 2, 546–47; *ibid.*, III, iv, 1167–69. On Feb. 14, Paymaster Edmund E. Paulding telegraphed to Lt. Col. Theodore S. Bowers. "We have positive assurances from the Treasury Department that money will be furnished during this month for the payment to December 31st— Please instruct the Adjutant Generals of the various commands to have the making up of the rolls of February 28th deferred, as we probably will not be able to complete the December payment until after the 28th inst—The Armies of the Potomac and James will be first paid unless you otherwise request—" ALS (telegram sent), DNA, RG 107, Telegrams Collected (Unbound). See *O.R.*, I, xlvi, part 2, 554.

To Maj. Gen. Edward R. S. Canby

City Point, Va, Feb.y 13th *1864*5.

MAJ. GEN. E. R. S. CANBY
COMD.G MIL. DIV. W. MISS.
GENERAL,

A copy of your letter to the Sec. of War, pointing out the prejudice to the service which will necessarily follow the opening of trade with the states in rebellion,[1] has been submitted to me. You will perceive that Par. V of *"Executive Order"* of Sept. 24th/64 leaves a wide discretion to Military commanders in the matter of trade with these states. Entertaining the same viuws expressed in your letter I have put a stop to supplies going out, through Norfolk Va, to Lee's Army. In this I have been sustained by the President and the Sec. of War, eliciting from the latter the enclosed telegraphic dispatch.[2]

Under this authority I authorize you to restrict trade, and the bringing out of southern products, within the limits of your command, as you think will best secure the interests of the public service. I have always believed that entire non-intercourse with "people in rebellion" would prove the most speedy way to bring about a permanently peace. This view has been expressed by me, officially, over and over again. I know that people who do not serve with the Armies in the field naturally think the more trade we have the better able we will be to support the expenses of Government. Speculators who have trade permits, universally a worse class of people with an Army than the worst rebels falling within our lines, do all they can to stimulate this opinion.—Make your own orders governing this matter, basing them upon Par. 5 of *"Executive Orders"* of Sept. 24th 1864, and upon the authority here given.

It may be well for you to authorize a certain amount of trade within our lines and also the bringing out of southern products in

---

FEBRUARY 13, 1865 — 419

rear of positions permanently held by us. This however I do not direct.

Very respectfully
your obt. svt
U. S. GRANT
Lt. Gn

ALS, deCoppet Collection, NjP. *O.R.*, I, xlviii, part 1, 829–30. On March 7, 1865, Maj. Gen. Edward R. S. Canby, Fort Gaines, Ala., wrote to USG. "I have the honor to acknowledge the receipt of a copy of your communication of the 13th instant, and its enclosures. The receipt of the original was acknowledged from New Orleans, and I now enclose a copy of the General Order issued in pursuance of your instructions." LS, DNA, RG 108, Letters Received. *O.R.*, I, xlviii, part 1, 1107. The enclosure is *ibid.*, pp. 1062–63.

1. See *ibid.*, I, xli, part 4, 785–93.
2. See telegram to Edwin M. Stanton, Feb. 7, 1865.

To Maj. Gen. George H. Thomas

City Point, Va, Feb.y 13th 1864 5.

MAJ. GEN. G. H. THOMAS,
COMD.G DEPT. OF THE CUM.D
GENERAL,

General Canby is preparing a movement from Mobile Bay, against Mobile and the interior of Alabama. His force will consist of about 20.000 men besides A. J. Smith's comman[d]. The Cavalry you have sent to Canby will be debarked at Vicksburg[.] It, with the available Cavalry already in that section, will move from there Eastward in co-operation. Hood's Army has been terribly reduced by the severe punishment you gave it in Tennessee, by desertions consequent upon their defeat, and now by the withdrawel of many of them to oppose Sherman. I take it a large portion of the Infantry has been so withdrawn. It is so asserted in the Richmond papers and a Member of the rebel Congress said a few days since in a speach that one half of it had been brought to South

Carolina to oppose Sherman. This being true, or even if it is not true, Canby's movement will attract all the attention of the enemy and leave an advance from your standpoint easy. I think it advisable therefore that you prepare as much of a Cavalry force as you can spare and hold it in readiness to go south. The object would be threefold, first; to attract as much of the enemy's force as possible to insure success to Canby, second; to destroy the enemy's lines of communication and Military resources, Third; to destroy or capture their forces brought into the field. Tuscaloosa and Selma probably would be the points to direct the expedition against. This however would not be so important as the mere fact of penetrating deep into Alabama. Discretion should be left with the officer commanding the expedition to go where, according to the information he may receive, he will best secure the objects named above.

Now that your force has been so much depleted I do not know what number of men you can put into the field. If not more than 5,000 men however, all Cavalry, I think it will be sufficient.

It is not desirable that you should start this expedition until the one leaving Vicksburg has been three or four days out, or even a week. I do not know when it will start but will inform you, by telegraph, as soon as I learn. If you should hear, through other sources, before hearing from me you can act on the information received.

To insure success your Cavalry should go with as little wagon train as possible, relying upon the country for supplies. I would also reduce the number of guns to a battery, or the number of batteries, and put the extra teams to the guns taken. No gun or Caisson should start with less than eight horses.

Please inform me by telegraph, on receipt of this, what force you think you will be able to send under these directions.

> Very respectfully
> your obt. svt.
> U. S. GRANT
> Lt. Gen.

ALS, Murray J. Smith Collection, PCarlA. The letter was also telegraphed to Maj. Gen. George H. Thomas, which may account for the fact that all copies are

dated Feb. 14, 1865. Telegram received (marked as sent at 1:00 p.m., received
at 2:45 p.m.), DNA, RG 107, Telegrams Collected (Bound); copies, *ibid.*, Telegrams Received in Cipher; *ibid.*, RG 108, Letters Sent; DLC-USG, V, 46, 73,
108. *O.R.*, I, xxxiv, part 1, 45–46; *ibid.*, I, xxxvi, part 1, 49–50; *ibid.*, I, xxxviii,
part 1, 38; *ibid.*, I, xlix, part 1, 708–9. On Feb. 14, 8:00 p.m., Thomas telegraphed to USG. "Your telegram of 1 P. M. today received. I can send on the
expedition you propose, about (10.000) Ten thousand men. They are fully
equipped now with a battery to each Division composed of four guns six caissons
and each carriage drawn by eight horses. I will have the command in readiness
to move promptly upon receiving orders. I will be obliged to you if you will
notify me at least three or four days before you wish the movement to commence
as it takes about that length of time to get a despatch from here to Gen Wilsons
Headquarters; In the mean time I will prepare full instructions for the officer
who goes in Comd. of the expedition" Telegram received, DNA, RG 107, Telegrams Collected (Bound); (on Feb. 15) *ibid.*, RG 108, Letters Received; copies
(marked as received on Feb. 15, 1:40 a.m.), *ibid.*, RG 107, Telegrams Received
in Cipher; *ibid.*, RG 393, Dept. of the Cumberland, Telegrams Sent. *O.R.*, I,
xlix, part 1, 709.

On Feb. 15, 3:30 p.m., USG telegraphed to Thomas. "You may start the
Expedition from Eastport as soon after the twentieth (20th) instant as it can
get off." Copies, DLC-USG, V, 46, 73, 108; (marked as received at 4:30 p.m.)
DNA, RG 107, Telegrams Received in Cipher; *ibid.*, RG 108, Letters Sent; *ibid.*,
RG 393, Dept. of the Cumberland, Telegrams Received. *O.R.*, I, xlix, part 1,
716. At 10:00 p.m., Thomas telegraphed to USG. "Your telegram of 3 30 P M
is received. The expedition from Eastport will be ready to move promptly by the
time you design. I will try to keep you advised of the time the expedition from
Vicksburg starts" Telegram received, DNA, RG 107, Telegrams Collected
(Bound); (on Feb. 16) *ibid.*, RG 108, Letters Received; copies (marked as received on Feb. 16, 1:15 a.m.), *ibid.*, RG 107, Telegrams Received in Cipher;
ibid., RG 393, Dept. of the Cumberland, Telegrams Sent. *O.R.*, I, xlix, part 1,
717. On the same day, Thomas telegraphed to USG. "I have the honor to report
that last fall the second (2) Regiment Missouri Cavalry was ordered to Report
to me. Up to this time only a detachment of four (4) Companies have so reported
& a letter from Maj Genl G M Dodge of date Feby fourth (4) inst recd informs
me that the battallion is now with Maj Gen Stanley & that the balance of the
Regt has been ordered by Genl Canby & by Maj Genl Halleck to join that portion
of the command with Genl Canby. I am relying on this regt for Maj Genl Stoneman & if I obtain it will be able to give him a strong & good command" Telegram received (at 10:40 p.m.), DNA, RG 107, Telegrams Collected (Unbound); *ibid.*, Telegrams Collected (Bound). *O.R.*, I, xlix, part 1, 717. On Feb.
16, 11:30 a.m., USG telegraphed to Thomas. "As it is desirable to start Stoneman without delay, I think it advisable for him to go without waiting to get the
remainder of the 4th Mo Cav'y. Keep that portion of it in your command" Telegram received (at noon), DNA, RG 107, Telegrams Collected (Bound); *ibid.*,
Telegrams Collected (Unbound); copies, *ibid.*, Telegrams Received in Cipher;
ibid., RG 108, Letters Sent; *ibid.*, RG 393, Dept. of the Cumberland, Telegrams
Received; DLC-USG, V, 46, 73, 108. *O.R.*, I, xlix, part 1, 725. At 9:30 p.m.,
Thomas telegraphed to USG. "It seems to be now pretty certain that cheathams
and Lees Corps of Hoods army have left Miss and gone eastward. They left
Columbus and Tupelo about the 17th of January last & I have traced them

through different persons so regularly that I cannot longer doubt their having gone. The last person reported their having passed Opelika on the 27th January & all agree in reporting that they were going to S. C. I have also recd. two or three reports during the past week that Forrest is about to remove his troops to Georgia. If he has not already started I think my cavalry expedition from East-port will overtake him; It will be ready to start by the 20th Inst. I have taken measures to equip Gen Stoneman as rapidly as possible for his expedition and have substituted another regt. for the 4th Mo. Cav but would like to ~~have~~ get that regt as soon as possible, as I could make it very useful south of Chattanooga as there are a number of scouting parties of the enemy about Rome, Resecca, LaFayette and other towns in that region" Telegram received (on Feb. 17, 2:05 A.M.), DNA, RG 107, Telegrams Collected (Bound); *ibid.*, RG 108, Letters Received; copies, *ibid.*, RG 107, Telegrams Received in Cipher; *ibid.*, RG 393, Dept. of the Cumberland, Telegrams Received. *O.R.*, I, xlix, part 1, 725.

On Feb. 17, 5:30 P.M., USG telegraphed to Maj. Gen. Henry W. Halleck. "If the two Battalions of the 4th Mo. Cavalry ordered by Gen. Canby to Vicks-burg have not gone yet I would like to have them sent to Thomas. This would keep the regiment together and Gen. Thomas seems very desirous ~~to~~ of getting it." ALS (telegram sent), OClWHi; copies, DLC-USG, V, 46, 73, 108; (marked as received at 6:30 P.M.) DNA, RG 107, Telegrams Received in Cipher; *ibid.*, RG 108, Letters Sent. *O.R.*, I, xlix, part 1, 735.

On Feb. 20, 7:00 P.M. or 7:30 P.M., Thomas telegraphed to USG. "I start for Eastport today in order to get off the cavalry expedition as soon as possible" Telegram received (marked as sent at 7:00 P.M.), DNA, RG 107, Telegrams Collected (Bound); (marked as sent at 7:30 P.M.) *ibid.*, RG 108, Letters Re-ceived; copies (marked as sent at 7:00 P.M., received at 9:30 P.M.), *ibid.*, RG 107, Telegrams Received in Cipher; *ibid.*, RG 393, Dept. of the Cumberland, Telegrams Sent. Printed as sent at 7:30 P.M. in *O.R.*, I, xlix, part 1, 746.

On Feb. 27, 11:00 P.M., USG telegraphed to Thomas. "I have it from good authority that orders have gone from Richmond to the Commander at Mobile to hold that city to the last This will cause a concentration of the rebel forces in that quarter and make your cavalry expedition effective and easy, and will lead in the end to secure all we want without a long march into the interior by our Infantry forces." Telegram received (at 11:45 P.M.), DNA, RG 107, Telegrams Collected (Bound); *ibid.*, Telegrams Collected (Unbound); copies (marked as received at 12:00 P.M.), *ibid.*, Telegrams Received in Cipher; *ibid.*, RG 108, Letters Sent; (misdated Feb. 23) *ibid.*, RG 393, Dept. of the Cumberland, Tele-grams Received; DLC-USG, V, 46, 73, 108. *O.R.*, I, xlix, part 1, 755.

To Lt. Col. John E. Mulford

City Point Va, Feby 13th 1865

LT, COL, MULFORD
STR "NEW YORK" JONES LANDING

With the Steamers now at your Command you can Keep pris-oners at Varina to send through as fast as our men can be received in exchange, You might let Col, Ould know this so as to hasten the matter as much as possible,

U, S, GRANT
Lt, General

Telegram, copies, DLC-USG, V, 46, 73, 108; DNA, RG 108, Letters Sent; USG 3. *O.R.*, II, viii, 217. On Feb. 13, 1865, Lt. Col. John E. Mulford telegraphed to USG. "Your despatch relative to exchg received. I had today made arrangements for the Speedy delivery of all our men at and near Richmond. We are ice bound today but hope to relieved tomorrow." ALS (telegram sent), DNA, RG 107, Telegrams Collected (Unbound); telegram received, *ibid.*, RG 108, Letters Received.

On Feb. 11, C.S.A. Agent of Exchange Robert Ould wrote to USG. "I propose to deliver to you, by James River, Wilmington, or any other practicable points, all the Federal prisoners now in our custody, without delay, upon receiving an assurance from you that you will deliver an equal number of Confederate prisoners within a reasonable time. Of course, I would prefer that such reasonable time should be as early a day as will be practicable or convenient to you. I can deliver to you at Wilmington one thousand prisoners per day, commencing at any early date you may designate. I can have even a larger number in readiness at any named day. Deliveries of a like number per day, can be made at Cox's Wharf, on James River, at the same time. I will be obliged to you for an early answer." Copies, *ibid.*, RG 109, Ould Letterbook; Ould Letterbook, Archives Div., Virginia State Library, Richmond, Va. *O.R.*, II, viii, 206.

On Feb. 14, Bvt. Brig. Gen. William Hoffman telegraphed to USG. "There are steamers at Baltimore going through to City-Point. If it will not crowd Col. Mulford too much I will send 1500 prisoners by them." ALS (telegram sent), DNA, RG 107, Telegrams Collected (Unbound); telegram received, *ibid.*, RG 108, Letters Received. On the same day, USG telegraphed to Hoffman. "You can send the fifteen hundred 1500 prisoners to Col Mulford as you propose in your telegram of this date. He is ready to receive them." Telegram received (at 3:50 P.M.), *ibid.*, RG 107, Telegrams Collected (Bound); *ibid.*, RG 249, Letters Received; copies, *ibid.*, RG 108, Letters Sent; DLC-USG, V, 46, 73, 108; USG 3. At 2:40 P.M., Mulford had telegraphed to Lt. Col. Theodore S. Bowers. "I can receive the fifteen hundred prisnrs refered to by Col Hoffmn when will they reach here, leave Baltimore" Telegram sent, DNA, RG 107, Telegrams Collected (Unbound); telegram received, *ibid.*, RG 108, Letters Received.

On Feb. 17, USG twice telegraphed to Hoffman. "Have the fifteen hundred (1500) prisoners of whom you telegraphed on the fifteenth (15) started yet Col Mulford is ready for them." "Col Mulford will be here most of the time to receive any prisoners you may send, in his absence or at any time you can consign prisoners to Genl M R Patrick Provost Marshal General Who will take charge of them and deliver them to Col Mulford at the earliest practicable moment" Telegrams received (at 12:15 P.M. and 7:05 P.M.), *ibid.*, RG 107, Telegrams Collected (Bound); *ibid.*, RG 249, Letters Received; copies, *ibid.*, RG 108, Letters Sent; DLC-USG, V, 46, 73, 108; USG 3. At noon and 2:35 P.M., Hoffman telegraphed to USG. "Please inform me whether any officer has been designated to attend to the duties of Col. Mulford at City-Point in his absence. I have frequent occasion to send individual prisoners to him for

special exchange and I would respectfully suggest that some officer should be
present to receive them and all other prisoners." "One thousand prisoners have
left Baltimore for City-Point. Fifteen hundred will leave Point Lookout tomorrow." ALS (telegrams sent), DNA, RG 107, Telegrams Collected (Bound);
telegrams received (at noon and 2:55 P.M.), *ibid.*, RG 108, Letters Received.

On Feb. 14, Mulford wrote to Bowers. "I have the honor to inform you that
I have this day held a conference with Hon R. Ould Confed Agent for Exchange
upon the subject of the release of a class of prisoners known as 'Merchant Service
Men', consisting principally of persons captured on our inland waters while engaged in the U. S. transport service, many of whom have been prisoners for a
long period, extending in some instances through quite two years—and now that
other exchanges are being consumated, this class whose claims have for a long
time been practically ignored have in my opinion a legitimate demand upon our
attention. The result of my conference with Mr Ould was an agreement, subject
to the approval of Lieut General Grant Commanding Armies of the United
States, for the release & exchange of this class of prisoners upon the conditions
provided by the Cartel of July 22d 1862, which defines the grades; & establishes
the rates of equivalents, on the basis of naval captures This I believe to be a
just and equitable arrangement and respectfully submit the matter for the consideration of the Lieut General, awaiting his instructions on the subject . . ."
ALS, *ibid. O.R.*, II, viii, 219. On Feb. 15, Bowers wrote to Mulford. "Your
communication of date 14th inst in relation to the exchange of a class of prisoners, known as 'Merchant Service Men,' is received, The agreement with Judge
Ould, for the release and exchange of this class of prisoners upon the conditions
provided by the Cartel of July 22d 1862, is approved, and you will carry out the
same as speedily as practicable" Copies, DLC-USG, V, 46, 73, 108; DNA, RG
108, Letters Sent; USG 3. *O.R.*, II, viii, 227–28.

On Feb. 17, 8:30 P.M., USG telegraphed to Maj. Gen. Henry W. Halleck.
"I am told that prisoners coming from the North to be exchanged enquire particularly about the priveleges extended to deserters under the provisions of special
order No. 3. of Jan. 4th 1865. from these HdQrs. Would it not be well to have
the order circulated at all the prison camps?" Telegram received (at 10:00 P.M.),
DNA, RG 249, Letters Received; copies, *ibid.*, RG 107, Telegrams Received in
Cipher; *ibid.*, RG 108, Letters Sent; DLC-USG, V, 46, 73, 108; USG 3. *O.R.*,
II, viii, 242. On Feb. 18, Col. Edward D. Townsend telegraphed to USG. "In
your telegram of seventeenth to Genl Halleck about deserters special order number three of Jany four (4) 1865 is referred to. No copy of this order has been
received in any of the offices here if you will please cause a copy to be sent it
will be cilrculated as you desire" Telegram received (at 12:45 P.M.), DNA,
RG 108, Letters Received; copy, *ibid.*, RG 94, Letters Sent. On Feb. 19, USG
wrote to Townsend. "Herewith I send you copies of Special Orders. No 3. current
Series. as per your request of yesterday by telegraph." LS, *ibid.*, RG 249, Letters
Received. See *O.R.*, I, xlvi, part 2, 828–29.

To Brig. Gen. Lorenzo Thomas

(Cipher)   City Point, Va, Feb.y 14th *18645*. [*11:00* A.M.]
ADJ. GEN. OF THE ARMY, WASHINGTON,
Lt. Col. Duff, formerly Act. Inspector Gen. on my Staff, is in
Washington ordered there to be Mustered out of service by reason
of expiration of his term of service. If it is decided that he is in
service still I wish him ordered to his regiment at once. I do not
want him to remain in Washington as an officer.

U. S. GRANT
Lt. Gen.

ALS (telegram sent), CSmH; telegram received (at 1:00 P.M.), DNA, RG 94,
Record & Pension Office, Document File, G206 (VS) 1865; *ibid.*, RG 107, Telegrams Collected (Bound). On Feb. 15, 1865, Col. Edward D. Townsend telegraphed to USG. "Dispatch of 14th received. Lieutenant Colonel Duff second
(2nd) Illinois Artillery, was advised by letter January twentieth (20th) that
term of service would expire on the twenty ninth (29th) January, and that he
could not be remustered, the regiment not being Veteran He is not now, considered in the service of the United-States." Telegram sent, *ibid.*, Telegrams
Collected (Unbound). On the same day, Lt. Col. Theodore S. Bowers transmitted this telegram to William L. Duff, Washington, D. C., adding: "In consequence of the receipt of the preceding telegram, Your application for a leave
of absence from these Headquarters cannot be entertained" Copies, DLC-USG,
V, 46, 73, 108; DNA, RG 108, Letters Sent.

To Edwin M. Stanton

City Point, Va, Feb.y 15th *18645*.

HON. E. M. STANTON,
SEC. OF WAR,
SIR:
I have examined the ration prepared by Prof. E. N. Horsford
and without being prepared to give an opinion as to its value, or
the practiability of using it advantageously, I am so impressed with
the importance of reducing the bulk and weight of the Army ration, that I would recommend a fair test be given it.—I would sug-

gest that the Com.y Gen. be directed to order half a million rations to be distributed at points from which expeditions will be fitted out to penetrate far into the enemy's territory.

It would only be on expeditions where it would be desirable to take supplies for as long a period as possible, and with as little transportation as could be got along with, that it would be advisable to use the concentrated ration.

> Very respectfully
> your obt. svt.
> U. S. GRANT
> Lt. Gn.

ALS, DNA, RG 108, Letters Received, W181 1865. Eben N. Horsford, born in 1818 at Moscow, N. Y., educated at Rensselaer Polytechnic Institute and in Germany, taught chemistry at Harvard before resigning in 1863. See Samuel Rezneck, "Horsford's 'Marching Ration' for the Civil War Army," *Military Affairs,* XXXIII, 1 (April, 1969), 249–55.

To Edwin M. Stanton

City Point, Va, Feb.y 15th *1864*5.

HON. E. M. STANTON,
SEC. OF WAR,
SIR:

Enclosed I send you a letter from Mrs. Shirley, of Vicksburg Miss. applying to me for my influance to obtain for her son a Cadets appointment. This is one of the most deserving cases that can be found in the whole South. As Mrs. Shirley states her husband, and in fact the whole family, were Union people from the start "in the strongest sense of the term." They have lost all their property as stated by Mrs. Shirley. At the breaking out of they rebellion Mr. S. had two sons, the oldest about Eighteen then. To prevent him being forced into the rebel service, against his principles, he was sent North to volunteer on the side of the Union. He did so volunteer as a private soldier. The boy who Mrs. Shirley now desires to send to West Point shew the most decided loyalty on the advance of our troops upon Vicksburg. For several days from the commencement of the siege he kept his place in the ~~ra~~front rank among our men, gun in hand, and only desisted after repeated orders to do so.

I hope the President will find it practicable to appoint Robert Quincy Shirley, from the State of Miss. If this cannot be then from some place where a vacancy exists.

> Very respectfully
> your obt. svt.
> U. S. GRANT
> Lt. Gn.

ALS, DNA, RG 94, Cadet Applications. Enclosed was a letter of Oct. 3, 1864, from Adeline Shirley, Vicksburg, to USG. "Will you pardon me for asking you to take an interest in my humble affairs? My object is to learn if I could obtain your influence to have my son placed as a student at West Point. He is sixteen years of age, of a vigorous and healthy frame, and willing to be useful to his country. You may possibly remember our family: we were the occupants of the 'White House,' which stood outside of the Rebel fortifications at Vicksburg. You will recollect the destruction of our property, the house being on the battle field. All we have left is a plantation now in the possession of Rebels, and of course lost to us. The government of the United States has not yet paid us for what was destroyed, by their army near this place. I am unable to finish the education of the boy, for whom I would ask you to interest yourself, by a few words of recommendation to President Lincoln. My husband died three weeks after the surrender of Vicksburg; he was a Union man in the strongest sense of the term, and stood firm for his country, in her darkest hour: even to the wreck of his fortune. While he lost his life from the fatigue which he endured, at the time of the siege. There has not I believe been any youths, sent from Mississippi to West Point, for more than three years. May it not be a happy omen of peace and reunion, should the President look favorably upon my application, that a native of this erring State, should now desire to be educated, among those who are hereafter, to defend the *whole nation*, from revolution and anarchy. Once more I would beg your pardon, for the liberty I have taken in addressing you. . . . P S. The name of the son for whom I wish to ask this favor of the President, is Robert Quincy Shirley, now at school at Mt Vernon New Hampshire." ALS, *ibid.*

On June 16, 1865, USG telegraphed to the commanding officer, Vicksburg. "Furnish transportation to Cadet Shirley from Vicksburg to West Point New York. Mrs. Shirley, the mother resides in Vicksburg," ALS (telegram sent), *ibid.*, RG 107, Telegrams Collected (Bound); telegram sent, *ibid.* See *PUSG*, 9, 75–77. Robert Q. Shirley did not graduate from USMA.

To Maj. Gen. Edward R. S. Canby

City Point, Va. Feb.y 15th 18645.

MAJ. GEN. E. R. S. CANBY,
COMD.G MILⱡ. DIV. W. MISS,
GENERAL,

If Mobile f[a]lls into your hands after a defence of the place treat all property etaken as fairly belonging to the Government. Listen to no claims of citizens, or speculators having trade permits, but take all cotton and such other articles as have been used to sustain Southern credit and ship them to New York, to the Quartermaster there, to be disposed of under the directions of the Sec. of War. Let Treasury Agts have nothing to do with your captures. They have no business with the Army if you desire to be clear of them. It is only after the President declares, by proclaimation, a port to be open that the Treasury Dept. has rights, and thens they are subject to the Military Authorities.

Should Mobile surrender without opposition you will treat all property you may declare captured as here directed. But it will be discretionary with you to respect such private claims to property as you may deem proper and judicious. In no case however permit the claims of aspeculators, with trade permits, to cover property falling within your hands. If they have made investments in property whilst still in the hands of the enemy ait has been with the hope of very great gain and they take all the chances of loss incident to a state of war.

Very respectfully
your obt. svt.
U. S. GRANT
Lt. Gn.

ALS, DNA, RG 393, Div. of West Miss., Letters Received. *O.R.*, I, xlix, part 1, 723. Lt. Col. Theodore S. Bowers endorsed a copy of this letter. "Major General J. M. Schofield, Commanding Dept. of North C[aro]lina, will be governed by the instructions given Maj. Gen. Canby in all cases to which they apply—" Copy, DLC-Joseph R. Hawley. On March 1, 1865, Maj. Gen. Edward R. S. Canby wrote to USG. "I have the honor to acknowledge the receipt of your communication of the 15th ultimo. The policy indicated in that letter has been adopted with regard to all property that falls into our hands as the result of military operations. The same rule will be followed with regard to Pensacola, which may become an important auxiliary base of operations. The proclamation of the President making it a free port and market for products has not been made effective by the appointment of the necessary Treasury Officers, and I have refused permits and clearances except for Army and Navy supplies; and no trade or intercourse will be allowed, pending military operations in this neighborhood." LS, DNA, RG 108, Letters Received. *O.R.*, I, xlix, part 1, 811–12.

To Isaac N. Morris

City Point, Virginia, Feb. 15th, 1865

Every thing looks to me to be very favorable for a speedy termination of the war. The people of the South are ready for it if they can get clear of their leaders. It is hard to predict what will become of them, the leaders, whether they will flee the country or whether the people will forcibly depose them and take the matter in their own hands. One or the other will likely occur if our Spring Campaign is as successful as I have every hope it will be.

Yours Truly.
U. S. GRANT.

Quincy Herald (weekly), Feb. 27, 1865; *Ponca City News*, Sept. 28, 1924.

To Gen. Robert E. Lee

City Point Va. Feby 16th *18645*.

GENERAL R. E. LEE
COMD'G C. S. ARMY
GENERAL,

Enclosed I send you communication from W. R. Beall, relating to James Monoheim [*Monnehause*], with endorsement thereon, and an extract from the Richmond Examiner, dated December 8th 1864, containing statement of the capture of thirty seven (37) union citizens and their commitment to "Castle Thunder", to be held as hostages for the good treatment and return of Confederate citizens alleged to have been captured by us.

Previous to the receipt of the enclosed communication, and before my attention was called to the extract from the "Richmond Examiner," I directed the release of all prisoners held by Military Authority within the Department of Virginia and North Carolina against whom sufficient evidence could not be found to convict them of the offences with which they stand charged, and also such as were imprisoned without proper charges, if any shuch there were.

Similar orders were intended to be given throughout the entire Military Command of the United States, but before such orders are now given, I desire information as to the truth of the statement of the "Richmond Examiner" before referred to, and if true, the names of the persons held by us, for whom they were seized and held as hostages, and when and where captured, that their cases may be inquired into, and the proper action had as to each.

I would respectfully propose the release and exchange of all citizen prisoners now held by Military Authority, except those under charges of being spies, or under conviction for offences under the laws of War, on both sides.

> Very Respectfully
> Your Obt. Svt.
> U. S. GRANT
> Lt. Gen

Copies, DLC-USG, V, 46, 73, 108; DNA, RG 94, Record & Pension Office, 520701; *ibid.*, RG 108, Letters Sent. *O.R.*, II, viii, 236. On Feb. 18, 1865, Gen. Robert E. Lee wrote to USG. "I have received your letter of the 16th inst: and have submitted your proposition to release citizens held as prisoners by either party to the Secretary of War. I shall be glad if some arrangement can be made to relieve such persons from unnecessary suffering. I have no knowledge of the facts mentioned in the extract from the newspaper, but will direct inquiry to be made. I gave no order for the arrest of any citizen, and if it be true that those mentioned were taken by any of our forces, I presume they are held as hostages generally for persons of the same class in the custody of the Federal Authorities, and not for particular individuals." LS, Washington and Lee University, Lexington, Va. *O.R.*, II, viii, 261. On Feb. 21, Lee wrote to USG. "I am informed by the Secretary of War, to whom the proposition relative to citizen prisoners contained in your letter of the 16th instant was submitted, that our commissioners of exchange have already received instructions to effect an arrangement with those of the United States similar to that proposed by you. And I am also informed that it is intended that the release of citizen prisoners held by the Confederate authorities shall immediately follow the exchange of military prisoners now in progress. This fact renders it unnecessary to reply more fully to your specific question with reference to the prisoners referred to in your letter, and I hope there will be no difficulty in relieving all such prisoners on both sides." *Ibid.*, p. 282.

To Maj. Gen. Ethan A. Hitchcock

City Point Va
10 30 P M Feb 16th 1865

MAJ GEN E A HITCHCOCK

I see it stated in the papers, that when some prisoners in the west were paroled to be sent forward for exchange, those who preferred northern prisons, to a return to the rebel service, were invited to step to the front: I think this wrong. Those who do not wish to go back are the ones whom it is most desireable to exchange; If they do not wish to serve in the rebel army, they can return to us after exchange, & avoid it

U S GRANT
Lt Gen

Telegram received (at 11:30 P.M.), DNA, RG 107, Telegrams Collected (Bound); *ibid.*, Letters Received; copies, *ibid.*, Telegrams Received in Cipher; *ibid.*, RG 108, Letters Sent; *ibid.*, Letters Received; DLC-USG, V, 46, 73, 108; USG 3. *O.R.*, II, viii, 234. See *ibid.*, pp. 239–40.

To Maj. Gen. Henry W. Halleck

City Point Va, Feby 16th 1865 [*noon*]

MAJ, GEN, HALLECK
WASHINGTON

Our prisoners in the South, will probably be delivered to us as fast as they can be got through without reference to the number received from us, To expedite this delivery I have authorized those West of the Miss, to be delivered at any point on the River, those in the South West at Mobile and those in N. C. at Wilmington or Richmond. Their equivalents will be delivered on the James River. Please notify Canby and Schofield of this and direct them to receive all prisoners delivered to them   Canby had better send all that are delivered to him, on the Miss, to Benton Barracks to be paid and furloughed   Those received at Mobile can be sent either there or to Annapolis according to the direction transports may be taking at the time of their delivery. Schofield of course will send all he receives to Annapolis.

U. S. GRANT

Lieut, Gen,

Telegram, copies, DLC-USG, V, 46, 73, 108; (marked as received at 2:00 P.M.) DNA, RG 107, Telegrams Received in Cipher; *ibid.*, RG 108, Letters Sent; *ibid.*, RG 249, Letters Received; USG 3; DLC-John M. Schofield. *O.R.*, II, viii, 235.

On Feb. 16, 1865, USG telegraphed to Lt. Col. John E. Mulford. "In arranging to receive prisoners at Wilmington agree to receive none there but those who are physically able to bear a sea voyage on ordinary transports   all the sick and disabled should be brought to the James river for dilivery" Telegram received, DNA, RG 107, Telegrams Collected (Unbound); copies, *ibid.*, RG 108, Letters Sent; DLC-USG, V, 46, 73, 108; USG 3. *O.R.*, II, viii, 235. An undated telegram from Mulford to USG may have been sent in reply. "Your despatch recd, I will make the arrangemt you direct in regard to invalid persons" ALS (telegram sent), DNA, RG 107, Telegrams Collected (Unbound).

To Maj. Gen. Henry W. Halleck

———

City Point Va, Feby 16th 1865 [7:30 P.M.]

MAJ, GEN, HALLECK
WASHINGTON

There is no necessity ofor sending supplies to Port Royal for the use of Shermans Army. There is scarcely a possibility of Shermans requiring supplies from Port Royal and if he should we would hear through Rebel sources in time to send them on Shipboard intended for Georgetown to him,   By having a good supply on hand for the troops in the Dept, of the South they could alway's supply Sherman for a few day's until more could reach him,

U. S. GRANT

Lieut, General

Telegram, copies, DLC-USG, V, 46, 73, 108; DNA, RG 92, Consolidated Correspondence, Supplies; (marked as received at 10:00 P.M.) *ibid.*, RG 107, Telegrams Received in Cipher; *ibid.*, RG 108, Letters Sent. Printed as received at 10:30 P.M. in *O.R.*, I, xlvii, part 2, 442–43. On Feb. 16, 1865, 5:00 P.M., Maj. Gen. Henry W. Halleck had telegraphed to USG. "I have just learned from Genl Meigs & the Com. Genl. that requisitions for sixty days supplies are being filled & sent to Port Royal, & that similar requisitions have just been recieved from Genl Schofield to be sent to Beaufort N. C. This does not agree with my understanding with Genl Sherman. I understood from him that shipments to Port Royal for his army were to cease as soon as he should reach the interior of South Carolina, and that the remainder of his supplies should be ready to meet him at Georgetown S. C. Cape Fear River or Newberne, N. C. It will not be possible to accumulate sufficient supplies at all these points, nor will it be possible to keep supplies on ocean transports, as they are exceedingly scarce. Moreover, supplies can be sent from New York & Fort Monroe to any point north of Georgetown much sooner than from Port Royal. We shall hear of Sherman's whereabouts much sooner than they will at Port Royal, and can send him supplies sooner than we can send word to the Port Royal. It therefore seems to me that to send such a large amount to Port Royal now will result in enormous expense & great inconvenience. By direction of the Secty of War I refer this matter for your instructions" ALS (telegram sent), DNA, RG 107, Telegrams Collected (Bound); telegram received, *ibid.*; *ibid.*, RG 108, Letters Received. *O.R.*, I, xlvii, part 2, 442.

To Maj. Gen. George H. Thomas

City Point Va
11 30 P M Fe[b] 16 1865

Maj Gen Geo H Thomas
Nashville Tenn

Arrangements have been entered into for the exchange of prisoners until one or the other party is exhausted of all on hand

You may receive all Forrest will send you and receipt for them, forwarding them to Benton Barracks for parole until exchanged Their equivalents will be delivered here to Col Ould or will be sent out from Eastport with his consent.

If he will not deliver them so, you may send clothing to them— I would agree to no trade being opened with the south, except such portion as comes within our lines, and then only enough to prevent suffering. If you deliver any prisoners, they must be paroled until

declared exchanged by proper authority under the Cartel of Sixty
two 62   What you receive will be paroled in like manner—

U S GRANT

Lt Gen

Telegram received, DNA, RG 107, Telegrams Collected (Bound); *ibid.*, Tele-
grams Collected (Unbound); copies (marked as received on Feb. 17, 1865, 1:00
A.M.), *ibid.*, Telegrams Received in Cipher; *ibid.*, RG 108, Letters Sent; (incomplete) *ibid.*, RG 249, Letters Received; (misdated Feb. 17) *ibid.*, RG 393,
Dept. of the Cumberland, Telegrams Received; DLC-USG, V, 46, 73, 108; USG
3. Printed as received on Feb. 17, 9:00 A.M., in *O.R.*, I, xlix, part 1, 725–26. On
Feb. 16, 4:50 P.M., Maj. Gen. George H. Thomas telegraphed to USG. "Gen.
Forrest through Gen Wilson says that he is willing and anxious to have us send
clothing to our prisoners confined in Mississippi and Alabama   he represents
them as suffering & guarantees safe transmittal & delivery of everything sent to
them   They number about seven thousand (7000),   He wishes also to make an
exchange of prisoners now in their hands or who may hereafter be taken. Is also
desirous of allowing the people to send their Cotton within our lines and take
out nothing but necessaries of life." Telegram received, DNA, RG 108, Letters
Received. *O.R.*, II, viii, 238. The telegram received was transmitted via Washington, D. C., with the name of Maj. Gen. Henry W. Halleck cancelled; the telegram is printed as addressed to Halleck *ibid.*, I, xlix, part 1, 725.

To Edwin M. Stanton

———

City Point Va, Feby 17th 1865 [*8:30* P.M.]

HON, E, M, STANTON
SEC, OF WAR
WASHINGTON D, C,

The Rebel Flag Boat "William Allison" whilst on her upward
trip from Cox Landing this afternoon was blown up by a Torpedo
The boat went down almost immediately   Our Pickets saw no sur-
vivors from her   There were no Prisoners a-board at the time,
This catastrophy pobably arrose from one of the enemy's own
Torpedo's which has been in the water for a long time,

U, S, GRANT

Lieut, Genl,

Telegram, copies, DLC-USG, V, 46, 73, 108; (marked as received at 10:00
P.M.) DNA, RG 107, Telegrams Received in Cipher; *ibid.*, RG 108, Letters Sent.

O.R., I, xlvi, part 2, 574. On Feb. 17, 1865, Maj. Gen. Edward O. C. Ord telegraphed to USG, then twice to Brig. Gen. John A. Rawlins. "Have just heard by signal from the tower crows nest that the rebel flag of truce boat was blown up by one of their own torpedoes just below Cox ferry She was going up Have not heard the particulars will send them when I do" Telegram received (at 6:25 P.M.), DNA, RG 108, Letters Received. "It was the flag boat 'William Allison' which was blown up. She went down almost immediately, there were no prisoners going up in her, another rebel Steamboat was near. No survivors were seen by our pickets—" "I have just learned that 2000 blankets 20 cases shoes & blouses and about 40 boxes express freight for the Indiana prisoners went aboard the Allison today for our soldiers prisoners south. Capt Hatch exchange officer the medical Director from Richmond & from twelwe to twenty of the rebel ambalance committee were also aboard" Telegrams received (the second at 10:40 P.M.), *ibid.* The first is in *O.R.*, I, xlvi, part 2, 579. See telegram to Edwin M. Stanton, Feb. 18, 1865.

On Feb. 17, 11:00 A.M., USG telegraphed to Secretary of War Edwin M. Stanton. "If you will allow me to stop the Bay line of Steamers from runing to Norfolk and to make proper regulations for the carrying of passengers, freight &c. I think evils now existing may be cured." ALS (telegram sent), CSmH; copies, DLC-USG, V, 46, 73, 108; (marked as received at noon) DNA, RG 107, Telegrams Received in Cipher; *ibid.*, RG 108, Letters Sent. *O.R.*, I, xlvi, part 2, 574. At 1:45 P.M., Stanton telegraphed to USG. "You are authorized to stop the Bay line of Steamers from runing to Norfold and to make such regulations for carry passengers freight &c as you deem proper" ALS (telegram sent), DNA, RG 107, Telegrams Collected (Bound); telegram received (at 1:50 P.M.), *ibid.*, RG 108, Letters Received. *O.R.*, I, xlvi, part 2, 574.

To Edwin M. Stanton

City Point. Va. February 17th *1864*5.

HON. EDWIN M. STANTON
SECRETARY OF WAR,
WASHINGTON, D. C.
SIR:

The late Edward C. Washington 13th United States Infantry, who fell at the head of his Regiment in the assault on Vicksburg, May 1863, left a son who is now of the proper age to enter the Military Academy,—which he is desirous of doing. His mother, too, (widow of the late Capt. Washington) is exceedingly anxious for his appointment. I am informed that he is of correct habits and well-fitted by education for the place. In consideration of these facts I earnestly recommend that Reade M. Washington, of Chambersburg, Franklin County, Pennsylvania, Son of the late Captain Washington, U. S. A., be appointed a Cadet to the United States Military Academy at West Point.

> I have the honor to be, Sir,
> Very Respectfully
> Your Ob't. Servant
> U. S. GRANT
> Lieutenant General.

LS, DNA, RG 94, Cadet Applications. Reade M. Washington attended USMA 1865–67.

To Maj. Gen. George G. Meade

By Telegraph from City Point
Dated Feby 17 *18645*

To MAJ GENL MEADE

Have you ascertained the Cause of the musketry firing last night Supposed to be on the 9th Corps front

> U. S. GRANT
> Lt Genl

Telegram received (at 10:00 A.M.), DNA, RG 94, War Records Office, Army of the Potomac; copy, Meade Papers, PHi. *O.R.*, I, xlvi, part 2, 575. On Feb. 17, 1865, 10:20 A.M., Maj. Gen. George G. Meade telegraphed to USG. "No special report has been made of the musketry firing last night—I presume it to have been confined to picket firing, made more lively by the artillery practice during the day. This was brought on I understand by our batteries on the right, shelling some camps of the enemy in the morning, the enemy returning the compliment in the afternoon. I have sent officers to investigate the matter.—Fifty Six deserters have come in during the last two days They all concur that their rations are very short, and that there is great discontent among the men.—" ALS (telegram sent), DNA, RG 94, War Records Office, Army of the Potomac; telegram received, *ibid.*, RG 108, Letters Received. *O.R.*, I, xlvi, part 2, 575. On the same day, Maj. Gen. Edward O. C. Ord telegraphed to USG. "Following just received 'Hatchers Feb 17th BRIG GENL TURNER Chfstaff—I have the honor to report that the enemy attempted to drive in my picket at a point opposite Dutton where the lines are closest but were repulsed. The attacking column consisted of ten companies of Stewarts Brigade, a few volleys from my men stampeded them. Two dead rebels many hats and muskets found in front of our lines this morning. This occurred at half past one a m. Twelve deserters came in during the night four of them were of the attack. They report that their men would not fight and that they scattered at our first fire. Their object was to drive us back, we being too near at that point. The deserters report some wounded in the affair—E FER-RERO Bt Maj. Genl 9. more deserters just in making twenty one on Ferreros front—" Telegram received, DNA, RG 108, Letters Received. *O.R.*, I, xlvi, part 2, 582.

On Feb. 18, 6:00 P.M., USG telegraphed to Ord. "If you have any shells filled with Greek Fire I wish you would ~~experim~~ experiment with a few of them on the Abbattis of the enemy and see if it can be set on fire." ALS (telegram sent), CSmH; telegram received (at 6:30 P.M.), Ord Papers, CU-B. *O.R.*, I, xlvi, part 2, 588. At 7:00 P.M., Ord telegraphed to USG. "Have only a few shells, hundred pounders, and no guns of that cal. facing the enemys abattis near enough" Telegram received, DNA, RG 108, Letters Received. *O.R.*, I, xlvi, part 2, 588. At 3:50 P.M., Ord had telegraphed to Brig. Gen. John A. Rawlins. "Thirty-eight deserters in yesterday—forty-three to-day—on my front." *Ibid.*

To Edwin M. Stanton

City Point Va, Feby 18th 1865 [*1:30* P.M.]

HON E. M. STANTON
SEC OF WAR
WASHINGTON

The only further particulars learned from the Rebel Steamer destroyed yesterday by a torpedo is that she had on, at the time, besides the crew, The Medical Director from Richmond Capt. Hatch Asst. Agent of Exchange, and from twelve to twenty of the Ambulance Committee, She also had on board 2.000 blankits, 20 cases Shoes, and blouses, and about 40 boxes Express frieght for our prisoners South, I had prohibited the ~~Army~~ buying of percussion torpedoes by the Army and Commodore Radford[1] informs me that the Navy have laid none such there. There is but little doubt but that the accident occurred from a torpedo that has been a long time in the water, and propably, shifted from it's original position by freshet. I have not yet learened whether any of the passengers or crew escaped,

U. S. GRANT
Lieut, Gen,

Telegram, copies, DLC-USG, V, 46, 73, 108; (marked as received at 2:40 P.M.) DNA, RG 107, Telegrams Received in Cipher; *ibid.*, RG 108, Letters Sent.

Printed as sent at 2:00 P.M. in *O.R.*, I, xlvi, part 2, 583–84. See telegram to Edwin M. Stanton, Feb. 17, 1865.

1. William Radford, born in Va. in 1808, stepson of explorer William Clark, entered the U.S. Navy as midshipman on March 1, 1825. Following the sinking of his ship, the U.S.S. *Cumberland*, by the C.S.S. *Virginia* (*Merrimack*), he spent two years as executive officer of the Brooklyn Navy Yard, during which he was promoted to commodore as of April 24, 1863. Returning from the second Fort Fisher expedition, he was assigned to command the James River Div. See telegrams to Edwin M. Stanton and to Gustavus V. Fox, Jan. 24, 1865; telegram to Edwin M. Stanton, Feb. 25, 1865.

To Edwin M. Stanton

(Cipher) City Point, Va, Feb.y 18th *1864*5.
Hon. E. M. Stanton, Sec. of War, Washington
The Richmond Dispatch of this morning says Sherman entered Columbia yesterday morning and its fall necessitates it presumes the fall of Charleston which it think likely is already being evacuated.
U. S. Grant
Lt. Gn.

ALS (telegram sent), OClWHi; copies, DLC-USG, V, 46, 73, 108; DNA, RG 108, Letters Sent. *O.R.*, I, xlvii, part 2, 472. On Feb. 18, 1865, Maj. Gen. Godfrey Weitzel telegraphed to Lt. Col. Theodore S. Bowers. "The Richmond Dispatch just rec'd says Sherman entered Columbia yesterday morning and that ~~the~~ its fall necessitates it presumes the fall of Charleston, which it thinks likely is already being evacuated" ALS (telegram sent), DNA, RG 107, Telegrams Collected (Unbound). Also on Feb. 18, USG telegraphed to Secretary of War Edwin M. Stanton transmitting reports from the Richmond newspapers of events in S. C. *O.R.*, I, xlvii, part 2, 472–73.

On Feb. 19, Stanton telegraphed to USG. "I congratulate you on the news from South Carolina. I have directed your order in respect to deserters to be printed in large handbills and posted in every Camp & distributed on the boats." ALS (telegram sent), DNA, RG 107, Telegrams Collected (Bound); telegram received (at 12:30 P.M.), *ibid.*, RG 108, Letters Received. *O.R.*, I, xlvii, part 2, 484.

On Feb. 20, USG telegraphed to Stanton. "The following dispatch just received . . . 'The Richmond Examiner of today just received says Charleston was evacuated on tuesday last G Weitzel M Genl" Telegram received (at 12:30 P.M.), DLC-Robert T. Lincoln; copies, DLC-USG, V, 46, 73, 108; DNA, RG 108, Letters Sent. *O.R.*, I, xlvi, part 2, 596. On the same day, USG also transmitted this message to Maj. Gen. George G. Meade. Copies (2), Meade Papers, PHi.

To Maj. Gen. Henry W. Halleck

(Cipher)   City Point, Va, Feb.y 18th 1865 [*4:30* P.M.]
MAJ. GN. HALLECK, WASHINGTON

With Charleston in our hands, which I now believe assured to us, Gilmore will be able to spare a large part of his force. Direct him the moment that takes place to Garrison the seaport Harbors he deems most important for us to hold with minimum numbers and send all surplus troops to Cape Fear river. If he should receive other instructions from Sherman he will be guided by them. He should send none but White troops out of his Dept.

U. S. GRANT
Lt. Gen.

ALS (telegram sent), OClWHi; copies, DLC-USG, V, 46, 73, 108; (marked as received at 4:45 P.M.) DNA, RG 107, Telegrams Received in Cipher; *ibid.*, RG 108, Letters Sent. Printed as received at 5:00 P.M. in *O.R.*, I, xlvii, part 2, 473.

To Maj. Gen. Henry W. Halleck

Head Quarters Armies of the United States
City Point Va. February 18th 1865
MAJ. GEN. H. W. HALLECK
CHIEF OF STAFF OF THE ARMY
WASHINGTON D. C.
GENERAL:

Your communication of the 15th inst. with enclosure, calling my attention to the fact that advantage is being taken by General Beall Confederate Agent, of the recent agreement between Judge Ould and myself, to supply Rebel prisoners with new uniforms and blankets, is received. The arrangement for the relief of prisoners of war was made at a time when exchanges could not be made, and under it I see see no way to prevent rebel prisoners from being clothed. Having, however, a very large excess of prisoners over the enemy, we can, in making exchanges, select those who have not been furnished with new clothing or blankets. By this means but a very limited number of rebel soldiers will be returned with new uniforms. Should it become necessary prisoners for exchange can be required to turn their blankets over to their comrades who remain

Please give orders to Gen. Hoffman accordingly

Very Respectfully
Your Obt Servant
U. S. GRANT
Lieutenant General

Copies, DLC-USG, V, 46, 73, 108; DNA, RG 108, Letters Sent; *ibid.*, Letters Received; *ibid.*, RG 249, Letters Received; USG 3. *O.R.*, II, viii, 257. On Feb. 20, 1865, Maj. Gen. Henry W. Halleck endorsed this letter. "Respectfully referred to Bvt Brig Genl Hoffman. The Secty of War directs that the recommendations of Lt Genl Grant be carried out." AES, DNA, RG 249, Letters Received. *O.R.*, II, viii, 257. On Feb. 15, Halleck had written to USG. "Information has been received here from various sources, that the proceeds of the thousand bales of cotton sent from Mobile are to used to supply the rebel prisoners of war, now being exchanged with new uniforms and blankets, so that they can return to the field fully clothed and supplied in the United States! By direction of the Sec'y of War I enclose herewith a copy of a letter, referring to a contract by the rebel General Beall in New York for Twenty thousand grey coats and pants, and twenty thousand blankets. The Secretary of War does not see how, under the agreement between yourself and Mr. Ould this can be prevented and directs me to refer the matter to you for your action or suggestions." LS, DNA, RG 108, Letters Received. *O.R.*, II, viii, 227. The enclosure is *ibid.*

On Feb. 17, Halleck wrote to USG. "I am directed by the Sec'y. of War to forward to you the enclosed letter of General Beall, and to say that General Vance has been released on parole to assist General Beall and also that three officers have been sent to the prison depots, as agreed upon. It will be seen from this letter, that all the proceeds of the rebel cotton are devoted to supplying the rebel prisoners with new clothing, shoes and blankets. Not a cent is expended for provisions. The result is that we feed their prisoners, and permit the rebel government to send cotton within our lines, free of all charge, to purchase and carry back the means of fitting out their own men for the field. Under these circumstances, the Sec'y of War is not disposed to sanction the admission of any more cotton on the same terms." LS, DNA, RG 108, Letters Received. *O.R.*, II, viii, 241. The enclosure is *ibid.*, pp. 241–42.

On Feb. 17, USG endorsed a bundle of documents. "The within official copies of papers on the subject of shipping Confederate Cotton at Mobile are respectfully furnished for the information of Judge Ro. Ould. Agent of Exchange C. S. A." ES, DNA, RG 109, Secretary of War, Letters Received. *O.R.*, II, viii, 240. The enclosures are listed *ibid.*

To Lt. Col. John E. Mulford

City Point, Va, Feb.y 18th *18645*.

LT. COL. MULFORD, AGT. OF EXCHANGE, JONES LANDING

The following dispatch has just been received from Gen. Hoffman in reply to one from me in relation to prisoners in in close confinement.[1]

"The only prisoner in Irons at Johnson's Island is a Citizen prisoner Thomas F. Berry who was so confined last night for killing Lt. H. Morgan a prisoner of War. Shall Berry be tried by Commission or sent forward for Exchange?"

(Signed) WM HOFFMAN
C. G. P.[2]

Please notify Col. Ould of this. I shall direct that Berry be tried.[3]

U. S. GRANT
Lt. Gen.

ALS (telegram sent), CSmH; copies, DLC-USG, V, 46, 73, 108; DNA, RG 108, Letters Sent; USG 3.

On Feb. 15, 1865, 8:30 P.M., USG telegraphed to Secretary of War Edwin M. Stanton. "Will you please have Commo. Buchanan sent here for exchange? We will be able to release some of our sailors from southern prisons with him." Telegram received (at 9:20 P.M.), DNA, RG 249, Letters Received; copies, *ibid.*, RG 107, Telegrams Received in Cipher; *ibid.*, RG 108, Letters Sent; DLC-USG, V, 46, 73, 108. *O.R.*, II, viii, 226.

1. On Feb. 15, 9:00 P.M., USG telegraphed to Stanton. "The Rebel Agt of Exchange says, he understands that Campbell, Mars [*Marr*], and others are still in irons at Johnson's Island, Will you please direct Gen, Hoffman to furnish me a list of rebel prisoners who are still so confined and under what order's so that I may know whether such complaint's are well founded" Copies, DLC-USG, V, 46, 73, 108; (marked as received at 10:00 P.M.) DNA, RG 107, Telegrams Received in Cipher; *ibid.*, RG 108, Letters Sent; DLC-Edwin M. Stanton. *O.R.*, II, viii, 226. See *ibid.*, pp. 226–27. On Feb. 17, 9:00 P.M., USG telegraphed to Bvt. Brig. Gen. William Hoffman. "Please forward as soon as possible all rebel prisoners who are or have been in close confinement or in irons for special exchange for the same class of prisoners in the South." ALS (telegram sent), CSmH; telegram received (marked as sent at 8:30 P.M., received at 10:00 P.M.), DNA, RG 107, Telegrams Collected (Bound); *ibid.*, RG 249, Letters Received. *O.R.*, II, viii, 242.

2. ALS (telegram sent), DNA, RG 107, Telegrams Collected (Unbound);

telegram received, *ibid.*, RG 108, Letters Received. *O.R.*, II, viii, 258. On Feb.
20, 12:30 P.M., Maj. Gen. Henry W. Halleck telegraphed to USG. "Genl Hoffman reports in answer to your telegram of the 15th that there were then no
prisoners of war in irons at Johnson's-Island. On the 17th Thomas F Berry was
placed in irons for killing another prisoner, viz, Lieut Harlin Morgan." ALS
(telegram sent), DNA, RG 107, Telegrams Collected (Bound); telegram received, *ibid.*; *ibid.*, RG 108, Letters Received. *O.R.*, II, viii, 270.

3. On Feb. 18, 6:00 P.M., USG telegraphed to Hoffman. "Thos. F. Berry
now in confinement at Johnson's Island for the murder of Morgan a prisoner of
war may be tried where he is." Telegram received (at 7:00 P.M.), DNA, RG
107, Telegrams Collected (Bound); *ibid.*, RG 249, Letters Received; copies,
ibid., RG 107, Telegrams Received in Cipher; *ibid.*, RG 108, Letters Sent; USG
3. *O.R.*, II, viii, 258.

To Richard J. Oglesby

City Point, Va, Feb.y 18th 18645.

DEAR GOVERNOR,

I write to ask you to tender to Capt. Alfred T. Smith, of the
8th U. S. Infantry the appointment of Col. in one of the new Illinois
Regiments, if any are to be raised. Capt. Smith is a son of Gen. Jno.
E. Smith, and son-in-law of Medical Inspector Kittoe, both of
whom you favorably know.

Capt. Smith has been at West Point as an Asst. Prof. of Mathematics & Tactics throughout the war and is exceedingly anxious to
see some service. His regiment is reduced to but few men and is in
the North besides, so that if relieved from duty at West Point he
would simply command a handful of men doing garrison duty.

I you can grant this request you will confer a great favor on
some of your warmest friends and will also give to an Illinois
regiment a valuable and educated commander.

Yours Truly
U. S. GRANT
Lt. Gn.

HIS EXCELLENCY R. OGLESBY
GOV. OF ILL.

ALS, Oglesby Papers, IHi. Alfred T. Smith, USMA 1860, was appointed col.,
156th Ill., as of April 4, 1865. See letter to Edward D. Kittoe, Feb. 24, 1865.

On March 6, 4:00 P.M., USG telegraphed to Secretary of War Edwin M.
Stanton. "Capt, A, T, Smith 8th U, S, Infantry, now on duty at West Point,
having been appointed Colonel of one of the new Regiments of Illinois Vols, I

would respectfully ask that leave of absence be granted to him to accept the appointment His Regiment I understand is at Chicago ready to take the field" Copies, DLC-USG, V, 46, 74, 108; DNA, RG 108, Letters Sent.

To William H. Seward

City Point, Va, Feb.y 19th *1865*

HON. W. H. SEWARD,
SEC. OF STATE,
DEAR SIR:

I am in receipt of "Copy" of Col. Bilbo's letter of the 14th inst. in relation to the return of Ex. Gov. Foote to the United States at any time he chooses to return within the next three months, addressed to you.[1] I know nothing of Governor Foote personally; but soon after the fall of Vicksburg I received a letter from a gentleman in St. Paul, Min. who had been a resident of the former place for ten years prior to the war, giving me the status of the leading men in the state of Mississippi. He spoke of Foote as a Union Man and although he had taken a seat in the Rebel Senate he believed it was for the purpose of retaining a place of influance where, at the right time, he could use it advantageously for restoring peace and Union.—I believe no harm could come to our cause from the exercise of Executive clemency in his case and think much good might arise from it. We have every reason to believe, in fact know, that even if he is not disposed to do what Col. Bilbo says he is there is still a large class of the deligations from the states named by him who are advocates of peace on such terms as they can get. Would it not be well to let them see, by an example, that, notwithstanding the President's Proclaimation excludes them from its benefits, yet those who freely and voluntarily return to their allegiance will be forgiven and restored to their rights as citizens? I do not profess to be a judge of the best civil policy to pursue to restore peace and the integrity of the Union, my duty being to apply force to accomplish this end. But Col. Bilbo's letter, or a copy of it, being refered to me I take it as an invitation to give my views, and do so for what they are worth, without a desire or wish that they should be adopted against the views of those whose dutiey it is to study this phase of the question. The St. Paul letter here refered to, I think, is in my private desk in Washington. If you would like to see it I will direct Capt. Leet, my A. A. G. in the city, to look it up and give it to you.

> Very respectfully
> your obt. svt.
> U. S. GRANT
> Lt. Gen.

ALS, Seward Papers, NRU. On Feb. 26, 1865, 11:00 A.M., USG telegraphed to Secretary of State William H. Seward. "My Adj. Gen. in Washington has failed to find the St. Paul letter ref[e]rred to in my letter and which you wish to see." ALS (telegram sent), Kohns Collection, NN; copies, DLC-USG, V, 46, 74, 108; DNA, RG 108, Letters Sent.

1. On Feb. 14, William N. Bilbo, St. Nicholas Hotel, wrote to Seward. "I have written this by the urgent solicitation of Gov Foote of Tenn with whom I had an interview previous to his departure for Europe. He begs that you permit him to return to the United States within the next three months, whenever *he* may deem it most advisable because he said, there was a solemn compact entered in to between the almost entire Congressional Delegation from Tennessee nearly a majority of that from N. Carolina Georgia and Alabama, and a portion from Mississippi and Virginia that if peace was not restored then that they would in defiance of Davis and the War faction stump their respective states for an immediate reunion with the Federal States. He further stated to me that every sagacious or well informed citizen of the South at the period of his leaving believed the Rebel States were exhausted in all the indispensable resources of war, and must yield before the expiration of six months if we in the North prosecuted the war with vigor and courage. Gov Foote spoke of you in the kindest manner and said while his memory remained, he would never forget the kindness which you evinced to himself and family. Foote to my own knowledge even down to the commencement of hostilities was a strong Unionist in Tenn, and was President of the last Union meeting held in the city of Nashville His hatred to Jef Davis and his Administration has ever been as it is now unabated and uncompromising. Thus I have written you as I promised him" Copy, *ibid.*, Letters Received. *O.R.*, I, xlvi, part 2, 561. For Bilbo, a Nashville lawyer and newspaperman, see Johnson, *Papers*, III, 503; Lincoln, *Works*, VIII, 226.

To Edwin M. Stanton

(Cipher)   City Point, Va, Feb.y 19th 1865 [*10:00 P.M.*]
HON. E. M. STANTON, SEC. OF WAR, WASHINGTON

I would most decidedly oppose enlisting prisoners of War, with bounties. The most determined men against us would be the first to enlist for the sake of the money and would returning with it to their friends. I would make no special objection to trying the experiment of one or two regiments raised without bounty but even this would be risky. The men who want ~~are~~ to enlist are those who really it is most desirable to exchange first. If they want to enter our service in good faith they can return under the Presidents Amnesty proclaimation, and my order, and become loyal citizens and help fight on the side of peace.

U. S. GRANT

Lt. Gn

ALS, PPRF. *O.R.*, III, iv, 1185. On Feb. 19, 1865, Secretary of War Edwin M. Stanton telegraphed to USG. "I send you a telegram from General Hooker and the Commandant of Camp Douglas about enlisting rebels prisoners. Please let me know whether you think any more rebels prisoners should be enlisted on our side" ALS (telegram sent), DNA, RG 107, Telegrams Collected (Bound); telegram received (at 9:20 P.M.), *ibid.*, RG 108, Letters Received. *O.R.*, III, iv, 1185. The enclosure is *ibid.*

To Maj. Gen. John M. Schofield

City Point Va, Feby 19th 1865

MAJ, GEN, J. M. SCHOFIELD
COMDG DEPT, OF N, C,
GENERAL,

Your two letters of the 15th inst, are just recieved, Shermans instructions were probably given before he knew what force we would have to operate with in North Carolina. At all events in pursuing the course directed by me, you accomplish what Sherman directs The object is to open [c]ommunication between the Sea coast and Goldsboro by rail so as to meet Sherman with supplies for his Army and to put at his disposal an available force, If you succeed in the capture of Wilmington you will probably secure the road almost complete, from Newbern it would have to be rebuilt entire, At the former place you would be better supplied with storage, It also gives you the advantage of a road bearing Southwest which after all might prove the one necessary to open first,

It will be well to have Palmer push on in pursuance of Sherman instructions and at the same time direct your attention to Wilmington,   You will either capture the place or hold a considerable force of the enemy from Shermans front,   The last news from Sherman direct was on the 7th inst,   I directed a copy of that dispatch sent to you,   He was then encountering bads roads, and much water, and was not [c]ertain but these causes would force him to turn upon Charleston,   In that case he would want his supplies sent to Bulls Bay,   Richmond papers of yesterday however announce his capture of Columbia on the morning of the 17th   As he was then across the Congaree, it is not likely that he will turn back,

This success will probably force the evacuation of Charleston In that case Gilmore will have a disposable force of ten or twelve thousand men which I have directed him to send to you,

Should you find an advance on Wilmington impracticable keep up such a threatening attitude that the enemy will be compelled to retain there all the force he now has, and push on the Colum from New bern,

I will send you a Canvass pontoon train immediately if it can be raised[1]

> Very Respectfully
> Your obt svt
> U, S, GRANT
> Lieut, Gen,

Copies, DLC-USG, V, 46, 73, 108; DNA, RG 108, Letters Sent. *O.R.*, I, xlvii, part 2, 492. On Feb. 15, 1865, Maj. Gen. John M. Schofield twice wrote to USG, once to Brig. Gen. John A. Rawlins. "Genl Sherman's instructions to me, through Genl Foster, a copy of which I enclose, make the capture of Kingston of primary importance, and seem to regard that of Wilmington as secondary, while your instructions, under which I am acting, make the capture of Wilmington the first object. The difference will be immaterial if I succeed in making any considerable advance along the Wilmington and Goldsboro R. R. before Genl Sherman comes up. If not, it occurs to me that it may embarrass Genl Sherman if he does not know exactly what I am doing, and to what point he must look for supplies. My object is simply to call your attention to this matter, in case it may have escaped your notice, so that if practicable to communicate with Genl Sherman he may be informed. I think with you that Wilmington should be taken first, for I can not safely calculate on making a juncture with Genl Sherman at any point further North." "On the 11th, after landing one division of the 23d Corps, I pushed forward Genl Terrys line East of Cape Fear River and found the enemy in a strongly intrenched position, opposite Fort Anderson, running from the river to Masonboro Sound. In the advance we lost about sixty in killed and wounded, and captured 54 prisoners. Information obtained by Genl Comstock after you were here shows that the enemy's line West of the river runs from Fort Anderson to a pond, formed by daming Orton Creek, and runing back into a swamp some eight or nine miles in length, so that Fort Anderson can not be turned without going around that swamp. Not deeming the force I then had sufficient for such a move I directed my attention to the possibility of turning the enemy's position by crossing Masonboro Sound. Genl Comstock made a reconnoissance ~~for~~ on the 11th, from which the move seemed quite practicable. The plan was to land pontoons and Navy small boats on the beach about two miles South of Masonboro Inlet, haul them across the peninsula to the Sound at a place where it is only about three hundred yards wide, march the troops along the beach to the point of crossing, and transfer them to the main land before daylight in the morning. All arrangements were made for executing the plan on the 12th, but in the afternoon a North East wind sprang up, which rendered such operations impossible. The wind has continued to blow from the Sea since that time. Yesterday I succeeded, after much difficulty, in getting the pontoon wagons ashore, and determined to make the attempt to haul them along the beach to the point where we could cross the sound. The teams made such slow progress, that at Midnight I became satisfied we could not reach the point in time to commence the crossing before daylight, and hence could not reasonably expect success. I therefore abandoned the enterprise. This plan was a favorite one with Genl Comstock and, I believe, had the wind been favorable, would undoubtedly have been successful. At all events we have lost nothing by making the attempt. My second division commenced to arrive yesterday and I can now commence operations West of the river without further delay. The enemy's camps indicate some increase of his force since I arrived here, but I have no definite information on the subject. I have no information from Genl Palmer later than the 10th He ought to be moving about this time." "The pontoon train I now have is so heavy that I fear it will cause serious delays in operations over the bad roads which prevail in this country. If you can send me some of the cloth batteaux I think it will facilitate my operations." ALS, DNA, RG 108, Letters Received. *O.R.*, I, xlvii, part 2, 436–38. The enclosure in the first is *ibid.*, p. 163.

1. On Feb. 19, 5:15 P.M., USG telegraphed to Maj. Gen. Henry W. Halleck. "If there is any Canvass Pontoons in Washington or New York please send Gen. Schofield enough for about 800 feet of bridging. The pontoons he has are to heavy for the roads at this season." ALS (telegram sent), MH; copies, DLC-USG, V, 46, 73, 108; DLC-John M. Schofield; (marked as received at 6:00 P.M.) DNA, RG 107, Telegrams Received in Cipher; *ibid.*, RG 108, Letters Sent. *O.R.*, I, xlvii, part 2, 485. On Feb. 20, 11:00 A.M., Halleck telegraphed to USG. "The last of Schofield's troops will get off to-day. Canvas-pontons will be sent from here and New York. Deficiency in length of bridging will be supplied as soon as possible." ALS (telegram sent), DNA, RG 107, Telegrams Collected (Bound); telegram received, *ibid.*; *ibid.*, RG 108, Letters Received. *O.R.*, I, xlvii, part 2, 501. On the same day, USG telegraphed to Schofield. "Gen Halleck telegraphs me at eleven (11) A M to day that the 'last of your Troops will get off Today—Canvas pontons will be sent from Washington and New York and the deficiency in length of bridging will be supplied as soon as possible" Telegram received (at 12:50 P.M.), DNA, RG 107, Telegrams Collected (Bound); copies, *ibid.*, RG 108, Letters Sent; *ibid.*, RG 393, Dept. of N. C., Telegrams Received; DLC-USG, V, 46, 73, 108. *O.R.*, I, xlvii, part 2, 509. At the same time, USG

telegraphed to the operator. "Please put up the above dispatch and deliver to Lt Wilbur on board steamer Neptune who left here this morning & will reach Fort Monroe during the afternoon on his way to Ft Fisher." Telegram received, DNA, RG 107, Telegrams Collected (Bound). On Feb. 22, Brig. Gen. Richard Delafield, chief of engineers, telegraphed and wrote to USG. "Your order for a bridge equipage for General Schofield is filled and the supplies are now going on board the transports in this city for Wilmington" LS (telegram sent), *ibid.*, Telegrams Collected (Unbound); telegram received (at 2:55 P.M.), *ibid.*, RG 108, Letters Received. "Your order of the 19th inst. for a bridge equipage for Gen. Schofield communicated to this Department by Gen Halleck Chief of Staff, has been filled as follows: 50 canvas boats: 19 boat wagons (16′ reach) 30 chess wagons (9′ reach); and a full supply of balks and chesses and army wagons for the transportation of the balks and chesses. These supplies are now going on board the transports at this city for Wilmington, N. C." LS, *ibid. O.R.*, I, xlvii, part 2, 526.

To Brig. Gen. Rufus Ingalls

City Point, Va. Feby 19, 1865

BRIG. GEN. R. INGALLS.
WASHINGTON. D. C.

The Department here is entirely out of Coal. Mulford's flag of truce boats are unable to go down the river for want of fuel. Please see whether coal cannot be hurried forward.

U. S. GRANT
Lt. Gen.

Telegram sent, DNA, RG 107, Telegrams Collected (Unbound); telegram received (at 12:48 P.M.), *ibid.*, Telegrams Collected (Bound). *O.R.*, I, xlvi, part 2, 593. On Feb. 19, 1865, Brig. Gen. Rufus Ingalls, Washington, D. C., telegraphed to USG. "I have been assured that every possible effort has been made to supply us with coal—There are large quantities on the way—If it be not at City Point the Flag of truce boats must stop to coal at Fortress Monroe—" ALS (telegram sent), DNA, RG 107, Telegrams Collected (Unbound); telegram received, *ibid.*, RG 108, Letters Received.

On Feb. 20, Col. S. Lockwood Brown, Washington, telegraphed to USG. "Your dispatch to Genl Ingalls has been referred to this office Five hundred and eighty three (583) tons of coal for City-Point left Fort-Monroe this morning for City, P Three thousand six hundred (3600) tons left Cape Henlopen for Fort-Monroe on the 19th inst. and will probably reach Fort-Monroe to-night. There is great delay and difficulty in forwarding coal on account of ice in Northern ports." ALS (telegram sent), *ibid.*, RG 107, Telegrams Collected (Unbound); telegram received, *ibid.*, RG 108, Letters Received. On the same day, Ingalls telegraphed to USG. "Genl Meigs says that nearly four thousand tons of coal left the Delaware this day with a fair wind for Fortress-Monroe—He also

says that forage for North-Carolina has been shipped—I leave this evening—"
ALS (telegram sent), *ibid.*, RG 107, Telegrams Collected (Unbound); telegram
received, *ibid.*, RG 108, Letters Received.

To Edwin M. Stanton

City Point, Va, Feb.y 20th *1865*

HON. E. M. STANTON,
SEC. OF WAR,
SIR:

Whilst in Washington on my last visit I took occasion to examine "Copies" of all the "Official" correspondence between Major
H. D. Wallen, 7th U. S. Infantry, and Adj. Gen. Thomas on the
occasion of the Major being ordered to New Mexico. The correspondence on the part of Wallen is creditable to him. ~~and~~ It shew
a desire to get into the field where he might have an opportunity of
earning promotion. It would seem that he was pushed off to New
Mexico where but a hanfull of his regiment was serving whilst the
greater part of it was serving in the East, most, if not all the time,
commanded by his junior. It really seems to me, from a fair examination of these papers, that Maj. Wallen has been harshly dealt
with. I may not know all the circumstances however. If I am right
I would earnestly recommend, as a partial reward for the past disappointment which Maj. Wallen has suffered, and for services
rendered by him in New Mexico, as testified to by General Carlton,
that he be Breveted Lieut. Col. and Colonel, in the Regular Army.

I spoke to the President on this subject whilst I was in the City
and he requested me to make this statement in writing. I will be
pleased therefore if you will lay this before him if the appointments
asked can not be given without.

I shall really feel pleased if you will have Major Wallen Breveted up to a Colonelcy.

Very respectfully
your obt. svt.
U. S. GRANT
Lt. Gn.

ALS, DNA, RG 94, ACP, 681 ACP 1874. On Dec. 27, 1864, someone, perhaps Maj. Henry D. Wallen, prepared a lengthy unsigned memorandum concerning mistreatment of Wallen, attributing this to his Southern origins. "This want of Confidence in the loyalty and patriotism of Major Wallen, after a life-time of faithful service, and, too, without an arrest or reproach of any Kind, was doubless brought about by Adjutant General Thomas, U. S. Army, who stated to Lieut. Genl. General Grant, and perhaps, also, to the President, and the Hon. Secy. of War, that Major Wallen had *threatened to resign and go South, if he was not promoted.*" *Ibid.,* 1328W CB 1865. See *Calendar,* May 30, 1864.

To Maj. Gen. Henry W. Halleck

City Point, Feby 20th 1865 [*11:30* A.M.]

MAJ, GEN, HALLECK
WASHINGTON

It will not do for Canby to risk [*William F.*] Smith with any Military Command whatever   The moment Canby should differ with him in judgment as to what is to be done, and he would be obliged to differ or yield *to him* entirely he would get no further service out of him but on the contrary he would be a Clog,   Let Smith continue on the same duty as he has been detailed for

U, S, GRANT
Lieut, Genl,

Telegram, copies, DLC-USG, V, 46, 73, 108; (marked as received at 11:45 A.M.) DNA, RG 107, Telegrams Received in Cipher; *ibid.,* RG 108, Letters Sent. *O.R.,* I, xlviii, part 1, 917. See *ibid.,* pp. 463–64, 830, 1001–2.

To Maj. Gen. Henry W. Halleck

City Point. Va. February. 20 *1865*

MAJ. GEN. H. W. HALLECK,
CHIEF OF STAFF OF THE ARMY
WASHINGTON, D. C.
GENERAL:

Herewith I respectfully return the papers referred to me in the case of Brigadier General J. G. Lawman, U. S. Vols. with the following statement:

Gen. Lawman was relieved from duty in front of Jackson, Miss, in July, 1863, by Maj. Gen Sherman, at the request of Maj. Gen. Ord, who at the time or soon thereafter preferred charges against him. Copies of these charges were sent to Gen. Lawman, then at his home, with directions to him to report to Headquarters at Vicksburg. He reported accordingly, but his Division being then at Natchez, as well as most of the witnesses in his case, he was ordered there to await the convening of a Court for his trial; but the movement of the Army of the Tennessee from Vicksburg to reinforce the Army of the Cumberland at Chattanooga, made it impracticable to convene the Court. My appointment to the command of the Military Division of the Mississippi, left the disposition of Gen. Lawman's case with Maj. Gen. Sherman, who succeeded me in the command of the Department of the Tennessee, and there is no doubt but the continued activity and movement of the troops to which the witnesses, as well as the officers who would most naturally be detailed to constitute the Court, belonged, has prevented his trial. There certainly has been, nor is, no disposition to deny to Gen. Lawman a full investigation and hearing in the matter of which he stands charged, as soon as it can be done without detriment to the public service. In honest bravery and devotion to his country no man stands higher than Gen. Lawman. At Belmont. Fort Donelson, Shiloh and the Hatchie he won the commendations of his superiors for great gallantry; but while there was no lack of confidence in his bravery, and going into a fight when ordered, there was an entire want of confidence in his judgement if thrown however partially upon his own resources. For this reason I cannot recommend him for assignment to a command in the front.

Very Respectfully
Your Obedient Servant
U. S. GRANT
Lieutenant General.

LS, DNA, RG 94, Generals' Papers and Books, Jacob G. Lauman. On Feb. 4, 1865, George C. Lauman, Burlington, Iowa, wrote to U.S. Representative James F. Wilson of Iowa. "I take the liberty of addressing you, on a subject of deep interest to myself, but of little to the public generally, and in asking your assistance, I must beg it as a personal favor.—My Brother Jacob G Lauman, as you are probably aware, tindered his services to his country, at an early period of this unfortunate Rebellion, and served on the various Battle fields of the south-west, until the battle of Jackson, where misfortune befel him, and he was relieved of Command. Since that time he has not ceased to ask for an investigation of the affair, and feels confident of his ability to disprove the charges brought against him, could an opportunity be granted him.—His health has become so shattered by an attack of Paralysis, that he has no hope whatever of recovery,—and yet feels that to resign his commission, without a trial, is equivalent to admitting the truthfulness of the charges.—I am therefore *very anxious* that *something* should be done in the matter,—feeling as I do, that he may die suddenly, at any moment, —For the sake of his children, as well as his own, justice should be done, while he is living.—I have already written to Senator Grimes on the subject, and earnestly wish that if in any way you can forward my object you will be inclined to do so.—I am exceedingly desirous that something should be accomplished, before the adjournment of Congress." LS, *ibid.* On Feb. 17, Maj. Gen. Henry W. Halleck referred this letter to USG. AES, *ibid.* See letter to Maj. Gen. William T. Sherman, July 11, 1863. On Aug. 24, 1865, Brig. Gen. Jacob G. Lauman submitted his resignation. ALS, DNA, RG 94, ACP, 366L CB 1865. On Aug. 24, Maj. Gen. William T. Sherman endorsed this letter. "Respectfully forwarded & recommended—General Lauman did good service from the begining of the War until the capture of Vicksburg: Since he has been suffering from a wound and disability. In resigning he should be complimented by a Brevet as Maj Genl. for 'Vicksburg' " AES, *ibid.* On Nov. 1, USG endorsed this letter. "Approved and respectfully forwarded to the Secretary of War." ES, *ibid.* Lauman received the bvt. appointment.

To Maj. Gen. George G. Meade

City Point, Va, Feb.y 20th 1865

MAJ. GN. MEADE,

Rebel papers of Saturday gave full particulars of Sherman's entrance into Columbia on the morning of the 17th and sayid they supposed the evacuation of Charleston had already commenced. I will have the Bulliten prepared for Washington sent to you every evening hereafter.[1]

Desertions on Ord's front have been on the increase since the return of the "pPeace commissioners." They have been more numerous on his front than yours so far.[2]

U. S. GRANT
Lt. Gn.

ALS (telegram sent), CSmH; telegram received (at 12:30 P.M.), DNA, RG 94, War Records Office, Army of the Potomac. *O.R.*, I, xlvi, part 2, 597.

On Feb. 20, 1865, 10:20 A.M. and 11:30 A.M., Maj. Gen. George G. Meade telegraphed to USG. "I have nothing of particular importance to report—every thing being quiet along my lines—Within the last few days Two flags of truce have been received one from Genl. Heth asking for the bodies of two officers buried within our present lines—These bodies were found & delivered on the picket line under a flag—The second was Genl Finnegan also asking for a body— It was ascertained the officer referred to was not dead, but was at City Point wounded—an answer to that effect was sent to Genl. Finnegan.—The Provost Marshall's report this morning shows Fortiny Nine (49) deserters as having been received during the preceeding 24 hours—Nothing of importance elicited from them.—" "Deserters from Bushrod Johnstons division, report that a des- patch was yesterday received to the effect 'that Columbia was in our possession, our cavalry in Winsboro' & that Charleston had been evacuated'—I forward this for what it is worth.—" ALS (telegrams sent), DNA, RG 94, War Records Office, Army of the Potomac; telegrams received (the second marked as received at 10:30 A.M.), *ibid.*, RG 108, Letters Received. *O.R.*, I, xlvi, part 2, 596–97.

At 1:00 P.M., Meade telegraphed to USG. "I congratulate you most heartily, on the successful working of your plans, as proved by the evacuation of Charles- ton & the occupation of Columbia & Winsboro—I shall be very much obliged to you for your promised copy of the daily bulletin made up from the Richmond journals. . . . The firing now going is our batteries shelling the enemys working parties putting up abbattis—The enemy replies.—" ALS (telegram sent), DNA, RG 94, War Records Office, Army of the Potomac; telegram received (at 1:00 P.M.), *ibid.*, RG 108, Letters Received. *O.R.*, I, xlvi, part 2, 597.

Also on Feb. 20, USG telegraphed to Meade and Maj. Gen. Edward O. C. Ord. "I am in receipt of copy of a dispatch from Adm.l Dahlgren to the Sec. of the Navy announcing the evacuation of Charleston and that he was runing up to take possession—Please fire a salute at 12 m. to-morrow for the capture of that place & Columbia." ALS (telegram sent), OClWHi; telegram received (at 9:00 P.M.), DNA, RG 94, War Records Office, Army of the Potomac; Ord Papers, CU-B. *O.R.*, I, xlvi, part 2, 598.

1. On Feb. 20, USG sent to Meade the daily summary of news extracted from the Richmond newspapers, which Meade transmitted to his corps com- manders. Telegram received, DNA, RG 393, 2nd Army Corps, 1st Div., Tele- grams Received; *ibid.*, 5th Corps, 3rd Div., 3rd Brigade, Telegrams Received; William C. Banning, Silver Spring, Md.; copy, Meade Papers, PHi. *O.R.*, I, xlvi, part 2, 599–600; (addressed to Secretary of War Edwin M. Stanton) *ibid.*, I, xlvii, part 2, 499–500. Through the closing months of the Civil War, telegrams providing daily summaries of information from Richmond newspapers were sent in USG's name to Stanton. USG's phraseology in his telegram to Meade, the absence of copies in USG's letterbooks, and the preparation of similar telegrams by staff officers during USG's absences indicate that these telegrams were rou- tinely prepared by the staff. For that reason, those available in the *O.R.* have been omitted from these volumes. On Feb. 21, USG telegraphed to Meade and to Ord transmitting a telegram of Feb. 18 from Maj. Gen. Quincy A. Gillmore to Maj. Gen. Henry W. Halleck announcing the fall of Charleston. Telegram re- ceived, Ord Papers, CU-B; (2) DNA, RG 107, Telegrams Collected (Un- bound); *ibid.*, RG 108, Letters Received; *ibid.*, RG 393, 2nd Army Corps, 1st Div., Telegrams Received; copies, *ibid.*, 9th Army Corps, 1st Div., 3rd Brigade,

Telegrams Received; (2) Meade Papers, PHi. The telegram transmitted is in *O.R.*, I, xlvii, part 2, 483–84.

2. On Feb. 20, USG telegraphed to Brig. Gen. John W. Turner, chief of staff for Ord. "Please report the number of deserters received the last 24 hours by the Army of the James." ALS (telegram sent), Kohns Collection, NN; telegram received, DNA, RG 393, Dept. of Va. and N. C., Telegrams Received. On the same day, noon, Turner telegraphed to USG. "Forty-two deserters have come in since yesterday morning." *O.R.*, I, xlvi, part 2, 605. Also on Feb. 20, USG telegraphed to Stanton. "Desertion from the enemy is on the increase, Number arrived f within our lines the last 24 hours is 91. Their testimony is that many more go to their homes than come within our lines." Telegram received (at 12:10 P.M.), DLC-Robert T. Lincoln; copies, DLC-USG, V, 46, 73, 108; DNA, RG 108, Letters Sent. *O.R.*, I, xlvi, part 2, 596.

On Feb. 21, USG telegraphed to Turner. "Please send by telegraph the number of deserters coming in on your front in the last twenty four hours. You will also hereafter send to these Hdqrs immediately after your reports are rec'd the number of deserters coming in daily." Telegram received, Ord Papers, CU-B. On the same day, 10:20 P.M., Turner telegraphed to USG. "Twenty-four deserters have come in since my report of yesterday morning. Will send daily reports as directed." *O.R.*, I, xlvi, part 2, 618.

From that day through March 27, Turner, followed by Bvt. Brig. Gen. Theodore Read, sent daily statements to USG's hd. qrs. of deserters entering the lines of the Army of the James. They reported nine on Feb. 22, twenty-eight on Feb. 23, twenty-six on Feb. 24, twenty-one on Feb. 25, thirteen on Feb. 26, eight on Feb. 27, twenty-five on Feb. 28, fourteen on March 1, eighteen on March 2, forty-six on March 3, eight on March 4, twenty-five on March 5, six on March 6, thirty-six on March 7, twenty-two on March 8, twenty-six on March 9, twenty-three on March 10, thirty-three on March 11, fourteen on March 14, forty-four on March 17, thirty-six on March 18, sixteen on March 19, twenty-three on March 20, twenty-nine on March 21, forty-nine on March 22, eleven on March 24, thirteen on March 25, twenty on March 26, and eight on March 27. *Ibid.*, pp. 647, 663, 698, 710, 722, 733, 775, 790, 815, 831, 846, 880, 891, 906, 917, 929, 977; *ibid.*, I, xlvi, part 3, 21, 31, 42, 55, 65, 78, 100, 161, 188, 208.

To Maj. Gen. George G. Meade

By Telegraph from City Point 2 30 P M
Dated Feby 20th *1864*5.

To MAJOR GEN MEADE

I believe under the right sort of Commander Greggs Cavalry could now push out striking the South Side railroad at some point between Petersburg and Burksville, crossing the Danville road between the latter place and the Appomattox and the South side road again West of Burksville—From thence they could push

South West heading the streams in Virginia until they reach North Carolina where they could turn SouthWest and push on until it joins either Sherman or Schofield which ever proves most practicable—They could destroy the railroad as they cross but should not stop in Virginia to do any extensive damage—In case you think of a General who can be trusted with this I could send you some of Gen Ords Cavalry to do picket duty until a Division could be brought from the Valley

U S GRANT
Lt Gen

Telegram received, DNA, RG 94, War Records Office, Army of the Potomac; copies, *ibid.*, RG 108, Letters Sent; DLC-USG, V, 46, 73, 108; (2) Meade Papers, PHi. *O.R.*, I, xlvi, part 2, 598. On Feb. 20, 1865, 4:35 P.M., Bvt. Maj. Gen. Alexander S. Webb, chief of staff for Maj. Gen. George G. Meade, telegraphed to USG. "Your despatch of 2 30 p m. in cipher to Gen Meade is just received. General Meade is out, but is expected back in an hour." Copy, DNA, RG 393, Army of the Potomac, Letters Sent. *O.R.*, I, xlvi, part 2, 598. At 9:30 P.M., Meade telegraphed to USG. "Genl. Getty is I expect the best officer to entrust with the duty you propose—I will see him tomorrow—The roads at present are very bad & the streams all full—The cavalry could not take any wagons, artillery or ponton train—and if they do not stop to do any damage to the R. Rds it appears to me the effect of the movement will only be to re-inforce the army they join;—except they will undoubtedly stir up the country thro' which they pass—How long will it take to get a Division here to take their places—I am moderate in my cavalry wants but do not like to be without any.—" ALS (telegram sent), DNA, RG 94, War Records Office, Army of the Potomac; telegram received, *ibid.*, RG 108, Letters Received. *O.R.*, I, xlvi, part 2, 598. On the same day, USG telegraphed to Meade. "If I take Cavalry from you other will be ordered to take its place the moment that is decided on—It would probably take a week to move a Div from the Valley—" Telegram received (at 11:15 P.M.), DNA, RG 94, War Records Office, Army of the Potomac; copies, *ibid.*, RG 108, Letters Sent; DLC-USG, V, 46, 73, 108; (2) Meade Papers, PHi. *O.R.*, I, xlvi, part 2, 599.

At 10:30 P.M., Meade telegraphed to USG. "It has just been reported to me that among the deserters who came in yesterday were (27) Twenty seven from one company nearly all bringing their arms with them—They say another company will probably come in tonight—I would like to have some more of your printed orders to distribute among them.—" ALS (telegram sent), DNA, RG 94, War Records Office, Army of the Potomac; telegram received (at 10:40 P.M.), *ibid.*, RG 108, Letters Received. *O.R.*, I, xlvi, part 2, 599. On the same day, USG telegraphed to Meade. "The orders you request will be sent out to you in the morning." ALS (telegram sent), Kohns Collection, NN; copies, DLC-USG, V, 46, 73, 108; DNA, RG 108, Letters Sent. *O.R.*, I, xlvi, part 2, 599.

To Maj. Gen. John M. Schofield

———

City Point—
Feb 20th [186]5

MAJ GEN J. M. SCHOFIELD
FT FISHER

The rebel Government Will deliver a large number of our prisoners to us near Wilmington during the present and ensuing Week —If our agent of exchange is not there receive them & forward to Annapolis Do not allow this exchange of prisoners to interefere in any manner with your proposed Military operations—Relieve Gen Meagher to proceed to his place of residence and report by letter to the adjt Genl for orders[1]—Richmond papers of today report that Charleston was evacuated on the 14th—Gen Sherman is in possession of Columbia—Beauregard is falling back towards Charlotte N. C. where he is expected by the enemy to make a stand —The advance of Sherman is reported at Winnsboro.

U. S. GRANT
Lt Gen

Telegram received, DNA, RG 107, Telegrams Collected (Bound); copies, *ibid.*, RG 108, Letters Sent; *ibid.*, RG 393, Dept. of N. C., Letters Received; DLC-USG, V, 46, 73, 108; (incomplete) USG 3. *O.R.*, I, xlvii, part 2, 509. Also on Feb. 20, 1865, USG telegraphed to the operator. "Please put up above for Gen Schofield and deliver to Lieut Wilbur on Steamer Neptune and inform Capt James A Q M that the boat need not be longer detained" Telegram received, DNA, RG 107, Telegrams Collected (Bound).

1. On Feb. 5, 3:30 P.M., USG telegraphed to Maj. Gen. Henry W. Halleck. "Please inform me what portion of Schofield's Command, if any, have sailed." ALS (telegram sent), Kohns Collection, NN; copies, DLC-USG, V, 46, 73, 108; (marked as received at 4:15 P.M.) DNA, RG 107, Telegrams Received in Cipher; *ibid.*, RG 108, Letters Sent; (marked as received at 4:20 P.M.) DLC-John M. Schofield. *O.R.*, I, xlvii, part 2, 306. At 6:30 P.M., Halleck telegraphed to USG. "One division of the 23d corps sailed yesterday, numbering five or six thousand. Also over two thousand of Meagher's division are off. The remainder of his force will embark as soon as they can be collected. They are in utter confusion, & he seems to be ignorant of what troops he has, or where they are. It is strange that Genl Thomas should have intrusted men to such an officer." ALS (telegram sent), DNA, RG 107, Telegrams Collected (Bound); telegram received, *ibid.*; *ibid.*, RG 108, Letters Received. *O.R.*, I, xlvii, part 2, 306. On Feb.

6, 10:30 A.M., USG telegraphed to Halleck. "If Meagher has lost his men it will be well to send some officer from Washington to look after them and to relieve Meagher. If he has lost his men it will afford a favorable pretext for doing what the service would have lost nothing by having done long since, dismissing him." ALS (telegram sent), CSmH; copies, DLC-USG, V, 46, 73, 108; (marked as received at 11:15 A.M.) DNA, RG 107, Telegrams Received in Cipher; *ibid.*, RG 108, Letters Sent. *O.R.*, I, xlvii, part 2, 318. On Feb. 8, Brig. Gen. Innis N. Palmer, New Berne, N. C., wrote to USG. "I have the honor to enclose herewith an official copy of a communication I have considered necessary to address to Maj Gen Meigs   No regular communication has yet been established between these Head Quarters and Hilton Head and for this reason and from the fact that I believe these matters should receive immediate attention, I communicate direct." Copy, DNA, RG 393, Dept. of Va. and N. C., Letters Sent. On Feb. 10, 8:45 A.M., Col. Ralph C. Webster, Fort Monroe, telegraphed to USG. "The following has just been recd from Genl Palmer, addressed to you. Feb 8th 9. P. M. 'The troops of Meaghers Division are just arriving at Morehead. They have no transportation." ALS (telegram sent), *ibid.*, Military Div. of the Miss., Letters Received; telegram received (marked as sent at 9:00 A.M., received at 9:30 A.M.), *ibid.*, RG 107, Telegrams Collected (Bound); *ibid.*, Telegrams Collected (Unbound); *ibid.*, RG 108, Letters Received. *O.R.*, I, xlvii, part 2, 383. On Feb. 9, Maj. Robert N. Scott wrote to Halleck accusing Brig. Gen. Thomas F. Meagher of drunkenness at Annapolis while moving troops, and, on Feb. 11, USG endorsed this letter. "I would respectfull[y] recommend that Brig. Gen. T. F. Meagher, for the condition of his command in coming from Tenn. to Annapolis, and for his condition on receipt of orders for their further movement be mustered out of the service." AES, The Scriptorium, Beverly Hills, Calif. On Feb. 20, 10:00 A.M., USG telegraphed to Halleck. "Has Gen. Meagher been dismissed? If he has not I think it will be well to relieve him from duty. Brig. Gn. Hugh Ewing, now on his way to Washington might be ordered to take his place." ALS (telegram sent), CSmH; copies, DLC-USG, V, 46, 73, 108; DNA, RG 94, Letters Received, 204A 1865; (marked as received at 10:10 A.M.) *ibid.*, RG 107, Telegrams Received in Cipher; *ibid.*, RG 108, Letters Sent. *O.R.*, I, xlvii, part 2, 501. At 2:00 P.M., Halleck telegraphed to USG. "The President has not acted on Meagher. The Secty of War thinks you had better order Schofield to relieve & send him home." ALS (telegram sent), DNA, RG 107, Telegrams Collected (Bound); telegram received, *ibid.*; *ibid.*, RG 108, Letters Received. *O.R.*, I, xlvii, part 2, 501.

To Maj. Gen. Philip H. Sheridan

(Cipher)   City Point, Va, Feby 20th 18645. [*1:00* P.M.]
MAJ. GEN. SHERIDAN, WINCHESTER VA.

As soon as it is possible to travel I think you will have no difficulty about reaching Lynchburg with a Cavalry force alone. From

there you could destroy the rail-roads and Canal in every direction
so as to be of no further use to the rebellion this coming Spring or,
I believe, during the existence of the rebellion. Sufficient Cavalry
should be left behind to look after Mosby's gang. From Lynchburg, if information you might get there would justify it, you could
strike South, heading the streams in Virginia to the Westward of
Danville, and push on and join Sherman. This additional raid with
one now about starting from East Tennessee under Stoneman
numbering four or five thousand Cavalry, one from Vicksburg
numbering seven or Eight thousand Cavalry, one from East Port
Miss, Ten thousand Cav.y. ~~and~~ Canby from Mobile Bay with
about Thirty Eight thousand mixed troops, the three latter pushing for Tuscaloosa, Selma & Montgomery, and Sherman with a
large army eating out the vitals of South Carolina, is all that will
be wanted to leave nothing for the Rebellion to stand upon. I would
advise you to overcome great obsticles to accomplish this. Charleston was evacuated on Teusday[1] last.

U. S. GRANT
Lt. Gn.

ALS (telegram sent), PPRF; copies, DLC-USG, V, 46, 73, 108; DNA, RG 108,
Letters Sent. *O.R.*, I, xxxiv, part 1, 46; *ibid.*, I, xxxvi, part 1, 50; *ibid.*, I, xxxviii,
part 1, 39; *ibid.*, I, xlvi, part 2, 605–6. On Feb. 20, 1865, Maj. Gen. Philip H.
Sheridan telegraphed to USG. "Scouts which I had up the valley, have returned,
and report that Wickham's Cavly: Brigade (4 Regts) left for Greenville N. C.
last saturday week—and that it is probable that Paynes brigade would also go—
It is the common talk, that Richmond will be evacuated—Lee falling back to
Danville—During January and February, my scouting parties have had little
brushes with Guerr~~il~~illas; capturing over (150) one hundred and fifty officers
and men—these affairs have all been small and were not reported in detail—On
the 18th inst: one of my parties captured (40) forty of mosby's men, and about
(100) one hundred horses, but in getting off with their plunder they were
attacked and nearly all the prisoners recaptured and some of our own men were
also taken; we never can tell how many, as they make their escape and come in—
The snow is still on the ground here, nearly afoot deep—and the weather has
continued bad up to the present time." Telegram sent, DNA, RG 107, Telegrams
Collected (Unbound); telegram received (at 11:40 A.M.), *ibid.*, Telegrams Collected (Bound); (at noon) *ibid.*, RG 108, Letters Received. *O.R.*, I, xlvi, part
2, 605.

1. Feb. 14. C.S.A. forces evacuated Charleston on Feb. 17.

To Lt. Col. John E. Mulford

City Point, Va, Feb.y 20th *18645*.
LT. COL. MULFORD, AGT. OF EX. JONES LANDING.
Please notify Col. Ould that I have refered his communication in relation to the confinement of C. C. Clay, "and another prominent citizen," to Gen. Thomas with directions to release them if they are in confinement. I have ordered all prisoners of war who are or have been in close confinement, or Irons, here for exchange. I do not think any are now so confined. I have however forwarded Col. Oul's communications in relation to particular cases reported to him and if they are confined as he thinks they will be released. His information proved incorrect in regard to those reported to be in close confinement on Johnson's Island.

U. S. GRANT
Lt. Gn

ALS (telegram sent), CSmH; copies, DLC-USG, V, 46, 73, 108; DNA, RG 108, Letters Sent; USG 3. On Jan. 18, 1865, C.S.A. Agent of Exchange Robert Ould wrote to Lt. Col. John E. Mulford concerning the arrest of Clement C. Clay, Sr. LS, DNA, RG 109, Papers Relating to the Exchange and Treatment of Prisoners, File 32, Case 15. *O.R.*, II, viii, 86–87. Endorsements indicate that Clay was released before the papers arrived.

On Feb. 20, USG telegraphed to Mulford. "Are you getting any of our prisoners from Richmond to-day? Especially are any of them arriving from Danville and North Carolina?" ALS (telegram sent), Kohns Collection, NN; copies, DLC-USG, V, 46, 73, 108; DNA, RG 108, Letters Sent; USG 3. On the same day, Mulford, Varina, Va., telegraphed to USG. "Danville Prisoners will all be in Richmd by tomorrow night, I expect to receive fifteen hundred of our men including One Hundred Officers tomorrow, have delivered fifteen hundred to Mr Ould today. There will be ten to fifteen thousand of our men delivered at Wilmington this week The agt has gone there to attend to it—No receipts of our men here today" ALS (telegram sent), DNA, RG 107, Telegrams Collected (Unbound); telegram received, *ibid.*, RG 108, Letters Received.

Calendar

1864, Nov. 16. To managing committee, Sailors' Fair, Boston. "I have just shipped per Adams' Express a box of trophies from the battle field to your address, which please accept as a donation from the armies operating against Richmond to the Sailors' Fair, held in your city. Hoping the offering may prove an acceptable one, and that it will contribute to the benevolent and patriotic purpose designed by your fair, I subscribe myself . . ."—*New York Herald*, Nov. 22, 1864.

1864, Nov. 16. Brig. Gen. Richard Delafield, chief of engineers, to USG. "I have the honor to transmit herewith one copy of the 'Map of Part of the Military Department of the South, &c., for your use."—Copy, DNA, RG 77, Letters Sent.

1864, Nov. 17, 12:25 P.M. Maj. Robert Williams, AGO, to USG. "Paragraph forty four (44) of Special Orders three hundred and eighty three (383) of November 4th from this Office, directing Captain F. Gerker Commissary Subsistence of Volunteers, to repair to Augusta, Maine, and relieve Captain W. S. Dodge Commissary Subsistence of Volunteers, has been revoked."—LS (telegram sent), DNA, RG 107, Telegrams Collected (Unbound); telegram received, *ibid.*, RG 108, Letters Received.

1864, Nov. 17. Maj. Gen. Henry W. Halleck to USG. "Respectfully forwarded to Lt Genl Grant for his information. Advices from other sources indicate that many of our foreign troops & substitutes, prisoners of war, are joining the Rebel service."—AES, DNA, RG 108, Letters Received. *O.R.*, II, vii, 1123. Written on a letter of Nov. 12 from Maj. Gen. John G. Foster, Hilton Head, S. C., to Halleck discussing, and forwarding documents concerning, U.S. soldiers who had been captured, taken an oath of allegiance, and joined C.S.A. regts.—ALS, DNA, RG 108, Letters Received. *O.R.*, II, vii, 1122–23.

1864, Nov. 17. Maj. Gen. Henry W. Halleck to USG. "In the absence of the Secty of War, these papers are forwarded to Lt Genl Grant for his action."—AES, DNA, RG 108, Letters Received. Written on a letter of Nov. 9 from Governor Thomas E. Bramlette of Ky. to Secretary of War Edwin M. Stanton. "The enclosed statement of Doctors Gardner and Harper, Surgeon and Asst. Surgeon of the 30th and 13th Ky., was handed me by Doctor Gardner, after a long conversation with him in reference to the brutal outrages witnessed by him, and in part set forth in this communication This cut-throat, Champ Ferguson, holds a commission in the rebel army, but plays the part of murderer and robber. He moves with the confederate forces, and they are responsible for his butcheries. Lieut. Smith, wounded at Saltville and prisoner, who was murdered as detailed by Dr. Gardner, I have known from his infancy. He was a noble specimen of a brave and patriotic Kentuckean. Most of the others murdered were colored troops. Surely our Government should make an official demand upon the confed-

erate authorities, to surrender up this man Capt. Champ Ferguson, for punishment. I know of more than thirty citizens brutally murdered by this man,
while in the confederate service. They were murdered because of their
loyalty. Old and unoffending men have fallen under his murderous hand.
The confederate authorities cannot escape the responsibility of his acts
except by surrendering him up to our authorities. I respectfully but earnestly urge upon you to take steps to arrest the career of this confederate
brute."—Copy, *ibid.* The statements enclosed are *ibid.*

1864, Nov. 17.   Maj. Gen. Philip H. Sheridan, Newtown, Va., to Capt.
George K. Leet. "Keep your scouts on the alert at Gordonsville or on the
Rail road in that vicinity. It is very necessary for the next ten days"—Telegram received (on Nov. 18, 9:00 A.M.), DNA, RG 107, Telegrams Collected (Bound); copies (2—marked as sent at 4:30 P.M.), DLC-Philip H.
Sheridan. *O.R.*, I, xliii, part 2, 637. On Nov. 18, Leet, Washington, D. C.,
telegraphed to Sheridan. "Your dispatch of yesterday is received. Scouts
have been directed to go out tomorrow morning and use every effort to
obtain information from Gordonsville & vicinity. They will be kept active."
—ALS (telegram sent), DNA, RG 107, Telegrams Collected (Bound).
O.R., I, xliii, part 2, 641. Later telegrams exchanged between Leet and
Sheridan, Nov. 23–Dec. 8, concerning scouting are *ibid.*, pp. 662, 666–67,
677, 725, 744, 756–57.

1864, Nov. 18.   Asst. Secretary of War Charles A. Dana to USG. "Respectfully referred to Lieut: General U S. Grant."—ES, DNA, RG 94,
Letters Received, 540E 1864. Written on a letter of Oct. 13 from Charles
M. Eustis, Paris, to Secretary of War Edwin M. Stanton disclosing the
code used by the C.S.A. Signal Corps.—Copy, *ibid.*

1864, Nov. 20.   To Brig. Gen. John A. Rawlins. "Mr. Geo. C. Wood &
Mr. Geo. Bliss, Jr. visit City Point as representatives of the Thanksgiving
Committee of the City, and to distribute the bounties of good people of this
section among our troops. Please envite these gentlemen to take up their
quarters with us during their stay at Hd Qrs. and give them every facility
both for carrying out the object of their mission and also of seeing."—ALS,
MHi.

1864, Nov. 22.   Brig. Gen. John A. Rawlins to Maj. Gen. George G.
Meade. "Please order a Regiment of Colored troops of your Command to
report to Post Commander at City Point for fatigue duty &C in the Quarter
Masters Department"—Telegram received (at 8:50 P.M.), DNA, RG 393,
Army of the Potomac, Cav. Corps, Letters Received; copies (2), Meade
Papers, PHi. *O.R.*, I, xlii, part 3, 680.

1864, Nov. 25.   Maj. Gen. John A. Dix to USG. "Thomas Firman 10th
New-York Vols. discharged by Special Order War Dept. A. G. O. No 409

dated Nov. 21. 1864. was accidentally forwarded to that Regiment on the 17th inst. I will thank you to return him to these Head Quarters, furnishing him with transportation."—Copies, DNA, RG 393, Dept. of the East, Telegrams Sent; *ibid.*, 2nd Army Corps, Telegrams Received.

1864, Nov. 26. USG endorsement. "Respectfully returned to the Hon. Sec'y. of War, and attention invited to endorsement of Brig. Gen. Ingalls, Chief Q. M. etc. and accompanying reports."—ES, DNA, RG 92, Letters Received from Depts. and Bureaus. Written on a letter of Oct. 3 from Brig. Gen. Rufus Ingalls to Bvt. Maj. Gen. Montgomery C. Meigs requesting forage.—Copy, *ibid.* On Nov. 25, Ingalls endorsed this letter. "Respectfully returned to LtGenl. Grant. Commdg. Armies U. S. for his information. Copies of certain telegrams and extract from letter are herewith accompanying, to show in part what my action has been. Genl. Meigs receives a Report of Forage from me daily showing the amount on hand and the number of animals. I have done all in my power during the year past to have the proper amount of forage shipped to the front. We make no purchases here. Col. Buren in New York City is charged with the buying and shipping of forage under the orders of the Quartermaster General. Both of these Officers are informed of our wants. Genl. Butler might have ascertained the facts on inquiring of his Chief Quartermaster or at these Hd. Qrs. without communicating *direct* with the War Department. The Quartermaster General is presumed to be responsible for the supplying of forage. Unless vigorous measures are enforced there will be suffering for want of Hay. I would respectfully request the Lieut. General to give orders in the premises."—ES, *ibid.* On the same day, 11:10 A.M., Asst. Secretary of War Charles A. Dana telegraphed to USG. "Major Genl Butler telegraphs that the Battery & Cavalry horses in his Command are suffering for hay and that the Govt is losing large sums in the depreciation of these horses from this Cause The secty of war desires that you should Cause immediate inspection to be made of the Q Ms dept in order to ascertain the extent of the evil Complained of & who is responsible for its existance & that you report the result to this dept"—Telegram received, *ibid.*; *ibid.*, RG 107, Telegrams Collected (Bound). *O.R.*, I, xlii, part 3, 703. USG endorsed the telegram received. "Refered to Brig. Gen. R. Ingalls, Chief Q. M. for report"—AES, DNA, RG 92, Letters Received from Depts. and Bureaus. See *O.R.*, I, xlii, part 3, 700–1, 703–4.

1864, Nov. 26, 10:48 P.M. Maj. Gen. Winfield S. Hancock to Brig. Gen. John A. Rawlins. "I would suggest that it might be better to order Col [Morg]an to report to me in Washington at once without waiting for the my order, instead of extending his leave. During the few days before I enter on my duties he will assist me in getting up my back reports—"—ALS (telegram sent), DNA, RG 107, Telegrams Collected (Unbound); telegram received, *ibid.*, RG 108, Letters Received. *O.R.*, I, xlii, part 3, 712. On Nov. 27, Rawlins telegraphed to Maj. Gen. George G. Meade. "Gen.

Hancock telegraphs from Fort Monroe, that he wishes Lieut. Col. Morgan ordered to report to him, or if that can not be done to have his leave of absence extended for ten days, that he may have his assistance in the getting up of his back reports. He supposes it will be all satisfactory to you and Gen. Humphreys and but for the many matters on his mind, when he left, would have made the application to you. Please communicate your pleasure in this matter to these Head Quarters."—Copies, DLC-USG, V, 45, 70, 107; DNA, RG 108, Letters Sent. On the same day, Meade telegraphed to Rawlins. "I have [*no*] objection to the proposed extension of Lt. Col. Morgans leave for 10 days, but I should object to his separation from the 2d A. C. for any length of time as he is the Inspr. Gen. appointed for that Corps & if Gen Hancock is very desirous of having the service of Lt Col. Morgan which I can readily understand I would suggest Lt. Col. Morgan being appointed Inspr. Gen. of the new Corps Gen H is about to organize in which case he would ~w~ vacate his present position in the 2d A C. & the new commander of that Corps could select a suitable officer to be appointed in his place"—Telegram received (misdated Nov. 26), *ibid.*, Letters Received; copy (dated Nov. 27), *ibid.*, RG 393, 2nd Army Corps, Telegrams Received. On Nov. 28, 3:15 P.M., Rawlins telegraphed to Hancock. "The order for Col. Morgan to report to you, has not been issued, but his leave of absence has been extended ten (10) days. You will have to procure an order from the Sec. of War, transferring Col. Morgan from the 2d Army Corps, so as to have his position in that Corps vacant, that it may be filled by Gen'l. Humphrey's. Otherwise he will have to remain with the Corps."—Telegrams received (2), *ibid.*, RG 107, Telegrams Collected (Unbound); copies, *ibid.*, RG 108, Letters Sent; DLC-USG, V, 45, 70, 107. *O.R.*, I, xlii, part 3, 726. See *ibid.*, p. 807.

1864, Nov. 27. USG endorsement. "Respectfully forwarded."—AES, DNA, RG 94, ACP, 1352M CB 1864. Written on a letter of Nov. 24 from Maj. Gen. George G. Meade to Secretary of War Edwin M. Stanton requesting that all members of his staff be given bvt. appointments one grade above their current rank.—LS, *ibid.*

1864, Nov. 27. USG endorsement. "Respectfully forwarded to the Secretary of War, and attention invited to the endorsement hereon of Brvt Maj. Gen A. H. Terry, of which I approve, and therefore recommend that general Orders and instructions from the Adjutant General's Office be so modified as to permit the Muster-out of service of each man at the date of the expiration of his own term of enlistment, as provided in the last paragraph of General Orders No. 243, of date Aug. 9. 1864. A. G. O., for new organizations."—ES, DNA, RG 94, Vol. Service Div., Letters Received, W3318 (VS) 1864. Written on a letter of Oct. 25 from Capt. Lewis C. Hunt, 67th Ohio, to Capt. Wilberforce Nevin discussing the issue of whether soldiers enlisted for three years should be discharged on the basis of the date they were mustered into service or the date the regt. was mustered.—LS, *ibid.* On Nov. 15, Bvt. Maj. Gen. Alfred H. Terry endorsed this letter. "Respectfully forwarded to Lt. Col T. S. Bowers A. A. G. The date fixed by the War Department for the muster out of the original members of this regiment is ~~is~~ January 10th 1865, January 10th 1862 being the time when the organization of the regiment was completed by the consolidation of two imperfect organizations. But it appears that many of the men were *mustered into the service of the United States* in the months of October, November, & December 1862 & that there was no remuster when the consolidation took place. Consequently the men within named and some who have already served three years from the date of the only muster into service which they have ever had. I respectfully submit that the contract of enlistment is an individual contract and that the contract which one man may make for himself can in no wise be affected by the contract which another man may make for himself. If A. contracts to serve three ye[ars] from *the date of his muster into service* [he] cannot be held for three years and one month because 'B.' who has made a similar contract did not comme[nce his term] of service until two months after A commenced his. I also submit that no Orders of the War Department can legally vary the contract of enlist[ment] after it has once been made; neither can they vary the Statute law which fixes the three years as the longest period for which a man can ever voluntarily contract to serve. It seems to me that the men within named are entitled to be mustered out now, and while I recommend their discharge as an act of justice to them I also recommend it as a matt[er] of policy: the discontent caused by t[he] detention affects not only themselves but o[thers] who are not now entitled to their discharge but who fear that when their term shall have expired they will be held to a long[er] service. To such a degree does this disconte[nt] affect the discipline & efficiency of the regiment that I should not place much dependence upon it in action. It has been an excellent regiment & still would be such were the evil remov[ed.]"—ES, *ibid.*

On Jan. 23, 1865, Maj. Samuel Breck, AGO, wrote to USG. "I have the honor to acknowledge the receipt of the papers forwarded by you from Capt. Lewis C. Hunt, Commd'g 67th Ohio Vols, who requests that certain men of that command be mustered out of service from date of enlistment and not that of their muster-in In reply I have the honor to inform you that the papers in the case have been submitted to the Secretary of War who decides that no change can be made in existing regulations on this subject"—LS, *ibid.*, RG 108, Letters Received.

1864, Nov. 27. Maj. Gen. Philip H. Sheridan, Kernstown, Va., to Lt. Col. Theodore S. Bowers. "I respectfully request that Colonel A. Piper 10th N. Y. Heavy Artillery, now on duty at Hd Qrs 18th A. C., be ordered to report to me, immediately. The Colonel has made application to me to be ordered here, and inasmuch as his regiment is serving with my command, and I am great need of his services as Chf of Artillery, I have no hesitancy in making this request."—LS (telegram sent), DNA, RG 107, Telegrams Collected (Unbound); telegram received, *ibid.*; *ibid.*, RG 108, Letters Received. *O.R.*, I, xliii, part 2, 677. See *ibid.*, p. 772.

1864, Nov. 28–30. USG endorsement. "Respy returned. There are serious objections to any portion of the army engaging in trade. When so engaged but little active service can be expected. If this cotton can be gotten and under the auspices of the Treasury Department, I am entirely willing and would much prefer that the enemy should be paid for it in whiskey than in currency"—Copy, DLC-USG, V, 58. Written on a letter of Aug. 11 from Brig. Gen. Innis N. Palmer, New Berne, N. C., to Secretary of War Edwin M. Stanton proposing to trade whiskey for cotton.—*O.R.*, I, xlii, part 2, 123–24. Some time between Nov. 30 and Dec. 2, USG endorsed a communication concerning the promotion of Palmer. "Respy forwarded to the Secretary of War. I am not sufficiently familiar with General Palmers services to approve this application"—Copy, DLC-USG, V, 58.

1864, Nov. 28. Secretary of State William H. Seward to USG introducing his son.—Stan. V. Henkels, Catalogue No. 1194, June 8, 1917, p. 91.

1864, Nov. 28. Col. Reece M. Newport, chief q. m., Baltimore Depot, to Bvt. Maj. Gen. Montgomery C. Meigs. "I have the honor to enclose herewith, a letter of Lieut. General Grant, recommending that the Schooner 'Champion,' and her owner, Capt. M. P. Morse, be employed by the Government, with an endorsement of Gen'l Ingalls, authorizing Col. Bradley to employ the vessel and her Commander. Also a letter to me from Col. Bradley, earnestly requesting that the vessel be Chartered here. Capt W. L. James, a. q. m., Fort Monroe, states, by way of endorsement on Col. Bradley's letter, that the vessel can be usefully employed at that point. She is not needed here, and the rate allowed according to tonnage would not meet the expenses of running the vessel according to Capt. Morse's statement. I respectfully refer the matter to you for consideration and favorable action."— LS, DNA, RG 92, Letters Received Relating to Chartered Vessels.

1864, Nov. 28. U.S. Senator John Sherman of Ohio to USG. "At the suggestion of Col. Hardie I write you direct to see if it is possible for you to secure the release or special exchange of Major Wm. Stanhope Marshall— 5th Iowa Vols. now a Prisoner with the Rebels—He is a relative of my wife —has been over a year a prisoner & is now or was recently in Charlestown S. C. He is a gallant Soldier & I very much hope General that you can & will secure his exchange—"—ALS, USG 3. See *O.R.*, II, vii, 881.

1864, Nov. 29. Capt. George K. Leet, Washington, D. C., to Lt. Col. Theodore S. Bowers. "Scouts succeeded in reaching our Agent by lower route last night & returned today. They report that only Kershaws Division of Earlys command has gone to Richmond—It is rumored that Early will endeavor to withdraw all his forces from the Valley—A battle is expected shortly at Richmond and women and children are being moved from there & Petersburg to other points for safety. . . . Copy to Gen. Sheridan"—ALS (telegram sent), DNA, RG 107, Telegrams Collected (Bound); copy, Meade Papers, PHi. Printed (probably incorrectly) as sent by Maj. Gen. Henry W. Halleck to Bowers in *O.R.*, I, xliii, part 2, 694.

1864, DEC. USG note. "I can give no sentiments, as you ask, except a hope for a speedy suppression of rebellion."—ANS (facsimile), Kenneth W. Rendell, Inc., Catalogue 89 [1973], p. 35.

1864, DEC. 2. USG endorsement. "Respectfully returned—Not approved." —ES, DNA, RG 107, Letters Received, F1207 1864. Written on a memorandum of Nov. 29 concerning Mrs. Mary J. Fitzpatrick, who requested permission to join her husband, a farmer and foreign noncombatant, at Petersburg. The Fitzpatricks had lived at Fredericksburg when the town was bombarded; at that time Mrs. Fitzpatrick had received permission to live in the North.—*Ibid.*

1864, DEC. 2. Brig. Gen. Charles K. Graham to USG. "The enemy fired upon a working party in one of our advanced works and the firing extended along the line. It has ceased. To-day the enemy fired upon our pickets under orders as we ascertained from a deserter to do so if the colored division was on duty. The firing was stopped by our artillery evidently doing some mischief."—ALS (telegram sent), DNA, RG 107, Telegrams Collected (Unbound). An undated telegram from Graham to USG may have been sent the same day. "The enemy opened on a working party at one of the Redans on this front and it extended to along their picket line—The firing has almost entirely ceased."—ALS (telegram sent), *ibid.*

1864, DEC. 2. Special Orders No. 141, Armies of the U.S. "Col George H. Sharp, 120th Regt. New York Vols, is announced as Assistant Provost Marshal General, Armies operating against Richmond, and will report to Brig Gen. M. R. Patrick, Provost Mar. General, for duty."—Copies, DLC-USG, V, 57, 62, 63, 64. *O.R.*, I, xlii, part 3, 779.

1864, DEC. 3. Secretary of War Edwin M. Stanton to USG. "I enclose herewith a letter addressed to Mr Henry Massie, in at Charlottesville in Virginia, with the request that you will cause it to be forwarded to the Rebel Agent for Exchange for transmission to Mr Massie."—Copy, DNA, RG 107, Letters Received, M3299 1864. Related correspondence is *ibid.*

1864, DEC. 3, 2:30 P.M. Maj. Gen. George G. Meade to USG. "(Confidential) . . . The only corps I could assign Col French to, would be the 2d

—I am of the opinion this would not be agreeable to Maj. Genl. Humphreys tho' I have not referred the question to him.—In view of the previous high command held in this army by Col French, and the circumstances attending his separation from it—I think his return to it would be neither expedient or politic—Can he not be assigned to the Army of the James, or some detachment from it.—"—ALS (telegram sent), DNA, RG 393, Army of the Potomac, Telegrams Sent; telegram received, *ibid.*, RG 108, Letters Received. See *O.R.*, I, xlvi, part 2, 52.

1864, DEC. 5, noon.   To Secretary of War Edwin M. Stanton. "I would respectfully request the suspension of special order 425 paragraph 25 detaching the Medical Director of the 2nd Corps—This officer can not well be replaced in the field at present"—Telegram received (at 1:00 P.M.), DNA, RG 107, Telegrams Collected (Bound); copy, *ibid.*, Telegrams Received in Cipher. On the same day, 1:15 P.M., Maj. Gen. George G. Meade telegraphed to Brig. Gen. John A. Rawlins. "Surgeon Doherty is a faithful & meritorious officer who has been continuously in the field since the commencement of the war & in my judgement is entitled the relaxation which his assignment to Maj. Genl. Hancock will give him—I should not have objected to his transfer had the question been referred to me—My object in alluding to his order was to show the principle being practiced of removing these officers without asking how it would affect the public service and to base my suggestion that the Dept should be asked to make such reference before ordering away others, as I was informed that a considerable number of staff & other officers were expecting orders to report to Maj. Genl. Hancock—I am not apprised that these expectations was were based on any thing Maj. Genl. Hancock has said or done, but I thought it prudent to suggest this step being taken as it is natural both Genl. H & the department should be desirous of getting the most efficient officers in the new corps—In this I am desirous of accomodating Genl. H as far as my knowledge of the wants of the service will admit & I shall cheerfully give my consent to the transfer of any officer whom Maj. Genl—Humphreys or any other Corps Comdr. says can be spared—If the despatch in the case of Surgeon Doherty is not sent I would advise its being retained   Surgeon D. under the orders of the War Dept—sent to him direct, in advance by telegraph in advance of the printed ordre left here several days ago.—"—ALS (telegram sent), *ibid.*, RG 94, War Records Office, Army of the Potomac; copy, Meade Papers, PHi. *O.R.*, I, xlii, part 3, 806. On Dec. 6, Meade wrote to USG's hd. qrs. requesting revocation of the order sending Asst. Surgeon Charles Smart to the 1st Army Corps, which USG endorsed between Dec. 7 and 9. "Respy forwarded to the Sec of War, with the request that the order in the case of asst surgeon Smart, U. S A. be revoked, or at least suspended for the present. The Medical Director of this Corps has been ordered to report to General Hancock, which ought to be sufficient for the present"—Copy, DLC-USG, V, 58.

1864, DEC. 5.   To Joseph H. Choate. "Your favor inviting me to be present at the meeting of your society on the 22d inst. is received. My duties are such that it would be impossible for me to make any appointment so far ahead, and especially so when it would take me from the armies in the [fi]eld. Please make my excuses to the New England Society for not accepting this kind invitation to be present with them on the 22d of December." —*New York Herald*, Dec. 23, 1864. Written in response to an invitation of the New England Society, New York City, to a commemorative ceremony.

1864, DEC. 5.   To Isaac F. Quinby. "I have found your letter giving the name of your son in full and will attend to making application for his appointment in the ⊞Navy at once. As soon as the result is known will inform you. I great haste yours Truly"—ALS, DLC-USG, I, B. On Dec. 9, Secretary of the Navy Gideon Welles wrote to USG. "Your letter of the 5th inst. recommending De Hart Goldsborough Quimby for appointment to the Naval Academy, is received. In reply I have to state that the appointments are all made for the present Academic year, which commenced on the 1st of October. Master Quimby's name will be entered on the list of applicants however, and the application will be considered when appointments for the next year are to be made."—Copy, DNA, RG 45, Miscellaneous Letters Sent. De Hart G. Quimby attended the U.S. Naval Academy 1865–66, then received a commission as 2nd lt., 5th Inf.

1864, DEC. 5.   Special Orders No. 143, Armies of the U.S. "The four (4) companies of the 184th Regiment NewYork Vols, now in the 1st Brigade 3d Division 6th Army Corps, are hereby transferred from the 6th Corps to the Army of the James, and will proceed to Harrisons Landing, and join the six Companies of the Regiment, on duty there. The Quarter Masters Department will furnish necessary transportation."—Copies, DLC-USG, V, 57, 62, 63, 64. *O.R.*, I, xlii, part 3, 809.

1864, DEC. 6.   Brig. Gen. Charles K. Graham, Jamestown Island, Va., to Maj. Gen. Benjamin F. Butler, copy to USG. "The Rebels burnt a sutlers schooner and Captured the Propeller Lizzie Freeman off Pagan Creek between 11 & 12 oclock last night. Capt Sawtelle supt of Prison labor was on board of a barge in tow of the Freeman at the time. He escaped uninjured but one Colored soldier was Killed. Two wounded besides the Mate of the barge. The steamer put off either for the Chickahominy or Nansemond. Capt. Fitch was near at the time this boat went alongside of the burning Schooner but did not board the barge   As the rebels had escaped he went immediately to smithfield to see operator with other parties landed last night to look out after the party Committing this mischief. The wounded men will be sent up in the Mail boat   If the Jessup is within call dispatch here immediately to the mouth of the Chickahominy. My boat is aground but as soon as she is off I will go to the Nansemond. The Foster will return to Smithfield The whole Country to the southward of Pagan's Creek should be scoured"—Telegram received, DNA, RG 108, Letters Received. *O.R.,* I, xlii, part 3, 840–41.

1864, DEC. 6. Lt. Col. Cyrus B. Comstock to Brig. Gen. Seth Williams, adjt. for Maj. Gen. George G. Meade. "Can you tell whether General Upton has been ordered away from the Sixth Corps to Tennessee or elsewhere?"— Printed as received at 12:10 P.M. in *O.R.,* I, xlii, part 3, 820. On the same day, Williams twice wrote to Comstock. "At this moment I am unable to answer your inquiry about General Upton, but I will endeavor to ascertain from Generals Seymour and Wheaton whether the order you allude to has been issued." "General Seymour informs me that about the 1st of December General Upton was with the Army of the Shenandoah, and soon to leave for Tennessee, where it was understood he was to have a division of cavalry."— *Ibid.* After recovering from wounds received at the battle of Winchester (Sept. 19), Bvt. Maj. Gen. Emory Upton commanded the 4th Div., Cav. Corps, Military Div. of the Miss.—*Ibid.,* I, xlv, part 2, 173.

1864, DEC. 7. USG endorsement. "Respectfully refered to the Sec. of War. I know nothing of his case and do not want to call to the field any one whose services are required elswhere or who is unfit for duty when he comes."—AES, Mrs. Walter Love, Flint, Mich. Written on a letter of Dec. 1 from Judge David Wilmot, U.S. Court of Claims, to USG. "Capt. G. B Overton of the 14 Infantry, was seriously wounded in the thigh, a little above the knee at Chancellorsville. A part of the bone was carried away, and the ball still remains in the leg. He has most wonderfully recovered, but is still unable for the field. He has for six months been upon detached service at Rochester N. Y—mustering and disbursing Officer. Your recent order calls him into the field—By advice of the Secty of War, I ask of you a suspension of your late order in his case. I know the Captain well—he is a brave and faithful officer, and does not seek to avoid any service that he is able to perform."—ALS, *ibid.*

1864, DEC. 8. USG endorsement. "Approved and respectfully forwarded to the Adjutant General of the Army"—ES, DNA, RG 94, Letters Received, 2494S 1864. Written on a letter of Nov. 28 from 1st Lt. James Stewart, 4th Art., Fort Dushane, Va., to Brig. Gen. Lorenzo Thomas requesting assignment to his battery.—ALS, *ibid.*

1864, DEC. 8, 3:00 P.M. Rear Admiral David D. Porter, Norfolk, to USG. "Miami has been ordered to City Point—Three Gunboats to patrol the River between Pagan Creek, Ragged Island Creek, and Point of Rocks. All the vessels will row guard at night, and every precaution taken to prevent surprise. There are now 65 rebel sailors with 10 cart loads of powder at Smithfield on or near Pagan's Creek. They came from Richmond around by Franklin These are the men doing the damage."—ALS (telegram sent), CSmH; telegram received, DNA, RG 108, Letters Received. *O.R.*, I, xlii, part 3, 864; *O.R.* (Navy), I, xi, 155.

1864, DEC. 9. USG endorsement. "Respectfully returned. The services of this officer are not required."—ES, DNA, RG 107, Letters Received, M3262 1864. Written on a copy of a letter of Nov. 26 from Asst. Secretary of War Charles A. Dana to Maj. Gen. W. MacAlpine enclosing a letter of Nov. 23 from MacAlpine, Washington, D. C., tendering his services to suppress the rebellion.—Copy, *ibid.*

1864, DEC. 9. C.S.A. Agent of Exchange Robert Ould to USG. "It seems that General Butler has been informed that my flag-of-truce boat would be at Boulware's Wharf, on James River, to-morrow. It will be impossible for me to be at that point to-morrow, and I cannot now state when I will be."— *O.R.*, II, vii, 1206.

1864, DEC. 10. To q. m. "Do you know whether the Steamer Martin has passed Ft Monroe or not. If she has not, please notify me when she does."— Copy (press), DNA, RG 107, Telegrams Collected (Bound). On the same day, 5:01 P.M., Col. Ralph C. Webster, Fort Monroe, telegraphed to USG. "The Martin passed here at 4.30"—ALS (telegram sent), *ibid.*, Telegrams Collected (Unbound). An undated and unaddressed telegram from USG may have been sent the same day. "Operator will please ask operator at Newport News if Steamer *Martin* has left there"—Charles Hamilton Auction 41, April 23, 1970, no. 84. A telegram dated only "10th," 5:15 P.M., "N News," from Lt. Col. Frederick T. Dent to USG may also have been sent on Dec. 10. "The fog is so thick that we cannot run, will wait here until it clears a little and then go on."—Telegram received, DNA, RG 107, Telegrams Collected (Bound).

1864, DEC. 10. Lt. Col. Theodore S. Bowers to Maj. Gen. Lewis Wallace. "Get one of the regular regiments of infantry of your command in readiness to come to City-Point immedy, on receipt of orders,"—Telegram, copy, DNA, RG 393, Middle Dept., Telegrams Sent (Press). *O.R.*, I, xliii, part 2, 775. On the same day, Wallace telegraphed to Bowers. "Your Telegram rec'd—The regular Troops are now distributed all over this Dept. but one regiment can be ready to leave Annapolis in forty-eight hours or as soon as they can be collected at that point—It will leave that large camp almost without a guard but I will do th my utmost to execute your order promptly and send other Troops there. I have been obliged to send some of the regulars to the Eastern shore their presence being very necessary there—"— ALS (telegram sent), DNA, RG 107, Telegrams Collected (Unbound); telegram received (at 11:50 P.M.), *ibid.*, RG 108, Letters Received. *O.R.*, I, xliii, part 2, 775.

1864, DEC. 10.   Mrs. P. D. White, Warrenton, N. C., to USG. "I have
the honor to apply for a passport for myself and five children to pass through
your lines by flag of truce to New York City—from which point I desire to
sail directly for Liverpool. My intention is to remain in England during the
War for the purpose of educating my children. By granting the above request you will confer a great favor on . . ."—ALS, OClWHi. On Dec. 31,
C.S.A. Agent of Exchange Robert Ould endorsed this letter. "Respectfully
referred to Lt. Gen. Grant—If consistent with Gen. Grant's Sense of duty,
he will confer a great favor upon a worthy lady, by complying with her request—"—AES, *ibid.* Mrs. White was probably Priscilla White, mother of
nine children, married to John White, a merchant of Warrenton, appointed
N. C. commissioner to sell cotton bonds and purchase supplies in Europe.—
1860 U.S. Census, Warren County, N. C.; Frontis W. Johnston, ed., *The
Papers of Zebulon Baird Vance* (Raleigh, 1963), I, 288–89.

1864, DEC. 11.   Bvt. Maj. Gen. Montgomery C. Meigs to USG. "Very
Stringent orders for vigilance against incendiarism have lately been given
by the War Department. Gen Rucker reported that he had about 120 Rebel
deserters Employed & that he thought them a very unsafe class of men
about the Depot in these times. As they were Employed under your orders
directing Employment in the Qur Mrs Dept at places where they would
not be Exposed to capture to be given to rebel deserters who desired it, I
did not feel at liberty to direct their discharge but forwarded the letter of
Gen Rucker to the Secretary of War with the remark Endorsed that they
were Employed under the order referred to   It was returned to me with a
severe rebuke & with instructions to give such orders as I thought the service
of the Qur Mrs Dept in Washington at this time required without regard
to any antecedent orders of yours. I ~~have~~ instructed Gen Rucker to discharge immediately all rebel deserters for whom he was not willing to be
responsible & I wrote this note lest it may be represented to you that I am
disregarding your orders & you may misunderstand my ~~intention~~ action as
much as I regret to find the Secretary has. Wishing you prosperity & success . . ."—ADfS, DLC-Montgomery C. Meigs. On Dec. 9, Brig. Gen. Daniel H. Rucker wrote to Meigs questioning the wisdom of the employment of
some 120 C.S.A. deserters by the Q. M. Dept. in Washington.—Copy, DNA,
RG 107, Letters Received from Bureaus. On Dec. 10, Meigs endorsed this
letter to Secretary of War Edwin M. Stanton noting that the deserters were
employed by order of USG.—Copy, *ibid.* On the same day, Stanton endorsed
this letter. "Referred back to the QuarterMaster General whose duty it is
to give his subordinates such instructions as in his opinion the safety of the
service in the department under his charge may require and not to endeavour to shift responsibility upon the Secretary of War in relation to the
details of the QuarterMaster department. It cannot be possible that the
QuarterMaster General can construe General Grant's order so as to retain
in the QuarterMaster's employment persons who are dangerous to the ser-

vice. The Quarter Master General is directed to give such instructions to General Rucker as in the opinion of the QuarterMaster General the safety of the QuarterMaster's service in Washington requires at the present time without regard to any antecedent orders of General Grant."—Copy, *ibid.*

1864, DEC. 11. Lt. Col. Theodore S. Bowers to Brig. Gen. Marsena R. Patrick, provost marshal. "You will receive, take charge of, and distribute as heretofore all recruits forwarded from camps of rendez-vous, and that arrive at City Point for the Armies operating against Richmond, until further orders from these HeadQuarters"—Copies, DLC-USG, V, 45, 71, 107; DNA, RG 108, Letters Sent; *ibid.*, RG 393, Army of the Potomac, Staff Officers, Letters Received. *O.R.*, I, xlii, part 3, 954.

1864, DEC. 14. To President Abraham Lincoln. "Respectfully forwarded to the President for his information."—Telegram received (at 5:10 P.M.), DLC-Robert T. Lincoln; (press) DNA, RG 107, Telegrams Collected (Bound). USG enclosed a telegram of 3:30 P.M. from Maj. Gen. George G. Meade to USG. "I yesterday remitted the sentence in the case of John McNulty alias Joseph Riley Company E. 6th New Hampshire Vols and beg leave to refer to my letter to you in the case. The record will be forwarded to the President as directed"—Telegram received, *ibid.* Earlier on the same day, Lincoln telegraphed to USG. "Please have execution of John McNulty, *alias* Joseph Riley, Co. E 6. N. H. Vols. suspended, and record sent to me." —ALS (telegram sent), *ibid.* Lincoln, *Works*, VIII, 167. On Dec. 13, Meade wrote to USG. "Your letter asking for a reprieve in the case of Private Reilly, 6th N. H. vols., sentenced and ordered to be hung on Friday next, December 16th, has been referred by me to the Judge Advocate of this army, who has endorsed on it as follows: 'John McNulty, alias Joseph Reilley, Company "E," 6th N. H. vols., plead guilty to the charge, 'Deserting to the enemy.' He is 23 years old; a substitute, enlisted June 2nd 1864; received pay to August 31st 1864; deserted from the picket line near Pegram House October 15th 1864: is represented as having been a steady, honest and faithful soldier; was in several engagements, and in one attracted the particular notice of his captain by his good behavior.' When acting on this case my attention was drawn to the statement of the prisoner that he had deserted in consequence of a letter received from his wife, and I furthermore observed that he had been arrested near Harper's Ferry, soon after his desertion, instead of in Tennessee as most of the other deserters had been; still my conviction being firm that desertion to the enemy should be punished with death—the frequency and increase of this crime at this time in this army, together with the fact that four others were similarly sentenced at the same time, and that the prisoner's statement was not corroborated by any evidence,—I deemed it my duty to order the execution of the sentence. In consideration of your wishes and of the good character given the prisoner prior to his offence, I will now accept the statement of himself and wife, and have accordingly ordered him reprieved and returned to duty."—Copy, DNA, RG 393, Army of the Potomac, Letters Sent.

1864, DEC. 14.   USG endorsement. "Approved and respectfully returned to the Adjutant General of the Army."—ES, DNA, RG 94, ACP, D658 CB 1864. Written on a letter of Nov. 21 from Maj. Gen. Napoleon J. T. Dana, Vicksburg, to Lt. Col. Christian T. Christensen, adjt. for Maj. Gen. Edward R. S. Canby, recommending Col. Embury D. Osband, 3rd Colored Cav., for appointment as bvt. brig. gen.—ALS, *ibid.* On Feb. 1, 1865, Osband was nominated as bvt. brig. gen. to rank from Oct. 5, 1864.

1864, DEC. 14.   USG endorsement. "Approved and respectfully forwarded to the Adjutant General of the Army. Cap't. Benedict has not sufficiently recovered from wounds received in battle, for active field duty."—ES, DNA, RG 94, Letters Received, 1725C 1864. Written on a letter of the same day from Capt. Avery B. Cain, 4th Inf., City Point, to Brig. Gen. Lorenzo Thomas requesting that 2nd Lt. Thomas F. Quinn be returned to his regt. from recruiting service and replaced by Capt. Abner R. Benedict.—LS, *ibid.*

1864, DEC. 14.   Col. Edward D. Townsend, AGO, to USG. "I have the honor to request that you will furnish for the information of this office a list of Generals Officers of the General Staff, and acting Staff Officers on duty at the Headquarters Armies of the United States during the month of August 1864."—Copy, DNA, RG 94, Enlisted Branch, Letters Sent.

1864, DEC. 20.   To Secretary of War Edwin M. Stanton. "The Richmond 'Dispatch' of today has the following. 'From South Western Virginia. Telegrams received yesterday from Lynchburg contain the latest intelligence we have from the raiders on the line of the Virginia and East Tennessee Rail Road. From the latest of these it appears that the yankees on Saturday having come to Max Meadows ten (10) miles this side of Wytheville turned back towards Abingdon destroying property of all kinds as they went. As they were returning Col Witcher struck them at Adkins on Saturday evening about 4 o.clock and fought them till night. Adkins is a point on the Rail Road seven miles this side of Marion.   the result of Col. Witchers fight is not given. It is believed that the enemy has succeeded in destroying the Machinery at the Lead works, the report that that point was guarded by Genl Vaughan being untrue. From the celerity of their movements it is doubtful whether the Enemy have any artillery and some think that for the lack of this arm they have not and will not attack the salt works. The statements of the telegraphs mentioned are based on information telegraphed to Lynchburg by officers of the Va & Tennessee R. R. one of whom escaped from the enemy at Glade Springs and the other went out from Lynchburg on an Engine to make a reconnoissance. These officers also report that the Enemy has destroyed every bridge on the Rail Road between Glade Spring and Max Meadows' "—Telegram received (at 3:30 P.M.), DNA, RG 107, Telegrams Collected (Bound). *O.R.*, I, xlv, part 2, 284.

1864, DEC. 20. To Secretary of War Edwin M. Stanton. "I would respectfully recommend Edwin Harlan, late a Capt. in the 21st Ill. Vol. Infantry, the regiment of which I was Colonel, for the position of Lieut. Col. in one of the new regiments being raised for the First Army Corps, Capt. Harland served faithfully for the three years he was mustered into the service and is now out of service only by the expiration of his term of service."—ALS, DNA, RG 94, ACP, H43 CB 1865. No appointment followed, but Edwin Harlan was appointed capt. and commissary as of Jan. 25, 1865.

1864, DEC. 20. Maj. Gen. Henry W. Halleck to USG. "I am directed by the Secretary of War to transmit to you the enclosed papers from the Chief Engineer. Order No 32 of the Engineer Department was issued by the authority of the Secretary of War, and is merely an order enforceing existing Army Regulations. To permit the taking of photographic views or plans of any portion of forts or military defenses, except for official purposes, is deemed a violation of Regulations and Orders. The Secretary therefore directs that you will take the proper measures to enforce the authority of the Government, by seizing all photographs and negatives of any part of Fort Monroe or its approaches. The papers to be returned for file."—LS, DNA, RG 108, Letters Sent (Press). On Jan. 21, 1865, Col. Joseph Roberts, 3rd Pa. Art., Fort Monroe, endorsed this letter. "Respy returned. The photographer referred to by Col Brewerton is Alexander Gardner, styling himself—'Photographer of the Army of the Potomac, corner of 7th and D streets, Washington D. C.' He has published a catalogue of 'Photographic incidents of the War' which was printed sept 1863 at Washington —by 'H. Polkinhorn, Printer.' The negatives referred to are beyond my control, but are no doubt at Mr Gardners photographic gallery in Washington. I am under the impression that he took no views of the batteries of Ft. Monroe, but merely of groups of individuals, of some of the quarters, and of the 15 inch gun, called the 'Lincoln Gun' No violation of Engineer order No. 32 will be permitted hereafter."—Copy, DLC-USG, V, 58. On Jan. 28, USG endorsed this letter. "Respy returned to Maj Gen Halleck, Ch of staff of the army, Washington, D. C. and attention invited to report endorsed hereon. Orders have been issued to prevent the taking of photographic views of forts and defenses hereafter, except for military purposes"—Copy, *ibid.*

1864, DEC. 21. USG endorsement. "Respectfully forwarded to the Secretary of War, with the earnest recommendation that William H. Morgan, late Col. of the 25th Reg't. Indiana Vols. be given a Regiment in the new Corps. Col. Morgan has a fine military record, and is the Officer who displayed such conspicuous gallantry at Davis' Mills Miss. in Dec. 1862"— ES, DNA, RG 94, Vol. Service Div., 6911 (VS) 1879. Written on a letter of Nov. 5 from William H. Morgan, Cincinnati, to Brig. Gen. John A. Rawlins. "Learning that you arrived at St. Louis on the evening of the 4th inst., and that you did not pass through this city as I had hoped and expected, I have concluded to *write* you in reference to a matter of no little or ordinary importance to me, and shall do so with the hope that your personal attention may be drawn to, and your interest enlisted in the matter to be presented. Desiring to be as brief as possible, I will commence by saying that my connection with the army was severed nearly four months ago, owing to the expiration of my term of service, and that I am now and have been for some time exceedingly anxious to return to it again. When I reported at Indianapolis I found so many applicants for regimental commands that I did not make application for another regiment, but concluded at the earnest solicitation of friends to engage in civil persuits again, and finally moved to and commenced business in this city. I am, however, restless and greatly dissatisfied, and can expect no relief but by returning again to the army, and this I hope to accomplish through and the General-in-Chief—I have been informed and may have been deceived, though I think not, that Genl Grant is friendly disposed towards me, that he once urged my promotion, and but recently expressed his regrets that his effort had failed to secure my advancement and thereby the continuance of my services as an officer in the Army. Believing this information to be correct, it is reasonable to suppose that the General would be willing to do something for me, if advised of my wishes and desires, and I ask this favor of you prompted soto do by the kindness received from you in the past—My military education, experience and ability are probably well known to you and Genl Grant, but if desired the testimonials of the officers under whom I have served can be presented—Can I, therefore, hope for advancement or assistance from the quarter indicated? If you please I would be happy to know your views in reference thereto, and as soon as convenient."—ALS, *ibid*. Morgan was appointed col., 3rd Veteran Inf., as of Jan. 10, 1865.

1864, Dec. 21. Brig. Gen. Richard Delafield, chief of engineers, to USG asking for information which could lead to bvt. commissions for engineer officers.—ALS, DNA, RG 108, Letters Received.

1864, Dec. 21, 12:30 p.m. Maj. Gen. George G. Meade to USG. "Twenty three deserters came in yesterday—they do not communicate any thing of importance—A contraband who came in from Hicksford reports the enemy busily engaged in repairing the Welden R. Rd between the Meherrin & the Nottoway—also that the enemys cavalry are suffering for the want of forage since the destruction of the road, and that a large part of the cavalry has been sent to Bellefield tho' a considerable force remains at Stony Creek—"—ALS (telegram sent), DNA, RG 94, War Records Office, Army of the Potomac; telegram received (at 12:35 p.m.), *ibid*., RG 108, Letters Received. *O.R.*, I, xlii, part 3, 1050–51. On Dec. 22, noon, Meade telegraphed to USG. "Six deserters are reported as coming in yesterday—no information of any movement of the enemy has been obtained from them.— Two men deserted from the 2d corps picket line to the enemy last night— There is nothing else of any consequence to communicate from this Army. —"—ALS (telegram sent), DNA, RG 94, War Records Office, Army of the Potomac; telegram received, *ibid.*, RG 108, Letters Received. *O.R.*, I, xlii, part 3, 1056. On Dec. 23, 1:00 P.M., Meade telegraphed to USG. "Nineteen deserters are reported this morning as coming from the enemy into the lines of the 9th & 2d corps—And two deserters from the 2d corps to the enemy—The enemy's deserters report the establishment of a new mortar battery in front of Fort Morton—The attention of the Engineers & artillery have been directed to this matter.—I have a Richmond paper of the 22d—extracts from which are not forwarded as it is presumed you have seen it"—ALS (telegram sent), DNA, RG 94, War Records Office, Army of the Potomac; telegram received (at 1:00 P.M.), *ibid.*, RG 108, Letters Received. *O.R.*, I, xlii, part 3, 1062.

1864, DEC. 21, noon. Maj. Gen. Edward O. C. Ord to USG. "A Deserter in this morning from 28th Georgia—Colquitts Brigade—Hokes Division, states that one Brigade Kirtlands—left for North Carolina yesterday A. M. Fields—Kershaws Bartons—and remainder of Hokes Divisions—Still in my Front—the Rebels are granting furloughs two to every hundred men—"—ALS (telegram sent), DNA, RG 107, Telegrams Collected (Unbound); telegram received (at noon), *ibid.*, RG 108, Letters Received. *O.R.*, I, xlii, part 3, 1054. On the same day, Ord telegraphed to Lt. Col. Theodore S. Bowers. "The following despatch has just been recd from Bermuda. To ASST ADJT GENL. I have the honor ~~to report~~ to report the arrival of part of the Staff of 2d Brigade 1st Infty Div army of West Va with about fifteen Enlisted men in Charge of Horses & Baggage belonging to Brigade Hd Qurs. We are in advance of Colonel Wm. B. Curtis Comdg 2d Brigade and his Command and await your orders. Signed H. R. McCORD A A A G—' I know nothing of the force Referred to"—Telegram received (at 6:40 P.M.), DNA, RG 108, Letters Received. *O.R.*, I, xlii, part 3, 1054. On the same day, Bowers telegraphed to Ord. "The troops you refer to are the advance of reinforcements from the valley now on the way with orders to report to you. When they get here you are expected with a part of them to relieve the troops recently sent from here to Bermuda Hundred and let them come back—"—Telegram received, DNA, RG 393, Army of the Potomac, Cav. Corps, Telegrams Received; copies, *ibid.*, RG 108, Letters Sent; DLC-USG, V, 45, 71, 107. *O.R.*, I, xlii, part 3, 1054. On Dec. 22, Ord twice telegraphed to USG. "Deserters from Calkitt's brigade say that the balance of the Division (Hoke's) was to have left this morning for the South ~~and w~~ or West they went thro' Richmond avoiding the pontoon bridge."—ALS (telegram sent), DNA, RG 107, Telegrams Collected (Unbound); telegram received, *ibid.*, RG 108, Letters Received. *O.R.*, I, xlii, part 3, 1060. "Another brigade of Hoke's Division ha~~ves~~ been sent south and was met on the cars south of Petresburg by a deserter now here. I have a deserter here who has been a long time at Charlotte N. C. and can give you valuable information about that place and Columbia N. C."—ALS (telegram sent), DNA, RG 107, Telegrams Collected (Unbound); *ibid.*, RG 393, Army of the Potomac, Cav. Corps, Telegrams Received; telegram received, *ibid.*, RG 108, Letters Received. *O.R.*, I, xlii, part 3, 1060. On Dec. 25, Brig. Gen. John W. Turner, chief of staff for Ord, telegraphed to USG. "Gen Ferrero reports as follows—Huntons Brigade of Pickets Division left for ~~Georgeville~~ordonsville on Friday morning last by Rail—13 men reported frozen to death on the cars six 6 Deserters came in during the night. The 31st u. s. c. t. has returned also the balance of Col Wells Brig"—ALS (telegram sent), DNA, RG 107, Telegrams Collected (Unbound); telegram received (at 10:20 A.M.), *ibid.*, RG 108, Letters Received. *O.R.*, I, xlii, part 3, 1076.

1864, DEC. 23.   USG endorsement. "Approved and respectfully forwarded to the Secretary of War."—ES, DNA, RG 94, ACP, K20 CB 1869. Written on a letter of Nov. 22 from Lt. Col. William T. Clark, Louisville, to Secretary of War Edwin M. Stanton recommending Capt. Kilburn Knox for promotion to bvt. maj.—ALS, *ibid.* Knox was so promoted, to date from July 22, the date of death of Maj. Gen. James B. McPherson, on whose staff he had served.

1864, DEC. 23.   USG endorsement. "Respectfully forwarded to the Hon. Secy. of War with the remark that the Lt. Genl. is of the opinion that there is much merit in the inventions of Col King, and he would recommend that a Board be appointed to investigate and report upon its merits and adaptability to the service"—ES, DNA, RG 94, Letters Received, 2314W 1864. Written on a report of Dec. 21 of a board of officers headed by Lt. Col. Frederick T. Dent examining "cavalry raiding equipment" invented by Lt. Col. Walter King, 4th Mo. Cav.—DS, *ibid.* On Dec. 20, King, City Point, wrote to Brig. Gen. John A. Rawlins asking that his inventions receive consideration.—ALS, *ibid.*

1864, DEC. 23–27.   USG endorsement. "Respy. forwarded to the Sec of War. It appears that 2d Lieut George de Charms, 54th Regt Ohio Vols. was killed at the battle of Pittsburg Landing while in command of his Company, and that his mother is not able to recieve pension because he was not mustered into the service—I therefore request that the necessary order be issued recognizing him as properly in the service, which will enable the mother to draw the pension. In the early stages of the service—and especially in the West—mustering was little understood, and hence mistakes of this kind occured frequently"—Copy, DLC-USG, V, 58. Written on a letter of Brig. Gen. Thomas Kilby Smith recommending a pension for the mother of 2nd Lt. George de Charms, 54th Ohio.—*Ibid.*

1864, DEC. 23.   USG endorsement. "James H. Burdick (then) 1st Lieutenant of the 1st Mich. Battery, served as Act'g. Ordnance Officer in the Dis't. of the Tenn. for over 3 months, whilst I was in Command, and discharged the duties of position with promptness, fidelity and ability. His habits were exemplary and his conduct that of an honorable, intelligent and efficient Officer   I cordially recommend him to the favorable consideration of the Government."—ES, DNA, RG 59, Letters of Application and Recommendation. Written on a letter of Dec. 3 from Capt. James H. Burdick, 1st Mich. Light Art. and act. chief of art., Dept. of the Gulf, New Orleans, to Brig. Gen. John A. Rawlins. "I have the honor to state that my term of service as a commissioned officer Vols expires in January next, and that I purpose making application to be appointed Military Storekeeper of Ordnance. You will recollect me as Lieut Burdick who had the charge of the Ordnance for General Grants Army whilst operating against Vicksburg in 1863, and I respectfully request that you do me the honor to send me such recommendation as to my qualifications for the position alluded to as you deem me worthy of, and if proper, would also respectfully request that you ask the Lieut General Comdg the U S. Army for some such testimonial as he may from recollection of me think me deserving of. I would say further that I have served as an Acting Ordnance Officer for over two and one half years and from my experience think I am competent to discharge my duties as a Military Store Keeper with credit to myself and to the satisfaction of the Ordnance Department."—ALS, *ibid.* On Oct. 4, 1871, Burdick, Yankton, Dakota Territory, sent this letter to Secretary of State Hamilton Fish in connection with his application for the post of secretary of Dakota Territory.—ALS, *ibid.* On the same day, Burdick wrote to USG. "I have the honor to state that, having been informed that a vacancy would probably soon occur in the office of Secretary of Dakota Territory, I have today addressed the Honorable Secretary of State, expressing my willingness to accept an appointment to that office if by your favorable consideration and continued friendly confidence I should be so honored. You will probably remember me as Acting Ordnance Officer under your command in the Department of the Tennesee in your operations against Vicksburg, and since the war as a resident in Alabama. Some papers are submitted with my letter to the Hon. Secretary of State."—ALS, *ibid.* On Dec. 19, 1872, Burdick was confirmed as marshal of Dakota Territory.

1864, DEC. 23.   Maj. Gen. Henry W. Halleck to USG. "In view of the complaint and remonstrance of Mr. Tassara, Envoy Extraordinary and Minister Plenipotentiary of Her Catholic Majesty, the Secretary of War directs that the military authorities of the United States conducting flags of truce, will neither receive nor convey any communication whatever, issued from or directed to any Spanish authority or agent, unless the same shall be unsealed."—LS, DNA, RG 108, Letters Received. *O.R.*, I, xlii, part 3, 1062.

1864, DEC. 24.   USG endorsement. "Approved and respectfully returned" —ES, DNA, RG 94, ACP, L516 CB 1863. Written on a lengthy letter of Feb. 20 from Brig. Gen. Michael K. Lawler to U.S. Senator Lyman Trumbull of Ill. requesting promotion to bvt. maj. gen.—ALS, *ibid.* Lawler was not promoted during the war.

1864, DEC. 24.   Brig. Gen. Richard Delafield, chief of engineers, to USG. "I transmit herewith for your information a Map of the Eastern portion of the Military Department of N. Carolina, prepared in this Department."— Copy, DNA, RG 77, Letters Sent.

1864, DEC. 24.   Special Orders No. 156, Armies of the U.S. "The Seige Train of the Armies operating against Richmond, commanded by Bvt. Brig. Gen. H. L. Abott is hereby permanently attached to the Army of the Potomac and will report accordingly."—Copies, DLC-USG, V, 57, 62, 63, 64. *O.R.*, I, xlii, part 3, 1070.

1864, DEC. 25.   To Maj. Gen. Edward O. C. Ord. "Has Miss Humphreys and the lady with her been permitted to pass the rebel lines? There are two more ladies here and two young men with the passes of the President wishing to go through. There does not seem to be any necessity of sending them up if they are not going to be received."—ALS (telegram sent), CSmH; copies, DLC-USG, V, 45, 71, 107; DNA, RG 108, Letters Sent. At 12:50 A.M. (time or date possibly incorrect), Ord telegraphed to Brig. Gen. John A. Rawlins. "The enemy have treated the application of Miss Humphreys and friend to pass into Richmond—with contemptuous silence—I have no idea they will be allowed to go and I think no other appl similar applications should be allowed on this front—"—ALS (telegram sent), *ibid.*, RG 107, Telegrams Collected (Unbound); telegram received, *ibid.*, RG 108, Letters Received.

1864, DEC. 26.   To Secretary of War Edwin M. Stanton. "The Richmond papers of today contain the following from Gordonsville—'The following official telegram was recd at the War Dept Saturday night. Head Qrs Army N Va Dec 24th—HON JAMES A SEDDON—Genl Fitz Lee reports that the force which attacked Lomax yesterday consisted of two Divisions of the Enemys Cavalry under Genl Torbert—Genl Lomax was posted across the Madison turnpike two and a half miles from Gordonsville the enemy was handsomely repulsed and retired about three (3) P M leaving some of his dead on the field. He travelled too rapidly last night to engage his rear having passed Jacks Shop—twelve miles from Gordonsville one hour after dark. Thirty two prisoners captured at Liberty Mills on the 22d being unable to Keep up on their retreat were liberated—Genl Lomaxs loss was slight. Signed R E LEE—From South Western Va—The following official dispatch was recd at the War Dept Saturday night Head Qrs Army N Va Dec 24th—HON JAS A SEDDON. Genl Breckinridge reports that the enemy after having been roughly handled in the engagements of Saturday and Sunday near Marion many having been Killed and wounded gained possession of Saltville during the night of the 20th—The garrison retreated up Rice Valley—His advance arrived at Daylight on the 21st and the enemy retired that night & the morning 22d towards Hectors Gap. They are being pursued Our troops are bearing the fatigue and exposure with great cheerfulness the damage to the Salt works can soon be repaired. Many bridges and Depots on the railroad have been burned—Signed R E LEE—From South Western Va—Interesting Particulars of the raid—The Lynchburg Virg[in]ian of the 22d ult has from an authentic source the following account of the raid in southwestern Va—on monday the 12th the enemy Since ascertained to consist of Genl Stonemans and Burbridge[s] forces concentrated at Beans station advanced eastward vaughn was at greenville & dukes brigade at Rogersville The movement was rapid & duke being in their route was forced back to Kingsport where on the 13th he was a attacked & suffered a repulse the enemy thus got ahead of Vaughn & on the morning of the 14th he entered Abingdon Duke falling back towards Abingdon—Genl Breckinridge at Wytheville apprised of the advance at once began to concentrate his troops for the defence of Saltville on the afternoon of the 14th he started by train for that point himself [a]rriving at Glade Springs that night late He barely escaped capture & reached Saltville next morning—The enemy reaching Glade Spring shortly after daylight on the 15th the force of the enemy after leaving Abingdon divided into two columns one threatening Saltville the other going to Glade Spring and towards Wytheville at three P M the enemy entered Marion twenty six (26) miles west of Wytheville & despatched a force which was sent southeast toward the Lead mines meanwhile Genl Vaughn leaving Bristol to his left arrived in front of Marion supposing the main column had gone to the Lead mines pursued the detachment with his main force leaving Col Gillespie with the remainder of his command at Marion—On the morning of the 16th at daylight Col Gillespie was attacked repulsed retreating towards Wytheville sixteen (16) miles distant. There were no troops at this point—The rail road superintendent having failed to send them from Dublin for want of cars also but a portion of the stores could be removed from Wytheville. The retreat of Gillespie was so rapid and the pursuit of the enemy so close that the former arrived at Wytheville at half past eleven A M & passed through the town in a stampede all efforts to rally them failing the enemy appeared at 1 P M videttes approaching very cautiously—Major Johnson a a G of Breckenridges staff with a half dozen officers & men remained & by standing picket at the west end of the town in sight of the Yankees detained them from coming in for two (2) hours—The town was by this time cleared— At three P M Maj Johnston having withdrawn to the east of the town Genl Gillum sent in a flag of truce which Maj Johnston recd through Capt Sample & Maj McMahon of Genl Breckinrdges staff. The unconditional surrender of the town was demanded with ~~guantee~~ guarantee of security to private property & Citizens—Maj Johnston replied agreeing to surrender the town on these conditions provided he was allowed half an hour in which to withdraw his forces After much deliberation Gen Gillums declined to give the time asked but to respect private property & citizens—Maj Johnston having thus gained more than an hour for the retreating & cavalry ~~ret~~ & trains withdrew his forces six (6) all told & came on towards Dublin—The enemy adhered to his terms & disturbed no private property—When Gillum

found out the ruse which had been practiced upon him he was more amused
than incensed—On saturday morning before daylight the enemy after burning the Rail Road Depot Ordnane & Medical & ~~bu materials~~ buildings retreated as he came first sending a detachment of two hundred to the Lead
mines. Genl Vaughen was at this important point but believing exaggerated
reports of the enemys strength retreated on his approach—[T]he damage
to the mines was slight & can soon be repaired. The enemy retired towards
Marion doubtless to effect a junction with the main force & capture Saltville
but at last accounts this important point was safe & Genl Breckinridge has
repulsed the enemy on several accasions—The Raid is ably conducted the
force moving rapidly & doing but little pillaging—From Wilmington—Wilmington Dec 24th   Seventy (70) vessels of the enemys fleet are reported
off Fort Fisher this morning   no demonstrations of landing yet. The weather
is mild and WNW. A. Yankee Gun Boat grounded last night fnear Ft Fisher
& was blown up by the enemy. Second Dispatch. Wilmington Dec 24th—
The Yankee Gunboats were repulsed six miles below Ft Branch on the Roanoke River on friday. Col Whitford was seriously wounded. The fight is
expected to be renewed this morning."—Telegram received (at 11:10
P.M.), DNA, RG 107, Telegrams Collected (Bound).

1864, Dec. 28.   To Secretary of War Edwin M. Stanton. "The Richmond
papers contain the following items from Georgia—'The latest official advices from Georgia indicate that sherman has already followed up the occupation of savannah by sending a force of cavalry artillery and infantry upon
an expedition whose destination can only be guessed at from the direction
in which it has moved. These troops are reported to have gone towards the
Altamaha river & we shall no doubt next hear that they have crossed that
stream and are moving to south western Georgia in quest of the prisoners
of war who were supposed to be at Andersonville. Shermans programme
for his grand campaign northward seems to be no secret   he will start from
Port Royal and move straight on Branchvil[le] the point of Junction between the Georgian & Carolinian railroads   he then proposes to follow the
main lines of railroad towards Virginia stealing & murdering as much as
he can by the way   All very fine but if sherman proposes Lee disposes.
From Wilmington—The following official dispatch was recd last night.
Wilmington Dec 27th 3 P M   to His Excy the Presidt of the Confederate States. The enemy has reembarked under cover of his fleet   his
movement is not developed   I have visited Fort Fisher & find the damage
slight except the buildings not necessary for defence   only two guns disabled   The works remaining indicate that the bombardment was very heavy
Maj Genl Whiting Comdg the Defences at the mouth of the river Col Lamb
Comd'g the fort & the officers & men composing the garrison deserve especial commendation for the gallantry efficiency & fortitude displayed under
very trying circumstances   signed Braxton Bragg—From south western
Va—The Lynchburg Virginian has the following additional in relation to
the Capture of the salt works announced officially on yesterday—We had

been led to hope that these important works were safe but the sources from which their reported Capture comes leaves us no room to doubt its correctness they were occupied by the enemy on tuesday the twentieth and held by them as is stated until thursday when they retreated towards Bristol— We learn that the place was held by about two hundred Reserves under Col Preston the most of whom escaped Capture the works are reported to be but little damaged & we understand that persons who have visited them since the occupation by the enemy think they can be put in working order again by the first of February—A large quantity of salt already gotten out was destroyed and all [t]he buildings at the place were burned several pieces of artillery were also captured by them but they got but little else of any Kind. Genl Breckenridge at the last accounts was at saltville preparing to follow the enemy on [t]heir retreat beyond Continued skirmishing with their Rear Guard no further fighting has taken place than that already reported—A Gentleman who passed over the [r]ailroad from Bristol to Glade [s]pring after the enemy advanced says the bridges between these places are all burned but that the track [i]s uninjured"—Telegram received (at 7:05 P.M.), DNA, RG 107, Telegrams Collected (Bound); *ibid.*, Telegrams Collected (Unbound). *O.R.*, I, xliv, 825–26.

1864, DEC. 28–31.   USG endorsement. "Respy, forwarded to the Sec of War, with the earnest recommendation that Capt D D Wiley, Depot Commissary at City Point, who is a most efficient and deserving officer, may be breveted a major from the 1st day of August"—Copy, DLC-USG, V, 58. Written on a letter of Dec. 23 from Lt. Col. Michael R. Morgan recommending a bvt. promotion for Capt. Daniel D. Wiley.—*Ibid.* On Dec. 12, President Abraham Lincoln had nominated Wiley as bvt. maj. as of Aug. 1.

1864, DEC. 29.   To Brig. Gen. Joseph D. Webster. "Please relieve Capt Sidney A. Stockdale, Provost Marshal, and order him to report to me in person."—Copies, DLC-USG, V, 45, 71, 107; DNA, RG 108, Letters Sent.

1864, DEC. 29, 12:15 P.M.   Maj. Gen. George G. Meade to USG. "There was considerable firing principally mortars along the line of the 9th corps yesterday it being kept up till 9. P. M. Twenty deserters from the enemy are this morning reported, but no information of any importance received from them.—"—ALS (telegram sent—at 12:30 P.M.), DNA, RG 94, War Records Office, Army of the Potomac; telegram received, *ibid.*, RG 108, Letters Received. *O.R.*, I, xlii, part 3, 1092.

1864, DEC. 30.   USG endorsement approving an expedition.—American Art Association, Anderson Galleries, Inc., Sale No. 407, Jan. 17–18, 1934, p. 79. Written on a letter of Dec. 29 from Col. George H. Sharpe to Lt. Col. Theodore S. Bowers discussing an expedition to Fredericksburg to capture C.S.A. Lt. Col. John S. Mosby.—*Ibid.*

1864, DEC. 30. Maj. Samuel Breck, AGO, to USG. "I have the honor to acknowledge the receipt of a communication from Robert M Scott Co "B" 5th U. S. Cav. formerly of Co "K" 8th Pa Res. Cav. forwarded by you to this office the 29th ulto—stating that his term of service has expired, and requesting to be furnished with his Descriptive List, to enable him to be mustered out of service. In reply I have the honor to inform you that, the records on file in this Office, show that this man enlisted in the Regular Army, Novr 3d 1862, to serve three years. Also, that he deserted from Baltimore Md. Dec 9th 1862. On the muster roll of Company "B" 5th U. S. Cav for the months of Sepr and October 1864, he is reported 'Joined from General Depot Sepr 24th 1864'. From these reports it appears that this soldier, has to make good the time lost by desertion, (nearly two years) and his term of service will not therefore expire until some time in the year 1867."—LS, DNA, RG 108, Letters Received.

1864, DEC. 30. Capt. George K. Leet to Lt. Col. Theodore S. Bowers. "Our Scouts visited the Old man last night and returned this morning, with report, that reinforcements, supposed to be part of One Division and a Brigade from another, were sent from Richmond to Hood on Wednesday last. Early remains at Staunton, with no change in his numbers."—ALS (telegram sent), DNA, RG 107, Telegrams Collected (Bound). Printed (probably incorrectly) as sent by Maj. Gen. Henry W. Halleck to Bowers in *O.R.*, I, xlii, part 3, 1101.

1864, DEC. 30. Maj. Gen. Winfield S. Hancock to Carr B. White, Georgetown, Ohio. "I have been furnished with a copy of your letter to the Adjutant General declining the appointment of Colonel in the First Corps. I regret that you did not feel at liberty to accept the appointment. It was made solely on the recommendation of Lieut. General Grant who asked that you might be made the senior Colonel of the Corps in order that you might have command of the First Brigade. General Grant stated that the application was made by him without your knowledge. The appointment was made as requested by General Grant and had you concluded to accept I think your prospect for further promotion would have been unusually good."— Copy, DNA, RG 393, 1st Army Corps, Letters Sent.

1864, DEC. 31, 9:00 P.M. To Secretary of War Edwin M. Stanton. "The augusta papers Say that the Georgia [C]entral Railroad will be completed [t]hrough to Social Circle by the fifteenth of January the rest of the road from there to [A]tlanta is so badly used that unless the Govt will furnish men and means it [c]annot be repaired. A Soldier of fFields Division complains bitterly in a letter to the Editor of the Examiner of the suffering among the men for want of clothing. He says many of us are almost destitute of pants. The Enquirer says there is a very general murmuring in private letters from the Army because of their failure to receive their pay. A Telegram from Genl Beauregards says it is reported [t]hat the column of the enemy which proceeded as far as the Altamaha bridge on the Gulf Railroad has returned to Savannah. The Augusta Constitutionalist [l]earns on good authority that a large number of the galvanized Yankees who recently took the oath of allegiance to [t]he Confederate Govt Joined our Army and were sent to Savannah have gone over to [t]he enemy. Before deserting our ranks they conspired to Kill their officers and ~~going~~ in a body to the enemy but the plot was discovered and seven of the ringleaders were tried and shot. The others returned to Savannah. From Wilmington—Wilmington North Carolina Dec 30th 1864—Genl Bragg has issued a congratulatory order on the defeat of [t]he enemys grand armada before Wilmington paying a merited compliment to Genls Whiting and Kirkland Col Lamb and officers and men engaged. The enemys attack the first day lasted five hours on the second day seven hours firing altogether over twenty thousand shots from fifty nine vessels. The Confederates responded with six hundred and sixty two shots the first day and six hundred the second. Our loss is three Killed and fifty five wounded. The ground in front and rear of the fort is covered with shells & is torn in deep pits—Two guns in [t]he fort burst two were dismounted by ourselves and two by the enemys fire yet the fort is unhurt—Scouts report [t]hat Butler made a speech at Newbern [s]aying he would eat his christmas dinner in Wilmington—It is reported that a part of a negro regiment and [t]he fifth regt of regulars were lost in [t]he gale. The Expedition up Roanoke river has returned   Signed P W A—"—Telegram received (on Jan. 1, 1865, 10:10 A.M.), DNA, RG 107, Telegrams Collected (Bound).

1864, Dec. 31.   USG endorsement. "The accompanying papers are respectfully submitted to the Secretary of War. The Mailboats were so encumbered with private freight that it became necessary to prohibit their carrying any. The consequence is that large amounts of Express and other freight and goods for the Army have accumulated at Washington and Fort Monroe which cannot be brought forward. Sutlers are now unable to bring forward their supplies as the number of schooners at City Point is limited to the capacity of the harbor. I believe it would be to the interest of the service to permit a couple of vessels to run on private account under close military regulations. If the War Department would prefer having nothing to do with the subject, and have no objections I will cause a line to be established that will supply the want herein mentioned"—ES, DNA, RG 107, Irregular Series, Letters Received. Written on papers concerning a proposal by Hinckley and Kidder, Boston, to establish a steamboat line between Washington and City Point.—*Ibid.*

1864, Dec. 31.   Oliver Cox to USG. "I had the honor some months ago to address you regarding a plan for *Secret Communication* which I claim as the inventor. By your direction I submitted it to Capt Leet who has, as he has informed me, brought it to your notice through Col Babcock. The other week I had an interview with Col Geo. H. Sharpe A P. M. G. at his request,

at which time I entered into a full explination of the system; and I also sub-
mited another Invention of mine for Signaling from an enemy's camp or
teritory, the original papers of both plans being now in the possession of
Col Sharpe. If either one or both of these have any merit and can be used
to the advantage of the Govermt. the knowledge of which will be a source of
great satisfaction to me. All I wish is an Acknowledgement of their merits if
any they have, from under *your own* signature which favor I doubt not you
will grant. Please address *No- 170 K st Washington D. C.*"—ALS, DLC-
USG, I, B. On Feb. 5, 1865, Col. George H. Sharpe endorsed this letter
with a statement that he had successfully used the cipher devised by Cox
but had not tested the signal system.—AES, *ibid.* On Feb. 6, Lt. Col. Theodore S. Bowers endorsed this letter. "Respectfully returned to Mr Cox. and
attention invited to the endorsements hereon, as the only report that can be
made on the subject at present. Gen. Grant has not had leisure to give these
ciphers a personal examination, but has confidence in the judgement of Col.
Sharpe."—AES, *ibid.* On Jan. 28, 1867, Cox wrote to USG concerning his
invention of a substance which would cause enemy gunpowder to explode
unexpectedly.—ALS, DNA, RG 156, Correspondence Concerning Inventions. On Jan. 30, USG endorsed this letter. "Respectfully refered to the
Chief of Ordnance."—AES, *ibid.*

[1864?].   USG note. "Direct Adj. Gen. authorize Gen. Hartranft to delay
departing for duty until further orders."—Stan. V. Henkèls, Catalogue No.
1194, June 8, 1917, p. 22.

[1865?].   "A friend of the family" to USG. "I make thus bold to appeal to
your Kindness of heart in behalf of two young friends who are Strill Prisonrs
of War, Lieut James D Gale of Huger Battery Co D of Norfolk Va who is
at Johnsons Island Block 11 Co 23 and Private Ashland C. Gales of same
at Point Lookout Md Co A. 4 Division. I make this appeal particularly in
behalf of the Mother who is in dilicate health and wishes to see her Sons
before she dies. I am satisfied that all that is necessary for you to know is
the facts to move your sympathies. In consideration of their youth & other
circumstances for which they are not responsible will you not have them
released? I doubt not you will"—AL, DNA, RG 109, Prisoners' Oaths and
Paroles, Johnson's Island.

1865, [JAN.].   U.S. Senator Charles Sumner of Mass. to USG introducing
Auguste Laugel.—Auguste Laugel, "A Frenchman's Diary in our Civil-
War Time," *The Nation*, 75, No. 1936 (Aug. 7, 1902), 108.

1865, JAN. 1.   To Brig. Gen. Joseph K. Barnes, surgeon gen. "Upon investigation I find that neither the Western Metropolis or Ben De Ford are
in the James River   I learn that both boats went to Alexandria several days
ago under orders from the Medical Dept"—Telegram received (at 5:30
P.M.), DNA, RG 107, Telegrams Collected (Bound); copies, *ibid.*, RG

108, Letters Sent; DLC-USG, V, 46, 71, 107. On Dec. 31, 1864, 10:30
A.M., Barnes telegraphed to USG. "If the hospital transports western Me-
tropolis & Ben Deford Can be spared will you please order them to report
to Maj Genl sherman at savannah for transfer of sick & wounded to N Y
These steamships were taken for an urgent military necessity on Dec 9th
by Maj Genl Butler & are supposed to have returned to Fortress Monroe"—
Telegram received, DNA, RG 107, Telegrams Collected (Unbound); *ibid.*,
RG 108, Letters Received.

1865, JAN. 2, 12:30 P.M.   Maj. Gen. Henry W. Halleck to USG. "A pre-
tended deserter reports that Lee has constructed a dam on the James river
by means of which he expects to inundate a part of your works. I did not see
him so as to learn any of the particulars of his story."—ALS (telegram
sent), DNA, RG 107, Telegrams Collected (Bound); telegram received,
ibid.; *ibid.*, RG 108, Letters Received. *O.R.*, I, xlvi, part 2, 11.

1865, JAN. 3.   Bvt. Brig. Gen. James Gwyn to USG. "Your telegram is
received and will be attended to; Wrote Miss Redden on the subject today"
—ALS (telegram sent—misdated 1864), DNA, RG 107, Telegrams Collected (Unbound).

1865, JAN. 4, 6:00 P.M.   Maj. Gen. Philip H. Sheridan to USG. "I transmit the following information, obtained from deserters ~~who~~ that left Richmond last Wednesday [*Dec. 28*], and just arrived at this place—it may
corroborate information which you have already recd—Gordon', Pegram' &
Grimes', Divisions went from the valley to Petersburg, and went into the
trenches—Pegram came out to Gordonsville when the Cavly was in that
vicinity—then returned to Richmond, and all three (3) of the Div: went
south of Richmond—Whartons Division is at Fishers ville, between Waynesboro, and Stanton—Rosser is at Lexington—Lomax on the Rapidan River—
The Div: ~~which~~ that went south lost very heavily by desertion—It is reported
that there is about (2) two months supplies in Richmond, and that they
are preparing for a siege, and that the supplies coming are Flour and Bacon
and that they are all coming from the south—"—ALS (telegram sent),
DNA, RG 107, Telegrams Collected (Unbound); telegram received, *ibid.*;
ibid., Telegrams Collected (Bound); (at 6:55 P.M.) *ibid.*, RG 108, Letters
Received. *O.R.*, I, xlvi, part 2, 36.

1865, JAN. 5, 10:45 A.M.   President Abraham Lincoln to USG. "Richard
T. Jacob, Lieutenant Governor of Kentucky, is at the Spotswood-House in
~~Richmont~~ Richmond under an order of Gen. Burbridge not to return to Ken-
tucky—Please communicate leave to him to pass your lines, and come to me
here at Washington."—ALS (telegram sent), DNA, RG 107, Telegrams
Collected (Bound); telegram received (at 11:04 A.M.), *ibid.*, RG 108,
Letters Received. *O.R.*, II, viii, 23. Lincoln, *Works*, VIII, 198. See *ibid.*,
pp. 120, 182–83, 222; *SED*, 38-2-16.

1865, JAN. 5.   Brig. Gen. John A. Rawlins to Asst. Secretary of War Charles A. Dana. "The Richmond papers of today contain the following items—'Sherman's movements; from the following telegrams, received on Monday night, it will be seen that Sherman has crossed the Savannah River and is moving northward towards Charleston. Charleston, Jany 2d 65. The enemy have landed in force on the South Carolina side of the Savannah River, and are driving in our pickets towards Hardeeville.' W. J. HARDEE Hardeeville is a station on the Charleston and Savannah Railroad, twenty (20) miles from Savannah. Shermans present objective point is Branch-ville, the point of junction, on the Charleston and Savannah, with the Au-gusta R. R. We have heard no estimate of his forces but presume he has been reinforced by Foster's command from Port Royal and perhaps by all the Yankee troops from Morris Island and thereabouts. We infer, from what is said by the Yankee papers, that he has left only a brigade of Infan-try in Savannah which with the assistance of the Navy he thinks will be able to hold the city. Genl. R. S. Ripley has been ordered to the Army of Tennessee. The Georgia militia after nobly sustaining the State passed through Augusta on the 28th of December. Wilmington Jany 4th 1865 Late news from Newbern & Beaufort reports that Butler's army & Porters fleet have gone to Hampton Roads or perhaps to City Point. Only one thou-sand troops are at Moorehead City. It was reported at Newbern that the Yankees lost five vessels sunk and fifteen disabled, all their horses and artil-lery, and much ammunition and baggage, in the late gale. Only the disabled vessels were left at Beaufort. Hood heard from at last! An official despatch from Gen. Hood dated Corinth Dec. 26th was received at the War Depart-ment last night. Gen. Hood states that the army has recrossed the Tennessee River without material loss since the battle in front of Nashville.' Jackson Dec. 19th 64. Major Watson, just from Shreveport, reports the death of Maj. Gen. Price at Dooley's Ferry, Lafayette Co., Ark., on the first inst. of apoplexy. The gallant Semmes! This gallant and distinguished officer, com-mander of the famous "Alabama" arrived in Jackson, Miss. on 17th inst. He is in fine health and spirits and expresses the opinion that the war will soon end. He came by way of Texas, and is accompanied by his son. We may expect him in Richmond this week.' "—Telegram received (at 8:30 P.M.), DNA, RG 107, Telegrams Collected (Bound).

1865, JAN. 5, 12:50 P.M.   Col. Edward D. Townsend, AGO, to USG. "The Secretary of War desires you to forward as soon as convenient copies of correspondence conducted by yourself on the subject of the following Resolution of the House of Representatives. Resolved, That, if not incom-patible with the public interest all communications in reference to the exchange of prisoners not heretofore published—be communicated to this House by the Secretary of War   Please acknowledge receipt"—Telegram sent, DNA, RG 107, Telegrams Collected (Unbound); telegram received, *ibid.*, RG 108, Letters Received. On the same day, Brig. Gen. John A. Rawlins telegraphed to Townsend. "Your telegram asking for copies of correspondence in reference to exchange of prisoners, just received. Genl Grant has gone to Fort Monroe but the matter will be attended to at once"—Telegram received, *ibid.*, RG 94, Letters Received, 8A 1865; *ibid.*, RG 107, Telegrams Collected (Unbound); copies, *ibid.*, RG 108, Letters Sent; DLC-USG, V, 46, 71, 107. On the same day, Rawlins wrote to Maj. Gen. Benjamin F. Butler. "The following communication has just been received by telegraph: . . . You will please forward to these Headquarters, at the earliest possible moment, all communications between yourself as Agent of Exchange, and Judge Ould, Agent on the part of the Confederacy, on the subject of exchange of prisoners, and especially in all matters touching the same referred to you from these Headquarters."—LS, DLC-Benjamin F. Butler.

On Jan. 11, Rawlins telegraphed to Maj. Gen. Edward O. C. Ord. "On the 5th inst Genl Butler was directed in a written communication to forward to these Head Quarters copies of all correspondence with the Rebels on the subject of exchange of prisoners—Has any progress been made towards furnishing this report—Have you any information on the subject" —Telegram received (at 11:00 A.M.), Ord Papers, CU-B. On the same day, Ord telegraphed to USG. "I have no information at all from Gen Butler or any other Source on the subject of Exchange of prisoners. I am informed by Lt Col Smith A A G here that this correspondence was entrusted to Capt. Puffer A D C he and it I presume are at Ft Monroe. Col Mulford is at Aikens. Will Call on you tonight or tomorrow"—Telegram received (at 6:20 P.M.), DNA, RG 108, Letters Received. On Feb. 5, Lt. Col. Theodore S. Bowers wrote to Lt. Col. John E. Mulford. "You will please furnish a full and detailed report to these Head Quarters of the action of Maj, Gen, B, F, Butler, in relation to the exchange of prisoners of War so far as you have any knowledge, of such action, together with your own action, during the time he had the matter in hand,"—Copies, DLC-USG, V, 46, 72, 108; DNA, RG 108, Letters Sent; USG 3.

1865, JAN. 6. To Asst. Secretary of War Charles A. Dana. "The Richmond papers of today have the following items—'Augusta Jany 5 1865. Kilpatrick has not crossed the Altamaha but is supposed to be on the Carolina side of the Savannah River—Hudson Virginia paper report that Forrest has been killed by one of his own men—A Yankee raid on the Mobile & Ohio R. R. tore up miles of the track near Varona. A private letter says that Genl Price is not dead—It is currently rumored here that Genl Hood is dead— From Charleston—Charleston Jany 5th.—No further movements of the enemy are reported today. His force is still concentrating and are assembling between Hardeeville and the Savannah River. There is no truth in their reported advance on Grahamville The reported deaths of Genls Hood and Forrest are not confirmed—From Savannah we learn that Genl Sherman is pursuing a very ~~concili~~ conciliatory policy towards the people in Savannah, and has issued a proclamation permitting planters to bring in their produce [as] usual, and holds out inducements for them to do so—This looks as if he feels perfectly secure and meant to make all the friends he could—The Charleston Mercury understands that Sherman has given [the] citizens of Savannah fifteen days to settle up their bank and other accounts which are to be balanced in Confederate Treasury notes. If this really is true, there will be but few open accounts in Savannah after the fifteen days of grace expires—Everybody & everybodys relation will be eager to square up at once. Gen Hood being now safely across the Tennessee beyond all doubt, we await with some interest the details of his future motions. Thomas will endeavor by all practicable means to prevent him if possible, but, delay him at all events from proceeding to Charleston, or any other point on the prospective line of Shermans march Whether it be the object of Hood to march to the defence of Charleston, remains to be seen. If such is his determination we may anticipate more severe fighting between the rival armies of Tennessee—Meanwhile Shermans march northward from Savannah does not appear to be making very rapid headway—Possibly the weather has been unpropitious, or other and more important causes have combined to impede his advance upon Charleston. We have nothing of interest from that quarter' "—Telegrams received (2—at 12:00 P.M.), DNA, RG 107, Telegrams Collected (Bound).

1865, JAN. 6. Maj. Gen. David Hunter, Washington, D. C., to USG. "Will you not ask Mr. Satnton to give me a command against wilmington? I will take fort fisher or leave my bones on the Sands."—Telegram received, DNA, RG 108, Letters Received. *O.R.*, I, xlvi, part 2, 53.

1865, JAN. 7. To President Abraham Lincoln. "In reply to your dispatch of this morning I have to state that Gen'l Griffin commanding 2nd Division 9th Army Corps telegraphs me that private Waterman Thornton one hundred seventy ninth (179) New York Volunteers was executed yesterday in accordance with sentence of a Genl Court Martial promulgated in Genl Orders number One (1) of date January 2nd from Head Qrs Army of the Potomac for desertion to the enemy"—Telegram received (on Jan. 8, 8:55 A.M.), DLC-Robert T. Lincoln; DNA, RG 107, Telegrams Collected (Bound); *ibid.*, Telegrams Collected (Unbound); copies, *ibid.*, RG 108, Letters Sent; DLC-USG, V, 46, 71, 107. On Jan. 6, 7:20 P.M., Lincoln had telegraphed to USG. "If there is a man at City-Point, by the name of Waterman Thornton who is in trouble about desertion, please have his case briefly stated to me & do not let him be executed meantime"—ALS (telegram sent), DNA, RG 107, Telegrams Collected (Bound); telegram received, *ibid.*, Telegrams Collected (Unbound); (on Jan. 7, 10:30 A.M.) *ibid.*, RG 108, Letters Received. Lincoln, *Works*, VIII, 203.

1865, JAN. 7. USG endorsement. "Respy returned to the A G. of the Army with report. The practice of arresting persons on suspicion of being deserters, and forwarding them to City Point without examination or evidence of desertion requires correction. Men are recd here daily who have been arrested upon the charge of desertion, taken to the Pro. Mar. who pays the fee allowed by law, and forwards the prisoners to this place without any examination (or evidence) or information in the case. After a thorough investigation here, perhaps requiring weeks the parties prove that they are civilians and have never been in the service. The detectives who arrested them, did so, simply to obtain the reward   More care on the part of the Pro. Marshals at the North would prevent many of these cases. I trust the attention of Gen Fry will be called to this subject; and that orders will be issued requiring Pro. Marshals to examine into the cases of every deserter recieved by them, and forward with each, notes of all facts relating to him that can be obtained. By this means, improper arrests can in most cases be prevented, or the parties making them punished"—Copy, DLC-USG, V, 58. Written on a letter of Nov. 27, 1864, from Henry Campbell and others, City Point, to President Abraham Lincoln stating that they had been wrongfully imprisoned as deserters. On Jan. 26, 1865, Brig. Gen. James B. Fry wrote to Brig. Gen. John A. Rawlins. "I have the honor to acknowledge the receipt of a communication addressed to his Excellency the President, dated November 27th 1864, signed by Henry Campell, John Williams, John Brown, George Hawkins, Francis Conrad, John P. Robinson, James Ward. Matthew J. Boyce, Robert Whitman, C. F. Belmont and V. Simonson. stating that they had been 'wrongfully imprisoned on the suspicion of being deserters from the Army of the United States, and been detained from three to Six months without having been brought before any Military Court to investigate our respective cases,' with the report of Brig. Gen'l. W. R. Patrick, Provost Marshal General of the 'Armies operating against Richmond,' and the indorsement of Lieutenant General Grant, dated the 7th instant, directing my attention to the practice of arresting persons on suspicion of being deserters; and requesting that orders be issued, requiring Provost Marshals to examine into the case of every deserter received by them,—and forward with each, notes of all facts relating to him that can be obtained,—I have the honor herewith to inclose copies of such pargraphs of the regulations of this Bureau, as relate to this subject, and which District Provost Marshals have been instructed to observe. I also inclose a copy of a letter of instructions of this date, which has been sent to all Provost Marshals of Districts and Acting Assistant Provost Marshals General of States,—which it is hoped will accomplish the desired result. I shall endeavor to see that these provisions are strictly conformed to, and in the mean time, will take pains to investigate all special cases of the character complained of, that may be brought to my notice. Should the General-in-Chief deem it proper to suggest any further regulation or instruction in connection with this subject, I would be pleased to carry them into execution."—LS, DNA, RG 108, Letters Received. The enclosures are *ibid.*

1865, JAN. 7. Maj. Gen. John A. Dix to USG. "Respectfully referred to Lieut. Genl. Grant. The writer is very desirous of being permitted to go home by way of Petersburgh, I am confident his statement is true, and send

his application with my approval."—AES, OCIWHi. Written on an undated letter from M. D. McIntyre to Dix. "Having been induced to sacrifice
my property, and leave my home and friends under false pretenses, by a
man who has proved himself a *Villain*; I find myself in New York without
friends and money, and being an invalid of heart-disease; I am told by the
best of Physicians that I am liable to die at any moment. Having a daughter
eleven years old, I desire to return to my friends in Montgomery-Ala. that I
may die in peace, and leave my child with her relations. If you will sir,
obtain a permit through the War Department for the most speedy return,
I shall be under obligations which I can never repay, but I hope you will
receive a just reward from high Heaven who hears the cry of the Widow
and Orphan."—ALS, *ibid.*

1865, JAN. 7. Maj. Gen. George G. Meade, Philadelphia, to USG. "I
today saw Dr. Hewson who is attending on Genl. Robt. Tyler—He told me
he was very desirous that Genl Tyler should remain here for a few weeks
longer to undergo an operation, which he the Dr. believes will give him
great relief—Genl. Tylers condition is such that he has been reported fit to
travel and will therefore have to leave, unless he can be placed on some light
duty, or granted an extension of his leave.—I understand he will probably
apply to you to order him here for light duty, and I have written this note,
to give you my opinion that his case is a meritorious one, and that I think
he should be permitted to remain here for the purpose mentioned. Dr. Hewson is a private physician, and his certificate will not cover Genl. Tylers
remaining—The Post surgeon Dr. Neil reports him able to travel—but as
the operation proposed is to be executed by another—he is not called upon
to refer to it in his report & certificate—"—ALS (misdated 1864), Porter
Collection, USMA. *O.R.*, I, xlvi, part 2, 67. On the same day, Brig. Gen.
Robert O. Tyler, Philadelphia, wrote to Brig. Gen. John A. Rawlins asking
to be assigned to Maj. Gen. George Cadwalader and enclosing Meade's
letter.—*Ibid.*, pp. 66–67. On Jan. 18, Lt. Col. Theodore S. Bowers telegraphed to Tyler. "Report to Maj. Gen. Cadwallader for duty"—Copies,
DLC-USG, V, 46, 72, 107; DNA, RG 108, Letters Sent. *O.R.*, I, xlvi, part
2, 176.

1865, JAN. 7. William Cowan, Carbondale, Ill., to USG. "I appeal to you
to sustain me under your gen Orders No "10". I came to Memphis last Feb.
and took the oath under your Orders No "10" in good faith & have lived up
to the requirements of of said Orders. The Benefits of that order & the order
itself has been respected by all Commanders at Memphis, until Gen Dana
took Command of the Department of the Miss. In his special Orders No
"226" he requires all Rebel deserters to join the Enrolled Mititia of the
District of West Tenn, or leave the department; making no provisions for
those persons living in the department. The only alternative for them is to
join the Militia or be banished from their *Homes* during the War His
special orders No "226" Conflicts materially with *your Gen* Orders No

"10". I am now banned from my family & home (Memphis) by his special Orders No "226." Under no Circumstances will Gen Dana allow a Rebel deserter to live in Memphis save by Enrolling in the Militia. I respectfully ask you to modify Gen Dana's Special orders No "226" so as to protect me & others who have taken the oath under your Gen Order No "10" His (Gen Danas) special *orders* No "226" has greatly impaired the moral effect of your Orders No 10 Pardon me for troubling you with this Communication This is a matter of interest to me and all men of the same Class."—ALS, DNA, RG 108, Letters Received. On Feb. 7, Lt. Col. Theodore S. Bowers endorsed this letter. "Respectfully referred to Maj. Gen. Dana, comdg. Dept. of Mississippi, and special attention invited to par. 6 of G. O., No 10, Hdqrs. Milty Div of the Miss., dated Dec 12 1863, and also to marked paragraph of the accompanying S. O., No 3 from these Headqrs., by which it will be seen that it is the established policy of the U. S. Government to exempt all deserters delivering themselves up under said orders from military service, particularly 'forced military duty' or service endangering them to capture—All military commanders have been required to carry out in good faith the principles of these orders"—ES, *ibid.* On Feb. 14, Maj. Gen. Napoleon J. T. Dana, Memphis, endorsed this letter. "Respectfully returned. The number of Rebel deserters who have flocked to Memphis and other posts, has been so great that it has been a necessity to bring them under military surveillance or remove them. Enrolling them has served the double purpose of surveillance and of making them useful for local *defenses* in an extraordinary emergency such as has often existed at Memphis and may arise at other posts. The enclosed copy of an endorsement which has been approved by the Secretary of War, seems to justify the reasoning which has been applied to the solution of a very difficult problem. In order however to silence complaints and remove a seeming obstacle in the way of rebel desertion, the enclosed order No 23, has been issued, and attention is invited to it. A copy of previous order, No 11, on the subject and which was distributed in the country in this vicinity, is also enclosed and attention invited to it."—ES, *ibid.*

1865, JAN. 8. USG endorsement. "Respectfully referred to the Adjutant General of the Army. My time will not permit me to examine this new system of tactics, and it may be advisabl[e] if any proper board be in session that this system be referred to them for examination and report."—ES, DNA, RG 107, Letters Received from Bureaus. Written on a letter of Jan. 5 from William H. Morris, "Home Journal office," New York City, to USG. "I send by this mail a copy of my Infantry Tactics, which I respectfully request you to accept. In preparing this system of tactics my object has been to increase the efficiency of our troops by *systematising* the movements *now generally employed*—resulting from *necessity*—but which are *not* presented in any other work. On the ground that 'every thing which is superfluous is worse than useless,' I have omitted all movements and explanations which are unimportant *for the field*. The modifications consist chiefly in changing the march of subdivisions by their front to the march by their *flank*—the only practicable means in woods—and always *shortest* lines. I respectfully request a board of officers, composed of those who have had recent experience, to examine this system with a view to its adoption by our infantry. Considering that I have reduced the work to two small volumes; and that the commands have been shortened, and that the movements have been so simplified that new troops can master the subject in half the time required to learn the intricate and impracticable movements of former systems, I feel satisfied, if you can spare time from your many ~~important~~ responsible duties to give the subject attention, that you will see its importance."—ALS, *ibid.* On Jan. 5, Morris wrote a similar letter to Secretary of War Edwin M. Stanton, endorsed by USG on Jan. 13. "Respectfully returned to Maj. Gen'l. Halleck Chief of Staff. A similar communication from Gen'l. Morris was referred by me a few days since to the Adjutant General with the remark that my time did not permit me to examine into the merits of Morris' Tactics, but suggested that if a proper Board were in session in Washington, that the new system of Tactics be referred to them for investigation and report."—ES, *ibid.*, RG 108, Letters Received. On Feb. 4, Morris wrote to USG. "Some weeks ago I sent by mail, directed to you, a copy of my Simplified Infantry Tactics. As I have never heard of their having reached you, I send another set by Colonel Badeau, who was kind enough to say that he would deliver them in person. It is so generally admitted in our Armies that the prescribed tactics are unsuited to the wants of our service, that I can make the statement without the fear of refutation. The long marches our troops have to make; the wooded country they have to manoeuvre in, and the necessity for simple, rapid and practicable movements, have so modified the former systems, that the government tactics no longer teach the movements as *now* executed in the field. Learning these facts from my own experience, I have undertaken to supply the great want: —a system of tactics explaining the *present* usages of the service, and from which every thing superfluous and useless has been excluded. I have labored incessantly on this work for two years, in order to arrange it in the most concise, clear and progressive manner. I have published it at my own expense—which has been considerable, owing to the tabular arrangement of the 2d Volume. It therefore does not seem to me to be asking too much, to request that my system of tactics may be officially examined for the service. In answer to the presept, that 'it is always dangerous to change a system of tactics during a war' I can state that I do not seek to change the tactics, but I am trying to have a text-book ~~as knowle~~ authorised, which will teach tactics *as they now are*, in order to ensure uniformity among old and new troops. A large numbers of the State Adjutant Generals have already written to me expressing their approval of the work and desire to adopt it. They are satisfied that it will save much study, labor and time, and much increase the efficiency of their troops. The Herald, Times, Tribune, Army and Navy Journal, United service Journal, and other leading papers commend the book in the most unqualified terms. A number of general officers of distinction have written me letters expressing their warm approval. I select, from the many I have received, one from Major General G. K. Warren, commanding 5th Army Corps, who is considered one of the best practical tacticians in service. Major General Meade wrote me last month, that he had ordered a board of general officers to examine my book.—Should their report be favorable—which I cannot doubt—may I request that you will forward it to the War Department with your endorsement asking that it may be 'Authorised' for our Infantry?"—ALS, USG 3. On the same day, Morris wrote to Lt. Col. Adam Badeau asking him to deliver the letter to USG.—ALS, *ibid.* Morris, USMA 1851, resigned from the U.S. Army in 1854 to join his father in editing the *Home Journal.* He reentered the army as capt. and adjt. as of Aug. 20, 1861, and was appointed brig. gen. as of Nov. 29, 1862. Wounded at the battle of Spotsylvania on May 9, 1864, he was mustered out on Aug. 24, then wrote *Field Tactics for Infantry* (New York, 1864). On March 21, 1866, U.S. Senator Edwin D. Morgan of N. Y. wrote to USG urging Morris's reappointment to the U.S. Army, but no action followed.—LS, DNA, RG 94, ACP, M838 CB 1878.

1865, JAN. 8. To Maj. Gen. Napoleon J. T. Dana. "You will on receipt of this revoke par five of special order number ten dated Vicksburg Miss December first Eighteen sixty four. You will cause a copy of the order of revocation to be delivered to the family injured by implication and also one sent to these Hd Qrs"—Telegram received (press), DNA, RG 107, Telegrams Collected (Bound); copies, *ibid.,* RG 108, Letters Sent; DLC-USG, V, 46, 71, 107. The order read: "Anna Lum, of Vicksburg Miss, supposed to be a spinster, about twenty years of age, after applying for a pass in various quarters and being refused, clandestinely and by fraud left Vicksburg on 29th ulto., in company with one Clark Wright. The following is the report of the Provost Marshal on the affair; 'I learn from members of the Lum family, who have been examined by me this morning, that Miss Anna Lum left in company with and in charge of one Clark Wright, formerly a Colonel in the United States service, It appears that the family did not know she was going until a short time before she left, they knew she had been refused a pass, but Clark Wright came up in the evening with a carriage and stated to them that it was all right and Miss Lum could now go with him; that he then took her away in the carriage and that was the last they saw of her. The records in the pass office show that on 28th ulto., Clark Wright obtained a pass to Cairo, Wright either smuggled Miss Lum on board the steamer without a pass or must have inserted the name of his wife in said pass, and passed Miss Lum as such on board the boat. Both of the above named persons will be arrested wherever found within the limits of this command at any future time, and will be imprisoned at either Cairo, Columbus, Memphis, Vicksburg or Natchez, until report is made to these Head Quarters and orders received in regard to them."— Copy, DNA, RG 393, District of West Tenn. and Vicksburg, Special Orders. On Jan. 12, Dana wrote to USG. "I feel that I take great liberty in

presuming to address you personally but hope you will find room to pardon
it on the score that it is due to myself to make explaination   Yesterday I
received your telegraphic order to revoke my special order regarding Miss
Anna Lum and I immediately obeyed it,   I ask your indulgence now to
listen unofficially to my explaination so that your own mind may be convinced that I ought to have credit for the motive which actuated me   Until
a few day's ago I was not aware that the family possessed any peculiar
interest with yourself or General Rawlins   Early in October I made a Cavalry expedition to Fayette and Woodville,   on that trip letters were found
which went to prove that the two young grand-daughters of Mrs Lum held
communications with prisoners in the jail and correspondence with rebel
officers outside the lines,   The former fact I had before been aware of,   On
my return from that expedition I remonstrated sevearly, warmly, perhaps
harshly with the old lady about the conduct of the young women and cautioned her that she must take care of them or they would surely get into
trouble   I have no wish to give you all my impressions but merely to do
myself the justice to show you that I did not act whimsically or without
deliberation. Late in November I was compelled to banish five females from
the lines, one of themses a Mrs Foulkes; had previously been imprisoned in
New Orleans and was known to be one of a number who held traiterous
communications with the enemy and carried on a business of smuggling
letters and goods,—They were sent out across the Big Black by my Cavalry
force, when the expedition which destroyed the Mississippi Central Road
started,   Arriving at the Big Black Mrs Foulkes pleaded illness and wished
to be left behind whilst the other four went on, and afterward proposed to
Col. Osband, if allowed to return to make important disclosures and point
out important documents in Vicksburg, which the Provost Marshal was
informed of, and Col. Osband believed, seriously implicated and compromised one or both of the Miss Lums,   At this junction Miss Anna Lum
suddenly applied to the Pro. Mar. for a pass to go North. He therefore
wrote me a note stating that it was supposed Mrs Foulke would make disclosures concerning her and asked if she should have a pass,   I replied No.
not till Mrs F. came in; Miss Lum then came to my house saw my aAid,
and I refused her admittence to my office,   She then went across the street
to the lodging room of Capt. Dana another Aid who then came to me to
renew the solicitation for a pass which I refused,   I was informed that she
afterward went to the Post Commissary and made another attempt to get a
pass from him. You may then imagine my surprise when a couple of days
afterward it was reported to me that she had treated the Military authority
with contempt and had left the City in company with one Clark Wright in
defiance of it. I considered that if a proper vindication were not made by a
suitable punishment that all other females and all other males would be
encouraged to show a similar contempt for order and restraint"—Copy,
ibid., Dept. of Miss., Letters Sent. On Jan. 13, Dana, Memphis, telegraphed
to USG. "Your telegraph of Eighth is recd & has been fully complied with"—
Telegram received (press), *ibid.*, RG 107, Telegrams Collected (Bound).

On Jan. 23, USG wrote to Dana. "Acknowledges receipt of communication from Hd. Qrs. Dept. of Miss. dated Jany. 12th 1865. States that the order directed to be revoked was only objectionable so far as it reflected upon the chastity of the young lady effected. Does not expect personal relatives to be protected in wrong doing, if Miss Lum is guilty as charged, she should be punished as any other young lady guilty of like offence."—*Ibid.*, RG 393, Dept. of Miss., Register of Letters Received. See *PUSG*, 9, 77*n*–78*n*.

On Feb. 8, Lt. Col. Theodore S. Bowers twice wrote to Dana. "You will please direct that the real estate, buildings, and property of Mrs Ann Lum, of Vicksburg, Miss, in consideration of protection given her for the same by Lieutenant General Grant, while Major General in command of the Department of the Tennessee, and of her loyalty, be exempted from the operation of your order relating to the rates of rent in Vicksburg, Mississippi, of date September 24 1864, and signed by your then Provost Marshal; and you will permit Mrs Ann Lum to collect her rents as per agreements with her tenants at the time of and prior to the date of said order."— LS, DNA, RG 109, Union Provost Marshals' File of Papers Relating to Individual Civilians. "The enclosed printed copy of an order relating to the rates of rents in the City of Vicksburg, Miss, of date Sept, 24th 1864, issued by the then Provost Marshal of that place by your direction, has just come to the attention of the Lieutenant General It does not meet with his approval You will therefore cause its immediate revocation. Loyal persons, including those that have been disloyal but who have availed themselves of the Presidents Amnesty Proclamation, resident in the City of Vicksburg should be permitted the same priveledges in the rental of their property as if they resided in the Loyal States of the North, while the property of disloyal persons should be taken possession of and used or rented to the highest bidder for the benefit of the Government. Such was the practice in the Department of the Tennessee of which your Department formed a part."— Copies, DLC-USG, V, 46, 73, 108; DNA, RG 108, Letters Sent.

1865, JAN. 9.   USG endorsement. "Respectfully returned. Under existing regulations each Division in the Armies operating against Richmond is allowed one wagon for the exclusive purpose of carrying arms and armorer's tools. To furnish each regiment a wagon for this purpose is unnecessary and would add largely to the present cumbersome, but necessary trains, The appointment of an officer in each regiment as Ordnance Officer is impracticable. Each Company Commander now receives ten dollars a month for taking charge of Arms and other property, and it is the fault of the Regimental Commander if he is not held to a strict accountability."—ES, DNA, RG 94, 5640 1864. Written on a letter of Nov. 18, 1864, from Col. Llewellyn P. Haskell, 41st Colored, to Brig. Gen. Alexander B. Dyer, chief of ordnance, concerning surplus ordnance and ordnance stores.—ALS, *ibid.*

1865, JAN. 9.   USG endorsement. "Respectfully returned; with the remark that all permits for Embalming Surgeons within the lines of the

Armies operating against Richmond have been revoked and the Surgeons ordered without the lines"—ES, DNA, RG 94, Letters Received, 2195S 1864. Written on a sheaf of papers concerning charges of extortion against an embalmer, Dr. Richard Burr.—*Ibid.* On the same day, Lt. Col. Theodore S. Bowers wrote to Brig. Gen. Marsena R. Patrick, provost marshal. "The Lieut. Gen'l directs that all permits for Embalming Surgeons within the lines of the Armies operating against Richmond be immediately revoked, and that you will order the Surgeons with all their apparatus and Stock to proceed north without the lines of these Armies"—Copies, DLC-USG, V, 46, 71, 107; DNA, RG 108, Letters Sent. On the same day, Bowers issued Special Orders No. 7. "All embalming surgeons having been excluded from the lines of the Armies operating against Richmond, the friends and relatives of officers and soldiers are hereby notified that hereafter the bodies of officers and soldiers who die at general or base hospitals, can be embalmed without charge upon making personal application to the Chief medical officer of hospitals. Applications for the embalming of officers and soldiers who die at the division hospitals at the front, or on the feild of battle, must be made to the Medical Director of the Corps to which such officers or soldiers belonged."—Copies, DLC-USG, V, 57, 63, 64, 65. *O.R.,* I, xlvi, part 2, 76.

1865, JAN. 9.   Maj. Gen. Henry W. Halleck to USG. "A Bill, endorsed by yourself, Genl Meade, other Genl officers, & heads of Bureaus, was last year submitted to Congress by the Secty of War and favourably by the Mily committees, To regulate and equalize the rank and pay of Chiefs of the different Staff Depts. The enclosed Bill is a copy with the adition of the second *proviso* which seems necessary to prevent existing abuses. If approved by you please return with your endorsement, to by submitted to the Secty of War, with other recommendations."—ALS, DNA, RG 108, Letters Sent (Press). A copy of the bill is *ibid.,* Letters Received.

1865, JAN. 10.   Bvt. Maj. Gen. Henry J. Hunt to Brig. Gen. John A. Rawlins suggesting changes in the organization of the art. of the Army of the Potomac.—Copy (unsigned), DNA, RG 108, Letters Received. *O.R.,* I, xlvi, part 2, 83–88.

1865, JAN. 11.   USG endorsement. "Respectfully forwarded to the Adjutant General of the Army, with the request that the wihin named officers be ordered to their proper Command, if their services can be spared"—ES, DNA, RG 94, Letters Received, V2 1865. Written on a letter of Jan. 3 from Maj. Gen. Benjamin F. Butler requesting the reassignment of certain officers.—LS, *ibid.*

1865, JAN. 11.   Secretary of War Edwin M. Stanton to USG. "I return herewith the draft of an order proposed to be issued by you. It has my cordial approval"—ALS, DNA, RG 108, Letters Received.

1865, JAN. 11, 8:20 P.M.   Maj. Gen. Edward O. C. Ord to USG. "but one paper just received—have telegrapd to know the cause of non receipt of others—Only item it contains is . . ."—ALS (telegram sent, misdated 1864, ellipses in the original), DNA, RG 107, Telegrams Collected (Unbound).

1865, JAN. 12, 1:00 P.M.   To Asst. Secretary of War Charles A. Dana. "I would respectfully recommend Capt. Robt. N. Scott for the appointment of A. A. G. made vacant by the death of Maj. Perkins. Will you do me the favor to lay this matter before the President."—ALS (telegram sent), CSmH; telegram received (marked as sent at 12:15 P.M., received at 5:00 P.M.), DNA, RG 107, Telegrams Collected (Bound). On Jan. 13, 1:00 P.M., Dana telegraphed to USG. "No appointment will be made of an assistant adjutant General until Mr. Stanton returns. My impression is that there is no vacancy the appointment of Major Bowers having provided for this very place."—ALS (telegram sent), *ibid.*; telegram received, *ibid.*, RG 108, Letters Received.

1865, JAN. 12.   To Asst. Secretary of War Charles A. Dana. "Richmond papers just received. They say that; 'There is no telegraphic news from any quarter owing to the lines being down between Greensboro and Danville. The freshet of the late rains has been very great along the Piedmont R. R and is said to have washed away a couple of bridges which will be repaired in a few days' "—Telegram received (at 8:45 P.M.), DNA, RG 107, Telegrams Collected (Bound). *O.R.*, I, xlvi, part 2, 104.

1865, JAN. 12, 1:00 P.M.   To Maj. Gen. Henry W. Halleck. "If Col. W. A. Nichols can be spared I wish you would have him ordered to the Army of the Potomac as A. A. G. I have relieved Gen. Williams and put him on my Staff as Inspector Gen. having particular duties which I have selected him to perform."—ALS (telegram sent), CSmH; telegram received (at 5:00 P.M.), DNA, RG 107, Telegrams Collected (Bound). Printed as sent at 12:15 P.M., received at 1:00 P.M., in *O.R.*, I, xlvi, part 2, 105. See *ibid.*, pp. 93, 107. On Jan. 13, 11:50 A.M., Halleck telegraphed to USG. "The War Dept cannot spare Col Nichols till the return of Genl Townsend, who is expected early next week. Will that answer your purpose?"—ALS (telegram sent), DNA, RG 107, Telegrams Collected (Bound); telegram received, *ibid.*; *ibid.*, RG 108, Letters Received. *O.R.*, I, xlvi, part 2, 113. On the same day, USG telegraphed to Maj. Gen. George G. Meade transmitting Halleck's telegram.—Telegram received (at 4:45 P.M.), DNA, RG 94, War Records Office, Army of the Potomac; copy, Meade Papers, PHi.
 On Jan. 11, Brig. Gen. John A. Rawlins had telegraphed to Meade. "Gen. Grant desires that you will please send gen. Williams down. The order in the case will be sent you tomorrow"—Telegram received (at 5:45 P.M.), DNA, RG 94, War Records Office, Army of the Potomac; copies, *ibid.*, RG 108, Letters Sent; DLC-USG, V, 46, 71, 107; Meade Papers, PHi. *O.R.*, I, xlvi, part 2, 93. On Jan. 12, USG telegraphed to Meade.

"Would you like to have Col. R. Williams A. A. G. ordered to report to you? If so I will ask to have him so ordered."—ALS (telegram sent), Kohns Collection, NN; telegram received (at 11:00 A.M.), DNA, RG 94, War Records Office, Army of the Potomac. At 12:30 P.M., Meade telegraphed to USG. "I do not think Col Williams A. A G. would suit the position of chief of the Dept in this army—If I could have a choice Col. W. A Nichols as an officer whose experience in the field would render him a valuable adjunct.—is the man I would select."—ALS (telegram sent—misdated Dec. 12, 1864), *ibid.*, RG 393, Army of the Potomac, Telegrams Sent; telegram received (dated Jan. 12, 1865), *ibid.*, RG 108, Letters Received. On the same day, USG telegraphed to Meade. "I will ask to have Col. Nichols sent to you as A. A. Gen. of the Army of the Potomac. In telegraphing you this morning I could only think of Ruggles & Williams who were available and thought the latter would be the most acceptable."—ALS (telegram sent), CSmH; telegram received (at 1:20 P.M.), DNA, RG 94, War Records Office, Army of the Potomac.

1865, JAN. 12.   Secretary of the Interior John P. Usher to USG. "I transmit to you herewith, a copy of a letter that I have, this day, addressed to the Hon: the Secretary of War, which contains the views of this Department upon the subject to which it relates—A copy of my last annual report, is also transmitted; to pages 7 and 8 of which, your attention is respectfully invited."—LS, DNA, RG 108, Letters Received. *O.R.*, I, xlviii, part 1, 498. The enclosure discussed the removal of Indians along the route of the Union Pacific Railroad.—*Ibid.*, pp. 498–99.

1865, JAN. 13.   To President Abraham Lincoln. "Maj Gen Ord telegraphs that nothing is known of the conviction of Henry Stork, but if sentence be has been pronounced & the man be alive, he will have its execution stayed—" —ALS (telegram sent), Lamon Papers, CSmH; telegram received (press), DNA, RG 107, Telegrams Collected (Bound). On Jan. 12, Lincoln had telegraphed to USG. "If Henry Stork of, 5th Pa. Cavalry has been convicted of desertion, and is not yet executed, please stay till further order & send record."—ALS (telegram sent), *ibid.*; copy, *ibid.*, RG 94, Letters Received, 36P 1864. Lincoln, *Works*, VIII, 212. On the same day, Lt. Col. Theodore S. Bowers telegraphed to Maj. Gen. Edward O. C. Ord. "The following dispatch Just recd   Please furnish any information on the subject you may have,"—Telegram received, Ord Papers, CU-B; copies, DLC-USG, V, 46, 71, 107; DNA, RG 108, Letters Sent. On the same day, Ord telegraphed to USG. "Nothing known of the Sentence of death of such a person, Will have it Stayed should such have been pronounced & the man be alive" —Telegram received, *ibid.*, Letters Received. On Jan. 17, USG telegraphed to Lincoln. "All that is known of Henry Stork fifth Penna Cavly is that notice was received from Col Cross Qr Mr at Pittsburg that he had paid reward for his apprehension on the fifteenth (15) of October   he has not yet been received. Should he be tried the Proceedings in the case will be forwarded"—Telegram received (press), *ibid.*, RG 107, Telegrams Collected (Bound); copies, *ibid.*, RG 108, Letters Sent; DLC-USG, V, 46, 71, 107. See Lincoln, *Works*, VIII, 213n.

1865, JAN. 13.   To Asst. Secretary of War Charles A. Dana. "The Richmond papers today have the following items, Sherman's movements! The Charleston Courier of the 5th says the latest account from the road Thursday night stated that the enemy this side of the Savannah river, had retired towards night, and our picket lines to Hardeeville were re-established, Wednesday morning the enemy advanced & drove in our pickets. A later report from Grahamville Wednesday evening states that the enemy was moving in force on the Perrysburg road below Sisters Ferry, A flag of truce communication was held at Port Royal Ferry Wednesday afternoon for the purpose of exchanging letters and official documents. The Courier of the 6th says, an authentic dispatch received Thursday evening states that there had been no new movement of the enemy during the day, His forces were still crossing the river & assembling between there & Hardeeville. Our cavalry still picket near Hardeeville. The Mercury of the 7th says, Yesterday morning the Yankees in unknown force, are reported to have crossed New river on the road to Grahamville. Their main body however is still in the neighborhood of Hardeeville As yet their object is not developed but Wheeler is closely watching their movements, The Georgia Central R. R.! This road has been repaired from Macon to Gordon, & the hands are now at work on the Milledgeville & Gordon road, which is expected to be completed to the vicinity of Milledgeville in a week or ten days. A temporary bridge made of flats has been thrown across the Oconee at Milledgeville. Defences of Mobile! The Augusta Chronicle says a correspondent who has had an opportunity of examining the defences of Mobile expresses the opinion that there is not a better fortified place on the continent, & says not less than sixty millions of dollars have been expended in placing her in her present impregnable condition. Ten thousand men can successfully hold it for an indefinite period against five times the number. Our correspondent says he has no fears for the safety of the place. Rumor was current this morning that Goldsboro N. C. had been captured by the enemy, This cannot be true as official dispatches were rec'd last night from Goldsboro in which no mention is made of the proximity of the enemy. The blockade of the highways leading from Richmond by military order it is said has had the effect to seriously diminish the number of market carts that have heretofore thronged the market, and threatens to cut short the daily supply of provisions, Yesterday the Mayor of Richmond made a visit to the lines below and the Hd Qrs of the Comd'g Genl. with the view it is said of obtaining a relaxation or removal of the embargo in order that the citizens may be relieved & the markets supplied. We understand that the object of barring a free passage of the highways was to check the exodus of the negroes of Richmond & carrying second hand information to the Enemy's lines. This is stopping at the spiggot and letting it escape at the bung hole. The runaway negroes will take to the fields, woods & by-paths, the wagons of the market men cannot.' "—Telegram received (at 6:00 P.M.), DNA, RG 107, Telegrams Collected (Bound).

1865, JAN. 13. George H. Stuart to USG. "The Annual Meeting of the U. S. Christian Commission occurs in the City of Washington on Thursday Jan. 28th, & days following, according to Enclosed Circular. At the Public Anniversary on Sunday Evening, Jan. 29th, the Hon. Secretary Seward has signified his willingness to preside. Addresses are expected from distinguished representatives of the Military & Naval Service, as well as by gentlemen prominent in Church & State. Your known interest in our work, & the sense of our honest endeavor to aid in the successful accomplishment of the operations you so worthily lead, embolden me to invite your attendance at the above Anniversary, if compatible with pressing public duties. If, beside your attendance, you could give a few words of public approval,— (I remember your Magnanimity & reluctance to anything like public manifestations),—they would much help the cause of the Commission, which we believe to be the cause of the Country & of Christianity. If your personal presence is impossible, may I ask a response by letter with permission to read it at the Anniversary? . . ."—LS, DNA, RG 94, U.S. Christian Commission, Letters Sent (Press).

1865, JAN. 14. To Asst. Secretary of War Charles A. Dana. "Today's Richmond papers have the following items. 'From Wilmington! An official dispatch received Yesterday says about 50 vessels are in sight, mostly opposite the point of the former landing of the Enemy. The weather is fair and the sea smooth. There was a report last night that the Enemy's fleet had begun the bombardment of Fort Fisher, There was however no official dispatch on the subject. They will find the fort in much better condition for resistance than when Butler made his [at]tempt upon it. The Horse Marines at work! We learn upon good authority that a detachment of Confederate Cavalry recently captured a Yankee Gunboat on the Potomac We would like to name the gallant command of which they are a part, but deem it prudent not to do so. Damage to the Piedmont R R! The Danville Register learns that the heavy rains of yesterday washed down the trestle work on the Piedmont R. R. between Reidsville and Benaja, and between Greensboro and Sepinaw, so that the trains cannot pass over that portion of the road, It will require several days to repair the damage done. The water supply.! The freshet in the James has interfered with the City Water works and the supply has been cut off for two days, As the high tide is now rapidly falling water communication will doubtless be resumed today or tomorrow. It is a little paradoxical that when water is so plentiful it should be so scarce, At present it is, "Water, water Every where, but not a drop to drink" An Editorial says the Piedmont connection will be in running order today or tomorrow, It is urged that the gauge of the Piedmont link, (48 miles) between Richmond & Augusta, be changed, so as to have a single gauge between Richmond & Atlanta. Ex. Govr. H. S. Foote of Tenn. & member of the Confederate Congress was arrested on the 12th at Occoquan attempting to go North.' "—Telegram received, DNA, RG 107, Telegrams Collected (Bound). On the same day, Lt. Col. Theodore S. Bowers telegraphed to Maj. Gen. George G. Meade transmitting the news from Wilmington.—Telegram received (at 10:45 P.M.), *ibid.*, RG 94, War Records Office, Army of the Potomac; copy, Meade Papers, PHi. *O.R.*, I, xlvi, part 2, 126. On the same day, Brig. Gen. Charles Devens had telegraphed to USG transmitting this information.—ALS (telegram sent), DNA, RG 107, Telegrams Collected (Unbound). *O.R.*, I, xlvi, part 2, 128.

1865, JAN. 14. Peter M. Dox, Huntsville, Ala., to USG. "If such a man as Genl J. D. Webster now at Nashville, who combines *Civis* with Military Capacity, could be placed in charge of the District of North Alabama, it would do a great deal of good at this time. The people here, in my opinion, under wise management, are ready for the work of reconstruction—In this opinion our best Union men concur. Hoods' disasters have operated like a charm, Every body seems submissive—Can you not assist in sending us Webster to govern us? Col: Lyon who commands the post at Huntsville knows our people well and comprehends their wants at this time—He is, by the way, the best Post commander I ever knew, & ought to be placed in command of a District extending from Decatur to Stevenson. Give him that District, with the power and rank of a Brig: Genl.,—with Webster to supervise, as commanding all North Alabama, & the best of results would speedily follow. I write to you on this subject because I believe you will do justice to my motive in writing. I have made many unrequited sacrifices for the Sake of our glorious Union; And, God Knows, I am ready to make more —But, I am sick of our present condition, and I believe this people are sick of it—With a firm, wise hand at the helmm here, I believe, that, so far at least as North Alabama is concerned, the work of reconstruction would be an easy one. Mrs Dox joins me in regards to yourself & Mrs Grant—"—ALS, DNA, RG 108, Letters Received. Dox, a lawyer in N. Y. before moving to Ala., was a brother-in-law of Dr. Charles A. Pope of St. Louis, a friend of the Dent family. See *PUSG*, 10, 528–29.

1865, JAN. 14. Mayer Lehman and I. T. Tichenor, Richmond, Va., to USG. "We have the honor to announce to you that the State of Alabama has appropriated Hufive hundred thousand dollars for the relief of prisoners from that State held by your Government The Undersigned having been appointed Agents for the purpose of carrying into Effect the design of this appropriation most respectfully ask through you permission to proceed to the United States on the object of our mission Having obtained permission from the Confederate Government to Ship cotton to the amount of this appropriation we are instructed by the Governor of Alabama to ask permission to pass it through the blockade We would further State that it would be agreeable to the Governor of Alabama if a vessel of the United

States should be permitted to carry this cotton to the port of New York to be there Sold and the proceeds applied to the purchase of blankets clothing and such other things as may be needed for the comfort of prisoners from that state. We beg leave to suggest mMobile bay as the point from which this cotton may be shipped We deem it proper to state that our mission is confined strictly to the object stated. It embraces nothing of a military or political nature and if permitted to carry out the design of our State we will cheerfully submit to such rules regulations and paroles as are usual in such cases. We well know that a gallant Soldier must feel for those brave men who by the fortunes of war are held as prisoners exposed to the rigors of a climate to which they are not accustomed the severities of which are augmented by the privations necessarily attendant upon their condition We ask this favor with confidence assured that your sympathies with the unfortunate brave will lead you to do all in your power to promote the benevolent design entrusted to us by the State of Alabama—"—LS, DNA, RG 108, Letters Received. *O.R.,* II, viii, 69–70, 166. On Feb. 1, Lehman and Tichenor wrote to USG. "we had the honor to forward to you on the 14th of January by flag of truce boat an application for permission to proceed to the United States for the purpose of supplying the wants of prisoners from the State of Alabama. The closing of that mode of communication by the ice on the river has induced our government to grant us permission to communicate with you by another channel We enclose a copy (substantially) of our former letter and as it is a matter of the highest interest to the Government and people of our State most respectfully ask that we may be permitted to confer with you in person in regard to it. If such an interview should be deemed by you inconsistent with the interests of your Governmt or inconvenient to yourself we would be pleased to recieve your decision on our application of the 14th Ultimo"—LS, DNA, RG 108, Letters Received. *O.R.,* II, viii, 166. See Isaac Markens, "Mayer Lehman in Correspondence with Gen. U. S. Grant, Jefferson Davis and Gov. T. H. Watts, of Alabama," *Publications of the American Jewish Historical Society,* 20 (Baltimore, 1911), 154–57.

1865, JAN. 16.   To Asst. Secretary of War Charles A. Dana. "The Richmond papers today have the following items. 'Wilmington Jan 13. 1865. The Yankee fleet consisting of about 60 vessels attacked Fort Fisher this morning about 7 o'clk   The bombardment lasted all day   The Yankees landed a force about 5 miles above Ft. Fisher on the coast this morning. No particulars rec'd from Genl Whiting who is comd'g at the Fort. Editorial— The great winds of Saturday brought down the telegraph poles on the Southern lines & we are without information from Wilmington later than the 13th. On that day 60 vessels of the Yankee fleet attack Ft. Fisher at 7 o'clk in the morning & kept up a tremendous fire throughout the forenoon. During this bombardment they landed troops in unknown force 5 miles above Ft. Fisher. Genl Whiting is in command at the fort. This Expedition is believed to be under the sole command of Porter who has gone to show what he can do without Butler. All the Monitors on the coast have been collected for the purpose & it is said to be Porter's intention if the attack on the fort fails to attempt running them past them to see if Wilmington cannot be taken in the same way that New Orleans was taken—Later—We learn late last night that the enemy continued his fire on Ft. Fisher throughout Saturday and Sunday, but without the least injury to the fort. The party which landed above are endeavoring to throw up fortifications, but are obstructed by the Confederate Artillery. Charleston Jan 14. The enemy's force about Hardee-ville have retired back to the Savannah river. There is some doubt whether troops had been sent to Beaufort. There are no indications of an advance this way. Charleston Jan. 13. Intelligent persons from Savannah state that the late meeting there numbered about 300, of whom 100 were Jews 75 Irish and the remainder men of Northern birth & shaky politicians, who no more represent the people of Savannah than a dozen deserters represent Lee's Army. Second Dispatch! Charleston Jan. 15. 250 refugees arrived here last night from Savannah. The Yankees were busy removing obstruc-tions from the river & say they will soon move on Augusta, Branchville & Charleston   No movement has been made as yet, though refugees think there will be soon. Sherman & his officers threaten to reduce Charleston & South Carolina to desolation,   His rule in Savannah for policy continues mild. He has written a letter to the citizens saying the only way to have peace is to send members to the United States Congress & return to the Union & that it is ridiculous to think of any other kind of reconstruction, The refugees brought out such servants & baggage as they desired. Many negroes were returning to their masters   A fire was discovered at Salisbury N. C on the morning of the 13th about 11 o'clk in the vacant store room in the 'Gov W. Brown' building near the property of J. H. Ennis. It spread with great rapidity to the right & left involving almost every wooden build-ing in the block,   Murphy's three story brick building arrested the flames on the south and Ennis' brick buildings now occupied by the Commissary Dept. arrested them on the North. The buildings of the Qr. Mrs. Dept. &c were destroyed with some property, but how much is yet unknown. The loss of movable property either public or private was not very great   The fire is believed to have been the work of an incendiary. Canton Miss. Dec. 31. The Federal Cavalry force under Gen. Grierson who had been operating on the Mobile & Ohio Railroad with some success until driven off by our forces under Gen Gholsom, captured Bellefonte Miss, on the night of the 30th after destroying the Barkstone factory. They divided on the morning of the 31st, the main body ~~going~~ moving on Grenada which it is supposed they burned. The other column struck the Central R. R. 20 miles South of Grenada at Winona where they burned the depot,   They then moved South destroying the R. R. & buildings. At sunset today they were at West Station Col. W. A. Broadwell Chief of the Cotton Bureau Trans. Miss. Dept. has purchased and introduced into the Dept. pledging payment in cotton, 23,800 pairs of blankets 60.000 pairs of shoes, 150.000 yards shirting & towels, 150.000 pounds of powder, 200 000 pounds of lead, 5.000.000 percussion

caps and a large quantity of guns, 1540,000 yards grey army cloth &
Satinell & a large quantity of hardware, Copper, Saltpetre, & a great Quan-
tity of small stores. Gov. Foote is still at Fredericksburg on his parole.' "—
Telegram received (at 6:00 P.M.), DNA, RG 107, Telegrams Collected
(Bound).

1865, JAN. 16, 3:30 P.M.   Asst. Secretary of War Charles A. Dana to
USG. "Reports have lately reached this department th of an extensive trade
with the rebels carried on through Norfolk. One of these reports estimates
the amount sent out from within our lines there at one hundred thousand
dollars daily. Provisions for Lee's army are said to be the main article of
export. Boats are said to be sent through on each side with unbroken cargoes. Gen. Butler who has just arrived here renews the statement general
statement without specifying any amount of business. He says the trade is
carried on under the recent orders of the Treasury department for buying
the products of the rebel states and allowing one fourth of the value to go
back in supplies. He has shown me a memorandum which he says is in the
handwriting of a rebel quarter master respecting proposals to exchange
cotton for provisions upon this basis. It is also reported from the West that
extensive arrangements have been made to supply the rebel armies there
with food & other necessaries from within our lines under cover of the
same treasury orders. Please cause the facts at Norfolk to be investigated,
and advise this department what action is requisite you deem to be necessary
in the premises upon military grounds."—ALS (telegram sent), DNA, RG
107, Telegrams Collected (Bound); telegram received, *ibid.*, RG 108, Letters Received. *O.R.*, I, xlvi, part 2, 144–45. On Jan. 19, Maj. Gen. Edward
O. C. Ord wrote to USG. "private . . . I propose after thinking the matter
over about the huge illicit trade *reported*—to order a Military Commission,
with power to call for papers and persons—have them after investigating
thoroughly—*try*, and sentence parties they may deem guilty—Genl Gordon
shrewd & fond of such hunting—and Col Potter of the 12th N Hampshire,
and Major Read—A A Gl—late of Brooks Staff—I propose as members—I
think this report of 100,000$ a day food &c sent to rebels is a sword with
two edges, and if not guarded against may be used by politicians   Butler is
not the only one aimed at by it—hence I propose taking the bull by the
horns—if we can fasten the matter upon Either Treasury or Benj— Fs—
agents—clap them in the guard house, and the politicians will find they
have started the wrong rabbit—with as bushy tail—and as soon as some
Treasury scamp is in the guard house or prison *they* will have to let him
out—I write to you in regard to this matter—rather than telegraph for *all*,
our telegrams are viséed at Washington—What do you think of my proposition—I am not afraid to try it and think the Commission will do—if you
can suggest a better man than Gordon for the leader—please do so—He was
in conversation with me before the 2d Wilmington Expedition started very
emphatic—in his statements of what Curtis told him might and ought to
have been done by the first expedition—"—ALS, DNA, RG 108, Letters

Received. *O.R.*, I, xlvi, part 2, 181. On the same day, Ord issued Special Orders No. 19, convening this commission; the full report is in DNA, RG 153, OO-2145.

On Jan. 23, Ord wrote to Brig. Gen. John A. Rawlins. "I have the honor to enclose herewith a letter from Major Read Recorder of the Commission now sitting at Norfolk for the investigation of frauds committed in this Department, asking that the proceedings of a General Court Martial which considered the same subject may be sent to the Commission for their instruction and guidance. I enclose also a Memorandum made by Major Stackpole, who was the Judge Advocate of the Court Martial referred to, showing the nature of the cases tried before the Court and their probable bearing on the cases now being examined by the Commission. It will be seen from the letter of Major Read that the proceedings are now in the hands of General Marston who went to Washington with General Butler and is supposed to be now there. I have the honor to request that he be directed to forward them to Major Read, at Norfolk."—LS, *ibid.*, RG 393, Dept. of Va. and N. C., Letters Received. The enclosures are *ibid.* On Jan. 24, USG endorsed the letter. "Respectfully referred to Maj Gen Halleck Chief of Staff, who will please ascertain the custodian of the proceedings referred to, and order their return to Maj Gen E. O. C. Ord,"—ES, *ibid.*

On March 20, USG wrote to Secretary of War Edwin M. Stanton. "I have the honor to transmit herewith the proceedings of a Military Commission, of which Brig, Gen, Gordon, is President, held at Norfolk Va, for the purpose of investigating and inquiring into the subject of alleged contraband trade, and abuses, under the Treasury, Trade, regulations, This Commission was ordered in pursuance of a telegram from the War Dept, of date Jan'y 16th, 1865,"—Copies, DLC-USG, V, 46, 75, 108; DNA, RG 108, Letters Sent. At 11:00 A.M., Stanton telegraphed to USG. "I saw General Gordon at Norfolk. He is content to remain in command there and unless you think differently it seems to me he will do better than any one else. Hartsuff will not be a good assignment to that place in my judgment." —ALS (telegram sent), *ibid.*, RG 107, Telegrams Collected (Bound); telegram received, *ibid.*, RG 108, Letters Received. *O.R.*, I, xlvi, part 3, 50.

The commission recommended that eleven persons, including George W. Lane and U.S. Asst. Treasury Agent Benjamin H. Morse, be held for trial. On Feb. 17, Brig. Gen. Innis N. Palmer, New Berne, N. C., wrote to Chandler and Walker, Norfolk. "Your letter of the 11th inst. making enquiry concerning the draft given by me in favor of George W. Lane is received. In reply I will state that on or about the 22nd ultimo, I had a conversation with Lieut. Gen. Grant concerning the cargo of goods recently carried through our lines to the Confederacy by Mr. Lane, During that conversation, Gen. Grant directed me to enquire if this money for which [t]he draft was given had been paid, and if it had not, to stop the payment of it, until Lane's case could be investigated, I obeyed my instructions, and I had heard nothing of the matter since until the receipt of your letter, The money which I was first directed to restore to Mr. Lane is still on deposite

with J. W. Warren & Son, of New York, and I presume that when Mr.
Lane has fully acquitted himself of all intentions of wrong in his recent
trading with the enemy in this state, I will be directed to see that this money
is paid him,"—Copy, DNA, RG 393, Dept. of N. C., Letters Received. On
March 27, Lt. Col. Theodore S. Bowers endorsed this letter. "As the within
case of G. W. Lane has been fully investigated by a Military Commission
convened by Maj. Gen Butler, while Comdg the Dept. of Va. and N. C.,
and the proceedings thereof approved of by him, the same will be considered as final; and the finding of said Commission and Gen. Butler's orders
therein will not be interfered with."—Copies, *ibid.*; DLC-USG, V, 58. On
Feb. 27, Lane wrote to USG. "The undersigned would beg to call your
attention to the statement of facts below made, and respectfully ask that an
order be issued directing, Brig. Gen. I. N. Palmer, to pay over to the undersigned the amount of the Draft originally drawn by him in my favor."—
Copy, DNA, RG 393, Dept. of N. C., Letters Received. A petition from
Lane and others, released on bond from arrest, was endorsed by USG on
May 6. "Respectfully forwarded to the Secty of War, to know what action
should be had in these cases. The report of the Military Commission before
which they were investigated was forwarded to the War Depatment on
the 20th of March 1865."—Copies, *ibid.*, RG 108, Letters Received; DLC-
USG, V, 58. On April 27, Palmer wrote to USG. "I desire as a matter of
protection to myself, to call your attention to some facts, in relation to the
case of Mr. G. W. Lane, who recently appealed to you for the restoration
of some money, the proceeds of cotton ordered to be confiscated. In the
endorsement on this appeal, made by Colonel Bowers, and which was sent
to me, it is stated, that 'the Lieut. Gen. has no desire, to interfere with the
decision by General Butler,' and I of course ordered the money restored at
once. From the manner in which the endorsement is worded, I am induced
to believe, that a conversation which I had with you on board the steamer
at Fort Monroe, concerning this man Lane, has escaped you[r] memory,
and it is very necessary that I should bring it to your remembrance. We
were in a hurried conversation, at which I think Gen. Ord was present,
speaking among other things of the contraband trade in Eastern Virginia,
and North Carolina, and I menteniond the case of Lane, which appeared to
me one of the worst. I mentioned that the property confiscated by my order,
had been ordered to be restored, and you asked me if the restoration had
been made I replied, that I presumed it had, as I had sent a draft to New
York for the money, but a short time previously. I said that I could ascertain by telegraph if the draft, had been paid, and I understood you to say
decidedly, that if the money had not been paid, it ought to be retained for
the present, Lane was just about to be arrested to be brought before the
board, of which General Gordon, had been appointed President, and which
was organized to inquire into all the contraband trade. I immediately made
inquiry if the draft had been paid, and was informed, that it had not, I
then stopped the payment, stating that it was done by your direction. Lane
now states as I am informed that you recently stated that you never had any

conversation with me in regard to the matter: that you utterly denied that I had stated to you anything about the contraband trade &c. Thus he has not only made it appear, that to injure him, I had made a false statement, but he has set up a claim for $900 damages. Lane's counsel, in this matter, is a sharp unscrupulous lawyer in Norfolk by name Chandler, and I believe they are determined to make trouble for me if they can. I desire therefore to know if you have seen anything in my action in this case, that you do not approve, and whether Lane has any reason for making the statements he has."—Copy, DNA, RG 393, Army of the Ohio, Dept. of N. C., Letters Received. On May 12, USG endorsed this letter. "The conversation within alluded to, had not at the date of the endorsement referred to, nor has it now, escaped my mind. Your statement of it, and my direction for your action, in the premises is correct in every particular, and the endorsed order for the carrying out of Gen. Butler's order, was, and is, no manner intended as a censure upon you It was made upon my being apprised of the fact that Gen. Butler's order was based upon the findings of a Military Commission, and upon mature consideration I deemed it best not to interfere with it. If Mr. Lane, or any one for him, states that I have at any time denied having the conversation referred to touching this matter, or the subject of contraband trade at Norfolk, he or the person so stating it speaks what is not the fact."—Copies, *ibid.*; DLC-USG, V, 58. See Lincoln, *Works*, VII, 258; *ibid.*, VIII, 368, 395; *Private and Official Correspondence of Gen. Benjamin F. Butler* (n.p., 1917), V, 556, 557, 564, 576–83; *HRC*, 38-2-24; Charles C. Nott and Samuel H. Huntington, *Cases Decided in the Court of Claims ... at the December Term for 1866 ...* (Washington, 1868), II, 184–206; John William Wallace, *Cases Argued and Adjudged in the Supreme Court ... December Terms, 1868 and 1869* (New York, 1904), VIII, 185–201; Ludwell H. Johnson, "Contraband Trade during the Last Year of the Civil War," *Mississippi Valley Historical Review*, XLIX, 4 (March, 1963), 646–52.

On June 3, Morse, Philadelphia, wrote to USG. "During the month of Feby last I was summoned as a witness to appear before a Commission at Norfolk. Va of which Genl Gordon was Chairman and after giving testimony before sd Commission was orderd under Bonds for $50.000. which was not Convenient for me to give and I was Confined in the quarters of the Provost Marshal. Upon the 3d day one of the Commissioners visited me and asked what amt I was willing to give, I gave $10.000. and was not allowed to leave the City of Norfolk until I made application to you and recd permission to go at my pleasure This Bond is still upon me and I respectfully ask an unconditional discharge."—ALS, DNA, RG 108, Letters Received. On June 23, Rawlins endorsed this letter. "Respectfully referred to Major Gen A H Terry Comdg Dept Virginia who will, if it has not already been done, please order the release from arrest of the within named parties, and the cancelling of the bonds or personal recognizances they have entered into in pursuance of the requirements of the military Commission of which Brig Gen Gordon was chairman."—ES, *ibid.* See *Calendar*, Sept. 30, 1864.

1865, JAN. 16.   Asst. Secretary of the Navy Gustavus V. Fox to USG. "A
fast Steamer leaves here tomorrow afternoon at 4 P. M. for the Fleet off
Wilmington. She can touch off Fort Monroe Wednesday [*Jan. 18*] morning,
to take despatches or any officers if you desire it"—Copy, DNA, RG 45,
Miscellaneous Letters Sent. *O.R.* (Navy), I, xi, 603.

1865, JAN. 16.   Maj. Gen. Edward O. C. Ord to USG. "I find Genl Turner
has been detained here by a summons, to go to Washington—by the Committee—If you think his presence necessary while I am absent, I will send
him up now—I shall return during the to night—"—ALS, MOLLUS-Mass.
Collection, PCarlA.

1865, JAN. 17.   To Maj. Gen. Henry W. Halleck. "Please call the attention of the Surgeon General to the necessity of sending a Hospital Steamer
to Fort Fisher for the purpose of taking care of our wounded"—Telegram
received (at 2:15 P.M.), DNA, RG 107, Telegrams Collected (Bound);
copies, *ibid.*, RG 108, Letters Sent; DLC-USG, V, 46, 71, 107. *O.R.*, I,
xlvi, part 2, 159.

1865, JAN. 17.   Postmaster Gen. William Dennison to USG. "I have just
received the following dispatch from W. A. Carter special agent of this Department, represented to me as a reliable man, namely   Ft Bridger Jany
16   To. P. M. GENERAL   'The vital interests of the country especially
those of the overland mail and telegraph lines demand that the protection
of the overland route be assigned to one (1) man,   I but express the universal desire of all the Territories concerned, in respectfully Submitting
that a Department of the Plains be created and the command be assigned
to Brigadier General T. Edw. Conner who will keep open our communication' "—Copy, DNA, RG 28, Letters Sent by the Postmaster Gen.

1865, JAN. 18, 8:00 P.M.   To Secretary of War Edwin M. Stanton. "I
transmit the only news found in todays Richmond Papers. 'No official news.
The telegraph line from Richmond to Mobile is notw in working order but
neither official news despatch nor press report from any quarter was received over the wires today. There seems to have been no foundation for the
report that General Breckinridge had been appointed Secy of War. He is in
the City on business connected with his command in South Western Va.
General D H Hill passed through Augusta yesterday going south. The
order for Mr Footes discharge reached Fredericksburg on yesterday. He is
expected to reach the City this evening. He is said to have prepared a speech
for delivery in Richmond' "—Telegram received (at 8:15 P.M.), DNA, RG
107, Telegrams Collected (Bound).

1865, JAN. [18–21].   USG endorsement. "Respy returned and special
attention invited to accompanying report. It will be seen that the men were

forwarded ten days ago. Since then I have ordered that all similar case be tried here, where witness can be readily called. The abuses practiced by guards of the V. R. C. bringing forward recruits is astounding. Unless I can prevent these outrages by summarily punishing the guilty here, I will be compelled to recommend that more reliable troops be assigned to the duty of bringing forward recruits"—Copy, DLC-USG, V, 58. Written on a letter of Col. George H. Sharpe concerning the arrest of a detachment of the 22nd Veteran Reserve Corps.—*Ibid.*

1865, JAN. 18, 1:00 P.M. Asst. Secretary of War Charles A. Dana to USG. "(Confidential) Mr. Clay, rebel agent in Canada said to a confidential friend last week that if Fort Fisher fell it would be their policy to hold Wilmington at all hazards, even if they had to give up both Petersburg and Richmond, for Wilmington was of more importance to them than the other places. It would be hard, he said, even to live without Wilmington. Richmond was not necessary to Wilmington; but Wilmington was indispensable to Richmond. These were his very words but whether they were his own conclusions or the substance of information recd. from Richmond my informant can't tell"—Telegram received, DNA, RG 108, Letters Received. *O.R.,* I, xlvi, part 2, 170.

1865, JAN. 18. Brig. Gen. James B. Fry, provost marshal gen., to USG. "I am informed that Lieut' Col' Duff, and perhaps other Officers, are making inspections in the different States, in connection with the Recruiting and forwarding of men. As the information obtained by these inspections, may be of use to me, in my Official duties, I respectfully request, if consistent with your views, that I may be furnished with copies of the Inspection Reports referred to, and any tabular statements which may accompany them." —LS, DNA, RG 108, Letters Received. On Jan. 20, Brig. Gen. John A. Rawlins wrote to Fry. "I have the honor to acknowledge the reciept of your letter to Lt, Gen, Grant under date of the 18th, and to reply that the reports obtained by Lieut, Col, Duff A, I G, from the State of Ohio, Indiana and Illinois were a few days since forwarded to the Adjutant General of the for their proper reference"—Copies, *ibid.,* Letters Sent; DLC-USG, V, 46, 72, 107.

1865, JAN. 18. Maj. Thomas M. Vincent, AGO, to USG. "I have the honor to acknowledge the receipt of your reference of the letter of Brig. General Joseph R. Hawley, requesting that Colonel Joseph C. Abbott, 7th New Hampshire Volunteers, be retained in service for the unexpired portion of three years from his last muster, November 17. 1863. In reply, I am directed to inform you that a previous application in this case was received, which was decided by a letter from this Office of the 30th ultimo. to General Ord, copy herewith, The case has again been carefully considered, and no departure from the decision of the 30th ultimo, and Circular No. 36, series of 1864. can be made."—LS, DNA, RG 108, Letters Received. The enclosure is *ibid.*

1865, JAN. 18.   William M. Clark, Norfolk, to USG. "I would like a pass to visit City Point   my brother is sick in the Hospital   I cannot obtain it here   would like to start tomorrow morning from Old Point"—Telegram received, DNA, RG 107, Telegrams Collected (Unbound).

1865, JAN. 18.   J. S. Moore, Baltimore, to USG. "To shew you that your attack on Genl Butler is not unnoticed, I can assure you on the authority of *the whole loyal public North* that your treatment of this element—the union men—will not be bourne much longer. The abuse of that General shall not proceed from *such a source.* Only think what patience we have already had with you! You crossed the Rapidan with a larger force than Napoleon had to invade Russia with. Where are they now? You confront the rebel Genl Lee now with a larger force ~~now~~ than Wellington gained the battle of Waterloo with, and your chief occupation seems to be to 'fire salutes' for the victory of others. Please take a hint. . . . If Genl Butler were to declare the government dissolved under Mr Lincoln, and assume the Presideny himself, the army and the people *would sustain him*"—ALS, DLC-Robert T. Lincoln. USG endorsed this letter: "For the President"—AE, *ibid.*

1865, JAN. 19.   To Secretary of War Edwin M. Stanton. "The Richmond Dispatch has the following telegram. Charleston Jany 15. A heavy force of the enemy advanced from Beaufort yesterday morning against Pocotaligo which place was evacuated last night by Genl McLaws. Refuges from savannah report one corps of Shermans army gone to Wilmington & that the cotton in savannah has been or will be confiscated. Second dispatch 'Charleston Jany 16th   After abandoning pocotaligo our forces took position behind the Combahee river   no further movement was made yesterday The enemy is beleived to be aiming at Branchville. Two Monitors were sunk last night in this harbor probably by torpedoes. They lie about eight hundred yards from Fort Sumter towards Sullivans Island   their smoke stacks only are visible.' Third dispatch   Charleston Jany 17th   'Deserters & prisoners report the force that advanced from Beaufort to consist of the 15th & 17th Corps with Little artillery or baggage train & that Sherman was moving by rail road with the remainder of his army artillery trains etc. They report also that Charleston is their destination. The enemy advanced within 2 miles of Combahee yesterday [a]nd and then retired. ~~Charleston Jany 17~~ From the Whig   Charleston Jany 17   A Yankee monitor on picket duty between Fort Moultrie & Fort Sumter was sunk last night supposed by a torpedo   only the smoke stack is left above the water. A Yankee deserter reports that the force on the line of the Salkahatchie consists of the seventeenth & part of the fifteenth corps. Their destination is said to be Charleston   A Considerable body of the enemys Infantry moved up about noon within two & half miles of the Combahee bridge, but afterwards retired to their intrenchments at Gardners Corner   Nothing. We have to repeat. The same old tune. No official despatches containing news of Public interest received today ˙Telegraphic lines working in every direction The late rain and freshets' The wilmington Journal says that on Wednesday night some seventy feet of the Rail Road bridge over the Roanoke river at Weldon was washed away. We have not learned which part of the bridge suffered but lean to the impression that it was on the northern side. The salisbury watchman in an article on the same subject says neither of the rail roads have escaped serious damage. We learn that the central road has been materially injured between this place and High Point. The Danville Register of tuesday states that the trains would pass over the Piedmont road to Greensboro the next day (wednesday) the damage done the track by the recent freshet having been repaired. The Examiner says it is positively stated in the War Dept that no particulars whatever of the fall of Fort Fisher have yet been received. Capt Raphael Semmes has arrived in Richmond. Conventions of citizens in S. C. are asking to have Genl Johnston placed in command of their state forces to resist Sherman It was Generally understood yesterday that the rebel senate in secret session passed resolutions recommending that Genl Lee be put in command of all the armies of the Confederacy & that Johnston be restored to the command of the army of the Tenn Rumors are still rife of a change in the reb war Dept"—Telegram received (at 5:45 P.M.), DNA, RG 107, Telegrams Collected (Bound).

1865, JAN. 19. To Col. James A. Hardie. "There is no objection to coming to City Point"—Telegram received (press), DNA, RG 107, Telegrams Collected (Bound). On the same day, Hardie twice telegraphed to USG. "Hon. James T. Hale M. C, asks that Mrs Beech, wife of Captain Beach, C.-S. be permitted to visit City-Point. Is there any objection?" "The Secretary of the Interior asks a pass for Mrs Captain J. C. Paine from Baltimore to Head-Quarters 9th Army Corps, to visit her husband. The Assistant Secretary of War directs me to request an expression of your views as to the propriety of granting this application—"—LS (telegrams sent), *ibid.* On the same day, USG telegraphed to Hardie. "Owing to the fact that the armies are liable to move at any moment the army commanders have deemed it judicious to prohibit ladies from visiting the front as their presence there might cause serious embarrassment in case of a move. In Mrs Paynes case however a pass may be given for a limited time"— Telegram received (press), *ibid.*; copies, *ibid.*, RG 108, Letters Sent; DLC-USG, V, 46, 72, 107.

1865, JAN. 19. To Maj. Gen. Christopher C. Augur. "Please send the men convicted of desertion and sentenced to be shot referred to in your dispatch of this date to Genl Patrick at this place"—Telegram received (press), DNA, RG 107, Telegrams Collected (Bound); copies (entered as sent by Brig. Gen. John A. Rawlins), *ibid.*, RG 108, Letters Sent; (entered as written by USG) DLC-USG, V, 46, 72, 107. At 3:20 P.M., Augur had telegraphed to USG. "There are now at Alexandria some twenty men who have recently been tried and convicted of desertion to the enemy, and sentenced to be shot or hung, at such time and place as you may direct within the limits of the Camp of the Army of the Potomac. Shall I send them to Genl Patrick with the orders in their cases?"—ALS (telegram sent), DNA, RG 107, Telegrams Collected (Unbound); telegram received, *ibid.*, RG 108, Letters Received.

1865, JAN. 19. USG endorsement. "Respectfully returned. I would request that this application be denied."—ES, DNA, RG 107, Letters Received, A78 1865. Written on a petition of Jan. 6 of Milton Austin, Boston, asking permission to enter army lines to take away the refuse of the slaughterhouses.—ADS, *ibid.*

1865, JAN. 19. Brig. Gen. John A. Rawlins to Maj. Gen. George G. Meade. "At your request the order releiving Genl, Seymour from duty will be revoked, You may deliver to him however the order rel[e]iving him, if it has not already been sent him,"—Copies, DLC-USG, V, (misdated 1868) 46, 72, 107; DNA, RG 108, Letters Sent. *O.R.*, I, xlvi, part 2, 177. At 11:00 A.M., Meade telegraphed to Rawlins. "Genl. Seymour's order was delivered to him last night & all publicity given to the fact of its issue.—I can not but feel gratified at its proposed revocation at my request—If I had not been convinced there was no intention on Genl. Seymour's part to do wrong, I would never have interposed—His letter was wrong & will be misconstrued—He admits this but disclaims any design to give such construction—He has already been severely punished and the publicity given to his order will have a salutary effect on the army—"—ALS (telegram sent), DNA, RG 94, War Records Office, Army of the Potomac; telegram received, *ibid.*, RG 108, Letters Received. *O.R.*, I, xlvi, part 2, 177. For orders relieving Brig. Gen. Truman Seymour and their revocation, see *ibid.*, pp. 172, 178. On Jan. 5, Seymour wrote to the editor, *New York Times*, that the impossibility of destroying fortifications by naval gunfire justified Maj. Gen. Benjamin F. Butler's failure to capture Fort Fisher.—*New York Times*, Jan. 16, 1865.

1865, JAN. 19. Brig. Gen. Solomon Meredith, Paducah, to Brig. Gen. John A. Rawlins. "I have the honor to request that Brigd Genl. E. S. Bragg 1st Brigade, 3d Division 5th Army Corps may be ordered to report to me for duty for the purpose of commanding Post of Columbus Ky. I have forwarded an application to the Secretary of War on this subject. General Bragg Served with me in the Same Brigade in the Army of the Potomac for nearly three years and is an Officer of high military qualities and executive ability which is greatly required in a commanding Officer for that Post. I have no Officer of Sufficient rank that I can place in that position in my District and with the view of procuring a competent Officer for this position I have the honor, to make the above request"—LS, NNP.

1865, JAN. 20. President Abraham Lincoln to USG. "If Thomas Lamplugh, of the first Delaware Regiment, has been sentenced to death, and is not yet executed, suspend & report the case to me."—ALS (telegram sent), DNA, RG 107, Telegrams Collected (Bound). Lincoln, *Works*, VIII, 226. On the same day, Brig. Gen. John A. Rawlins telegraphed to Lincoln transmitting a telegram of 8:45 P.M. from Maj. Gen. George G. Meade. "The proceeding in the case of private Lemplough first (1st) Delaware Vols will be forwarded to the President and action in the case suspended, till his orders are received"—Telegram received (at 9:20 P.M.), DLC-Robert T. Lincoln; DNA, RG 107, Telegrams Collected (Bound); copies, *ibid.*, RG 108, Letters Sent; DLC-USG, V, 46, 72, 107. See Lincoln, *Works*, VIII, 227*n*.

1865, JAN. 20. Brig. Gen. John A. Rawlins to Secretary of War Edwin M. Stanton. "The following dispatch is taken from todays Richmond Whig. 'Charleston January 17th—We have nothing direct from General Wheeler. One of the line of couriers who left from below McBrides Brigade yesterday morning, reports that the enemy are still below. Deserters who have come in on that side report that two (2) Corps had crossed at Port Royal. The Courier says there was cavalry, artillery and Infantry coming from Cossawatchie. The forces of the enemy are believed to be concentrating above McPhersonville.' Second dispatch 'Charleston Jan'y 18th. The enemy made a move in the direction of the Conbahee River yesterday. It is believed to be nothing but a feint. All quiet there today. Nothing from any other point.' It also reports a destructive fire on Sunday night last at Augusta Ga, burning over Four hundred (400) bales of Cotton. On monday evening another fire occurred at Hamburg opposite Augusta in which from fifteen hundred 1500 to two thousand 2000 bales of Cotton belonging to the Government was burned.' The Examiner says that 'there have been some recent dispositions of the rebel forces in the South and West, the details of which are inadmissable.' The Charleston mercury states that 'A large number of reinforcements had arrived in that City.' The resolutions which were referred to yesterday as having passed the Confederate Senate creating the Office of Commander in Chief of all the armies of the Confederacy [a]nd recommending the reinstatement of Gen Johnston have been passed by the latter branch of the Confederate Congress. The Oconee R R Bridge is reported finished and passenger trains will soon pass over it."—Telegram received (at 5:35 P.M.), DNA, RG 107, Telegrams Collected (Bound).

1865, JAN. 21. Heinrich Tiedeman, M.D., Philadelphia, to USG. "Please read the enclosed certificates and spent a few moments to investigate why this Capt. Dilger is overlooked and, forgotten in a maner which is almost alike ingratitude and an insult. You as a soldier and a gentleman must appreciate acknowledge and reward the valor of a brave and able comrad in arms and this confidence to you—renders me bold enough to direct these lines to you without any ceremonies."—ALS, DNA, RG 108, Letters Received. Enclosed was a sheaf of copies of statements praising Capt. Hubert Dilger, Battery I, 1st Ohio Art., Tiedeman's son-in-law.—*Ibid.*

1865, JAN. 23. To Secretary of War Edwin M. Stanton. "The Richmond Whig has the following. The Augusta Constitutionalist of the seventeenth (17) says that for several days the streets of that City have been thronged with fugitives from S. C. accompanied by their families flocks herds cattle servants and stock of all kinds   There seems to be a general Exodus from the Old palmetto state and the planters in the Dist of Barnwell especially are fleeing from what they conceive to be the wrath to come. Safety and security from the inroads of the Yankees are being sought in the interior of Georgia   The following dispatch was read in the N. C. senate on Wednesday last. 'HON MILES M BANE speaker state   Wilmington has not fallen nor not likely to fall   N. C. will do her duty & all will be well with an honest effort This town can be held. For Gods sake let the legislature come up to the crisis   Dont despair of the republic' (signed) E D HALL   Persons who left Wilmington on Wednesday say that our forces had fallen back within Eight (8) miles of the town and that General Terry had demanded a surrender giving General Bragg until yesterday (19th) to decide upon what he would do. The removal of all public property was going on as fast as possible & we doubt not but every preparation was being made to fall back —Persons from there say that all is confusion at Wilmington and that nothing can be heard as to the fighting that has taken place the casualties or any thing of kind   The Genl impression was that the place would go and that most of the people would remain and go with it. Of the freshet last week the Charleston mercury says that between this city and Columbia the long trestle work on the South Carolina Rail Road at Kingsville was washed away. At Chester on the Columbia and Charlotte Rail Road heavy losses were sustained and the track greatly damaged which by proper Exertions Can be repaired in three (3) weeks time. On saturday last two hundred & fifty (250) Yankee deserters were started from Richmond through the lines Enroute for the north by the usual way"—Telegram received (at 7:10 P.M.), DNA, RG 107, Telegrams Collected (Bound).

1865, JAN. 23. USG endorsement. "Respectfully forwarded to Maj Gen Halleck, who who will order the two Batteries, named by Gen Meade in his Endorsement as being at Camp Barry, to join the 6th Corps in the Army of the Potomac."—ES, DNA, RG 94, Letters Received, 101H 1865. Written on a letter of Jan. 12 from Bvt. Maj. Gen. Henry J. Hunt to Bvt. Lt. Col. Simon F. Barstow requesting that batteries be sent from Washington to the Army of the Potomac.—LS, *ibid.*

1865, JAN. 23, 10:30 P.M. Maj. Gen. George G. Meade to USG. "I have notified Col Duane to have ready 500 feet of bridging with wagons & mules & subject to your order.—Will you require any engineer troops to accompany the train—If so how many companies—I should think two would be ample—"—ALS (telegram sent), DNA, RG 94, War Records Office, Army of the Potomac; telegram received, *ibid.*, RG 108, Letters Received. *O.R.*, I, xlvi, part 2, 207. On Jan. 24, USG twice wrote to Meade. "Please have Col. Duane and one of his assistants report here to me this morning for duty for the next two days They can come down with you this morning." "You will please send in the five hundred feet of bridging with the wagons and mules, and also two Companies of Engineers to accompany them, You will call upon Gen. Ingalls for transportation,"—Copies, DLC-USG, V, 46, 72, 108; DNA, RG 108, Letters Sent. *O.R.*, I, xlvi, part 2, 227. On the same day, USG telegraphed to Maj. Gen. John G. Parke. "Please inform Col. Duane's assistant that instead of 500 feet of Pontoon train, six hundred will be required. Send that amount to City Point for shipment."—ALS (telegram sent), CSmH; copies, DLC-USG, V, 46, 72, 108; DNA, RG 108, Letters Sent.

1865, JAN. 23, noon. Brig. Gen. John A. Rawlins to USG. "Saturday's Richmond Examiner states positively that Mr Seddon Secy of War has resigned and if any nomination has been made of his successor it has not yet been acted on. There is nothing at the War Dept of shermans movements later than already reported Genl Hardee telegraphed thursday to the Dept that there was nothing of interest to communicate"—Telegram received (at 12:30 P.M.), DNA, RG 107, Telegrams Collected (Bound); copy, *ibid.*, RG 94, War Records Office, Army of the Potomac. *O.R.*, I, xlvi, part 2, 206.

1865, JAN. 24. To Secretary of War Edwin M. Stanton. "Richmond papers rec'd. News scanty—The freshets in the South have been very damaging to railroads & other property. Dispatch reports that maj. Gen. Gordon has been placed in command of the 2nd Corps lately commanded by Lt. Gen. Early. No appointment has yet been made for Secy of War. indeed Mr. Seddons resignation has not been accepted. It is rumored that Mr Benjamin has sent in his resignation."—Telegram received (at 8:30 P.M.), DNA, RG 107, Telegrams Collected (Bound).

1865, JAN. 24. USG endorsement. "Respectfully forwarded to the Secretary of War"—ES, DNA, RG 94, ACP, T18 CB 1865. Written on a letter of Jan. 21 from Maj. Gen. Alfred H. Terry, Fort Fisher, N. C., to Brig. Gen. John A. Rawlins recommending the promotion of Col. George S. Dodge for services during the Fort Fisher expedition.—ALS, *ibid.* On Jan. 22, Bvt. Brig. Gen. Cyrus B. Comstock wrote to Rawlins. "When the Sec. of War asked Gen. Terry for names for promotion the latter omitted the name of Col. Dodge Chf Qr. Mr. but has since specially recommended him. The Qr. Mr.'s affairs have been admirably managed in this expedition, especially the worst part, that is the seagoing part & the credit of it is due to Dodge who has shown forethought, skill & untiring energy. As the rewards for the success of the expedition are distributed his work should, as all important to its success, be remembered & I hope the geneal will approve Terry's recommendation. There is nothing new here, everything being as when I wrote day before yesterday. The admiral has not moved any higher up the river yet. He has another letter from Sherman who was at Pocotaligo I am told. I wish some of you would write & tell me the news—this correspondence is getting awfully one sided. Remember me to all."—ALS, *ibid.*, RG 108, Letters Sent by Comstock. On Jan. 23, Terry wrote to Rawlins recommending a bvt. promotion in the U.S. Army for Brig. Gen. (and Bvt. Maj. Gen.) Adelbert Ames, which USG favorably endorsed on Jan. 25.— *O.R.*, I, li, part 1, 1200. On Jan. 19, Ames wrote to Secretary of War Edwin M. Stanton recommending a promotion for Capt. Charles A. Carleton, adjt. for Ames.—LS, DNA, RG 94, ACP, T18 CB 1865. On Jan. 25, USG endorsed this letter favorably.—ES, *ibid.* On Jan. 18, Bvt. Brig. Gen. Albert M. Blackman, Fort Fisher, commanding 27th Colored, wrote to Brig. Gen. Lorenzo Thomas asking assignment at his bvt. rank.—ALS, *ibid.*, B51 CB 1865. On Jan. 25, USG endorsed this letter favorably.—ES, *ibid.* On Feb. 13, USG favorably endorsed two letters from Terry requesting additional bvts. and promotions for officers at Fort Fisher.—ES, *ibid.*, T38 CB 1865.

1865, JAN. 24.   To Bvt. Maj. Gen. John G. Barnard. "You have permission to stay."—Telegram received (at 1:10 P.M.), DNA, RG 107, Telegrams Collected (Bound); copies, *ibid.*, RG 108, Letters Sent; DLC-USG, V, 46, 72, 108. On Jan. 24, Barnard, Washington, D. C., had telegraphed to USG. "I have a good deal of old business &c to finish up.—Would like to stay till Friday, but can come down at once, if you need me. . . . Direct answer to No 10 16½ Street."—ALS (telegram sent), DNA, RG 107, Telegrams Collected (Unbound). On Feb. 2, 5:30 P.M., Barnard, Fort Monroe, telegraphed to Brig. Gen. John A. Rawlins. "Just arrived—Shall leave for City Point about 9 this P. M."—ALS (telegram sent), *ibid.*

1865, JAN. 24.   To Maj. Gen. George G. Meade. "Please direct Col. Duane to send his Photographers to Fort Fisher to report to Gen. Comstock for duty until the works about Cape Fear River are photographed"—Copies, DLC-USG, V, 46, 72, 108; DNA, RG 108, Letters Sent. *O.R.*, I, xlvi, part 2, 227.

1865, JAN. 24.   To U.S. Senator Zachariah Chandler of Mich. "Gen, Peirce has permission, and he has been notified."—Copies, DLC-USG, V, 46, 72, 108; DNA, RG 108, Letters Sent. On the same day, Tuesday, Lt. Col. Ely S. Parker telegraphed to Maj. Gen. Andrew A. Humphreys. "At the request of Senator Chandler Rep— Kellogg permission is granted Brig, Gen B, R, Peirce to visit Washington   Please notify him and say that he is expected there by thursday,"—Copies, *ibid.*; *ibid.*, RG 393, 2nd Army Corps, Telegrams Received. On Jan. 30, Col. James A. Hardie telegraphed to USG. "Brig. Genl B. R. Pierce asks extension of leave for five days—Can it be granted?"—LS (telegram sent), *ibid.*, RG 107, Telegrams Collected

(Bound). On the same day, Lt. Col. Theodore S. Bowers telegraphed to Hardie. "Your dispatch in relation to Gen. Pierce was in the absence of Gen Grant referred to ~~G~~Maj. Gen J. G. Parke, Army Potomac, who objects to the ~~extend~~ extension of Gen Pierces leave of absence"—ALS (telegram sent), *ibid.*, Telegrams Collected (Unbound); telegram received (at 2:40 P.M.), *ibid.*, Telegrams Collected (Bound).

1865, JAN. 24.   President Abraham Lincoln to USG. "If Newell W. Root, of 1 Conn. Heavy Artillery is under sentence of death please telegraph me briefly the circumstances—"—ALS (telegram sent), DNA, RG 107, Telegrams Collected (Bound). Lincoln, *Works*, VIII, 235. On Jan. 25, 12:30 P.M., USG telegraphed to Lincoln. "The following is the report in the case of Newell W. Root"—Telegram received (at 3:15 P.M.), DLC-Robert T. Lincoln; DNA, RG 107, Telegrams Collected (Bound); copies, *ibid.*, Telegrams Received in Cipher; *ibid.*, RG 108, Letters Sent; DLC-USG, V, 46, 72, 108. USG enclosed a report of Capt. P. T. Whitehead, judge advocate, to Brig. Gen. Marsena R. Patrick. "I have the honor to report in regard to Private Newell W. Root alias Geo H. Harris Co H 1st Conn Heavy Artillery, that he was tried by this Court on Dec 19th 1864 & convicted of 'deserting to the Enemy' & sentenced to be hung. His sentence is approved by General Meade & ordered to be carried into effect at City Point on Friday 27th inst under the directions of Provost Marshal General. The facts in the case show that Root deserted to the Enemy near Dutch Gap & gave himself up to the rebels as a union deserter; was released under Rebel order No 65 and on making his way through to ~~Lexington~~ Louisa Ky represented himself as a rebel deserter for the purpose of getting out of the service, he gave the name of Harris & came to City Point in arrest under that name. Capt Dimock Co H. 1st Conn Artillery proves that Root left camp on James River without authority and never returned. Private Potts same Company proves that he saw Root near the canal on that day and asked him if he was going back to camp, Root answered that, he was not going back so much as he was! Potts never saw him after that until on trial. The fact of Roots giving himself up as a deserter is proven by his own statement made voluntarily to the examining officer. In his statement he claims to have been captured and that he then represented to his captors that he was a deserter and also that when he was sent from Richmond and released near Pound Gap he was advised by others with him to pass for a rebel deserter when he entered our lines in Kentucky"—Copies, *ibid.* On the same day, 10:25 P.M., Lincoln telegraphed to USG. "Having received the report in the case of Newell W. Root, I do not interfere further in the case."—ALS (telegram sent), DNA, RG 107, Telegrams Collected (Bound). Lincoln, *Works*, VIII, 237.

1865, JAN. 24.   Bvt. Maj. Gen. Edward Ferrero to USG. "I returned it by Mail—"—ALS (telegram sent), DNA, RG 107, Telegrams Collected (Unbound).

1865, JAN. 24.   Brig. Gen. John A. Rawlins to Maj. Gen. John Gibbon.
"A party of 20 men & 2   have started under command of Capt Brook 3
Penna Cavalry to Capture some scouts of the enemy—As they may have to
return through your line please inform your officers of Cavalry Pickets of
the fact"—Telegram received, Ord Papers, CU-B.

1865, JAN. 24, 7:00 P.M.   Maj. Gen. Philip H. Sheridan, Winchester,
Va., to USG. "I wish to fit up a canvas ponton bridge for the cavalry of this
military Div.n and want a company of Pontoneers to take charge of it—will
you have the kindness to order a Co to me from the Army of the Potomac—
I should like to have the same company and officers that I had with me on
my expedition in June"—Telegram received (at 7:20 P.M.), DNA, RG
107, Telegrams Collected (Bound); *ibid.*, RG 108, Letters Received;
copies, *ibid.*, RG 107, Telegrams Received in Cipher; (2) DLC-Philip H.
Sheridan. Printed as addressed to Brig. Gen. John A. Rawlins in *O.R.*, I,
xlvi, part 2, 252. At 9:35 P.M., Lt. Col. Ely S. Parker telegraphed to Maj.
Gen. John G. Parke. "You will order one Company of Pontoniers to the Valley of the Shenandoah to report to Maj Gen Sheridan. The Genl would be
pleased to have the same company & officers that were with him on his
expedition last June."—Telegram received, DNA, RG 94, War Records
Office, Army of the Potomac; copies, *ibid.*, RG 108, Letters Sent; DLC-
USG, V, 46, 72, 108; Meade Papers, PHi. *O.R.*, I, xlvi, part 2, 228. On
Jan. 25, 10:40 A.M., Sheridan telegraphed to Rawlins. "Capt Follwell 50th
New York Vols. Engrs. was the officer who had charge of the bridge train
for me last summer & is the officer that I should like detailed with his Company to report to me"—Telegram received, DNA, RG 107, Telegrams Collected (Unbound); *ibid.*, RG 108, Letters Received. *O.R.*, I, xlvi, part
2, 264.

1865, JAN. 24.   Col. James L. Donaldson to USG. "I hope you will not
deem me troublesome if I ask you to advocate the confirmation of my brevet
of Brgadier General now before the Senate. It was given for 'meretorious
and distinguished Services in the Qmr. Dept in the campaign terminating
in the fall of Atlanta.' None better than yourself know what I did to make
that campaign a success, and what difficulties I had to Encounter and overcome—After the initiation of the campaign under Sherman, I organized my
Employes into a Military force, and was prepared to defend Nashville if
not too heavily attacked, and so well was Genl Thomas pleased with the
organzation after reviewing it that he gave me a position in his inner line
to hold during the recent battles before Nashville, and I occupied it three
days and nights with five thousand men—He has also given me the 15th &
17th Colored regiments U. S. Troops, so that in fact, I have a military
command as well as a staff position—The War Department has sent me
commissions (without pay or rations) for my military organzation—Hoping
my dear General that you can assist me, and tendering you my hearty
congratulations on recent Events which are due solely to yourself."—ALS,

DNA, RG 393, Dept. of the Cumberland, Provost Marshal, Letters Sent. Donaldson was confirmed on Feb. 14.

1865, JAN. 25, 3:00 P.M.   Secretary of War Edwin M. Stanton to USG. "The following is from Hon. M. F. Odell and is forwarded for your information. 'I have [j]ust had a conversation with a deserter from the rebel army, who has been in the "works" on the *North Side* of the James over twelve months. He left them last monday week Jan. 9th. He says the rebels are *mining for Harrison,* a work taken from them last fall and still held by our men. He has been on the spot and seen the *mine.* I know the man, he is *reliable.* He also says, that obstructions of a formadable character are now placed in the James river just above "Dutch Gap Canal." ' "—LS, DNA, RG 107, Telegrams Collected (Bound); telegram received, *ibid.,* RG 108, Letters Received.

1865, JAN. 25.   Maj. Gen. Philip H. Sheridan to USG. "On my arrival here I investigated the case of the man of the 15th New Jersey Regiment of whom you spoke to me, and find that he was restored to duty by Major General Wright Commanding 6th Corps. The man was present with his Regiment and it is thought there is authority for so doing, A copy of General Wrights order was sent you immediately after the receipt of your letter on the subject"—Copies, DNA, RG 393, Middle Military Div., Letters Sent; DLC-Philip H. Sheridan. Possibly related is a USG endorsement to Sheridan of Jan. 31. "Referred to Maj Gen Sheridan. This is the case I wrote to you about from Burlington, N. J. and requested you to ask the President to pardon. Please attend to and have the man discharged the service"—Copy, DLC-USG, V, 58. Written on a letter of Jan. 23 from Mrs. Elisha Ettarger [?], Burlington, N. J., asking that her brother, John Leeson, 15th N. J., be released from prison.—*Ibid.*

1865, JAN. 25.   Brig. Gen. Philip St. George Cooke, New York City, to USG. "I have two daughters, one a widow, with infant children suffering for clothing—I propose sending them a box, of two cubic feet or less, containing clothing and nothing other, contraband, on honor: unless letters of affection only, from their mother(?). The box to be sent to *you,* 'from PSGC';—with the request that you have it marked 'For Mrs Charles Brewer or Mrs J. E. B. Stuart; care of _____'—Genl. Lee or Mr Ould; by flag of truce. My feelings & strong motive must be my only justification, for attempting thus to trouble you, & to consume even a moment of your so valuable time. (Such things, I know, have been allowed.) An Aide, D. C. can write me if you approve & assent."—ALS, DNA, RG 108, Miscellaneous Papers.

1865, JAN. 25.   Lt. Col. Ely S. Parker to Brig. Gen. Rufus Ingalls. "You will please direct the Quarter Master at Ft, Monroe to furnish transportation for all supplies now at the Fort, or that may hereafter arrive to New

York consigned to Wm N. R. Beall C, S, A, Agent, when sent by the
Southern Authorities or contributed from other sources for distribution
among the southern prisoners confined in the North,   Individual contribu-
tions for prisoners confined at Point Lookout Md, will be sent ~~direct~~ by the
Quartermaster direct to that place"—Copies, DLC-USG, V, 46, 72, 108;
DNA, RG 108, Letters Sent.

1865, JAN. 26.   To President Abraham Lincoln. "The following just recd
Will forward proceedings as soon as recd"—Telegram received (at 1:35
P.M.), DLC-Robert T. Lincoln. USG appended a telegram of the same day
from Maj. Gen. John G. Parke. "No proceedings in the case of Wm A Jeffs
Co "B" fifty sixth (56) Mass Vols have been recd at these HdQuarters   In
case the sentence should be death the proceedings will be forwarded you"—
ALS (telegram sent), DNA, RG 393, Army of the Potomac, Miscellaneous
Letters Received; copies, *ibid.*, Letters Sent; DLC-Robert T. Lincoln. On
the same day, Lincoln had telegraphed to USG. "Suspend execution of death
sentence of William H. Jeffs Company B Fifty sixth Massachusetts volunteers until further orders, and forward record of trial for examination."—
Telegram sent, DNA, RG 107, Telegrams Collected (Bound); copy, *ibid.*,
RG 94, Letters Received, 102P 1865. Lincoln, *Works*, VIII, 239. See
ibid., p. 245.

1865, JAN. 26.   USG endorsement. "Respectfully forwarded to the Secretary of War, with the request that the order herein referred to be postponed until the close of the War. The practice of selling confiscated property
near the garrisons in the revolted states, brings into the Army a class of
speculators whose influence is worse than that of the most virulent Secessionist & takes from the Government in a single quarter more actual cash
than is realized by the Treasury by the sale of the property"—ES, DNA,
RG 107, Letters Received from Bureaus. Written on a letter of Jan. 23
from Maj. Gen. Edward O. C. Ord to Secretary of the Treasury William
P. Fessenden protesting the sale of timberland near Norfolk and Portsmouth.—LS, *ibid.*

1865, JAN. 26.   To Maj. Gen. John G. Parke. "The above just received
—Please send proceedings to these Head Quarters."—Telegram sent, DNA,
RG 108, Letters Received; telegram received (at 4:15 P.M.), *ibid.*, RG
393, Army of the Potomac, Miscellaneous Letters Received. At the foot of
the telegram received is a memorandum. "Simon J. Shaffer alias Samuel
Jefferson, 15th New York Engineers, to be shot at 12 m. Jany 27th under
direction Genl. Benham, City Point."—*Ibid.* On the same day, USG tele-
graphed to Parke. "The person referred to by the President is probably
Simon J. Shaffer 15th N. Y. Engrs."—Telegram sent, *ibid.*, RG 108, Letters
Received; telegram received (at 4:15 P.M.), *ibid.*, RG 393, Army of the
Potomac, Miscellaneous Letters Received.   On the same day, 3:30 P.M.,
President Abraham Lincoln had telegraphed to USG. "Suspend execution

of Hamel Shaffer ordered to be shot at City-Point tomorrow, until further orders, and forward record of trial for examination"—Telegram sent, *ibid.*, RG 107, Telegrams Collected (Bound); telegram received (at 3:45 P.M.), *ibid.*, RG 108, Letters Received. Lincoln, *Works*, VIII, 239. On Jan. 27, Lt. Col. Ely S. Parker telegraphed to Lincoln. "In compliance with telegraphic order of 3,30 P. M. 26th inst I have the honor to forward 'Proceedings of General Court Martial' in the case of Simon J. Shaffer alias Samuel Jefferson 15th Regt, N. Y. Eng'rs"—Copies, DLC-USG, V, 46, 72, 108; DNA, RG 108, Letters Sent. On Feb. 6, 1:25 P.M., Lincoln telegraphed to USG. "Suspend execution in case of Simon J. Schaffer 15th N. Y. Engineers until further orders and send me the record."—LS (telegram sent), *ibid.*, RG 107, Telegrams Collected (Bound). Lincoln, *Works*, VIII, 263. On the same day, USG telegraphed to Lincoln. "The execution in the case of simon J schaffer 15th N Y Engineers was suspended until further orders on the 27th January and the Record was forwarded to Washington on the following day"—Telegram received (at 4:45 P.M.), DLC-Robert T. Lincoln; DNA, RG 107, Telegrams Collected (Bound); copies, *ibid.*, RG 108, Letters Sent; DLC-USG, V, 46, 72, 108. On the same day, 2:05 P.M., USG transmitted this telegram to Maj. Gen. George G. Meade, adding a note. "Please comply with above order"—Telegram received, DNA, RG 393, Army of the Potomac, Miscellaneous Letters Received.

1865, JAN. 26.   Christopher Thorssen, Cincinnati, "formerly 9th O. V. I.," to USG. "The papers tell us that the fate of our suffering prisoners in the south is now placed in your hands. You are a soldier and will feel for them. For three years I have battled for my country, and am now disabled, a cripple. Is it too much, when I now ask this country to give me bak my brother, the only hope and comfort left to me, who is now prisoner for over 16 month, being taken at the battle of Chicamauga. There may be more in the same condition and I am not praying for a special exchange, but I implore you, General, if you have it in your power, open these prisons doors, send our brothers home into our arms, and brighter laurels will crown your brow, than if you won a glorious battle and the poeple will bless you not only as its greatest general but as its best and noblest of men."—ALS, DNA, RG 108, Miscellaneous Papers.

1865, JAN. 27.   To President Abraham Lincoln. "Maj Gen Parke furnishes the following information in relation to Barney Rouke 15th N. Y. Engineers of whom you telegraphed this morning"—Telegram received (at 4:15 P.M.), DLC-Robert T. Lincoln; DNA, RG 107, Telegrams Collected (Bound); copies, *ibid.*, RG 108, Letters Sent; DLC-USG, V, 46, 72, 108. The telegram included a message of Jan. 27 from Maj. Gen. John G. Parke to Lt. Col. Theodore S. Bowers. "Private Barney Rouke 15th N. Y. Engineers was not sentenced capitally—His sentence to be dishonorably discharged the service of the U. S. and to be confined at hard labor for the period of ten (10) years in the Penitentiary at Albany N. Y. or in such other prison as the Proper Authorities may direct was approved & the record forwarded Jany 2nd 1865 to the Judge Advocate General for reference to the Secretary of War for designation of place of confinement"—Copies, *ibid.* On the same day, 11:35 A.M., Lincoln had telegraphed to USG. "Stay execution in case of Barney Rourke 15th New York Engineers until record can be examined here."—Telegram sent, DNA, RG 107, Telegrams Collected (Bound); telegram received, *ibid.*, RG 94, Letters Received, 108P 1865. Lincoln, *Works*, VIII, 240. Since USG's telegram was sent from City Point after his departure, it was presumably sent by a staff officer in USG's name.

1865, JAN. 27. To Capt. George K. Leet from Fort Monroe. "Please purchase for me, and send bill to City Point, Sixteen yards of cheap carpeting, one Bolster and two pillows. These articles can be sent by Express or in charge of Mail Messenger as you deem best. Gen. Rawlins and myself are just on our way to Fort Fisher. Will be back probably in four days."—Stan. V. Henkels, Catalogue No. 1194, June 8, 1917, no. 221. A document of Feb. 4 listed in the same catalogue as written by "Mr. Benners" to "Captain Bowers, Chief of Staff," might possibly have been written by Lt. Col. Theodore S. Bowers to Leet. "Gen. Grant thinks the bills you sent him amount to $28.75, but he has mislaid them. He encloses herewith $30.00. He can't make change. Says you shall go to an Oyster Saloon and eat a plate of oysters for him, for the difference."—*Ibid.*, no. 230.

1865, JAN. 27. Brig. Gen. James Totten, Mo. State Militia, New Orleans, to USG. "I have the honor to ask a few moments of your valuable time and attention to the case of a friend and warm admirer of your own. When you were in this City, in September 1863, the gentleman to whom I have reference attended you, at the request of General Banks, when injured at a review at Carrollton. I mention this fact to call him to your mind and to assure you in befriending him you will only be doing a service to a gentleman, your friend, and one who has done you a small service and stands ready to serve you again. The gentleman I refer to is Dr I. V. C. Smith, Ex-Mayor of Boston, a learned man and highly accomplished Surgeon &c, Dr Smith was for some time Professor of Anatomy in the New York Medical College; he was afterwards sent to New Orleans to manage the Christian Commission in the Department of the Gulf, and served as a Surgeon in the St James' U. S. Hospital at the same time. He was then Commissioned Lieut-Colonel by General Banks because of his professional services in organizing an institution for the insane. Last Season he performed the duties of Medical Inspector, and subsequently was appointed Commissioner of Health in New Orleans. In August last Dr Smith left the Army, but is still acting as Supervisor of the institution for the insane. The Dr now delivers, gratuitously, three lectures weekly before Army and Navy Surgeons for their improvement in their professional services. General Banks made efforts to have Doctor Smith appointed a Medical Inspector in the Army, but had not the power to do so. The Doctor is still managing the manifold interests of the Christian Commission without any compensation; but having a family to support, and having had to sacrifice property to a considerable extent, he is desirous of being appointed a Medical Inspector in the Volunteer Service, in order that he may have some means of living and providing for his family. If General Grant can by his great influence, aid the Doctor in procuring the appointment indicated, he will not only secure to the Service a most competent Medical Officer and estimable gentleman; but likewise confer a lasting favor upon that gentleman himself, and many other friends; . . ."—LS, DNA, RG 108, Letters Received.

1865, JAN. 27.   Henry W. Bellows, U.S. Sanitary Commission, New York City, to USG. "There is not a day in which I am not in receipt of agonizing appeals from relatives and friends, for the relief of our misused prisoners. It is stated that you now have full authority to regulate the matter by conference with Gen. Lee! Is this so? And what expectations can you hold out to the country of any special improvement in the case of our Prisoners in Rebel Hands, except by seizing their prison houses? Does any opportunity exist of forwarding boxes or stores to the Prisoners, at Richmond, at Danville, at Andersonville? If these inquiries were not every day made of me, as President of the Sanitary Commission, I should not trouble you to give me reliable information, that I may aid in alleviating the horrible anxiety that burdens the homes & hearts of the country. Any words you say on this subject, will be welcomed with profound confidence & gratitude. If you can say any thing encouraging or consoling to the Nation, or give any hope of our prisoners obtaining any relief, either from our enemy, or from our own Government, I beseech you to do it speedily."—ALS, DNA, RG 108, Miscellaneous Papers.

1865, JAN. 30.   Maj. Gen. Philip H. Sheridan to USG. "Would it be proper to let me know where Genl Grovers div is   Gen Birge & several other officers have applied to me to know where to Join their commands"—Telegram received, DNA, RG 107, Telegrams Collected (Unbound); (press) *ibid.*, Telegrams Collected (Bound). *O.R.*, I, xlvi, part 2, 307. On Jan. 31, Lt. Col. Theodore S. Bowers telegraphed to Sheridan. "Gen, Grovers Division has gone to Savanah Ga, and will constitute a part of the permanent garrison of that place"—Copies, DLC-USG, V, 46, 72, 108; DNA, RG 108, Letters Sent.

1865, JAN. 31.   To Secretary of War Edwin M. Stanton. "The following dispatches are taken from todays Richmond Whig. 'Charleston Jany 29th   Our scouts report that the Enemy infantry infantry are camped near Enniss Cross Roads on the road leading toward Grahamsville & on the road towards Sisters Ferry   A reconnoitering force was reported within four (4) miles of Robertsville this morning   A small party of Yankees landed on Little Britain Island near Legears Saturday night & were driven off   Jackson Miss Jany 28th—Twenty three (23) houses six hundred (600) bales cotton commissary Quartermaster & other stores were burned at Summit this morning   The fire was accidental   The "Examiner" states that Gen Hardee telegraphs that all attempts of the Enemy to cross the Cumbahee had so far failed   General Dick Tayler telegraphs that most of Thomas army is reported to have marched west from Columbia to Clifton on the Tennessee River and that a portion of their forces including A J Smiths are said to be in the vicinity of Huntsville & Eastport   There is no Change in the fleet of mobile   The Enemy is still leaving Pascagoula' "—Telegram received (at 6:00 P.M.), DNA, RG 107, Telegrams Collected (Bound).

1865, [FEB.].   USG endorsement. "I know nothing of this young applicant cadets app[oint]ment myself but the endorsements he has are such as to recommend him highly."—AES, DNA, RG 94, Cadet Applications. Written on a letter of Jan. 4 from Bvt. Maj. Gen. Nelson A. Miles to President Abraham Lincoln. "I have the honor to recommend Mr Edmund Zalinski, of Seneca Falls, N. Y. for the appointment of cadet in the Military Academy at West Point. He is a young man of superior intelligence, and fine education, and shows great zeal and aptness in the attainment of Military Knowledge. He has been acting for several months, in the capacity of Volunteer Aide-de-camp upon my Staff, always proving himself competent for the performance of the duties imposed upon him, and, when under fire, has given evidence of courage of a high order. He possesses qualities which, if developed, would, in my opinion, make of him a superior officer, and I respectfully urge that this request be favorably considered."—LS, *ibid.* Maj. Gen. Andrew A. Humphreys and Maj. Gen. Winfield S. Hancock were among those adding favorable endorsements. On Feb. 22, Lincoln endorsed this letter. "West-Point—*file.*"—AES, *ibid.* Edmund L. Zalinski was appointed 2nd lt., 2nd N. Y. Art., as of Feb. 23, 1865, and 2nd lt., 2nd Art., as of Feb. 23, 1866.

1865, FEB. 1, 5:00 P.M.   To Brig. Gen. Henry W. Wessells, commissary gen. of prisoners. "Please send Lt. Col. Jones, 57th N. C. from Johnston's Island to Fort Delaware for exchange by next Flag of Truce. I ask this because of his kindness to our men confined in the South where he commanded as attested by officers who were under his charge."—ALS (telegram sent), OClWHi; telegram received (on Feb. 2, 4:35 A.M.), DNA, RG 107, Telegrams Collected (Bound); *ibid.*, RG 249, Letters Received. On Feb. 4, Bvt. Brig. Gen. William Hoffman, who had replaced Wessells as commissary gen. of prisoners, wrote to USG. "I have the honor to inform you that Lieut Col Jones, 57th North Carolina Regiment, a prisoner of War confined at Johnson's Island, has been ordered to be sent for exchange, in compliance with your request, by telegram, of the 2nd inst. He will be sent to report to Lieut Col J. E. Mulford, Agent for Exchange, Fortress Monroe, Va."—ALS, *ibid.*, RG 108, Letters Received.

1865, FEB. 1. USG endorsement. "Refered to Chief of Signal Corps."—AES, DNA, RG 111, Letters Received. Written on a letter of Jan. 30 from William M. Marshall, Philadelphia, to USG discussing his invention of a method of "magnifying light" which could be used for the signal service.—ALS, *ibid.*

1865, FEB. 2. To Secretary of War Edwin M. Stanton. "The following despatch is taken from the Richmond Whig of today—'Charleston January 31st—All the movements of the enemy indicate that Augusta & Branchville are their points of destination The twentieth (20th) Army Corps occupies Robertsville This place is about fifty (50) miles above Savannah & five (5) miles from the river A heavy force of Infantry, Artillery, & Cavalry is reported encamped near the Junction of the Saltkelcher & Old Union road. this force is believed to ~~be~~ consist of the fifteenth (15) & sixteenth (16) A Corps Yesterday morning the enemy advanced in considerable force of Infantry and Artillery from White Point & Drove in our skirmish line three (3) miles to Kings Creek our Infantry afterwards advanced and drove the enemy back to White Point re.establishing our picket line Since this all has been quiet on the Combahee at that point The enemy made a demonstration on our position defending the Pontoon bridge over the Saltkehatchie this afternoon but without result It is reported that they burnt McPhersonsville last night This village is five (5) miles northwest of Pocataligo The Examiner reports that this morning about two hundred & fifty (250) of the enemys deserters under order sixty five (65) were started for a point on the Hostile lines to go to their homes'."—Telegram received (at 5:50 P.M.), DNA, RG 107, Telegrams Collected (Bound). On Feb. 3 and 4, USG transmitted to Stanton additional news reported in the *Richmond Whig* from Charleston.—*O.R.,* I, xlvii, part 2, 285, 294.

On Feb. 2, USG telegraphed to Stanton. "The Richmond Whig has the following (copy of Gen. Ord's telegram) The Examiner reports that this morning about 250 of the Enemy's deserters under order 65 were started for a point on the hostile lines to go to their homes—"—Telegram received (at 6:00 P.M.), DNA, RG 107, Telegrams Collected (Bound).

1865, FEB. 2. Special Orders No. 24, Armies of the U.S. "Brig. Gen. S. Williams, acting Inspector General Armies of the United States, will proceed without delay, to the Department of the South, and make a thorough inspection of military affairs in that Department. All military authorities are ~~requested~~ required to afford him every facility in the execution of this order. Bvt. Captain C. W. Woolsey, Acting Aid-de-Camp will accompany Brig. Gen. S. Williams, Acting Inspector General, on his tour of inspection" —Copies, DLC-USG, V, 57, 63, 64, 65. *O.R.,* I, xlvii, part 2, 205.

1865, FEB. 3. Maj. Gen. George G. Meade to Lt. Col. Theodore S. Bowers. "Col Dent promised to give me a pass for Mrs. Robertson, the wife of a rebel in Charleston—Mrs. R belongs to one of our most loyal families in Philada and altho married in the South, is desirous of leaving the Confederacy with her children & living with her family in Philada—I do not believe she has any purpose but the one stated above, nor will she in any way abuse the privilege thus granted to her in case the favor of a pass is accorded—I send an open letter for her in which you can place the pass & forward it by flag of truce—I also forward a letter from her brother in law in Philada at whose request I write—Iff this pass can be given I shall esteem it a personal favor—"—ALS, OClWHi.

1865, FEB. 3.   Special Orders No. 25, Armies of the U.S. "The following organizations are hereby assigned to the Army of the Potomac, Maj. Gen. Geo. G. Meade, Commanding: 11th Regt. U. S. Infantry 1st Battln Maine SharpShooters. Halls Indpdt Battln Michigan SharpShooters."—Copies, DLC-USG, V, 57, 63, 64, 65. *O.R.*, I, xlvi, part 2, 362. On Feb. 4, Lt. Col. Ely S. Parker wrote to Governor Samuel Cony of Maine. "I am directed by the Lieut Genl, Com'dg to request you to report to these Head Quarters, at thes earliest moment pacticable whether it is intended to fill up the 1st Regt Maine Sharp Shooters, and if so how soon it is expected that this will be accomplished, Its efficiency in the field is very much dependent upon its numbers, hence the above inquiries,"—Copies, DLC-USG, V, 46, 72, 108; DNA, RG 108, Letters Sent. For correspondence concerning the 11th Inf., see *O.R.*, I, xlvi, part 2, 205, 449, 478.

1865, FEB. 3.   John Beamish, Memphis, to USG. "Will you oblige me by letting me know if you consider forcing a man (under penalty of again leaving Home) into the Militia liable to Meet the Confederate forces at any time a violation of your Special Orders No 82 (a Copy of which is Inclosed) or not I came into the U. S. Lines and gave my self up in good faith under that order beleiving I would be allowed to stay at Home in Memphis with my family but by the decission of Brig Genl Dustan Comg the Militia and Maj Genl Dana the last of which I received through Col Young A. P. Ml Genl I shall be compelled to leave again It being out of all Reason to suppose that I after—deserting the Confederate Army to live with my family in peace would take up Arms (even in the Militia) against my former Comrades knowing the penalty also in case of capture. I have a Militia pass for 15 days and trust that your answer will arrive in time and do away with the painful necessity of my again leaving home"—ALS, DNA, RG 109, Unfiled Papers and Slips. On Feb. 13, Lt. Col. Theodore S. Bowers endorsed this letter. "Respectfully referred to Maj Gen N. J. T. Dana, Comd'g Dept of the Miss."—ES, *ibid.*

1865, FEB. 4.   USG endorsement. "Respy returned to the Com Genl, U S A. and attention invited to endorsement hereon by Col M R. Morgan, Cf. Comry. Armies operating against Richmond as all the report necessary on this case. Complaints like those within are nearly always without foundation."—Copy, DLC-USG, V, 58. Written on a report of Lt. Col. Michael R. Morgan concerning a complaint that soldiers did not get enough to eat.— *Ibid.*

1865, FEB. 4. Peter F. Schliecker, Union League, Norfolk, to USG. "I have been appointed one of a Committee of Investigation by our Union League to Collect information as regards disloyal & unworthy Office holders in this department & we feel it our duty to inform you *knowing* that *you* will give us any necessary assistance to purge our Community of such disgracefull impositions as have been *&* *are now* being practiced on us greatly to the detriment of our Govt—We would respectfully suggest that three or more Commissions be appointed by you to aid us in the discharge of our duty and most respectfully Suggest the names of our Brothers of the League John H Boston Jas H Nall Z Sykes Patrick Offalton J C. Somers & T P. Crowell all of whom have stood the test & who even during the rebel reign here were firm in the Cause of our Country & who were imprisoned & persecuted for the sake of the Union   these are some of the few and staunch & reliable Union men and as our League has unanimously determined to assist & use our utmost exertions to elect '*true & reliable Union men*' & *none* others to all Offices of profit or trust from the lowest to the highest   The Loyall portion of this Community are in constant jeopardy of our Lives as threats are made & we have to Contend Constantly for our Union rights & to endeavour to thwart the designs of *Traitors* (and those who have but lately taken the Oath to our Govt & would *not* have taken it then (as they say) untill Compelled by Military law)   Many of whom who have since taken the Oath applied for & almost invaribly obtained responsible offices & positions   the Evidence is so great to prove their unfitness & disloyalty—that if you desire it, we will send   We beg your invaluable instruction & *Help* in this matter. We respectfully furnish you with Certificates proving the *disloyal*[ty] & immorality of the holder of one of the most responsi[ble] positions in our midst viz that of the 'Agent of the Commissions of the *Poor* & Keeper of the City Alms House.—The unworthy & disloyall incumbent who has acted with Others to organize parties & aposistion to endeavour to break up our Union League & our Govt   (Thomas D Williams) by Repeated malignant & Rebellious acts as well as words—now holds the responsible position before named greatly detrimenta[l] to the interests of the Loyall & worthy Poor & our Gov't. There is another of the many important subjects that we (as the Sworn Supporters of our Govt) wish to bring to your notice (Tho' you may be posted on this Matter) & that is the Question of Civil Gov't. The importance of which you can plainly see *has not* & *will not* aid our Goverment in the restoration of the Union because the Executive Gov. Pierpoint & some of his Staff & Coadjutors who appointed W W Wing (formerly P. Master here) as Treasurer of the State of Va (& *After* he Wing had been dismissed from the P. Office for disloyalty & Perjury to Our Goverment in that he the said Wing acted as an Agent for & did assist Rebels (who had not taken the Oath) to redeem their Property & he

Wing received *Bribes* for so doing.—L W Webb Auditor Public Accts & Geo P. Kneller who acted as Serjt at Arms at House of Representatives both of whom were Unanimously Expelled from Our League & from the Society of reliable Union men for disloyalty to our Gov't. & disgracefull remarks against our Gov't Military The above will Exhibit a birds Eye view of what an awfull reign of Terror would exist if we had (what these unprincipled men call) Civil Goverment by the influence of Pierpoint & his Coadjutors. The above is only a few cases of hundreds of similar acts, and as we the Loyall League intend to do our utmost to purge out all such imposters, Petitions have been sent to for our approval for the resolution of Civil Gov't but invariably *we have* & intend to disapprove of such Petitions, *untill* we the League can organize it on a *Firm & Loyall Basis* This man Williams was Appointed by the Military July 18/64 through the Military Commission For the Poor (as the Agent,) is still retained in Office in *spite* of the *unrebutted* & Sworn Certificates of Five of our most responsible & tried unconditional Union men & supporters of the Gov't We the League want Help from you to assist us in the full & fearless discharge of our duties We apply to you particularly as we Love & respect you & can fully confide in your deliberations We would respectfully invoke your favorable Consideratio[n] & aid us in our Efforts to assist Our Beneficent Goverment in the restoration of Our Glorious Union"—ALS, DNA, RG 109, Union Provost Marshals' File of Papers Relating to Individual Civilians. See *Calendar,* June 5, 1863.

1865, FEB. 5.   Maj. Gen. Edward O. C. Ord to Lt. Col. Horace Porter. "I enclose you sundry papers bearing on the subject of management of Negro Affairs in this Department the reports of Captains Brown and Wilder may give you some insight into the amount of their responsibilities, Lt Col White's report has not been sent in yet as soon as it is you will receive a Copy of it. The subject to which I wish your attention called—are the farms and schools of and the issues of rations and clothing, to the Colored people —the farms and schools should if possible be supported from the labor of the farms, and as few rations issued to the Colored population as consistent with their ability to earn their own bread. Clothing is now sent in large quantities from the north but there is no responsibility in regard to its issue —And I am informed that in many instances it is sold. returns of such sales and of the proceeds there from should be made—and if proceeds are returned to the donors—such fact should be proven and published—various reports have reached me in regard to expenditures by the Quarter Master Dept for fuel forage and other articles reported purchased from the Bureau of negro affairs—which articles it is stated in some instances cost more to haul than they could be bought for,—the relations between the Quarter Master Department and the Beurau of negro affairs should be strictly examined—And the Books of the Savings Bank Norfolk should also be Carefully overhauled—that it may be known who are the Depositers, what becomes of funds of deceased, or discharged soldiers—what amount if any has been called for by depositers and the necessity for such a bank and its proffit to the Colored Soldiers reported—The Condition of the Colored schools—actual number of students—course of studies health of pupils and the expense of the system stated—with a report as to who are the teachers how paid, fed, and lodged, Should you require the services of an assistant or clerks please call on Lt Col Smith A. A. Genl Hd Quarters of the Dept and he will detail them,"—Copy, Ord Papers, CU-B.

1865, FEB. 6.   John Swinton, *New York Times,* to USG. "I respectfully and earnestly ask the Lieutenant General, in behalf of a deeply distressed mother and family, that he will give directions that one of the special exchanges be made in favor of Capt. G. W. Whitman 51st New York Vol.— and another in favor of Lieut. S. Pooley 51st N. Y. Vols. The former has been in active service for four years, has borne himself bravely in battles east and west, including Vicksburg and Jackson, and has an aged widowed mother in deepest distress. Both of the above officers have been promoted from the ranks for brave conduct on the field, and both are now, or were lately, in C. S. Military Prison, Danville, Va. In giving the order of release the Lieutenant General will be gratefully remembered by the prisoners, by their parents and friends, and by his Devoted admirer"—Horace Traubel, *With Walt Whitman in Camden* (New York, 1915), II, 426–27. A reported reply of Feb. 13 from Lt. Col. Ely S. Parker to Swinton cannot be located.—Jerome M. Loving, ed., *Civil War Letters of George Washington Whitman* (Durham, 1975), p. 22n.

1865, FEB. 7.   USG endorsement. "Approved and recommended. Col. Kent is personally known to me since September 1861. He entered the service as a private, and has won his way to his present position by faithful and honest service. He is brave, intelligent, capable, and would fitly fill the position for which he is recommended."—ES, DNA, RG 94, ACP, 231K CB 1865. Written on a letter of Dec. 31, 1864, from Brig. Gen. Michael K. Lawler, Memphis, to President Abraham Lincoln recommending Col. Loren Kent, 29th Ill., for appointment as brig. gen.—LS, *ibid.*

1865, FEB. 7.   USG endorsement. "Respectfully forwarded to the Adjutant General of the Army, Not approved. These papers would have been returned to Gen. Foster to be forwarded through the proper military channel, but for the fact that among them is a letter from Gen. Foster to the Adjt Genl, transmitting them. How they got out of the regular channel I am unable to say."—ES, DNA, RG 94, ACP, V55 CB 1865. Written on a letter of Jan. 9 from Bvt. Brig. Gen. Milton S. Littlefield, Hilton Head, S. C., to Brig. Gen. Lorenzo Thomas recommending Col. Charles H. Van Wyck, 56th N. Y., for appointment as brig. gen.—ALS, *ibid.* On Jan. 30, Governor Reuben E. Fenton of N. Y. endorsed this letter. "Respectfully referred to Lieut Genl U. S Grant with request that he give the same such direction & indorsement as he deems proper."—ES, *ibid.*

1865, FEB. 7. USG endorsement. "Respectfully returned. No stipulation has been entered into between Judge Ould and myself authorizing contributions to Confederate prisoners of war from friends within our lines, nor would I consent to such an arrangement."—*O.R.*, II, viii, 140. Written on a letter of Jan. 28 from Brig. Gen. Halbert E. Paine to Maj. Gen. Henry W. Halleck, which Halleck endorsed to USG on Jan. 31.—*Ibid.*, pp. 139–40.

1865, FEB. 7. USG endorsement. "I know of no instance officially of interference by officers of the Departmt with hospital steamers, save as may be inferred from the within case of the steamer 'Cosmopolitan' Unofficially however I heard that General Butler had a hospital steamer for his Head Qrs on the Fort Fisher expedition. By what authority I know not. So generally does the right of the Medical Department to control these boats seem to be recognized that I see no particular necessity for publishing the order asked for, nor do I see any objection to it. The steamer 'Cosmopolitan' should be returned, if she has not already been to the Medical Department" —Copy, DLC-USG, V, 58. Written on a letter of Jan. 23 from Brig. Gen. Joseph K. Barnes, surgeon gen., to Secretary of War Edwin M. Stanton.— *Ibid.*

1865, FEB. 7. USG endorsement. "Respy returned to Maj Gen E. O. C. Ord, Comdg. Department of Virginia, with the information that it is deemed inexpedient to apply to the President to close the port of Norfolk: that his authority as a military commander to regulate trade is undoubted: that he is specially authorized and directed to prohibit in orders, if he has not already done so, merchandize of any kind from passing Norfolk or Portsmouth, or elsewhere, in his Department to the interior, under penalty of seizure and confiscation of the property and stock, and fine and imprisonment of the offenders"—Copy, DLC-USG, V, 58. Written on a letter of Feb. 2 from Maj. Gen. Edward O. C. Ord recommending the closing of the port of Norfolk.—*Ibid.*

1865, FEB. 7. Mary Duncan, New York City, to Lt. Col. Adam Badeau. "In relation to our recent conversation respecting the shameful outrages that have been perpe≠trated by the troops at Natchez—I feel called on to inform you that recent letters give tidings of the *great* reform instituted in said place—under the rule of Genl Davidson & it seems that the citizens are greatly pleased with the reformations already worked through Genl D's. orders.—Therefore—it is probable that *if* thefts & murders *again* occur— that they will meet their appropriate punishment,—& that military rule will no longer be a shadow of the substance. Let me entreat you, however, to try & have the sentence of my Father's murderers duly carried into execution! For—I should think that Genl Grant could have the order promptly obeyed, & such delay & injustice are indeed *hard* to bear. Thanks for your

kind note, & with cordial regards to our good friend Genl Grant—. . . Did
the Genl ever receive the letter I addressed him Last month?"—ALS, USG
3. On Feb. 25, Maj. Gen. Napoleon J. T. Dana, Memphis, wrote to Lt. Col.
Theodore S. Bowers. "Your endorsement of the 17th inst, inclosing Copy of
Genl Order No 38. of 1864 from Hd Qrs Depmt and Army of the Tenn,
relating to execution of two murderers of the father of Mrs Duncan is received—This is the first Copy of that order which has been seen in this
Command & no authority has ever been received for the execution of these
men—I have forwarded it to Brig Genl Davidson Commanding the District
of Natchez with orders to execute the order—"—ALS, DNA, RG 108, Letters Received. On March 6, Brig. Gen. John W. Davidson endorsed to USG
a copy of General Orders No. 11, District of Natchez, March 3, concerning
the execution; a copy of the death certificate; and a copy of a letter of March
4 from Davidson to Dana reporting compliance with orders.—*Ibid.* On
March 11, Dana wrote to Brig. Gen. John A. Rawlins. "I have the honor
to report that, in obedience to orders from the Lieutenant General Commanding, privates David Geer and Alexander McBride of Company I.,
28th Regiment Illinois Volunteer Infantry, convicted before a General Court
Martial of the Murder of Mr Sergeant, and sentenced 'to be shot to death
with musketry', were executed, in the manner prescribed, on Saturday the
4th day of March 1865 at Natchez Miss."—LS, *ibid.* On May 10, 1864,
four soldiers of the 28th Ill., believing that George W. Sargent of Natchez
kept four or five thousand dollars at home, guided by one of his former
slaves who had enlisted in the 6th U.S. Heavy Art., attempted to break
into Sargent's mansion. Sargent encountered the soldiers on the gallery of
Gloucester, and was mortally wounded while attempting to give the alarm.
—Court-martial records, *ibid.,* RG 153, LL 2874.

1865, FEB. 8.   USG endorsement. "I would recommend the promotion of
Col. Bouton to Brevet Brig. Gen. and await Gn. Sherman's recommendation
for further promotion."—AES, DNA, RG 94, ACP, B147 CB 1865. Written on a petition of Sept. 2, 1864, from officers of the 1st Brigade, U.S.
Colored, to Brig. Gen. Lorenzo Thomas urging that Col. Edward Bouton,
59th Colored, commanding the brigade, be appointed brig. gen.—D, *ibid.*
On Feb. 23, 1865, President Abraham Lincoln endorsed the petition. "A
good set of recommendations respectfully submitted to the Secretary of
War."—AES, *ibid.*

1865, FEB. 8.   To operator, Fort Monroe. "Please say to Mrs. Ord that
Mrs. Grant can not go to Fortress Monroe this evening."—ALS (telegram
sent), DLC-Samuel K. Rupley.

1865, FEB. 8, 11:01 P.M.   Maj. Gen. John G. Parke to USG. "Firing is
on right of our line—No: 4 & Fort McGilvery—No musketry—Presume it
was caused by our Batteries opening on working parties—or upon Cars

running upon Richmond R. Road—Nothing more than usual—"—ALS (telegram sent), DNA, RG 393, Army of the Potomac, Miscellaneous Letters Received; copy, *ibid.,* 9th Army Corps, Telegrams Sent.

1865, FEB. 8.   Lt. Col. Ely S. Parker to S. Hopkins Emmery. "I am directed by the Lieutenant General Commanding, to acknowledge the receipt of yours of the 1st February '65; and to say that every exertion is now being made to effect a general exchange of all prisoners now held North and South. Owing however to the difficulty of moving large bodies of men in the South, by reason of the bad condition of the railroads and other highways much delay will be experienced before our men can reach a place where we can receive them. Your letter has been referred to Col. J. E. Mulford, Assistant Agent of Exchange. Supplies or money packages for prisoners in the South can be sent directed care of Lieut Col. Jno. E. Mulford, Fort Monroe, Va. Asst Agent of Exchange, Fort Monroe, Va."—ALS, OCIWHi.

1865, FEB. 8.   George H. Stuart to USG. "I have the honor to introduce to you the Rev. Edward P. Smith, the present General Field Agent of the U. S. Christian Commission in charge of the work in the armies operating against Richmond, newly elected, in place of John A. Cole, Esq., the former agent. Rev. Mr. Smith has been director of the operations of the Commission in the armies of the Cumberland and Tennessee and enters upon his new sphere of labor with the highest confidence of the Commission. I beg leave to ask for him the courtesy and exertions of the officers under your command—as these were once extended by yourself in the west—and have followed the course of our work since its commencement."—LS, DNA, RG 94, U.S. Christian Commission, Letters Sent (Press).

1865, FEB. 9.   USG endorsement. "Respectfully forwarded and recommended. Capt. Stockdale entered the service as an enlisted man at the commencement of the War and has served continuously since that time, rising to his present position by honest merit. His fine business habits and qualifications, and strict integrity, fit him admirably for the position for which he is hereby recommended, and the duties of which he is now discharging. I make this recommendation from my own personal knowledge of Captain Stockdales merits."—ES, DNA, RG 94, ACP, 105M CB 1865. Written on a letter of Jan. 20 from Lt. Col. Michael R. Morgan to USG recommending Capt. Sidney A. Stockdale, 103rd Ill., for appointment as capt. and commissary.—LS, *ibid.* No appointment followed.

1865, FEB. 9.   USG endorsement. "Respectfully forwarded and recommended. This officer was recommended for the same position some time since & it is earnestly hoped that this appointment, deserving as it certainly is, may be made."—ES, DNA, RG 94, ACP, C1156 CB 1863. Written on a letter of Feb. 8 from Lt. Col. Michael R. Morgan to USG recommending

1st Lt. Thomas J. Cate, 36th Colored, for appointment as capt. and commissary.—LS, *ibid.* No appointment followed.

1865, FEB. 9.   President Abraham Lincoln to USG. "Suspend execution of death sentence of Hugh F. Riley, eleventh Mass Vols. now in front of Petersburg, until further orders, and forward record for examination."— Telegram sent, DNA, RG 107, Telegrams Collected (Bound). Lincoln, *Works,* VIII, 274. USG had left for Washington; Lt. Col. Theodore S. Bowers transmitted the message to Maj. Gen. George G. Meade.—Telegram received (at 3:50 P.M.), DNA, RG 393, Army of the Potomac, Miscellaneous Letters Received.

1865, FEB. 9, 11:30 A.M.   Maj. Gen. Edward O. C. Ord to USG. "I understand that Capt Walbridge Qur Master at Bermuda hundred has been relieved by orders from Washington and ordered to dep't. of south. I respectfully ~~request~~ represent that Capt Walbridge is one of our best Quartermasters and to relieve him would be a serious detriment to this army. I understand that Gen Ingalls did not direct this"—Telegram received (at 11:35 A.M.), DNA, RG 108, Letters Received.

1865, FEB. 9.   Maj. Gen. Edward O. C. Ord to USG. "Can I get a strong Regt of Cavalry from Genl Gregg to scout the south side of James river from Fort Powhatan ~~from the Army of the Potomac~~—I hear a torpedo party —500 strong has started ~~down~~ from near Peters burg—"—ADfS (telegram sent), Ord Papers, CU-B. On the same day, Lt. Col. Theodore S. Bowers telegraphed to Ord. "Your cipher dispatch of 12. m to Gen Grant did not reach here until after he had left."—Telegram received, *ibid.*

1865, FEB. 9.   Governor James Y. Smith of R. I. to USG. "In accordance with a resolution of the General Assembly of this State, I have the honor to enclose to you a copy of a Resolution of thanks passed by that body. I avail myself of this oppertunity, to unite with our Legislature in tendering You my own thanks for the many brilliant victories which have, on so many occasions, crowned the army of the United States while under your command."—LS, USG 3. A copy of the resolution is *ibid.*

1865, FEB. 13, 11:30 P.M.   To Secretary of War Edwin M. Stanton transmitting news copied from Richmond newspapers.—*O.R.,* I, xlvii, part 2, 405. Similar telegrams of Feb. 14, 15, 16, and 17 are *ibid.,* pp. 416–17, 428, 441–42, 455.

1865, FEB. 13.   USG endorsement. "Respy. referred to Maj Gen E. R. S. Canby, comdg. Mil. Div. West Mississippi, who will please give such directions as will insure proper respect to any safe-guards given by me while in the command (immediate) of the forces operating on the Mississippi, or by any other officer duly authorized to grant them, unless the parties hold-

ing them have, since the date of such safe guards conducted themselves in
such a manner as to forfeit them unfit to hold them."—Copy, DLC-USG,
V, 58. Written on a letter of Jan. 26 from Brig. Gen. Lorenzo Thomas,
Vicksburg, stating that safeguards given by USG while in Miss. had been
disregarded.—*Ibid.; ibid.,* V, 49.

1865, FEB. 13.   Asst. Secretary of the Navy Gustavus V. Fox to USG. "I
inclose herewith a letter from several of our officers who are now confined
in Libby Prison and ask that their cases may be brought up for exchange.
With one exception—that of Acting Master Shulze—they were engaged in
the destruction of the rebel ram Albemarle, on which occasion they were
captured. They are brave and deserving fellows, and I hope you may be able
to effect their exchange."—*O.R.,* II, viii, 214. The enclosures are *ibid.*

1865, FEB. 13.   Jeremiah Clemens, West Philadelphia, to USG. "I have
just learned by letters from home that my kidnapping connexion Mr Daniels
has escaped from Huntsville & is now in the vicinity of Nashville   The
probability is that he will be making his way to Memphis or Arkansas
where he will try to get in with some roving band of Guerillas as he is
perfectly worthless & has no means of making a living otherwise   The first
time I meet him I will save the Government all trouble in regard to him
But in the meantime I am afraid of anothers kidnapping raid   His Sister in
law writes me that he is the most utterly dispicable, & unprincipled man
she has ever met   My health is very bad   I was attacked in Washington
with inflammatory catarrh the symptoms of which were so threatening that
the Physicians deemed it advisable to pack me off home, & to the care of
my own Physician   The trip completely prostrated me—& even now I am
mending very slowly. I hope to be able to write you tomorrow thanking you
for your kindness & explaining Ala matters"—ALS, DNA, RG 109, Union
Provost Marshals' File of Papers Relating to Individual Civilians. On Feb.
15, Lt. Col. Theodore S. Bowers endorsed this letter. "Respectfully referred
to Maj. Gen. George H. Thomas, Com'd'g Dept Cumberland, in connexion
with a paper on the same subject heretofore referred."—AES, *ibid.* On Feb.
6, Lt. Col. Ely S. Parker prepared a pass. "Permission is hereby granted
Jere Clemens to take to Huntsville Alabama such articles of household
furniture, bedding, medicines, and provisions as may be necessary for the
use of his own family and for the supply of such Negroes as may still remain
upon his plantation,"—Copies, *ibid.,* RG 108, Letters Sent; DLC-USG, V,
46, 72, 108.

1865, FEB. 14.   USG endorsement. "Respy referred to Col Jno. E. Mulford, agent of Exchange, who will please confer with Judge Ould, Confederate Agent of Exchange, on this case and report the results to the Lieut
General. It is supposed that this case comes under the recent agreement for
the exchange of all prisoners held in close confinement."—Copy, DLC-USG,
V, 58. Written on documents concerning Col. Charles S. Hanson, 37th Ky.,

captured by C.S.A. forces and charged with cruelty to prisoners and violation of parole, probably those documents printed in *O.R.*, II, viii, 154–56, 184–87.

1865, FEB. 15, 11:00 A.M.   To Maj. Gen. Henry W. Halleck. "Brig, Gen, Robt. O. Tyler will be a good man to send to West Ky, to relieve Meredith, Tyler is in Philadelphia,"—Telegram, copies, DLC-USG, V, 46, 73, 108; (marked as received at 11:25 A.M.) DNA, RG 107, Telegrams Received in Cipher; *ibid.*, RG 108, Letters Sent. *O.R.*, I, xlix, part 1, 716. At 1:35 P.M., Halleck telegraphed to USG. "Genl R. O. Tyler's last report was unfit for field duty. Genl Thomas was directed to designate an officer to take Genl Meredith's place."—ALS (telegram sent), DNA, RG 107, Telegrams Collected (Bound); telegram received, *ibid.*; (at 2:35 P.M.) *ibid.*, RG 108, Letters Received. *O.R.*, I, xlix, part 1, 716. Maj. Gen. George H. Thomas succeeded in persuading the War Dept. to revoke the order removing Brig. Gen. Solomon Meredith from command of the District of Western Ky.—*Ibid.*, pp. 701, 702, 717, 726.

1865, FEB. 15.   USG endorsement. "I earnestly recommend the appointment of Col. Bachelder to the position of Capt. & A. Q. M. in the regular Army. It is with officers of such qualifications that it is desirable we should fill up the standing Army."—AES, DNA, RG 94, ACP, 2833 ACP 1877. Written on a letter of Feb. 8 from Col. Richard N. Batchelder, chief q. m., Army of the Potomac, to President Abraham Lincoln asking an appointment as capt. and q. m. in the U.S. Army.—ALS, *ibid.* Brig. Gen. Rufus Ingalls and Maj. Gen. George G. Meade had already endorsed the letter favorably, and the appointment was made as of Feb. 16.

1865, FEB. 16.   USG endorsement. "Respy. forwarded. The fact that colored regiments can easily be kept full, and that the officers of these regiments have much more labor to perform than officers of white troops, should entitle this communication to careful consideration"—Copy, DLC-USG, V, 58. Written on a letter of Feb. 15 from Maj. Gen. Godfrey Weitzel requesting "revocation of G. O. 182. AG June 20th 1863 so far as it relates to Colored Regiments"—*Ibid.*, V, 49.

1865, FEB. 16, midnight.   To Maj. Gen. Winfield S. Hancock. "If you desire it Maj Gen Shurz can be ordered to report to you to assist in raising your corps and to command a Division when raised—I think he might be of much service in the West in raising troops"—Telegram received (on Feb. 17, 1:15 A.M.), DNA, RG 94, Generals' Papers and Books, Schurz; copies, *ibid.*, RG 107, Telegrams Received in Cipher; *ibid.*, RG 108, Letters Sent; DLC-USG, V, 46, 73, 108. *O.R.*, I, xlvi, part 2, 573. On Feb. 18, Hancock telegraphed to USG. "A sufficient number of officers who have heretofore served with me, ~~and~~ have applied, to fill the prominent commands. If the decision should be left with me I would prefer appointing them though I have no doubt the officer you mention would be of ~~some~~ service in the North West in recruiting."—LS (telegram sent), DNA, RG 107, Telegrams Collected (Unbound); telegram received, *ibid.*, RG 108, Letters Received. *O.R.*, I, xlvi, part 2, 591. On the same day, Brig. Gen. John A. Rawlins telegraphed to Hancock. "Maj, Gen, Carl Schurz U. S. Vols, has been ordered to report to you to aid in recruiting your Corps with especial reference to his operating ~~in~~ for this purpose in the Northwest, If when the organization of the Corps is completed, you should prefer some other Officer to command General Schurz can be assigned to duty elsewhere"—Copies, DLC-USG, V, 46, 73, 108; DNA, RG 108, Letters Sent. *O.R.*, I, xlvi, part 2, 592. The orders are *ibid.* On March 6, Lt. Col. Theodore S. Bowers wrote to Maj. Gen. Carl Schurz. "Lieutenant General Grant directs me to respectfully acknowledge the receipt by him of your letter of date 26th February, and to say to you in reply that upon the completion of your present duties, you will be ordered to report to Major General W. T. Sherman as you request As soon as you are ready to go to Sherman please notify these Headquarters, and the necessary orders will be sent you at once"—LS, DLC-Carl Schurz. *O.R.*, I, xlvii, part 2, 712. The orders are *ibid.*, I, xlvi, part 3, 395; *ibid.*, I, xlvii, part 3, 75. According to a traditional account in the family of a former clerk of Maj. Gen. William T. Sherman, USG sent Schurz to Sherman with an envelope apparently filled with dispatches but which contained old newspapers and a note from USG. "Can you use this man? I have no place for him." Sherman returned Schurz to USG with an envelope containing the same newspapers and a note. "I can't either."—*New York Times*, Oct. 11, 1969. The story cannot be verified, and Sherman kept Schurz, who served as chief of staff to Maj. Gen. Henry W. Slocum in the last days of the war. See *Reminiscences of Carl Schurz* (New York, 1907–8), III, 108–11.

1865, FEB. 16.   President Abraham Lincoln to USG. "Suspend execution of death sentence of George W. Brown, Company A fifteenth New-York Engineers, now at City-Point, until further orders, and forward record for examination"—Telegram sent, DNA, RG 107, Telegrams Collected (Bound); telegram received (at 11:15 A.M.), *ibid.*, Telegrams Collected (Unbound). Lincoln, *Works*, VIII, 301. At 11:45 A.M., USG endorsed the telegram received to Maj. Gen. George G. Meade. "The above just received & is forwarded for your action—"—ES, DNA, RG 107, Telegrams Collected (Unbound). On the same day, Meade twice telegraphed to Lincoln. "Your telegram to Liut Gen Grant, suspending execution of sentence in case of Private Geo. W. Brown, Fifteenth 15 N. Y. Engineers, received. There is no such person as Geo. W. Brown—but there is a Private Geo. Rock—alias Geo Rock Brown, Fifteenth 15 N. Y. Engineers to be executed tomorrow. Presuming he is meant, I have ordered the suspension of the execution of his sentence. The records in his case are with the Judge Advocate General, and have already been acted on by you. His execution was suspended last fall by your order, and the order for his execution tomorrow, was based on one from the War Department ordering it to take place." "Private George Rocke, or George Rock Brown, company A Fifteenth 15 New York Engineers was sentenced to be shot on Friday the twenty eighth (28) day of October 1864. Execution of sentence was suspended until November fourth (4) 1864—and again suspended until further orders by direction of the President. The order suspending the execution was cancelled by Special Orders Number Fifty two (52) Paragraph One 1 of Feby first (1) 1865 from War Department, and the prisoner was ordered to be executed on Friday February Seventeenth 17 1865 by Special orders No: Thirty nine 39 of February ninth 9 1865 Head Quarters Army of Potomac. Today the sentence has been again suspended in obedience to a telegram of this date from the President directing suspension of the execution of Geo W Brown Co A Fifteenth 15 N Y Engineers, there being no person of the latter name under sentence, or in this company. The record in this case was forwarded to the Judge Advocate General, October Sixteenth 16 1864."— Telegrams received, *ibid.*; (at 6:10 P.M. and 10:10 P.M.—two of the second) *ibid.*, Telegrams Collected (Bound).

1865, FEB. 16. President Abraham Lincoln to USG. "Suspend execution of death sentence of Charles Love, Seventh New-Hampshire Vols. at City-Point until further orders, and forward record for examination"—Telegram sent, DNA, RG 107, Telegrams Collected (Bound); telegram received, *ibid.*, Telegrams Collected (Unbound). Lincoln, *Works*, VIII, 302. See *ibid.*, p. 243. On the same day, Lt. Col. Theodore S. Bowers endorsed this telegram to Maj. Gen. Edward O. C. Ord.—AES, DNA, RG 107, Telegrams Collected (Unbound); telegram received (at 2:50 P.M.), Ord Papers, CU-B.

1865, FEB. 17. USG endorsement. "Respectfully forwarded to the Sec. of War with the recommendation that the Judge Advocate General be requestd to examine the case refered to within and give an opinion. If I am not mistaken the most of the Court and witnesses in this case were persons who immediately after the trial left the service to join the rebel Army."—AES, DNA, RG 94, ACP, 16V CB 1865. Written on a letter of Feb. 15 from William K. Van Bokkelen, City Point, to Lt. Col. Theodore S. Bowers. "I would ask that if not incompatible with the views of the Lieut General, he would give me a letter to the Hon Secy of War requesting him to cause the Judge Advocate General to review the proceedings of a General Court held against me and acted on in April 1861. My object is to get the opinion of Genl Holt on the case and if favorable (of which I have no doubt) to endeavor to have the decision laid aside If the Lieut General approves please direct to me at 58 Pearl Street New York"—ALS, *ibid.* On Feb. 25, Judge Advocate Gen. Joseph Holt endorsed this letter. "Respectfully referred to the Secretary of War. The writer of the within communication to Lieut Gen Grant, (W. K. Van Bokkelin) was a Captain and Asst. q. m. in the U. S. Army, convicted by a Gen: Court Martial convened in 1860, of 'violating the 39th Art of War' and 'Rendering incorrect accounts to the Government,' and sentenced to be cashiered. The sentence was confirmed by the President, as appears by Gen Order of the War Dept. No 18 dated May 8. 1861. The Court was composed of eight officers four of whom it is found left the service and went South, but this fact does not, it is conceived, raise any question favorable or otherwise to Bokkelin, the evidence upon which the findings rest being deemed clear and conclusive as to his guilt. There are on file in this office the records of a Court of Inquiry, convened in 1856, to investigate his transactions; of a Court Martial, convened to try him in 1857; and of two others, appointed in 1860; and an examination of these leads to an unfavorable estimate of his character. No further action in the case is recommended."—ES, *ibid.* On March 10, Bvt. Lt. Col. Samuel F. Chalfin, AGO, sent USG a copy of Holt's opinion.—LS, *ibid.*, RG 108, Letters Received. Van Bokkelen, USG's classmate (USMA 1843), was never restored to duty.

1865, FEB. 17.   USG endorsement. "I think it will be well to adopt the plan proposed by Gov Fletcher for the protection of Missouri the ensuing years, that is, to let the Governor call out for one year the number of men Gen Dodge thinks will be necessary to protect the state. Men who have been in the service are worth much more than new volunteers, and infinitely more than those obtained by draft, where so many are disloyal"—Copy, DLC-USG, V, 58. *O.R.*, I, xlviii, part 1, 696. Written on a letter of Jan. 31 from Maj. Gen. Grenville M. Dodge, St. Louis, to Secretary of War Edwin M. Stanton discussing his need for troops and the desirability of accepting the proposition of Governor Thomas C. Fletcher of Mo. to fill the quota of his state with militia.—LS, DNA, RG 108, Letters Received. *O.R.*, I, xlviii, part 1, 694–95. On Feb. 21, Maj. Gen. Henry W. Halleck wrote to USG. "The Secty of War directs me to return to you the enclosed papers with the information that there is a law forbidding the adoption of any plan like that of Governor Fletcher for substituting militia for calls under the draft. The Secretary had therefore been obliged to decline the acceptance of Gov.s Fletchers proposal, and the papers were referred for your information in regard to Genl. Dodges views of the probable military necessities of that Dept., and in order that measures might be taken accordingly."—LS, DNA, RG 108, Letters Received. *O.R.*, I, xlviii, part 1, 925. On Feb. 24, USG endorsed this letter. "Respectfully returned. The reports of Gen. Dodge, and Gov. Fletcher, of Mo. were referred to me in the hand writing of the Secretary of War, for my 'report and opinion' I believed, and believe still, the proposition of Gov. Fletcher is the best we can do for the interests of the service. The troops he will call out will be turned over to United States authority, and will form a part of the national forces. As defenders of Missouri they will go into Kansas or Arkansas as may be necessary, in pursuit of invaders. If it is still decided that these troops can not be received, it will be advisable to send all troops raised in Missouri by draft to other sections of country to serve, and supply their places from Thomas' Army, giving

him new troops now being raised to take the place of those thus taken from
him"—ES, DNA, RG 108, Letters Received. *O.R.*, I, xlviii, part 1, 925–26.

1865, FEB. 17.   USG endorsement. "Respy. referred to Maj Gen Meade,
Comdg A of P. with the information that the intention of S. O. 8. from
these Head Qrs was that the Comdg Generals of the Army of Potomac and
of the James should each designate one or more regiments of their respective commands to which the Provost Marshal General could assign men
now in barracks at City Point, without anything to show for what regiments
they were intended. In many cases this information may be recieved hereafter, and it may become necessary to transfer to other regiments, and it
was intended to leave the whole matter in the hands of the Provost Marshal
General. By reference to S. O. 8. it will be seen that the object was to put
men in service who have been in the barrack for months (because it was
impossible to ascertain where they belongd) under condition that it would
render it practicable to transfer them in the event it became necessary to do
so."—Copy, DLC-USG, V, 58. Written on a letter of Brig. Gen. Marsena
R. Patrick concerning the assignment of recruits.—*Ibid.*

1865, FEB. 17.   Lt. Col. Theodore S. Bowers to Maj. Gen. Edward O. C.
Ord. "You will please direct the Commission now sitting at Norfolk to inquire into the management of the 'New Regime' New's paper published in
that City, and ascertain how, by whom, and by whose authority the same
has been carried on,   Also whether any Commissioned, Non-Commissioned,
Officer's or Enlisted men, have by detail or otherwise been engaged upon
it"—Copies, DLC-USG, V, 46, 73, 108; DNA, RG 108, Letters Sent.

1865, FEB. 17.   Brig. Gen. Charles K. Graham, Point of Rocks, Va., to
Lt. Col. Theodore S. Bowers. "The authority to recruit the Thirteenth New
York Artillery was obtained by Major-General Foster from the Governor
of that State. It was expressly stated, I have always understood, that the
Third Battalion should consist of seamen, for marine artillery and army
gun-boat service, and the men were even uniformed and armed to adapt
them for that duty. The Reno, Parke, Foster, and Burnside were built to be
manned by this battalion. The First and Second Battalions are doing duty
in this department. Three batteries I believe are on the Bermuda line. To
transfer the officers and men, most of whom are seamen, to land service
would, I believe, occasion great dissatisfaction."—*O.R.*, I, xlvi, part 2, 582.
On Feb. 19, Maj. Gen. Edward O. C. Ord telegraphed to Brig. Gen. John
A. Rawlins. "The following recd from Genl Gordon   *By Telegraph from*
Norfolk   *Dated* Feby. 19 *18645. To* MAJ. GEN. ORD—Gen Palmer has
ordered the troops at Coanjack to report to him   They are two 2 Companies
one 1 of them white thirteenth 13 N. Y. H. A. The other Colored all under
Major McLaughlen   both theese Companies belong to regiments in this
command   Many applications have been made to have these men releived
from Gen. Palmers command but evidently Gen. Palmer does not intend to

do so We cannot prevent smuggling with the force here even with those at Coanjack. about five hundred 500 men have reported about one thousand 1000 more are needed. (signed) GEO. N. GORDON Br. Genl"—LS (telegram sent), DNA, RG 107, Telegrams Collected (Unbound); telegram received, *ibid.*, RG 108, Letters Received. *O.R.*, I, xlvi, part 2, 594. On the same day, Bowers wrote to Brig. Gen. Innis N. Palmer. "You will immediately relieve the two Companies (Commanded by Maj Laughlin) belonging to Regiments serving in the Dept, of Virginia, and order them to report at once to Brig Gen, Gordon at Norfolk Va,"—Copies, DLC-USG, V, 46, 73, 108; DNA, RG 108, Letters Sent. *O.R.*, I, xlvii, part 2, 498. On the same day, Rawlins telegraphed to Ord. "Gen Palmer has been directed to to releive the two companies mentioned in Gen Gordons despatch, and order them to report to Gen Gordon at Norfolk immediately."—Telegram received, DNA, RG 94, War Records Office, Miscellaneous War Records; copies, *ibid.*, RG 108, Letters Sent; DLC-USG, V, 46, 73, 108. *O.R.*, I, xlvi, part 2, 594.

1865, FEB. 17. Bvt. Maj. Peter S. Michie to Lt. Col. Theodore S. Bowers. "I am in receipt of an order from Army Hd Qrs by direction of Genl Grant, relieving Detachments of the 15th N Y. Engrs. serving with this army and later a telegram from Genl Barnard saying that Capt Luby's command will remain with me for the present I represented to Genl Barnard this morning that I would require this Detachment to man the four (4) Ponton trains he ordered me to prepare for the spring campaign—and hence his telegram in ignorance I presume of the order issued from your Hd Qrs To carry out his orders in regard to Ponton trains it is necessary to have theise detachment and hence I ask for instructions as to which order I shall obey"—ALS (telegram sent), DNA, RG 107, Telegrams Collected (Unbound). *O.R.*, I, xlvi, part 2, 580. On the same day, Bowers wrote to Michie. "It was supposed by the Lieutenant General that you could take care of your Pontoons by details from the Engineer Regiment under your Command, If it is impossible to do this, he will consent to you retaining the men of the 15th New York Engineers It is very desirable however that they be returned to their proper command,"—Copies, DLC-USG, V, 46, 73, 108; DNA, RG 108, Letters Sent. *O.R.*, I, xlvi, part 2, 580. On the same day, Michie telegraphed to Bowers. "I have only 565 Engrs—for duty in this army—at Ft. Monroe, New-berne N. C. & Bermuda—and with the Army—265 of these are one year recruits that go out by November—Every-day all but 70 or 80 are on detail and there is not much work required—at present. They have had no rest since May. I will not be able to do without the detachment which I shall reserve exclulsively for Ponton Duty, if permitted"—ALS (telegram sent), DNA, RG 107, Telegrams Collected (Unbound); telegram received (at 10:55 P.M.), *ibid.*, RG 108, Letters Received. *O.R.*, I, xlvi, part 2, 580. On Feb. 18, Bowers wrote to Michie. "In consideration of your dispatch of last evening, the Lieutenant General consents to your retaining the detachment of the 15th New York Engineers until further orders"—Copies,

DLC-USG, V, 46, 73, 108; DNA, RG 108, Letters Sent. *O.R.*, I, xlvi, part 2, 588. On Feb. 21, Brig. Gen. John W. Turner, chief of staff for Maj. Gen. Edward O. C. Ord, telegraphed to USG. "Your dispatch is recd The detachment of the 15th N. Y. Engineers now with this Army are the only Experienced pontooneers in it. The 1 N. Y. Engineers are very much depleted and somewhat disorganized and could neither furnish Officers or men for pontoon trains.—It would seriously cripple if not and greatly delay the organization of the trains ordered by Gen Bernard by taking these men away now, and in my opinion great risks would be incurred in not having them these trains ready in the event of this Army moveing soon—For the number of trains ordered this Detachment furnishes scarcely a sufficiency" —Telegram received (at 7:30 P.M.), DNA, RG 107, Telegrams Collected (Unbound). *O.R.*, I, xlvi, part 2, 617.

1865, FEB. 17.   Jesse Roberds, Anna, Ill., former capt., 31st Ill., to USG. "In your Order Compensating Soldiers who Ran the Blockaid at Vickesburg Miss I was allowed pay as principal Engineear on the Steamer Harrison and I have Neaver Reced any thing   please Set fourth In My papers the amount that I was allowed and what Q M Will pay the same and Send My papers Backe to Anna Ills."—ALS, DNA, RG 393, Dept. of the Tenn., Miscellaneous Letters Received.

1865, FEB. 18.   Maj. Gen. John Pope, Milwaukee, Wis., to USG. "I have no Adjt Genl. I need for the Division Adjt Genl an experienced Officer well acquainted with such duties. Lt Col Jno. L. Sprague of the Army who is now with the army in front of Richmond is eminently qualified for the position and as he is besides an old friend I request earnestly that you order him to report to me in St Louis"—Telegram received, DNA, RG 108, Letters Received. On the same day, the request was granted through Special Orders No. 35, Armies of the U.S.—Copies, DLC-USG, V, 57, 63, 64, 65.

1865, FEB. 19.   USG endorsement. "Respectfully returned. I recommend that the proposition of the Mayor of Baltimore for keeping the inmates of Prince George County, Virginia Poor House, be accepted until some better arrangement can be made."—ES, DNA, RG 94, Letters Received, 271M 1865. Written on a sheaf of papers indicating that the city of Baltimore would accept the fifteen inmates if paid thirty-five cents per day for each. —*Ibid.*

1865, FEB. 20.   USG endorsement. "Respy referred to Brig Gen W. Hoffman, Comy Gen of Prisoners wih the request he will furnish any information he may have in relation to this man"—Copy, DLC-USG, V, 58. Written on a letter of Feb. 15 from C.S.A. Agent of Exchange Robert Ould to Lt. Col. John E. Mulford concerning the imprisonment of Lt. Edward S. Ruggles.—*Ibid.*; *ibid.*, V, 49. Bvt. Brig. Gen. William Hoffman later endorsed this letter. "Respy returned to Lt Gen U. S. Grant, Comdg U S. A.   E. S.

Ruggles 2d Lt. signal Corps, was captured at Fort Adams, Miss. Oct 13, 1864, and is now a prisoner of war at New Orleans, La."—Copy, *ibid.*, V, 58.

1865, FEB. 20.   USG endorsement. "Respy returned. I concur in the views expressed by Gen Halleck, and recommend that the within proposition be not approved"—Copy, DLC-USG, V, 58. Written on a letter of Governor Samuel J. Crawford of Kan. asking authority to raise a regt.—*Ibid.*

1865, FEB. 20.   Maj. Gen. Winfield S. Hancock to USG. "You will remember that in the list of recommendations for brevets for the Army of the Potomac last fall, Lieut Col. Morgan, Chief of my Staff and Ass't Inspector General, was recommended for appointment as full Brigadier General by yourself and General Meade. This appointment was not made, but Colonel Morgan received the appointment of Brevet Brigadier General. I was informed at the War Department that there were few vacancies and that Colonel Morgan being a Staff Officer must give way to Commanders of Troops who had been recommended for promotion. You may remember saying to me subsequently that you would have Colonel Morgan promoted when I was in a position to assign him to a command in the 1st Corps. Colonel Morgan is anxious to command Troops and if he is promoted I will assign him to duty to command the 1st Brigade, unless you should order him elsewhere. As he has served for Three years with the Army of the Potomac, he tells me if the matter is left to his choice he would prefer some new field, say General Sherman's Army. Major General Slocum applied nearly two years since to have Colonel Morgan promoted and assigned to a Brigade in his Corps. It is not necessary for me to reopen Colonel Morgan's case in this letter.—I will merely say that in General Warren's Official report of the battle of Bristoe, Octr, 14, 1863, he recommends in strong terms Colonel Morgan's promotion. General Warren also specially recommended him last fall. Major General Couch, formerly in command of the Second Corps has also recommended his promotion. I have recommended him many times, not only in my official reports but on special occasions. All his recommendations are unsought and the result of his valuable service in the field. Though now a Staff Officer, he has commanded troops, having been Commandant of Artillery of the Second Corps for more than a year. The immediate occasion of this letter is that General Morgan cannot take command ion his brevet rank as he would then be obliged to give up his appointment as Asst. Inspector General and would draw pay as Captain only. I trust that before the expiration of the present Congress, General Morgan may receive his appointment so that he can get command of troops in the Spring campaign."—LS, DNA, RG 108, Letters Received. *O.R.*, I, xlvi, part 2, 606–7. See *ibid.*, pp. 724–25. On March 14, Lt. Col. Theodore S. Bowers wrote to Hancock. "Referring to your letter of date 20th February, recommending the appointment of Lieutenant Colonel Morgan of your Staff as Brigadier General of Volunteers, General Grant directs me to

say to you that there is at present no vacancy in the number of Brigadier
General[s] allowed by law, and that until some vacancy does occur, nothing
can be done in the case,"—Copies, DLC-USG, V, 46, 74, 108; DNA, RG
108, Letters Sent. *O.R.*, I, xlvi, part 2, 982.

1865, FEB. 20. Jacob Levison, asst. sergeant-at-arms, Assembly Cham-
ber, Carson City, Nev., to USG. "Allow, that from the hights of the Sierra
Nevada's, a faint voice of patriotism, and admiration, may reach you upon
the glorious path of renown and honor, which will bring your name down
to posterity, with the great predecessors of our cherished Union. And in the
fervor of these, my feelings I beg leave to name my newly born son, after
so illustrious a Citizen the one I now have the honor to address, with the
sincerest esteem, . . ."—LS, USG 3.

Index

Chicago Historical Society, Chicago, Ill.: documents in, 10n (3), 12n–13n, 13n–14n, 21, 24, 57n, 60n, 276–77
Chickahominy River (Va.), 471
Chickamauga, Ga., battle of, 525
Chihuahua, Mexico, 251n
Choate, Joseph H. (of N.Y.): letter to, Dec. 5, 1864, 471
Chowan River (N.C.), 65, 333n, 384n
Chrismer, Wayde, Bel Air, Md.: document owned by, 163
Christensen, Christian T. (U.S. Army), 476
Cincinnati, Ohio, 3n, 81n, 149, 153, 154n, 243n, 291, 379n, 477, 525
Cincinnati Commercial (newspaper), 154n
Cincinnati Gazette (newspaper), 29n
City Point, Va.: troop movements at, 4 and n, 5, 35, 111n, 122n, 161n, 162n, 317n, 372n, 473, 475, 543; visitors to, 15 and n, 26n, 152, 210n, 220n, 264n, 276n, 290n, 322n, 414n, 514, 515; USG at, 44, 123n, 127n, 184n, 242n, 331n, 407, 413n; French warship goes to, 48n; depot at, 68n, 69n, 122n, 340, 448n, 485, 487, 519; provost marshal at, 98n; Negro troops at, 121n, 464; Negroes sent to, 201n; ships at, 208n, 305n, 308n, 319n, 423n, 472; post office at, 221 and n; prisoners sent to, 264n, 374n, 375n, 385 and n, 386n, 390, 424n, 453n, 492, 493, 521, 524–25, 540, 541; threatened, 304n, 319 and n; negotiations at, 338n; mentioned, 13, 143n, 172n, 173n, 175n, 282n, 291, 303n, 336n, 361, 405, 480, 490, 520, 526
Clark, William (explorer), 438n
Clark, William C. (of Norfolk), 514
Clark, William T. (U.S. Army), 89 and n, 90n, 480
Clarke, Capt. (C.S. Army), 244
Clay, Clement C., Jr. (C.S.A. agent), 377, 378n, 513
Clay, Clement C., Sr. (of Ala.), 459 and n
Clemens, Jeremiah (of Ala.), 538
Clements House, Va., 373n
Clendenin, David R. (Ill. Vols.), 285n
Clifton, Tenn., 528
Coal, 176n, 206 and n, 207n, 226n, 229n, 248n, 249n, 297, 408, 448 and n

Cobb's Hill (Va.), 363n
Coffee, 383, 385n
Cohasset, Mass., 329n
Coinjock, N.C., 543, 544
Colburn, Richard T. (newspaper correspondent), 52n
Cole, John A. (U.S. Christian Commission), 536
Colorado (U.S. Navy), 156n, 157n
Colquitt, Alfred H. (C.S. Army), 100n, 278n, 479
Columbia, S.C.: defended, 40, 259; William T. Sherman threatens, 75n, 131n, 170n, 171n, 172n, 294, 295n, 296n, 343; prisoners paroled from, 136; resident of, 137; captured, 438 and n, 446, 452, 453n, 456; information about, 479; railroad to, 518
Columbia, Tenn., 24n, 135n, 188n, 528
Columbia Carolinian (newspaper), 244
Columbia University, New York, N.Y.: document in, 162n
Columbus, Ky., 497, 516
Columbus, Miss., 209n, 421n
Combahee River (S.C.), 257, 377n, 380n, 381n, 514, 517, 528, 529
Commodore Barney (U.S. Navy), 319n
Commodore Morris (U.S. Navy), 319n
Comstock, Cyrus B. (staff officer of USG): staff duties of, 31n, 377n, 472; on Fort Fisher expedition, 197, 198n–99n, 228n, 229n, 230n–33n, 236n, 243n, 276–77, 277n–79n, 377n, 401, 408; promoted, 233n; on reconnaissance, 447n; recommends promotion, 519–20; photographers report to, 520
Confederate States Congress, 144, 419–20, 443, 444n, 505, 515, 517
Congaree River (S.C.), 295n, 446
Connecticut Volunteers, 521
Connor, Patrick E. (U.S. Army), 202n, 512
Conrad, Francis (prisoner), 493
Conrad, Joseph S. (U.S. Army), 150n
Conscription: of Negroes, 20n; provides unreliable troops, 35n, 400; praised by USG, 143; by C.S.A., 144, 402, 463; ordered, 144n; of correspondent, 224n, 408–9; in Ind., 285n; in Mo., 542
Cony, Samuel (Gov. of Maine), 530
Cook, John (U.S. Army), 16, 17n

Mattapony River (Va.), 111*n*
Maury, Dabney H. (C.S. Army), 236*n*, 268, 269*n*
Maximilian (Emperor of Mexico): C.S.A. dealings with, 250, 288*n*, 289*n*, 290*n*; finances of, 252*n*; mentioned, 283*n*, 285*n*, 287*n*
Max Meadows, Va., 476
Maynadier, William (U.S. Army), 254*n*
Mayo, Joseph (mayor of Richmond), 503
Mazatlan, Mexico, 253*n*
Meade, George G. (U.S. Army): in Petersburg campaign, 5*n*, 10 and *n*, 12 and *n*, 13*n*, 14*n*, 26*n*, 40, 40*n*–42*n*, 41, 43–44, 43*n*, 44*n*, 45*n*–46*n*, 60*n*, 85*n*, 86 and *n*, 87*n*, 92 and *n*, 108 and *n*, 109*n*, 120, 121*n*–22*n*, 136*n*, 159*n*, 164*n*, 192*n*, 231*n*, 400, 436 and *n*, 453*n*, 454–55, 455*n*, 464, 469–70, 478–79, 485, 518–19, 530, 543; visits USG, 25, 26*n*, 264*n*–65*n*, 364*n*; sends expedition down Weldon Railroad, 30, 30*n*–31*n*, 55–56, 55*n*, 64–65, 65*n*–67*n*, 81, 81*n*–82*n*, 84–85, 85*n*–86*n*, 92, 93*n*–94*n*, 96–97, 97–98, 97*n*, 98*n*, 99*n*, 104*n*–5*n*, 105, 105*n*–6*n*, 120*n*; informed of USG's absence, 37*n*, 280, 305*n*, 386*n*–87*n*, 396*n*; war news sent to, 40, 54*n*, 66*n*, 126*n*, 158*n*, 164*n*, 230*n*, 438*n*, 452, 453*n*, 505; and Roger A. Pryor, 42*n*; reports desertions, 43*n*; staff of, 81*n*, 145*n*, 500, 501–2; requests relief of James H. Ledlie, 87*n*; angry about Henry G. Thomas, 103, 103*n*–4*n*; approves resignation, 116*n*–17*n*; in battle of the Crater, 135–36, 136*n*, 139, 142, 142*n*–43*n*, 399 and *n*; deals with civilians, 166 and *n*, 529–30; orders court-martial, 264 and *n*; at Philadelphia, 264*n*, 338*n*, 494; relieves John Gibbon, 272*n*; praised by USG, 299, 300; promotion of, 299 and *n*, 300, 322*n*; informed about C.S.A. commissioners, 346*n*–47*n*; in battle of Hatcher's Run, 363–64, 364*n*, 365, 365*n*–66*n*, 372, 372*n*–74*n*, 382, 382*n*–83*n*, 387, 387*n*–88*n*, 391–92, 392*n*, 394; sends staff officers to Winfield S. Hancock, 465–66, 470; recommends promotions, 466, 539, 546; approves death sentence, 475, 521; assists Robert O. Tyler,

494; examines book on tactics, 497; revokes order relieving Truman Seymour, 516; suspends executions, 517, 525, 537, 540–41; instructed about photographers, 520; mentioned, 167, 472
—Correspondence from USG: telegram to, Nov. 17, 1864, 5*n*; telegram to, Nov. 25, 1864, 25; telegram to, Nov. 25, 1864, 26*n*; telegram to, Nov. 28, 1864, 30; telegram to, [Nov. 27], 1864, 31*n*; telegram to, Nov. 29, 1864, 37*n*; telegram to, Dec. 2, 1864, 37*n*; telegrams to, Nov. 30, 1864 (2), 40; telegram to, Nov. 30, 1864, 41; endorsement to, Nov. 30, 1864, 43–44; endorsement to, Nov. 30, 1864, 43*n*; letter to, Nov. 30, 1864, 43*n*; telegram to, Dec. 1, 1864, 54*n*; telegram to, Dec. 3, 1864, 55; telegram to, Dec. 3, 1864, 55–56; letter to, Dec. 5, 1864, 64–65; telegram to, Dec. 5, 1864, 66*n*; telegram to, Dec. 5, 1864, 66*n*–67*n*; telegram to, Dec. 11, 1864, 67*n*; telegram to, Dec. 7, 1864, 81; telegram to, Dec. 7, 1864, 82*n*; telegram to, Dec. 8, 1864, 84–85; telegram to, Dec. 8, 1864, 85*n*; telegram to, Dec. 8, 1864, 86; telegram to, Dec. 8, 1864, 86*n*; telegram to, Dec. 8, 1864, 87*n*; telegrams to, Dec. 9, 1864 (2), 92; telegram to, Dec. 9, 1864, 93*n*; telegram to, Dec. 9, 1864, 94*n*; telegram to, Dec. 10, 1864, 96–97; telegram to, Dec. 10, 1864, 97–98; telegram to, Dec. 10, 1864, 97*n*; telegram to, Dec. 10, 1864, 98; telegram to, Dec. 10, 1864, 98*n*; telegram to, Dec. 11, 1864, 105; telegram to, Dec. 12, 1864, 108; telegram to, Dec. 12, 1864, 108*n*; telegram to, Dec. 12, 1864, 109*n*; telegram to, Dec. 7, 1864, 117*n*; telegram to, Dec. 14, 1864, 120; telegram to, Dec. 13, 1864, 120*n*; telegram to, Dec. 14, 1864, 121*n*; telegram to, Dec. 19, 1864, 135–36; telegram to, Dec. 23, 1864, 158*n*; telegram to, Dec. 25, 1864, 164*n*; telegram to, Dec. 25, 1864, 164*n*–65*n*; telegram to, Dec. 25, 1864, 166; telegram to, Jan. 13, 1865, 183*n*; telegram to, Jan. 18, 1865, 183*n*; telegram to, Jan. 14, 1865, 264; telegram to, Jan. 6, 1865, 264*n*; telegram to, Jan. 13, 1865,